The Violin

The Violin

A SOCIAL HISTORY OF THE WORLD'S
MOST VERSATILE INSTRUMENT

DAVID SCHOENBAUM

W. W. NORTON & COMPANY

New York • London

For information about permission to reproduce selections from this book,
write to Permissions, W. W. Norton & Company, Inc.,
500 Fifth Avenue, New York, NY 10110

For information about special discounts for bulk purchases, please contact
W. W. Norton Special Sales at specialsales@wwnorton.com or 800-233-4830

Manufacturing by RR Donnelley, Harrisonburg, VA
Book design by JAM Design
Production manager: Julia Druskin

"Don't Let That Horse" by Lawrence Ferlinghetti (p. 521), from *A Coney Island of the Mind*, copyright © 1958 by Lawrence Ferlinghetti. Reprinted by permission of New Directions Publishing Corp.

Library of Congress Cataloging-in-Publication Data

Schoenbaum, David.
The violin : a social history of the world's most versatile instrument / David
Schoenbaum. — First edition.
pages ; cm
Includes bibliographical references and index.
ISBN 978-0-393-08440-5 (hardcover)
1. Violin. 2. Violin—History. I. Title.
ML800.S326 2012
787.209—dc23

2012033866

W. W. Norton & Company, Inc.
500 Fifth Avenue, New York, N.Y. 10110
www.wwnorton.com

W. W. Norton & Company Ltd.
Castle House, 75/76 Wells Street, London W1T 3QT

1 2 3 4 5 6 7 8 9 0

FOR

YAEL, NATAN, CHARLOTTE, AND LOUISA

CONTENTS

ACKNOWLEDGMENTS

SOME YEARS AGO, when the St. Louis Symphony invited Liu Yang, a gifted young Chinese violinist by way of Cincinnati, to play the Nielsen concerto, I had a welcome opportunity to visit my friends John and Fay Scandrett. I'd known John and Fay since graduate school in Madison, where John, an impassioned amateur cellist, was a doctoral candidate in physics when he wasn't playing quartets. We regularly crowded into their tiny apartment below the Presbyterian student center to sight-read Haydn till midnight, while baby Claire, who would grow up to play the piccolo professionally, slept undisturbed through the din. Now and then, we even got together in John's lab over the noon hour.

With my visit impending, Fay mentioned to a neighbor that I was working on a social history of the violin. "What's that?" the neighbor asked. Fay did her best to explain. "Who'd want to read that?" the neighbor replied.

It was a fair question. But for me, at least, the answer was simple. I did. The violin had been around for nearly five hundred years. Like the Western music that was reconstructed around it, it had become one of the world's great export products. People in all kinds of places had found ways to play it in all kinds of ways. Deep into its fifth century, it worked as well for indie rock as it did for "Turkey in the Straw" and the monumental chaconne Bach appended to his D Minor solo violin partita. But how and why, and what did this tell us about the world?

My curiosity went back to fourth grade, when Raymond P. Wiegers, a large man with a booming voice, visited my class ex officio. Like many American cities of the day, Milwaukee was serious about its public schools. Mr. Wiegers's job was music education. The system even provided instruments. When Mr. Wiegers asked for volunteers, I raised my hand. To this day, I don't know why. But it was fine with my parents, and it never occurred to me to drop out. It turned out to be one of the most consequential decisions of my life.

By the time I was sixteen, lessons with Mr. Wiegers had led to lessons with his successors, Hans Muenzer and Florizel von Reuter. Muenzer had studied with Hans Sitt, a pillar of the Leipzig conservatory in its golden age. Reuter was an American-born prodigy and enthusiastic spiritualist, with a colorful and distinguished European career, who had played at the White House for President William McKinley and had a soft spot for Paganini.[1] As an undergraduate in Madison, I drifted into the gravitational field of Rudolf Kolisch, whose quartet was one of the great ones of the interwar years. In 1944, he accepted a job at the University of Wisconsin because he needed one. When John and I played for fun, we played with our friends. When Kolisch played for fun, which he had in his younger years, he played with his brother-in-law, Arnold Schoenberg, and Anton von Webern, icons of twentieth-century music.[2]

In taste, style, and temperament, Muenzer, Reuter, and Kolisch were from different planets. But all three were Central Europeans, serious professionals, heirs to a great tradition, far from home in every sense, and reduced directly or indirectly to teaching me. I was approaching midlife as a professional historian before the larger implications of this finally hit me with help from a review assignment. Joseph Wechsberg, a wonderful writer with his own colorful Central European past and special relationship to the violin, had published an expansive series of *New Yorker* pieces on the violin scene that had been republished as a book.[3] There was obviously a story here that went back to at least the sixteenth century. I then realized that, for all the titles on violins and violinists extending over furlongs of library shelf, no one, including Wechsberg, had yet written it.

A family occasion in 1993 was a convenient excuse to propose the idea to Don Lamm, then president of W. W. Norton, who was nice enough to take me to lunch. To my lasting gratitude and delight, he not only liked the idea, he tracked me to a motel in Westchester County before the afternoon was over.

Neither of us realized that a book with four chapters would turn into four books that caused me to wonder in bleaker moments whether I might be working on a giant obituary. The depth and breadth of my ignorance about how violins are made and sold were clear from the beginning. What came as a surprise was the eggshell fragility of what I thought I knew about players and playing. Getting this right led me to places I never thought I'd see, people I never thought I'd meet, languages I never thought I'd speak or read, and things I never learned in graduate school. It also took years longer than my publisher, my wife, or I ever imagined.

After five previous books extending across most of the twentieth century, I was less surprised by the village of makers, dealers, players, teachers, and accessory personnel it took to connect me with so many intersecting worlds. But I've never been so grateful to so many people in so my many ways. My wife, who has become an old hand at this, leads the list. Don Lamm, who was there when this all began, and Drake McFeely, his successor at the finish line, are only a step behind. Like all good editors, Jeff Shreve, Janet Byrne, and Nancy Wolff have done what they could to save me from myself.

I am grateful to the German-American Fulbright Commission and the Netherlands Institute for Advanced Study for money and to the University of Iowa for time. I am deeply indebted to the Landesarchiv Berlin, Thomas Ertelt of the Staatliches Institut für Musikforschung, Berlin, Dietmar Schenk and Karen Krukowsky of the Universität der Künste, Berlin, and Ed Shreeves, Jody Falconer, Ruthann McTyre, and Amy McBeth of the University of Iowa Libraries for resources, archivalia, and patience.

For source materials not otherwise available, or that I'd not even been aware of, I'm indebted to Chip Averwater, Bernice Singer Baron, Robert Bein, Charles Beare, Willem Bouman, Paul Childs, James Christensen, Paul Cohen, John Dilworth, Rachel Donadio, Rosa Fain, Dave Fulton, Helmut Gabel, Claire Givens, Peter Greiner, Roger Hargrave, Peter Harstad, Brian Harvey, Ben Hebbert, Rachel Baron Heimovics Braun, Ron Humphrey, Sergei Kapterev, Judith Kirsch, John Koster, Udo Kretzschmann, Leopold La Fosse, Angelika Legde-Jaskolla, Erin Lehman, Philip Margolis, Ruthann McTyre, John Milnes, Don Mowatt, Richard E. Myers, Mark Mueller, David Nadler, Elena Ostleitner, Annette Otterstedt, Mark Peterson, Gabriella Poggi, Christopher Reuning, Greg Riley, Josef Schwarz, Lynn Sargeant, Margaret Shipman, John Sidgwick, Gary Sturm, Henry Turner, Peter van Dam, William Weber, Rüdiger Wittke, Peter Zazofsky, Mrs. Sandra de Laszlo and Caroline Corbeau of the De Laszlo Archive Trust, and Jennifer Ring of the Bowers Museum of Cultural Art.

For interviews, information, and general collegiality, I am grateful to those who made themselves available with patience, good humor, and unmatched expertise: Alexander Abramovich, Ayke Agus, Gregg T. Alf,

Lynn Armour, Chip Averwater, Charles Avsharian, Dmitry Badiarov, Joan
Balter, Eric Booth, Margaret Downie Banks, Bernice Singer Baron, James
Beament, Charles Beare, Ingeborg Behncke, Robert Bein, Constance
Hoffman Berman, Matthieu Besseling, Sean Bishop, Willem Blokbergen,
Dieter Boden, Beatrix Borchard, Leon Botstein, Willem Bouman, Kerry
Boylan, Rachel Baron Heimovics Braun, Henry Breitrose, Peter Brem,
Zakhar Bron, Nigel Brown, Bonny Buckley, Richard Caplan, Tina Carri-
ère, Susan Demler Catalano, Choon-Jin Chang, Roger Chase, James Chris-
tensen, Mark Churchill, Floriana Colabattista, Anne Cole, Michael Cope,
Jeffrey Cox, Joseph Curtin, Michael Darnton, Dorothy DeLay, Andrew
Dipper, John Dilworth, Eugene Drucker, Christiane Edinger, Cyril
Ehrlich, Heidrun Eichler, Martin Eifler, Linda Anne Engelhardt, Toby
Faber, Rosa Fain, Isabelle Faust, David Finckel, Michael Fleming, Guust
François, Robert Freeman, Todd French, David Fulton, Geoffrey Fushi,
Diana Gannett, David Garrett, Madurai Ginanasundaram, Bernd Gell-
ermann, Frances Gillham, Ivry Gitlis, Claire Givens, Raymond F. Glover,
Rachel Goldstein, Peter Greiner, Ilan Gronich, Andreas Grütter, Bruno
Guastalla, Ida Haendel, Don Haines, Gisela Hammig, Roger Hargrave,
Brian Harvey, Joji Hattori, Jay Heifetz, David Hempel, Peter Herrmann,
Julian Hersh, Stefan Hersh, Klaus Heymann, Ulf Hoelscher, Wolfgang
Höritsch, Andrew Hooker, Peter Horner, Regina Imatdinova, Tim Ingles,
Anne Inglis, Peter Jaffe, D. Martin Jenni, V.N. Jog, Maya Jouravel, David
Juritz, Joachim Kaiser, Serge Karpovich, Philip J. Kass, Ani Kavafian,
Ida Kavafian, Anastasia Khitruk, Benny Kim, Wonmi Kim, Dai-Sil Kim
Gibson, Alix Kirsta, Peter Klein, Jürgen Kocka, Renate Köckert, Jennifer
Koh, John Koster, Allan Kozinn, Udo Kretzschmann, Jerome Kuehl, Laura
LaCombe, Jaime Laredo, André Larson, Harold Laster, Joel Lazar, Claude
Lebet, Norman Lebrecht, Carol Lee, Erin Lehman, Florian Leonhardt, Wal-
ter Levin, S. B. Lewis, Li Dan, Joseph Lin, Liu Yang, Margot Lurie, Diet-
mar Machold, Hans Maile, John Malyon, Andrew Manze, Mike Margolin,
Philip Margolis, Humphrey Maud, Margaret Mehl, Eduard Melkus, John
Menninger, Henry Meyer, Amanda Mitchell-Boyask, Geraldo Modern,
John Monroe, Kenneth Morris, Mark Mueller, James Murphy, Yfrah Nea-
man, Miguel Negri, Jack Neihausen, Christine Nelson, Amy Ng, Takako
Nishizaki, Franz Xaver Ohnesorg, Elmar Oliveira, Annette Otterstedt,
Helena Percas de Ponseti, Mark Peterson, Stewart Pollens, Larissa Pop-
kova, Christoph Poppen, Tully Potter, David Powell, Doris Bogen Preucil,
William Preucil, Jason Price, Peter Pulzer, Guy Rabut, David Rattray, Jim

Reck, Matthew Reichert, Ruggiero Ricci, Marcel Richters, David Rivinus, Ronald Robboy, Patrick Robin, Duane Rosengard, Linda Roth, Michel Roy, Naomi Sadler, Michel Samson, Martijn Sanders, Nahma Sandrow, Steve Sanford, Keith Sarver, Kurt Sassmannshaus, Edmund Savage, Claire Scandrett, John Scandrett, Cornelia Schmid, Wendie Schneider, Michael Schoenbaum, Robert Schwartz, Josef Schwarz, Bijan Sepanji, Philip Setzer, Karen Shaffer, Eudice Shapiro, Carla Shapreau, Thomas Shires, John Sidgwick, Marc Silverstein, Dmitry Sitkovetsky, Robert Sklar, Paul Smith, Alvin Snider, Eileen Soskin, Arnold Steinhardt, Hellmut Stern, Ethan Stone, Helen Strilec, Gary Sturm, Thomas A. Suits, Christian Tetzlaff, John Topham, Gayane Torosyan, Sherrie Tucker, Henry Turner, Brigitte Unger, Russell Valentino, Josef Vedral, Maxim Viktorov, Bart Visser, John Vornle, Melvin Wachowiak, Jutta Walcher, Joshua Walden, Mark Warner, William Weber, Krzysztof Wegrzyn, Donald Weilerstein, Elmar Weingarten, Michael Weisshaar, Eduard Weissmann, Graham Wells, Daniela Wiehen, Jon Whiteley, Mark Wilhelm, Wanda Wilkomirska, Stephen Wright, Neil Whitehead, Reiko Miyasaka Yabushita, Vera Negri Zamagni, Peter Zazofsky, Robert Zimansky, and Samuel Zygmuntowicz.

INTRODUCTION
The Global Instrument

~

O N OCTOBER 5, 1962, the word *globalisation* made its English-language debut in the London weekly *The Spectator*.[1] But for anyone interested in the violin, the phenomenon, like the instrument, had been around since at least the middle of the sixteenth century.[2]

As early as 1768, Jean-Jacques Rousseau's *Dictionnaire de Musique* declared that "There is no instrument from which one obtains a more varied and universal expression."[3] Rousseau was never the easiest man in the world to agree with. But it is hard to fault his assessment.

Till well into its adolescence, the instrument's structure, even its name, were up for grabs. Known as *skrzypce* in Poland, it was called *ffidil* in Wales, *smuikas* in Lithuania, *biola* in Java. In Transylvania, they built it with three strings, in southwest Moldavia with seven. In southwestern Norway, home of the *hardingfele*, they added four or five resonating strings that vibrated sympathetically when the four primary strings were bowed.[4] Portuguese traders hauled it along from Angola to Sumatra. Celts from the Highlands to the Appalachians, Cajuns from Nova Scotia to Louisiana, could hardly get enough of it. "In Iran," declared *Grove's Dictionary of Music*, the music world's *Britannica*, "the violin is the only Western instrument to be admitted without reservation into traditional music because it is possible to play the whole of *kamanche* repertory on it." As far back as 1683, it was reported that no Hungarian gentleman was seen without a gypsy fiddler.[5] For the Waraos of Venezuela's Orinoco Delta, the love affair with the violin went back to the early eighteenth century, when they discovered that the instrument they called the *sekeseke* was as adaptable to fertility ceremonies as it was to tribal happy hours.[6]

Depending on where and when, it might be supplemented by drums, trumpets, gongs, bagpipes, mandolins, double basses, accordions, pianos and harps. In time, it would even include record players. Yet measured by what was to come, its variety and universality were only beginning to take shape.

Ironically, no one could say for sure when and where its story began. By the end of the twentieth century, there was general agreement that the violin appeared sometime between Columbus's first voyage in 1492 and the birth of Shakespeare in 1564. Like the potato, it seems to have proliferated, first across Europe, then beyond it, as Europe itself proliferated. But while the potato was clearly a New World product, the violin, for all anyone could tell, just happened.

A friend of Jean-Philippe Rameau and court composer to Louis XV, Jean Benjamin de Laborde (1734–1794) became the first to address the question of its modern provenance while working on his four-volume *Essai sur la musique ancienne et moderne*. He assigned colleagues and associates to comb the archives, then patiently—and in vain—waited a year. In the end, he yielded to his publisher and let his book appear in 1780 without an answer. "Knowing so little about something is very close to knowing nothing at all,"[7] he acknowledged wistfully. The violin was not an invention but "a growth, a survival of the fittest," the Rev. H. R. Haweis explained a century later.[8]

Since at least the nineteenth century, prototypes, cognates, and antecedents have been on view in museums and private collections from the great European capitals to the National Music Museum in Vermillion, South Dakota. Their workmanship ranges from the heartbreakingly lovely to the this-can't-be-serious, their authenticity from the proven to the conjectural to the mythological. On the threshold of the twenty-first century, genealogical traces had been found from Britain to Poland, and morphological affinities from the Alps to the Po Valley. But a conclusively demonstrable evolutionary chain remains as elusive as ever.

Whatever its origins, its impact on Western culture has been as radical in its way as that of the printing press or the steam engine. Within a few lifetimes, makers, players, composers and collectors had taken the violin to heart as one of the great breakthroughs in the history of culture, even technology. By the end of the seventeenth century, it had rerouted the course of both instrument and music making, leaving a trail of musical forms and ensembles—orchestra and string quartet, symphony, concerto, and sonata—that reached around the world. They still defined the musical landscape three centuries later.

Whoever they might be, its creators had evidently taken what the scientist and musicologist Sir James Beament called "the extraordinary properties of trees and waste material from animals, of hearing, and of musical people," mixed well, and produced a winner. A world-class entomologist and Fellow of the Royal Society, as well as an amateur bass player, self-taught acoustician, and violin-maker's spouse and father, Beament marveled at an "improbable object which has not been changed significantly since it was evolved by trial and error."

His uncommonly helpful introduction demystified the spruce and maple that are the instrument's primary materials; the vibrating strings that are its motor; the varnish that preserves the wood; the glue that holds it together, as well as the neural processes it activates in its players and listeners. Like predecessors from Mongolia to Egypt, it remained a box of air, designed to amplify a vibrating string. But no previous box had shown itself to be so comprehensively adaptable and desirable to so many people in so many ways, while appealing to virtually every sensory organ but the tongue.[9]

Five centuries after its appearance, it remained one of the few baroque objects still in common daily use.[10] In 1983, Don Haines, a University of Iowa violinist in a billowing tunic, delivered Vittorio Monti's ever-popular "Csárdás" to a cheering crowd at a Big 10 football game, accompanied by the University of Iowa marching band. In 2009, Glenn Donnellan, a violinist with the National Symphony, tricked out a Louisville Slugger, Derek Jeter model, with strings, bridge, pegs, and an electronic pickup, and fiddled "The Star-Spangled Banner" for a delighted crowd at Washington's Nationals Park and YouTube viewers around the world.[11]

The new instrument merged design and materials, science, art, and craftsmanship in a marriage seemingly made in heaven. Like a baby, the violin could be made virtually anywhere. Legend to the contrary, the younger Giuseppe Guarneri (1698-1744), known as del Gesù, did not make violins in jail. But Geoffrey Allison, a U.S. Army medic who brought wood with him to Iraq and ordered more from a war zone, made six violins alongside his bunk during a thirteen-month tour in 2005–6.[12] If empirical experience pointed to maple and spruce as the optimal raw materials for the purpose, whalebone, matchsticks, and aluminum could also do the job. Confined to a German POW camp, Clair Cline, an American flier shot down over Holland in World War II, produced a violin from bed slats.[13]

Portable and resilient, the instrument was also startlingly tough. A plane crash in 1949 that silenced the violinist Ginette Neveu also silenced her Stradivari. A crash in 1953 that killed the violinist Jacques Thibaud silenced his. But the same year, a 1743 Carrodus Guarneri (named for the British violinist John Carrodus) survived the New Mexico car crash that killed its owner, the Austro-American Ossy Renardy; and a 1732 Stradivari known as the Red Diamond survived near drowning off the coast of California.

Swept out to sea by a freak storm as its owner, Sascha Jacobsen, then concertmaster of the Los Angeles Philharmonic, drove home, the Red Diamond was discovered the next day on a beach three miles to the north by a music-loving lawyer. His wife had meanwhile heard the news of its loss on the radio. They immediately rushed the waterlogged Strad to Hans Weisshaar, a protégé of the legendary restorer Simone Fernando Sacconi, and the only world-class restorer west of Chicago. Patience and some seven hundred hours of work saved the Red Diamond, while incidentally turning Weisshaar into a legend of the profession.[14] In 2008, the young German-American David Garrett slipped on a flight of stairs at London's Barbican Centre and landed on his 1772 Guadagnini. In this case, it was estimated that J&A Beare in London would need eight months and £60,000 to do what needed doing. Despite three major and several minor cracks, there was never any doubt that the Guadagnini would recover.[15]

The instrument's fretless design allowed unimpeded movement over a four-octave continuum of pitches, correct or otherwise. Four strings, tuned in fifths, accommodated the diatonic scale to four fingers. They also simplified movement from string to string. Arches and sides, "substantially over-engineered, as so many things in the past sensibly were," as Beament noted,[16] accommodated the odd stresses imposed by the downward thrust of the bridge. By 1840, the year of the Italian violinist and composer Niccolò Paganini's death, string tensions imposed a stress equivalent to 35–44 kilograms. They were to go back down to 25–30 kilograms; but this was still the equivalent in weight of an eight- or nine-year-old child on an instrument whose total weight (pegs, bridge, strings, and tailpiece included) is 450–500 grams. Given a great instrument with modern strings and correct alignment of its seventy or so parts, the engineering paid off in a tone—as insinuating as the voice of conscience or the serpent in Eden, and as complex and individual as wine—that could still be heard over large orchestras in spaces as large as London's 5,226-seat Royal Albert Hall.

Add the bow. Long, short, straight, or curved in either direction, it allowed a range of color and articulation equally adaptable to church, theater, courtly entertainment, salon, saloon, and country crossroads. The only limits were the imagination of the composer and the performer. Half a century before Johann Sebastian Bach's benchmark solo sonatas and partitas, the virtuoso-composer Heinrich Ignaz Franz Biber (1644–1704) showed musical Salzburg how bow and violin together could manage chords, even multiple voices, in every key. A century later, Paganini and innumerable successors showed dazzled audiences from the Hebrides to St. Petersburg how the left as well as the right hand could pluck strings, in principle combining some of the more spectacular effects of the lute and harp.

Furious in the 1870s about federal troops coming to evict him from a homestead built on land reserved for the Osage nation, Charles Ingalls, Laura Ingalls Wilder's father, shouldered his fiddle and met them with a rousing chorus of "The Battle Cry of Freedom."[17] But the fiddle would have met the challenge just as well had he opted for a gavotte, waltz, polka, reel, foxtrot, mambo, or raga. The product of an African-American tradition reaching back to slavery, the Kansas City Blues Strummers's 1926 recording of "Broken Bed Blues"[18] documents still more things in heaven and earth than were dreamt of in European fiddle philosophy.

Standing or sitting, for better or worse, at any latitude, longitude, or time of day, the violin could be played solo or in groups, by royalty or rustics, artists or entertainers, professionals or amateurs, adults or children, men or women, American slaves or Russians serfs. Compelled to compensate for an early childhood injury and carpal tunnel syndrome, Rudolf Kolisch, a mid-twentieth-century champion of new music, and Reinhard Goebel, a late twentieth-century champion of early music, even played it the other way around, with the violin in the right hand and the bow in the left.

Above all, the violin could sing like nothing to date save the human voice. "Is it not strange," Shakespeare's Benedick observes sourly at an extended house party, "that sheeps' guts should hale souls out of men's bodies?"[19] With f-holes superimposed on a nude female back, Man Ray's iconic photo of 1924 compares the violin to a woman. "Like the notes of a fiddle, she sweetly, sweetly raises the spirits, and charms our ears," says Macheath, the antihero of John Gay's "Beggar's Opera (1728)," comparing a woman to the violin.[20]

As early as 1540, violins were played professionally in a string band imported from Italy by King Henry VIII as accompaniment at courtly dances.[21] In 1603, they were heard at the funeral of Queen Elizabeth.[22] Four years later, for the first time ever, Claudio Monteverdi, a native of Cremona and the era's greatest composer, deployed a trio of violins to make a dramatic point in *Orfeo*, the first great opera. "Né temer déi ché sopra un'aurea cetra/Sol di corde soavi armo le dita . . . " ("Fear not, noble god, for I arm my fingers only with the sweet strings on a golden lyre . . . "), says the title character. Associated till now with "lively, popular but definitely down-market dance music,"[23] the violin had suddenly become the key to the gates of hell. From there to the end of his career, it remained a fixture in Monteverdi's orchestrations, as in *Il Ritorno d'Ulisse in Patria* of 1639–40, where it scores again, this time when Ulysses draws his bow on his wife's suitors.

By 1750, the violin and its siblings, the viola and cello, had effectively driven the viols, lutes, lyres, and all other historical contenders into attics, museums, and oblivion, where they would remain till the rediscovery of early music on early instruments about 150 years later. First useful, then indispensable, to virtually any ensemble for any purpose short of a military band, the violin had already reached the boundaries of Europe and beyond by Rousseau's time. Even as he wrote, itinerant Italians in St. Petersburg were training locals to play Italian music on Italian violins, while Thomas Jefferson and his brother, Randolph, took up the instrument in colonial Virginia.[24]

Brian Harvey notes that military officers, like doctors, lawyers, and ecclesiastics, were regular customers of William Forster (1739–1808), a respected London violin maker.[25] Patrick O'Brian, a historical novelist of exemplary punctiliousness, let his main characters, Aubrey and Maturin, take their instruments and duets aboard, before weighing anchor and taking on Napoleon in a series that reached twenty volumes before his death in 2000.[26]

What went around came around. Josh Antonia Emidy, or Emidee, born in West Africa around 1770 and first carried off to Brazil as a slave and then brought to Portugal, became a good enough violinist to join the orchestra of the Lisbon Opera. Officers and crew of the British frigate *Indefatigable*, on shore leave in the Portuguese capital, were so impressed that they shanghaied him to be their ship's fiddler. Five years later, he was finally allowed to go ashore at Falmouth, where he seems to have played, taught, conducted, composed, and even inspired one local pupil to fervent antislavery activism, before his death in 1835.[27]

By the mid-nineteenth century, local players had introduced the violin to south Indian Carnatic music.[28] By the end of the twentieth century, India's most distinguished classical violinist acknowledged regretfully that his violin bore much of the responsibility for driving the viol-like saringhi into near extinction.[29]

By the end of the twentieth century, careers that had once been guild-ish, picturesque, and random had long since become as global as Coca-Cola. In 1967, for the first time since its creation in 1939, New York's Leventritt competition produced two winners, neither American nor European, from half a world apart. Known to the world as Pinky, Pinchas Zukerman, the eighteen-year-old from Tel Aviv, was already the third generation of a mostly male Russian-Jewish cohort who had made the twentieth-century violin world their own. Known to her teacher as Cookie, Chung Kyung-wha, the nineteen-year-old from Seoul, would soon be recognized as the founding mother of a predominantly female East Asian cohort that showed every promise of becoming its twenty-first-century successor.[30] Both had come to New York to study at the same school, Juilliard, with the same teacher, Ivan Galamian, an Iranian-born, Russian-trained Armenian who fled the Bolshevik Revolution for Paris before coming to the United States in 1937.

Would it have surprised Rousseau that an instrument, already more varied and universal than any other in his lifetime, had only become more varied and universal after his death? Probably not. Within a generation of his death, the bow had been fundamentally re-engineered for big play-ers, playing bigger pieces with bigger orchestras in bigger halls. Virtually every surviving old instrument worth owning had been retrofitted with a longer neck, tilted to allow for increased string tension, and a substantially heavier bass bar, to produce more, and a more brilliant, sound.

By the end of the eighteenth century, violin making itself had prolifer-ated across Italy and Europe. As the twentieth century dawned, Alsatian, Bavarian, Saxon, and Japanese makers flooded Eastern Europe, America, and then the world with affordable, factory-made instruments that Amer-icans could buy from the Sears, Roebuck catalogue. On the eve of the twenty-first century, an aspiring Suzuki parent could buy an entry-level Chinese fiddle over the counter at a Taoist temple in Suzhou, or the main street music store in Parma, the city where Paganini is buried. Shar Products, an Armenian-American family business in Ann Arbor, Michigan, that had become a kind of L.L. Bean of string instrument supplies, sold them online.

The familiar multipliers of a bourgeois age—urban growth, rising incomes, social mobility, professionalization, cultural snobbery, self-improvement, immigration, colonial expansion—only amplified the violin's variety and universality. New wealth and new cities created new audiences. New orchestras, operas, theaters, dance halls, as well as the movies, created new jobs for the graduates of new conservatories. New immigrants brought instruments, tastes, traditions, skills, and ambitions for their kids. European soldiers, administrators, businesspeople, doctors, teachers, missionaries spread their currencies, languages, guns, bacilli, locomotives, religions, and music to ever more non-European places.

Western music was, in fact, among the most characteristic, appealing, and potentially universal of all European products, the great German sociologist Max Weber argued in an essay-length appendix to his monumental *Society and Economy*. Knowledgeable, elliptical, and dense with undeveloped ideas, Weber's argument can only make the reader regret that he died without turning it into a book.[31] What he had in mind was the piano, an industrial product that spread the tempered diatonic scale around the world as efficiently as British looms and locomotives had spread the inch and the British thermal unit. But the dynamic that favored the piano also favored the essentially pre-industrial violin. Over almost half a millennium, it had taken root in Europe and North America; in Russia, from St. Petersburg to Odessa and Siberia; in Latin America, from Mexico to Argentina; in East Asia, from Korea to Singapore; in the Middle East and western Asia, from Israel to Turkey but also Christian Armenia, including an Armenian diaspora extending from Beirut to California.

On the threshold of the twenty-first century, the violin was as ubiquitous as McDonald's, with listed dealers and makers from every continent and at least forty-four countries.[32] Arvel Bird, a Native American Celtic violinist of Shivwit Paiute and Scottish ancestry, toured America from Chesapeake, Virginia, to Portland, Oregon, with his band, Many Tribes, One Fire, and sold many, many CDs.[33] With the end of apartheid, the violin also showed up in non-white South Africa, where a cohort of dedicated teachers, with the help of corporate sponsors, was hard at work trying to make Soweto the new Odessa.[34]

From cost to culture, there were plenty of contingent explanations for the violin's absence, rejection, or at least scarcity between Bombay and the Jordan River. There were at least as many to account for its welcome almost everywhere else. There was the appeal of identification with winners. There was its potential for adding value to marriageable daughters. There was the protean adaptability that allowed it to coexist with the Uzbek ghijak and nearly bury the Kazakh qobyz.[35] There was the all-points modernization strategy, pioneered by Japan since the 1870s, that had made Western music as Japanese as baseball and now extended from South Korea to Malaysia.[36]

In 1997 Petronas, the Malaysian national oil company, recruited a new symphony orchestra for a new concert hall, itself an accessory to the Petronas Towers in Kuala Lumpur, then the world's tallest building. Recruitment was subcontracted to IMG, a London management with global reach. Global management produced a British manager and a Dutch conductor. Global auditions produced a global orchestra. For the moment, Malaysians were hardly represented.

In part, the new orchestra seemed a response to one in Singapore.[37] In part, it looked like one more step in a national modernization strategy. Queried by an interested interviewer, a Malaysian diplomat conceded that this was the first he'd heard of the new orchestra. He then recalled that ten years earlier Petronas had imported Jackie Stewart and a Formula One racing team before there were local tracks and drivers.[38]

On the other hand, market research pointed to a Southeast Asian field of dreams, where people really would come, if a hall were built and an orchestra recruited. It was even imaginable that local players would one day play in it. In 1915, the Boston Symphony's thirty-fourth season, only eight of its players were American-born. In 1973, most of its players were native, and their conductor was Japanese. Founded in 1879 as the Shanghai Municipal Public Band, the Shanghai Municipal Orchestra accepted its first Chinese as an unpaid volunteer in 1927.[39] Founded as a mostly British ensemble in 1974, the Hong Kong Philharmonic employed three Chinese as associate concertmasters, and an almost exclusively Asian violin section a generation later.

Yet for all the tectonic changes that transformed the musical, cultural, social, and political landscapes over nearly five centuries, three propositions seemed unshakeable. According to the first, the violin appeared in Italy, spontaneous and full-blown. According to the second, the best violins, in ascending order of goodness, were Italian, Italian-built before 1800, and

Italian from Cremona. (According to the third, the rank order had never been, and could never be, any different.) All three propositions were arguable, unhistorical, and misleading. But they had at least one great and common virtue. They pointed to the story of where the violin really did come from, how the Italian violin came to be regarded as *the* violin, and who and what turned it, like no other instrument, into a global collectible, talisman, and icon.

BOOK I

Making It

HERE IS NO shortage of material for anyone interested in what the musicologist David Boyden called ". . . the fascinating, arcane and baffling world of the violin."[1] In summer 2002, a keyword search for "violin" in the Library of Congress's online catalogue produced 9,976 titles. A follow-up in the more expansive Research Libraries Information Network produced 104,881.

From Alf to Zygmuntowicz, a Google search led to every imaginable dimension of the instrument's impact and the people associated with it. Among 855 listings were makers and sellers of violins and bows of every kind and quality, dealers in related goods and services, from horsehair and massage to endoscopic surgery, players from baroque to bluegrass, teachers for every age and level of skill, museum collections, online auctions, iconography, discographies, and stolen instrument directories, the majority with sound, high-resolution graphics, and links to still more websites, most of them in English.

Any serious research library also offered monographs, manuals, methods, memoirs, medical advice, and catalogues. There was how-to literature extending from Dr. Suzuki's "Twinkle, Twinkle" for toddlers to Heinrich Wilhelm Ernst's polyphonic studies for the violin's equivalent of .350 hitters, 3.55 milers, and winners of the Wimbledon singles. There were stories and novels extending from Lloyd Moss's *Zin! Zin! Zin! A Violin*[2] for readers four to eight to the gothic and potentially R-rated. There were court reports and price lists going back at least to the nineteenth century, and player biographies and instrument histories going back to the seventeenth. Wax cylinder recordings of Joseph Joachim (1831–1907) and Maud Powell (1868–1920) were now available on CDs and CD-ROMs. Brief impressions of Fritz Kreisler (1875–1962) and Eugène Ysaÿe (1858–1931), filmed in the era of Rudolph Valentino and *The Perils of Pauline*, were available in VHS and DVD and on YouTube. Yet the violin's origins were still as obscure and suggestive as they were for Laborde.

If many titles can be called, few could be chosen as reliable, despite the best efforts of their authors. The question of how the violin evolved and where it came from had engaged, fascinated, and puzzled pioneer investigators from François-Joseph Fétis, the nineteenth-century polymath and conservatory builder, to Curt Sachs, the father of modern organology a century later. Of deepest interest to George Hart, the great Victorian expert and a major London dealer, it was of no less interest to amateurs like the Rev. H. R. Haweis and the novelist Charles Reade, who pursued it with much the same gusto that contemporaries like Thomas Henry Huxley and Bishop Samuel Wilberforce brought to the origin of species.

Fétis in Brussels and Joseph Joachim, a virtuoso turned professor in Berlin, made sure that new conservatories acquired instruments in the same way the newly endowed museums acquired bones, fossils, and rocks. Konstantin Tretiakov, a pioneer industrialist, collector, and philanthropist, not only made over some thirty old Italian instruments to Nikolai Rubinstein, the director of the Moscow conservatory, but commissioned new instruments from the French violin makers Georges Chanot and Auguste Bernardel.[3]

In 1872, much of respectable Britain showed up at what would soon become London's Victoria and Albert Museum to see and be seen at a benchmark exhibition of pre-1800 European lutherie. The organizing committee of forty-five included the queen's second son, the Duke of Edinburgh; Jean-Baptiste Vuillaume, the great French violin maker; Mr. A. Sullivan, the composer; and M. Ambroise Thomas, director of the Paris Conservatory. For those who couldn't make it, the *Pall Mall Gazette*, an evening daily, hired Reade to cover it in some fourteen thousand words. A decade later, the museum acquired a collection that its website still pointed to with pride in 2010, when it also announced that the collection would be dispersed to other museums or relocated in permanent storage to accommodate the V&A's growing collection of fashions and costumes.[4]

The acquisition testified to the breadth and depth of Victorian public interest. In 1882, Carl Engel, a wealthy German collector and amateur music historian, died in London, leaving an unpublished study of the violin and its ancestors and 201 instruments, among them Northumberland bagpipes, a Spanish bandurria, a Norwegian Hardanger fiddle, a heap of viols, and what was believed to be a sixteenth-century German violin.[5] His nephew and executor, Carl Peters, later an unsuccessful English Channel swimmer and pioneer of what would become German East Africa, saw to publication of the study.[6] He then sold "the stuff," as the violin maker, restorer, and historian John Dilworth would refer to it a few generations later,[7] to the Victoria & Albert. The purchase price, £556/6s, was enough at the time to buy a Stradivari.[8]

The collection was still a challenge to researchers a century later. The sources themselves were one problem. Strewn like glacial moraine across much of Europe, they include instruments, pieces of instrument, furniture samples, text references in a buffet of languages, and images in virtually every medium but photography.

Qualified historians were the other. All kinds of disciplines—political history, medieval history, art history, geology, paleology, chemistry—had been professionalized since the mid-nineteenth century. But violin history, the domain of artisan-dealers since the late eighteenth century, was still in amateur hands well into the twentieth century.

The conjunction of workbench perspective and amateur enthusiasm left lasting marks. Energized by the glory of a still recent Cremonese past and the risks and opportunities of the turbulent Parisian present, pioneer investigators, whose lives reached from the sunset of the ancien régime to the coming of the railroad and telegraph, blazed the trail of violin history.

Laborde, a court official, who fell victim to the guillotine in 1794, contributed a definitive anthology of what was known to date. Sébastien-André Sibire, a cleric who provided the necessary liturgical utensils for King Louis XVI's final mass and survived the Revolution,[9] published *La Chélomonie ou le parfait luthier*,[10] an essay on violin making aimed at an audience that took reconnection with the great Italian tradition at least as seriously as the victories of Napoleon. Fétis, who knew everyone worth knowing, left monographs on Paganini and J.-B. Vuillaume, a superstar violin maker and dealer,[11] whose shaky credibility is roughly equivalent to Mason Locke Weems's version of George Washington, and William Herndon's of his onetime law partner, Abraham Lincoln. But unlike the first trio, who wrote history, a second trio, of Ignazio Cozio di Salabue (1755–1840), Luigi Tarisio (c. 1790–1854), and Vuillaume (1798–1875), actually made it.

In 1771, the young Count Cozio, a Piedmontese landowner, inherited a notable collection of classic instruments from his father. The experience turned him into a major collector in his own right. He had a lively interest in trading and dealing, and a determination to learn everything possible about the great Cremonese makers and their shops while there was still living memory of them.

In 1824, as Cozio's interest faded, the equally obsessive Luigi Tarisio, from a family as plebian as Cozio's was patrician, began acquiring items from Cozio's collection. From 1827 until his death in 1854, he then marketed them, and as many other classic instruments as he could find, in Paris.[12] His strategy was classically simple: buy cheap in Italy, where the instruments now enjoyed little apparent worth, then sell dear north of the Alps, where dealers couldn't get enough of them. What might have happened if Cozio had gone straight from the military academy to the Piedmontese local history that was the passion of his old age,[13] or Tarisio had been run over by a stagecoach en route from Milan to Paris, is the violin world equivalent of what might have happened had the French won at Waterloo or the Confederates at Gettysburg.

The trade was ". . . perhaps the only craft in the world in which the old is more consistently admired than the new, and the maintenance more difficult than the construction,"[14] Sibire declared, quoting the great French violin maker Nicolas Lupot (1758–1824). From Tarisio on, violin history as construed and constructed by himself and Cozio became canonic as it was passed from dealer to dealer and generation to generation like a family album.

Their vision inevitably reflected their own age of heroic individuals, ascendant nations, and worshipful regard for the Italy of the Renaissance. A century would pass before it was seriously challenged. As late as 1984, the editor of an otherwise respectable handbook still attributed the violin to "an unknown Italian genius, somewhere near Milan, [who] conceived and built the first violin" sometime ". . . during the early 1500's."[15] As late as 2002, a website listed in Google still offered a high-resolution view of the "famous Duomo Apse in the birthplace of the violin, Cremona."[16]

Meanwhile, a platoon of presumptive inventors, some famous, some not, fell to new research. Among them were the Brescian patriarch Gasparo Bertolotti, also known as da Salò (1540–1609), the Cremonese patriarch Andrea Amati[17] (c. 1505–1577), Caspar Tieffenbrucker (1514–c. 1571), a Bavarian known to French and Italians as Gaspard Duiffoprugcar, and Jean Kerlino, a Breton, who may or may not have been invented by Vuillaume.[18] "Better no facts at all than spurious ones," an early twentieth-century commentator wrote.[19]

In time, Cozio and Tarisio would be succeeded by professionals of real distinction, just not as professional historians. Margaret Lindsay Murray, who pioneered astronomical spectroscopy with her spouse, Sir William Huggins, wrote a groundbreaking monograph on the Brescian master

Giovanni Paolo Maggini (c. 1580–c. 1630).[20] Fascinated by an inherited cello, Brian Harvey, author of the standard text on auction law as a professor at the University of Birmingham, produced an exemplary social history of the violin in Britain and was the coauthor of the standard work on violin fraud.[21] A bass player in the Philadelphia Orchestra, Duane Rosengard parlayed curiosity about his own instrument into codiscovery of the great Antonio Stradivari's will and a benchmark biography of Giovanni Battista Guadagnini (1711–1786).[22]

Still others wrote violin history as local history. Carlo Bonetti, a retired army officer, unearthed archival documentation on Stradivari that no one had seen for four hundred years.[23] Bernhard Zoebisch, a dentist in Markneukirchen, produced a model history of violin making in the Vogtland.[24]

On the eve of the twentieth century, the three Hill brothers of London, the era's emblematic dealers, launched a new scholarly epoch with a series of handsomely produced and lovingly illustrated monographs on the emblematic makers that they sold directly to subscribers. They were still available in paperback and prominent on every serious dealer's bookshelf a century later.[25] For the first time, oral tradition was supplemented by archival research, much of it by hired researchers. That the Hills were the publishers was another novelty. Successors made the subscriber monograph a trade staple.

The first of the Hill set appeared in 1892, its authorship outsourced to Lady Huggins, whose appreciative sponsors named a 1707 Strad in her honor.[26] The Hills themselves did the others, Stradivari in 1902, the Guarneris in 1931. A volume on the Amatis, though apparently intended, never made it to publication.[27] It was the first time since the instruments were built that anybody had not only deplored but documented the "indiscriminate abuse" inflicted on old instruments that was "unfortunately all the rage at the time," as a grateful Italian noted a century later.[28]

The next leap, to the threshold of academic historiography, would have to await another generation. In 1965, David Boyden, a University of California musicologist, published *The History of Violin Playing from Its Origins to 1761*. A resourcefully documented, imaginatively argued, and engagingly written overview of violin, bow, maker, player, composer, market, and audience from the earliest documented beginnings to the introduction of the modern bow, it launched another epoch. Yet another generation later, Sylvette Milliot showed what a professional musicologist, raised in the shadow of the Annales school of French social history, could accomplish with multiple generations of Chanot-Chardons, the family of French makers.[29] But there were few historians to match her.

Instead, as John Dilworth noted, violin history remained the preserve of three complementary but essentially adversarial constituencies that came to it by different routes for different reasons.[30] From Vuillaume to modern authorities like Charles Beare, the late twentieth century's flagship dealer, or Philip J. Kass, a Philadelphia-based expert and appraiser, the first and oldest of them came directly from the trade. Relative newcomers, the second, like Dilworth and his English contemporaries Roger Hargrave and Andrew Dipper, were makers, copyists, and restorers. The third, from Fétis to his fearlessly tough-minded Belgian successor Karel Moens a century and a half later, were curators with academic credentials.

All three shared an interest in provenance and authenticity. But, as Dilworth was quick to point out, each also regarded the others with deep and plausible suspicion. Dealers wanted to sell things. Makers and restorers wanted to make the unplayable playable and create credible alternatives to the dealers' ever more expensive originals. Curators and musicologists wanted to get the story right and keep things as they were.

Charles Beare's experience in the late 1990s with an unreconstructed violin by the Bolognese Carlo Tononi showed what could happen when curatorial scruple collided with the facts of life. As a fourth-generation dealer with a profound sense of history as well as a profound respect for his product, Beare would have liked nothing better than to sell it as he found it to an early music player. But early music players, he acknowledged regretfully, were an "impecunious lot" and he had rent, salaries, insurance, heat and light to consider. After waiting in vain for a customer, he finally did what generations of predecessors had done. He fitted the Tononi with a modern scroll and neck and sold it without a problem. But unlike most of his predecessors, he included the original neck in the package, on the chance that a future owner might want to consider a retrofit.[31]

The limits of professional synergy could be seen again at a symposium in Washington in early 2001. The object this time was to decode the decorations that distinguish a small but notable collection of Stradivaris, built between 1687 and 1722 and bequeathed to the Smithsonian's Museum of American History in 1997 by Herbert R. Axelrod, a New Jersey collector and patron.[32] So far as anyone could tell, it was the first time a group like this had ever got together for the purpose. Panelists, including curators, dealers, art historians, even a materials expert, were rounded up from Tokyo, Chicago, and Philadelphia.

The answer was of particular interest to Gary Sturm, curator of instruments in the Smithsonian's Division of Cultural History. Apart from a few random examples and an analogous set in Madrid, the collection is virtually unique. Of the hundreds of stringed instruments Stradivari produced, only eleven were ornamented.[33] Yet the motifs were a mystery, perhaps because they were so obvious to Stradivari and his contemporaries that an explanation seemed unnecessary.

The heraldry and decorative arts experts spotted clues but had no definitive answer. The dealers were knowledgeable about the architecture and anatomy of Stradivari instruments. They also knew whose hands the instruments had passed through, could certify their authenticity, assess their state of preservation and, of course, estimate their market value. But decorations were something they didn't think or particularly care about. So there was no answer from them, either.

Due to a fiscal crunch that hit the Smithsonian a few weeks later, there was no follow-up conference. Six years would pass before Stewart Pollens, who had not even been there, answered the question, at least to a point. Once curator of instruments at New York's Metropolitan Museum and now a private consultant, he located the source of the decorations in a collection of embroidery and sewing patterns published in Venice in 1567.[34]

Energized by a bull market, a change in musical taste, and increasingly informed curiosity, new research was meanwhile both sought and rewarded as never before. Since the nineteenth century, prices had consistently risen or leveled off, and since the 1960s, they had soared dramatically. Since World War II, interest in music written before 1800 had also soared.[35] The demand for old violins to buy and old violins to play rose in tandem.

As growing demand chased limited supply, authenticity inevitably became an issue, and credible expertise became a crucial comparative advantage. Born of an eminently practical concern for assuring customers that they really got what they paid ever more for, demand for research in the lives, methods, and business practices of first-, second-, then third-tier old masters soared, too. The new global market, extending beyond anything the Hills ever imagined, only confirmed that knowledge could be money as well as power. Dealers, makers, restorers, and curators alike had reason to be pleased.

Where there were old violins, there was likely to be restoration. Pummeled and perspired on by players, abused and neglected by collectors, relished by woodworms, held hostage by humidity, oxidation, and their own built-in stresses, and victimized by disastrous repairs and nominal improvements, virtually all instruments older than their owners had begged for attention since Tarisio first brought them to Paris. For the first time, demand for historically informed restoration coincided with some real possibility of achieving it.[36]

Quality copies were another option. Be they acknowledged or covert, good, bad, or off the assembly line, there had been a market for them since Italian instruments became the gold standard. Copies by British masters such as Bernhard Simon Fendt (1800–1852), the wonderfully colorful John Lott (1804–1870), and the legendary Voller family had come to be appreciated for their own sake, and Vuillaumes, once scorned as phony Stradivaris, were cherished as original Vuillaumes. With their exhaustively researched, thoughtfully modified, exquisitely reproduced, and convincingly antiqued copies of the classics, Sam Zygmuntowicz argued in 1995, modern makers like himself, born in 1956, and his contemporaries Dilworth and Hargrave, were latter-day Vuillaumes with what was essentially a four-point program. The first was to satisfy demand for a scarce commodity that had already lost much of its original substance en route through innumerable hands, shops, and repairs. The second was to educate themselves in historical techniques and modern materials. The third was to advance their technical skills by raising the bar to ever more challenging levels. The last was to increase acceptance of new instruments by buffering their unfamiliarity.[37]

The coming of the early music players only added to the fun. By the end of the twentieth century, orchestra rosters, complete with instrument listings, had become a regular feature of early music performance. With their juxtaposition of old old instruments and new old instruments —". . . Jacopo Brandini, Pisa, 1793, David Rubio, Cambridge, 1989, David Tecchler, Rome 1780, German 1750, George Stoppani, 1989 . . . "[38]—they were often as entertaining as the performance.

Museums from Berlin, Brussels, Paris, Oxford, South Kensington, and Vienna to Moscow, Taipei and Vermillion, South Dakota, completed the virtuous circle. Institutions created to preserve history had now become places where it was made. Energetic, underemployed, and academically certified early music players looked to them for jobs. They made it their mission to decode the relics, masterpieces, and indeterminate artifacts entrusted to their care. Historically minded violin makers, who were often their peers and contemporaries, looked to them for material and insights. "Wandering the many floors of the museum put me in mind of a Victorian fossil," Dilworth reflected after a tour of the Brussels Museum. "Does this rib belong here, and is this antediluvian-looking multi-string hulk a true ancestor, an evolutionary dead-end or an outright fake?"[39]

"My whole life is about getting these wonderful things out of their cases and making them understandable," explained Annette Otterstedt, a curator at Berlin's Historical Instrument Museum, when asked what she did. "This is why I ask for accurate reconstruction, because it recovers a lost skill that we can always use, if our hands and heads aren't to become vestigial."[40]

The results were engagingly paradoxical. At the frontier of a five-hundred-year-old profession, contemporary makers now built old instruments with modern technologies, even composite materials, and marketed them on the Internet. Meanwhile, like human evolution, the origins of the instrument, along with generations of received wisdom, were pushed back ever further into the past.

"The violin was not born of a single parent, but evolved from several early in the sixteenth century," Boyden wrote in 1965.[41] Otterstedt added a generation later: "What we know . . . is that neither a painter, nor an inspired discoverer 'invented the hallowed form of the violin,' but that it resulted from a process extending over centuries, whose diversity we should welcome, not repress."[42]

A STAR IS BORN

THE SEARCH FOR the origins would lead to a new world of tangled genealogy, evolving architecture, alternative models, and a landfill, where generations of received wisdom came to rest. Yet virtually all routes lead back
to the sawmill and the Silk Road.

Known in Roman times, the sawmill had apparently been forgotten
for most of a millennium before its cautious reappearance in the twelfth
century. But it seems to have spread rather quickly from the fourteenth
century on. With finished boards and planks now generally available,
woodworking skills proliferated,[43] leading to whole new trades, crafts, and
branches, which sorted themselves out in guilds.

Furniture, cabinet, and box making are practical examples.[44] Instrument making was a natural spin-off, with a hereditary link to box making
still evident as late as 1716, when one Giovanni Guidante, also known as
Fiorino, identified himself in a Bolognese court document as a maker of
violins and tobacco boxes.[45] In some places, like Strasbourg, instrument
makers were accepted as joiners or box makers. In others, like Nuremberg, joiners worked hard to keep them out. In still others, like Augsburg,
the trades collided. In 1559, charges were brought against a lutemaker
who took jobs associated with box making. Three years later, charges were
brought against a violin maker, who outsourced violin parts to a joiner.[46]
The same year, in Füssen, a lute-making center on the edge of the Alps,
instrument makers formed their own guild to protect themselves from
competition, at least partly engendered by themselves.[47]

Rediscovered on the threshold of the twenty-first century as antiquity's
Internet, the Silk Road, too, went back to Roman times. Till the discovery
of the New World some 1,500 years later, it linked China with Byzantine
Constantinople, also known as Ottoman Istanbul. Via Central Asia, the

Caspian Sea, and the Persian Gulf, it then merged with another, predominantly Islamic distribution system, extending to the Atlantic.

While traffic favored goods of all kinds, there was also a robust commerce in arts, skills, and ideas, including music. Various plucked and bowed string instruments along the route such as the dombra, rebab, and Persian spiked fiddle are still in use from Uzbekistan to Queens.[48] Others, like the lute and rebec, surfaced in Moorish Spain, where they coexisted with the vihuela, another imported product, possibly from France or Flanders.[49] In Spain, all three found their way to Sephardic Jews, who took them along when they decamped to Lombardy and the Veneto, southern Germany, the Netherlands, and Britain after their expulsion from Spain in 1492.[50]

The harpsichordist and musicologist Thurston Dart (1921–1971) inferred that the plucked vihuela de mano and bowed vielle then generated a hybrid—in effect, a bowed guitar. With Spanish illustrations to confirm its point of departure, the hybrid made its way to Italy, possibly with Catalans en route to Rome, or just as possibly with Sephardic Jewish refugees en route to Venice or Milan.[51]

The best of all possible sources would be surviving instruments. But in the real world, where makers and restorers downsized, refinished, regraduated, and cannibalized old instruments for centuries, few survived at all, let alone intact, according to Karel Moens, the Antwerp curator, whose investigations made him the avenging angel of the new violin history.[52]

An authentic and virtually unreconstructed sixteenth-century ensemble in the restored gothic cathedral of Freiberg, a Saxon town on the flank of the Erzgebirge, was a rare exception. As dear to organologists as a perfectly preserved brontosaurus might be to paleontologists, it included a small three-stringed and a large four-stringed violin, a viola, and a small and a large three-stringed bass.[53] The style was as consistent with the homemade models typical of itinerant player-makers as it was different from the Cremonese product that would become standard. It remained common to cheap German instruments as late as 1900.[54]

At the other end of the authenticity scale are twenty-odd surviving instruments, known or assumed to be the work of Andrea Amati (c. 1505–1577), Cremona's founding patriarch, whose birthdate itself is a matter of conjecture. In 2007, a consort of specialists, including a maker-historian, an art historian, an instrument historian, an electrochemist, and a dealer-publisher met in Cremona to commemorate the five hundredth anniversary—give or take a few years—of Amati's birth. They agreed that he had been a solid citizen, an inspired craftsman, and an exemplary businessman. Virtually everything else was up for grabs, even including a generally acceptable translation of an apparently programmatic Latin slogan painted on five of the surviving instruments. Who ordered them, and when and where they were painted, remained a mystery.

The other notable challenge was a legendary ensemble of twelve large and twelve small violins, six violas, and eight cellos, of which eight more surviving instruments were supposed to be a part. Presumably bought by or for the court of Charles IX (1550–1574) of France, they had generated a substantial literature, from Sibire to the Hills, who bequeathed a violin and viola, assumed to come from the French royal collection, to the Ashmolean Museum in Oxford.

The instruments were historically associated with the formidable Catherine de' Medici (1519–1589), who left her native Florence at fourteen to marry into the French court, where she became queen consort of King Henry II, then regent on behalf of her ten-year-old son, Charles IX. With a passion for dance and ritual and allegorical entertainment that virtually assured demand for violins and full employment for violinists,[55] she had effectively turned the French court into a colony of Italian culture by the middle of the sixteenth century. How the instruments were commissioned and paid for, and how many were made and delivered, remains a question.

Moens and others have expressed skepticism about the connection to Cremona, the size of the order, and the capacity of Amati's shop. But there are more or less plausible answers to his reservations. In 1816, Cozio claimed ownership of a three-stringed violin by Andrea Amati, a credible indicator of its antiquity. In 1898, Gaetano Sgarabotto (1878–1959), a distinguished Italian violin maker, reportedly repaired another. A royal Tour de France between 1562 and 1564 left behind a trail of monumental arches and allegorical columns that matched the iconography on the presumed Amati violins.[56] Records confirm that in 1572, when Amati's was still the only known shop in Cremona, a French court player was dispatched with 50 lire to buy a Cremonese violin "for the service of the king."[57] Between 1555 and 1573, the roster of imported Italian violinists at the French court grew from five or six to thirty, a credible metric of demand.[58] At a production rate of one month for a violin and three for a cello, and family members, apprentices in various stages of training, and hired staff to back up the master, it was also possible for the shop to handle an order of this size within ten years.[59]

Whether the nominal Amatis still on view in England, Italy, and the United States are what they claim to be was another question. Moens, who examined them, noted significant structural inconsistencies among them. He also found indications that all of them had been repeatedly, heavily, and anonymously worked on, as well as countless inconsistencies between nineteenth-century descriptions and what was now on view.[60] Whatever its outcome, it could at least be argued that the debate was its own reward. If the Charles IX instruments were authentic, so much the better. If not, the debate was an incentive and launching pad for more research.

For modern researchers, surviving images and texts have been at least a helpful supplement to surviving instruments. By a happy coincidence, the origins of the violin coincide with the introduction of printing. Three canonic handbooks confirm and document the violin's arrival and progress.

The first is by Martin Agricola (c. 1486–1556), a German Protestant, whose handbook of contemporary usage, *Musica Instrumentalis Deudsch*, went through four printings between 1529 and 1542, followed by a revised version in 1545. Of particular interest are references to a fretless instrument, tuned in fifths, that shows up as one of a family of four, and can even be played with vibrato. A woodcut in the first edition shows a three-stringed Polish instrument, startlingly similar to one painted almost concurrently by Gaudenzio Ferrari of Vercelli in northern Italy.[61]

The second is by Philibert Jambe de Fer (c. 1515–c. 1566), a Protestant from Lyon, who composed psalms, organized the music for the entry of the fourteen-year-old Charles IX into the author's hometown, and published his landmark of organology, *Epitome musical des tons, sons et accordz, es voix humaines, fleustes d'Alleman, fleustes à neuf trous, violes & violons*, in 1556. "Why do you call one type of instrument viols and the other violins?" the author asks rhetorically. "We call viols those with which gentlemen, merchants, and other virtuous people pass their time . . . ," is the answer. "The other type is called violin; it is commonly used for dancing and with good reason, for it is much easier to tune." The instrument is conveniently portable, "a very necessary thing while leading [*conduisant*] wedding processions or mummeries." But it is little used, he adds, save by "those who make a living from it through their labor."[62]

The third is an overview of contemporary instruments by Michael Praetorius (1571–1621), a prodigiously energetic German organist who was also a hymn composer, amateur theologian, and pioneer musicologist. "And since everyone knows about the violin family, it is unnecessary to indicate or write anything further about it," the author remarks in a much-cited passage from the second volume of his four-volume *De Organographia*, published in 1618. Within three generations, a three-string innovation, first spotted concurrently in Magdeburg and Vercelli, had become a four-string part of the landscape. The fitness that favored the survival of this particular species and the dynamic that favored the transfer of its technology were still worth thinking about four centuries later.

At least part of the answer was disarmingly simple. Even in an early modern Europe, where most people lived and died without ever seeing the world beyond the horizon, cities stayed within their walls, and enterprise of every kind was cocooned within the constraints of a feudal constitution, people, things, and ideas got around. Networks born of war brought Spanish, French, and Austrian armies to Italy. Networks born of commerce brought Tyrolean instrument makers from the Alpine village of Füssen to Venice, Rome, and Padua.[63] Networks born of art brought the composer Orlando di Lasso to successive jobs in Mantua, Milan, Palermo, Naples, Rome, Antwerp, and Munich.[64]

A second factor was a sea change from choral to instrumental polyphony that transformed both the violin and demand for it as it changed the course of European music. While cause and effect chase one another's tail, comparison of the well-documented court of Ferarra in the last quarter of the fifteenth century with the equally well-documented court of Munich a century later is at least an indicator of how, where, and when the sea change occurred.

Notable, under Duke Ercole I, for civic improvements and an intricate foreign policy, Ferrara was also conspicuous for the duke's old-fashioned piety, his court musicians, and his attention to his children's music lessons. His daughter and successor, Isabella d'Este, marchesa of Mantua from age sixteen and one of Renaissance Italy's most remarkable women, was at least as serious about music as he was.[65]

With its full schedule of liturgical observances, Carnival, jousts, horse races, university openings, and receptions for distinguished visitors, the court offered occasions enough for music. The demands of civic display account for the growth of a corps of trumpeters from six to ten between 1471 and 1478, plus four new wind players and a trombonist. Then came strings, an acknowledged Ferrarese specialty.[66] By the 1490s, Isabella's agent reported the use of larger instruments in ensembles of up to six.[67] By 1511, Holman estimates, a violin consort was operating in Ferrara.[68]

In Munich, random violinists with German names were engaged solo from at least 1519, while ensembles already prospered in the more cosmo-politan Nuremberg and Augsburg. Forty years later, concurrent with the arrival of the great composer Orlando di Lasso, Munich violinists came in sets, had Italian names, and played motets and madrigals as well as dance tunes from written music. Court records recommended Italian instru-ments, and Italian connections are plausible. Yet contemporary engravings still show violinists with instruments reminiscent of the professionally made but distinctly un-Italian ones in Freiburg.[69]

Over the next century, as court ensembles grew, violinists also appeared in the private sector, primarily as dance players. French, German, and Dutch painters and engravers regularly linked the violin to sex, booze, gluttony, stupidity, dishonesty, and indolence. Italians continued to associate it with the respectability and social cachet of court, theater, and church.[70]

A third factor in the triumph of the violin was a slow-motion trans-formation in instrument making. Evidence from the court to the street corner both north and south of the Alps points to demand for something new and better from the primeval soup of existing instruments. When the violin eventually arrived, professionals seem to have been quick to appreci-ate it. But Jambe de Fer to the contrary, they seem to have played the new instrument interchangeably with the viol. So long as both were in demand, Tyrolean, then Italian, makers made viols and violins interchangeably too. But they arrived at different solutions by different routes.

For no one could say how long, instruments held to the chest or on the shoulder had been scooped out of a single block like a little boat or canoe, though bigger instruments were necessarily made from multiple pieces. The maker then added a neck, a belly, and, in the case of larger instru-ments, a back.[71]

In an era when only guild members were allowed to use nails and glue, guildless instrument makers learned to slot the pieces into grooves and hold their products together together with pegs and dowels.[72] Moens points to vestiges of that past still visible in the extended corners where the violin's ribs meet, in the way its back and belly overhang the ribs, in its round shoulders and the way they join the neck. Though makers grew increasingly sophisticated, this technique seems to have remained standard operating procedure for both viols and violins made north of the Alps.

From there it spilled over into Italy from the Tyrol, while the technique that Moens refers to as "archaic" survived in folk instruments into the twentieth century.[73]

Bigger ensembles and instruments changed the equation. There were places where the trade flourished with professional demand, and cognate guilds coexisted and even cooperated. There were other places where instrument makers joined what they couldn't beat—for example, the local box makers. There were still more places where they organized informally.

There was also Füssen, where quality materials and skilled, seasonably underemployed labor merged in a critical mass with major merchant traffic, killing time while negotiating transshipment from road to water transport. Strategically located on a major north-south trade route, Füssen was a particular favorite of Maximilian I, the music-loving Holy Roman Emperor. Between 1497 and his death in 1517, Maximilian twice invaded Italy and waged coalition war against Venice. During virtually the same years, a stream of south German lute makers, with privileged access to the same best-quality fir and maple that went into best-quality Bavarian and Tyrolean furniture,[74] established themselves in northern Italy.

By 1500, an established diaspora of lute makers from Füssen had become a glory of Bologna.[75] By midcentury, the Tieffenbrucker family had set up shop in both France and Italy. Within a century, Italian techniques and Italian-style violins, built like lutes around inner forms by practitioners of a craft still known in France and Italy as lute making, were making their way back north.

There is no clear evidence that Italian apprentices in fact learned lute making from immigrant German masters. According to Elia Santoro, a journalist turned violin historian, the new technique reached Cremona and more generally the lower Po Valley via Venice in the early sixteenth century.[76] There is also no evidence that Italian lute makers were quick to apply the technique to violins. Ironically, the few contemporary references to Italian violins point to local versions of the northern variety.

Yet irrespective of where it came from and how it got there, the new technique was adopted with results that superseded all others in a culture and country where the violin enjoyed respect and status. For the next 250 years, Italy and the violin would enjoy a special relationship.[77]

THE GOLDEN AGE

$\backsim$

THE SPECIAL RELATIONSHIP began, as so often, with geography. Europe yearned for silk and spices. Italy linked demand with supply. The mercantile role transformed a natural entrepôt into a producer in its own right, whose very vices somehow turned themselves into virtuous circles.

Between the twelfth and sixteenth centuries, even as its duchies, city-republics and mini-principalities inextricably entangled themselves in the conflicting claims and aspirations of Roman popes and German emperors, the peninsula's flourishing towns redefined urbanity, invented diplomacy, helped revolutionize warfare, and transformed international relations.[78] Foreigners of every kind came to pray, fight, plunder, learn, buy, sell, to marvel at native ingenuity in every form, from the fork to the Sistine Chapel ceiling, to see the future, and to see the past.[79]

In time, Italians would appreciate that 1492, the year that Columbus discovered a new hemisphere; the Spanish-born Rodrigo Borgia was elected pope in Rome; Ferdinand of Aragon and Isabella of Castile conquered Granada in their joint capacity as king and queen of Spain; and Lorenzo Medici, or Lorenzo the Magnificent, died in Florence, was a watershed for them, too.

The message would be awhile in arriving. In the meantime, over a short to middle run that extended from the twelfth to the sixteenth century and continued to make Venetian establishmentarians twice as rich as their Amsterdam peers well into the seventeenth, a commodified, monetized economy generated capital, real growth, and discretionary income. Even the mercenaries known as condottieri turned out to be economic multipliers, transferring wealth to little towns like Urbino, Mantua, and Ferrara via the energetic little courts that contracted their military services. Trade, manufactures, banking, tax farming, sale of knighthoods and church offices, even other people's wars, paid off. So did land, particularly from the mid-seventeenth century on, as the North Italian manufacturing and service economy sloped off in a deflationary spiral that was to continue for two hundred years.[80] In contrast to many other places, landowners still preferred to live in town, so rural wealth continued to concentrate in urban hands.

Meanwhile, remarkably, war itself worked like a peace bonus, as belligerents adapted to the contingencies of capital-intensive mercenary forces, including the ascendancy of the defensive and cautious use of troops.[81] Richard Goldthwaite, an expert on the period, notes, for example, how Spanish and papal forces built military infrastructure in Lombardy, a first payoff. They paid in New World silver, a second payoff. By keeping other powers out of northern Italy, they kept the area comparatively stable, a third payoff, especially at a time when Italy's neighbors north of the Alps were headed for a century and more of religious civil warfare.[82]

Perhaps most remarkable, they even bore the costs of maintaining and defending their Italian protectorates. In many places, including Brescia and Cremona, sixteenth-century economic life went on as though the new masters were hardly there. The Venetian establishment actually paid less in taxes than it earned on loans.

At other times in other places, even butchers, bakers, and candlestick makers put their money in capital investments, industrial development, or foreign adventures. But all three presupposed an investor-friendly civil order, economies of scale, political will, bureaucratic initiative, and technological sophistication. All were beyond Italian reach. Instead, Italians who could afford it invested in art of every kind, public and domestic, as well as beautiful, well-made, and durable things meant to be used close to home. These were then included in daughters' dowries, bequeathed to heirs, and eventually passed on to grandchildren's grandchildren. Housing and the church, artists and artisans, were all among the beneficiaries. Like the glory of any number of the arts and crafts at which Italians excelled, Italian violin making had a good deal to do with the way supply responded to demand in a society in which inherited wealth and discretionary income coexisted with limited investment opportunities.

Yet the uniqueness of Italy only begins to cover the uniqueness of Brescia and, still more, of Cremona, the Lombard towns where the new violin seems first to have flowered. Their physical location between the Alps and the Po Valley is again an obvious place to start. Maple and spruce, the basic materials most favored by violin makers then and since, were easily available in both towns.[83] Both towns had access to waterways, a crucial comparative advantage in an era when it could cost up to twenty times as much to transport a given load by land as by water.[84] Though hard to imagine as navigable today, Brescia's stream, the Mella, flowed south-ward from the Alps. Cremona had the Po, Italy's closest approximation of a Rhine or Mississippi, linking all points between Turin and the Adri-atic. Each town, like Füssen, was also a natural exit on sixteenth-century Europe's equivalent of a north-south interstate, linking rich southern Germany with rich northern Italy. At a historical moment when Füssen was exporting instruments and makers to much of northern Italy, and Venice was changing the course of music history, while incidentally making itself "the unchallenged capital of instrumental music,"[85] a glance at the map confirms where the trade axes intersected.

History followed geography. Between the fifth and fifteenth centuries, Attila the Hun, Charlemagne, the Emperors Frederick II and Henry VII, as well as nearby Verona and Milan all laid claim to Brescia, before Filippo Visconti, the viscount of Milan, finally sold it to Venice in 1426. Save for a relatively brief French presence between 1512 and 1520, the city remained Venetian till French troops showed up again under Napoleon.

Locals could at least console themselves that a place so attractive to others must have got some things right, music among them. In 1500 there were fourteen identifiable stringed instrument makers in Brescia, includ-ing at least one supplier to Isabella's court in Mantua. The instruments, in turn, were part of a larger musical scene, including makers of wind and keyboard as well as stringed instruments, and players were taken suffi-ciently seriously that city council records in 1508 refer to a board of exam-iners established to certify their professionalism.[86]

The French assault in 1512 inflicted damage from which the city never recovered.[87] Yet instrument making seems to have risen rocketlike from the disaster. Within a half generation of what Lady Huggins refers to as "a terrible siege and sack,"[88] Brescian makers were again producing instru-ments that looked to one local writer as though created by nature rather than by human hand.[89] In 1527, Zanetto Micheli established a business that would extend over three generations and continue some eighty years. Little over a generation later, a first world-class violin maker, Gasparo Ber-tolotti (1540–1609), known as da Salò for the town he came from, had appeared on the local scene. Himself the son and nephew of makers, Berto-lotti would then pass the torch to Giovanni Paolo Maggini (1580–c. 1631), a second world-class maker, greater even than himself.

By 1561, Brescia was a town of over 41,000—compared to Florence's estimated 59,000 and Bologna's 72,000[90]—where music poured from every church and monastery, churches maintained orchestras, and the rapport between makers, players, and composers could be as close as father and son.[91] Meanwhile, as Ravasio notes, there was a revealing evolution in nomenclature. Till the middle of the fifteenth century, "violino" seems to have referred generically to stringed instruments played with a bow. Between 1578 and 1600, Bertolotti is specifically associated with violins, although he also produced violas and basses still highly regarded centuries later.[92]

In many ways the very model of an early seventeenth-century master, Maggini was born to a sixty-two-year-old landlord father who seems to have moved the family to Brescia when an elder son went into business there as a shoemaker, then remained till Paolo opened his first shop in his mid-twenties. A decade or so later, Paolo married a furrier's daughter. He fathered ten children; only four would survive him. His tax assessments for 1617–26 testify to a comfortable income from his wife's dowry and his father's estate but above all a thriving business in wood and strings as well as instruments. The proceeds not only supported a proliferating family. They maintained a second accredited master as full-time employee, a second house and shop, and three farms, with enough money left over to loan at 5 percent.[93]

Then nemesis struck again. Between 1628 and 1630, war, famine, and finally plague struck northern Italy, killing not only Maggini but the Brescian instrument trade. Some forty years would pass before Giovanni Battista Rogeri, arriving from Cremona, would open a new shop in Brescia, where he was succeeded by his son. By then, the city's historic moment had come and gone. Maggini left a son, Carlo, age six, as heir.

The plague also cost Cremona an estimated two-thirds of its population,[94] including Girolamo Amati, Andrea's son, two Amati daughters, an Amati son-in-law, and Girolamo's wife. But Nicolò (b. 1596), the youngest of Girolamo's three sons and the ninth of some twelve children, survived, if only barely. His survival made all the difference.

A few years after Maggini's death, the scientist Galileo Galilei, himself a musician's son, asked a Venetian friend to consult a knowledgeable professional on how to find a Brescian violin for his nephew, an orchestra player at the court of the Elector of Bavaria. The friend consulted the composer Claudio Monteverdi, a native Cremonese but also a string player and pioneer orchestrator, with fifty years of professional experience. Brescian violins were easy to get and a third the price of Cremona violins, Monteverdi told him. But the Cremonese were incomparably better. He also offered to look into the matter personally.[95] In the end, Galileo got a Cremonese instrument—a "singularly successful one," he was assured—for 15 ducats, handling and shipping not included. Monteverdi's position on Cremonese superiority was soon taken for given throughout Italy and the profession.

Like Brescia's, Cremona's location made it both attractive and hazardous. The Po, just beyond its gates, sometimes descended from the Alps to the Adriatic at flood stage. A pontoon bridge there connected Europe's north with Europe's south. But favorable location came at a price. In the wake of the Roman Empire, the city was repeatedly flattened by invading Goths and Huns. In the so-called High Middle Ages, its attractiveness to successive Hohenstaufen emperors made it a ping-pong ball in the open-ended war of Guelphs and Ghibellines. As Italy's intramural wars morphed into European proxy wars, Cremona found itself a hinge between three of the new era's great powers, Spain, Austria, and France.

Imperial favor was another mixed blessing. Between 1499 and 1535, a crucial generation in the genesis of the violin, the city changed hands three times. At last, after sixty-five years of locally devastating Franco-Spanish competition, the treaty of Cateau-Cambrésis turned Cremona into a cultural center of Spanish-dominated northern Italy.[96] Spanish hegemony continued until the threshold of the eighteenth century, a period that just happens to include nearly the full cycle of classical Cremonese violin making.

The baroque politics of dynastic hegemony then leveraged the death of a childless monarch into the War of the Spanish Succession. This time, Cremona found itself between the France of Louis XIV, which seized it in 1701, and imperial Austria, which claimed it de facto in 1706 and de jure in 1713. In 1733 the French returned in operations linked to the War of the Polish Succession. In contrast to their Napoleonic grandsons some sixty years later, their political demands were moderate. Reduced by half from what it was 150 years earlier, Cremona was now a city of 20,000, where a garrison of 12,000, a fifth of the whole French expeditionary force, inevitably weighed heavily on local resources and sent prices soaring.[97]

In fact, the city seems to have been grateful for the relative law and order of Spanish rule. As though impervious even to siege, flood, famine, and plague, Cremona's economy chugged on resiliently till at least the middle of the seventeenth century. The new governors were not only tol-

erant of existing urban establishments. They were to some degree dependent on them for expertise and credit.[98] Local entrepreneurs bought wool
and cotton, which local producers turned into textiles and local merchants
exported. Local woodcarvers, cabinetmakers, joiners, and carpenters turned
materials from the Alps and Adriatic into furniture and the spectacular
choir of the local cathedral,[99] then covered them with what Simone Sacconi
believed was the same varnish used later on Amati violins.[100]

As elsewhere in the neighborhood, music was highly regarded. Organized activity at the local cathedral went back to 1247. From at least 1427,
the city not only employed wind players, including bagpipers, but recruited
them like football players. As elsewhere, where art and craft cohabited, a
culture of string players and instrument makers also grew and flowered.
Galeazzo Sireni learned to make carriages and sedan chairs from his father,
taught himself to make instruments, and wrote four-part songs.[101] The
arrival of Venetian Jews only added to the mix in a town already well
endowed with woodworking skills, a passion for music, and a preexisting
community of Jewish music and dance teachers, textile merchants, junk
dealers, money lenders, printers, booksellers, and jewelers, whose antecedents went back to the thirteenth century.[102]

It took some four hundred years and a serendipitous discovery by Carlo
Bonetti to show how these pieces may have fit. In 1526, with Cremona again
facing devastation and pillage, civic officials responded with a quick survey
of male heads available for military service. The artisan count reported one
Io Giovanni Liunardo da Martinengo, 50, in the Maggio Porta Pertusia
neighborhood, as well as an Andrea and an Io Antonio, no family name
indicated, living in his house. Martinengo is identified as a lute maker and
"pater." Andrea and Giovanni Antonio are identified as "famey." [103]

Since "pater" in the local dialect could mean both junk dealer, a characteristically Jewish occupation, and a master acting in loco parentis, Martinengo's job description has puzzled modern investigators, uncertain how
such an odd couple of occupations could coexist under one roof. "Famey," in
turn, suggests dependents or family members. Yet the young men appear
to have been sons of Master Gottardo Amati. What Gottardo was master
of is just one more unanswered question.[104]

Either way, a case can be made for "pater." As the assimilated son of
Moise, one of the immigrant Venetian bankers of 1499, Martinengo may
well have carried on a family business that included police auctions as
well as moneylending. As the only lute maker in a pre-industrial town

with a rigorous corporate social order, he could as plausibly have taken on apprentices in a contractual relationship that made them dependents by definition.

While little is known of Andrea's origins, training, and professional pedigree, they sufficed, as Hargrave notes, to make him "probably the first, certainly the first known, and arguably the most important Cremonese violin maker."[105] Scraps and inferences teased from notarial documents,[106] plus a scattering of instruments, many of them heavily altered, suggest that he had established himself as husband, father, and master sometime between his appearance in the military census in 1526 and his debut as lessee of a house with shop space in 1538. By the time of his death in 1577, he had advanced to role model and patriarch.

His coming of age and certified mastery coincided with Cremona's return to a Spanish administration made only the more visible by royal visits in 1541 and 1549. These coincided in turn with a proliferation of churches and convents, a boom in the decorative and musical arts, and what soon showed promise of becoming a bull market for what Denis Stevens calls the "neat four-cylinder machines with greater horsepower and very low rosin consumption"[107] that were to be the Amati family's lasting achievement and legacy.

The economic historian Carlo Cipolla, who knew how the story came out, would rightly identify export dependency, uncompetitive prices, and structural bottlenecks as long-term causes of secular decline.[108] Yet to the sixteenth-century equivalent of Wall Street, the merger of Italian civic vitality with Spanish power and market share could well have looked like a winner. The combination of corporate regulation, artisan craftsmanship, and family business assured both a support system for the maker and quality control for the consumer. For the upscale patron likely to buy or order an Amati instrument, price was no object. A virtually seamless musical culture with Italy at its center made demand potentially global. The Pax Hispanica not only linked Cremona to the world's most powerful court, with branches from Brussels to Peru, but to the Roman papacy, home office of another global enterprise. After decades of devastation by contending armies, it looked to many, and especially the urban establishment, like a good thing in itself.[109]

By 1576, census takers reported a growing community of 36,000, with some fifty parishes, five with links to instrumentalists, forty teachers, including music and dance teachers, and one instrument maker. In 1583 string players took their place in the cathedral's sacred concerts.[110] Andrea was dead, but three daughters were comfortably provided for, and two sons were ready to continue where he had stopped. In a 1628 memo, the composer Heinrich Schütz urged his employer, the Elector of Saxony, to buy two violins and three violas, most probably from Andrea's son Girolamo, "considering that when such makers are gone, violins of that quality will be unavailable."[111]

Actually, the family was just warming up. Andrea's grandson and great-grandson would be emblematic makers too. Going on five hundred years later, Amati instruments still gave pleasure and instruction to players, listeners, makers, and museumgoers, not to mention dealers. They also left a paper trail, as baffling as it was essential to successive generations of dealers, trying to make sense of what they were looking at as prices rose and rose.

Known to posterity as the Brothers Amati, Girolamo and his elder brother Antonio could as easily have been half-brothers. With as many as twenty-one years between them, they would go their separate ways in 1588, eleven years after their father's death. As with much of the family history, the cause of the split remains a mystery. The settlement is a matter of surviving, if elliptically Latinized, record. The notary stipulated ingeniously that one brother would divide the objects in question on a given Thursday. The other would then appear on Friday to choose his share. Antonio ended up with his brother's half claim to a second house in the neighborhood; it housed the family and shop. Tools and patterns were split between them, implying that both intended to go on making instruments. Financial penalties, a hint of hard feelings, were set for non-compliance. From there till Antonio's death in 1607, the brothers seem to have stopped working together. Yet the common label survived till Girolamo's death in 1630.

Solo or in tandem, they left a substantial collection of instruments of all kinds and sizes whose workmanship inspired imitators, acknowledged and otherwise, well into the eighteenth century, and puzzlement as well as admiration ever after. The obvious question, all the more urgent with growing expertise and escalating prices, was who made what.

A major clue was there all along, but its potential was only discovered incrementally, beginning in the late nineteenth century. This was the Stati d'Anime, a family registry commissioned by the Council of Trent in 1563. Every year, on Easter Monday, the parish priest went door to door, counting and recording his parishioners. The practice continued into the Napoleonic era.

The registry was uneven. To complicate things, the so-called Isola, the compact neighborhood where a significant contingent of woodworkers[112] cohabited for centuries, was subdivided in three parishes. Though surviving records for San Matteo, the Stradivari family parish, are notoriously weak, San Faustino, the Amatis' parish, is impressively strong, despite the absence of records for the crucial post-plague years 1630–41, and for 1670–79, which include the last years of Nicolò's life. Yet it took some three hundred years, plus the patience, ingenuity, and energy of Kass, then employed by William Moennig & Son in Philadelphia, and Carlo Chiesa, a Milanese maker and researcher, to show what could be done with it.

The result is as much the portrait of a milieu as of a family. At its heart is a tract of seventeen houses, on both sides of a street where Amatis, Stradivaris, Guarneris, Bergonzis, Rugeris, Storionis, and Cerutis coexisted. Among them, in midblock, is the Casa Amati, with several wings, a shop, and a courtyard, inherited from Nicolò's father and grandfather.[113] Around them are neighbors, whose names recur in both one another's and the city's histories as landlords, tenants, marriage and legal witnesses, godparents, in-laws, fellow makers, musicians, and the owner of a popular theater. Then come the core family, relatives, apprentices, servants, and hired hands. Over forty years, the aggregate occupancy of the Casa Amati would rise from five to as many as eleven.

Nicolò, the third-generation patriarch, who restored the family fortunes after a season of disasters and invested prudently in real estate, is front and center. Then comes an older half-sister, perhaps a widowed survivor of the plague, with successive generations of her own family. There is Lucrezia Pagliari, the twenty-six-year-year-old woman Nicolò married when he was forty-eight. There are the six—of nine—children who reached adulthood. The firstborn, Girolamo, died at three. He was followed a year later by another Girolamo, the last son and the only one to join the business. Known as Hieronymus II, he would die without male heirs at ninety-one. Of five siblings, three joined religious orders, as would innumerable of their Bergonzi and Stradivari peers in a town where priests, monks and nuns made up a startling 10 percent of the early seventeenth-century population.

Flanking the family are two or three servants, a few as young as ten; hired hands, presumably engaged to produce such necessary but unglamorous accessories as pegs, fingerboards, bridges, bass bars, even scrolls;[114] and apprentices from outside the family. Over forty years, there seem to have been as many as seventeen, mostly from other instrument-making centers like Padua, Bologna, Milan, and Venice. Those who could then went on to open their own shops, establish the Amati style and model in other towns, and transform it into a global standard.

Three apprentices stand out. One of the most notable is Andrea Guarneri, who opened Cremona's second shop around 1650[115] and founded his own three-generational dynasty. Another, Giacomo Railich, was deputized to acquire new violin-making skills for the benefit of a respected family lute business that would relocate and diversify from Füssen to Naples, Padua, Brescia, and Venice.[116] The most tantalizing apprentice, if he was one, is Antonio Stradivari. Early instruments reflect Amati influence, but the Amati style left its marks on everyone. The Easter Monday census shows no sign of him. Coming from a local family, he had no reason to live in the master's house, and Cremona was full of parishes other than San Faustino.

Hill colleagues and nineteenth-century biographers reported confirmations of an Amati apprenticeship. But the Hills never saw any evidence of them. An early Strad, with a label identifying the maker as Amati-trained, was understandable cause for jubilation; but there is no mention of Amati on a label dated a year later, or any found since.[117] Yet who can imagine that the greatest maker of them all taught himself or that, in a corporate order as hierarchical as the Church, he could have opened a shop if he had? Given Cremona's options, if not the Amati shop, where would he have gone?

Only a little less mysterious, his later life can be reduced to four data. He lived a long and productive life. He made an impressive number of extraordinary instruments for a demanding clientele. He left a large family and a substantial estate. He could write, which was not at all a given at the time. Virtually everything else is guesswork.

Save for apparent consensus about his father's name, the family history is a cipher. Bonetti and his coauthors, Agostino Cavalcabò and the legal historian Ugo Gualazzini, note that nonresidents had to apply for citizenship in the presence of witnesses when opening a shop. In Stradivari's case, no such petition has been found.[118] Even his age takes a butterfly course. Successive census returns between 1668 and 1678 actually report him growing younger.[119] His wives' birthdates were duly noted at marriage. His own, presumably between 1644 and 1649, was not. Why? Renzo Bacchetta speculates that vital statistics for 1647–49 were lost when renewed belligerency between France's Modenese and Spain's Milanese proxies led to a flow of refugees that included Stradivari's mother.[120] As the Hills say of his apprenticeship, "The questions, we fear, can never be answered."[121]

It is known that he was producing instruments by 1667. Few seem to have been made—or have survived from—before 1680. There might have been more, Beare speculates. Possibly early instruments went to hard users like working musicians. Possibly their owners postdated them by a decade or two to enhance their value.[122] In any case, this, too, remains a mystery.

His first marriage, in 1667, may or may not have been early, even precocious, for a young artisan without family or property. Andrea Amati was over thirty when he first married. His grandson Nicolò was approaching fifty. It was true that Pietro Guarneri married at twenty-two, and Giuseppe Guarneri del Gesù at twenty-four.[123] Unlike Stradivari, both had established fathers.

On the other hand, the four- or nine-year age difference between Stradivari and his first wife, Francesca Ferraboschi, surely was uncommon. At twenty-seven, she was already a widow, her brother having shot her first husband with a crossbow under circumstances that caused him to be exiled, though he was later allowed to return to Cremona. The 1659 Easter Monday census, listing Ferraboschis just four houses down the street from the Amatis, is a clue to how she and Stradivari might have met.[124] The arrival of a first child five months after the wedding might explain the marriage, though recovery of her dowry might explain it, too. Meanwhile, her ex-father-in-law sued successfully for custody of the two young granddaughters from her previous marriage.[125]

It was a dramatic way to start. There is no hint of anything to match it in the remaining seventy years of Stradivari's life. On the contrary, he seems to have gone about his business in the most literal way, progressively growing into a mature, an old, and then a very old master. The business clearly flourished. In 1680, for 2,000 lire down on 7,000 total, he acquired a house and a shop, surrounded by neighbors of his own or complementary trades. By 1684, the property was paid off.[126] At the time of his death, he had evidently leveraged a superlative product, an upscale clientele, and an international reputation into a substantial fortune. In thirty-one years of marriage, Ferraboschi produced two daughters and four sons. Of these, four reached adulthood, including two sons who would spend their working lives in the family shop.

On her death, Ferraboschi was honored with a funeral and procession whose itemized bill includes the parish priest and a mass, fourteen additional priests, a choir boy, thirty-six Dominican fathers, sixteen Franciscan fathers, thirty-one fathers of Sant'Angelo, twenty-seven fathers of San Luca, twenty-one fathers of San Salvatore, nineteen fathers of San Francesco, unspecified numbers of orphans and beggars "with hat," and fees for administration and for sixteen torch-bearers, bells, draperies, and gravediggers.

A little more than a year later, Stradivari married Antonia Maria Zambelli, 35, of whom nothing else is known. The second marriage produced another daughter and four more sons, the last born in 1708, when Zambelli was forty-four and Stradivari between fifty-nine and sixty-four. In 1737, both died, Zambelli in March, Stradivari nine months later. They were buried in a chapel of the parish church, San Domenico, where Stradivari had acquired a tomb from a family of Cremonese gentry eight years earlier, substituting his name for theirs on the tombstone.[127] This time there was no record of funeral arrangements. A will, dated 1729, was found serendipitously in 1995 when its discoverers, Chiesa and Rosengard, were hunting for traces of Stradivari's younger contemporary, Giuseppe Guarneri.[128]

The longest autograph yet found from any classical maker, the will is an *insalata mista* of family album, business history, and social document. Counting Zambelli, there were eight living heirs when the will was drafted. Stradivari was at pains to see justice done, but self-evidently within the parameters of a patriarchal social order that would survive well into the twentieth century. Zambelli was named heir to her clothing, bed linens, and half her jewelry. A later codicil left her money and household effects as well. She was otherwise declared the responsibility of her two surviving sons. In the event of remarriage, the inheritance would lapse. But her death in advance of Stradivari's took care of that part.

The three of seven surviving children who joined religious orders constituted another category of heirs. There was to be an annuity for Francesca Maria, a nun, who had entered the same convent as a granddaughter of Andrea Guarneri in 1719 and been supported since by interest on her dowry. Fixed income on a home mortgage loan to the latest generation of Amatis was reserved for Alessandro, a priest—a son from the first marriage. Fixed income on a half-share in a pastry shop was reserved for Giuseppe, also a priest (and a son from the second marriage).

Annunciata Caterina, also known as Caterina Annunziata, unmarried and sixty-three at her father's death, inherited clothing, household linens, jewelry, and the income on two rather substantial loans going back to 1714. The youngest child, Paolo, already set up in a dry goods partnership and still under the age of thirty at his father's death, was to get a substantial cash payment if he opened his own business. He was otherwise to get an equivalent amount in cash and household effects, as well as six presumably finished violins.

That left Francesco (b. 1671) and Omobono (b. 1679), the sons from the first marriage, who had spent their lives in the family shop. Omobono, the more gregarious, had taken off as an eighteen-year-old for Naples, then Italy's greatest city, and Europe's third greatest after London and Paris. His father had maintained him there for two and a half years, although he had apparently never forgiven him for leaving home. Forty years later he assessed Omobono post facto for his upkeep. Like his half-brother Paolo, Omobono inherited six violins. That was all that shows up in the will. The rest of the estate, including the shop, its reputation, finished instruments, wood, tools, and patterns, and the house with its contents minus disbursements, went to Francesco, the dutiful elder brother and eldest surviving child, who was also named his father's executor.

The will is the closest existing approximation of a portrait. But it is equally interesting for what it implies about a family, culture, society, even relative values and orders of magnitude. The respective annual payments of 150 and 300 lire to the two clerical sons, as well as 170 for Annunziata Caterina and 100 for Francesca, tell what it cost to maintain an older and a younger priest, a nun, and an aging, unmarried daughter. The valuation of six violins at 1,000 lire total, or something over 150 lire apiece, tells something about a priest's annual upkeep relative to the contemporary price of a Strad, but also about Stradivari's income. Over forty-six years as an independent maker, the Hills estimated, Stradivari produced 1,116 instruments, including 960 violins.[129] Multiplied by 150, then divided by 46, the result is a gross annual average of 3,130 lire, without even factoring for the violas, cellos, viols, lutes, guitars, mandolins, harps, and whatever else may have emerged from the shop. Like his peers, Stradivari then invested a share of the net in loans, real estate, and collateral enterprises. Though conjectural and crude like virtually everything else we know about Stradivari, the figure suggests not only how well he did but how he dominated the local market.

Whether in cash or kind, the 6,000 lire reserved for Paolo's future says something about the relative costs of a Stradivari and a start-up business.

Four years after drafting his will, Stradivari would pay 25,000 lire to buy
his youngest son a junior partnership in a local textile firm. Annunziata
Caterina's annuity, indirectly derived from a 5 percent return on credits
extended many years before, is another indicator of her father's net worth.
In 1680, Stradivari bought his house for 7,000 lire. In 1714, he lent 12,000
lire, a figure well in excess of his house's value, even allowing for mild
inflation.[130] A year later, Giuseppe Guarneri, Stradivari's junior by some
twenty years and a major maker in his own right, had to borrow 1,000 lire.
He then defaulted on the loan.

The secrets of Stradivari's success have haunted the popular imagination since his death.[131] From Félix Savart, the pioneer nineteenth-century
physicist, on, his materials have been a prime suspect, be they natural,
enhanced by season,[132] climate[133] or mineralization,[134] baked, or chemically
doctored.[135] Mathematically based acoustical principles, orally transmit-
ted and lost from view with the passing of the guilds, are close behind.[136]
But nothing conclusive has been found to confirm that any of these has
any merit.

Varnish has been a perennial favorite[137] since at least 1859, when Giacomo Stradivari, a direct descendant, told Vuillaume about a formula copied from a vanished family Bible. Vuillaume volunteered to test the formula
in confidence and to report the results. He then returned to Paris with what
was claimed to be a portrait of the master. Passed on to his daughter, it
eventually made its way to the Hills, who concluded, after conferring with
Lady Huggins, that it was probably a portrait of the young Monteverdi.[138]

The great varnish hunt was ultimately a dead end. Victorians hoped
to reach the magic essence by direct contact with Stradivari's spirit.[139] Successors a century later could search for it among up to six hundred Google
entries. But they might as well have been searching for Hammett's Maltese falcon or Citizen Kane's Rosebud, according to Joseph Curtin of Ann
Arbor, Michigan, a serious acoustician and accomplished maker. Neither
more nor less than plant oil and tree resin, the nominal secret was at most
a personal variation of the varnish used by Stradivari's neighbors and competitors, Curtin reported.[140] In 2009, an elaborate Franco-German analysis
of tiny fragments of varnish from five instruments at Paris's Musée de la
Musique reached the same conclusion.[141] The real secret, Simone Fernando
Sacconi concluded after a lifetime of study and hands-on experience, was
that there was none. Stradivari did what his peers and contemporaries did,
just more and better.[142]

That his career was a benchmark, an Indian summer, a glorious sunset, and a coda, was implied, though unstated. Over the course of his wonderfully long and productive working life, Cremona steadily lost population and manufacturing base, while Italy lost comparative advantage and export markets to more dynamic and better-located north and west European neighbors.[143] The next generation of Stradivaris was virtually a metaphor of the world they inherited. Two had already died without issue as more or less young adults, including Giulia, a daughter who had married well with a generous dowry in 1689.[144] Of the seven survivors, three joined monastic orders or made careers in the church, among them two from the second marriage. The propensity for the church, even on this scale, was in fact unremarkable in Catholic Europe. But the three nonclerical survivors from the first marriage were single, too, either approaching or beyond retirement age on their father's death. Of the four nonclerical survivors from both marriages, only Paolo, the youngest, married.

At the same time, a proliferating violin trade had followed demand to new musical centers at home and abroad, while Stradivari's very success, as Chiesa and Rosengard note, inadvertently pushed his competitors to the wall.[145] The local consequences could be seen at the Guarneri house just a few steps down the street.

Like his father, the elder Giuseppe filius Andreae, Bartolomeo Giuseppe Guarneri spent most of his working life in Stradivari's shadow. Born in Cremona in 1698, he also died there seven years after Stradivari. Some twenty years before his birth, his uncle Pietro Guarneri, both a player and maker, left for Mantua, where he joined the court orchestra, made relatively few but first-class instruments, enjoyed a local monopoly as supplier of strings and accessories, and left a comfortable estate.[146] A generation later, Giuseppe's brother, a second Pietro Guarneri, followed his uncle's example. Unlike their Cremonese peers, Venetian makers, players, composers, and publishers could barely keep up with the demand from churches, theaters, opera houses, academies, private patrons, melomaniac amateurs, as well as the *ospedali*, the legendary girls' boarding schools, for bigger orchestras, more concerts, new pieces, printed music, and instruments of every kind.[147] By 1725, the younger Pietro had established himself in Venice, where he married in 1728. He fathered five sons and five daughters between 1729 and 1743. None followed him into the business. He died in 1762, survived by his widow, at least one son, of whom nothing else is known, and a legacy of still-coveted instruments, including some wonderful cellos, as well as a violin dated 1734 that the Hills thought he might have made collaboratively with his stay-at-home brother.[148]

There is no evidence that the younger Giuseppe ever left Cremona, although his choice of maple hints at a possible Venetian supplier.[149] Still, the world came to him in the form of French customers and a Viennese wife who, remarkable for the time, may have been a maker, too.[150] The conjunction of France and Austria under his roof effectively described Cremona in his lifetime. Virtually on arrival in 1733, a local violinist later recalled, a French colonel from Avignon tried to buy the Stradivaris that the master's son Paolo would later sell to the Spanish court. Though nothing came of the sale, the bid confirms at least that the occupiers were aware that there was more to Cremona than strategic geography.

The arrival of the French was soon followed by the arrival of professional players and visiting officials, who interacted with the local professionals in what seems to have been the first such club in generations. Since most were violinists with links to local makers, it seems plausible that Guarneri, still in his midthirties and by far the youngest maker in town, offered competitive prices and buyer-friendly terms.[151]

The final decade of his life seems, at least, to have brought some modest success. Surviving instruments show him at the top of his form. The Hills estimate that he may have built as many as 250 violins, though no known violas or cellos, over a relatively short working lifetime; but as of 1931 they knew only 147 of them. In 1998, Robert Bein, the Chicago dealer, knew of 132, including two recently, mysteriously, even amazingly arrived from post-Soviet Russia, with no indication of where they had been and what they might have been doing since the October Revolution.[152]

In the meantime, twenty-five of his violins had converged from around the world at New York's Metropolitan Museum for a show and symposium commemorating the 250th anniversary of Guarneri's death. The idea originated with Hargrave, Dilworth, and Stewart Pollens, the Metropolitan's instrument conservator, over a dinner in London's Soho. They then recruited Peter Biddulph, a major London dealer, to lead the way to the Metropolitan. Surrounded by security, Hargrave and Dilworth had nonetheless to collect the instruments themselves, hand-carry them to New York, and even assemble the show because "we were the ones with the insurance cover," as Hargrave recalled with implied exclamation points. There was a series of gallery talks by the violin trade's equivalent of the

College of Cardinals, while a platoon of world-class virtuosi showed what the instruments could do.[153]

The celebration was the more remarkable for a maker hardly known beyond Cremona's city limits in his lifetime. Like his brother, Giuseppe left no shop or known apprentices. His only apparent heir was his wife, who remarried, left town, and vanished from history. It was 1776 before a Cremonese merchant offered Cozio one of his instruments at 75 percent the price of a Giovanni Battista Guadagnini, Cozio's current favorite. By 1827, when Tarisio first appeared in Paris, both Paganini and his 1742 Guarneri had become famous all over Europe. But two generations had passed since anyone had actually known the man who made the instrument Paganini called "The Cannon." It was only in the 1850s that Guarneri prices finally caught up with Stradivaris.[154]

Giuseppe was now referred to as del Gesù for the stylized cross and devotional letters IHS he stamped on his labels after 1733. It was apparently meant to distinguish the younger Giuseppe from his father. Whether anything more was intended is yet another mystery. He had also become an urban legend as a kind of Villon or Cellini of the violin, who had served time for dispatching a fellow maker in a brawl. According to one version, an assist from the jailer's sympathetic daughter had even made it possible for him to continue working behind bars.[155]

Ironically, research inspired by the Metropolitan show reveals a dutiful son and solid citizen securely plugged into neighborhood business and social and parish networks. His basic problem seems to have been neither more nor less than cash flow. The problem dated back to his father and was ultimately rooted in the local economy. Possibly the last cohort trained the old-fashioned Cremonese way, the Guarneri sons presumably learned the family trade from their father, who had nothing to pay them, despite rent on a second house, inherited from his mother. Yet surviving traces of the younger Giuseppe reflect a respectable, even enterprising young man, who married and left home at twenty-four, leased an inn at age thirty, sold the lease at a small profit, and opened a violin shop. Beginning in 1732, he even employed his father.

By 1735, things had brightened up to the point that the elder Guarneri could resume interest payments on loans taken out to buy his brother's share of their father's house. Then the Austrians returned to Cremona and imposed a punitive new tax to support the local garrison, and the economy plunged again. Father, son, and daughter-in-law once more had to move into the same house. Of the 2,500 lire Guarneri realized on the sale of the lease, 2,000 went to retiring his father's loans. To pay for his mother's funeral, he had to take out a loan himself. Until his death in 1740, the elder Guarneri was actually dependent on his son. By agreement with his brother in Venice, the younger Giuseppe then sold his grandfather's house, effectively ending a family business reaching back to 1653. Of 3,000 lire from the sale, half went to retiring debts. Giuseppe and his brother split the rest between them.[156] A few years later, he died, preceded by Stradivari in 1737, Girolamo Amati, who died in 1740, and the Stradivari sons, who died within a year, in 1742 and 1743. In 1747, Carlo Bergonzi, the last great Cremonese maker, also died. In a society and economy where real estate was the most reliable indicator of wealth, they were the last Cremonese makers to own property. Though Lorenzo Storioni (1744–1816) and a century of Cerutis would confirm that it was not the end of good local making,[157] it was certainly the end of an era. Ironically, Enrico Ceruti, the last link to the great tradition, was the first and last Cremonese maker to leave a portrait, a photo taken on his deathbed in 1883.

"Drive me, please, to the house of Stradivari," H. R. Haweis, the fiddle-loving Victorian cleric, told the cabbie on his arrival in Cremona in 1880. "Who?" said the cabbie. "Stradivari, the great violin-maker," Haweis answered. "They don't make violins here anymore," the cabbie replied.[158] S. Domenico, the site of Stradivari's grave, had already been leveled in 1868–69 by a hundred workers with picks and shovels, who first turned the church into rubble, then turned the rubble into a Po embankment. The rediscovery of the grave, a by-product of the demolition, was remarkable enough to be reported in the local paper.[159] At least the tombstone was salvaged. After some years in a municipal storage space, it was eventually relocated to the Piazza Roma, in a park built on the original site, where it still took some looking to find it, and finally in the local museum.[160]

The museum is also home to a collection of Stradivari artifacts, paper and wood models, tools, even a Mantegazza brothers stamp for turning out phony Stradivari labels. They only got there in 1930, after passing through many hands. Even then, it took the tenacity and eloquence of their sixth owner, Giuseppe Fiorini, a Roman maker and Sacconi's mentor, to get the museum to take them,[161] and few visitors are likely to quibble with the writer Victoria Finlay's characterization of the museum as "one of the most boring museums about an interesting subject in the whole of Europe."[162]

As late as 1925, the Casa Guarneri and the neighborhood around it were still there for the Hills to photograph.[163] They too were gone by 1937,[164] when a local initiative, enthusiastically promoted by Roberto Farinacci, the city's Fascist chieftain, and personally approved by Mussolini, led to an international show, commemorating the bicentennial of Stradivari's death. Of the forty-one exhibited Strads, Sacconi brought as many as fifteen from New York. An estimated hundred thousand visitors, a third foreign, showed up to see the Italian Old Masters. An estimated thirty-five thousand, half from abroad, stayed on to see the work of 119 Italian moderns.[165]

Things then turned dark again. Arriving for a first worshipful visit in 1961, Charles Beare found a plaque where the Stradivari house had stood, as well as a bar that was later transformed into a hamburger joint. It was 1962 before the city finally invested £17,000 in a Strad of its own, the 1715 "Cremonese," to show off at City Hall. One of an estimated fourteen that had belonged to Joseph Joachim, the great nineteenth-century virtuoso, it was acquired from Hill's.[166]

IN THEORY, CREMONA'S loss should have been Venice's gain. Six-teenth- and seventeenth-century Venetians produced plenty of elegant viols, liras, guitars, lutes, and theorbos. But violin making was a slow starter. Makers with distinctly un-Italian names like Straub and Kaiser had surfaced by 1675. They were followed by a trail of gifted Italians, including a few who developed their woodworking skills on wooden shoes. Unlike the Cremonese makers, virtually all the Venetian makers were migrants who headed for Venice as others would one day head for Paris, Berlin, or Chicago.

Though relatively short-lived, the Venetian era was memorable while it lasted. By 1715, the guild counted six members, already an impres-sive figure in a town of some 40,000. But at least three major nonguild makers were also at work. The first was Mateo Goffriller, a Tyrolean, who apparently avoided the guild, with its expectation that instruments be labeled, to beat taxes. When a minor competitor died in 1733, the second, Domenico Montagnana, was sent to inventory the estate. Mon-tagnana, whose shop generated enough business to employ at least five and enough income to invest at 3.5 percent and buy his daughters Rialto apartments,[167] found a hundred German fiddles, which he appraised at a lira and a half each. Two obvious lessons emerge from the story. The first is demand for violins in general, including cheap imports. The second is a parallel demand for good, even great, violins from people who could afford to buy them.[168]

Yet, as in Cremona, the sun seems already to have been setting by midcentury. The third great Venetian, Santo Serafino, for reasons unclear, stopped work in 1744. His nephew Giorgio, who married into, and prospered in, the Montagnana shop,[169] died in 1775. Pietro Guarneri was the last of a Venetian as well as a Cremonese line. By 1793, when Napoleon arrived in Venice, there were still 260 guilds. But the violin makers' guild was down to its last member.

The inadvertent price of empire was arguably among the reasons. In 1740–41, Empress Maria Theresa's imperial Austria lost Silesia to Prussia, a kingdom on the make. As is often the case, military contingency led to economic reform. In an era of ascendant mercantilism, the result was higher taxes, forced exports, and more power for the central government in Vienna. The net losers included Italian artisan enterprise in both Cremona and Venice, and the local gentry who were among its best and steadiest customers.[170]

The retrenchment in violin making was hardly confined to Austrian Italy.[171] The limits of demand would seem to be a second reason. In 1669, the great Tyrolean maker Jakob Stainer produced four violas for the cathedral in Moravian Olmütz (now Olomouc). Where was the cathedral likely to find something better, and how soon was it likely to need more? Barring fire, flood, burglary, or a misdirected rocket, bomb, or cannonball, who needed to replace a Montagnana, a Santo Serafino, or a Pietro Guarneri? A serious professional maker could turn out as many as twenty violins a year, eight hundred over a working lifetime. René Vannes's *Dictionnaire universel des Luthiers*,[172] a standard reference work, lists sixty makers in Cremona alone by the middle of the eighteenth century. A few, like the earlier Amatis, Andrea Guarneri, or Stradivari, could work on commission, sell to collectors, and set their own prices. But with the inevitable priority of feeding themselves, and what Walter Kolneder delicately refers to as "their not infrequently large families,"[173] most needed to produce ahead. The question was how many Italian violins the market could absorb, and how much people could or were willing to pay for them.

A likely third reason was the decline of Venice itself. The city had been on the slippery slope since the fifteenth century, when the Turks overran Constantinople and Columbus discovered America. Then came war after war with the Ottomans, glorious victories, artistic triumphs, but also military and commercial decline, oligarchical entropy, and the creeping irrelevance of what had once been a miniature superpower. With the Treaty of Campo Formio in 1797, Napoleon turned the city over to the Austrians after a thousand years of independence. It was not only the end of an era in violin making.

But as acted out and virtually personified by Giovanni Battista Guadagnini, it was that, too, though some two hundred years would pass before his remarkable career would be fully understood and appreciated.[174] The reef of myth and error that had meanwhile formed around his name was no less remarkable. He was not, in fact, a maker's son, a Cremona native, a Stradivari apprentice, as was often assumed, in part with his own acquiescence and participation. Least of all was he two different people with a common name.

The reality was colorful enough. He was born on the edge of the Apennines in 1711, in Bilegno, a village barely discernible on maps, on a tiny tributary of the Po, upriver from Cremona. Once more, his early years are a guess. One clue at least suggests a tangible negative. A lifelong illiterate, he had obviously not gone to school.

While still young he left for Piacenza, a river town of 27,000, home to the Farnese family court of Piacenza-Parma, a client of the Spanish crown. By the mid-1730s, his father had successively operated an inn, a butcher shop, and a bakery there, but not a violin shop. At twenty-seven, Guadagnini married.

His affiliation with a woodworking guild in 1748 was reasonable grounds for Rosengard to infer his employment as a woodworker. But he was making violins at least two years earlier, and hints of professional activity go back still further. Though the law required a four-year apprenticeship for violin makers, there are no surviving indications of where or when he completed one. He had seen and learned from a number of Strads that passed through his hands late in life. Whether labels describing him as "alumnus Antonii Stradivari" are his own idea or someone else's, they are not to be taken literally.

Over some forty years, his professional life was essentially a fantasy on four recurring themes. Family, as usual, was a big one. He was in regular contact with players. Beyond any other major maker, he was a pawn on the eighteenth-century chessboard, regularly picked up and moved by wars, treaties, dynastic marriages, and princely fortunes. More clearly and suggestively than any maker to date, his fortunes were also directly linked to the future of the market.

Coincidence may also have played its part. In 1740, Guadagnini and his wife seem to have shared quarters with a woodworker married to a violinist's daughter. Within a year, he was apparently keeping company with local string players and making violins around an internal form. That his circle included the Ferrari brothers was obviously good for business. Sons of a local cheese dealer, they were respectively concertmaster and a promising young cellist in the court orchestra. By 1743, he seems to have been producing beyond local demand.

More complicated in its consequences was the War of the Austrian Succession. A Spanish siege and short-lived victory brought Prince Felipe, a violin-loving general, an elaborate victory celebration attended by the prince's Farnese mother, and an entourage of celebrated violinists, including one from Cremona. But the siege may also have contributed to the death of Guadagnini's father in 1746, leaving the son responsible for his stepmother and half-siblings, in addition to his own wife and three children. The Austrians returned, followed by an epidemic that killed Guadagnini's wife. He quickly married his earlier neighbor's younger sister, the violinist's daughter, who was herself widowed with children at twenty-two. She died almost as quickly, leading in 1747 to Guadagnini's third marriage, this time with the daughter of an apothecary.

In 1748, the Treaty of Aachen ended the War of the Austrian Succession, returning Piacenza to Spain. With the waning of Cremona, Guadagnini, still under forty and twice widowed in two years, had his own, his second wife's, and his father's family to take care of. He was also the most important maker in the Po Valley. A year later, they all moved to Milan, where his friend Ferrari had joined the formidable orchestra of the ducal court as principal cellist, composers and virtuosi flourished, and middle and upper class amateurs, to quote Rosengard, displayed "an almost maniacal enthusiasm" for recreational ensembles.[175]

Within a few years, his shop was the busiest in a market that already supported established makers like the Testore brothers and Landolfi, as well as a contingent of small-bore competitors. Over the next nine years, by Rosengard's estimate, his production of at least a hundred violins, including about a dozen dated 1758 and labeled "Cremona," plus at least a half dozen characteristically user-friendly cellos,[176] may have approached the output of all other local makers combined.

At this point, politics seems to have intervened again. The Peace of Aachen turned Felipe, the violin-loving Spanish infante, into a Duke of

Parma. Felipe's 1739 marriage to Louise Elizabeth, a daughter of France's Louis XV, turned his court into an Italian Versailles. His appointment of the French Guillaume du Tillot as general intendant transformed his capital of 32,000 into an outpost of the Enlightenment, a seedbed of artisanal industry, and a center of French, then Italian opera. A gifted technocrat as well as a music lover, Tillot wanted a role model artisan and the best available maker and repairman for an orchestra recruited from as far away as Paris. Presumably recommended by the Ferrari brothers, who had moved to Parma in the early 1750's, Guadagnini moved again, arriving in Parma in 1759.

The clincher might well have been a tenured position at 1200 lire a year, about a fifth of the going orchestra salary and equivalent to the earnings of a palace doorman or shoemaker. It was still the most stable income he would know, a rare achievement for a working artisan, and enough to marry off three daughters, one of them to Tillot's valet. But a family of seven dependents still faced a cash-flow problem, as French subsidies fell victim to royal extravagance and losing wars, the death of the music-loving Duke Felipe brought a less art-minded heir to the title, and Tillot was dismissed in 1771. The solution was one more move, this time to Turin. Though Rosengard estimates moving costs as high as 28,000 lire, the ducal court saw Guadagnini off with a severance package of 3,600 lire. He left three daughters and "many grandchildren" behind.[177]

On the face of it, the new venue was attractive as the capital of a mini-kingdom, transformed from a duchy by the Treaty of Utrecht. It was conveniently close to France, an established market for Italian violins. Under a royal administration with foreign policy ambitions, it was bureaucratically enterprising and economically active. A respectable tradition of local violin making went back to 1647, when a couple of German émigrés set up shop and turned it into a success.[178] Gaetano Pugnani, the era's reigning virtuoso and a native son, had recently returned from London to take charge of the royal orchestra. There was no serious violin shop to compete with.

The crucial relationship again seems to have been pure windfall. In 1773, the eighteen-year-old Count Cozio di Salabue discovered the sixty-two-year-old Guadagnini, and vice versa. Cozio was understandably attracted to a man he had reason to believe knew the Cremonese scene. Guadagnini, who evidently felt that a Cremona connection was crucial to his livelihood and reputation, did nothing to disabuse him. Even his family bought into the story, and Guadagnini swore to its veracity under oath.

It was not an easy relationship, but it was remarkably consequential. Within a year, the young gentleman was discreetly but heavily engaged in buying, selling, and collecting Old Master violins through agents and intermediaries, while underwriting brand-new Old Masters from Guadagnini. Both as proxy and consultant, the older man represented and advised the younger in ever more elaborate transactions, though there is no evidence that Cozio's acquisition of Stradivari's tools and models was among them. Guadagnini then fitted out Cozio's acquisitions with new fingerboards, necks, and bass bars for resale.

Between 1774 and 1776, he also turned out at least fifty violins of his own at the rate of about one per month, plus two violas and two or three cellos. The instruments included a few labeled "Guadagnini Cremonen" and even "Dominus I[gnatius] A[lessandro] Cotii"[179]—that is, Cozio. They were apparently meant as trading material for Cozio's agent Anselmi. Forty-eight Guadagnini violins, two violas and two cellos, and a mixed bag of seventeen Guarneris, Amatis, Bergonzis, Cappas, Rugeris, and a Stainer, still in Cozio's possession on his death in 1840, are credible evidence that the plan did not work out.[180] In late 1776, Cozio asked Guadagnini to build his instruments around Stradivari forms. Obviously determined to make authentic Guadagninis, not facsimile Strads, Guadagnini refused. A year later, the relationship ended, leaving behind a trail of recrimination that would eventually show up in Cozio's journals.

From 1777 to his death in 1786, Guadagnini continued making Guadagninis as a self-employed producer. He left a large family, a small estate, and no will. The remaining inventory included bows, mandolins, and guitar rosettes, testifying to a multi-purpose shop, as well as a mattress Guadagnini once received from Cozio as payment in kind.

The shop's subsequent fate was both an extended epilogue to his own career and the kind of intergenerational saga that would inspire a thousand novels. His sons established themselves as Turin's leading guitar makers, despite fourteen years of French annexation, punitive taxation, and revolutionary sanctions that effectively wiped out the theaters and titled amateurs, who were their basic clientele. In the aftermath of the French retreat, a grandson, Gaetano II, succeeded to the business at twenty. Literate and educated, as Giovanni Battista was not, he reconnected and catered to the old clientele, made, repaired, and traded in instruments, did well on investments, and left an impressive inventory on his death at fifty-seven. His son, Antonio, an excellent maker, who also succeeded to the business at twenty, turned it once more into an incubator of distinguished local violin making[181] before passing it on to one more generation, Giovanni Battista's great-great-grandson, Francesco, another respected maker. About two hundred years after the first Guadagnini began making violins, the loss of a last son at sea in World War II finally turned an exemplary family business into history.[182]

OVER THE HILLS
AND FAR AWAY

MEANWHILE, VIOLIN MAKING continued elsewhere, in part because it had never stopped. By 1650, Italian-model violins had surfaced in Amsterdam. Within a generation, Stradivari's contemporaries were producing Dutch Amatis the way New York's Garment District would turn out Diors three centuries later. The labels were a token of respect, not consumer fraud, according to Fred Lindeman, the Amsterdam dealer. The idea, the musicologist Johan Giskes infers, was to recover market share by creating local versions of an Italian designer model.[183]

Direct influence was a favored explanation for how it was done. Italian violins surface in Amsterdam insurance records by 1660, and Cremonese violins in a 1671 auction catalogue.[184] But modern research shows no traces of Italian makers in Amsterdam or aspiring Dutch makers in Italy.

A case can be made for indirect influence. Francis Lupo, a player-maker from a Sephardic Jewish family that made its way from Italy to England and back to the continent, married a widow. Her son, Cornelius Kleynman, a very good maker, might well have learned the trade from his new stepfather.[185] Hendrik Jacobs, the most notable Dutch maker, lived around the corner. His early instruments resemble Kleynman's. He, too, married a widow and acquired a stepson, Pieter Rombouts, who became the second notable Dutch maker. His instruments resemble Jacobs's.

But the likeliest explanation seems to be civic rather than family history. Late-sixteenth-century Amsterdam was one of several Lowlands commercial centers, with a population of some 30,000. By 1670, it had grown to 200,000, leaving Bruges and Antwerp in the dust. Its trade networks extended from Indonesia to Italy. Immigrants and refugees arrived from as far away as the Iberian Peninsula and the Baltic coast.

Though there were no violin makers among them, there were also plenty of Italians, both resident and visitors, and plenty of Italian cultural influence. Unsurprisingly, the first golden age of Dutch violin making runs more or less parallel to the fortunes of the city and the mercantile republic of which it was part. In 1600, there were six stringed instrument makers for a population of about 50,000. By 1622, there were at least ten for a population of about 100,000, including one who specifically called himself a "violin maker." By 1650, virtually all makers referred to themselves that way, despite product lines that included lutes, citterns, harps, gambas, the pocket-sized dance master's fiddles known as pochettes, and harpsichords.[186]

Meanwhile, the instrument worked its way up the social ladder from fiddlers to professionals to the gentleman-amateurs, who built townhouses and hired Dutch masters to paint their family portraits. As playing and making went their separate ways, both adapted their supply to the demand of rich and poor, farmers and burgers, amateur orchestras, theater managers, family entertainments, even church concerts. By 1700, local publishers had put Italian music on the market before it was available in Italy.[187] Painting and music converged too, as players painted, artists bought instruments, and instrument makers' sons went into the art business.[188]

Rombouts's death in 1728 marks the end of the first golden age, as Dutch making shut down for the same reasons that were shutting down making in Italy. With demand saturated by domestic and foreign suppliers alike, the natural course for the next generation was repairing and dealing. A second golden age, heavily influenced by French makers, soon dawned in The Hague, the second capital of the Netherlands and a diplomatic center. This time, the demand side was made up of Masonic lodges, literary circles, reform and political clubs, and music societies, in a town already situated where Italian and German virtuosi regularly stopped off en route to or from England.[189]

Born in 1724 in a German village just across the border, Johannes Theodorus Cuypers seems to have come from nowhere. He surfaced as a citizen of The Hague in 1752.[190] What he did till then is, once again, unknowable. But somewhere, presumably from a French luthier resident in The Hague, he had learned to make good-quality and still desirable Strad-based instruments. He left three clues to the past and immediate future of the trade. With no apparent link to Italy, the Italian model had become the gold standard of European making. The interaction of players, teachers, and makers had made the violin a fact of middle-class life.

A combination of French cultural and entrepreneurial reach had made the French violin, with its extended neck and bass bar, the middle-class version of the Italian violin.

England, as so often, was both generic and a case unto itself. Energized by growing demand for players and instruments, English making combined foreign inspiration with immigrant talent and local genius to produce a legacy of world-class shops and a stockpile of good instruments. The trouble and expense of shipping from the continent, combined with the royal family's soft spot for the instrument, made cello-making a specialty. The earliest known English cello appeared in Oxford in 1672.[191]

While the shops became an international standard, the instruments, save for cellos and bows, were barely known past Dover. But they were cherished at home, if often with a hint of defensiveness. "Without at all detracting from the real excellence of Wm. Forster's instruments . . . we may confidently assert that the great Cremona Makers have had no rivals," a Victorian writer warned aspiring buyers. ". . . Wm. Forster's Violoncellos have, however (in England at any rate) been held in high esteem both by players and amateurs, and have realized good prices."[192]

Not only were continental dealers ignorant about English instruments, Arthur Hill noted grimly in 1911. They did all they could to keep their heirs ignorant about them by switching labels whenever they got their hands on one. Hill had just sold the legendary Fritz Kreisler a violin by Daniel Parker, a London maker who lived in the first half of the eighteenth century. The delighted Kreisler, who had played it in public the night before, found it as good as his del Gesù. But he also wanted the label gone so he could claim it as a product of the eighteenth-century Mantuan master Tomaso Balestrieri when he took it back to Germany.[193] At a party in New York thirty years later, he proudly showed it off to his colleague, the great Nathan Milstein. The nominal Balestieri had meanwhile become the "Parker Strad," he explained, because "[i]t sounds so good."[194]

Between the peaks there were extended periods of stagnation during which local making took what Charles Beare called a W-shaped course.[195] The first peak included a critical mass of gifted makers on the threshold of the eighteenth century. The second comprised a squad of equally gifted, often colorful, and better-documented copyists toward the middle of the nineteenth century. About 150 years would pass before the W reached a third peak—in a late twentieth-century cohort whose skill as restorers and inspired copyists was recognized and valued as far away as Minneapolis and Bremen.

The roots of all three reached back to a consort of viols, an ensemble first seen in Mantua in 1495 and enthusiastically welcomed in England within a generation. By 1600, violins seem to have been well established, though they took some getting used to. Thomas Mace, a contemporary lutenist and music writer, deplored "their "High Priz'd Noise fit to make a man's Ear Glow." Yet well before he died, one writer's "scoulding violins" had become another writer's "chearful violin," whose "Silver Sounds . . . so divinely sweet" could make the listener "dissolve in tears and prayers at Chloe's feet."[196]

Roger North, an uncommonly shrewd and thoughtful observer, attributed the violin's success to the "the very good tone that instrument commands" and to its potential for playing half-tones and even double stops in tune. He was also quick to link the instrument's potential to the player who "understands the capacity and extent of the instruments, as well as the dexterity that belongs to them."[197] He was especially impressed by Nicola Matteis, an Italian who reached London via Germany and "held the company by the ears with that force and variety for more than an hour together, that there was scarce a whisper in the room, tho' filled with company."[198]

In contrast to Holland, England's Italian connection was direct as well as ancient. The earliest players, recruited from Italy for Henry VIII's string band, not only brought their instruments; they might even have made them. By Purcell's time, the traditional player-maker had long since yielded to a division of labor between two virtually autonomous professions. The likelihood that the newer immigrants played or acquired English instruments still approaches zero. It can be reasonably assumed that young Gasparo Visconti, a native Cremonese who knew and had even worked with Stradivari, was playing a Strad when he arrived in London on the threshold of the eighteenth century.

The court orchestra was already importing Cremonese instruments in 1637, when John Woodrington, a local maker, produced a "new Cremonia Vyolin," obviously inspired by an imported original. From midcentury on, the player or gentleman who could afford one either bought Italian or a Stainer by the great Amati-influenced Tyrolean. According to Beare, the popularity of Stainers then caused them to be so widely, not to mention badly and cheaply, copied that they threw British making into a half-century trough.[199]

As early as 1704, Stradivari's long shadow could be seen in the work of Barak Norman, one of the first important British makers.[200] It was only toward the turn of the nineteenth century that the superstars—Giovanni

Battista Viotti, then Niccolò Paganini—showed what a Strad or del Gesù, with its newly extended fingerboard and reinforced bass bar, could do. From there on, demand for homemade Stainers gave way to a taste for homemade Strads from off-the-rack to concert quality.[201]

Like top-quality playing, top-quality making remained heavily dependent on Italian and German imports. One of the earliest violins made in England was built by Jacob Rayman, a native of Füssen, who settled in London around 1625.[202] Vincenzo Panormo, regarded by Beare, Dilworth, and Kass as "the most important English maker of his time," was actually a Sicilian who worked in France for decades before leaving revolutionary Paris in his fifties to establish himself in London.[203]

The question is why native talent took so long to arrive. By the middle of the sixteenth century, there were English viols of exemplary elegance and technical sophistication, as well as buyers prepared to pay top shilling for them.[204] Yet up to a century and a half would pass before domestic violins of equivalent elegance and sophistication appeared on the English market.

Writing in 1726, North hints, at least, at a possible explanation. "The use of the violin has bin little . . . except by common fiddlers," he noted.[205] Yet the gentlemanly preference for the viol was only one obstacle to serious violin making in a society that continued well into the twentieth century to discriminate more rigorously than most between gentlemen and players. The social status of the crafts was also arguably an obstacle. "It is a remarkable fact, and shows in a strong light the difference of manners and customs in different countries," Pearce sighed, "that both Amati and Stradivarius seem to have been of ancient and honourable families, and yet notwithstanding their adopting an avocation which would in England be thought to tarnish an old family name, they lived and died respected and honoured by their fellow citizens."[206]

The Puritan interlude would seem to be another obstacle. A scourge of gentlemen and their consorts, the Puritans were at least as suspicious of musicians and what Mace called their "frisks." Harvey reports a whole windfall of cabinet makers from Holland, France, and Germany whose Italian and Tyrolean-influenced skills might have gone into violin making had they not been Calvinists. He also documents a contemporary violin made of metal. Apparently not unique, it was possibly played, imaginably made, and almost certainly owned by John Bunyan, a tinker, or metalworker, before he became a Baptist, took up preaching, and turned his attention to *The Pilgrim's Progress*.

Still, according to North, many preferred "to fiddle at home, than to go out, and be knockt on the head abroad."[207] As public music languished, domestic music seems actually to have flourished. The receding tide of revolution left a critical mass of amateur violinists collectively keen for methods, manuals, instruments, and music to play on them.

Yet ironically, the same circumstances that discouraged an indigenous Stradivari and inhibited a native violin industry made importing and dealing increasingly remunerative. Born of an eclectic network of mutual protection societies in the shadow of London Bridge, the trade followed the city westward to the worlds of Defoe, Hogarth, and Samuel Smiles, the prophet of early Victorian self-help.

Meanwhile, aspiring makers like the Forster, Dodd, and Kennedy families gravitated from the provinces to the big city, where they and their descendants would dominate the market for several generations. Some did well. In 1725, George Miller Hare died wealthy as proprietor of a shop in St. Paul's Church Yard. In 1741, the same year that Henry Fielding collected £183 from his publisher for *Joseph Andrews*, whose country curate, wife, and six children subsist on an annual income of £23, Peter Wamsley insured his Piccadilly shop for £1,000.[208] By the end of the century, Richard Duke, the most admired maker of his time, had parlayed his flourishing shop into a special relationship with the Duke of Gloucester, private lodgings in Old Gloucester Street, and workshops in Gloucester Place. On the threshold of the nineteenth century, John Betts, Duke's foreman and himself a respected maker, employed the still more respected Panormo, as well as Henry Lockey Hill, whose grandsons would turn a family shop into the violin trade's Ritz.

Indeterminate hundreds of other makers fell into the "They also serve who only stand and wait" category or slipped through the cracks of poverty and epidemic disease. John Kennedy was jailed for debt. So was Matthew Hardie, the "Scottish Stradivari," a former joiner and army veteran. John Dodd, the bow maker, drank himself to death. Of four violin-making sons of the gifted Bernhard Simon Fendt, an émigré from Füssen, only Bernhard Jr. reached middle age.

Still others, like John Lott (1804–1870), lived raffish and colorful lives. As the son and brother of violin makers, Lott learned the craft from his father and practiced briefly until, as Charles Reade wrote, "the fiddle trade took one of those chills all fancy trades are subject to."[209] Lott also survived, if only barely, a brief but dramatic career as a fireworks artist and

another as an itinerant actor; talked himself into a theater orchestra, where
he soaped his bow, allowing him to be seen, but not heard; and toured
Europe and America as keeper to a temperamental and ultimately homicidal circus elephant.

Between engagements, he learned to paint beechwood to look like oak,
maple, or walnut. The skill stood him in good stead a few years later as
demand for quality copies took off like railroad stocks. By the late 1840s,
Lott was copying Guarneris with such success that Yehudi Menuhin's first
wife bought him one as an original a century later. Late in life, when
Menuhin wanted to sell it, Beare had to tell him it was a copy. It ended a
friendship of many years, Beare remembered sadly.[210]

Lott himself might have applauded the Voller brothers, William and
Arthur, and their father, Charles, a cabdriver who had wandered into violin making via music teaching, the perfume trade, and the navy. By the
mid 1880s, they were copying Italian instruments for Hart & Son, a leading London dealer. In 1899, Meredith Morris, who would write a directory
of British Makers,[211] acknowledged a Voller del Gesù as "almost impossible
to distinguish from the original."[212] Voller copies, not necessarily identified
as such, were meanwhile selling nicely in Italy.

Self-employed homeworkers in successively better neighborhoods, the
brothers outsourced label making at sixpence each to a neighbor's son with
a gift for calligraphy. The rest of the job—dendrochronologically correct
wood, varnish, aging, simulated cracks, even ingeniously archaic indications of previous ownership—they handled themselves at an estimated
rate of about ten instruments a year. On the eve of the twentieth century, a
London shipping firm with a sideline in violins launched a Voller copy on
what would be a sixty-year career as a Strad.[213] Hamma & Co., Germany's
most prominent dealer, established a relationship with the Vollers that
would survive World War I. Beginning in 1920, they would do business
with Wurlitzer in New York.

Low-profile before the war, and scarcely noted after, they were never
fully lost from view. Major dealers bought their product at good prices.
Major players sought them out for repairs and commissions. William, who
died in 1933 at seventy-nine, left his wife a respectably middle-class estate.
Posterity, perhaps unfairly, questioned their character; but nobody questioned their skill. Ironically, a commemorative symposium in 2002 had
to be canceled for lack of borrowable "first choice instruments to make a
first rate exhibition."[214] It was hard to believe that there was a shortage of

owners. The problem seemed rather to be a shortage of owners willing to admit it.

Walter Mayson (1835–1904), who took up full-time making at thirty-nine after losing his job with a Manchester shipping company, produced a reported 810 instruments in a working life half as long as Stradivari's. Among them were twenty-seven violas and twenty-one cellos, several with Boer War and other patriotic associations, a few with bas-relief backs. Mayson married again after a first wife, courted six years, died in child-birth. He then spent years paying off the mortgage on a house he couldn't afford to live in that was eventually sold at a loss.

Meanwhile, he turned out a steady stream of essays, poems, and a novel to supplement his modest income. In 1888, he won an Australian com-petition but failed to collect the gold medal because the organizers went broke. In 1899, he agreed to a series of articles for *The Strad* that were col-lected and republished in book form but which lost money. When local admirers got together to present a collection of his best work to royal museums in Salford and London, they managed to buy one instrument posthumously.[215]

Edward Heron-Allen (1861–1943), well-connected from birth, was as fortunate as Mayson was luckless. An Edwardian of Michelangelesque many-sidedness, he was still a schoolboy at Harrow when an interest in Soho, where his father practiced law, led to an interest in the neighbor-hood's violin shops. He sought out Georges Chanot, the London-based son of a Parisian family active in the trade since the 1820s, for an informal apprenticeship. He even paid for it himself.

He made at least two instruments. But while still in his twenties, he was encouraged by Sir Richard Burton, an even more colorful figure than himself, to write about the violin instead. A manual on how to make one, dedicated to the Duke of Edinburgh, appeared in *Amateur Work Illustrated*, an over-the-counter magazine. Republished as a book, it was still listed by Amazon 120 years later.[216] In the early 1970s, John Dilworth dropped plans to matriculate at the University of Brighton and enrolled at the newly created violin school in Newark, near Nottingham, after discovering Edward Heron-Allen in his school library. On the threshold of her teens, Anne Cole, an American maker, used it to teach herself, after discovering it in Albuquerque, New Mexico.[217]

As maker-lawyer-author, Heron-Allen wrote with particular author-ity on current litigation, edited the *Violin Times*, and joined the Hills, the elder Hart, and Reade as one of Britain's few acknowledged experts.[218] He also toured the United States, where he lectured on palmistry; published papers on marine biology; got himself elected to the Royal Society and the Academy of Saint Cecilia; translated the Persian poet Baba Tahir and practiced law; produced pseudonymous occult fiction and genteel pornography in limited editions; trained neighborhood Boy Scouts for Home Guard service in the event of war; served as a Middle East expert in the War Office when World War I actually came; kept a voluminous and fascinating diary of how the war transformed the world around him;[219] and took a serious interest in Buddhism.[220]

Still, while London dealers and English gentlemen defined the instrument's mystique and market, French and German artisans redirected its course. The process reached back to the sixteenth century, when Mirecourt in Lorraine and Mittenwald in Bavaria began producing instruments at popular prices for a regional market. A century later, Markneukirchen in Saxony joined the game. Like Cremona, all three were strategically located, welcomed a variety of crafts, numbered both church and state among their customers, and were aware of what was happening south of the Alps.

As Italian supply declined and European demand increased, all three towns, none larger than a few thousand people, turned themselves into cottage industrial Detroits. The transformation democratized the Strad in much the way that Henry Ford democratized the Rolls-Royce. In principle, each town aspired to a product line extending from the family sedan to the economy model. French makers were quick to establish themselves at the Mercedes end. Fairly or otherwise, that left the Germans, and especially Markneukirchen, with the Volkswagens, even Model Ts.

On the eve of the twentieth century, Arthur Hill reminded himself almost daily that German was a synonym for cheap, incompetent, and fraudulent. In the interstices of the Aspen Festival a century later, Joan Balter, a Berkeley, California, dealer, patiently explained to Chinese parents, shopping for their growing daughter, that they would pay a triple premium for an Italian label, double for a French, and single for a Mittenwald, provided that it was handmade and sufficiently old.[221] The discerning collector, on the lookout for a Markneukirchen equivalent, found it at weekend flea markets.[222]

But the similarities outweighed the differences. Comparative advantage in all three towns began with raw materials. Both French and German makers enjoyed easy access to quality pine and spruce. In 1870, more than a quarter of Bismarck's new Germany was covered by forests, a space larger than half of the United Kingdom. On the eve of World War I, Germany's forests still employed more people than its pace-setter chemical industry. France was equally fortunate. It not only had expanses of communal forest in the Alps, Vosges, Jura, and Pyrenees but tropical hardwoods like ebony and pernambuco as a colonial spin-off.[223]

Again in contrast to Britain, the artisan infrastructure in all three towns remained intact and recognizable long after the guilds had been officially abolished. By 1850, three of every five Britons were employed in manufacturing, and of the two-fifths still farming, large numbers were landless. A generation later, two-thirds of their French neighbors were still on the land, more than half were still rural in 1911, and some 80 percent of them were peasant smallholders.[224] The story was essentially the same in Bavaria, the Tyrol, and the Saxon Vogtland, where extensive pools of rural family labor were grateful for seasonal employment that Britons had left behind by the mid-nineteenth century.

Mirecourt, generic in many ways, was a ducal residence town with a good location. But two comparative advantages might have caught the eye of an eighteenth-century MBA. One was the complementarity of its principal trades, the second its easy access to Paris.

With the encouragement and patronage of the Dukes of Lorraine, local makers produced armor, leather goods, textiles, and lace. After the Thirty Years' War devastated the town, a new duke hauled it back from the brink. By 1725, there were reportedly ten violin shops in Mirecourt. Seven years later, their owners prevailed on "François, by the grace of God Duke of Lorraine and of Bar, King of Jerusalem, etc." to charter a guild.[225] By 1748, the ten shops had nonetheless grown to sixty.

On the eve of the Revolution, a lace and drapery enterprise operated by the Ladies of the Monastery of Poussay employed as many as a thousand women in a town of seven or eight thousand while incidentally supporting the instrument trade. The connection went back at least as far as 1629, when it occurred to the splendidly named Dieudonné Montfort, a local lace merchant, to diversify his product line. From the shop door to the distribution network, the lace and instrument economies would meet and merge for the next few centuries. Nine Chanots would make and sell violins in France and seven more in England before the line finally ended in 1981.[226]

The Revolutionary era was another blow to Mirecourt. In 1806, Mayor

Jacques Lullier lamented that the blockade and naval war had cost his town as many as five hundred export-dependent jobs. Yet smallholder peasants and artisan families were among the Revolution's long-term winners. Before its glow finally faded, violin making would employ up to 80 percent of the working population.[227]

As in Italy, the family dimension is striking. On its appearance in 1932, Vannes's *Dictionnaire universel des Luthiers* listed 830 local masters, including 23 Jacquots going back to 1580 and 25 Vuillaumes going back to 1625. Between 1620 and 1954, there would be eight generations of violin-making Mangenots.[228]

The stability of the profession is striking.[229] Binding in law, the seventeen articles of the Mirecourt charter elaborated privileges, duties, procedures, ranks, offices, and above all constraints on competition as codified and stratified as the ancien régime, and only a little less durable. They survived in their original form till 1776, when Anne-Robert-Jacques Turgot, the royal finance minister, abolished the guilds, including the examiners, who decided who was qualified to open a shop. As a believer in the newly fashionable doctrine of deregulation, Turgot also cut the fees for opening a shop by almost three-quarters, including tax, guild dues, honoraria for the examiners and guild president, and administrative costs. Yet as late as 2002, the long shadow of corporate regulation still fell on the British-trained Hargrave, one of the most accomplished of modern masters, when the German guild charged him with claiming and practicing mastery without their license.

Hierarchical, patriarchal, and meritocratic, the unreconstructed guild was actually an anticipation of where the Revolution was headed. At the foot of the totem pole was the apprentice, exclusively male, usually between twelve and fifteen. Adults were rare, foreigners uncommon. A contract was drawn up before a notary. Most apprentices came from modest and, at least in the eighteenth century, illiterate, peasant, artisan, and shopkeeper families. Those who could afford the one to five hundred livres a year for six years' tuition and room and board paid half up front, the rest over the remaining three years. Apprentices were expected to provide their own clothes, bedding, and shoes.

Guild regulations required that apprentices be spaced at least four years apart so that there could never be more than two in any given shop at any given time. It was claimed, and perhaps sincerely believed, that the incoming apprentice needed four years of one-on-one instruction; but the statute was also meant to constrain the better-fixed from getting a jump on the competition by engaging a shopful of apprentices.

Families who couldn't afford to pay signed over their sons as supplementary domestic help. In an era without electricity, running water, and central heating, the boys worked off their indenture in household chores. Meanwhile they learned the trade five days a week, twelve to fifteen hours a day, with two ninety-minute meal breaks; there was a ten-hour workday on Saturdays. With Sundays, some thirty church holidays, and Saturday evenings off, the work year came to about 240 very long days. Accommodation would improve considerably by the mid-nineteenth century. But on the threshold of the eighteenth, according to Sylvette Milliot, in a shop that opened onto the street, with a second room that served as kitchen and bedroom for the master and his family, the apprentice lived in "the attic in the best cases." [230] With exemptions for sons-in-law and sons of fellow makers, the final test was a so-called masterpiece, often something less than a full-size instrument. Assuming that it passed the examiners, the newly qualified craftsman then paid his registration fee—17 livres in 1715, 18 in 1730—and picked up his certificate.

Employed in a reasonably successful shop at six livres a day, three in cash, three as room and board, he could hope to pay off his apprenticeship within ten years. At least in theory, he could then open a shop of his own. Only a few did or could afford to. The normal course was to work for wages in the same or another shop, where it was taken for given that he was qualified for any job that came through the door.

Limited only by preference and volume, the master could now take on as many such employees as he wished. In principle, the employee could stay indefinitely, provided only that he wanted to and the employer wanted to keep him. In the event the master died, an assistant frequently married his widow, often his business manager, despite sometimes significant age differences. Marie-Jeanne Zeltener, who successively married four assistants, outlived at least three, among them Louis Guersan (c. 1700–1770), whose shop—"near the Comédie-Française," as his labels emphasize—was the Hill's of eighteenth-century Paris. Zeltener left a wardrobe of thirty-one dresses and petticoats valued at 2,600 livres.[231]

With its multiple fees, the expense of buying, renting, and outfitting the premises, and the obligatory opening gala, the step from artisan to shop owner was a big one. The artisan was now a merchant, though guild regulations restricted him to one shop and obliged him to sell in person on the premises, reserving off-premise sales to itinerant peddlers. Wood and other raw material acquisitions were also subject to review—to make sure that no one cornered the market at an advantageous price and resold at a markup. So far as possible, competition was confined to the quality of the product. Particular jobs like gilding and inlays were sometimes outsourced, though there were makers capable of delivering scrolls whose points formed daisies or ended in an elegant seashell.

Success, as Milliot notes, was a function of bench skills, business sense, and the market. The first, to a point, were within guild control. The second, like math, language, and musical and athletic skills, was something some people had and others didn't. The third, like the weather, was beyond anyone's control.

Then there was luck. The last decades of the ancien régime were famously bad for the French crown's credit rating, but they were springtime in Paris—and Potsdam and Parma—for the violin trade. The professional clientele was only the beginning. Then came the player's colleagues and pupils, the officials who managed his orchestra and its instruments, not to mention employers like Louis XV's wife, Marie Leczinska, with her three weekly musicales and a troop of musically gifted children, including the Dauphin and Mme. Adelaïde, both enthusiastic violinists.

Guersan, the second child of a weaver who died young and left him nothing, set the pace for social mobility. In business at twenty-five, he had already moved to a more elegant neighborhood by age thirty, where his customers included the virtuoso Leclair, the composers Guillemain and Rameau, and the young Prince de Guéménée, a serious amateur cellist. In 1754, he was named "Violin Maker to Monseigneur the Dauphin," the later Louis XVI.

The "near the Comédie-Française" on his labels was a signal that extended far beyond location. Personal charm, A-list social connections, favorable terms of trade and credit, elegant receptions in elegant reception rooms, technical skill in adjustments and restoration—he had and did them all. Conversion of gambas to cellos was a specialty. The process of turning a baroque nightingale into the kind of violin that Paganini called his Cannon by substituting large for small bass bars and longer, angled fingerboards for short, straight ones was already well under way by the middle of the eighteenth century.

By 1776, the year Turgot abolished the guilds and the American colonies declared their independence, both the supply and demand sides might have been designed by Adam Smith, whose *Wealth of Nations* appeared the same year. A growing pool of increasingly skilled labor exploited comparative advantages in materials and market access. A growing pool of middle-class and upper-class consumers found good and very good instruments at affordable prices.

If unskilled laborers struggled to make their way at 100–300 livres a year, the wage equivalent of a lower-end apprenticeship fee, the certified worker could now look forward to 700 livres, the equivalent of an entry-level Latin teacher's salary, equal to or better than what fellow artisans earned in other skilled crafts. An independent maker could earn 1,000–3,000 livres, the salary of an assistant tutor to a princely family, and enough to live on without having to worry about renting rooms or other supplementary income. At 3,000 livres, life became positively comfortable. With 5,000 the generally accepted threshold of bourgeois status, a few makers earned as much as 5,500, allowing them to invest in rental properties like their Cremona peers, spend their Sundays raising fruits and vegetables in the spacious gardens of their country houses, and enjoy furniture, wardrobes, paintings and libraries, with a social status unknown to their parents and grandparents.

For some of the most prominent figures in the trade, even the Revolution seemed rather an inconvenience than a major disruption. In 1790, Jean-Henri Naderman, another "violin maker to the Queen," replaced the sign on his shop with one more suitable to a world of liberty, equality, and fraternity. The new sign read "To Apollo." But it could as plausibly have read "Prudence, Pragmatism, and Publishing." The last, a sideline since 1777, now became his principal activity, as an inventory, previously limited to literature for harp and keyboard, expanded to include music for wind bands and a "Marche des Marseillois" in eight parts.[232]

Georges Cousineau found it prudent to substitute his own "Violin Maker to the Queen" with "Cousineau, Father and Son, Violin Merchants, Paris." Yet despite a résumé that explicitly identified his son Jacques-Georges as "harp teacher to the Queen," the Committee of Public Safety hired Cousineau *fils* to help inventory instruments left behind by émigrés. Meanwhile, Cousineau *père* speculated in confiscated real estate while continuing to market violins against stiff Parisian competition as far away as Portugal.

Left with a fistful of mortgages on his father's death in 1800, Jacques-Georges still managed to get himself named "Violin maker to Her Majesty the Empress," and "Harp advisor to the Empress Josephine" in 1805. The first title, at least, survived the imperial divorce, and the accession of a new empress, Marie-Louise. Prudence won again as the winds blew in from Waterloo, and with them the returning Bourbons. On his mother's death certificate in 1815, Cousineau declared himself "Violin maker to the Sovereign" and "son of the former violin maker to the Queen."

The cautionary exception was Léopold Renaudin, a respected maker who left Mirecourt for Paris at sixteen and seems to have made innumerable customers happy by cutting their old instruments down to more modern and user-friendly sizes, a practice that would become something of a Parisian specialty in the next century. Just forty on the eve of the Revolution, he repaired basses for the Royal Academy, rented guitars to the Opéra, and produced his own version of the Strads increasingly popular with visiting soloists. A year later, he was elected to his neighborhood council.

From there on, his career took a turn unique not only in French violin making but probably the history of the trade. In August 1793, his colleagues elected him to the city council, where he was co-opted by Maximilien Robespierre, the lawyer turned revolutionary, who gave the world the concept of "terror." Within weeks, Robespierre's demands on the revolutionary tribunal caused the number of jurors to grow from sixteen to thirty.

Among the new jurors was Renaudin, who soon found himself judging such famous defendants as the queen, the Girondins, Jacques Hébert, Georges-Jacques Danton, and Camille Desmoulins. He never wanted to acquit anybody, a witness later quoted him saying at his trial. A new law only accelerated the tribunal's pace. Between March 10, 1793, and June 10, 1794, there were 1,220 executions. In the seven weeks that followed, there were 1,376. On July 27, rebels in the National Assembly, fearing that they would be next, drew the line and challenged Robespierre and his associates to step down. Renaudin's shop was sealed, and Renaudin turned himself in to the police. The next day Robespierre was tried and executed. Four days later charges were brought against Fouquier-Tinville, his chief prosecutor, and other officers of the tribunal.

In March 1795, Renaudin, still jailed without charges despite various initiatives by his increasingly destitute wife, testified as circumspectly as possible on his relationship to Robespierre. Over the course of marathon proceedings in March and April, eight witnesses spoke in his defense, among them a doctor, a dentist, a music teacher, a trio of artisans, and the president of his local council. Speaking for himself, Renaudin took the same line as Fouquier, who insisted that he was just following orders. With tears in his voice, a reporter noted, he also declared his affection for his wife and emphasized his parental obligations. The court was unmoved. Asked whether the defendants initiated or were only accessories to a miscarriage of justice, the jury found only Fouquier an initiator. But asked if thirty-one accomplices had acted with conscious malice, the court convicted and sentenced sixteen to death, among them Renaudin.[233]

Even the peak of the Terror could not deter Nicolas Lupot, "the French Stradivari," from settling in Paris in 1794 and opening a shop, where he not only "created the standard by which the rest of the great French school is judged," according to Beare and Milliot,[234] but set exemplary standards of political navigation. In 1813, with Napoleon already on a slippery slope without brakes, Lupot was appointed violin maker to the imperial chapel. Only three years later, he was appointed violin maker to the royal school of music, soon to become the Conservatory.[235]

The bonanza would have to wait a generation till the troops came home from Waterloo, the Bourbons came home from exile, and the historical dust settled. But things would only get better as the physical and human capital created before the Revolution and salted away in real estate, day-to-day repairs, and pragmatic survival paid off in its aftermath. The Paris sky was already brightening by 1818, when J. B. Vuillaume arrived from Mirecourt at twenty with six livres in his pocket. He was followed by three brothers. For at least three generations, they and their peers would dominate Europe as Napoleon never did. On the threshold of the twenty-first century, their shadows could still be seen on New York's West Fifty-fourth Street, where René Morel (1932–2011) and Gael Français still did what their ancestors began in Mirecourt a quarter of a millennium earlier.

The principle behind the new French hegemony was simple. Since Andrea Amati, violins had gravitated to power and money. Before and after the Revolution, power and money gravitated to Paris. The third step was obvious, but the mechanisms that made it work were not.

The first synergy was the dynamic that carried Italian players and instruments—as well as Italian chefs, painters, sculptors, landscape architects, dancing masters, and virtually every other art and craft—northward since at least the Medicis; and French scholars, artists, churchmen, salesmen, and above all soldiers southward since at least Charles VIII. The combination made it virtually inevitable that French players and collectors should be both among the first to discover, buy, expropriate, covet, marry into, and learn from Italian violins, with particular attention to Strads, from at least 1770.

The second synergy was the musical connection that made Paris a violin capital as Italy, with plenty of indirect help from French statesmen and generals, was shutting down. London and Vienna were magnetic, too; but neither could match the self-supporting infrastructure of amateur and professional players, collectors, teachers, concert managers, and patrons that assembled around the newly founded Conservatoire and its Italian director, Luigi Cherubini, a French citizen since the 1790s. Also unmatched were the depth of inventory, variety of choice, and technical expertise available from an estimated thirty Parisian dealers, nineteen instrument makers, five bow makers, and five string makers, by the 1830s.[236]

The third synergy, a legacy of Louis XIV, the Revolution, and Napoleon alike, was the intrinsically French cuvée of conservatism and emancipation, capital and province, that transformed ambitious young violin makers into characters in a Balzac novel and made the complementarity of supply-side Mirecourt and demand-side Paris a national model. Paris looked to Mirecourt for instruments, bows, and accessories, as well as staff and apprentices, Mirecourt looked to Paris for orders. Traffic between them was unceasing. A rigorous division of labor, often with family members, went on at both ends.

The model Mircourtien, invariably male, left for Paris in his teens, where he now worked ten to twelve hours daily, three hundred days a year for four years, beginning at 7:00 a.m., winter and summer, for 4 francs a day. On completion of his apprenticeship, his daily earnings rose to 7 francs—provided he wasn't on piecework.[237] At least in principle, misery's reward was an independent existence, a family business, and eventual return to a comfortable retirement, often enough in Mirecourt.

There were significant differences of emphasis. While a dozen or so Paris makers aimed for the carriage trade, Mirecourt aimed for the mass market. If Parisians exported an estimated 12 percent of their product, Mirecourtiens exported three-quarters and upward of their voluminously larger production. In 1839, Charles Buthod's shop in Mirecourt, aiming for volume, produced perhaps 900 instruments a year. Vuillaume's shop in Paris produced 150.[238]

The real breakthrough would wait another generation. In 1857, twenty-four-year-old Louis Emile Jérome Thibouville-Lamy, whose family had been in instrument making since 1790, joined Husson-Bouthod

& Thibouville, a family firm. Within a decade, he had taken over as sole proprietor. A decade later, he had rationalized and industrialized production, exhibited 5-, 10-, and 20-franc violins in Vienna, and established four factories, with an aggregate work force of 420. Among them was one in Mirecourt whose annual output was 25,000–30,000 instruments, elaborately sorted by style and cost of materials. Thibouville's catalogue for 1867 offered a menu of 28 violin bows and 48 violins. By 1900, his Mirecourt competitor Drögemeyer had widened the choice of models to 360.[239]

THE UPPER END of French making can be seen in two histories, one individual, the other collective. The individual is Vuillaume, "this whale of the violin trade," "this Rastignac," as Emanuel Jaeger apostrophized him on the occasion of his bicentennial.[240] The collective is the Chanot, then Chanot-Chandon, family, whose successive generations mirror not only the experience of a trade, profession, culture, even a nation, from the sunset of the ancien régime to the mid-twentieth century.

Respectful competitors in life, both emerged from the eighteenth-century Enlightenment, still fertile in the Napoleonic afterglow. In 1817, Félix Savart, a twenty-six-year-old doctor, more interested in acoustics than in patients, invented a trapezoidal violin, a kind of balalaika look-alike, with vertical, pencil-straight sound holes. As the first violin consciously based on mathematical models, it lent itself to serial production by makers seriously convinced that the violin was capable of still greater perfection than the empirical Cremonese had already conferred on it.[241] It never caught on.

The same year that Savart presented his trapezoid, the music section of the Royal Academy of Fine Arts auditioned another innovation. This one was guitar-shaped, with the scroll turned not toward but away from the player. A few years later, its maker, François Chanot, would prove that his instrument could even accommodate a fifth string and double as a viola.[242]

Like Savart, Chanot was a scientist, resolved to tease out the theoretical principles of a fundamentally intuitive and empirical craft. He came from Mirecourt, where his father, Joseph, also made violins. Born in 1788, he meant to go into the family business. Instead, he entered the Polytechnique at nineteen, graduated as a marine engineer, and worked his way up to captain and designer of a seventy-four-gun ship.

The Battle of Waterloo ended a half-decade of impressive upward mobility. Effective January 1, 1816, he was dismissed from the service, suspected of anti-Bourbon views. His appeal rejected, and with no obvious alternative in view, he left Paris with a lump settlement of 1,750 francs and went home to Mirecourt.

His return to Paris, with his pilot model and a paper explaining it, brought him a ten-year patent and what looked like a promising second career. He had produced a quartet plus bass; got Pierre Baillot, the reigning king of French violinists, to demonstrate what his instrument would do; established a company in Mirecourt to meet Parisian demand; even persuaded Nicholas-Antoine Lété, the organ-building son of another Mirecourt clan, to invest 20,000 francs in the enterprise. The navy then reinstated him. Leaving the company to his partners, he returned to the service.

Four years in the violin business showed promise. But they had scarcely begun to pay off. Though well-made, competitively priced at 300 francs, and respectfully received by the string faculty of the Conservatoire, Chanot's product would soon be a candidate for the instrument museum.[243] He nonetheless left a double legacy. Half was his younger brother Georges, dispatched to Paris to help look out for François's children. The other half was Vuillaume, who had left Mirecourt to help in the Paris shop.

What would distinguish Vuillaume over the next half-century was a unique capacity to define himself and make his way. Like millions of contemporaries, he would spend his working life on one of the world's great political fault lines. Yet three revolutions, a second Napoleonic coup d'état, a Prussian siege, and at least one civil war seem to have caused him nothing worse than a bit of incidental inconvenience during the Commune of 1870, when it seemed prudent to leave Paris for his daughter's estate.[244]

Like millions of contemporaries, he would also spend his working life at the junction of two eras. On the threshold of his career, the Enlightenment belief in science that brought him to Paris gave way to the Romantic passion for history. Rothschilds and Pereires rounded out their sets of newly acquired antiques with impeccably crafted contemporary facsimiles.[245] Each in its way, the Palace of Westminster, Paddington Station, Neuschwanstein, and the new Hungarian parliament building bore witness to a high summer of reverence for the past. Yet few would bridge the worlds of practical innovation and historical rediscovery, and do so well by it, as Vuillaume.

"Get rich by hard work, thrift and honesty," King Louis Philippe's prime minister, François Guizot, enjoined his Norman constituents in 1841. Vuillaume had been acting out Guizot's advice for twenty years. Since 1838, he had bought a first house for 80,000 francs, then another nearby for 120,000 francs. Like all such investments since that of Nicolò Amati, the second house was intended as a cash cow. In 1843, for another 38,000 francs, he added a country house, complete with extensive gardens and outbuildings, where he would eventually retire, while incidentally avoiding the Parisian excise tax on imported wood.[246] A few years later, he added a third town-house, adjacent to the others, this one for 72,200 francs, at a time when even the greatest Strads could still be had for 5,000–7,000 francs.[247]

The hard part in Vuillaume's view was not so much earning money as keeping it. He mastered that skill, too. Thrifty enough to deny his wife a carriage long after they could afford a fleet of them, he took the bus. But he married off his daughters with 1,000-franc dowries—plus one écu, or gold coin, for each of them from the two he brought from Mirecourt on his arrival in Paris in 1818.[248] As sensitive to the real estate and securities market as he was to the quality of timber in old chalets, and the practical potential of whole trees seasoned with the bark left on, he also served as investment counselor to his Brussels-based brother.[249]

In his memoir, David Laurie, the Glasgow dealer, who regularly did business with the Vuillaumes, recalls a Thursday at the country home and shop where the aging Jean-Baptiste made himself available for a weekly open house and office hour. He found the proprietor, already a legend, cheerfully selling his patented varnish to starstruck violin makers. Of course, Vuillaume confided after the visitors had left, it was not the varnish he used himself.[250]

Nonetheless as committed to the satisfaction of his customers as he was to the quality of his product, Vuillaume did equally well by both, while exporting an estimated 75 percent of his output.[251] Beginning with Paganini, whose Guarneri he reportedly opened in the presence of its horrified owner,[252] he worked with and for the era's great ones, including the Norwegian virtuoso Ole Bull,[253] the Belgian virtuoso Charles-Auguste de Bériot, and his son-in-law Jean-Delphin Alard, a professor at the Conservatory. In 1851, he exhibited nine copies and won the highest prize at the Great Exhibition in London. On his return home, he was met with the rosette of the Legion of Honor.[254]

He had already laid the foundation of his success within a few years, even months, of his arrival in Paris. As certain as Chanot and Savart that the violin was still a work in progress, he realized that it was the Italian past that the public clamored for. He made it his mission to give them what they wanted. With amateur collectors snatching up Old Italians as many as three or four at a time, the challenge was selling instruments that players, too, could afford.

His solution was wonderfully simple. For those who could pay for them, there would be Old Italians by Old Italians. For those who couldn't, there would be Old Italians by Vuillaume, at prices beginning at 200 francs. Even this was no small investment in a country of some 30 million, where only 200,000 men paid the 200 francs a year in direct taxes that qualified them to vote. But it compared favorably with the going rate for Strads. "Look, you're going to get an exact reproduction of a Strad, varnish, sound, etc.," Morel paraphrased the maker at his bicentennial symposium. "Nobody can tell the difference, my instruments sell for 500–800 francs, so why buy a Strad that you can't get for under 6000–8000?"[255] He meant it, too, asking, and evidently getting, nearly three times as much for his Strad, Guarneri, and Amati copies as currently asked for original Mantegazzas, Balestrieris, and Gragnanis.[256]

By the time he died, at seventy-six, he had produced some three thousand instruments, all numbered and branded as confirmation of his own part in their manufacture. Of these, 464 alone were produced between the years 1842 and 1850,[257] a total and average that far exceeded Stradivari's over a substantially longer working life. The multiplier was Vuillaume's support staff, hired to play Francesco and Omobono, the Stradivari sons, to a Parisian Stradivari with two daughters and no sons.

Priced and graded according to the cost of materials, Vuillaume's instruments were scrupulous but creative copies of the major Italian makers as interpreted by a man who felt himself in every way their peer. The best were of concert quality. According to Millant, Paganini's protégé Camillo Sivori made a distinguished career on a Vuillaume copy of Paganini's famous Guarneri "Cannon" that was itself one of many. In 1946, Fritz Kreisler played it.[258] In the days of extended sea voyages, cautious Europeans frequently left their Strads at home and toured the United States with a Vuillaume. A century later, according to René Morel, Aaron Rosand reversed the procedure. Leaving his Guarneri at home, he toured Europe and the world with a different Vuillaume Guarneri. Over nine months, while his Guarneri was in Morel's shop, Ruggiero Ricci toured with a Vuillaume Maggini that had belonged to Kreisler. He returned to New York with reviews full of admiration for the instrument's marvelous tone.[259]

All the while, Vuillaume maintained a steady stream of genuinely ingenious experiments and patented innovations. Among them were the octobass, a bass to end all basses, standing over 11 ft. (3.45 m.) high, with a C an octave below the cello C; a hollow steel bow tested by de Bériot and even declared "infinitely preferable and much superior to those made of wood" by Paganini;[260] a bow that allowed an itinerant virtuoso to rehair it without professional help by snapping in a prepackaged module; a contralto viola; a seven-string cello or piano substitute, called the heptacorde, designed to accompany recitative; an automatic (that is, chin-operated) mute that spared the player inconvenient hand motion; and a frazing machine that shaped violin tops and backs for the economy model of his later years.[261]

None was a commercial success. But a corps of former employees—among them the violin makers Hippolyte Silvestre, Honoré Derazey, Charles Buthod, Charles Adolphe Maucotel, Joseph Germain and Telesphore Barbe; and the bow makers Clement Eulry, J. P. M. Persoit, Dominique, François and Charles Peccatte, Joseph Fonclause, Nicolas Maline, Pierre Simon, F. N. Voirin, and Hermann Richard Pfretzschner—were among his most successful students of the trade.[262]

The distinction was hard-earned. Even by the prevailing standard of 4 francs a day for common labor, Vuillaume seems to have been an outstandingly tight-fisted employer. Proud of his own humble beginnings, when he regularly lunched on a boiled pear, he started employees at 3 francs, providing housing in a storeroom. Yet thanks to Vuillaume's shop, Milliot notes without irony, the French school became a worthy heir of the Italian one, and Fétis could declare in more ways than he probably intended that Paris was the Cremona of the nineteenth century.[263]

While Vuillaume broke ground for the middle-class Strad and the modern market, the descendants of Joseph Chanot were also busy, in part purveying instruments to the middle class, in part joining it. François, the polytechnicien and naval officer, clearly set the pace. His brother Georges was not far behind. Active to a Stradivarian age, he would live to worry whether his grandson, the family's fourth Georges, born in 1870, would make it to his baccalauréat, and Le Figaro would note his death in 1883.[264]

Though it is uncertain when the first Georges arrived, he opened his first Paris shop in 1821 in a neighborhood of townhouses, only recently developed for commercial use. Two years later, at twenty-two, he started a family with Marie-Florentine Sophie Demolliens, four years his senior. In

1827, with the birth of a son, Auguste Adolphe, the couple married and legitimated the daughter born four years earlier.

An 1828 bill of sale for a Guarneri cello confirms that Georges already knew where to look for inventory, recognized an authentic Old Italian when he saw it, and found customers for his product. More remarkable, an 1827 violin, exhibited at the year's Exposition des Produits de l'Industrie française, confirms that his wife, too, was a maker. As the only known woman maker of her time, she produced at least three violins. The first, with a Latin inscription, enameled depictions of angelic and historic figures playing ancient instruments against a gothic façade, and an allegorical minstrel pursued by a demon, was evidently snapped up in short order by an unidentified Paris maker. The first project led to a second, commissioned by an English amateur, at the suggestion of a Viotti protégé.[265]

Surviving records testify to a steady trade with both Mirecourt and Paris suppliers in strings, cases, and bows to supplement Chanot's Italian copies. Ever on the lookout for buyers, he also invested in English and German lessons. He then set out for the frontiers, leaving his wife, young Auguste, and the family maid, Rose Chardon, to mind the store. In 1841, he added Spain and Portugal to his itinerary.

A visit to London paid off with a connection to Charles Reade. A visit to Berlin led to the Prussian king's concertmaster, who gave Chanot his Strad to repair, and a local dealer, who bought his Strad copy. When the dealer moved on to Philadelphia, a 150-kg consignment of Chanot violins, cases, strings, and scores followed him. With time off for medals at French industrial expositions in 1839, 1844, and 1849, Chanot then turned his sights on St. Petersburg, where he consigned three violins to local dealers before returning via Dresden, Leipzig, Vienna, and Hamburg. Between 1845 and 1858, his foreign clientele equaled his domestic one, including steady customers in Zurich, Berlin, St. Petersburg, and Istanbul, as well as the French diaspora in Brussels, Amsterdam, Aachen, and Maucotel in London, another Mirecourt native, who not only looked to Chanot as a supplier but sent him 3,000 francs from a local French customer to invest in Sardinian railroad stocks.[266]

In 1847, after three moves in twenty-six years, he relocated the shop in new and stable premises that it would continue to occupy till 1888, and the family moved into four increasingly well-furnished rooms on the fourth floor of the same house. About thirty-five years would pass before the coming of running water and a bathroom.[267] But even the landlord, a

Comte de Labord, who was also a parliamentary deputy, suggests that the move was upward mobility in more than the physical sense.

Milliot points to three indicators of success. One was a vigorous and revealing trade not only in Old Italian instruments, damaged or cannibalized by countless previous dealers and collectors, but the freshly crafted parts needed to restore them. Another was an inventory, including six Guarneris, four Ruggeris, three Landolfis, two Gaglianos, and a Maggini. The third index was an investment portfolio, including Romanian, Sardinian, Piedmontese, and Alsatian railroad stocks. Between 1847 and 1859, the business generated an estimated 5,000 francs, the equivalent at the time of one or two Strads. The investments, by comparison, generated an estimated 9,800 francs for Chanot, plus 6,200 more for Antoinette, the maid's sister.[268]

Yet even as the business flourished, the domestic scene encountered heavy weather. In 1840, Florentine lost her mind. Relocated to an outbuilding of a sister's house in her native village, she became intermittently difficult, even violent. Back in Paris, the family managed as best it could without her. Chanot personally escorted Auguste Adolphe to London to learn the trade from John Turner, a respected dealer as well as a steady customer. Surviving correspondence confirms a cordial welcome, a nine- to ten-hour workday, roast beef, potatoes and beer enough to hold the young Chanot from lunch till breakfast the next morning, and a yearning for French books in a town where he had few friends and winters seemed particularly long and dark. An industry-wide cash-flow problem then caused him to return to his father's business, where he distinguished himself as a bow maker and restorer. In 1848, Auguste was upset by the coming of Napoléon III. Stagestruck like many young men, he also fantasized about a career writing for the theater. But, again representative of his era, he died of tuberculosis at twenty-seven.

Georges II was more of a challenge. Initially reluctant to join the business at all, he learned to make bows, revealed a precocious aptitude for the trade on a debut sales trip to London, and returned home more difficult than when he left. When a job opened at Maucotel's, his grateful father sent him back to London, where he quickly became involved with a girl and was challenged to a duel.

Swept away by another English girl, he resolved to stay in London, where he fathered Georges III and opened his own shop in 1857–58. A year later, his mother died, and his father married Antoinette, who had meanwhile borne him a son, Joseph Chardon. For reasons no longer apparent, he was not formally legitimated. But it was agreed that he would take over the shop progressively, beginning at eighteen, and share the property, under his mother's supervision, while Georges, now sixty, retired to a 6,000-franc property between Paris and Versailles, and conveniently close to a railroad station.

In 1868 the shop, with a window to the street, was officially renamed Chanot-Chardon. Two years later, Joseph and the employee he only married some weeks later produced another Georges, this one Georges IV. The war with Prussia that broke out soon afterward brought business to a halt for several months. Neither a republican like his first two children nor a Bonapartist like the third, Georges looked on in dismay as Napoleon III was deposed. His regime had at least been good for business.

It was July 1871 before the Paris shop reopened, at first slowly, then with increasing success as the country absorbed the cost of defeat and reparations. A year later, when the famous Gillott collection came up for auction in London, Joseph was one of the few foreigners to buy, though cautiously, given the weakness of the franc.

Business as usual seems nonetheless to have been good enough. Customers included the Belgian virtuosi Henri Vieuxtemps and Hubert Léonard, and the composer Camille Saint-Saëns, as well as innumerable lawyers, teachers, and architects, who looked to the House of Chanot for reliable expertise, skillful restorations, and setups.

Meanwhile, a new generation had come of age. Trained in Paris, Frederick, the elder, tried and failed to set up shop in the ferociously competitive London market. His brother Georges Adolphe succeeded in Manchester, where he immediately sold a Strad cello consigned to him by Joseph. He then vindicated the family honor by taking a gold medal at the 1885 London Exposition.

Back in Paris, Joseph enlisted Georges IV, the first of the family to attend a lycée, in another generation of partnership. Now known as Chardon & Fils, the firm lived in comfortable symbiosis with a loyal clientele of teachers, orchestra players, and amateurs extending as far as Réunion and Rostov-on-Don. Restorations and appraisals were still a reliable moneymaker, but the stars had long vanished from the customer list, sales of old Italian instruments were now rare, and making, too, had become both discretionary and marginal.

A forty-four-year-old reserve quartermaster on the eve of World War

I, Georges IV passed the long, sad war years making fourteen violins and four violas and poking around Les Halles in search of windfalls. His son André, a volunteer in 1914, was appreciated as a cellist and workman in his own right. He survived the war to manage the French Tenth Army orchestra in occupied Mainz, then returned to Paris and the family business.

The postwar years brought a modest prosperity, as well as an apartment with a Gaveau piano and Japanese vases that Georges, the patriarch, could never have imagined. The demand side now included players from all the Paris orchestras as well as concertmasters from Helsinki to Istanbul, and foreign dealers from as far away as New York. André was a much-admired bow maker. In May 1937, the same month the Strad show opened in Cremona, the French guild, including Georges, pulled itself together for the Paris World's Fair, with the warm support of a bureaucracy determined "to exhibit new instruments, capable of showing America the value of the French creative genius, aided by our unmatched artisan violin makers, who are the envy of the world."[269]

In the aftermath of another calamitous war, the House of Chardon emerged once more under the direction of André and his sister Josephine. This was the last hurrah. In 1963, André died at sixty-six, leaving no heir but Josephine, also unmarried and already sixty-two. A distant echo of Florentine, she had taught herself to rehair bows, set up instruments, perform minor repairs, and buy instruments with the help of colleagues. She died, at eighty, after waiting on a customer.

The German scene was what France might have been had it consisted only of Mirecourt. At least till the end of the eighteenth century, German makers at home and abroad maintained respectable standards. They then opted for mass production. Yet even in Mittenwald and Markneukirchen, which stamped out violins as Detroit would stamp out cars, there continued to be good, even very good, violin makers, just as there were in Mirecourt.

A couple of centuries later, in the aftermath of unification with the West, dozens of appalled East German owners were told as gently as possible that what they thought were Old Italians were neither old nor Italian.[270] Serendipitously acquired by the West German Interior ministry in 1990, the East German state collection, too, consisted almost entirely of copies.[271] Ironically, the story could be read as a testimonial to German craftsmen whose instruments had delivered all that local concertmasters, products of one of the world's great orchestra cultures, had demanded of them over decades of professional playing.

Like Nicolò Amati and Stradivari, Jakob Stainer, the only German
mentioned in the same breath as his Italian contemporaries, is interesting
as a career, a template, and a historiographical puzzle. His paper trail is
unusually comprehensive. Letters and business records reflect a literacy not
typical of the trade or era, as well as a difficult personality. Court records
also reflect troubled times, made even more troubled by Stainer's impolitic
articulateness and heterodox reading.[272]

There are inevitably white spaces, too, beginning with the date of his
birth in Absam, a Tyrolean village, where there appeared to be no regular
priest in place to record such things until some thirty years after Stainer
was born. The earliest evidence of his existence, a documented inheritance
from a maternal great-grandmother's brother, dates from 1623. By this
time, according to Stainer's biographers, he was at least two, but more
probably six years old, born into a family of miserably poor workers and
miners astride the great imperial interstate between Verona and Augsburg.

Like his birth date, his education and training can only be inferred.
Even at the Tyrolean village level, schools existed, Latin was taught, church
music was cultivated, and miners and choirboys sang. Between 1624 and
1630, Stainer seems to have been a choirboy, possibly at the court in Innsbruck. To go by a 1669 letter, where he identifies violin playing as a useful
skill for makers, he may at least have had some lessons.

Where he learned his trade is another mystery. If the Innsbruck connection is valid, it might plausibly support an Italian connection. Traces
of Italian show up in Stainer's correspondence, as well as in other people's
recollections of him. But where he went and worked is anybody's guess.
Füssen might be a possibility had it not been hammered by the plague,
Swedish invaders, and the Thirty Years' War in the years when Stainer
would have been an apprentice. The Tyrol and Innsbruck were comparatively secure from predatory armies. He would have had to start there with
a cabinetmaker, because there was no major instrument maker.

The Amati look of his instruments hints at a Cremona connection, as
does a label dated Cremona 1645. It was discovered in 1910 in a violin that
was also labeled "Brothers Amati" and had already been sold as such to
a Viennese collector by Vuillaume in the 1850s. The Amati label can be
written off, since both brothers were long dead by 1645. But no Stainer
label was reported when the instrument was opened in 1892,[273] and the
instrument's "silvery" sound, lion's head substitute for a scroll, and German architecture are as suggestive of Venice as they are of Cremona, which
only leads back to Füssen and the Tyrol.

Given the family's poverty, how Stainer or his father might have paid for five or six years of room, board, and tuition is another open question. Guild rules allowed marriage with a master's daughter as an alternative to cash payment, but Stainer's wife seems to have been a miner's daughter, and they married in 1645, an estimated ten years after his apprenticeship would have ended.

His earliest known signed instrument dates from 1638, when he was around twenty.[274] His first documented sale, to the Salzburg court, dates from 1644. The next year he made a sale in Munich. The year after, there was a whole commission from the Innsbruck court, though an extended absence, presumably caused by his having to look for pigments in Venice, caused some of the work to be subcontracted to competitors, including a cousin of the court clock maker and the court violinist. By the early 1650s, a combination of family contingency, commercial success, and a modest inheritance from his father-in-law both allowed and required him to settle down. He had meanwhile applied successfully for a coat of arms, a modest status symbol that allowed him to testify in court without taking an oath. The design featured a mountain goat holding a violin, superimposed on the letters of his name.

He was also in increasing demand as a godfather; and a good enough credit risk that a local merchant, later a judge, lent him 150 florins, most probably to buy or renovate a house. The loan was five times what Stainer charged the Bavarian elector for an uncommonly elegant instrument, accessorized in ebony and ivory. In 1658, there was a commission from the Spanish court. In time, more would follow from Italy, Nuremberg, major monasteries, and the Archbishop of Bohemian Olomouc (Olmütz), who wanted a whole suite of two violins, four violas, two gambas, and a bass. Ferdinand de' Medici, the Tuscan prince, owned two Stainers. Antonio Veracini, the Tuscan virtuoso and composer, owned ten, comprising half of his collection.[275]

The same year, Stainer was named court servant by Ferdinand Karl, the Tyrolean archduke and a legendary spender with a Medici wife. The title fell short of court maker, but it qualified him to repair instruments and make himself known when itinerant virtuosi like William Young, the English court gambist, showed up at the music-loving court. The appointment lapsed with the archduke's death in 1662. There was eventual vindication: seven years later, the emperor conferred a similar appointment.

In 1659, an obscure brawl with a couple of farmers led to damage claims. In 1661, another court required Stainer to pay a contested bill of

50 florins. The putative home loan was still unpaid ten years later. Things only deteriorated from there.

Counter-Reformationist Austria was tolerant of many things but not of Protestants. Though not a Protestant, Stainer was suspected at least of knowing and sympathizing with some. According to one witness, he also owned, read, and discussed books disapproved of by the Catholic church, and eloquently at that, with acquaintances including a tailor, a tradesman, and a sawmill operator. In 1668, Stainer was called before a board of church officials, apparently to face heresy charges. The initial sentence, requiring the defendants to appear in sackcloth with candles, disavow their error, and reaffirm their Catholic faith, was reduced to a requirement that they burn their books. Stainer was nonetheless jailed—to prevent escape, one assumes. After pleading a contractual obligation to deliver instruments, he was released on bail. He was excommunicated, rearrested in 1669, and rereleased under protest only after an agreement to repent officially in church.

Through it all, business seems to have flourished, favored in part by his reputation for quality, in part by the growing taste for instrumental music. Cash flow was a perennial problem. Overextended himself, the archduke defaulted on payments. Ferdinand Stickler, dean of the parish church in Meran, who ordered a gamba in 1678, proposed paying in wine. For 16 thaler in cash instead of his usual fee of 20–30 thaler, Stainer agreed to throw in a lion's head instead of a scroll and take the instrument back if Stickler didn't like it.

In 1679 the Munich court advanced 150 florins for a consignment of instruments. This time, nemesis appeared as failing mental health, possibly bipolar disease. Senn estimates that Stickler's instrument was produced within a month, but Stainer reportedly had to be chained to the workbench. Meanwhile, phony Stainers proliferated, and a tide of debts rose around him. In 1682, he defaulted on interest payments and was placed in the custody of a court-ordered guardian. A year later he died. Little was left of the estate after the debts were paid, and his two surviving daughters ended their lives as domestics in the house of a deceased brother-in-law.

But there was a good deal more to his legacy. Till the coming of Viotti, the Strad, and a sea change in musical taste[276] more than a century later, Stainer's "silver-toned" violins would be the gold standard of the trade, admired as much abroad as they were at home. "The violins of Cremona are exceeded only by those of Stainer . . . whose instruments are remarkable for a full and piercing tone," the English musicologist Sir John Hawkins reported in his five-volume *General History of the Science and Practice of Music*, published in London in 1776. In Germany, Italy, and England, copyists scrambled to meet the demand for them. Successor makers from Augsburg to Mittenwald and Nuremberg to Prague were inspired by his example.

In Füssen, where Italian-style making went back to at least 1666, some eighty masters set up shop, and uncounted apprentices learned their trade over the course of the eighteenth century. In 1752, Johann Anton Gedler applied for citizenship as the fifteenth master in a town of 1,400. No problem, declared the city council, overruling the guild, and approving the application on grounds that current demand from Italy, France, and above all Germany could support a hundred masters. Local journeymen had no trouble finding jobs in Vienna, Olmütz, Breslau, and Prague. In 1769, a Munich master, the only violin maker in a town of 40,000, appealed to a baker acquaintance in Füssen to help find him an apprentice.[277]

In Nuremberg, Leonhard Mausiell, a native, sold Stainer-inspired violins and cellos to local churches, church schools, even city hall. The estate of a local merchant alone lists thirty-eight Mausiell violins, plus several more with Mausiell labels.[278] An otherwise uneventful history became more interesting with the coming of Leopold Widhalm, a gifted journeyman of Lower Austrian origins who took a job in the city's first shop and fathered a child with the master's daughter in 1745.

The practice was a fast track to citizenship so regularly trodden that the city council would eventually pass resolutions deploring the frequency of its use by Protestants as well as Catholics.[279] In any case, Mausiell and Michael Vogel, another local maker, were having none of it, and demanded action from the city council. Business was clearly an issue in a protected market, where Widhalm, the Catholic outsider, showed promise of becoming a serious competitor to Mausiell, already established for decades as the Protestant insider. But rank mattered, too, in a society so obsessed with status that it prescribed and codified the adjectives in obituaries and the allowable number of pallbearers.[280]

The solution was surprisingly simple. The council first denied Widhalm's claim to the family shop in Nuremberg. It then not only allowed the couple to resettle just outside the city walls in a more congenial neighborhood of soldiers, prostitutes, foreigners, religious sectarians, and other marginalized craftsmen but permitted Widhalm to take along his father-in-law's wood reserve. For the next thirty years, till his death in 1776, he restored lutes, added harps to his inventory, presumably sold his product to Catholic foundations, and reportedly exported to Spain, France, America, and Russia. He even recruited a local publisher and an imperial postal official as godfathers for his children. On his wife's death five years after his own, the house and business passed to two sons, who would eventually leave an estate estimated at more than 20,000 gulden, a respectable fortune in a market where Stradivaris were assessed at 125 gulden, Stainers at 75 to 150 gulden, Mausiells at 21 to 22 gulden, and Widhalms at 21 to 55 gulden.

If Nuremberg was Cremona as it might have been imagined by Wagner's Meistersinger, Mittenwald was Absam without Stainer. Another Alpine entrepôt and market town, it might have gravitated to cuckoo clocks and nativity scenes. That it didn't was the work of Mathias Klotz, born in 1653, who presumably returned to his native town a few years before Stainer's death after an apprenticeship with the lute maker Giovanni Railich in Padua. There is no evidence of any Stainer connection, but his product alone is a testimonial to Stainer's influence.

At work by 1684 in an ad hoc cartel of at least three makers,[281] he made good instruments, though probably not violins until they became fashionable some years later. He also marketed both his own and colleagues' instruments with energy and enterprise. His most notable achievement was an eight-generational dynasty of local makers, thirty-six altogether, that would extend past the middle of the twentieth century. A grateful community erected an idealized monument in his honor—in 1890, nearly 150 years after his passing.

What meanwhile defined Mittenwald was the progressive transformation of a handicraft into a cottage industry. The process was already well under way by 1800, when Napoleon's continental embargo cut off Britain, a favored market for Mittenwald products both before and afterward. By this time, autonomous makers, who peddled their wares at fairs and sold to monasteries, had been replaced by a handful of brokers who set up shop in metropolitan centers and tested their luck and risked their capital as far away as Russia and America.

Retailers supplied materials, contracted labor, and marketed the product. Pine was local. Maple, originally local, came increasingly from Bosnia, Herzogovina, and northern Turkey. Ebony, of course, was tropical. Gut strings were imported from Rome, Naples, Padua, even Markneukirchen, Mittenwald's competitor and subcontractor. Labor was tenaciously and comprehensively seasonal, in part because a smallholder population had hay to gather and wood to cut, in part because alternatives—forestry, waiting tables, bellhopping at a local hotel, even beating and gamekeeping for the Bavarian Prince Regent, the Grand Duke of Luxemburg, and Gustav Krupp von Bohlen-Halbach, the iron and steel baron—paid better. In a village of a few thousand, brokers maintained a cadre of some twenty to forty regular employees at a weekly wage of 15 to 25 marks. Irrespective of season, women were scarce until the varnish stage. Two hundred to two hundred fifty males were available for winter piece work, yielding roughly 8 to 12 marks of weekly income for workdays of twelve to fourteen hours. Given the option of forestry jobs at 3 to 4.5 marks daily, it was easy to see why violin making was seasonal.[282] Still, Ludwig Neuner, who spent six years with Vuillaume in Paris before returning to the family firm in 1884, employed up to two hundred to assemble a product line for a global clientele, marketed to American buyers at prices extending from $2.45 retail at the entry level to $108 a dozen wholesale for the upper-end model with the pearl-inlaid backs.

It was also easy to see why margins were tight. On the eve of the twentieth century, Mittenwald's volume was some twenty-five to thirty thousand instruments annually. In part, it owed its success to a pool of available, semiskilled labor, frugal use of materials, and a price structure so sensitive that it factored for transport costs, grocery prices, and insurance. But the linchpin was entrepreneurs, willing and able to pay a few marks for local products that would eventually retail at 5 to 300 marks, with an average between 30 and 70 marks; carry German customers for three to six months; and wait still longer for the checks from Russia and Latin America to arrive in the mail.

It was small wonder that skill levels sank with prices. In a process that effectively reduced making to four steps, Stainer's descendants built instrument bodies of back, top and ribs, and carved necks, varnished the assembled product, or set the instrument up. By the middle of the nineteenth century, virtually no one was left who knew how to build an entire instrument.

In 1858, Bavaria's King Maximilian II, a liberal with a soft spot for the arts and sciences, founded an *Unterrichts- und Musterwerkstatt*, a model teaching studio, where local fourteen- and fifteen-year-olds could essentially learn to do what their fathers did. The facility would slowly evolve into one of the world's oldest and most respected schools of violin making. But it was the brokerage firms, with their obvious stake in the status quo

at the intersection of demand and supply, that both funded it and supplied
it with basic materials.

It was 1888 before the curriculum finally extended to production of an
entire instrument. It was 1901 before the mission statement declared: "The
Mittenwald Violin Making School has the task of instructing its pupils in
the making of wooden instruments such that they can produce a complete
and marketable violin from the basic materials, and repair an old violin
so that it can again be used."[283] In the end, the economic consequences of
World War I finished off the local industry, though the Nazis tried in 1938
to resurrect the glory that was Mittenwald in much the same way, and for
the same reasons, that their allies in Italy tried in 1937 to resurrect the
glory of Cremona.[284]

The same year, Markneukirchen's unemployed were put to work on a
bit of local road construction known then and since as "the violin makers'
curve." Meanwhile, assiduous functionaries set about assembling twenty-
one autonomous guilds, seven of them made up of instrument makers,
under a common, Nazi umbrella. Undeterred by depressed export markets, increasing demand for skilled labor, and mobilization for World War
II, the consolidated guild still counted as many as 257 members as late as
1941,[285] the year Germany invaded the Soviet Union and declared war on
the United States.

It was all downhill from there. A postwar Communist regime declared
war on private enterprise. Those who could fled westward, leaving behind
the Kombinat Musikinstrumente, a socialized assembly line with some
1,200 employees in stringed instrument production alone, predominantly
aimed at the Soviet bloc.[286] Enough private initiative remained in 1970 to
erect a discreet but unmistakable monument to the unknown guild master in front of the local instrument museum. But the capitalist past that
had once made Markneukirchen one of the richest little communities in
Germany was practically an unmentionable.[287]

The roots of success went back to the sixteenth century, when readily
available pine and maple, a copper boom, and a Saxon court with a soft
spot for instrumental music led to an ascending curve of artisanal enterprise. Ironically, the same Thirty Years' War that devastated Füssen also
added to Markneukirchen's success. If the Counter-Reformation uncorked
a flow of Austrian refugees to Protestant Bohemia, the victory of the Catholic forces at the Battle of the White Mountain in 1620 only set them in
motion again, this time to neighboring Saxony. From there, the appeal of

civic identity, a weekly market, a transport-based service economy, even an elected judge and trial by jury, led to Markneukirchen, where a dozen Bohemian violin makers relocated between 1648 and 1677.[288]

In 1677 Duke Moritz of Saxony recognized "the honorable guild of the Neukirchen violin makers." Candidates for the master's certificate were expected to submit a violin, a gamba, and a cittern. For its part, the guild undertook to remunerate examiners with beer, brandy, and "a few dinner rolls," and to recognize successful examinees with a dinner that included "three pails of beer." Four years later, the violin dealer Heinrich Götz appeared on the local tax registry like the first robin in spring. What began as a sideline for wagoners soon became a lucrative business in its own right, with customers as far away as Warsaw, Strasbourg, and Scandinavia. By 1700, thirty local masters, including four of the original twelve Bohemians, were operating in a town of 6,000. In 1713, for a fee of 21 thaler, Elias Pfretzschner became the first dealer certified as a master.[289] By the mid-eighteenth century, the town's first exports were en route to North America via Nuremberg.[290] It was the guild's implosion and the ascendance of the dealers a century later, however, that would make Markneukirchen remarkable as well as rich.

The process began long before formal abolition in 1861. With its prohibition of out-of-town apprentices, the guild had been conceived as a kind of nonproliferation pact. At least initially, it paid off in extended family businesses and robust local patriotism. Extending across the generations, Vannes's directory lists fifteen Gliers, twenty Döllingers, twenty-six Gläsels and Fickers, and thirty-seven Gütters, figures impressive even by Mirecourt standards.[291]

Klingenthal, its competitor down the road, took out-of-town apprentices but required production on site. In contrast, Markneukirchen's charter was silent about out-of-town subcontracts. In 1828, Markneukirchen boasted 52 masters, 6 journeymen, and 10 apprentices. Forty wives and children were employed. Klingenthal, with 145 masters, employed 7 journeymen, 11 apprentices, and 17 girls and women. Each town produced around 7,000 violins a year. But while Klingenthal's product emerged from traditional shops, Markneukirchen's were already becoming little factories, with a growing concern for volume, a foothold in Russia, and a well-developed division of labor reaching back to 1710, when violin making spun off into collateral trades.[292] Among them were the import of raw materials, pegs, chin rests, bridges, necks, unvarnished bodies—modules, in effect—from specialist towns around the region, as well as independently incorporated bow and string making that were also destined for global prominence.

Perhaps the most notable of the new occupations was dealing, the crucial link between a Central European supplier and the world's first mass market. The industry was already in flower by the end of the eighteenth century. By the end of the nineteenth and early twentieth centuries, it would bring a U.S. consulate to Markneukirchen, a fanciful collection of Wilhelmine castles and Italianate villas to the hills overlooking its main street, and a cohort of entrepreneurial immigrants—Hammig, Möller, Wurlitzer, Mönnig—to flagship prominence in Berlin, Amsterdam, Cincinnati, New York, and Philadelphia.

As the local historian is quick to point out[293] and the exemplary local museum confirms, respectable artisanal craftsmanship never died out, and even flourished on the margins. Ayke Agus, an accomplished violinist as well as the great Jascha Heifetz's studio pianist, played a 1922 Ernst Heinrich Roth. The "old German violin" with "parts from various European shops" and a Storioni imprint, spectacularly played by the jazz artist and 2006 MacArthur "genius" Regina Carter, sounds suspiciously like a product of Markneukirchen.[294]

But Markneukirchen neither was nor aspired to be a Saxon Cremona. Beginning in 1834, traditional apprenticeship was supplemented by a trade school whose graduates were to transform the town into a world-renowned center for guitars, zithers, harmonicas, accordions and violins. By the end of the nineteenth century, 90 percent of the local production generated by 22 discrete occupational specialties was exported.

As early as 1870, milling machines, driven by gas-powered engines, cut fingerboards. The new machines showed such brilliant promise that a public company with over fifty employees was formed in 1907 to produce up to fifty-two thousand instrument bodies a year. It might have worked, had less mechanized shops not lowered their prices and earnings so far that even machines could no longer compete with them. Yet Markneukirchen still claimed 52 percent of the world's bowed and plucked instruments and 96 percent of its string market on the eve of World War I, and it had recovered most of its market share a decade after it. Even as they approached the slippery slope that would lead from the Great Depression and the rise of Hitler to forty years of communism and the fall of the Berlin Wall, 655 employees in 348 shops were producing bowed instruments. With subcontractors and specialties added, the totals reached 4,247 employees in 1,779 shops, whose livelihood depended on the willingness and ability of parents in faraway places to provide music lessons for their children.[295]

The faraway places included Japan, where the same need to modernize that led to battleships and baseball also led to an embrace of violins. A pioneer delegation of samurai, touring the West in the wake of the 1867 Meiji Restoration, returned deeply impressed by the uniform bowings of European orchestra players. In 1874 court musicians appealed to the Ministry of the Navy for Western training.

The first tentative examples of domestic violin making appeared around the same time. The decisive figure was Masakichi Suzuki, born in Nagoya, now a major industrial city, in 1859. The son of a samurai who took up business after the warrior class was abolished, and took up music teaching after the family business failed, Suzuki copied his first violin in 1887. Two years later, he cautiously showed his best product to Rudolf Dittrich, the resident German at the newly opened conservatory. By 1890, distributors in Osaka and Tokyo were selling Suzuki violins for half to a third the price of an imported one, although at half to a third the monthly wages of an entry-level teacher or policeman, this was still not cheap. By 1897, ten employees produced twelve hundred violins a year. By 1907, about a hundred employees with Suzuki-developed machines produced violins in the thousands. The real breakthrough came in 1914. With Mirecourt, Mittenwald, and Markneukirchen beyond reach for the duration, a staff of almost a thousand increased annual output to 150,000 violins and 500,000 bows.[296] Their similarity to the Markneukirchen product was not a coincidence.

That one or another Suzuki product made its way to Germany in the aftermath of the war completed the circle. In 1923, Suzuki's son Shinichi registered for the summer course at the Berlin Conservatory and stayed on to study with Karl Klingler, the onetime second violinist of the Joachim Quartet. In a letter, written in English, four years later, the elder Suzuki informed Georg Schünemann, the conservatory's deputy director, of his intention "to present one of my good violins every year in future, to good student who graduate your school, through your hand, if you like me to do so." Schünemann answered in the affirmative. Posted in January 1928, several Suzuki violins arrived duty-free in Berlin in March and were duly passed on to needy students.[297]

A little more than fifty years later, in a country where Nikon and Minolta had long since caught up with Vogtländer and Zeiss, Sony had

long since caught up with Grundig and Telefunken, and Toyota held its
own with Volkswagen, Soroku Murata founded the Tokyo Violin Making
School. A Mittenwald graduate whose copy of the "Hellier" Strad won a
gold medal from the Violin Association of America, he was distressed that
young Japanese could play and learn to play violins without leaving home,
while young Japanese who wanted to make and restore them still had to
go abroad.

For a fee equivalent to university tuition, plus a third again as much for
tools, eight to twelve students at a time could enroll in a four-year course
on the theory and practice of instrument making with a teacher, who made
a point of being addressed as "*oyakata*," a master of carpentry or handicraft
in the European sense, rather than "*sensei*," the teacher, guide, and instructor of judo, calligraphy, the tea ceremony, and the piano. Though Japanese musicians looked on homemade violins with the same disdain they
might show for Japanese Scotch,[298] admissions applications ran well ahead
of available places, at least till 2006, when no successor appeared to replace
its retiring founder.[299] But Tetsuo Matsuda, a Cremona graduate born in
a Japanese mountain village in 1945, continued to make elegant Guarneri
copies at his home in suburban Chicago, and to sell them through Bein
& Fushi, one of the world's great shops, on Michigan Avenue, one of the
world's great streets.[300]

By this time, a new cycle was under way across the East China Sea.
Like Christianity, Indian opium, and the bicycle, the violin reached China
with Western visitors. By the early 1930s, at least one Chinese player, Tan
Shu-zhen, had managed to work his way into the Shanghai orchestra,[301]
and Sito Fu-Quan, a co-founder of the Shanghai conservatory, had taught
himself how to make violins with the help of Heron-Allen's manual, Robert Alton's *Violin and Cello Building and Repairing* (London, 1923), and a
German trade delegation that told him how to order wood and tools from
Markneukirchen.

By the late 1940s, there were at least ten Western music stores in
Shanghai. In 1949, the year the People's Republic was proclaimed, a "New
China" instrument factory was founded too. A decade later, there were
an estimated fifty nationalized Chinese violin factories whose ascending production curve, undeflected and even encouraged by the vehement
anti-Westernism of the Cultural Revolution, peaked at some 345,000
instruments in 1977, about half of them for export. Tan, another of the
conservatory's founders, made sure that it included a workshop where

teachers and students could get instruments and repairs for free. He also channeled a government subsidy into Mongolian tree trunks, recruited a cadre of furniture makers and wood sculptors to copy Italian models from Heron-Allen's outlines, and organized short courses at fifteen factories around the country.

In 1978, Tan emerged from the depredations of the Cultural Revolution to resume where he had left off. With $125,000 from the Ministry of Culture to spend on good instruments, he was even dispatched to shop in the United States. He returned with three Pressendas and a Vuillaume, but also a conviction that the nation's resources would be better invested in a long march to domestic production. The result was a four-year curriculum in violin making for an annual class of ten, whose members were expected to play as well as their studio classmates and produce six or seven instruments while in residence. In 1980, two students were sent off to Mittenwald. In 1983, Zheng Quan, another rehabilitated casualty of the Cultural Revolution, was sent to Cremona. Four years later, with support from the Chinese embassy in Rome, he returned with a basic inventory of books, tools, and wood to establish the Research Center of Violin Making of the Central Conservatory of Music and to look into the availability of violin-quality domestic maple. In 1991, a Zheng violin placed first in a Cremona competition.[302] Meanwhile, the late twentieth-century version of the Markneukirchen Strad could be bought over the counter from Taoist temples in Souzhou to the main street of Parma, where Paganini is buried.

By the early twenty-first century, an estimated 50 to 80 percent of the student violins on the market were Chinese instruments of respectable quality and affordable price. Unable to compete with Chinese labor costs, European makers either looked to their machines or imported unfinished instruments from China, as Markneukirchen had once imported them from across the Bohemian border. They then finished them, added a label, and marketed them online, just as Markneukirchen had once finished imports, added a label, and marketed them through Sears, Roebuck. An estimated 60 percent of the Sino-European imports came with European labels. The rest were unapologetically Chinese; the Research Center of Violin Making of the Central Conservatory of Music and the Violin Makers Chapter of the China Musical Instrument Association announced their first international competition in spring 2010, and Western dealers asked without irony how Chinese makers had gotten so good so fast.[303]

THE ROAD NOT TAKEN

⌒

BY ANY STANDARD this side of the wheel, the alphabet, and the knife and fork, the global proliferation of the Italian violin is one of history's great success stories. But the history of *the* violin is more than the history of *a* violin.

Between 1957 and 1960, two acquisitions caught the attention of Olga Adelmann, a restorer at the Berlin Musical Instrument Museum. Serious attention was clearly indicated if they were to be identified, classified, and, ideally, restored to their original condition after—well, who even knew how many?—decades, even generations, of damage, bad repairs, and arbitrary alterations. What was their original condition? How could she restore them without knowing who owned them, who made them, and when and where they were made?

With their intarsia of folksy hearts, flowers, and geometrical patterns, the new specimens already stood out in any collection. They were just as notable for their broad fingerboards, oddly extended scrolls, and nominally archaic architecture, with extended corners, combined neck and upper block, almost vertical f-holes, and a bass bar carved directly from the top of the instrument rather than added separately. Closer to furniture than to lutherie, they were built as instruments were commonly built before the Italian method crossed the Alps. But there was nothing quaint, let alone primitive, about their workmanship.

It was equally clear to Adelmann that they had not only passed through a lot of shops but undergone major makeovers by people with a stake in selling them as Italian. The decorations made Brescia a popular cover. Of the two specimens at hand, one was transparently mislabeled as a Gasparo da Salò. The other had no apparent identity at all. Library sources were unhelpful. For the next thirty years, Adelmann pursued their provenance from Switzerland to Copenhagen and Brussels on vacation time and almost entirely at her own expense. Her efforts would eventually unearth twenty-one members of the same family as well as a surviving back and belly.

An unlikely Sherlock Holmes and still more improbable Javert, she nonetheless brought two inestimable qualifications to the project. One, as her colleague Annette Otterstedt noted after her death, was a Candide-like innocence and tenacity that she retained into old age, and which clearly sustained her long after peers and colleagues, including her employer, might have asked whether the search was worth the trouble.[304] The other was an uncommon technical skill, acquired by a fortuitous combination of circumstance and natural inclination.

Born in Berlin in 1913 to a painter mother and engineer father, Adelmann had gone to work for Otto Möckel, one of the city's better violin makers, on leaving school, and by sheer persistence persuaded him to teach her the craft. In 1940, with most male contemporaries in uniform or otherwise employed, she became the first German woman certified as a master violin maker. She then visited Cremona, where she met Sacconi, whose 'Secrets' of Stradivari she would one day translate. Ironically, on her return to Berlin, she made herself so useful to a subsequent employer that he impounded her tools when she wanted to leave and go into business for herself. Her solution was again characteristic both of herself and the times. She got herself to Markneukirchen, riding where necessary on top of overfilled railway carriages, and returned with the tools and materials she needed.

In a fourth-floor ruin in postwar Berlin, she finally set up shop with the help of a Berlin Philharmonic player, who even sent colleagues as customers. But she promptly went broke. "My job as a restaurateur in the Berlin Musical Instrument Museum was the luckiest turn in my life after inexperience in business caused me . . . to crash in the difficult 50s," she later wrote, "and then, for lack of alternatives, to work for a master guitar maker, which now turned out to be useful."[305]

By 1990, when she produced a first edition of her monograph, she had not only identified the mysterious acquisitions but discovered and named an extinct species. From here on, it would be known as Alemannic, for the Upper Rhenish intersection of Switzerland, Baden, and Alsace where the instruments had originated.

In 1995, there was a glorious moment when Choon-Jin Chang, the young associate principal violist of the Philadelphia Orchestra, appeared with his own instrument, a viola of ambiguous provenance. He had acquired it a year earlier from Moennig, the Philadelphia dealer, who had bought it from an amateur in Quebec and offered it as Brescian or Venetian at a respectable Italian price. On tour in Europe, Chang discovered the first edition of Adelmann's monograph in a London shop. Understandably curious about an instrument he had come to like better than any Amati or Guadagnini around him, he made a beeline for the Musical Instrument Museum on his arrival in Berlin.

For Adelmann and Otterstedt it must have been something like watching a visitor lead a woolly mammoth across the threshold on a leash. Chang's viola was heavily altered. But it was clearly a member of the Alemannic family, most probably a Frantz Straub built in the last quarter of the seventeenth century. He even played it for them, confirming to their delight that an Alemannic instrument could stand up to Italians in one of the world's elite orchestras. A year later, Adelmann's database had grown to thirty-three specimens. Among them were a cello-sized bass violin, six tenor violins, two soprano violins, and a communion table by the instrument maker Hans Krouchdaler, in use till 1889, that illuminated the common origins of all of them.

Otterstedt's reconstruction of their collective message was at once salutary and disarmingly straightforward. Their makers were neither perambulant players who made their own instruments, like colleagues from the Lowlands to Brescia, nor professional lute makers like their colleagues in Füssen. They seem, on the contrary, to have been solid citizens from the Upper Rhine, who lived between the mid-seventeenth and early eighteenth centuries, practiced a craft essentially derived from furniture making, and never left home. Straub, an exception, seems to have come from Füssen. But nothing in his product suggests exogenous origins.[306] Unlike relatives who gravitated to Italy, he seems to have studied and married locally, then settled down to father another generation of Black Forest makers. The rule is Krouchdaler, whose work not only included instruments of every size but, again to Otterstedt's delight, the 1678 communion table, confirming the proximity of instrument and furniture making, as well as the maker's place in the church establishment.[307]

Otterstedt notes that William Baker's shop in Oxford was producing similar instruments between 1669 and 1685. As far away as Poland, other shops were producing them, too. They were mostly interesting for what they weren't. Not viols, they were also not the genuinely archaic fiddles associated with dance masters and public entertainers. Though Italian instruments were already played and admired by London professionals, there is no hint in Baker's work that something important was going on in Italy.[308]

His instruments seem nonetheless to have appealed to post-Puritan Oxford's growing population of upscale amateurs. The Alemannic instruments appealed to a similar clientele, both Catholic and Protestant. By 1688, the Cistercian monastery of St. Urban had acquired a set from local makers. Over the next century, Calvinist school and college boys also discovered the joys of playing for fun. "There was no shortage of amateurs, a number of them fairly weak," Eduard Wölfflin noted of his predecessors a century later. This was especially true of string players, he added, "because countless old violins could be found in so many of the better houses."[309]

Surviving paintings, engravings, and inventories reveal that the instruments were as adaptable to popular dance music as to the pleasantly undemanding amateur chamber music cultivated in countless European salons and drawing rooms. In 1997, a quartet, including Otterstedt and her partner, the instrument maker Hans Reiners, put a set of Alemannic instruments through their paces at the Berlin Museum. Musicologically informed performances of Georg Muffat (1653–1704) and John Jenkins (1592–1678) gave some idea what the Alemannics' Cremonese cousins might have sounded like had they not been retooled for auditorium-filling sound on the eve of the nineteenth century. Chang's viola confirmed that they could also be refitted for Beethoven, Tchaikovsky, or Stravinsky.

All things being equal, Michael Fleming argues, there was nothing self-evident about the triumph, let alone superiority, of the Italian model after 1800.[310] But all things were not equal. Well into the eighteenth century, the Italian composers, soloists, and orchestras who set the musical pace also played Italian instruments. Alemannic makers made good instruments, too. But Italy set the fashions, and it was Italian that France and England wanted and sold.

By the beginning of the nineteenth century, players, composers, dealers, and collectors had made the Italian violin the universal market standard. Alemannic instruments drifted off into attics and museums, or circulated under deep cover as Brescians or Venetians. Left as they were built, Adelmann's discoveries were a credit to the world that created them.[311] But it was a small world. With the Italian model increasingly in demand where the money was, and imports undeterred by ad valorem duties as high as

20 percent,[312] there was little incentive to notice, let alone to seek and refit, the Alemannic version.

What remained was an urge to improve the Italian model that would flicker on intermittently through the nineteenth and on into the twentieth century. Agnostic about Italian perfection, undeterred, even inspired by the expansive dreams and abortive hopes of Savart, Joseph Chanot, and Vuillaume, innovators of every degree of ingenuity, practicality, and theoretical sophistication continued to build, cast, weld, hybridize, even invent, in an ongoing quest for a more adaptable, playable, or audible violin.

In the 1820s, the Viennese Johann Georg Stauffer, who also created a kind of bowed guitar he called the arpeggione, produced an elongated lozenge, with crescent C-holes parallel to the indented ribs known as the bouts. With its echoes of Savart, Chanot, the Biedermeier furniture of the period, and intimations of the Art Deco of a century later, its elegance still impresses. A decade later, Thomas Howell of Bristol, England, patented a guitar-shaped violin with a long neck, short body, and graduated ribs.[313] Yet despite good intentions and even good ideas, the road to the patent office invariably led to the museum, and the search for the future only confirmed that it had already happened.

Custodian of a formidable collection of Amatis, Strads, Guarneris, and Vuillaumes, the Smithsonian Institution's Museum of American History is also home to drawersful of early Americans, contemporary Italians, commercial Germans, and walk-ons like Gustav Henning of Boston, Miami, Denver, and Seattle, whose "deep, mellow and soulful" products were advertised in magazines and marketed by mail till he returned to his native Sweden, where he died in 1962.

Among the most interesting and certainly American of the Smithsonian's holdings is the "hollow back" or "Cradle of Harmony" violin, patented in 1852 by William Sidney Mount. Better known as a genre painter good enough for New York's Metropolitan Museum, Mount also invented a steamboat paddle wheel, a two-hulled sailboat, and a painting studio on wheels before his death in 1868. With its trapezoidal torso and pencil-straight sound holes, his violin could be a first cousin, even a *doppelgänger*, of Chanot's and Savart's. But there is no evidence of influence, direct or indirect.

In 1872, Michael Collins of Chelsea, Massachusetts, submitted his "echo viol," a gourd-shaped creation with two sound chambers, to the U.S. Patent Office. Forty years later, Charles R. Luscombe of Washington, D.C.,

appeared with a patent "fiddle," whose sixteen strings, tuned from middle
c to d', extended over sixteen bridges. Oscar Schmidt's ukelin, a hybrid
with bow and user's manual sold door-to-door, remained in production
from 1926 to 1964.

F. Bocker's "solophone" with attached fingerboard of 1893 was fitted
out with forty pushbuttons "to effect pitch changes without direct finger contact to the strings." W. A. Tuebner's undated bowed zither was
shaped like a mandolin. But the hybrid seems to have reached its zenith in
1897 with Franz Schwarzer, born in 1828 in what was then the Austrian
Olmütz. Successively a furniture maker, a zither maker, and a farmer in
Washington, Missouri, Schwarzer returned to instrument making after
his zithers won three gold medals at the 1873 Vienna Exposition. His
product line included guitars and mandolins as well as a concert violin
model zither, also available in cello form with viola tuning. They continued to sell into the 1950s, thirty years after the plant shut down. But
with 196 recorded sales of the violin and 14 of the cello model, they were
evidently not among his greatest hits.

Like hybrids, alternative materials consistently fired the imagination.
In 1891, Alfred Springer of Cincinnati was the first to patent an instrument made of aluminum, a material only recently commercially available
at affordable prices.[314] Beginning in the 1890s, Neill Merrill of New York's
Aluminum Music Instrument Company began fitting one-piece aluminum zithers, banjos, guitars, mandolins, and fiddles with spruce sound-
boards. In 1911, Felipe Fruman, identified in a contemporary newspaper
piece as a distinguished hairdresser of Morón, Argentina, invented a process for making violins out of bronze, steel, nickel, tin, and copper. In the
1930s, ALCOA in Buffalo, New York, began producing some 435 violins pressed from a single piece of aluminum for Joseph Maddy, an Ann
Arbor, Michigan, music teacher, and director of the National High School
Orchestra Camp, which would eventually grow into the Interlochen Center for the Arts.

Amplification was a favorite, too. In 1854, Sewall Short of New London, Connecticut, hollowed out the neck of a violin by Honoré Derazey
and fitted the bell of a horn over the pegbox. A half century later, a union
of bowed string and infant phonograph, named for its inventor, John
Matthias August Stroh, was a more sophisticated variation. Available in
"Home," "Concert," and "Professional" models, its linkage of bridge and
horn by a flexible aluminum diaphragm made it a dance band and outdoor

favorite as late as World War II. A century after its invention, variations of the Stroh violin, adapted to Transylvanian folk music and the indigenous needs of Myanmar, formerly Burma, were still reported in production.[315]

But after four hundred years of trial and error, the most interesting innovation was at the frontiers of science. In 1862, Hermann von Helmholtz published his *Lehre von den Tonempfindungen*.[316] Regularly updated till 1877, it energized, even revolutionized the study of hearing and acoustics. In 1891, Dr. Alfred Stelzner, probably the first stringed instrument designer with an advanced degree, took out a patent on a prototype sound box, theoretically applicable to the violin, viola, cello, contrabass, and violotta. The last, tuned an octave below the violin, was an entirely new instrument of his own invention, intended as an alternative or supplement to the viola.

While the patent was unspecific about the numerical values of the ellipses and parabolas at the heart of his design, the idea was clear. As a student of physics as well as music, Stelzner seems genuinely to have believed that he had discovered not only the principles that generations of predecessors had approached by trial and error but a new world. He then found an established maker in Wiesbaden to build a prototype, investors in Dresden to finance it, and a maker from Markneukirchen to produce it.

Though productivity would slow, initial output was impressive and public interest lively. While his violin maker shaped, mitred, purfled, and varnished some ninety-three instruments over twenty-eight months, Stelzner preached their virtues to any audience that would listen, sought media attention wherever it could be had, and even rounded up high-profile endorsements from the era's A-list violinists, Eugène Ysaÿe, Joseph Joachim, August Wilhelmj, and Emile Sauret, the cellist David Popper, and the composer Jules Massenet. Professional quartets performed on Stelzner instruments. Contemporary composers of modest distinction composed for them. Agents in Hamburg, Brussels, London, and New York pushed them, too.

But the bloom faded in short order. Two years after Stelzner's instruments made their debut at the 1892 Columbian exposition in Chicago, the firm was summoned for a bankruptcy hearing. An emergency appeal allowed production to resume till 1899. But bankruptcy and worse would follow. In 1906, at fifty-four, he shot himself.[317] He left a handful of instruments still on view in museums from Nuremberg to South Dakota, on sale from time to time in odd places, and good for an occasional session at musicology meetings.

Quality was among the less likely explanations for his failure. Like Adelmann's Alemannics, Stelzners are well made and fully functional; but creating demand for them was a serious challenge. While admired for its sound, the violotta was an armful, twice as deep from belly to back as a standard viola. Support from better composers might have helped. Even a Haydn, however, couldn't save the baryton, a cello-sized hybrid that was both plucked and bowed; nor could a Schubert save the arpeggione. It took more than the respectable but long-forgotten Felix Draeseke to save the violotta. Price was no advantage, either. Stelzners were decent value for what they cost—but that was no reason to buy one when French, even old Italian, violins of equivalent or superior quality could be had for the same price.

The search for an instrument informed by science nonetheless survived, though more than a generation would pass before it surfaced again in Cambridge, Massachusetts, where Frederick A. Saunders, a pioneer in atomic spectroscopy, a member of the National Academy of Sciences, and chairman of the Harvard physics department, also happened to be an amateur violinist-violist and president of the American Acoustical Society. Beginning in the 1930s, Saunders experimented with violins, measuring, analyzing, and comparing the response curves of hundreds of instruments from entry-level boxes to Jascha Heifetz's concert instrument, the Ferdinand-David Guarneri del Gesù, with Heifetz himself playing it.

In 1963, thirty-odd physicists, chemists, engineers, instrument makers, performers, composers, musicologists, patrons, and interested walk-ons gathered around a ping-pong table in his garden and agreed to carry on together as the Catgut Acoustical Society. While the name was meant to be funny, the organization was not. Over the next thirty years, with worldwide membership and a refereed journal, it would promote and institutionalize innovation like nothing yet in the long history of instrument making.[318]

If the garden belonged to Saunders, the gardener was Carleen Maley Hutchins, then fifty-two and still active forty years after the 1963 meeting. Born in 1911 to a Springfield, Massachusetts, accountant and his wife, Hutchins was as creative, colorful, and American as Vuillaume had been creative, colorful, and French. If Vuillaume stepped out of Balzac, Hutchins might have stepped out of a mid-Atlantic Willa Cather. Independent from early childhood, she bugled her way through summer Girl Scout camps and cultivated a taste for woodworking as a rare female presence in her high school shop class. She then studied biology at Cornell before being discouraged, like most women of her era, from attending medical school. Instead, she opted more conventionally for high school science teaching, and married after college.

A fortuitous meeting with Helen Rice, a colleague at New York's Brearley School, who would go on to create a worldwide directory of amateur chamber music players, redirected her life. Beginning on the trumpet and moving to the viola, a more traditional point of entry for adult amateurs, Hutchins joined Rice's circle in the mid-1940s. The next step in 1947, the year that Jackie Robinson broke baseball's color line, would turn her into a self-educated woman violin-maker-physicist, a species even more remarkable in historical perspective than an African-American second baseman. Dissatisfied with the viola she bought at Wurlitzer's, one of the city's bellwether shops, she resolved to make a better one herself. Rice offered to eat her hat if anything came of it. Two years later, she served up a hat-shaped cake to herself, Hutchins, and sixty friends.

Hutchins intended the viola as her last, as well as her first, project. It turned out to be only the beginning. The Rice connection paid off in more ways than cake. One was a six-year ad hoc apprenticeship with Karl Berger, a Swiss luthier with a shop facing Carnegie Hall. Another was an introduction to Saunders, leading to Hutchins's offer to build him the experimental instruments he needed for his research.

In the years that followed, Hutchins made her way from accessory to collaborator to autonomous researcher, retrofitted her house in Montclair, New Jersey, to accommodate a basement acoustical lab, and produced a steady flow of instruments, including the experimental Le Gruyère, with sixty-five holes punched in the ribs that could be plugged and unplugged in various combinations to test the interior resonance.[319] In 1959 she won a Guggenheim Fellowship, another first for a violin maker. In May 1962, *Time* hailed "the plump Montclair, N.J. housewife" who had needed "several years of electronic study" to master her measuring apparatus but counted professionals like Eugene Lehner, once of the legendary Kolisch Quartet, now of the Boston Symphony, among her customers. A few months later, she published her first article in *Scientific American*.[320] Meanwhile, in an upstairs room at Wurlitzer's, New York's top shop, she completed the violin-maker equivalent of graduate school with Sacconi. Over four years of tutorials, Sacconi allowed her to use his tools and patterns and taught her to find poplar for purfling, the decorative strip that lines a violin's upper plate, in old Chianti crates, and willow in old polo balls for the blocks at the corners of its bouts. He even let her take home the plates—the top and back—of the 1713 Wirth Strad to measure their response curve in her home lab.

By this time, she was well on the way to the octet of violins in graduated sizes, from tiny sopranino to contrabass, that would be her most notable achievement. The idea originated with Henry Brant, a professor at Bennington College, whose experiments with spatially separated groups and instrumentations ranging from clarinet, piano, and kitchen hardware to tin whistle and chamber ensemble led to thoughts about violins of all possible sizes in all possible registers.[321] In fact, many of the instruments he wanted had ancestors going back to Bach and even Praetorius. But nobody had seen one in real life or for at least two hundred years.

Hutchins's challenge was to reinvent them. The project would involve up to one hundred scientists, amateurs, and professional players over the better part of a decade. It would also lead to the rediscovery of Fred L. Dautrich, of Torrington, Connecticut, a kind of American Stelzner who, as far back as the 1920s and 1930s, had invented an alto vilonia, a tenor vilon, and a baritone vilono, to be played between the knees like a cello.

Hutchins's instruments made their debut in 1962 in a program of Brant before an audience from the Guggenheim Foundation. Beginning with a tiny treble violin, strung at tensions that called for a wire developed for NASA in the 1960s and required the player to wear safety glasses,[322] the consort extended to a six-foot contrabass violin, capable of sounds an octave below the cello. The violist Lillian Fuchs found the alto "exciting, but frightening," and meant it as a compliment. Brant, who combined the alto, tenor, and baritone with a normal violin in a standard quartet, found the ensemble "quite astounding." Three years later, the full set made its first public appearances at New York's Riverdale School and the 92nd Street Y in the presence of the ageless Leopold Stokowski, whose passion for innovation went back to the Philadelphia Orchestra fifty years earlier, and the *New York Times*, whose reporter thought some of the instruments showed promise.[323]

In time, the alto would be adopted for normal, horizontal use by a few professional violists, though its size appeared to be a challenge to anyone not built like a National Basketball Association point guard. Playing it vertically, the cellist Yo-Yo Ma chose it to record the Bartók viola concerto in 1994.[324] Hutchins's biographer, the musicologist and early musician Paul

Laird, has spoken up for the baritone as a baroque cello. On the eve of the twenty-first century, six sets were in use between San Diego, California, and St. Petersburg, Russia,[325] while others beat the now-familiar path to New York's Metropolitan Museum, the University of Edinburgh, Stockholm's Museet for Musik, and the National Music Museum in Vermillion, South Dakota.

Even Hutchins, who demonstrated and lectured on the octet some two hundred times and built or supervised construction of some ninety-four of its instruments, was skeptical that they would find a more permanent place. Her doubts were not only shared but raised a few orders of magnitude by John Schelleng, a former research director of Bell Labs, author of a classic article on the violin as circuit,[326] one of Catgut's co-founders, and an amateur cellist. The problem was not the introduction of new instruments but the development of conventional ones, Schelleng wrote Hutchins in 1974. ". . . the musician should be able to buy an almost top-notch instrument without making his father mortgage the farm." Audience interest was no proof of anything, he added. "The real person to reach . . . is the lass or lad hungry for a high-class instrument at a reasonable price on which to play the standard literature, [and] if possible make a living at it."[327]

But others continued to think outside the box. In the 1980s, Suzy Norris, a marine biologist's daughter who had learned the trade from Paul Schuback, a Barbados-born, Mittenwald-trained maker in Portland, Oregon, was so impressed by an Indian guru in New York that she invented the Suzalyne, an idiosyncratic union of violin and viola, with hints of the Indian *esraj* and Norwegian Hardanger fiddle, that combined five strings above the bridge with eight resonating strings below it. "I'll make the normal things too," Norris explained, "but I never want to stop doing the fun stuff."[328]

A few years later, David Rivinus, born in Turkey to an American Foreign Service family, took pity on a friend with persistent back pain and tendonitis. He took his cues from Otto Erdesz, a splendidly idiosyncratic Toronto-based Hungarian, who redesigned the viola's left side to make it easier for his then wife, the Israeli violist Rivka Golani, to reach the higher positions.[329] Rivinus reconfigured the whole instrument, shortening its length while maximizing the resonating chamber. He then called the result Pellegrina—pilgrim.

It looked "like an outsize pear stretched on the diagonal," Margalit Fox noted in the *New York Times*.[330] "A Daliesque, roller-coaster blend of taffy

laced with LSD," the self-defined freestyle fiddler Darol Anger called it in
the trade magazine *Strings*.[331] Isaac Stern wondered jocularly if it had been
left out too long in the sun. Spotting it for the first time in the hands of
Don Ehrlich, his assistant principal violist, Michael Tilson Thomas, the
conductor of the San Francisco Symphony, wondered if he might be hallu-
cinating. But while they may have laughed when Ehrlich sat down with his
viola, Rivinus's Pilgrim was among the first designs since Andrea Amati
to address the stress injuries that afflicted an estimated 65 to 70 percent
of professional orchestra players at some point in their careers. Ehrlich's
colleagues also liked the way it sounded. Sensitive to a profession whose
very dress code had barely changed since the Congress of Berlin, if not
the Congress of Vienna, Rivinus accommodated its inherent conservatism
with a more conventional model that nonetheless retained the Pellegrina's
advantages. "I'm the most reluctant revolutionary you can imagine," he
told Fox. "But someone came to me with a problem, and in great embarrassment, this is what I came up with."[332]

On the threshold of the violin's sixth century, Todd French, director
of a newly created Fine Musical Instrument Department at Butterfield
& Butterfield, a Bay Area auction house, exhibited other contemporary
American makers in Hollywood. Among the objects on display were
an asymmetrical blue violin by the New York maker-dealer Christophe
Landon and a Guarneri-based, Art Deco violin with a gold ball at the head
by Guy Rabut.

A veterinarian's son from Fontainebleau, Landon produced his first
asymmetrical violin in French Revolutionary red, white, and blue while
still an apprentice in Mirecourt. In the mid-1980s, he then set off for New
York, where he incidentally learned to play polo, almost certainly another
first for a violin maker. An artist-illustrator's son from Connecticut and
Landon's near contemporary, Rabut made his way to New York via a summer guitar course in Vermont and the full three-year program at the newly
opened Violin School of America in Salt Lake City. After a five-year tour
with René Morel at Jacques Français's shop on West Fifty-fourth Street,
he set up his own shop on the seventh floor of Carnegie Hall, where he
repaired and restored for an appreciative clientele before opting for full-
time making in a fifteenth-floor loft in lower Manhattan. But while both
he and Landon shared a passion for innovation, they left no doubt that
mainstream work in well-established shops was at least the stepmother of
their invention.

The Hollywood show also featured two instruments by Denny Ferrington, a displaced southerner and guitar maker from Pacific Palisades, whose blond, unblemished, and asymmetrical tear shapes were designed for potential mass production and easy access to the higher positions.[333] "If Stradivari and Guarneri were to wake up now and go to a violin convention, they'd be pissed!" Ferrington told an interviewer in 1996. " 'Man, you all've had 300 years and you're still making this?' "[334]

Landon acknowledged frustration that the Kronos Quartet, one of the era's most exuberantly innovative ensembles, remained "attached to their middle-range old instruments." Rivinus had at least got Hank Dutt, the Kronos violist, to give an instrument a serious look,[335] and found customers in the Turtle Island String Quartet, Welsh National Opera, Netherlands Radio Orchestra, and Boston Symphony. Rabut's projected quartet remained beyond the horizon, and while notable players were willing to try his Art Deco violin, it remained unsold.

Three years after the Hollywood show, Butterfield & Butterfield itself was gone, at least in the form generations had known. In 1999, it was acquired by eBay and in 2002 by Bonham's, a London auction house with an instrument department of its own. By this time, French was again playing the cello with the Los Angeles Opera, while marketing several lines of good but thoroughly conventional entry-level instruments, many Chinese, under a cluster of discreetly noncommittal labels. "The only thing people will pay money for is copies of antiques," Fan Tao, director of research at D'Addario, a major string manufacturer, reminded his colleagues, and Chinese workshops were getting better and better at making them at prices no individual maker could match.

Meanwhile, environmental legislation like America's Lacey Act complicated life for foreign as well as domestic producers by regulating both the import of such endangered materials as ebony, rosewood, and Bosnian maple and the export of finished products. Gibson, the guitar maker, had actually been raided by federal authorities. In principle, at least, the restrictions could include violins.[336] Innovation was indicated if makers hoped to survive, Tao emphasized. Of course, they would also have "to convince the buying public" to accept it, he added.[337]

BACK TO THE FUTURE

‿

YET FOR ALL that, the worst of times since Vuillaume showed promise of becoming the best of times since Guadagnini, thanks in part to science, in part to history, and in part to classical economics. After nearly a century in which professional violin making had come to seem as quaint and marginal as blacksmithing, the new makers were exceptional in many ways.

Stefan-Peter Greiner (b. 1966) was among the first of the new role models. Turned down by the venerable violin school in Mittenwald—in part, he inferred, because he was neither Bavarian nor Catholic, in part because he had worked on his first violin at fourteen and was not beginning from zero as the regulations envisioned[338]—he settled instead for an ad hoc apprenticeship with a Swedish maker in Bonn while concurrently studying varnishes and musicology at the University of Cologne.

Still in his early thirties, he wore elegant red vests with jeans and collarless white shirts; sold instruments to some of the era's top performers, including Christian Tetzlaff and the Alban Berg Quartet, struggled to keep his waiting list to four years, and named his son Antonio. To his delight, he even got the tax authorities to classify him as an artist with all the attendant advantages, rather than as a shopkeeper. Though himself a technological agnostic, Gregg Alf acknowledged respectfully that Hutchins had not only bonded physics and violin making like no one before her; she had gotten acousticians to disengage from classified research in submarine detection and return to their original subject.[339] Greiner, like Curtin, Alf's former partner, worked regularly with a professional physicist.

The new future was also informed by history, as market forces, driven by ever-growing demand for restoration and copies, led to ever-closer examination of archives and old instruments. Without help or even interest from the academic world, the payoff was a virtuous circle of research, publication, websites, summer camps, and annual meetings,[340] leading to more and better, yet still traditionally trained, makers, who in principle would produce more and better, yet still firmly traditional, instruments.

As far back as her initial decision to build a better viola, traditional instruments had actually stood tall among Hutchins's concerns. The octet, like most innovations, was an idea cast out to sea in a bottle. Time would tell whether the message reached posterity. For the here and now, she saw innovation as a means, not an end in itself. "It is possible for violin makers today, using technical information that's been developed over the last thirty years, to make fine violins every time," she declared. "There is no need to pay millions of dollars to get a good instrument."[341]

She not only spread the word from Montclair to China but took it personally to heart. In 1957, she confessed at an annual meeting of the American Association for the Advancement of Science that she had come to the aid of her friend Virginia Apgar, a Columbia University anesthesiology professor and amateur maker, who lusted after a perfectly seasoned curly maple shelf in a Presbyterian Hospital phone booth. The hospital had been uncooperative. The solution was half Charlie Chaplin, half a takeoff on Jules Dassin's classic film noir *Rififi*. Hutchins first copied the coveted shelf in a different material. She then took charge of the phone booth, while Apgar stood watch in her white lab coat, reminding Hutchins to drop a dime in the phone whenever a watchman appeared. To their dismay, the replacement shelf was a bit too long. Ever resourceful, Hutchins retired to a nearby restroom with the replacement shelf and a saw, while Apgar distracted a passing nurse, puzzled by the odd sounds coming from the restroom. It was the only time of day when repairmen could work there, Apgar reassured her. She then took the maple home and transformed it into a viola back.[342]

In 1982, the Chinese Ministry of Culture invited Hutchins to advise the infant violin industry in the wake of the Cultural Revolution and the visiting Isaac Stern. By 1999, about a half century after she started working, her output had reached an estimated 75 standard violins, 160 violas, and 12 cellos, in addition to purely experimental designs.[343]

Both published and personal, her example extended far beyond her workshop. Oberlin College and the Violin Society of America now ran summer workshops where contemporary makers like Dilworth and Zygmuntowicz coached registrants on tools, varnishes, and the latest word on computer-aided design,[344] while Curtin and Tao brought them up to speed on acoustics. Twenty years after Hutchins shed her light on China, it even shone forth from David Ouvry's Oxford webpage, where the former schoolteacher and Cambridge MA pointed with pride to the sine-wave generator he used to locate nodal points, and the frequency counter he used to measure pitches when crafting the wooden plates that would become violin backs and bellies.[345]

Ouvry's methods and technology were a measure of the distance traveled not only since William Baker, the Restoration fiddle maker, but since the Oxford of the early 1960s, when the city's closest approximation of a violin shop was a secondhand bookstore. Among other local novelties was a trio of young makers, respectively French, Canadian, and American, whose clientele of professionals, amateurs, and schoolchildren was reminiscent of Baker's. But their power tools were now as self-evident as central heating, and they made regular use of a binocular microscope when cleaning microcracks.[346]

Hutchins's influence was direct as well as indirect. Since the 1930s, teaching had come as naturally to her as woodwork. Saunders himself congratulated her on her first violin pupil in 1953. Between the late 1960s and the 1980s, she taught violin making and plate tuning a weekend or two a month to three to ten students at a time, till her collected protégés totaled some fifty.

Among them were a retired physics professor, a retired engineer, a retired research director at Lockheed Electronics, and a Washington economist; Deena Zalkind and Robert Spear, of Ithaca, New York, who set out, respectively, for medical school and a performing career before deciding instead to produce instruments good enough for the cellist Mstislav Rostropovich;[347] Gregg Alf and Joseph Curtin, of Ann Arbor, Michigan, who produced instruments good enough for Yehudi Menuhin, Ruggiero Ricci, and Elmar Oliveira;[348] a brace of guitar makers, a viola maker, and Diana Gannett, a multi-purpose string player and contrabass virtuosa who got interested in making after buying, and learning to love, Hutchins's first bass while teaching at Yale.

It was paradox enough that the rebirth of one of the world's most traditional crafts should coincide with a social, political, and cultural rebellion like none since 1848. But this time, generational rebellion and artisanal fortune were linked.

The numbers alone were striking. In 1976, there were no full-time makers left in Chicago, Robert Bein recalled a generation later. The *Strad*

Directory for 2004 listed as many as 10 shops in the city, plus seven in the suburbs, with more listings in 45 U.S. states. There were still more in 48 countries on every continent but Antarctica.[349] In Berlin alone, where Olga Adelmann was once grateful for salaried employment, there were 13. In Cremona, where Stradivari's contemporaries regarded a half dozen as a crowd, there were at least 54, and they now employed large numbers of women and non-Italians, as well as 120 students and apprentices. The most admired shop in town was, in fact, an Italian-Canadian-American co-production, founded in 1991 by Bruce Carlson, a onetime student of meteorology and a former U.S. naval officer who was also conservator of the civic collection.[350]

But the greatest of all leaps forward was arguably in quality. "There are probably more makers working today that can make good instruments than ever before," Oliveira declared in 1995.[351] A blue-collar prodigy from Connecticut with no dependable patronage or sponsorship, he was the first American to win a gold medal at the Soviet Union's Tchaikovsky competition. As one who had played many violins en route to his preferred concert instruments, including the 1726 Lady Stretton Guarneri del Gesù and its 1993 copy by Alf and Curtin,[352] he was a credible source.

In fact, the art had never died. By 1978, the year of Oliveira's Moscow triumph, dealers everywhere were busy rediscovering neglected nineteenth- and twentieth-century makers, among them the Torinese Giuseppe Rocca (1807–1865) and Annibale Fagnola (1866–1939), the Bolognese Ansaldo Poggi (1893–1984), and the Mantuan Stefano Scarampella (1843–1925), who had spent their working lives in the shadow of Guadagnini and the Cremonese patriarchs. By the end of the twentieth century, a flourishing monographic literature celebrated regional traditions from Liguria to Hungary.[353] "When you get tired ego-tripping, you should try some Rocca or Fagnola copies," the Philadelphia dealer Adolf Primavera told the young Sam after inspecting his copy of a Stradivari.[354]

Looking back, Zygmuntowicz acknowledged admiration, even awe, for more recent Old World mentors like the French-born Morel, who handled tools the way great players handle instruments.[355] The Brazilian-born Luiz Bellini (b. 1935), who worked with Sacconi at Wurlitzer's, and the Italian-born Sergio Peresson (1913–1991), who worked for Moennig, were positive role models. Peresson made, sold, and serviced instruments for Philadelphia Orchestra principals. Ruggiero Ricci, a lifelong collector, toured with a Guarneri copy he had begged Bellini to sell him.[356] Both makers had parlayed the visibility and patronage of major shops, a lifetime of restorations and adjustments, and day-and-night house-call availability to their clients. "I paid attention," Zygmuntowicz said.[357]

It was not so much that the art was an extinct species as that generations had passed since anyone could make a living making violins. Sacconi himself, already an icon to his contemporaries, averaged about one instrument annually over forty years. In more or less living memory, Carl G. Becker had created America's closest approximation of a Cremonese or Mirecourt-Parisian patriarchy. Beginning in the 1920s, he had contracted with his employer, William Lewis & Son of Chicago, to spend nine months a year repairing and restoring the classic instruments that made their way through Orchestra Hall just down the street from the shop. The other three months he made his own instruments, while passing the torch to his son, Carl F., who began at sixteen, and his grandchildren, Jennifer and Paul, who began at eleven and fifteen, respectively. Yet for instruments that would be regarded in his grandchildren's lifetime as some of the finest produced by an American, Bein estimated that Becker earned about a dollar an hour.[358] Peresson, the most successful American maker of his era, was approaching retirement before he set up his own shop.

"In endeavoring to get information regarding their life work from a number of contemporary American violin makers, the editor has had brought home to him forcibly the saying that 'art is modest,'" Alberto Bachmann reported in 1925 in his *Encyclopedia of the Violin*. Of ninety-two entries, seventy-six consisted only of a name and hometown. "It is difficult to believe that several refused information regarding their work even for encyclopedic purposes," he lamented.[359] A labor of passion produced almost sixty years later, Thomas Wenberg's one-of-a-kind *The Violin Makers of the United States* identified some 3,500 makers known to have produced a violin in the United States from the middle of the nineteenth to the late twentieth century. But the day jobs mentioned on virtually every page—among them "worked as a coal miner," "worked as a court reporter," "worked as a union representative," "worked as a cowboy, carpenter and building contractor," "worked as a mail carrier, doing his deliveries on horseback," "as a cabinet maker, clerical worker, slaughterhouse worker, trick cowboy, lasso handler, breaker of wild horses, sheepherder, cow puncher and blacksmith," "mechanical engineer by profession," "a chiropractor by profession," "operated the Ford auto dealership," "made the snowshoes Admiral Byrd wore on his expedition to the North Pole"—tell at least as much about the world they lived in.[360]

Of twenty-six British makers born between 1902 and 1948 and profiled in Mary Anne Alburger's 1979 collective biography, three are women, six made their way to the craft via furniture and woodwork, and ten more arrived via music, including conservatory study and professional orchestra playing. Among the rest are a former bank clerk, a former merchant seaman, and a former office machine technician. In a society still more class-conscious than many, her subjects extend from working-class to solidly middle-class, including a maker and a dealer who were, respectively, a Member and a Commander of the Order of the British Empire. Another was both daughter and wife of distinguished academics, each knighted, one a Fellow of the Royal Society. Only five had done more or less traditional apprenticeships, one as a furniture maker, another as a carpenter. Including the violin school graduates, who were among the youngest, only about a third had formal training as violin makers.

While economics was not a sufficient explanation for what they did and why they did it, it certainly seemed a necessary one. Between 1950 and 2000, world population soared from 2.5 to more than 6 billion. Average per capita income nearly tripled. It was inevitable that growing demand for a fixed supply would one day drive old instruments beyond the reach of all but the very rich. At least symbolically, that day arrived in 1971, when the 1721 Lady Blunt Strad broke the $200,000 barrier at Sotheby's in London. From there on, there was nowhere to go but up. There was virtually no direct connection between the sale of the Lady Blunt and the tidal wave associated with 1968. Yet what Paul Berman called the "utopian exhilaration" that "swept across the student universe and across several adult universes as well"[361] would be at least as significant a watershed in the violin-making revival. For as far back as anyone could remember, it seemed practically self-evident that violin making was an almost exclusively male, heavily local, traditional, unreflective, and self-referential craft, practiced for the most part by continental Europeans in blue smocks and steel-rimmed glasses. Now, on the foothills of young adulthood, a cohort of middle-class baby boomers, variously formed by the art school, the conservatory, the guitar class, and the hootenanny, appeared to have discovered it not merely as a vocational option but as a brave new world, even a promised land.

For the first time in over four hundred years, a subculture, whose professional identity and even family links reached back centuries, faced an entering class that could hardly be less like themselves. Americans and Britons, women, Jews, and college dropouts, their parents were profes-

sors, teachers, artists, photographers, veterinarians, wine growers, Holocaust survivors, and Spanish civil war veterans. Collectively, they seemed
a blend of the young Marx, in flight from capitalist alienation, and Benjamin Braddock, the title figure in the era's emblematic film, *The Graduate*,
in flight from a career in plastics.

"Pecuniary interests had nothing to do with what drove our generation
to aspire to make great looking and sounding violins," Carla Shapreau, a
San Francisco maker turned lawyer, explained.[362] Anne Cole recalled it as
"the hippy thing." Already a rarity by reason of gender, she was also the
daughter of a surgeon and an expressionist painter.[363] Baffled but game,
Zygmuntowicz's parents tried to arrange for him to apprentice with the
United Brotherhood of Carpenters.[364]

Temperamentally and biographically, the newcomers had little enough
in common. But save for the occasional pragmatist like Curtin, who considered air the maker's natural medium, and materials primarily a means
to an end,[365] they shared "a thing for wood,"[366] a tolerance for physical and
social distance, an aversion to hierarchy, and a free-spirited willingness to
take chances. A few decades later, Rabut was only half-amused that still
younger makers already regarded his as "the older generation." He looked
back wistfully on his cohort's collective indifference to the credit cards and
MBAs afforded by a favorable job market.[367]

Above all, they shared a passion for the art itself, expressed in a regard
bordering on the reverential for what Alf called the "icons of civilization"
created by the classical masters. "Who thought when I was learning to
carve a scroll I'd have to get so crafty at business?" he sighed.[368] Andrew
Dipper, a young Englishman, set out for Japan, found himself in Cremona,
and wound up translating Sacconi. "Violin making," he explained, "is an
attitude, not a profession."[369]

The third impulse came from the trade itself. In principle, good times
for dealers meant good times for repair departments and a golden age for
restorers able to bring back old instruments from the ravages of time, mal-
practice, and uninsulated attics. But the existing labor pool, much of it
drawn from prewar cohorts, was fading fast, and traditional on-site training had become prohibitively expensive in the booming economies and
labor markets that now extended from Munich to San Diego.[370] Both Mittenwald, a nineteenth-century foundation with a three-year curriculum,
and Cremona, another Sacconi legacy with a three- to five-year course, each
produced an annual cadre of graduates. Neither began to meet demand in

London, the trade's traditional center, and the United States, its new center of gravity.

The solution was a wave of institution-building like none to date. In 1972, David Hill, heir to one of the trade's flagship shops, Charles Beare, a Mittenwald product, whose family firm would soon be the Hills' successor, and the maker Wilfred Saunders helped create Newark, the first such British institution and the school that John Dilworth would attend. It offered a three-year course to an annual class of twelve with "a good level of basic woodworking skills."[371] The same year, the Silesian-born Peter Paul Prier, a Mittenwald graduate, created the Violin-Making School of America in Salt Lake City. Another first, it offered what would become a four-year course with an entering class of four that would later grow to twenty.

A generation after opening their doors, they had become an established part of the landscape, with elaborate curricula, a collective annual graduating class of about one hundred, and alumni associations across the globe. Similar schools would open in Chicago, Boston, Leeds, Tokyo, Wales, Sweden, Argentina, and at Indiana University, though others would shut down—victims, ironically, of the new schools' success in meeting the demand that had created them.

Approaching its third decade, Newark still enrolled its share of foreign applicants as well as domestic applicants in pursuit of a second, even third, career. But its approach was studiously conservative. "Our philosophy is to take the best instruments that have ever been made—the Strads and the Guarneris—and use these as models for our students," the director told an interviewer. "If we were asked where we'd like to be in ten years' time, we'd say we want to be doing the same thing as now, only better," a senior colleague added.[372] The "fiddle race," in which teams of four competed to produce a playable, unvarnished violin within three eight-hour days,[373] was a novelty that might have puzzled the Amatis. But the absence of power tools, a matter of principle at Newark, would have felt like home.

In addition to seven to fourteen hours a week of violin-making instruction by a senior faculty of seven, Cremona offered its hundred-odd registrants a more adventurous curriculum, including art and music history, commercial law and bookkeeping, Italian for registrants from at least thirty-nine foreign countries and all continents, English for non-native speakers, acoustics, and physical education. There was also an alternative curriculum in woodwork and design. Unlike Newark, Cremona was even equipped for electronic measurement. Salt Lake City's faculty of four—two violin makers, an artist, and a violin teacher—aimed for the basics, including instrument theory, history, construction, repair and setup, mechanical and artistic drawing, acoustics, music lessons, and orchestra. After three years of thirty-five-hour teaching weeks, at an annual fee roughly equivalent to state university tuition, candidates were expected to submit an unvarnished violin, a completed instrument, a mechanical drawing, an artistic drawing, pass an oral examination, and play a recital on the instrument they had completed.

If assembled for a collective photo, six women, including Ingeborg Behnke and Rena Makowski Weisshaar, would have stood out among the thirty-five otherwise male students in their class at Mittenwald. Joan Balter was the only female student in Salt Lake City. Behnke went on to a distinguished career as designated fixer, even wonder worker, to the string players of the Berlin Philharmonic, while Weisshaar settled in Los Angeles and went on to distinction as a competitor and judge at the annual meeting of the Violin Society of America.[374] Balter's summer studio at the Aspen Music Festival was now a one-stop support system for some of the world's major players. In 2004, the Entente Internationale des Maîtres Luthiers et Archetiers, the trade's College of Cardinals, still listed only 15 women among 164 men. Compared with 1967, when there was only one female member, it was a significant rate of growth.[375]

Unlike the Cremonese patriarchs, the modern makers also had public faces, many of them on websites of impressive range and sophistication. Media attention, both print and broadcast, was another given. If printed, the stories were likelier to show up in the style or features than in the arts or business sections. If broadcast, they surfaced in radio and TV magazines. Irrespective of medium, the story line was likely to be amazement that a craft, reflexively associated with dead Italians, had not only become relatively young and swingy but had gone high-tech.

Frequently well read, unfailingly articulate, even eloquent, the new makers were likely to feel and act like self-employed professionals, as much at home on the Web as at the supermarket. But their fascination with craft, tools, and materials, their interaction with players, plus the resolve of many to leave dealing, restoring, and repairing to others and to devote their lives to making, put them closer to the world of the Amatis than the world of the Chanots.

Though they could be divided into classicists and scientists, both groups were open-ended, and neither excluded the other. The classicists not only took their cues from history; a handful, among them Dilworth, Dipper, and Hargrave, wrote as well as emulated it. The scientists, like George Bissinger and Martin Schleske, believed in principle that an instrument gratifying to both maker and player could be built from a computer-generated "virtual Strad."

THE COMMON GOAL, as Hargrave saw it, was a violin both unique and "in the style of," that people would one day appreciate for its own sake as earlier generations learned to admire their Lotts and Vuillaumes. A near miss in 1992 at the Dorotheum, Vienna's historic auction house, where a locally celebrated violin tout had consigned Hargrave's copy of a Guarneri filius Andreae for sale as an original, was a measure of his success. Jacob Saunders, Hargrave's friend and Newark classmate, spotted it and blew the whistle. Hargrave was called to the scene to confirm the identification. Local papers made the most of the story.[376]

While the classicists looked for their cues in archives in Cremona or Venice, the scientists, many of them Catgut alumni directly or indirectly influenced by Hutchins, got themselves to labs like Bissinger's in North Carolina, where they borrowed Strads, tapped bridges, deployed 3-D scanning lasers, and mined data.[377] The violin is a sculpture not only in wood but in resonance, said Schleske, a Mittenwald graduate with years of postgraduate lab experience. He made his case with a bookshelf of technically sophisticated articles and color-coded computer simulations that measured both the response of an instrument and the auditory perception of the listener.[378]

Though not a physicist himself, Greiner learned early on what science was good for. A common interest in the violin and an acoustics class assignment at the University of Cologne led him to Heinrich Dünnwald, a professional physicist and Catgut veteran. In 1997, the two began working in tandem, turning a Jugendstil villa in leafy south Bonn into a celebrity address, and Greiner himself into the first violin maker to be advised by a practicing scientist and represented by an artists' management company.[379]

An hour's drive from Detroit, Curtin and Alf copied a 1728 Strad for a Los Angeles client with the help of nonstick rubber molds, epoxy resin castings, and an employee who had learned how to use them at General Motors. From there, their thoughts turned to 3-D laser scanners, capable of reducing even this scarcely perceptible contact with their model to a beam of light.[380]

A protégé of Erdesz and Hutchins, filled with "end of the millennium restlessness" and tired of feeling like a Civil War reenactor despite the new technologies, Curtin then went his own way. This time he looked to Gabriel Weinreich, a retired University of Michigan physicist, and Charles Besnainou, an Egyptian-born engineer at the Laboratoire d'Acoustique Musicale in Paris. Weinreich's contribution was the reciprocal bow, an ingenious package of computer, amplifier, loudspeaker, and phono cartridge that allowed for testing an instrument without the interposition of a living and inevitably idiosyncratic player.[381] Besnainou's was breakthrough experimentation in carbon fiber and composite instruments.

"Was this a direction I might follow with my own violin making?" Curtin asked. To him the answer was self-evident. The gleam in his eye only grew brighter in 2005 when the John D. and Catherine T. MacArthur Foundation declared him one of the year's twenty-five "geniuses" and gave him a $500,000 grant to spend as he wished over the next five years.[382] He was not the first violin maker to be declared a genius. But none had ever made it on quite this scale.

Did this mean that the four-hundred-year hegemony of dead Italian males was reaching its end, and that the world would again be made safe for the living maker? No one could say for sure. But there was room to be bullish; and sales to major orchestra players, high-profile ensembles like the Berg and Emerson quartets, and occasional soloists like Tetzlaff and Elmar Oliveira were reason to be hopeful

". . . new instruments are always to be avoided: if they have a good tone, it is almost sure to grow worse," a British customs manual reported in 1834.[383] Many players and conductors, too, still felt this way. A writer in search of conductors to interview found only one of seven, himself a brass player, even willing to talk about it.[384] Alf estimated that he spent up to 7.5 percent of his annual taxable income on the advertising and promotion needed to overcome inertial ancestor worship in a market where the sale of a single old Italian violin brought in more than Alf's net income from a year of making new ones.[385]

Yet that same market was also his ally. The kite effect that pulled the rest of the market along like a tail behind the ever higher-flying Cremonese allowed Alf and his peers to offer entry-level professionals career-quality instruments at half to a third the price of the most modest Old

Italian. A generation or two earlier, a young New York orchestra player could aspire to an upper West Side apartment and a Gagliano. The choice was now either/or. "I can't live in my viola," as one young player, the owner of two Rabuts, told their maker.[386] For the contemporary maker, structural hiccups like the 1997 Asian currency crash, which abruptly halved the purchasing power of ninety-two young South Koreans at Baltimore's Peabody Conservatory,[387] were an unanticipated bonus.

The early music scene was already a movable feast. A late twentieth-century growth sector set in a rust belt of nineteenth-century institutions, it generated jobs, players, and demand as far away as Tokyo. After two hundred years of modernization, *old* old instruments worth having were out of reach of its often young, enthusiastic, but mostly undercapitalized practitioners. *New* old instruments were both affordable and historically informed beyond anything previously known. In 2004, five of ten violinists, and two of three cellists in San Francisco's Philharmonia Baroque Orchestra, played baroque instruments made since 1987.[388] The same year, London's Becket Collection commissioned a Vivaldi Project of leading contemporary makers to produce nine Venetian violins, two violas, two cellos, and a bass. "We're aiming to re-create the experience of a concert in 18th-century Venice for both audience and players," said Elise Becket Smith, the collection's founder. "It's vital that the next generation of period-performance students can perform on suitable instruments."[389]

That makers like Alexander Rabinovich should appear in St. Petersburg to serve an ensemble like Musica Petropolitana was a treat in itself. Early music was rare enough in Western Europe in the years before World War I. It was virtually unknown in czarist Russia. Pursued with increasing expertise and passion in the West,[390] it remained virtually unknown in the Soviet Union. In a society where musical practice was politicized like everything else, its discovery both by Rabinovich and a handful of Leningrad Conservatory students in the late 1980s was perestroika in action.

As the son of a naval officer with a soft spot for practical invention, Rabinovich had picked up violin making from a classmate's father. With the help of anything he could find in museums and libraries, he continued by himself. Private making and selling were out of the question, and he covered his tracks from 1962 to the Gorbachev era with some forty-nine nominal jobs, from marine rescue to woodwind repair. Meanwhile, he scouted out dilapidated buildings, of which there was no shortage, in pursuit of wood. In 1989, Rabinovich packed up a couple of instruments, got himself to London, walked into the Royal Opera House, and managed within a couple of days to find a customer in the London Symphony. He then went home and looked for more customers. Revealing again of place and time, he listed himself in the *Strad Directory*. But he avoided listing himself locally, in part fearing the attention of tax collectors likely to claim 105 percent of his annual turnover, in part to escape the attention of totally ruthless armed robbers, who would take still more.[391]

The post-Communist transformation of Dmitry Badiarov was even more remarkable. Born in 1969 to a horn player father and a pedagogically gifted mother in Nalchik, a provincial capital on the northern edge of the Caucasus, he tumbled on woodworking at seven, a gifted Jewish violin teacher at eight, and a charismatic folklorist at eleven. The violin teacher piloted him to the Leningrad Conservatory, where he discovered baroque instruments and graduated with a diploma in performance. The folklorist's encouragement to find a Leningrad maker willing to teach him the craft led to Badiarov's first shop. There, like everybody around him, he did business in cash, kept a large trained dog, installed a bulletproof door and electronic security system, and screened and recorded all incoming phone calls to filter for strangers.[392]

By this time it was 1994. The next steps, respectively, were to study with the baroque violinist Sigiswald Kuijken; earn another diploma in performance; and open another shop, this time in Brussels, a much easier place to do business, where he made instruments for Kuijken's Petite Bande. He also married a classmate, a Japanese flautist, played in Mito dell'Arco, a Japanese early music quartet, and turned his website into a global research seminar on baroque iconography, style, and violin making.

Twelve years later, he informed his virtual clientele that he was moving to Japan, where he looked forward to teaching at a Tokyo violin school, taking charge of baroque instruments for a firm in Nagoya, and enjoying a climate more Cremonese, at least, than what he had known in Brussels.[393] But in 2011, returning to Holland and a better climate for early music, he opened a shop in The Hague. By coincidence, it was the day after Japan was hit by a record tsunami and earthquake. Yes, he had come a long way, Badiarov acknowledged, and that was just fine with his parents. Studiously unpolitical before 1992, they were just as skeptical about his chances in post-Communist Russia. "What could one believe, not being in the party, and living in Nalchik?" he asked.[394]

In the land of the Velvet Revolution, by comparison, the post-

Communist transformation was neither more nor less than a return to normalcy. Otokar Spidlen's shop in Prague, already in its second generation as the premier shop in a major musical capital, was expropriated by the Communists after their coup d'état of 1948. On the regime's collapse in 1989, it was returned to Premsyl, Otokar's son. Yet a semblance of normalcy prevailed even in the interim. Freelance artisans continued to work and market their product for hard currency through Artia, the state export agency, while Premsyl won prizes and served as a juror at competitions from Cremona to Salt Lake City, where his hosts, of course, paid his travel expenses. Though only family members were allowed to learn the trade, Premsyl's son Jan was allowed to study in Mittenwald. Unsurprisingly, he made a beeline for Beare's shop in London in 1989.

By this time, there was no Czech market left in the conventional sense. Before World War II, Czechoslovakia boasted an estimated five hundred makers. A half century later, there were an estimated thirty. During the forty-year Communist interregnum, Czech players, another export product, traveled, if they could, with two instruments and returned with one. Those who still had good instruments were reluctant to sell. Those without them did without, though good nineteenth-century instruments could be had for a fraction of Western prices. Yet only a few years later, hard currency and hard currency accounts, foreign commissions, and a substantial cut in export taxes had turned Prague back into a Central European city, where Jan Spidlen, a fourth-generation violin maker, again ran a Central European family business with his father.[395]

In Markneukirchen, just across the border, where a cohort of young German makers also rediscovered their collective past, Udo Kretzschmann's experience before and after 1989 virtually recapitulated the modern history of the town. Between 1716 and 1890, at least eight of his direct and ten of his indirect ancestors had been violin makers. Kretzschmann himself, a child of postwar East Germany, hoped to study mathematics at the university level. But his family attachment to the Protestant church, the regime's most persistent adversary, barred the way.

As an amateur violinist, he instead tried trade school, enrolling as an aspiring violin maker, or more accurately assembler, with the goal of leveraging his trade school certificate into a lateral university entry. It then came to him on the long march through prescribed courses in acoustics, aesthetics, and Marxism-Leninism that he really wanted to make violins. The solution, as usual, was a product of time and place. During the day, like generations before him, he assembled violins at the local factory, which employed 1,100 before the fall of the Berlin Wall and under 50 fifteen years later. When work was over, he dropped by for moonlight tutorials with one of the few surviving private makers.

In 1980, he joined the East German violin makers association for a visit to the Soviet state collection in Moscow, which the group was allowed to admire and examine for fifteen minutes. A few years later, he was certified a master, and was even permitted to work at home, after concluding that he would rather make real instruments at piecework rates than earn more assembling parts at the factory.

Then came historic 1989. Leaving his family while he made up for decades of lost time and travel, Kretzschmann hired out as ad hoc journeyman to shops in West Berlin, Hamburg, and Basel. He returned five years later to open his own shop in a town of 7,500, surrounded by as many as fifteen still younger makers resolved to do the same, among them two immediate neighbors.

After a decade of self-employment, he had acquired the survival skills of post-Communist life, including a computer, a serious car, and basic English. His repertory included violins, violas, and gambas, plus care and cultivation of a bilingual website. His work included repairs and restorations on school instruments, exhibitions in a town increasingly attractive to tourists, and occasional commissions from professionals and serious amateurs shopping for bargains.

While he dreamed of going up-market, great Italian models, familiar and accessible to Hargrave, Dilworth, Zygmuntowicz, and the other contemporary stars he admired from a distance, were hard to come by in small-town Saxony. The lengthening shadow of China,[396] as well as the long shadow of local history, when Markneukirchen was widely understood as another word for cheap, did not make things easier. Still, it was reasoned, if Chinese quality could improve dramatically in a generation, there was no reason why Markneukirchen's should not do the same.

For the moment, Markneukirchen again produced the solid, unpretentious instruments at affordable, if no longer East German, prices that had always been its comparative advantage.[397] Even if the new makers now had to market their product themselves, Kretzschmann couldn't imagine doing anything else. "Cheerful in hoping for customers, patient with the competition, continuing instant at the workbench," he described himself, in a neat paraphrase of Romans 12:12.[398]

LAST BUT NOT LEAST

THE STORY IS apocryphal but might as well be true. A dazzled music-lover approaches the unapproachable Jascha Heifetz after a concert. "Oh, Mr. Heifetz," the admirer burbles, "your violin sounds so wonderful." Heifetz peers thoughtfully at his Guarneri del Gesù. "I don't hear anything," he replies. The player is the obvious hero. Then comes the violin, followed at a discreet distance by its shadowy maker. The bow, a crucial accessory to the story, is nowhere to be seen.

In fact, as every teacher teaches and every player knows, the bow is what makes the instrument speak and sing. Without it, not even a Heifetz would be a Heifetz, and a Guarneri could as well be a four-string guitar. "Stroak; or else Play not at all," Thomas Mace declared, in *Musick's Monument*, as early as 1676. Yet of any twenty violinists who claim some knowledge of violins, "barely three take a similar interest in the bow," a writer on the subject reported credibly in 1922. "As for a perception of the characteristics of bows as works of art, which is the standard of the fiddle connoisseur, it hardly has any existence outside the small circle of bow makers," he added for emphasis.[399]

The same year, the Hills assigned Arthur Bultitude, a fourteen-year-old apprentice, to the bow department despite his spirited protests. At least according to oral tradition, the department went back to 1892, when Samuel Allen, the shop's only bow maker, walked out over a difference of opinion with his employer, Alfred Hill, on Home Rule for Ireland. Hill's solution was to reassign William Retford and William Napier from the case-making department. Neither had any experience with bow making, but they could at least console themselves that they had nothing to unlearn. Between them, they worked out a division of labor that survived till 1985. Different employees were responsible for different parts, which were then assembled. During World War I, older employees were replaced by teenagers fresh out of school, available cheap, and too young for the draft. In 1920, it was decided to number their work and identify the product accordingly.[400]

In the thirty-nine years between his arrival and 1961, when he left to open a shop of his own, Bultitude would produce thousands of bows stamped "W. E. Hill & Sons," train a follow-on generation of English bow makers, and become a legend among his peers. He then produced a few thousand more bows under his own name and sold them, too, as he reminded an interviewer. "I suppose . . . I showed some aptitude for small work, and perhaps a degree of patience beyond the ordinary," he reflected.[401] For his services to the trade, he was named a Member of the Most Excellent Order of the British Empire. It was the lowest of the order's five classes. But he shared it, at least, with the violin maker William Luff, a colleague at Hill's, and the Beatles.[402]

The so-called Bach bow was among the era's candidates for the proverbial fifteen minutes of fame. In the 1950s, Emil Telmányi, a Danish-based protégé of the Hungarian master Jenö Hubay and son-in-law of the composer Carl Nielsen, asked the Danish maker Kurt Vestergaard to build him a bow with a convex arch rising 10 cm from the hair and a thumb-operated lever that allowed him to vary its tension, depending on whether he wanted to play on one string or three or four. Armed with Vestergaard's creation, Telmányi then recorded Bach's sonatas and partitas for solo violin. The idea went back to the early twentieth-century musicologists Albert Schweitzer and Arnold Schering, who reasoned that if Bach wrote chords and polyphony, he meant them to be heard, even when played on four strings suspended over an arched bridge. The effect, as Jeremy Eichler described it, was like multiple violinists or a "dark-hued and mysterious" organ. Some listeners were reminded of an accordion. But it was like nothing ever heard by Bach himself. Conceived in the name of authenticity, Telmányi's Bach was rather a union of fantasy and literal-mindedness, neither more nor less authentic than Bach on a synthesizer or arranged for the Swingle Singers.[403]

While the violin served as motif and metaphor for generations of good and great poets and the viola for countless jokes, the real bow and its makers remained Cinderellas without a prince. A rare and exceptional invitation to the ball, Manuel Komroff's 1940 novel *The Magic Bow* and its 1947 movie spin-off[404] got no further than the title before the scenario turned it into a pumpkin. Stewart Granger played Paganini. Paganini played a Strad. The bow, as usual, played second fiddle. "I came to realize that I could buy a bow from one Fifty-seventh Street dealer and sell it at a profit to another just across the street," Paul Childs recalled of his New York student days in the late 1960s. Spotting lemons, Childs made lemonade, becoming the era's most respected expert on the bow and the people who made it.[405] It was only far into the twentieth century, when the prices for eighteenth- and nineteenth-century French bow makers began to soar like the prices for sixteenth- to eighteenth-century Italian violin makers before them, that bows at last got some respect.

There was no obvious justice or even logic in the general neglect. With its logarithmic curve,[406] elegant camber, precision mechanics, and jeweler's art, the bow was a marvel of functional design, and its maker a walking anthology of skills even a violin maker might envy. "It's a nice job, and has a lot in it, since it covers more than one medium," Bultitude explained with characteristic understatement. "You've got to be something of a silversmith, a goldsmith, you've got to work in tortoiseshell and ebony, and of course make the main thing, the stick."[407] Retford, the founding father of Hill's bow department, added cabinetmaker, toolmaker, engineer, even musician to the mix.[408] Henryk Kaston tuned Wanda Landowska's harpsichord, escaped German-occupied France, joined Albert Einstein for quartets, played thirty-five years in the Metropolitan Opera orchestra, and designed jewelry for the Vatican, Smithsonian, and Metropolitan museums while making bows for the likes of Heifetz, Isaac Stern, and Shlomo Mintz. He also found time to coauthor a breakthrough monograph on François Tourte, the bow maker equivalent of Stradivari.[409]

The elder Pietro Guarneri's estate included sixteen actual bows, both finished and unfinished. A letter to Tarisio from Paolo Stradivari, and designs found among his father's papers, suggest that Stradivari also made bows. But it went unremarked by contemporaries, and the existence of the drawings came as a surprise to the Hills.[410] Up to a century would pass before French and English makers would create bows now considered equivalent to the earliest Amatis, establish an autonomous craft, and identify their product.

The intervening years are as mysterious as the prehistory of the violin. Boyden's benchmark classic ends by design in 1761, the year Joseph-Barnabé Saint-Sevin, known professionally as l'Abbé le Fils, published his *Principes du Violon* in Paris. Sevin's manual would not only separate the old

Italian from the new French school of violin playing, it would mark the introduction of the new bow that would sweep away all predecessors even faster than the violin had.[411]

"We are entirely dependent on iconography for our knowledge of the sixteenth-century bow,"[412] Boyden notes of the absence of actual specimens. With minimal qualification, the same can be said for the seventeenth- and eighteenth-century bow. French, British, German, Italian, and Dutch images all reflect a work in progress. Tropical materials like snakewood were admired, but indigenous materials were in common use, too. Sticks might or might not be grooved or fluted. Though usually convex, bows could also be straight, and occasionally concave. Their length extended from 50 cm to 80 cm. The grip ranged from clenched fist to articulated fingers. While designed to play with the hand above the stick, they could also be played with the hand below it, as the gamba was always played and the contrabass is still played today. A variety of devices, including the thumb, kept the hair in place and modified its tension at the frog, the usually ebony, occasionally ivory, and exceptionally tortoiseshell box between the hair and the stick at the bow's lower end. A loop, knot, or wedge thrust into a mortised head held the hair in place at the tip.[413]

Graphics and manuals by the great players and bellwether teachers—Corelli, Veracini, Locatelli, Tartini, Geminiani, Leclair, Leopold Mozart—testify to firm views and current practice on how a bow should look, how it should be held, and what it should do; its weight, balance, length, strength, flexibility, and responsiveness to pressure; the role of fingers, wrists, arms, elbows, and shoulders. But the common denominator was rather the absence of one. Till well into the eighteenth century, French thumbs rested demonstratively on the hair, Italian thumbs on the underside of the stick. The seamless legato, firm attack, and virtually interchangeable up-and-down bow that have been universally taught since the nineteenth century, and were taken for given till new musicologists discovered old music, were still beyond the horizon.[414]

Yet there was no question that the bow was changing, just as the violin was changing. If the Abbé le Fils's manual of 1761 was one benchmark, Michel Woldemar's *Méthode pour le violon* of c. 1798 was another. To posterity's gratitude, Woldemar provided an illustration of four contemporary bows, reputedly from his own collection. Looked at in sequence, they document an evolution that had taken place since his birth in 1750. All were associated with prominent players, three of them prominent composers.

The first, short bow was identified with Arcangelo Corelli, who died in 1713; it was still in use at midcentury. At 61 cm or less, it really was short. It was also light, 37–42 g, with a slight convexity at the tip. But since c. 1720, it coexisted with a long bow of 69 cm to 72 cm, reportedly inspired by Giuseppe Tartini. Correspondingly heavier at 45 g to 56 g, it was still in use as late as 1800.

By this time, the future was at least in view. The new model was roughly the length of the long bow but a little higher and heavier. The stick was straight or slightly concave. Seen in profile, the head or tip resembled a hatchet. For those who could afford it, there might also be an ivory frog, elegant but fragile, with an indentation at the posterior as well as the anterior end, where the performer's thumb rested.

Later, when it had been superseded, it would be known as the "transitional" bow. Meanwhile, it was associated with Wilhelm Cramer (1746–1799), a second-generation player and wunderkind from Mannheim who joined his father's orchestra, the era's most admired ensemble, at a prodigious age, before leaving home for a solo career in Stuttgart. Paris came next, followed by twenty years in London, with a warm recommendation from Johann Christian Bach. But the "Cramer" bow was hardly specific to Cramer. First spotted in Italy around 1760, it soon showed up in Vienna, Paris, and London, where it was widely copied. Though its popularity peaked between 1772 and 1792, Ingres's famous pencil portrait in the Louvre confirms that it was still good enough for Paganini as late as 1819.

Remarkably, the future of the bow had arrived without him. "About 1785," as Werner Bachmann would write, "François Tourte (1747–1835) succeeded in producing in Paris a bow so remarkably satisfactory that it became the model in his own time and, with a few changes of detail, has continued as such."[415] With its overall length of 74–75 cm and average weight of 56 g, it was not only the fourth and last of Woldemar's set. Fétis, an informed and interested contemporary, if rarely the most reliable source, associated it with Viotti, whose sensational Paris debut in 1782 also established the Strad as a universal standard. Whether Viotti actually used Tourte's bow or the cognate model developed almost concurrently by Thomas Dodd in London is less certain.[416] But the technique implied in the thirty-one concertos he composed for himself, and an unfinished violin method partially published around 1840, leave no doubt that he might as well have. His successors and protégés—Rudolphe Kreutzer, Pierre Rode and Pierre Gaviniès—enshrined his technique in their études. Like the Tourte bow, they have remained the global standard.[417]

As with the violin, there was no eureka moment. But incremental changes had created a critical mass, this time in Paris, where people wanted services as well as goods. The changes included musical fashion, technology, raw materials, and social and even political organization. Italy had become a major exporter of both violins and violinists. Roads that once led to Brescia and Cremona now led to London, always keen for itinerant superstars, as well as to a pre-Revolutionary Paris that may have employed more string players than any other contemporary city.[418]

A new, classical style, a new standard of virtuosity, a new style of orchestral playing that demanded more and more discipline from more and more players, plus big-city audiences that wanted more sound in larger halls, all favored the long over the short bow.[419] They also pointed toward a still newer one that would bounce, respond immediately on contact with the string, and sustain a tone like a singer. Pernambuco, an imported Brazilian hardwood, was found to be tough, flexible, resilient, and affordable beyond anything previously available.[420] Innovations in metallurgy and mechanics led to the ferrule, a semicircular ring that spread 175 to 250 carefully matched horsehairs in a broad, even ribbon, and a retooled frog that allowed players to compensate for bad bow-hair days with the turn of a screw.[421] Co-optation of their guild in the 1770s by the *évantaillistes* and *tabletiers* (the makers of fans and fancy inlays) opened previously inaccessible metal- and woodworking skills to bow makers, allowing them to turn their product into collectibles by working gold, silver, tortoiseshell, and mother-of-pearl into their designs.[422]

François-Xavier Tourte (1747–1835), the prophet of the new bow, was born to a bow-making family and the spirit of the age. He was arguably less an innovator than an inspired synthesizer of improvements already in use in the family shop. But he devised a new process for scouring bow hairs with soap and bran water, and demonstrated that pernambuco need not be cut but could be heated and bent to shape, thereby preserving the fibers across the length of the stick.[423]

John Dodd (1752–1839), a London contemporary, seems to have hit on a similar combination a few years later. But Tourte would be recalled as a master craftsman, with a good location near the Pont Neuf, name recognition inherited from his father, a shop illuminated by natural light, and customers as distinguished as Viotti positively eager to walk up five floors.[424] Dodd would be remembered as a hard-drinking oddball and illiterate, "most regular in his irregular habits," who began as a fitter of gunlocks and maker of scales for weighing coins, scrounged for oyster shell, cadged the occasional silver spoon, and ended up, presumably indigent, in the Richmond workhouse.[425]

Though Tourte lived and worked within walking distance of the guillotine at the epicenter of the French Revolution, the only clear traces of the revolutionary era are seen in his son's career. As if resolved to act out Tocqueville's vision of the French Revolution as the triumph of the public sector, Louis-François Tourte entered the newly formed Conservatoire as a cello student in 1797. He then served in the Garde-Impériale-Musique from 1805 to 1809 and played in the orchestra of the Opéra from 1812 until his health-related retirement at fifty-two, three years after his father's death.[426]

Fétis notes Tourte's soft spot for fishing, presumably in the Seine just downstairs and out the door. Apart from bow making, it appears to have been his only interest. Sibire's appreciation of him as "the Stradivari of the genre"[427] is more comprehensive than the author may have anticipated or realized. Born ten years after Stradivari died, Tourte too would be impressively long-lived and, with an estimated two thousand bows, formidably productive.

He even resembled Stradivari in the absence of documentation on where and when he learned his trade. There is no record of an apprenticeship, completed or otherwise. That he was a native Parisian who lived at home is one possible explanation. That he was exempt from examination as son of a guild master is another. It could also be, as Fétis claimed, that he spent the formative years learning to make watches, a cognate skill to Dodd's scales and gunlocks, as well as a plausible preparation for bow making, before returning to the family shop.[428] Meanwhile, in tiny, woodsy Mirecourt alone, the number of bow-making establishments grew from five to eleven between 1758 and 1776.[429] Again like Stradivari, Tourte left lasting marks on a craft already in full bloom.

Material may have been a problem. "When he was working, we were continually at war with France, in consequence of which their maritime commerce was harassed by our ships," as Alfred Hill explained to an American amateur.[430] But customers were not. They included Pierre Baillot, Kreutzer, Rode, and the German virtuoso Ludwig Spohr, who built modern pedagogy on the bow he invented, as well as collectors of the sort who not only owned Strads but gave their name to them.[431] Recognition on a scale unmatched by any other bow maker was only a few steps behind. By the turn of the nineteenth century, Sibire had acknowledged him as a landmark. In 1818, he even achieved a degree of immortality Stradivari never attained, when his portrait appeared in a collection of engravings, flanked by Lupot, an artist's fanciful impression of Tieffenbrucker, and a pantheon of the era's great players from Leclair to Paganini.[432] Posthumous inclusion in Fétis's *Biographie universelle des musiciens* (1835–44), even his 1856 biography of Stradivari, was virtually automatic.

From the middle of the eighteenth century to at least the threshold of the twentieth, French hegemony in the bow was as complete as Italy's had been in the violin. In 1770 there were twenty-four known bow makers in France, two in England, and none at all in Germany. In 1810 the equivalent figures were eighteen, six, and three; in 1850, twenty-two, three, and twenty. In 1830, there were as many bow makers in Mirecourt and Markneukirchen as in all of England. It was only in 1870 that Germany caught up in bow making as it did in industrial development. Free-trade Britain, where lower-end bow making was no match for duty-free imports,[433] and upper-end bow making was essentially a London-based family niche, lagged far behind.[434]

Accessible, affordable material was certainly part of France's comparative advantage. Since the sixteenth century, pernambuco, coveted, imported, and regulated by Portuguese, Dutch, and French traders, had been a major source of red and violet dyes suitable for products as different as textiles, lacquers, cosmetics, toothpaste, and Easter eggs.[435] From the mid-eighteenth century, the wood's inherent strength, resilience, accessibility, and price had made it the preferred material of French bow makers. The barbell structure of the industry, with its ends in Mirecourt and Paris, added economies of scale and division of labor. By the mid-1840s, Nicolas Maire and a staff of fifteen in Mirecourt supplied four thousand bows a year to customers in Paris.[436]

Intentionally or otherwise, apprenticeship requirements widened the horizons of what was in many ways a federation of family businesses. Between 1730 and 1970, 80 percent of documented French apprentices left the family shop for some or all of their training, compared to 48 percent of their English, and 45 percent of their German peers.[437] For aspiring professionals, there were few better places to widen horizons than Paris, with its touring virtuosi, resident professionals, armies of students, and well-fixed amateurs.

The practically concurrent histories of the Tubbses, Pfretzschners, Kittels, and Peccattes tell relatively little about the bows they made. But they illuminate the experience and status of the subculture that produced them, as well as national differences that go well beyond the craft.

In Britain, where guild culture atrophied early, five generations of

Tubbses lived in the world Dickens wrote about, passing the craft from father to sons. Even James (1835–1921), the most distinguished, who crafted an estimated five thousand bows, spent a good part of his life producing anonymously for dealers. In 1862, a Tubbs bow won a gold medal for W. E. Hill at the International Exposition. James was nearly thirty, married and the father of a son, when he fell out with the Hills, opened his first shop, and went on to father eleven more children. Like Dodd, he was a legendary drinker.[438] Drinking and moonlighting are both plausible grounds for the split. He surely needed every penny he could get.

The 1880s were a good decade for Tubbs, possibly turning him into the first member of the family who actually made money in the trade. His customers included the London-based German virtuoso August Wilhelmj and Alfredo Piatti, the era's major cellist. The growing clientele for old Italian violins approached him for bows to play them with. The Duke of Edinburgh made him his bow maker by royal appointment. The 1885 Inventions Exposition awarded him a gold medal. But there is no particular evidence of social ascent, entrepreneurial spin-off, or even the obituary in the *Times* that conventionally marked the passing of a notable. A photo taken late in his life, after both his wife and the son who had taken over the business had died, show a tired old man working at a jumbled bench in a hat and overcoat.

In Germany, where an indestructible guild culture coexisted with entrepreneurial capitalism as in few other places, Carl Richard Pfretzschner of Markneukirchen passed on the craft to his son Hermann Richard. Barely three years after the Franco-Prussian war, Hermann Richard left for two years with Vuillaume in Paris. On his return, he put what he learned into practice and founded a firm that would still be operating five generations later. In 1901 Pfretzschner was appointed purveyor to the royal Saxon court in Dresden, a decade later to the grand ducal court of Saxe-Weimar, probably making him the first bow maker ever to achieve both honors. A century or so after Tourte, he was an example of, even a role model for, what a bow maker could do.

Ironically, Russia's answer to Pfretzschner was Nikolaus (Nicolaus) Ferder Kittel, a German from Markneukirchen or its environs. Reportedly Jewish, he set up an unpretentious shop in St. Petersburg in the 1820s, while still in his twenties. Jews were practically unknown in bow making and were practically barred from legal residence in St. Petersburg. But German tradesmen, like Paris fashions, were part of the landscape. Nicholas I, czar since 1825, appointed Kittel instrument maker to the court. Henri Vieuxtemps, appointed solo violinist to the court in 1846, discovered Kittel bows with such enthusiasm that all of St. Petersburg soon wanted one. On Kittel's death in 1868, his son Nicolai took over on the same unpretentious premises, where he was also appointed maker to the court and was commissioned to supply instruments as well as bows to the imperial orchestras.[439]

Like its counterparts in the West, the shop was especially admired for the skill of its employees, most of them German and all of them German speakers, like Heinrich Knopf, who later returned to Berlin and made Kittel bows there. Though the staff seem to have done most of the actual bow making, it hardly mattered. Good was good. Leopold Auer arrived in America with two Kittel bows. One of them, bequeathed to his most brilliant protégé, became Heifetz's favorite.[440] Rare was also rare. It was estimated in the 1960s that there were only 250–500 known Kittel bows in circulation, three-quarters of them in the United States. In 1999, a gold and tortoiseshell-mounted Kittel bow went on sale at Sotheby's with a presale estimate of £10,000–15,000. It sold for £51,000.[441]

But it was in France, where pre-industrial tradition merged almost seamlessly with bourgeois virtue, that the revolutionary bow most consistently produced the bourgeois bow maker. Successive generations of Peccattes are as representative of their time and place as successive generations of Guarneris. Born in Mirecourt in 1810, Dominique, the eldest, was recruited by François Vuillaume in 1826 to assist his brother, Jean-Baptiste, in Paris. The senior Vuillaume immediately put him to work producing bows stamped "Vuillaume à Paris." Exemption from military service four years later suggests that Vuillaume, who took money seriously, valued his services enough to buy him a substitute. In 1835, Vuillaume and Georges Chanot were witnesses at Peccatte's wedding. Before he was thirty, his bows were winning prizes.

In the mid-1840s he returned to Mirecourt to produce on his own, bought the family vineyard and house on the income from money loaned at 5 percent, and bought out his brother. In 1996, the year Childs's biography appeared, the house Peccatte had acquired at 3,850 pre-1848 francs sold for 150,000 modern ones. His bows meanwhile sold for upward of 300,000 francs. With dowries of 4,000 francs each, his daughters married a merchant from Epinal and a Vuillaume nephew. By the time Pecatte died in 1874, the market alone testified to the regard for his product.

Respected colleagues like Nicolas Maire sold to Chanot at 6 to 9 francs apiece. In 1869, a Joseph Henry bow went for 25 francs. Peccatte's last two, marketed posthumously by his widow, brought 41 francs each. Despite a recession in 1859–62 and the punitive economic consequences of the Franco-Prussian war, an eight-page inventory of his estate lists assets of 33,939 francs, including 1,232 liters of the 1871 vintage, 264 of the 1872, and 520 of the 1873.

François, his younger brother, both followed in his footsteps and went his own way. Born in 1821, he, too, went to Paris, and was exempted from military service in 1841. In late 1842, he returned to Mirecourt, married into a local luthier family soon afterward, and outsourced to a staff of four. Functional illiteracy, reflected in a dictated application to the local prefect for consideration as an entrant in the annual industrial competition, was obviously no handicap. Volume for the first full year of business fell just short of 13,000 francs, with expenses of about 6,000. His product, graded according to quality, was marketed at 1 to 50 francs, a cut or two below his competitor, Etienne Pajeot, thirty years his senior, who priced his between 15 and 100 francs. Demand nonetheless sufficed to buy him a house that sold for a respectable 3,500 francs on what was evidently his return to Paris in the early 1850s. He died there at thirty-four, leaving five children.

Charles, the last of them, was only five when his father died. Born in Mirecourt, he would be the longest-lived of the bow-making Peccattes, very possibly the first to go to school, the last to enter the family trade, as well as the third to be rejected for military service. According to military records he was literate, about five foot eight, and, even in Paris in the war year 1870, flunked the medical exam because of a hernia. Good enough to sell his bows to Vuillaume, he married in 1872, opened his own business in 1881, won prizes in Antwerp and Paris over the next decade, and set up shop in the upscale rue de Valois in 1885. On his death, twenty days before the Armistice in 1918, he left a modest estate.

It was the end of a chapter but not an era. "By no means unsatisfied" with the continental product but "averse to employ foreigners," as he reminisced several decades afterward, Alfred Hill "looked around for a good workman of British origin" and recruited the bow department that would become a glory of the shop. "I have always insisted on training our men from boyhood, in our own shops, a rule to which there has been no exception," he explained to an American customer in the market for a few Hill bows.[442]

A legend in his ninety-five-year lifetime, Retford personified its continuity. In 1893, as an eighteen-year-old, bored with the daily routine of rehairing ten bows for same-day pickup, he began planing sticks, the first step in transforming them into bows. He remained at the job till 1956, then continued at home for up to a dozen years, making still more bows for friends and fellow members of the Ealing Symphony.[443]

He had long since been department head when Bultitude signed on in 1922 as the newest member of a department of twelve. What had changed meanwhile was the traffic in German bows. In 1910, Retford remembered, Hill's sold about two hundred of them a year, bought duty-free at 10 shillings, then marketed at 21 shillings, almost half Retford's weekly salary. From 1914 till at least the mid-1920s, Hill's customers might buy British, French, or not at all. But they were unlikely to buy German.

For French bow makers, the economic consequences of the peace were at least tolerable, as domestic and colonial demand recovered and prewar customers reappeared from as far away as Japan and Australia. In 1910, France employed forty-eight documented bow makers, among them eighteen in Mirecourt and twenty-six, including Charles Peccatte, in Paris. In 1930, just past the peak of postwar recovery, the total had risen to fifty.[444] In Paris, at the upper end of the market, André Chardon, only the second bow maker in the five-generational family history, produced elegant bows in his father's shop. In Mirecourt, at the lower end, eight hundred wage and pieceworkers assembled over-the-counter bows for a wholesaler formed from the merger of three prewar firms.[445] With time out for a second war and a four-year occupation, production continued against worsening odds into the 1960s.

In Germany, where there had been sixty-six documented bow makers in 1910, there were only forty-one in 1930. In Markneukirchen alone, the numbers had shrunk from fifty-one to thirty-two, despite postwar recovery and even a bit of a boom. Just a few years later, unemployed bow makers were sure to be among the crews dispatched to build the "violin makers' curve" north of town. But save again for another war leading to a different occupation, life was unlikely to have changed much for established makers like the Nürnbergers and Pfretzschners. The Nürnbergers, another four-generational firm, enjoyed a special relationship to Wurlitzer in Cincinnati. They also sold a product good enough for Ysaÿe, Kreisler, and Oistrakh.[446] The real change came only afterward, for example, in 1958, when the current generation of Pfretzschners finally submitted to socialization, East German style.

West German production resumed about a decade later, borne aloft by the same rising prices, rediscovery of early music, and pursuit of happiness that were also transforming violin making. If the bow maker remained an unlikely candidate for the newspaper style section or the TV magazine, he—and increasingly she—at least showed promise of making it into the middle class. German-born Andreas Grütter, with a psychoanalyst father, a studio in Amsterdam, and a weakness for questions beginning with "why?," was a representative figure. So was Hans Reiners, who juggled a passion for early music with a day job as chief translator for the British garrison in Berlin before opening a studio specializing in antique flutes and pre-Tourte bows. The Norwegian-born Ole Kanestrom on Washington's Olympic peninsula had been a fishing guide and engineer with specialties in marine and industrial electronics before taking up bowmaking at forty-one. Elizabeth Vander Veer Shaak set up a personal Field of Dreams among the storefront churches and Chinese takeouts of Philadelphia's Germantown Avenue, after discovering the joys of bow making while working her way through grad school in audiology.[447]

But as with the violin makers, the back-to-the-future dimension was hard to overlook. In 1969, Etienne Vatelot invited Bernard Ouchard to create a bow-making course at the École Nationale de Lutherie, which was associated with the Lycée Jean-Baptiste Vuillaume in Mirecourt. As thousands of East Germans streamed westward over the Hungarian border just weeks before the fall of the Berlin Wall, a second Hermann Richard Pfretzschner packed up his firm and family in Markneukirchen and moved them to Bad Endorf, about 100 km from Mittenwald.

The turn of another century found whole cohorts of new makers in even more congenial places like Oxford, with its ancient university and vanished auto industry, and Port Townsend, on Washington's Olympic Peninsula, where 8,334 residents could see whales out the windows of lovingly preserved Victorian houses. No one in either town had ever expected to see a professional bow maker till an age of interconnectivity turned both into virtual Mirecourts, linked to a global guild with an estimated membership of two hundred.[448]

The new challenge was neither skills nor demand but the foundation of the craft itself. Pernambuco had once been plentiful nearly the entire length of the Brazilian coast, and as far as 150 km inland—reportedly so plentiful that, in Tourte's time, pernambuco logs covered 168 acres of central Paris.[449] On the eve of the twenty-first century, the Convention on International Trade in Endangered Species (CITES), noting that the original reserves had dwindled to 5 to 10 percent of their pre-Columbian volume, was seriously considering sanctions on pernambuco's further use.

The response, unprecedented in the history of the trade, was the International Pernambuco Conservation Initiative (IPCI). An ad hoc consortium of concerned bow makers, it was mobilized and guided by Marco Ciambelli, the Paris-based father of the Confédération des Métiers et des Utilisateurs des Ressources de la Nature (Comurnat), an NGO created to organize craftsmen from many fields to help preserve the natural materials they depended on.

Beginning in 2001, IPCI devoted itself to building wells and irrigation systems to save up to two thousand seedlings.[450] The next step was finding allies, among them the cacao farmers of Bahia, whose shade-loving product, it was hoped, would benefit from cohabitation with pernambuco, and the National Foundation for Pau-Brasil (Funbrasil), a local NGO that had already distributed three million seedlings since 1970. By 2003, the bow makers had reached working agreements with the Comissão Executiva do Plano da Lavoura Cacaueira (Ceplac), a cocoa-oriented research institute, supported by the Brazilian ministry of agriculture, and the Deutsche Gesellschaft für technische Zusammenarbeit, a German development agency that demonstrated its own bona fides by matching 100,000 euros already committed by IPCI.[451] "All of us, musicians, bow makers, instrument makers and music lovers alike, have profited from the wood pernambuco for centuries," Klaus Grünke, a bow maker, bow maker's son, and bow maker's brother, told the audience at a Viennese benefit concert in 2002. "It's time to give nature something back."[452]

Meanwhile, with thirty years to wait before the seedlings reached maturity, serious makers and even players turned their attention to alternatives. It was not the first time. On the eve of World War II, James Heddon's Sons Inc., of Dowagiac, Michigan, a manufacturer of fishing rods, golf clubs, and ski poles, introduced a line of extruded steel violin bows with cast aluminum heads and actually sold some until German bows returned to the market in the mid-1950s. In 1962, a family firm in the Bronx introduced a fiberglass option. But neither was intended for concert use.[453]

Inexpensive, adaptable, and virtually unbreakable, as well as warp- and weatherproof, carbon fiber, a mix of graphite and other fibers bound in an epoxy resin matrix and then molded, showed more promise.[454] In much the way the Acushnet Co. engaged the golfer Tiger Woods to use and endorse

their Titleist clubs and balls, Japan's Yamaha Corp. engaged the violinist
Pinchas Zukerman to develop and endorse a carbon fiber bow with faux
tortoiseshell frog and gold-plated fittings. A few years later, ever newer
designs and materials, including Kevlar, were in use by players as distinguished as Tetzlaff, Jaime Laredo, and Isabelle Faust.[455] The idea took
some getting used to. But so did aluminum baseball bats.

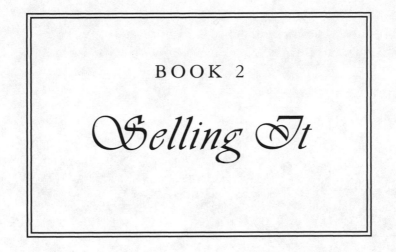

BOOK 2

Selling It

EANWHILE, THE TRADE went its own way. "Only the born violin dealer is really a violin dealer," said Albert Berr, a veteran German dealer, looking back on a lifetime in the business.[1] There were notable exceptions, from Tarisio to Robert Bein and Geoffrey Fushi. But it was at least convenient to be born a Chanot, Hill, Hamma, or Beare.

On the other hand, Berr's point could refer to a package of skills and aptitudes, like a gift for math, languages, or running marathons, that could happen to anyone, family or not. George Hart had it. William Ebsworth Hill had it, too, despite what Haweis called a "curious sort of inner otherwhereness,"[2] unimaginable in the patrician Hart.[3] But so did David Laurie, a onetime sailor, electro-plated hardware dealer, and father of eighteen whose daughter recalled how he had abandoned a flourishing oil business to pursue a "much more interesting, if less profitable" career in "fiddle-hunting."[4]

A self-made wholesaler, Laurie was "in no way connected by tradition with our calling," Hill's sons noted coldly[5] of a man they actually took to court in the early 1890s.[6] Yet even they acknowledged the "keen business sense and rare energy," that led Laurie to his "introduction to our shores of some of the finest existing examples of Stradivari's genius."[7] A century later, the dealer spectrum extended from British public school boy to American college dropout. There were also women, an innovation as sensational in its way as the admission of women to the military academies.

Common to the best of them were the patience of a Zen master, the tenacity of a distance runner, the nerves of a riverboat gambler, and the negotiating skills of a Henry Kissinger. Giovanni Morelli, the pioneer art historian, could tell a Botticelli original from a copy by virtually indiscernible differences in the turn of an earlobe or fingernail.[8] The born violin dealer could tell a Strad original from a copy by virtually indiscernible differences in the turn of an f-hole or a corner, and could remember instruments the way a born politician remembers faces.

Political skills were another part of the package. Depending on time and place, dealers might view their customers as artists, investors, aspiring patrons, "quite odd people who think it would be nice to acquire a Strad after striking it rich,"[9] or an easy mark. They might see the teachers who brought them business but also expected commissions as rainmakers or jackals. They might view their competitors as rogues and charlatans, and understand the market as a war of all against all. The urge to go it alone contended perennially with the opportunity for—or the necessity of—a joint venture. "Politics ain't beanbag," said Finley Peter Dunne's legendary Chicago barkeep, Mr. Dooley.[10] Neither was the violin trade. Yet it was hard to think of a major dealer who didn't share the "single-minded love of the violin for its own sake, as a thing of beauty, wonder, mystery" that Haweis attributed to W. E. Hill.[11]

Outsiders were as dazzled as they were baffled by it. "A class of people constitutionally on the make," said Haweis, the Church of England cleric, who knew and loved the violin like few of his contemporaries but had no illusions about the trade.[12] "I have come to the conclusion, 'after long years,'" he wrote, "that there are three things about which your averagely honest man has no conscience whatever—the first is a horse, the second is an umbrella, and the last, but not least, is a fiddle."[13]

For the historically minded, the trade resembled nothing so much as the Holy Roman Empire. It had its patriciate of upper-end dealers and auction houses, its middle class of family shops, and third estate of consultants, go-betweens and orchestra players, moonlighting from the trunks of their cars. By the late twentieth century, it had its eBay walk-ons.

Like the Empire, it was at once hierarchical, centrifugal, and anarchic. It had its emperors in Vuillaume, the Hills, Rembert Wurlitzer, and Charles Beare, whose certificates were virtually unchallengeable. It had its electors in the handful of shops, extending progressively around the world, that dealt in high-end instruments. It had its diet in the Entente Internationale des Maîtres Luthiers et Archetiers d'Art, founded in the wake of scandal in the 1950s by a self-selecting cluster of dealer-makers. It had its Guelphs and Ghibellines, locked in perennial and implacable rivalry with one another, and its de facto alliances of larger and smaller firms.

It even had its own version of *cujus regio, ejus religio*. In the sunset of a legendary career, Arthur Bultitude, Hill's legendary bow maker, recalled his interview with Alfred Hill in 1922. Was his father honest, sober, and hardworking, the fourteen-year-old Bultitude was asked? Were the family Church of England?[14] Generations later, Geoffrey Fushi, who displayed the Hill monographs in one twin bookcase and the collected works of L. Ron Hubbard in the other, cheerfully explained how Hubbard's Church of

Scientology contributed to the success of himself and his partner, Robert Bein,[15] and urged its virtues on new employees.

No one could say whether the violin trade, like the Holy Roman Empire, would last a thousand years. Bein, who was certainly among the violin empire's electors, foresaw the end game as early as 2001, at least where the game was understood to be the race for the old Italian instruments that had dominated the trade since the early nineteenth century.[16] But with almost five hundred years already behind it, it showed every promise of catching up with the Western Roman Empire (31 BCE–476 CE), despite its problems with credibility and pernambuco.

Its statics and dynamics were as complicated as its constitution. Perfect and imperfect competition, oligopoly, marginal utility, even rational expectations were in the mix, as was a history of practices the German critic Arnold Ehrlich referred to as "strikingly similar to fraud."[17] As early as 1899, he noted the bull market in old instruments, contrasted with the modest price of new ones. Many, in fact, were not Italian at all but good German copies. There was no evidence that critics or audiences heard any difference.

Players, understandably, thought about tone. But it was collectors, not players, who set the tone. What mattered was authenticity. Then came appearance and state of preservation. Tone failed even to finish in the money.[18] " . . . An instrument possessed of first-rate tonal quality but lacking in beauty of form, wood, or varnish sells for infinitely less than one with an attractive appearance," the dealer Alfred Hill advised an American client in 1932.[19] "I have seen collectors look for hours at a Strad they intended to buy, and never ask to hear it," the violinist Henri Temianka recalled in the 1970s.[20]

Stradivari and the younger Giuseppe Guarneri were the trade's magnetic north. From the early nineteenth century on, Strad models especially were copied as widely and self-evidently as the Garment District would copy Dior. The 1902 Sears, Roebuck catalogue offered "One of our Genuine Stradivarius Model Violins," complete with purfling, for $8. The "Special High Grade Genuine Stradivarius Model" could be had for $20.[21] A century later, the ripples could still be seen on the website of the National Music Museum in Vermillion, South Dakota, where a steady stream of correspondents wondered whether they might just possibly have struck gold in the attic or under the bed. "I have a violin labeled Stradivari," the generic inquiry began.[22] The answer was tactful but not encouraging.

Over two and a half centuries, their instruments had meanwhile passed through the hands of virtuosi from Spain to the Black Sea, French nobility *de l'épée, de la robe,* and *parvenue,* the Georgian gentry and Victorian middle class, Russian grand dukes, and Central European *Bildungsbürger.* Communist regimes in Poland, Czechoslovakia, and Hungary were eager to invest scarce reserves of hard currency in a Strad if it would help advance a local player in international competition.[23] In 1995, New York's Metropolitan Museum gathered twenty-five Guarneris for exhibition under a common roof. Among their owners were two of the century's great artists, the heir to a Mexican steel fortune, a vice president of Microsoft, a Chicago investor-collector, a winner of one of the world's most prestigious medical research awards, the chairman of a national commission on arthritis, museums in San Francisco and Taipei, and a Japanese foundation whose founder had helped colonize Manchuria in World War II, served three postwar years as a Class-A war criminal, and then built another fortune in powerboat racing.[24]

The path to their acquisition could be as casual as a trip to the supermarket or as elaborate as a dynastic marriage. On occasion, it could even take the form of a shootout at the O.K. Corral, where multiple sellers congregated, Strad in hand. With the presumptive buyer for once at an advantage, the sale went to the last dealer still standing.

Dietmar Machold was particularly proud of a sale that began with a call from a nominal trucking firm in West Berlin, advising him that the People's Democratic Republic of Korea (North Korea) was looking for a Strad. Undeterred by the likelihood that Western intelligence services were tapping his unsecured phone, he agreed to appear at the appointed time and place with a Strad and Roger Hargrave, at the time his restorer. A large black limousine picked them up at the famous Checkpoint Charlie and whisked them through the Wall. On their arrival at the North Korean embassy, they found seven competitors and the concertmaster of the Pyongyang Philharmonic already there. But it was Machold who got the business and paid in cash when the Koreans apparently decided that Beare's, his London competitor, was asking too little. A few years later, with thousands of North Koreans starving and global violin prices soaring, they still refused to sell, and continued to send their Strad to Machold in Tokyo for its scheduled service.[25] If the CIA really had listened in, there were evidently no hard feelings when Machold opened a New York shop in the mid-1990s.

In 2006, Beare evened the score when Jerry Kohl, an amateur guitarist who had made his fortune in upscale leather goods, decided that he would rather own a Strad than a Mark Rothko painting his daughter liked. After three months of inquiries he finally invited representatives from Beare's, Bein & Fushi, and Machold to show him what they had. Between them, they brought eight violins. Kohl himself added a ninth that had belonged to the comedian Jack Benny and had recently come on the market.

He then arranged for the concertmasters of the Los Angeles Philharmonic and the Los Angeles Chamber Orchestra to audition them, one after the other, for about eight hours total, at the city's new Disney Hall. The final choice came down to the 1712 Maria Teresa, consigned to Beare's by the family of the great Nathan Milstein, who had owned it for almost half a century, and the 1719 Duke of Alba, consigned to Bein & Fushi. In the end, Beare's won, reportedly at a non-negotiable price of $8 million. "My kids now own a part of history," Kohl told an interviewer contentedly.[26]

Commissions or consultant's fees are not uncommon in such negotiations, though Beare noticed that the usual two or three could easily grow to ten in dealings with the Japanese.[27] But unassisted deals are not unknown. Emil Herrmann, a major New York dealer before and after World War II, virtually sold the 1720 "Bavarian" Strad over the counter to a New York banker's daughter, who wanted to take up the violin, thought a Strad might be nice, and liked Bavaria.[28] Some years later, while working for Machold in Bremen, Hargrave had a similar experience when a funeral director from Nashville wandered into the shop, asked for a Strad, fiddled "The Orange Blossom Special" and liked what he heard. He then opened a suitcase to reveal a stash of bills, paid for his purchase in cash, and asked for directions to a cheap hotel.[29]

Whether the sale was simple or baroque, it was true, as Beare's associate Frances Gillham remarked, that compared to collector-quality art, even the asking price for a del Gesù is "a spit in the wind."[30] But a Strad is primarily a tool, equivalent in principle to a hammer or a tractor and susceptible like them to wear and tear. What made it art were skill, craftsmanship, and a patina of cultural association that combined to leverage it into the price class of a premium racehorse or an early, single-page sketch of Beethoven's Ninth, despite its utilitarian origins.[31] This still fell well short of a Mantegna at $28.5 million, let alone Edvard Munch's "The Scream" at $119.9 million.[32] But in the world of privately owned implements and utensils, there was nothing to match a Stradivari violin, unless it was a still rarer Strad cello or, rarest of all, a Strad viola.

Comparative pricing is admittedly a challenge. But the ratio of Strads to real estate over time is at least a serviceable metric. On his death in 1737, Stradivari left six violins each to two of his sons. Each set was valued at 1,000 lire, an average of 166.67 lire per instrument. A half century earlier, his house cost 7,000 lire.[33] With no evidence of significant inflation in the intervening years, this yields a house-to-violin ratio of about 1:42. In 1843, Vuillaume paid 38,000 francs for the suburban Paris property he would eventually retire to, including a three-story house and shop, a porter's lodge, a stable, and a garden with a small cottage. A year later, his competitor Gand sold the violinist-dancer Arthur Saint-Léon a Strad for 2,600 francs, yielding a house-to-violin ratio of slightly less than 1:15.[34] In 2011, Derek Jeter, the New York Yankees shortstop, built a seven-bedroom house on Florida's Tampa Bay for an estimated $7.7 million.[35] By this time, Kohl had paid $8 million for his Strad.

But 1:1 remained a moving target. In June 2011, an anonymous buyer paid $15.9 million, a new record, for the Lady Blunt Strad when it came up for auction a third time in barely forty years. Less than a decade later, following the death of its 104-year-old owner, Hugette Clark, daughter of Sen. William Andrews Clark of Montana, and his collector wife, Anna, a twelfth-floor Manhattan apartment came up for sale for the first time since 1925. With a princely view of Central Park, it was expected to bring as much as $25 million.[36]

Senior orchestra players, who had been lucky enough to buy old instruments in the mid-twentieth century and enjoy the late twentieth-century market, turned their instruments into retirement condos in Fort Lauderdale. Their successors, stretched for cash and credit to acquire what their predecessors had cashed in, appealed for help from parents, who took out second mortgages on their homes.[37]

An "alchemy of form, sound, and Italian origins, in which the real and the phony are deliciously mixed, supported in equal part by a flourishing trade, and the listener's inexhaustible and innocent need to dream," said Marie-France Calas, director of the Paris Museum of Music, in 1998.[38] The occasion was the bicentennial show commemorating the birth of Vuillaume, the father of the modern market. She was not the first to see the connections. But it took a knowledgeable French outsider to say it so elegantly.

PAYING THE PRICE

⌒

THE LOGIC CAN be found in any economics textbook. Supply and demand meet across the counter, exchange meaningful looks, and join in holy equilibrium. Berr, a veteran violin trade watcher, recalled an emblematic exchange sometime before 1915 between Franz Xaver Kerschsteiner, a Regensburg dealer, and a customer, who showed up one day with a violin that he had just bought for 600 marks. The figure corresponded at the time to what the average Prussian earned in a year.[39] The customer wanted to know what the instrument was worth. It was worth what the customer was willing to pay for it, Kerschsteiner told him.

How this worked at the highest level could be seen in the origins and development of the Strad market, beginning in the maker's lifetime. Elena Ferrari Bassazi makes a strong case that demand for Strads has followed the history of music. But she makes at least as strong a case that it has also followed money, power, and the changing profile of society's A-lists.[40]

Over time, the pursuit of Strads would be democratized and globalized like the pursuit of wealth. But in a world where prevailing taste favored the beautiful and durable, church and court favored music and pageantry, and an era of secular discovery favored collection of virtually everything collectible, three truths were self-evident early on. Some violins were worth more than others. Some people were not only willing but eager to pay the difference. The fewest of them were professional players.

Between Isabella of Castile on the eve of the sixteenth century and Philip II on the eve of the seventeenth, the royal Spanish inventory grew from barely 20 instruments, many bashed and battered, to 191, presumably new and shiny, and 44 of them with strings. By the seventeenth century, serious private collections flourished from Padua to Portugal and points north.

In 1998, a reconstruction of a specimen Dutch cabinet at Washington's National Gallery featured a painting by Frans Francken II and Jan Brueghel II, showing the Grand Duke Albert of Austria and his wife, Isabella, Infanta of Spain, at the center. Around them is a metaphorical universe of dogs and monkeys, fruit, flowers, shells, and minerals, several globes, a collection of glassware, classical sculpture in graduated sizes, contemporary paintings, swords, furniture, medals and medallions, printed books demonstratively opened on a table, as well as a lute, recorder, and two viols in an open cabinet at the rear. Around the painting are trophies from the nominal owner's own collection, among them a tabletop spinet, an elaborately inlaid ivory and tortoiseshell guitar, an ivory cornetto and recorder, a pochette, an Italian *chitarrino* with elaborately carved figures and foliage, and a 1678 Stainer viola, complete with a lion's head. Where demand like this existed, supply was never far behind. Whether the instruments were meant to be played is another question.

By the mid-seventeenth century, decorative flamboyance was on its way to obsolescence. Still, Nicolò Amati, whose violins certainly were meant to be played, inlaid at least two with small precious stones and fleurs-de-lys, and Stradivari, too, produced at least ten ornamented violins extending across most of his career.

Among the buyers were Prince Ferdinand, a son of Cosimo de' Medici, grand duke of Tuscany, who commissioned a quintet, and Cardinal Orsini, later Pope Benedict XIII. A third end user was Don Carlos, infante of Spain, the future King Carlos IV, who came by his quintet indirectly. Reportedly, Stradivari planned to present the instruments in person when King Philip V of Spain passed through Cremona in 1702. Nothing came of it, possibly because it seemed a bad idea to cozy up to a Bourbon before the War of the Spanish Succession was definitively settled.[41] The instruments were still in the shop when Stradivari died thirty-five years later. Another seventy-five years would pass before they finally made their way to Madrid with the help of a Spanish-based Cremonese cleric, probably a royal proxy, who bought them from Stradivari's son Paolo.[42]

An eighteenth-century collector, Marchese Vincenzo Carbonelli of Mantua, bought twenty-two violins, nine violas, and three cellos, among them ten Strads and assorted Amatis, Guarneris, Tononis, and Stainers, most probably for his house orchestra.[43] Though house concerts would survive until World War II and would even reappear a half century later, when wealthy patrons bought Cremonese instruments for loan to deserving young players, who contracted to play for the owners' guests, the con-

junction of contemporary instruments and contemporary music would not
be seen again till the coming of the saxophone and electric guitar.[44]

Carbonelli died in 1740. A century later, the scene looked much the
same. Cremona still trumped Brescia. Though Stradivari and the younger
Giuseppe Guarneri had trumped the earlier Amatis and Stainer, pursuit
of old, mostly Italian instruments was still the object of the game. But
instruments traded new in living memory were now traded as antiques,
and it was taken for given that they not only hadn't been, but couldn't
be, excelled.

On the face of it, there was also little change in the rules. At one time
or another, Paganini is believed to have owned eleven Strads, two unspecified Amatis, and four Guarneris, including his famous del Gesù Cannon.[45]
Over the course of Joseph Joachim's career, as many as fourteen Strad violins and one Strad viola passed through his hands, too.[46] Still, collectors
continued to make the market as they had in Carbonelli's day.

What distinguished the new collectors, be they private, public, corporate, or philanthropic, was the growing diversity of their venue, outlook,
and net worth.

The Soviet state collection, established in 1919, was a particularly
drastic example. With fifteen instruments by Stradivari, nine by various
Guarneris, and four by various Amatis, it was made up for the most part of
expropriations from owners now dead or in exile. By 1992, when it passed
to a reconstituted Russia, it had grown to some 350 items.[47]

A single 1690 Strad violin was a measure of the social distance covered
in twenty years. Its owner, Prince Felix Yossupov, one of the richest men
in Russia, left it behind with 183 other instruments[48] in late 1917, when
he fled the imperial capital a year after helping to assassinate the monk
Grigori Rasputin, whose baleful influence on the czarina was considered
a major factor in Russia's disastrous fortunes in the war. Ironically, the
assassination would restore his fortunes years later when he claimed successfully that MGM's 1932 film *Rasputin and the Empress* libeled his wife.[49]

The Yossupov Strad was meanwhile on loan to David Oistrakh, who
would become one of the greatest twentieth-century players. In 1937,
already an international prizewinner, Oistrakh took the violin to Brussels,[50] where he led a contingent of young Soviet violinists to five of the
year's six prizes at the first Queen Elisabeth competition.

The Western experience was less drastic but hardly deficient in color.
The names now attached to individual Strads and del Gesùs suggested the

world of old money and ancient titles that so often went with it. The Duke of Cambridge, for example, who owned five Strads that were probably bought for him by Viotti,[51] was the seventh son of King George III. The Duke of Edinburgh, a regular at Hill's and patron of the famous South Kensington violin show, was the second son of Queen Victoria. The reality behind more and more collections, though, was straight out of a nineteenth-century novel, where hard times coexisted with great expectations.

The frequency of French, and still more British, names and titles is an indicator of traffic flow but also of processes that were inexorably transforming new money into collections of Old Italians in unexpected places. Henri de Greffulhe, a probable model for Proust's Duc de Guermante, came from a banking family whose money went back to the French Revolution. His wife, the probable model for Proust's Duchesse de Guermantes, was a Princesse de Caraman-Chimay, concert producer to *tout* Paris, and a supporter of Captain Dreyfus. In 1882, Greffulhe acquired the 1709 Stradivari violin that would be named for him.[52] Marie Joseph Anatole Elie, Prince de Caraman-Chimay, was a Belgian parliamentarian and French Olympic fencer without much money. His wife, Clara Ward, the daughter of one of Michigan's earliest millionaires, later eloped with a Gypsy violinist. In the 1890s, the prince acquired the Stradivari cello named for Adrien-François Servais, considered by Berlioz to be the Paganini of cellists. More than a century would pass before both instruments were reunited at the Smithsonian Institution in Washington.

The tags, many created by the Hills, helped track and distinguish instruments by the same maker that frequently came back to them for resale, sometimes several times over. They also conferred a bit of added value for future buyers. But a major part of their charm was the immortality they conferred on previous owners. Some, like Lady Anne Blunt, a granddaughter of Lord Byron, self-made Arabist, breeder of Arabian horses, mathematician, chess player, and reportedly fluent in at least six languages as well as a gifted amateur violinist, were vivid figures in their lifetime.[53] Others, like Richard Bennett, a Lancashire mill owner who collected rare books and Chinese porcelains, as well as some of the world's most coveted violins, were practically invisible even to their contemporaries.

What they shared was a passion already undergoing a serious makeover by 1832, the year the House of Commons passed the First Reform Act. In the past, baroque collectors with ancient titles like Cozio and Carbonelli had paid old money for new instruments. For the present and future, until institutions with superior firepower entered the game, successors like the Duc de Camposelice, Baron Knoop, and Joseph Gillott, with new titles or no titles, lavished ever more new money on old and older ones.

On closer inspection, the Duc de Camposelice was Victor Ruebsaet, who leveraged a modestly successful career as a violinist and a tenor into a rewarding marriage. His wife, Isabella Eugénie Boyer, had been the last of two legal and three common-law wives of America's super-rich sewing machine manufacturer Isaac M. Singer and was the mother of six of his twenty-four children. Singer died in 1875. Four years later, Isabella's inheritance, considerable even after Singer's estate was divided in sixty parts, was the foundation of her marriage to Reubsaet.

In 1881, Ruebsaet acquired Italian nationality and an uncle's shaky title, conferred by the king himself. It is unlikely that this came cheap. The Belgian virtuoso Henri Vieuxtemps dedicated a new caprice to "Mr le Duc de Camposelice." The dedication led to a 1731 del Gesù for the duke to play it on and a gala musicale, attended by four hundred, where both the duke and duchess sang and the duke performed Wieniawski's "Légende," a popular encore piece. Over the next five years, the couple paid record prices for two full quartets of Strads, including a violin that had belonged to Vieuxtemps, and invited the city's leading performers to play them every week in the Camposelices' grand salon. In 1887 the duke died, after buying one last Strad at the then-stunning price of 30,000 francs. A few years later, considerably poorer than when she married Reubsaet, the duchess married again, contacted the leading dealers, and began to liquidate the collection.

The Knoop fortune rose parallel to the Duchesse de Camposelice's but continued to soar as hers sagged. Ludwig, the family patriarch, born untitled in 1821, left Bremen early for the cotton trade in Manchester. In 1846, a first son, Johann, was born. A year later, Knoop's company sent him to Russia to help a Moscow investor build the empire's first textile plant. Over the next twenty years, he built an entire Russian industry, established his own plant, one of Europe's largest, in what would be Estonia, and created a financial empire that included two banks and three insurance companies. In 1877 Czar Alexander II made him a baron.[54]

On the forty-hectare estate he had meanwhile acquired near Bremen, he built a Tudor country house large enough for his six children, sons-in-law, and domestic staff, while Johann, who would become the second baron and take over the family businesses on his father's death in 1894, began buying instruments. By 1918, when Johann died, a total of twenty-nine violins, violas, and cellos had passed through the family collection. It was remarkable enough that ten of his eighteen violins were Strads and four del Gesùs. It was amazing that four of his seven violas were Strads, a third of all Strad violas in the world.

Probably best qualified as very models of a modern collector were two unassuming men from the north of England: John Rutson, an active patron and board member of London's two leading conservatories, and Joseph Gillott, a Birmingham manufacturer. Rutson, a Cambridge-educated bachelor who seems to have lived on the income from a couple of landed estates, helped students through the Royal Academy of Music, lending and even giving them instruments from his personal collection. In 1890, he donated ten, including four Strads and three Amatis, directly to the academy. A little over a century later, with the help of several bequests and Dr. David Josefowitz's low-profile but impressively endowed Fridart Foundation, Rutson's nucleus had grown to some two hundred instruments, about half of them violins, probably the largest collection of its kind in the world.[55]

Unlike Rutson, Gillott seems to have collected for fun and profit. Born in Sheffield in 1799, he followed his father into the cutlery trade, where he worked his way up from knives to buckles and chains. His adaptation of machine presses to split and shape millions of steel pen-points made his fortune.[56] Beginning with some sixty European Old Masters, he first turned the proceeds into what may have been Britain's largest private art collection. Among the first to discover the Birmingham-based J. M. W. Turner, he then extended his buying to British contemporaries.[57]

It was the art collection that led to violins, when the writer Edwin Atherstone offered to trade "good fiddles" for three paintings, including a Rembrandt portrait. "Violins are often of extraordinary value as works of art," Atherstone assured him. Though this was news to Gillott, he agreed. A few months later, instruments in single and double cases began piling up in his picture gallery, among them nine by way of an elaborate trade with John Thomas Hart, the London maker-dealer who occasionally bought from Reade, the novelist, who frequently met Tarisio.[58] By the 1850s, Gillott had collected "upward of 500 instruments," possibly the largest private collection ever by a single individual. In 1872 he died.[59]

Summoned to catalogue the collection by Gillott's executors, George Hart, John Thomas's son and the era's reigning expert, was first struck by the sound of the key in the lock, an unmistakable signal that the room was seldom entered. The scene that followed must have been something like Carter's discovery of Tutankhamun's tomb. In the middle of the room, some seventy violins and violas in all possible conditions of repair were stacked on a table, and bows were laid out on the floor. Reaching into the pile at random, Hart pulled out a Guarneri filius Andreae viola.

But this was only the beginning. His inquiry after cellos sailed by the attendant. But "big fiddles" hit the mark, leading to a warehouse, where fifty cellos were neatly laid out in five rows among a heap of "unused lathes, statuary, antique pianos, parts of machinery, pictures and picture frames." There was still more in Gillott's bedroom. By the end of the day, the violin total alone stood at seven Strads, two Guarneris, one Bergonzi, two Amatis, and five more "of high class."[60]

On April 29, 1872, the instruments were put up for auction at Christie's. Though Vuillaume, who had planned to join the party, missed the date and arrived a day late, the lords of the London fiddle trade naturally showed up in force, among them the Hill family, Edward Withers and Hart, who bought a Strad for himself. Amateurs showed up, too, including Reade and the Earl of Harrington, who went home with an Andrea Guarneri violin and cello that would later bear his name.[61]

When the last hammer fell, the day's receipts stood at £4,195, in an era when a Nicolò Amati could still be had for £100 and the average annual earnings of a working-class family were about £80.[62] The Strad that would be known as the Gillott fetched £295, the other six £200 and down. A 1732 del Gesù went for £275. A 1741 Guarneri, sold to the senior Hart for £156, would later become the Vieuxtemps del Gesù.

Looking back a generation later, the Hills recalled the prices as average for the era. Meanwhile, European coal production and the world's monetary gold stock had more than doubled, world trade more than tripled, registered European steamship tonnage more than quadrupled, and both Germany and America rose to global economic power, while Strad values doubled, trebled, even quadrupled.

Over the same years, the inconspicuous Richard Bennett acquired the legendary Tuscan and Messiah as well as fourteen other Stradivari violins and nine del Gesùs, including five of the twenty-five exhibited in New York in 1995. "Short of robbing museums and institutions," it was a collection that could no longer be matched, Robert Bein noted respectfully a century later.[63] Yet, as the Hills noted at the time, only the very rich, like the von Mendelssohn brothers, with one, and the very, very rich like Knoop, with three, still owned complete Stradivari quartets,[64] and all of them were Germans.

The reality in violin collecting, as in steel production, naval building, and global market share, was that uncontested British supremacy was already going or gone. In its place was an exclusive international club, newly, but not *too* newly, monied, whose members, irrespective of nationality, were identical in gender, and basically similar in outlook, dress, and culture.

The circle was still primarily British. But it was increasingly open, with Germans like Knoop and the Mendelssohns already established, the French losing ground, the Russians moving up, and the Italians barely in the game. For the first time, there were even Americans, like the exuberantly named Royal De Forest Hawley, of Hartford, Connecticut, a "dealer in hardware, feed and general agricultural products," who "amassed a considerable fortune" before learning to read music at age fifty. A hobby player since childhood, Hawley was a regular customer of Hart's, fond of entertaining fellow fiddlers, including such distinguished performers as August Wilhelmj and Eduard Remenyi. "'Well, boys,' R. D. would remark to his guests, and soon the walls would echo to 'Money Musk,' 'Hull's Victory,' etc.," a friend remembered warmly.[65] Between 1876 and his death in 1893, six Stradivaris and two del Gesù violins had passed through his collection. His wife was urged to leave the collection to the Connecticut Historical Society but never got around to it. Instead, the collection passed to Ralph M. Granger, "a wealthy mine owner of California," who "erected a special music hall in his home at San Diego . . . and engaged the services of a violinist as curator."[66]

By this time, the torch and bug had passed to Dwight Partello, a U.S. consular and later Treasury official, who had first been exposed to violins as Hawley's guest. In 1892–93, the whole world could admire his growing collection at Chicago's Columbian exposition. Public-spirited to his death in 1920, he willed still more, including four Strads, three Nicolò Amatis, a del Gesù, and a Bergonzi, to the Smithsonian, with the stipulation that they "be placed in a separate case and suitably marked as the 'Partello Collection,' to be kept on exhibition perpetually." His less public-spirited daughters challenged the will and won. The instruments went first to Lyon & Healy, the Chicago dealers, then to the next generation of collectors.[67]

Irrespective of venue, the collectors seem to have spent an impressive number of their waking hours as well as a fair cut of their net worth in pursuit of instruments few of them played. From time to time, they even traded directly, and frequently acquired one another's instruments. But the trade was usually mediated by a dealer from an even tinier circle of peers and competitors, whom they consulted in much the same way that they consulted their lawyers and bankers.

What the circle was not built for were the shocks and aftershocks of World War I that would sweep European assets across the Atlantic, devastate Russia, and impoverish Central Europe. The war, the collapse of the mark, the short-lived reprise of the gold standard, the global depression, and the coming of the Nazis melted collections like Knoop's, inflated collections like Bennett's, and reshuffled the great violin collections like nothing since the coming of Tarisio.

Even by Hawley standards, it would be hard to think of a more demotic collector than Miles Frank Yount, of Beaumont, Texas. An Arkansas native who left school at fifteen, Yount switched in his midthirties from drilling for water to drilling for oil along the Gulf Coast of Texas. His efforts paid off in 1925 in one of the great strikes of the era. Over the next eight years, Yount's Spindletop field turned his company into the era's largest independent oil company.[68] It also turned Beaumont into a boomtown of 80,000, and Yount into an autodidactic connoisseur and violin collector and a University of Texas regent. A year later, a bad year for Strad sales anywhere, he bought two with help from Ernest Doring, then a salesman at Wurlitzer's in New York. One violin was evidently meant for his daughter, Mildred. Another was reserved for her teacher.

In March 1931, a consignment from Wurlitzer showed up at Yount's Beaumont home, accompanied by Paul Kochanski, one of the era's more distinguished players and a professor at Juilliard, who was invited to demonstrate them for family, friends, and invited guests.[69] The program combined a buffet of instruments with a menu of Kreisler arrangements, and Kochanski's own piece, "Flight," dedicated to Charles Lindbergh,[70] whose nonstop solo flight from New York to Paris had fired imaginations everywhere a few years earlier.

Yount's collection would eventually include a Stainer, a Guadagnini, Guarneris by Andrea and his son, Giuseppe, and a Montagnana. There might have been more,[71] but Yount died at fifty-three, his wife, Pansy, devoted herself to racehorses, and the violins returned to the market. There was then an extended time-out for World War II.

The postwar dollar allowed Henry Hottinger to do things that were no longer possible in sterling, francs, and marks and were unimaginable in rubles. A New York investment banker and co-founder of Wertheim & Co. in 1927, he began with a Strad in 1935. But another thirty-four violins were to follow, most of them after the war. Among these were fifteen Strads, one by Francesco, and eight Guarneris, including del Gesùs that had previously been owned by Viotti, Paganini, Joachim, Ysaÿe, and Kreisler. There was also a Stainer, and an Amati that claimed to be from the legendary collection of France's Charles IX.

For better or worse, however, the real beneficiaries of changing times were institutions. Both the German foreign ministry and the ministry of propaganda showed up as customers of Philipp Hammig, one of prewar Berlin's premier dealers.[72] Joachim von Ribbentrop, the foreign minister, was an amateur player.[73] His order may have been private. But the propaganda ministry, with aspirations to a large role in German concert life, was clearly there ex officio. By postwar estimate, it may have acquired as many as forty instruments to loan to demonstratively German young artists, as well as the conservatory professors, who were their teachers. Draft certificates, prepared in 1941, attest to the loans, express the wish that "the instrument may always resound to the honor of German art" and "proclaim to multitudes of Germans the honor of the German masters of the art, who play them." There was no clue to where the instruments came from. But in a country where Jewish fortunes and livelihoods had been systematically destroyed, Jewish property was systematically "Aryanized," and hundreds of thousands of Jews were desperate to emigrate, one source, at least, seems clear.

Instrument acquisition remained the order of the day as late as December 1943. By this time, the designated targets were occupied France and Belgium. Simple confiscation was considered, but it was also rejected by the ministry's music department. There was a revealing but inconclusive exchange about authorizing the German-operated Radio Paris to buy out the Paris dealers, harps and pianos included, through a German-owned French firm. Instead, 1.25 million marks were set aside for a commission of German buyers, including Fridolin Hamma, whose Stuttgart family had once done regular business with the Hills. Hamma seems, in fact, to have got to France, possibly more than once, as adviser and personal shopper to Ribbentrop, who wanted a Strad. According to a story current in the guild and happily recounted several times in Beare's postwar presence, Hamma treated his Paris colleagues to a first-class lunch at Ribbentrop's expense, then informed him that there was no Strad available. According to Hamma's report to the propaganda ministry, he had, in fact, been offered some interesting instruments. May and June 1944 found him busy outfitting the Bruckner Orchestra in Linz, the Austrian town dear to Hitler's heart. Whether any Paris violins ever got there, or anything came of the French connection at all, is unknown, and Hamma's denial of any serious effort to carry out his mission can neither be confirmed nor disproved.[74]

Meanwhile, an incomparably more benign bequest by the Hill family on the eve of World War II turned Britain's oldest public museum, Oxford's Ashmolean, into a significant collector of a very different kind. With one notable eighteenth-century exception, the Hill bequest was limited to the sixteenth and seventeenth centuries, reaching back to a violin and viola by Gasparo da Salò, and a violin and viola by Andrea Amati that the Hills believed to be from the Charles IX collection. The exception, housed in a glass case all its own, is the 1716 Strad known as the Messiah, probably the world's most famous violin. The collection came with an ironclad stipulation that the instruments be seen but not heard, and that the family retain control of who would be allowed to handle them.[75]

Philanthropic collecting took a significantly different course in Washington. Between 1924 and 1946, a critical mass of women patrons, another novelty, set about making a modest national capital a Stradivari capital. They also made sure that the instruments would be played, with the U.S. government as the unlikely trustee.

The process began with the conjunction of a wholesale grocery fortune and a passion for chamber music. On October 23, 1924, Elizabeth Sprague Coolidge, a Chicago heiress and talented amateur pianist, informed the Librarian of Congress of her intention to build the library an auditorium for chamber concerts and endow a trust fund to pay for them. Congress took only three months to agree to the auditorium. The trust fund, with no precedent in public law, took five weeks more. On March 3, 1925, President Coolidge—no relation—signed the enabling legislation. A year and five days after the letter of intent, the auditorium was dedicated with a series of five concerts. The Library of Congress concerts soon became a local institution.[76]

The instruments followed a decade later. This time the passion for chamber music was supported by a Worcester, Massachusetts, carpet-manufacturing fortune. In 1934, Gertrude Clarke Whittall, originally of Omaha, Nebraska, and widowed since 1926, settled in Washington, where her home musicales led her to the violinist Louis Krasner. Krasner then helped guide her to a quartet of Strads plus a third Stradivari violin and five Tourte bows. In 1935 she donated the instruments to the Library of Congress, with a further endowment to build a pavilion for them adjacent to the Coolidge Auditorium, and a sustaining fund to assure their use by a resident quartet. Beginning in 1936, the Whittall concerts became a Washington institution, and they continued uninterrupted through World War II, although the instruments were evacuated to Denison University, in Granville, Ohio, for the duration.[77] For Edward N. Waters, the longtime assistant chief of the Library's music division, the care and management of Mrs. Whittall could be as challenging as the care and management of the instruments and pavilion. But the benefactions kept coming.[78]

Two years later, the widow of Robert Somers Brookings, the founder of Washington's first think tank and heir to a St. Louis fortune, added his 1654 Nicolò Amati to the Library collection. In 1952, Fritz Kreisler, one of the twentieth century's bellwether artists and a naturalized American since 1943, topped it up with the donation of his 1733 del Gesù and what turned out to be a Hill bow, though it was presented as a Tourte.[79]

The third of the dowager patrons was Mrs. Anna E. Clark, second wife of William Andrews Clark, whose election by the Montana legislature to the U.S. Senate in 1899 and again in 1901 was a powerful argument for the Seventeenth Amendment.[80] A Francophile, art collector, her senior by thirty-nine years, and recently widowed, Clark had taken her on as a teenage protégée in the 1890s, first sending her to the girls' seminary in Deer Lodge, then to the Paris Conservatoire to study the harp. In 1904, they married. The certificate was predated to 1901 to legitimate two children born in the interim. After that, the couple settled down in Clark's 121-room pied-à-terre on Fifth Avenue at Seventy-seventh Street in New York, where they remained till his death, at eighty-six, in 1925.

A little over twenty years later, Mrs. Clark and Stradivari intersected some twenty blocks to the south. Since Clark's death, she had moved into a slightly more modest apartment overlooking Central Park, with maid, cook, secretary, and uniformed chauffeur. Known to attend two and even three concerts a day at Town Hall and Carnegie Hall, she also befriended the Belgian cellist Robert Maas, newly returned to New York after separation from the much-admired Pro Arte quartet on the eve of World War II. Maas led her to Emil Herrmann, the city's leading dealer.

For a quarter century, Herrmann had pursued a quartet of Strads that had once been Paganini's. A century earlier, Paganini's son Achille had consigned them to Vuillaume, who reluctantly sold them piecemeal.[81] It was April 1946 before Herrmann finally reassembled them. Among them was a 1724 violin that Cozio had bought from Paolo Stradivari and the viola that inspired Hector Berlioz's quasi-symphony *Harold in Italy*. He then got the players together with the instruments and Mrs. Clark, who wrote a check for $156,550,[82] together with the players. For the next twenty years, they toured as the Paganini Quartet. In 1949, Mrs. Clark returned with a quartet of Nicolò Amatis that would be used first by the Claremont Quartet and then the Tokyo Quartet, founded in 1969 by four young Japanese students at the Juilliard School in New York.

In 1966, the Paganini Quartet played its last concert. The next day, its first violinist, Henri Temianka, escorted the instruments to Washington, where he turned them over to the Corcoran Gallery. A block west of the White House, the museum was already home to a Clark Wing, built in 1928 to house seven hundred some objects from the late senator's art collection. Mrs. Clark wanted them, as well as the Amati set that was now at the museum, made available to active musicians.[83] She also stipulated that they remain inseparable.

Beginning with its chairman, David Lloyd Kreeger, himself a Strad-owning art collector,[84] the museum's music committee did its best to comply, adding its own stipulation that those who competed successfully for use of the instruments should show up regularly in Washington to play them at the Corcoran. In 1967, it awarded the instruments to the University of Iowa's faculty quartet, active concertizers with regular salaries and the backing of an established institution positively eager to cover maintenance and insurance.[85] In 1973, the instruments were reassigned to the first desk players of Washington's National Symphony. In the mid-1980s, they were reassigned again, this time to the Cleveland Quartet, which toured and recorded with them till its dissolution at the end of the 1994–95 season. Finally, in September 1995, it sold them to the Nippon Music Foundation for $15 million. The foundation then lent them to the Tokyo Quartet, still located in New York and down to its last two Japanese players, for the duration of its existence.[86] Between 1995 and 2002, the foundation added another eleven Stradivari violins, two del Gesù violins, and a second Stradivari cello to its collection.

Like the prizewinning Asian player, the Asian collector was by now no novelty. On June 3, 1971, at Sotheby's in London, Robin Loh, a Chinese oil trader and real estate developer from Singapore who already owned three Strads, outbid the world for a fourth, the Lady Blunt, that had once belonged to Bennett, Knoop, Vuillaume, and Cozio, as well as Lady Blunt herself. The seller was Sam Bloomfield, a retired Wichita, Kansas, aeronautics engineer, inventor, and aircraft manufacturer who now lived in California. The price, a new benchmark, was $200,000.

In 1968, C. M. Sin, a Hong Kong industrialist, who reportedly concluded after a comparative study of the collectibles market that violins lagged far behind Chinese porcelains, began cautiously with a Stainer. He then moved up to Strads. By 1972, seven Strads were already co-named Sin. In 1974 he acquired a del Gesù for $175,000. It was just another trophy for Sin. But it was a watershed moment in the life of the seller, Geoffrey Fushi of Chicago, still only thirty but on the threshold of a notable career. By the time Sin began to liquidate his collection, leaving Hong Kong like the British and resettling on the Isle of Wight in the 1990s, it was estimated that he had bought up to twenty Strads and owned as many as sixteen at one time.[87]

On the threshold of another new century, neither Sin nor anyone else thought Strads were underpriced, and collecting had established a few new benchmarks. The price makers were now Asian and American, and one of them, the Nippon Music Foundation, was an institution. Not only did more and more buy less and less. Contingent on the object, it might buy nothing at all. Leonardos were unavailable at any price, as David Fulton, the new era's premier collector, observed.[88]

Fulton had nonetheless done remarkably well even by historical standards. Like many collectors, he had begun to play the violin in his schooldays. Like relatively few, he was also good enough to play semiprofessionally. The moment of truth arrived in his college days. As concertmaster of the student orchestra at the University of Chicago, he was allowed to play a 1743 Testore, donated years before by a grateful alumnus. He took it to Henry Lewis, at the time Chicago's premier dealer, for nominal appraisal, and was allowed to try a Guadagnini and a Strad. He was still aglow a couple of decades later when a rediscovered classmate, en route to Chicago to pick up a Strad, invited him for the ride. He returned with a Pietro Guarneri of Mantua at a price exceeding the price of his house.

What would soon be the game changer was a market boom like none since the 1920s, favored by a technological breakthrough like none since the coming of the telegraph. Since college, Fulton had been a mathemati-

cian, an apprentice actuary, a statistician, and a computer scientist with a
tenured professorship at Ohio's Bowling Green State. He now turned to
entrepreneurship with a sense of time, place, and market that echoed Gillott. Consulting led to a contract with Fox Software and a joint venture
called Fox Holdings. By 1992, a mid-eighties start-up with six employees
had grown to three hundred. It was then acquired by Microsoft, where
Fulton became a vice president. In 1994, at forty-nine, he retired. Paying
for the Pietro Guarneri of Mantua was no longer a problem.

From then on, he had bigger objects in mind, including Pietro's nephew,
the third-generation Guarneri, who signed his instruments del Gesù. His
strategy was classically simple: pursuit of the best of the best, confirmed
by bombproof certificates and authentication. A decade after the Microsoft
takeover, he had collected a half dozen Strad and a half dozen del Gesù violins, violas by Andrea Guarneri and Gasparo da Salò, cellos by Stradivari
and Pietro Guarneri of Venice, and a formidable collection of Tourte and
Peccatte bows. He meanwhile acquired the respect of the world's leading
violin dealers, naturally including Beare, as well as the friendly interest,
even ad hoc camaraderie, of some of the world's great violinists. When
invited to join him for quartets in his living room, people rarely said no.

In 2001, Beare was asked to broker the sale of the 1709 Strad known,
since Vuillaume had compared its virginity to Joan of Arc's, as La Pucelle.
The seller, ninety-four years old, was Huguette Clark, daughter of the
late senator, whose mother, Anna, had presented it to her when Huguette
turned fifty. Beare immediately thought of Fulton, who agreed to buy
it sight-unseen at the requested price of $6 million. Fulton pushed back
on a confidentiality agreement that required not only that he not name
the seller but that he never play the instrument in the presence of someone else. Escorted up to Clark's Fifth Avenue apartment in the building's
freight elevator, Beare never met or even saw the seller.[89]

In a little manual for the inquiring violin buyer, first published in 1893
on the ascending slope of the great Victorian violin curve, Wm. C. Honeyman, the Scotch player-writer, sketched three perspectives on collecting.
He found Haweis "more sentimental than sound" for seeing collectors as
people who preserved "matchless gems from the wear and tear of constant
use." He acknowledged Heron-Allen's lawyerly-libertarian middle position
that people were entitled to spend their money as they pleased. He even
conceded "that all the violin collectors whom I have met have been singularly amiable and obliging men," though he added that "these have all

been players." He nonetheless regarded collectors as "the curse of violin players," whose selfishness and folly filled the market with restored Italian wrecks at ridiculous prices and put great instruments beyond the reach of even the best players.[90]

Speaking for himself as though to Honeyman at a century's remove, Fulton took the long view. "Personally, I've always viewed my violin collection as pure consumption," he said. He had bought his instruments to play as well as preserve, with no intention of realizing any added value. When the time came, he looked forward to finding the very best of the best an institutional home where they would be played but, above all, suitably maintained. The rest would eventually return to the market, contingent on the market. Liquidation, he estimated, would take ten to twenty years. In the meantime, his children, none of them violinists, would learn to be patient.[91]

THE FRENCH CONNECTION

⌒

"HAD THERE BEEN no 'fever' for Stradivari violins," Santoro observed in 1973, "there would probably have been little research into the Cremonese School, and the art of violin making that had flourished in Cremona since the early 16th century."[92] The argument was both original and true; but the same logic also led backwards. Without the research that Stradivari inspired, not least Santoro's own, we would not know much about the "fever" either, and how it made the modern violin market.

The second story begins where the first story stops. Till Stradivari's death, according to Santoro, makers were the supply side and local players, many of them organized in the city's three academies or musical clubs, the demand side. After Stradivari, things began to change. "Imitators, speculators, profiteers, collectors and researchers"[93] now became the main characters in the story. So did the Austrians and the local fiddle community who had known the great shops before they closed. Their collective impact would soon congeal into a nearly indestructible oral tradition.

Vienna's impact alone can hardly be overestimated. In 1736, Austria drove the Franco-Piedmontese out of Cremona. In 1738, it annexed Parma. Till at least the creation of an Italian kingdom more than a century later, Austria would dominate northern Italy as Spain had dominated it before.

Local considerations were important, too. As the legendary shops shut down, inventories receded, and the local economy sagged, players and teachers saw their chance. Violins had put Cremona on the map. Visitors from as far away as England were eager to get their hands on them. What could be more obvious than a second career as advisers, consultants, and proxies? And who more obvious to turn to for a product "sought like bread" than Paolo Stradivari, the great Antonio's increasingly cash-strapped youngest son, and Paolo's equally cash-strapped son Antonio II?[94]

For Paolo, who in 1771 was sixty-three and a partner in a well-situated but increasingly precarious dry goods business, the incentives were irresistible. His clientele, including the Austrian army and the local landed gentry, paid their bills increasingly late or not at all. He was already in failing health. He had no credit line in sight. His children included a monk, a nun, and a daughter whose dowry of 12,000 lire was half invested in the family business. Liquidation of assets all the way back to his father's shop can only have looked like his last best hope.

The incentives were at least as compelling for Antonio II, Paolo's second son, born in 1738, who fathered a family of six before his own death in 1789. At thirty-three, he had no known occupation. A codicil to Paolo's will excluded him from both the family business and his father's estate, as well as from an apartment in what had once been his grandfather's house that he hoped might yield some rent.

Since the shop had continued to operate for six to eight years after Stradivari's death, there was some likelihood of inventory to sell. The relatively unregulated state of the profession allowed proprietor-makers to sell not only their own work but the work of other makers under a house label. The law also assured the continuity of the house label for the life of the firm. Santoro surmises that both conditions favored traffic in unsold and unfinished—not to mention posthumous—Strads, made from Antonio's patterns. As addressee of solicitations from all over Europe, Cozio noted the proliferation of Strad and Amati copies going back to at least 1750.[95] His pursuit of real Strads and his fortuitous conjunction with the aging Paolo some three decades later pointed the way to the modern market.

By 1772, Paolo was negotiating the sale of the quintet his father once intended for personal presentation to Spain's Philip V. Surviving documentation authorizes payment in Spanish tender for the decorated quintet, plus two Stradivari violins; assures the instruments' authenticity; corroborates brokerage by a Brother Domenico and Brother Francesco of Madrid; and confirms that the twenty-four-year-old Prince Carlos is the end user.[96]

Meanwhile, like an aspiring Almaviva, the teenage count was courting Paolo with the help of multiple Figaros, including Giovanni Anselmi, a Turin dry goods dealer and Cozio's preferred associate and agent; the violin-making Mantegazzas of Milan; Guadagnini, the best imaginable technical adviser; and Francesco Diana ("Spagnoletto"), Cremona's reigning virtuoso. Provided that they were real, he wanted all the Strads and Amatis that he could get, in part for their own sake, in part to clone and trade as far away as Vienna and London,[97] though more than two hundred years would pass before the ample dimensions of his business model were fully recognized.[98] There were negotiations with Paolo till his death in 1775, then with Antonio II. There was even a brief reprise in 1801, the news somehow having failed to reach Cozio that the senior Antonio had already been dead for twelve years.[99]

The correspondence with Paolo refers vaguely to almost a hundred unsold instruments, including a couple of violas and cellos, still in Paolo's custody. But Santoro finds the number wildly inflated. In the end, Cozio came away with ten to twelve violins, possibly including the 1716 Strad that Vuillaume's son-in-law Alard would later call the Messiah.[100] Understandably, Paolo defended his father's authorship. But when challenged to produce a notarized affidavit, he evaded definitive certification, declaring that he only sold instruments by his father and half-brother Francesco.[101] Antonio II, who was not even born when his grandfather died and only seven when the shop shut down for good, was also consulted, but he was hardly qualified to confirm their authenticity.

In the end, reach exceeded grasp. Estates need managing. Austrian reforms, followed by Austrian reaction, only complicated the job. In 1796, French armies again swooped down on northern Italy, this time decked out in revolutionary red, white, and blue and led by a general, who assured his hungry soldiers that he was about to lead them into "the most fertile plains in the world," where they would find find honor, glory, and riches.[102] Cozio prudently arranged to leave his instruments with Carlo Carli, a Milanese friend, who was both a banker and a musical amateur.

A generation later, his youthful passion appears to have cooled to an abiding interest. In 1819, a hired clerk and his daughter helped him begin to sort the notes and correspondence on Cremonese violin making that would be scrutinized like the Rosetta stone 150 years later.[103] But the intended handbook never appeared, though he would live to eighty-five.[104]

Plans to sell the collection intact to a rich Cremonese as a step to reviving the city's glory also came to nothing,[105] most probably because rich Cremonese had gone the way of the great Cremonese violin makers. Instead, Carli was authorized to liquidate the collection ad hoc. In the summer of 1817, Paganini bought a 1724 Strad that he may have played in Cremona a year later.[106] In 1824, on the threshold of his own remarkable career, Tarisio showed up. He would remain a steady customer as long as there was something to buy and, as a rule, resell. All the while, Enrico Ceruti, a latter-day Cremonese maker, and a handful of Cremonese orchestra players beat the bushes for every old violin they could find and cornered the local market until at least the 1870s.[107]

The secrets of Tarisio's success seem to have consisted of a rare mix of salesmanly brilliance and autodidactic expertise, nourished by a passion so intense and single-minded that it left no room for any other. Contemporaries, holding up instruments at one end of a long room, looked on in awe as Tarisio, at the other end, identified what he had last seen decades earlier. "The man's whole soul was in fiddles," Reade reported admiringly.[108] Possibly trained as a carpenter and self-taught as a fiddler a half century after the Cremonese sunset, he had evidently spent his early years on the road in northern Italy, repairing furniture, fiddling for bed and breakfast, and working his way up to revarnishing journeyman instruments. He then traded them with villagers or country clergy who believed their old ones valueless, and restored the trade-ins in his attic room on the fourth floor of a seedy Milanese hotel improbably called the Hôtel des Delices. However he learned it, he clearly knew his business by the time he showed up at Carli's in his midthirties. He must also have made a credible impression. It was hard to imagine Cozio or his proxy opening the door, let alone selling a Strad, to "a little miser in search of who knows what," as Etienne Vatelot, the Paris dealer, would later observe.[109]

The turning point, by all accounts, was a chance conversation in Milan with a salesman and fellow collector recently returned from Paris. The man told him that old Italian instruments were both rare and sought after there. He wondered if Tarisio might not like to show the Paris dealers a bit of what he had. Taken by the idea, Tarisio reportedly set off from Milan with six violins. As usual, he traveled on foot, playing along the way in inns and taverns and sleeping in barns. It was a month before he reached the home of maker-dealer Jean-François Aldric, his first prospective customer. Money and instruments changed hands, but Tarisio left disappointed with the prices. He had yet to learn, Hart suspected, that he himself could create demand.[110]

When he next appeared in Paris, Tarisio made a point of arriving in a carriage, respectably dressed. He also called on Aldric's competition, including Thibout, Chanot, and Vuillaume. From here on, the price curve turned gratifyingly upward. With an auxiliary corps of local intermediaries engaged on commission, he meanwhile combed the Piedmont and northern Tuscany for anything he could take to Paris and, later, London. Over the next thirty years, the total would come to more than a thousand violins alone.[111]

His strategy for beating customs was at once simple and effective. Before crossing the border, he dismantled strings, pegs, bridges, and fingerboards and stuffed the disassembled instruments in bags. On arrival in Paris, he would find a hotel like the one in Milan, where he could hole up for two days and reassemble the instruments. He would then call on customers, who literally couldn't get enough. Vuillaume's reputation as a virtuoso of the wood graft and splice seems clearly linked to Tarisio, who regularly supplied him with opportunities to practice and perfect the art. One Strad viola was so badly damaged, according to Morel, that Vuillaume had to replace the belly. Resupply of authenticity-enhancing labels seems to have been another of Tarisio's services.[112]

Until his death in 1854, he visited Paris about twice a year, though the bottom of the barrel was increasingly in view. By 1853, Tarisio himself acknowledged that he was bringing "vegetables," and Chanot noted in a letter to his son Adolphe that at least two major Paris dealers, including Thibout, violin maker to the Opéra and the previous King Louis Philippe, no longer took his instruments on consignment.

He was nonetheless good for one last surprise. In January 1855, Vuillaume learned from a Milanese silk dealer passing through Paris that Tarisio had died. Saying nothing to anyone, he packed his bags and 100,000 francs and set off for the Hôtel des Delices at the maximal speed a transalpine winter allowed a coach to travel before the coming of the railroad. On his arrival in Milan four days later, neighbors confirmed that Tarisio had not been seen for a few days.

The story seems implausible. If Vuillaume needed four days to travel, so did his silk dealer informant. It followed that at least eight days had passed since Tarisio's death. If the silk dealer was aware of it, it seems odd that no one else was. Yet according to Vuillaume, so often the only source, nothing had happened in the interim. In any event, police were summoned, the door was forced, and, again by Vuillaume's account, Tarisio was found in bed, dead of a heart attack, with a violin in his arms.

Masterful as always, Vuillaume seized the initiative. Identifying himself as a business associate, he was allowed to take charge. The room was a jumble. Among the jumble was a heap of instruments, and among the heap were a bass by Gasparo da Salò and a number of Stradivari violins.

One of them, lodged in the bottom drawer of a rickety bureau, was the Messiah that Vuillaume would keep unsold until his death. Beside it was the del Gesù later named for his son-in-law, Delphin Alard.[113]

The next step was nailing down his option on the rest. Accompanied by Tarisio's sister, Vuillaume proceeded to the farm where Tarisio had settled her sons—"his yokel nephews," to quote Chanot—ten years earlier. Keen for ready cash and, again according to the canonic version, clueless about what they considered their uncle's junk, they settled for 80,000 francs in an era when a Strad could be had for 2,000 to 2,500 francs. Chanot, who knew something about peasants as well as violins, assessed the full estate, cash and property as well as instruments, at around 140,000 francs.[114] It was quite enough, in any case, to qualify Tarisio, the barefoot boy from Fontanetto d'Agogna, a niche in the violin dealer hall of fame. Meanwhile Vuillaume, the barefoot boy from Mirecourt, who would eventually join him in the violin dealer hall of fame, went home with a reported windfall of 144 to 246 instruments, among them as many as 24 Strads.[115]

Rewarded by a gain like none before or after, his venture left even as skilled and enterprising a competitor as his old friend and fellow Mirecourtien Chanot playing second fiddle. Milliot reports that Chanot himself got the shivers when Nicholas Vuillaume brought his big brother to inspect a Strad and Guarneri that Chanot wanted to sell him, knowing as he did that J.-B. "found nothing perfect, save what he sold himself." Vuillaume peered at the instruments through his spectacles, Chanot recalled, and said nothing likely to spoil the deal. The three men then went out for dinner, still a familiar part of major violin transactions a century and a half later, and Nicholas left for Brussels happy. Chanot, with 3,500 francs to show for the transaction, was happy, too. He was also clearly relieved to see that his expertise passed muster with "his colleague who was nonetheless his friend."[116]

The trade had reason to remember Vuillaume as every bit the peer of the superstars and conservatory professors who beat a path to his shop. Flanked by fellow lions like Beare and Morel, the old lion Vatelot commemorated him at the centennial celebration as a man who listened attentively, "sometimes with a gaiety lightly tinged with irony," avoided that "slightly obsequious complacency that many dealers display in talking to their clientele," and got customers to tell him things without revealing any himself. They nonetheless went away happy.[117]

Achille Paganini is a practical example. Born of his father's short-lived union with Antonia Bianchi, a Venetian opera singer, he was fifteen when his father died, leaving him the only heir to an estate estimated at 2 million francs. Among the assets were jewelry, furniture, a title allowing Achille to be addressed as baron, a heap of letters, a stack of musical autographs, a fine collection of instruments, of which the Stradivari quartet was only a part, and Vuillaume's address. Six years later, he decided to make use of the last to sell the quartet that would eventually make its way to New York, Washington, Iowa City, and, eventually, under Japanese ownership, back to New York.

The negotiations leading to the sale reveal a master of the trade at the top of his game. The negotiations would wander on for five years. Five more would pass before the last instrument finally reached a buyer. The process began in late fall 1846. Writing from his home in Genoa, Achille, who had evidently left the quartet with Vuillaume for repair, proposed a target price of 20,000 francs, with a 15 percent commission for the dealer. Given the condition of the instruments, the price was steep, Vuillaume replied, but he had done everything he could to restore them. He submitted a bill for 160 francs to cover the repairs, assured Achille that offers would be forwarded, and requested authorization to buy ads in the major papers.

Achille's asking price would not be seen again. Nearly three years later, the quartet remained unsold. But, at what could only have been Achille's request, Vuillaume reported that he had found him not only a first-rate accordion technician but a wonderful deal on a four-octave piano, at 200 francs plus 8 more for handling, that he was about to ship via Marseille. Six weeks later, in what looks like an additional customer service, he announced shipment of 12.5 meters of silk material at 168.75 francs, plus a cloak of velvet, silk, and wool lace at 150 francs. The instruments were still unsold.

In December 1850, more than four years after the negotiations began, there was another display of customer service. Vuillaume had spoken to Schonenberger, the publisher of Fétis's Paganini biography, who was willing to pay 6,000 francs for a number of unpublished Paganini compositions. Achille wanted 10,000. Proposing that Achille and Schonenberger split the difference, Vuillaume added that he was off to the London World's Fair, where he planned to offer Achille's quartet. But 20,000 francs was a lot of money, and Britain levied a 15 percent duty on imported violins. He again advised Achille to lower his price.

Three months later, with the manuscripts sold for 6,750 francs, and

Achille's price for the quartet downsized to 14,000, there had apparently been an offer of 12,000. Vuillaume proposed to match it, with no deduction for 232 francs already advanced for ads and repairs, and forfeit of his commission. Or, if he preferred, Achille, as the quartet's owner, could accompany Vuillaume to London and spare expense at customs.

When Achille said no, they were back to the question of how to declare them. If the instruments were as good as Achille believed them to be, Vuillaume warned him, he would have sold them individually years before at Achille's price. But only the viola was first-rate. The cello, at least, had scarcity value. The violins were okay but lacked the "splendor of varnish and richness of wood" that connoisseurs paid for.

Again writing from London, Vuillaume regretted Achille's failure to come along. Two dealers were interested but at well below Achille's price. Please advise, he said. The rest can be inferred from a consignment agreement dated September 10, 1851. Achille allowed Vuillaume to sell the instruments individually—2,500 francs each for the violins and viola and 5,000 for the cello. A year or two later, Vuillaume resold the violins to interested French amateurs. Though no prices are cited, it is hard to imagine that he took a loss. In 1856, according to Lebet, the cello went to a German amateur for 6,000 francs and the viola to an English amateur as part of a 9,000-franc package that included the 1736 Piatti Strad cello and a Vuillaume violin.[118] Here, too, the margin is guesswork, but a respectable profit can be inferred.

Chanot's career was a counterpoint to his old friend and competitor's. Endowed with the same peasant virtues—"common sense, patience, work ethic, thrift"—Chanot cultivated the comfortable amateur, developed his own special relationships with the French violin-maker diaspora, and placed his sons in London shops. If Vuillaume teased him by inviting him to stop by for a look—code, Milliot infers, for "see what I've just got from Tarisio"—Chanot got even. At an auction in Douai, he bid up an instrument dramatically, then dropped out, leaving Vuillaume to pay the inflated price.[119] For all that, civility and respect were never at risk. "Who will know the old Italian instruments when Chanot and I are gone?" Vuillaume asked.[120]

Like Vuillaume, he also opted for the upper end of the trade. "Believe me," he advised his son Adolphe, "there's no money to be made in this business, save in the old and the beautiful." He proposed three guidelines. The first rule was to diversify both inventory and skills—for example, by working and networking in London. The second rule was to lay away a reserve of good things even if they were expensive and might need time to sell. The third rule was to study and know the market—that is, follow the Strads. Local collectors wanted Italian violins, a London colleague told Chanot in 1852. Most of these were now in England. With so much available, there was little need to think about copies.[121]

THE RITZ OF VIOLIN SHOPS

FROM 1838 UNTIL the 1970s, the shop in central London founded by William Ebsworth Hill was the violin world's answer to the hotel in central Paris founded by César Ritz. In any town of a certain size there was likely to be a shop where one could buy a violin, just as there was likely to be a hotel across from the train station where one could get a room, dinner, and a drink. The difference was degree.

"There's no there there," Gertrude Stein famously said of Oakland, California. During the belle epoque, between the 1890s and World War I, Hill's, like the Ritz, was about as there as there could get. Ordinary dealers were happy to sell a couple of Stradivari violins in a year, even a lifetime. Most never sell one. In March 1891, the shop sold three in one week. A year later, it acquired three Strads—a violin, a viola, and a cello—in a single day. In 1893, Joachim and Piatti, the era's leading violinist and cellist, dropped in to look at three Strad violins, a Strad viola, and a Strad cello, all in the shop at the same time. In 1894, the shop was home, or at least a home away from home, to three Strad cellos.[122] With hundreds of Strad violins still in circulation at the end of the century, three in one place at one time was remarkable enough. But with possibly only fifty surviving Strad cellos, having three of them at one time was a thing of wonder.[123]

In time, both Hill's and the Ritz learned to tolerate comparison with newer enterprises like Herrmann and Wurlitzer, the Adlon, and the Waldorf, in more dynamic venues like Berlin and New York. But the novelty was minimal. The trade had always followed money and power. Where gross national product (GNP) and the middle class grew, the violin trade bloomed.

It was true that Hill and his sons brought a remarkable combination of technical skills, organizational discipline, and entrepreneurial zip. But their stock in trade was also the right product in the right place at the right time. In a golden age of live music and British supremacy, the violin was portable, sociable, affordable, and collectible in ways no other instrument could match.

As they had since the Restoration, touring superstars did their bit to enhance the violin's appeal. Paganini, almost fifty when he first appeared in London, made the violin exciting. Joachim, barely thirteen when he made his first appearance in London, made the violin respectable. In the midnight privacy of his diary, Arthur Hill dumped impartially on Frenchmen, Italians, Spaniards, Americans, Australians, and his fellow citizens, and hammered Jews and Germans with particular enthusiasm. But he was unfailingly respectful of Joachim.

Yet the real game changers were impersonal, among them the Industrial Revolution, which made Britons rich, and free trade, which put good and even great Italian violins within reach of people who had never dreamed of owning one. Walter Willson Cobbett, who would make his fortune in conveyor belts and brake linings, began to play at nine on a Guadagnini his father bought for £28. Over a life that spanned Hill's golden age, he tried a dozen Strads before dying as the owner of a del Gesù at almost ninety.[124]

The Industrial Revolution was remarkable above all for creating new wealth. As the first city of more than a million people on the eve of the nineteenth century, London had grown to an increasingly prosperous 6.5 million people on the eve of the twentieth. Over the half century between the 1830s, when W. E. Hill set up shop in colorfully unfashionable Soho, and the 1880s, when his sons set up shop on ever so fashionable Bond Street, British merchant shipping became so vast that it seemed only reasonable to measure global time from the Greenwich meridian, down river from London.

In 1890, the year that Emile Sauret, the newly appointed violin professor at the Royal Academy of Music, noted "a perfect craze for learning the fiddle,"[125] 20 percent of all world trade was British, and British trade exceeded French and German trade combined. Between 1860 and 1900, real wages increased by an estimated 75 percent, about a quarter of that in the century's last decade. Between 1876 and 1900, while annual per capita income in Germany rose from £24 to £32, annual per capita income in Britain rose from £28 to £51.[126]

Free trade both added and redistributed wealth. As Vuillaume was at pains to point out en route to the Great Exposition, imported French violins were taxed at 15 percent. Two years later, the Cobden-Chevalier treaty lowered the tariff to zero.[127] There were claims that free trade did to British violin makers what it did to British agriculture. One could argue this. Yet the McKinley Tariff Act of 1890, one of the steepest trade barriers on earth, had no apparent effect on homegrown Amatis, who continued to turn out American fiddles of every kind and quality, and Mirecourt violins would soon show up in every Sears, Roebuck catalogue.[128]

Whatever its impact on British makers, free trade paid off for dealers and customers both directly and indirectly. The direct impact was Adam Smith in real life: more choice at lower prices for a foreign product natives wanted. By the early 1880s, Hill's could offer the upper-end customer almost anything Italian at two- to four-digit prices. But it also offered decent French violins at £5.15.0 and instruments for beginners at £1.1.0, compared with trumpets at £5, clarinets at £2.14.0, and flutes at £1.12.0.[129]

The indirect connection was at least as significant but also counterintuitive. As domestic grain prices sank by half under the weight of overseas imports, paintings, tapestries, carpets, furniture, porcelain, and collectibles of every sort, the accumulated treasures of free trade's losers began making their way from the great country houses to the auction houses, where the new rich of commerce and industry were waiting to acquire them. With an unintended assist from the German armies that overran France and surrounded Paris in 1870 and 1871, London soon became—and would remain—the world's premier art entrepôt.[130] But while the Gillott sale was a big day for Christie's, the lag between art and instrument prices turned it into a one-day wonder. A century would pass before the auction houses found reason to reconsider.

The obvious winners were the dealers. Some, like the Hills and Hart & Son, were the trade's acknowledged aristocrats. But that still left plenty of room for more, including (as Arthur Hill noted with characteristic generosity) "Mr. Vaughan, the coffee house keeper and dabbler in fiddles, who went to Boston"; "that knowing amateur dealer Curtis of Blandford"; "Mr. Peat of Alfreton, who is one of the enterprising dealers in instruments of the cheap and nasty kind"; "Mr. Crompton, the dry salter who set up some years ago as a fiddle dealer in Manchester"; "Mr. J. Williams, dentist & violin dealer of Walsall"; and "Mr. Rhodes, the piratical dealer of Sheffield."[131] Parents were winners too, among them Jacob Bright, whose violist daughter aspired to an Amati, possibly even a Strad, and kept company with Joachim protégés.

Bright had been an MP for Manchester. His brother John, paired for eternity with his colleague Richard Cobden as a prophet of free trade, had been one, too. For those with a taste for such things, the conjunction of Brights, violins, and Manchester had a logic of its own. Home to 108 cotton mills in 1853 and still processor of 65 percent of the world's cotton sixty years later,[132] the city was not only the Vatican of free trade, but also home to a substantial German diaspora. As usual, where money came, culture followed. In 1857, Charles Hallé (Karl Halle) created Britain's first fully professional ensemble. A year later, it took up residence in the city's emblematic public space, the Free Trade Hall. In 1879, Georges Adolphe Chanot opened the first serious violin shop in the capital of industrial Britain.

The wealth that generated mass markets for soap,[133] tea, and newspapers also generated a market for music, violinists, and violins. In 1893, there were some fifty concerts a week in London alone and more professional orchestras in Manchester, Liverpool, and Bournemouth. Orchestras had grown in size as well as number. In the 1790s, Johann Peter Salomon organized a gala orchestra of forty, including sixteen violins, to play Haydn. A century later, Richard Strauss needed an orchestra of at least a hundred, including thirty-two violins, to play Strauss. Music halls, theaters, hotels, and restaurants also employed violinists, and there was a steady market for dances. In 1890, the professional directory listed 255 full-time violinists and violists in London. By 1900, the number had grown to 929, and it continued to rise gently before peaking in 1920 at 1,319.[134]

Most devoted of all, from the middle class and up, were the amateurs. They subscribed to the orchestra concerts, venerated the quartets, aspired to Italian fiddles as they aspired to chinoiserie and Persian carpets, reveled in musicales and *hausmusik*, sent their children to the new conservatories and private music schools, and made publishing and instrument dealing profitable. The phenomenon was European, and Britain was no exception.

Here too the growth rate was world class. Music was "utterly derogatory for a man in his social position," a scandalized dean of Christ Church, Oxford, informed the composer-music theorist Sir Frederick Ouseley in 1846. Gentlemen did classics and mathematics, the Rev. Edmund Fellowes's uncles told him as late as his own matriculation forty-three years later.[135] Yet within a decade, there was a school orchestra at Marlborough, one of the more illustrious public schools, and a violin teacher at Eton, who brought his young gentlemen to Hill's to try out a Ruggeri and a Montagnana.[136]

Where there were gentlemen, there were also ladies. In midcentury, the chances of seeing one with a violin case were about as good as the chances of seeing one with a polo mallet. It was claimed that Scots found the idea especially horrifying.[137] Yet by century's end, women attended Scottish universities, matriculated at Oxford, earned highest honors in classics and mathematics at Cambridge,[138] rode bicycles, and played tennis. It was hard to see why they should not play violins like Jacob Bright's daughter, the amateur, or even the Bohemian-born Wilma Neruda, now Lady Hallé, who had become an accomplished pro.

Though the suffrage might still be over the horizon, entries in Arthur Hill's diary testified to equal opportunity at Hill's.

Mrs. H. Brassey and her daughter called about going in for a better fiddle.

Mr. Muir MacKenzie called to us to find a good violin . . . for his niece.

A Dr. Crew of Higham Ferrers called with his daughter who has studied in Berlin with a violin for our opinion.

Viotti Collins called with his pupil, Miss Cheetham and her father. They selected the gold mounted Peccatte bow.[139]

Taunton, the Cheethams' hometown, was some decades closer to Jane Austen than to Cobden and Bright. Miss Cheetham was already the owner of a Tourte, a Guadagnini, and a Strad. Yet even for girls who didn't own Strads and Guadagninis, serious study was no longer a novelty, and conservatory training was at least a possibility. Joachim's studio in Berlin was a favored destination. So was the newly opened Royal College of Music, where Arthur Hill would campaign energetically and successfully to get Enrique Fernández Arbós appointed to a violin professorship left vacant after a professor was dismissed for sexual harassment.[140]

Hill himself had meanwhile been invited to join the Worshipful Company of Musicians, a born-again guild in the City of London, awakened to new life after decades of times so hard that it only survived by recruiting non-musicians. Since 1870, it had convinced even non-musician members that there was more to membership than the annual dinner. Hill's sponsors, Sir John Stainer, professor of music at Oxford after many years as organist of St. Paul's Cathedral, and Frederick Bridge, the organist of

Westminster Abbey, were more evidence that the violin trade had come a long way.

With its near-daily notations of comings and goings, supply and demand, Hill's diary is as representative of the era as *Mrs. Beeton's Book of Cookery and Household Management*. Family history is a matter of particular concern and fascination.[141] As the second of four sons to pilot the family firm into the modern era, Arthur cultivated a historical antiquity believed to date back at least to the Great Fire. A Hill's ad announced unblushingly in 1891:

> W. EBSWORTH HILL & SONS, Violin Makers and Sellers of ye Viol at No. 38, NEW BOND STREET, London, furnish all ye divers thyns for Stringed Instruments, especially Bows & eke Cases, chasteley wrought, & of excellent workmanship. All are made in theyre own Work-a-day Shoppes situate in Hanwell in ye fields, & ye best in Europe's Continent. There with hys famile dwells Master William Ebsworth Hill and supervyzes ye worke with ye assistance of hys four Sonnes, William, Arthur, Alfred, and eke Walter.[142]

A claim to descent from a "Mr. Hill ye instrument maker" mentioned in Samuel Pepys' diary[143] appeared to be a dead end.[144] But the link from the eighteenth century to the twentieth was unchallengeable. Joseph Hill (1715–1784) produced violins still valued in the 1990s. So did his son Henry Lockey (1774–1835), "an excellent craftsman, who brought up his children respectably, but left no heritage beyond his craftsmanship," as his grandson Alfred would recall of him.[145] Of his children, Henry (1808–1856) seems to have been the first of a long line of distinguished English violists. Henry's son, William Ebsworth, (1817–1895), who left school at fourteen, opened his first shop on Wardour Street seven years later. There he worked and raised a family. Some forty years would pass before the shop moved again. When it did, it would make violin history.

Since the seventeenth century, the winds of social change had carried the trade westward from London Bridge to St. Paul's to Soho. The next move carried Hill's to the latest desirable location in one of the world's most desirable cities. The new address was only a few minutes from Wardour Street in physical distance. But it was another world in what it said about the business. First at No. 30 and then No. 145 New Bond Street, the shop, in business from 1887 to 1974, finally succumbed to soaring rents.

To judge by the fiddle-loving Rev. Haweis, W. E. the founding father Hill, might have been a character out of George Eliot. With neither electricity nor family assistance, he "received one and all with the same mild and tolerant inattention," Haweis recalled. At least once he dismembered an ill-used Strad in front of its astonished owner, then ambled away as though he had already lost interest. But when the customer came back, it was probably in better shape than it had been since leaving Cremona. Before Hill "all was butchery," says Charles Beare the closest approximation of a late twentieth-century Hill. After him, England was the Promised Land of string instrument restoration, and it has remained so ever since.

To judge again by successive diary entries, the restoration skills came not a moment too soon.

We sent back today to Mr. Ward of Notting Hill his Joseph Guarnerius violin. The date of Mr. Ward's violin is 1735. Mr. Ward dropped the violin a short time ago, and then sent the bridge foot through the belly.

A letter from Partello saying a corner had got knocked off the Amati . . . , and when it fell out of the case, a visitor trod on it.

Mrs. Ogilvy has agreed to have her Strad violin restored, and she tells us the cause of the violin being cracked under the bridge. It appears a lady did not notice that it was lying on a sofa, and sat down upon it.[146]

Given the horrors that showed up in the shop with startling regularity, it comes as no surprise that "our fine," "our finest," "our handsomest," "our beautiful" cases are another recurring motif, or that "eke cases chasetely wrought" should have become a significant line of accessories, with testimonials from satisfied customers including Joachim, Neruda, and Willy Hess, who served as concertmaster in Hallé's Manchester orchestra.[147]

Hill's second claim to distinction was his reputation as "one of the few men whose judgment of a violin admitted of no appeal, and could be trusted to give an honest opinion." The trait was passed on to his sons and was absorbed in the collective self-image. It is noted in one diary entry: "A Mr. Gustav Lewie of Prague says that a friend of his, a professor at Vienna, tells him that we are the most honest people for violins." A customer from Fife, who appeared with her daughter in tow on the recommendation of an old Hill's customer she met in Cairo, "mentioned to Mrs. Haig that of all the dealers we were the only honest ones," it is noted in another.[148] There was a bit of midnight vanity in this, but more than simple conceit.

Ironically, what seems to have played the biggest role in turning W. E. Hill & Sons into a shop like none to date was the apparent indifference to current accounts and cash flow that assured that the senior Hill "was cheated left and right."[149] Unlike their father, the Hill sons combined a feel for the violin trade with a feel for business. The result was the first effective division of labor in what had been a series of sole proprietorships.

Their accession to the business seemed as natural as the migration of geese. W.E. saw to it that his sons left school as early as the law allowed. "Mr. Alfred" and "Mr. William," as the staff were instructed to address them,[150] were dispatched to learn the trade in Mirecourt. "Mr. Arthur" stayed home and "kept his eye in," losing no opportunity, as Haweis noted, "of acquiring a new fact, or a fiddle."[151] Walter, the youngest brother, died relatively young in 1905. But like their father, the older brothers were made to last, William to seventy, Alfred to seventy-eight, and Arthur to seventy-nine.

The shop that was their monument was the first of its kind the world had seen. Save for insurance, almost anything the customer might want could be had under one roof. Hill's bought, sold, repaired, restored, appraised, and certified the entire violin family, including bows, from entry level to world class, or a guinea (1 pound, 1 shilling) to £1,500 and up in contemporary prices.[152] Hill's also made instruments and bows that were sold under a house label, and manufactured cases and accessories. In the dawn of the early music revival, it took a shrewd interest in old instruments. It commissioned archival research in Cremona and Brescia and lined up subscribers for the authoritative monographs still in print a century later.[153]

The brothers were equals in the firm. Willie seems to have been more equal than his brothers in the hands-on work and management of the shops, where the bows, instruments, cases, and accessories were made. Alfred, who chatted up old ladies, pored over auction catalogues, haunted provincial antique shops, and scouted continental flea markets, beat the rest of the trade to the Camposelice collection.[154]

Arthur looked after business matters and managed the mail. They typically received anywhere from sixty to a hundred letters on any given day in the years 1890–1894.[155] The mail—from North and South America,

Jamaica, New Zealand, South Africa, Australia, much of Europe and the rest of Britain—was as remarkable for its provenance as its volume. Meanwhile, customers crowded through the doors: eighteen of them on one day in 1890 alone, among them a married couple, representatives of the Royal College and British Museum, and a lunch partner, who had come to pick up one of the brothers.[156]

But for the occasional concertmaster, the one demographic noticeably and consistently missing from Hill's midnight reflections are professional orchestra players in a city with more than a thousand active violinists and violists, and almost 250 active cellists in the directory for 1910.[157] Money is the most plausible explanation. Wages of £2 to £6 a week sufficed for a "fair living," according to *British Bandsman*, a contemporary trade publication.[158] But it was less likely to cover a £50 Testore, a £40 Rota, or a £30 Gagliano, the inventory that Hill's most liked to sell.

Over any given day, Arthur Hill encountered music royalty such as Ysaÿe, Joachim, Sarasate, and "Edward Elgar, the composer of Malvern"; concertmasters such as Hess and J. T. Carrodus (1836–1895), who gave his name to a del Gesù;[159] conspicuous numbers of active military officers, diplomats, and clergymen; as well as the children of business and professional families; occasional representatives of the City; a respectable cross-section of *Burke's Peerage*; occasional representatives of the *Almanach de Gotha*, including at least one Baron Rothschild; provincial Britons from all ends of England; diaspora Britons from the remotest corners of the Empire, with at least one "agreeable letter" of inquiry from the Philippines; an assortment of continentals from as far east as St. Petersburg; a repertory company of Henry Jamesian Americans; estate executors; his own and his customers' lawyers; an ongoing procession of dealers from home and abroad; and occasional auctioneers. There were cameo appearances by customs officials and officers of the law.

Notes to himself leave no doubt of some significant changes since the days when his father lost sight of the books.

> Lord Dunmore called and agreed to take over fine Rocca violin, but on the subject of paying had to address a few plain words to him. He left promising to leave £70 on account at the Carlton Club.
>
> A Miss Darcy called from Dublin, and after taking up some portion of our time, declined to pay ready money for her purchase, so somewhat to my regret, I was unable to do business with her.

Charles Fletcher here for about three hours, sold him a fine
Lupot violin for £85 on condition that he paid cash. This he has
agreed to do by selling out some American stock.[160]

Wardour Street was never like this. And it never offered this repertory of customer services, which included recommending a teacher or an
insurance underwriter; finding a violist for a customer's quartet; loaning a
debut recitalist an appropriate instrument; assessing the talent—presumably with caution—of a customer's child; helping a client buy a piano at
a generous discount; huddling with lawyers in a case of contested ownership; teaming up with the managers of a talented boy cellist to persuade
potential patrons to help buy an instrument; personally receiving customers at Paddington and Liverpool Street stations; arranging to hand-
carry Robert von Mendelssohn's new Strad viola to Berlin; even walking
"two nice American ladies" in St. James's Park.

Yet there is relatively little from the perspective of an accountant or
anything that might be of interest to an aspiring MBA. Employee memoirs
confirm a Victorian style of management, with close attention to haircuts,
sobriety, and church attendance. Employees were kept in departmental
niches to minimize the risk of independence, and they were kept away from
customers to minimize the temptation to moonlight. As late as the 1960s,
in the golden age of swinging London, a staff as large as twenty was likely
to get an earful if anyone dropped a "Mr." when addressing an employer,
and reminiscences of life in the shops on the grounds of the family home in
suburban Hanwell often recall the era's Ealing Studios comedies.[161]

The routine of deference may explain why shop relations go practically
unmentioned in Arthur's diary, although the volume and variety of goods
and services turned over on the premises imply a dramatic increase in staff
and payroll since the old days on Wardour Street. By the early 1890s, two
sisters as well as the four brothers seem to have worked in the shop. Then
came more personnel from outside the family, two of them in packing,
including a commissionaire who met trains in full livery, four employees
who made cases, and as many as eight more in the violin department,
including three apprentices.

Though prices are regularly noted, the bottom line is as discreetly
unmentioned as sex. Though the world sees a flourishing enterprise, profits have plunged from 20 percent to 12 percent, Arthur Hill notes with
understandable concern in 1892.[162] That profit margins on lower-end

instruments were minimal is easily understandable. But the upper end was also tight, and customer demand was clearly driving up prices. A Strad cello bought at £1,500 was sold at £1,600, and the difference had to be split with rainmakers who brokered the sale.[163]

"On a violin which is readily saleable at £300 to £500, a clever dealer can make a handsome profit; beyond that the profits become small by degrees and beautifully less," Edward Heron-Allen noted in the *Violin Times*. "The responsibility for this condition of things lies with the great players; so long as [they] insist on playing only on the violins of Stradivari the prices of Cremona violins will be maintained and wax higher yet; and the modern maker will starve."[164]

The modern maker part was arguable. In the 1890s as in the 1990s, the soaring prices on old instruments should have favored the makers of good new ones. But a high summer of collecting and a cresting wave of consumer aspiration were hard to challenge. The razor-thin margins on the sale of Guarneris and Strads in part explain Hill's interest in midrange instruments, his reluctance to extend credit, and the storms of midnight indignation that regularly overcame him as his thoughts turned to the commissions routinely demanded and expected by third parties of every kind.[165]

Still, the family's style of life leaves little doubt that the glass was always at least half full. In contrast to his introvert father, Alfred lived in Heath Lodge, a large house in Hanwell, where he served as a justice of the peace, presided over the Hanwell Orchestral Society, and chaired the neighborhood Conservative Association.[166] Arthur, who fly-fished, played tennis, tried (at least) to skate, and attended an occasional concert, the opera, or the theater, even traveled abroad, where he managed to combine pleasure with business. His descriptions of Germany, including a shared holiday with Stuttgart dealer and regular business associate Fridolin Hamma, are replete with Cook's tour images of beer gardens, military bands, and majestic views, not to mention Hamma himself, blasting away ineffectually but destructively on a hunting reserve he rented for £16 a year.[167]

Even a century later, much of Hill's world looks surprisingly familiar. The hegemony of the Old Italians remained established and unchallenged. The violin's appeal as tool, objet d'art, and collectible was reduced but still intact. Despite two world wars and the loss of an empire, London remained the world's violin capital. Even Hill's frustrations—the commission-hungry teachers, pandemic misrepresentation of makers and instruments, and prices people were prepared to pay his competitors—were touchingly familiar to Robert Bein, whose Chicago shop regularly bought and sold instruments that had once passed through Hill's.[168]

By the early 1890s, Hill's landscape was nonetheless shifting around him. He needed only to open his mail for inquiries "about the prices of our new instruments" from Dr. Green of Houston, Texas, a "long rambling letter" from Dr. Brimmer of Minneapolis, who wanted "a good fiddle of an ideal kind" but did not have a lot of money, the Amati for Dr. and Mrs. Bureell of Boston, or Mr. Ginn, a Boston publisher, referred by Prof. Joachim of Berlin, who wanted "a fine Strad" for his wife. There was also the "very rich American" student at the Berlin Conservatory, who thought she bought a Strad in mint condition from a local dealer. In fact, the instrument had already passed through many hands, including Hill's, who knew it to be a Rocca. "I am sorry anyone should be taken in with it," he acknowledged to himself. "But as long as it was only a German or American, I do not mind."[169]

With its intimations of Yankee-Teutonic greed, ignorance, suspicion, and guile, Hill's diary can also be read as a distant early warning of impending slippery slopes. "Thurlow Weed Barnes [a partner at Houghton Mifflin publishers, Boston] . . . we learn is the buyer of the Jupiter Strad," Hill notes in a characteristic passage. "This will be the first magnificent Strad violin taken to our knowledge to the States and vexed we are at its going, apart from the annoying fact of the Yankee having got it so cheap."[170]

His relationship to Hamma & Co., Hill's counterpart in Stuttgart, was about as warm. New by comparison, Hamma's went back to 1864, when its founding father, music teacher Fridolin, was introduced to a Strad by a pupil who had recently acquired one. Fridolin was so carried away by the experience that he resolved to go into the violin business. A year later he discovered Italy. While one son stayed home to mind the store, two others were posted to Naples and southward.

Over the next couple of decades, the Hammas turned up an estimated eight thousand instruments, some with original bows and cases. Looking back, an older Fridolin was as struck by what his grandfather, father, and their local associates had accomplished in Italy and Spain, as he was by a German market so undeveloped as to be almost blind to what Hamma & Co. had to offer. No wonder, he mused, that most of the instruments were sold to dealers in France and England.[171]

But that was then. Like Japan, followed by Korea, a century later, Germany had quickly become a moving target, with a steeply rising learning and demand curve and the money to nourish it. "Sent Hamma the perfect late Strad," Hill notes in 1891. "I don't like such a violin leaving the country and I hope therefore that its sale will be unsuccessful."[172] Still, business was business, and Hill's rose unflinchingly to the challenge. Did Hamma think he could sell six Strads? Hill would deliver the goods, but with a well-calculated sense of what the traffic would bear. "None of the dealers in Germany will be good enough judges to discover the sides are not by Strad and Germany is the only place for such inst[rument]s," he reports of a transaction soon afterward. "I certainly could not recommend such a violin to our English buyers."[173]

This was true, but it was also increasingly irrelevant. Germany came relatively late to concert life, conservatory training, and serious collecting, as it did to modern nationhood. But all three were in full flower by the early twentieth century. Berlin was especially thick with potential buyers, professional and amateur, who wanted instruments and could afford them.

By the early twentieth century, the great American orchestras and great American fortunes were also in place, as were audiences frantic for violins and violinists. Supply, both domestic and foreign, again followed demand. Soon to be a regular entry in Hill's diary, Victor Flechter, the first upper-end New York dealer, shows up as early as 1890, extending feelers to a Hill customer. If rascally is the epithet of choice in his debut appearance, its evolution from there—liar, swindler, "this Jew of a dealer," deadbeat, rogue, vagabond, "that tricky scoundrel"—is notable even by Hill standards. But it was again no obstacle to business through a proxy when the Jupiter Strad came back on the market in 1898.[174]

Within a generation, the Hills' comparative advantage in violin arbitrage, like industrial Britain's comparative advantage in iron, shipbuilding, and textiles, was in decline, but hardly eclipsed. World War I had almost delivered a knockout blow. Britain had not only survived but conquered. Hill's, too, made every effort to pick up where it had stopped in 1914, and Alfred Hill was still acknowledged globally as the expert's expert. In time, of course, the sun would also set on Hill's. The last serious hires were made around 1922.[175]

The process was incremental, even paradoxical. In 1925, as down payment on what America's first postwar president, Warren G. Harding, called "a return to normalcy," a newly elected Conservative government returned the pound to its prewar rate equal to $4.86. Tory blue to the tips of their toes, the Hills applauded, failing or refusing to see how it would ravage British exports and competitiveness, and diminish much of their prewar clientele.

It hardly followed that this was bad for Hill's or for the London art and antique dealers, auction houses, and restorative arts that targeted the same clientele. The return to the gold standard practically guaranteed that genteel Strad owners, already coping with postwar taxes and death duties, would be under still more pressure to sell to those who could better afford them.[176] Between Waterloo and 1914, Britons had bought the world's largest stash of old Italian violins. They now had the largest stash to sell.

If Victorian high noon, with occasional clouds, shines forth from Arthur's diary, its sunset can be seen in Alfred's correspondence, beginning in 1923, with Harrison Bowne Smith, a fourth-generation West Virginian in a three-piece suit. His George Washington Insurance Company was located in Charleston. He already owned a Lupot and an Albani from Hill's that Alfred considered "extremely nice." Over the next fourteen years, he would add a Strad and a Pietro Guarneri for himself; a child-sized Christian Hopf, personally chosen by Alfred, for his son; and a complement of Hill bows.

"If you take my advice, you will not trouble about a Tourte unless you have plenty of money to spare, for the Hill reproductions are equally good," Alfred informed him.[177] Accessories included Hill rosin, Hill pegs (despite America's new Smoot-Hawley tariffs that doubled their price), and a copy of the Hills' newly published Guarneri monograph. Among Smith's incidental acquisitions was a secondhand copy of *Readiana*,[178] a collection of pieces on subjects ranging from Stradivari to the persecution of Jews under Czar Alexander III, published shortly before novelist Reade's death. There may also have been a set of hunting prints. As attentive to full service as Vuillaume, Alfred had found the prints in a neighboring shop at Smith's request. He owned a few just like them, he added. Meanwhile, he sold Smith's brother, who was an amateur cellist, a Stainer and a Goffriller.

A passionate groupie, eager to learn more about the great ones like Kreisler and Heifetz from someone who actually knew them, Smith was an active amateur who invited family and friends whenever possible for an evening of Brahms's sextets. Above all, he was very American. In addition to being a serious reader of violin catalogues, he was also a serious reader of *Kiplinger's Letter*, a pioneer business newsletter first published in 1923. In time, both the catalogues and *Kiplinger's* would make their way to Hill, followed by random copies of *National Geographic, Reader's Digest,* photos of Smith's neighborhood ensemble and young children, and even songs composed by Smith's father. Attentive to his customer, Alfred replied that he had taken the photos home to show his family and passed on the songs to his sisters, who were "quite good amateur singers." Everyone found the children and their friends "fine, healthy little specimens of humanity," he reported. His sisters were also pleased with the songs.[179] He found the no-frills investment advice in *Kiplinger's* "racy." He also welcomed "serious" American violin literature, "for the perusal of same is often instructive and occasionally provokes a good laugh."

At least initially, Smith seemed a bit importunate, and Hill cool, businesslike, and minimally accommodating. "Banish from your mind the idea" that better deals are to be had in Germany or France because of the previous year's monetary convulsions, he wrote in January 1924. "This fallacy has enabled the unscrupulous sellers on the Continent to foist off on the unwary buyer a number of bad instruments at ridiculously high prices."[180]

The moment of truth arrived in early July 1927, when Hill notified Smith that "at my request, the owner of the 1690 'Stradivari' will be leaving the instrument here for a short time, so, if you care to come to London, you can see it." The instrument, once owned by Leopold Auer, had since been acquired by an Auer pupil who "happened to have the instrument with him in Paris when the Revolution broke out in his Native country, but owing to the change of fortune occasioned thereby, . . . was compelled to part with the violin."[181] From an unnamed Paris shop, it had then made its way to Richard Bennett in London, who showed up at Hill's proposing to trade it. In time, it would make its way to an anonymous member of Bein & Fushi's Stradivari Society.[182]

Smith seems to have boarded the next available liner, then gone home to think. "Cable me the one word, 'yes' or 'no,'" Hill fired off in mid-August. "I congratulate you on becoming the owner of the 1690 'Stradivari,'" read the follow-up on August 30.

Then and after, Hill's role was reminiscent by turns of the family doctor, lawyer, and financial counselor. Something of a violin hypochondriac, Smith wanted to know about small specks on his new trophy. "Spots of rosin, which we can easily remove," Hill answered reassuringly. "In fact, I am hoping that one of these days, you will bring the fiddle here again," he added, "for it is well that we should see it now and again in the same way you go to the dentist."[183]

Could Smith afford a Strad? "I admire your determination to do the right thing, for a fiddle, however fine it be, cannot replace wife and children, who certainly should come first!" Hill agreed. "At the same time, I can conscientiously assure you that, by purchasing the above fiddle, you will be making a good investment."[184] Should Smith consider trading his current Strad for another from a later, nominally more golden period? No, answered Hill, "for a fine example of early date may prove a more valuable possession than an indifferent specimen of later date." When Smith had made his fortune—"not an easy matter nowadays"—they would have another look. Till then, he was told he should be happy with what he had.[185]

As the correspondents kept one eye on the sky and one on the business pages, governments came and went, currencies rose and fell, and even the great Kreisler showed signs of wear. On the eve of Britain's 1931 general election, Hill looked forward, unsurprisingly, to the victory of the Conservative-dominated National Government. In the early dawn of the New Deal, both men were clearly baffled by a new U.S. president "in no way concerned as regards to the teaching of true Economics" and appalled by the new administration's "prodigal expenditure."[186]

Hill cautioned against South and West African gold shares, sent coupons to Charleston so Smith could collect for him on his U.S. bonds, and offered, in turn, to connect Smith with a reliable stockbroker in London. There was transatlantic consensus that art and music had come on hard times. "I have long felt that there is only one sound political alliance whereby the whole world will benefit and that is the alliance of all English-speaking peoples," Hill affirmed, despite reflexive skepticism about actually achieving it.

His brother, unaccustomed to health problems, was struggling with them, he reported in 1935, in a five-paragraph letter otherwise devoted to chin rests, the disposition of violins left by the recently deceased Paul Kochanski, and the most expeditious way for Smith to send him the dividends on his U.S. bonds. As for himself, he added, "I, thank God, am well and, as far as humanly possible, shall continue to carry on, for I am a firm believer in the old adage 'God helps those, who help themselves!'"

FROM MODERN
TO POSTMODERN

~

LOOKING BACK ON a long and eventful career, Emil Herrmann might have said the same. As the second son of a successful Frankfurt dealer, he was born into the trade like innumerable competitor-colleagues. His father, who had set up shop in 1890 and hired eight of Germany's best makers to produce a model he marketed as "Herrmann's Neue Solo Violine," took his sons in hand before they were ten, leading them from German to French to Italian violins, as well as making sure they learned to play. In 1902, the shop and the family moved to Berlin to concentrate on old instruments. Three years later, the seventeen-year-old Emil joined the firm as a partner and took to the road in a cutaway and top hat. To his father's delight, he sold his first Nicolò Amati at 21,000 marks—equal to about $5,000—a year later. In 1913 he opened his own shop. The next year he sold Reuven Heifetz the Tononi that would carry his prodigious son, Jascha, to instant celebrity on his arrival in New York in 1917.[187] Seven years later, under dramatically different circumstances, he would sell Reuven Heifetz the 1742 Ferdinand David del Gesù that Heifetz's son Jascha would play for the rest of his career.

In between came the war. Between March and August of 1915, Herrmann was drafted, sent to the Eastern Front, and taken prisoner by the Russians. Weeks later, he found himself in Siberia as the concertmaster of the camp orchestra and a violin teacher to his fellow prisoners. Then came the revolution, and the Bolsheviks, who let him play professionally in concerts and in cafés. Oddly enough, he married the third daughter of a Russian colonel and was allowed to leave at his own risk with what little cash he had earned and saved.

With a pianist and a fellow prisoner as manager, the young couple first made their way to Manchuria and China, and a modest concert series in previously German Tsingdao. This time, the earnings covered passage to Hamburg on a Japanese steamer. Five years after leaving Berlin, Herrmann was finally home again in ways neither the Hills nor the Chanots could have imagined, let alone matched.

Meanwhile, a rich, self-assured Germany had become a deeply divided and dysfunctional one. Herrmann's elder brother had been killed in the war. His father regarded his new daughter-in-law as an enemy alien. In 1922, when Herrmann struck out on his own again, the biggest item in his inventory was a single Guadagnini. Luck of a sort emerged from the ruins of the reichsmark. Asked to sell a del Gesù and a Strad for real money, he set out for London and Amsterdam and came back in triumph.

The next step, obvious in retrospect, was America. In 1923, Herrmann estimated there were possibly fifteen Strads in the whole United States. Thirty years later, some 250 Strads, and perhaps half of the five thousand to six thousand instruments that dealers referred to as "important" had migrated to a market where ownership tended to turn over substantially faster than in Europe.

Mindful that violins, as always, would follow the money, Herrmann not only made sure he was there to meet them, but, with his unique connection to newly impoverished Russian and German sellers, he also took an active part in helping them get there. As the great postwar inflation approached its crest, he set out for New York, Rochester, and Chicago with a consignment that included a Strad and a Nicolò Amati cello. He returned home with $15,000 in cash to a country where the mark would plunge from 400 to the dollar on July 1, 1922, to 4.2 trillion to the dollar in mid-November 1923.[188] It was enough to pay his staff $5 a week, a fortune under the circumstances, provided that they took care to exchange only $1 at a time.

The experience was so promising that Herrmann decided to return to and stay in America after the inflation subsided. It was his good fortune that German immigrants were among the least affected by the newly legislated immigration quotas. He teamed up with a German partner and established a beachhead as close as possible to Carnegie Hall. The new shop, possibly the first of its kind on Fifty-seventh Street, made him the first known dealer to operate concurrently on two continents. A few years later, he loaned a thirteen-year-old Yehudi Menuhin the 1733 Prince Khevenhüller Strad for a Carnegie Hall recital. Entranced by what he heard, Henry Goldman of the Goldman Sachs banking family bought Menuhin the instrument.[189]

By spring 1929, the shop had done so well that Herrmann established more beachheads in Chicago and San Francisco. Then came the crash. As was the case in 1923, it was an auspicious time to buy. But his capital had gone into the new shops, which he now had to shut down. The next few years were touch-and-go. As he told writer Joseph Wechsberg, he even had to pawn the family silver. Still, in 1935, when Henry Hottinger bought his first Strad, it was Herrmann he turned to. In February 1936, in a full-page ad with thirty-six photos set inside the back cover of the widely read *Musical America*, a pantheon of the era's great players identified themselves as Herrmann customers.

In 1937, the shop moved across the street into a cathedral-like, two-story space with vault capacity for 110 instruments. Herrmann was now the preeminent dealer with the best location in what was well on its way to becoming the world's music and financial capital. In 1938, he acquired a Connecticut farmhouse and property. By the early 1950s, Herrmann's purchase had grown into a 120-acre estate called Fiddledale and included a workshop, a chamber music pavilion, a swimming pool, a few natural lakes, a cocktail terrace, a barbecue terrace, parking space for twenty cars, and a bombproof vault with adjoining office and study, where Herrmann worked for years on an Amati biography. His wife would eventually pass the manuscript on to a Viennese publisher, but without a receipt or backup copy. It vanished without a trace when the publisher went out of business.[190]

In 1951, with overhead soaring, a war in Korea, both superpowers armed with nuclear weapons, and Manhattan presumably high on the Soviet target list, Herrmann moved full time to Connecticut with a few hundred selected instruments and several of his wife's Russian relatives. At a time when Strad prices in dollars were still in five figures, he estimated that he had sold more than $5 million worth of rare instruments since 1925.[191]

The party in New York went on without him. Simone Sacconi and Dario D'Attili, both natives of Rome, restorers of legendary skill, and pillars of Herrmann's success, relocated by prior consent to Wurlitzer's on West Fifty-fourth Street. Their arrival transformed a relatively new establishment with an illustrious pedigree into a Harvard of violin restoration and America's most distinguished violin shop.

Transplants themselves in 1853, the Wurlitzers had settled in Cincinnati, where a spring choral festival, two conservatories, and a cavernous

concert hall in a neighborhood still known as "Over the Rhine" made it
a kind of Ohio Düsseldorf. Within a decade, Rudolph, the family patriarch and the company's founder, had advanced from importer of German
instruments to producer of American ones, with a clientele that included
the Union Army. After the war he moved into piano manufacturing with
his brother in Chicago, where two sons turned their attention to auto-
mated instruments that would one day include the theater organ marketed
as "the Mighty Wurlitzer." But a third son, Rudolph, took off for Berlin,
where he studied violin with a member of the Joachim Quartet, violin
making with the curator of the new Berlin Conservatory collection, and
physics with the Nobel laureate Hermann von Helmholtz.

On his return, he built a violin department and hired Jay Freeman,
the era's leading American expert, from Chicago-based Lyon & Healy, his
only serious competitor in the United States. Seized in the mid-1920s by
a need to revive country fiddling, Henry Ford invited Emil Herrmann to
Detroit to show him assorted Strads and a del Gesù. He ended up buying
two Strads, still on display at his Dearborn Museum.[192] But he bought
them from Wurlitzer.

By this time, the torch was being passed to Rudolph's son, Rembert,
who began to learn the craft while still in school. In 1924, he dropped
out of Princeton with the family's consent and left for Europe. Over the
next two years, he met the Hills in London, Caressa in Paris, and Hamma
in Stuttgart, apprenticed with Amédée Dieudonné and negotiated with
local makers in Mirecourt, toured Italy and Germany, naturally including Markneukirchen, and examined violins extending from the sublime
to the ridiculous.[193] Full of ideas, including a Hill's-quality repair shop
as a way of getting people into the family's New York store, he returned
to Cincinnati as a vice president of the company. In 1937, he moved the
violin department to New York. In 1949, he declared its corporate independence.[194] "Most of the crooks in the business are not intentionally so,
but just plain ignorant," he wrote to his family from Mirecourt at age
twenty-one. The Hills were the scourge of such people, he reported. He
hoped that his own family might be the same in New York "and build up
a reputation of real knowledge and ability."[195] Charles Beare's judgment
that Wurlitzer "certificates are accepted universally" was about as close as
the trade comes to beatification.[196] Wurlitzer's premature death in 1963
qualified as news fit to print in both the *New York Times* and *Time*.[197] With
the acquisition of the Hottinger collection in 1965, the firm continued to

flourish under his wife's management. It only shut down after Simone Sacconi's death in 1974.

This time the mantle passed to Jacques Français, another European transplant, who had come to work at Wurlitzer's immediately after World War II. With deep family roots in the nineteenth-century Paris trade and a command of the craft acquired in prewar Mirecourt and Mittenwald, he returned in 1948 with a one-way ticket, $50 in cash, and a consignment of twenty violins, four cellos, and twenty-four bows.

Twenty years later, and minus the native ç, he was "the undisputed big dealer in the Big Apple," in Robert Bein's words, whose sales, client list, and force of personality—plus backup support from his fellow Mirecourtien, Sacconi alumnus, and nine-year Wurlitzer veteran René Morel[198]—qualified him for the dealers' "inner circle hall of fame."[199] In 1971, he exhibited French violins not seen publicly in France since 1900. Operating in the 1980s and '90s from Herrmann's old premises with Herrmann's files and a staff of eight, he sold six to ten Strads and del Gesùs a year, a market share estimated at up to half of global sales.[200] Like Herrmann's, his expertise was not widely admired by his peers. At the benchmark del Gesù show at New York's Metropolitan Museum in 1995, there were discreet smirks when Francais identified as genuine a del Gesù whose authenticity had been challenged by none less than Charles Beare. A dendrochronology exam proved Francais right.

YET EVEN AS the sons and grandsons of the great tradition established their beachheads, showed their flags, and made their fortunes in midtown Manhattan, tectonic changes already under way would transform the trade and the market within a generation. In 1960, a London orchestra player, who earned £1,000 a year, could buy a Guadagnini for £2,000, Beare remarked over lunch in 1997.[201] The player's successor, who earned £35,000 a year, would now be lucky to get one for £350,000. A few years later, David Juritz, concertmaster of the London Mozart Players, managed to get one for £250,000 in a rare direct transaction unmediated by a dealer. But it also took a winning lottery ticket, a good price on the Gagliano he had bought years earlier at £25,000 and expected Beare to sell for £100,000, and his wife's willingness to take out a second mortgage on the house.[202]

On June 3, 1971, the future made its debut before a full house at Sotheby's. Borne of at least four postwar scenarios, it featured a London auction, an Asian buyer, and the 1721 Lady Blunt Strad. Depending on how it was denominated, the winning bid was in the five or six digits. Irrespective of currency, it beat the previous record, which had been set three years earlier, by a factor of almost four.[203] The *New York Times* sent Harold C. Schonberg, its senior music writer. His story, including a phony portrait of Stradivari, covered four columns. At the *Times* of London the story made the front page.[204]

The new era had actually been in gestation since the mid-1940s, when the Bretton Woods agreement made the dollar the anchor of a new international monetary system, firmly established between the procrustean gold standard that prevailed before World War I and the beggar-thy-neighbor anarchy that followed it. In April 1948, the European Recovery Act (the Marshall Plan) committed the United States to the reconstruction of Europe on the condition that Europeans also help themselves.

Meanwhile, revolution in China and war in Korea accelerated the reconstruction of a demilitarized Japan, locked in an open-ended alliance with the United States. The end of the European empire led to trade liberalization and the opening of U.S. markets to integrate the newly independent Asian rim. In 1953, world exports were valued at $78 billion, in 1973 at $574 billion, and in 1982 at $1,845 billion.[205]

The European recovery and the rise of the Asian rim from South Korea to Singapore coincided with a third set of developments: the United States' deferred discovery of the welfare state, plus deployment of a half million soldiers in Vietnam, plunged the balance of trade and the U.S. federal budget into red ink and flooded the world with dollars. In 1945, half of all world output was American. By 1953 the United States' share had fallen to an estimated 44.7 percent, by 1980 to a more normal 31.5 percent. By 1960, the six-nation European Economic Community had reached trade parity with the United States. Between 1960 and 1980, Japan's share doubled, and its per capita GNP approached that of the United States.[206] In August 1971, the U.S. suspended gold convertibility and the dollar ceased to be almighty.

As the dollar sank to market rates and the world economy grew, the three earlier developments were subsumed in a fourth. Between 1950 and 1970, world auto production increased almost 3-fold, European auto production about 10-fold, and Japanese auto production about 1,500-fold.[207] In 1958, Pan American Airways introduced regular jet service between New York and Paris. The soaring appetite for cars, air travel, and growth in general, meant increased consumption of energy, above all oil. During the 1960s alone, while global population grew at 1.9 percent a year, global energy consumption grew at 5.6 percent. Between 1953 and 1970, coal's share of energy production fell from almost 70 percent to 45 percent, while oil's rose from 20 percent to 40 percent.[208]

The incidental cost was a dependency on the Middle East, which had some two-thirds of the world's proven oil reserves and a unique capacity for involving the rest of the world in its multiple conflicts. In 1960, five oil states founded the Organization of Petroleum-Exporting Countries (OPEC) to coordinate prices and production. In 1973, a Syrian-Egyptian declaration of war on Israel, plus deep regional frustration with a developed world accustomed to buying its oil cheap and selling its manufactures dear, led to retaliation. Arab producers declared an embargo against end users they considered friends of Israel. All producers raised prices as high as the traffic would bear. Taking 1970 = 100 as a baseline, world oil export prices in 1973 stood at 169. A year later they stood at 456. The Iranian Revolution toward the end of the decade, followed by the outbreak of the Iran-Iraq war, ratcheted them up still higher, to 782 in 1979 and 1,179 in 1981. In spring 1974, the annual rate of inflation in developed countries was 15 percent. It was still 8 percent at the end of the decade.[209]

The impact on the violin trade was diffuse, transformative, and global. As Europeans returned to the market and Asians discovered it, prices were quoted and checks accepted in a widening pool of currencies. Under the best imaginable circumstances, supply could only remain constant. Demand, on the other hand, was potentially open-ended. Inflation, with its powerful incentives to acquire real things, drove prices still higher. The beneficiaries were the sellers: on the one hand, a new generation of dealers, with a shared and increasingly sophisticated interest in history; on the other, the great London auction houses, whose history and unique location all but predestined them to see their chance.

What made the auction houses both useful and rich was their remarkable capacity for turning upper-end collectibles into quick cash for the seller and self-regard for the buyer. Energized by death, debt, and divorce and driven by changing fortunes, they were potentially viable, even attractive, in any European capital. But none could match the historical, cultural, linguistic, even physical proximity to the ever larger and richer power across the Atlantic that made London a particularly happy hunting ground from the mid-eighteenth century to the threshold of the twenty-first.

In its way, the history of the great auction houses was a history of the world since 1789. Desperate French aristocrats unloaded their collectibles, directly or indirectly, at Bonhams and Phillips. Sotheby's auctioned the library Napoleon took to St. Helena, negotiated a century later with central Europe's Jewish bankers and Soviet commissars, and cornered the amazing collections of Egypt's exiled King Farouk as Britain itself beat a retreat from Cairo in the 1950s.[210]

But it was the cresting wave of new prosperity after World War II—plus the charismatic leadership of Peter Wilson, a poor little rich boy with a profound understanding of what his peers wanted, needed, and feared—that made Sotheby's and its competitors a global address for nearly every known collectible, with violins at invitation-only, black-tie evening sales.

While violin auctions were not unknown, one could barely tell from company histories that instruments existed. Sotheby's classed them with furniture, Bonhams with tribal arts.[211] Dealers remembered the Gillott sale as a benchmark in the history of the trade. Christie's remembered that Gillott's instruments fetched £4,195 in one day, while his paintings, including a spectacular collection of Turners, had fetched about £165,000 over six. Three years before the Lady Blunt sale lit up the sky, the instrument turnover at Sotheby's approached £25,000. The same year, a single sale of art in Florence grossed more than £300,000.

The breakthrough to auction-house interest in violins and an instrument department at Sotheby's came in 1969, when a Canadian client brought in a large collection of what later turned out to be fakes. Graham Wells arrived soon after. An amateur woodwind player, he had first tried patent law and the paper trade with mixed success. He then joined Sotheby's as an administrator, the entry-level position. A colleague, who was nominally responsible for instruments, found them boring. Wells, who didn't, volunteered and was allowed to create Sotheby's first instrument department, learning the trade on the job by watching and talking to dealers. By the time he retired, he estimated that he had handled some eighty Strads, of which a few, among them the Lady Blunt, had come around twice.[212]

Thirty years after its creation, the department's annual sales reached £4 million to £5 million, compared with £8 million at their heady peak, when Sotheby's sold six hundred to seven hundred lots of instruments at a time.[213] It was a modest fraction of the $128,315,600 the company earned in May 1999 on the single sale of art that had belonged to John Hay Whitney, a former U.S. ambassador to Britain.[214] As Sotheby's continued to grow, such sums were not even enough to keep the department in the main building. But they were enough to justify its existence, and to fill a large room three times a year with clients bidding in multiple currencies.

This success inspired imitation. As the art student son of artist parents, Peter Horner signed on as an administrator at Sotheby's, where three years in the instrument department led to three more with Peter Biddulph, a major London dealer, and a fourth with Bein & Fushi in Chicago. After seven years, the duration of a classical apprenticeship, Horner returned to London, where he convinced Bonhams that there were instruments on the premises that might actually earn the company money. Like Wells before him, Horner saw his chance. He created an instrument department that offered professionals favorable terms and allowed players to try out an instrument for three days. Both were novelties, intended to create an edge in a trade where perennially underfunded musicians were regarded at least with caution, and consigned instruments could only be played for hours and were rarely taken out.[215]

The idiosyncratic discovery of instruments was probably seen to best effect at Christie's in January 1979, when the company welcomed the young and mobile Frances Gillham, who was short of conventional qualifications but had a musicology degree from Oxford. The daughter of professional flautists, she stoutly, if disingenuously, denied that she could type. She was named second in charge in an instrument department of two but soon advanced to number one.[216] She crashed through the glass ceiling and defied conventions to become the youngest member of the board, with bonuses and stock options, while still in her early thirties. By 1995, her Strad expertise was quoted respectfully in *Cigar Aficionado*.[217]

In seventeen years at Christie's, Gillham learned to cultivate dealers as potential customers as well as experts. She learned to watch estates to make sure that her reserves, the minimum acceptable bid on a given lot, were neither too high nor too low. She learned that she disliked staff meetings, consultations, and fixation on the bottom line. She also learned that she really liked to sell things.[218]

Yet try as she might, what she couldn't learn was how to get senior management to take instruments seriously. The moment of truth came in the mid-1990s, when her department was moved out of the main building on King Street, home turf for furniture, silver, jewelry, and fine art, and relocated to South Kensington among the stamp collections and antique motorcycles. Gillham refused the move and decamped for Beare's, where she soon became managing director.

The transition at Christie's could hardly have been more seamless. Gillham's successor, Jonathan Stone, also arrived with an arts degree. He too was an autodidact, though as the son of one of Yehudi Menuhin's concertmasters he had learned to talk the talk at the family dinner table. Like Gillham, he watched the competition to keep his prices competitive and took upper-end instruments to Beare's for setup when they came up for sale.

His results, like hers, were gratifying and more. Stone expected to sell 75–85 percent of his lots, despite an Asian currency panic. On April 1, 1998, he sold the 1727 Kreutzer Strad, whose previous owners included Vuillaume, Laurie, Hill's, Hamma, Wurlitzer, James H. Cecil Hozier, MP, Sen. William Andrew Clark, and George Kress, a Green Bay, Wisconsin, paper manufacturer, yachtsman, and amateur violinist, for £947,500, or $1.56 million at the prevailing exchange rate. Thirty years earlier, it had gone for $24,000. It was enough to buy a house, as a mystified Wisconsin neighbor remarked at the time. As a new auction house record, the sale enjoyed at least a flicker of media attention.[219] As was often the case, the bidder was a proxy. But within minutes of the sale it was known that the new owner was Maxim Vengerov, the dazzling young superstar from Novosibirsk, who had been making do for three years with a Strad on loan from an American patron.

Stone was both forthright and modest about the basic recipe for Christie's success. A well-documented Strad with a Wurlitzer certificate and Sacconi bridge was an obvious place to start. Hungry clients helped, too; in this case it was executors eager to liquidate Kress's estate with maximal efficiency, transparency and dispatch. Then came Christie's global name recognition and client network, a house organ that reached fifty thousand households, a highly professional home page, and two or three months' lead time to advertise the sale.[220] Soon afterward, Stone left the instrument department for a better job with a Japanese competitor. But ten years later, he was back and again setting records. This time it was as the international business director for Asian art in Hong Kong, by then considered third behind London and New York as the world's major art auction venue.[221]

The next victory lap was Sotheby's. On November 1, 2005, it announced the sale of a 1720 Carlo Bergonzi to Maxim Viktorov, chair of the Moscow-based Art of the Violin Foundation, with acknowledged links to a half dozen A-list museums and cultural institutions, its own Paganini competition, and fifteen instruments—including a Gagliano and a Tononi—already in its collection.[222] At £568,000, or $1.05 million, and with certification from Vuillaume that the instrument had once belonged to Paganini, the sale established a new and modestly interesting benchmark for the trade and the maker. That it had previously belonged to John Corigliano, the longtime concertmaster of the New York Philharmonic and father of the composer of the Oscar-winning score for *The Red Violin*, was of modest interest, too.[223]

But what caught the attention of news editors from Al Jazeera in Qatar to *The China Post* in Taiwan was less the purchase than the purchaser, pictured at his desk with a collection of leather-bound volumes, one clearly embossed with the imperial Russian double eagle. He was trim and artfully barbered, in designer glasses and a preppy zip-up shirt. His Legal Intelligence Group, a "non-commercial partnership" founded in 1995, had offices in Moscow, St. Petersburg, Dubai, Beijing, and London, and "projects in the sphere of the fuel and energy complex as well as electoral technology."[224] A consultant to Lukoil and BP, he had previously served as vice president of the Russian Fuel Union[225] and as banking council secretary for the Moscow region governor's office. As the Violin Foundation's patron and creator, he represented it ex officio.

Tim Ingles, Wells's successor, conceded that the Bergonzi was a relatively modest sale, even by instrument department measure. Then there was the $1 million that a post-Soviet billionaire donated to keep a Malevich painting in Russia in 2002, or the $100 million that another invested in Fabergé eggs in 2004.[226] Still, Viktorov was the first Russian since the revolution to buy such an instrument privately at Sotheby's, with every likelihood of more purchases to come.

Sure enough, as the dollar sank in February 2008 amid the U.S. housing crisis and as the price of oil reached record highs, Viktorov returned. This time he took home a privately brokered 1743 del Gesù. The price, reported to be "well in excess" of $3.54 million and maybe even close to double that, represented another new auction house record. A few weeks later, after trying out the new purchase himself with his pianist wife, he invited Pinchas Zukerman, accompanied by the Bolshoi Theater Orchestra, to show off what it could do before 160 invited guests at a private concert in Pashkov House, an elegantly restored neo-Palladian mansion that usually rented to select corporate clients for $100,000 a night. "Modern Russia is not just about oil and gas," the new owner explained. "It's about culture too." [227]

In the long run, it was nonetheless imaginable that the auction houses would again lose interest. The boom that led to the Lady Blunt and Kreutzer sales was also eroding the great private collections. The few remaining major collectors were likely to have special relationships with the few remaining upper-end dealers. Taxes—on income, inheritance, capital gains and anything else that might occur to a resourceful legislature or finance minister—could lead them, their heirs, or their executors as easily to institutional philanthropy as to an auction house.[228]

ENTER THE NEW dealers, who valued violins for their own sake and were in the trade for the duration. Beyond that, their similarity to their iconic predecessors grew ever more tenuous. After a century and a half of Atlantic hegemony, even their preferred venues—Chicago, Dallas, and Vienna, and affiliates in Zurich, Seattle, and the Asian rim—suggested new frontiers.

Arthur Hill might have been pleased by their respect for his family's achievement and legacy. He might have acknowledged their enterprise, diligence, and archival research. But given the impartial, lifelong, and clearly heartfelt disdain for Germans, Jews, Italians, Americans, most fellow dealers, and much of the human race that he expressed in page after page of his diaries, collegial regard is hard to imagine. Even Charles Beare, the closest approximation of a lineal heir, would probably have inspired ambivalence. Regard for Beare's associates and contemporaries could only have gone downhill from there.

In contrast to his generic disdain for others, Hill's ambivalence for Beare would be direct and personal, reaching back to 1865, when John Beare, a sometime music publisher and friend of Sir Edward Elgar, took up instrument dealing in London. In 1892, he set up shop in Soho with his younger son, Arthur, fresh back from studying the violin in Leipzig. In 1929, father and son were followed by Arthur's son William, fresh from a two-year apprenticeship in Mirecourt. Fresh from Mittenwald and Wurlitzer's, William's stepson Charles followed in 1961.

In 1992, Charles, the fourth-generation Beare, and a trio of colleagues in London and Chicago bought Arthur Hill's diaries from the fourth-generation Hills for £67,000.[229] For all of them, the exchange was an investment in intellectual capital. But for Beare, the symbolism, too, was hard to miss. From the 1890s on, it was in the nature of the trade that Beares and Hills would intersect. Like virtually everything that happened in the course of a working day, Arthur had noted the intersections with running commentary. His entries were rarely generous and never flattering.

At the same time, the sale confirmed how different the story had turned out from anything either family might have imagined. The year the diaries changed hands, the last of the Hill shop imploded in Hanwell, while J&A Beare observed its centennial in Soho. Charles Beare, Old Reptonian and Commander of the Order of the British Empire, had meanwhile become the first dealer to appear on an Honors List, and his son Peter, a fifth-generation Beare, had joined the business.

It was only on the threshold of another new century that John Beare's heirs moved west, but then on a scale beyond anything the Hills might have dreamed of. The new premises on Queen Anne Street were substantially larger, better lit, and conveniently located between the Wigmore Hall, the Royal College of Music, and the Bond Street underground station. There were also premises overseas in Dallas and New York and in cyberspace, including a Korean-language home page.[230]

On the queen's official birthday in 2008, J&A Beare, with £45 million in overseas sales in the previous three years, appeared among the winners of the Queen's Awards for Enterprise, shoulder-to-shoulder with BT Group Plc, Land Rover, and l'Anson Brothers of North Yorkshire, developer and manufacturer of a patented horse feed.[231]

In fact, save for birth, Beare came to the trade almost as naturally as the Hills. Like Alfred, he was both a maker and a dealer. Also like Alfred he learned by doing, and above all by seeing, in a shop that offered more to see than any other—110 Strads and 57 Guarneris alone during his time at Wurlitzer's.[232] Once more like Alfred and the patriarchal W.E., he remembered almost all of the instruments that passed through his hands. That many had been previously seen, certified, frequently worked over, and sold by the Hills, some several times over, was only natural too.

As successor to Hill's and Wurlitzer, he estimated that he sold an average of three or four Strads a year. But instrument sales by his estimate comprised only 20 percent of his business.[233] His research into Cremonese and Venetian makers carried on where the Hills had stopped.[234] It even extended to the Worshipful Company that the Hills had helped rescue from guildish oblivion.

While others might exceed Beare's volume, or match his scholarship, no one challenged his expertise. He had once asked his father how long it took to become an expert. Ten years, his father replied. He then asked how long it took before people acknowledged his father's expertise. Ten years, his father replied.[235] By the early 1980s, his expertise had acquired the authority of a Supreme Court ruling and his certificates had become the global gold standard.

Like sunlight behind the clouds, his presence could be felt even in his absence. In mid-November 1998, Bongartz, a Cologne auction firm, sold a nominal Stradivari to André Rieu, the Dutch entertainer, who bid by phone from Paris.[236] The reported hammer price was DM 2 million, at the time about $1.2 million. Within the hour, Rieu reportedly learned from an Amsterdam maker and a Basel dealer that his newly acquired Strad was a composite with a nineteenth-century French top.[237]

Christophe Landon, the latest French dealer-maker to set up in New York, was delighted with the story. "It proves that there are violins that sound like Strads, but everything happens in people's heads," he told an interviewer.[238] About a month later, no money had changed hands and Rieu returned the instrument to Bongartz with a complicated story about how Pierre Vidoudez, a Geneva maker and dealer who once owned the instrument, had allegedly misappropriated it from a previous German-Jewish owner, then certified and sold it as his own.[239]

The reality appeared to be quite different. The most recent owner was an unnamed European soloist, who had bought the instrument from Vidoudez with Vidoudez's certificate affirming it as an authentic Strad. Now approaching retirement, the soloist had consigned it to dealer Francais for six months with an asking price of $2.5 million. When there were no takers in New York, the owner turned to Europe. But no one there was willing to confirm Vidoudez's attribution. At this point the owner turned to Bongartz.[240]

Beare denied any part in the discovery of the instrument's French top that followed the Bongartz sale. But his reservations were shared by Vatelot in Paris, another cardinal in the violin world's curia, and were eventually confirmed by a dendrochronological exam that dated the top at circa 1832.[241] In the tiny world of violin trade watchers, the respective dots already shouted "Connect me!" Matthieu Besseling, the Amsterdam whistle-blower who first got to Rieu with the news, was close to Michel Samson, the European representative of Bein & Fushi in Chicago, who, as everyone knew, had a special relationship with Beare.

In fact, Beare insisted, he had recognized the instrument as a French composite and said so, when he first saw it at Vidoudez's some thirty years before. Vidoudez had nonetheless sold it as a Strad. "At the time I was evidently not worth taking notice of," Beare said.[242] He was nonetheless indignant that Bongartz had dumped the failure to sell on Vidoudez, who died in 1994 at eighty-seven[243] and could no longer defend himself, rather than come clean with the preemptive caveat that would have spared the whole embarrassment. In the end, the instrument was sold privately below the auction price, and Rieu found another Strad. But this time he kept the details to himself.[244]

Like a new wave film, the outcome of the story both encouraged and allowed for multiple interpretations. The first question was: sound or label? The instrument in question had been played for decades by violinists as distinguished as Mischa Elman without protest or complaint. Rieu obviously liked it too. Did it follow that a Strad by any other name would sound as sweet? Maybe. But obviously not to Rieu at the price he paid for it.

The next question was, how much is enough? Hellmut Stern, a long-time member of the Berlin Philharmonic and former Strad owner himself, liked to say that there are no bad Strads, just as there is no bad Mozart. But some are better than others in ways likely to influence their price. The "how much" question was particularly relevant when, as in this case, the Strad was fractional. Rieu's winning bid was half or less what the owner hoped to get in New York, and a third to a quarter what people were paying in Chicago and London for a Strad of collector quality. Was he actually getting a bargain?

The Hills had been party to just such a case. In a trade that frequently wears its memory on its sleeve, it was curious that no one referred to it. In 1883, Laurie sold James Johnstone, a Glasgow fish wholesaler and violin collector, a composite Strad, which had been assembled in Paris from parts recycled from less perfect composites bought from Hill's. Six years later, he inadvertently learned from Hill's what Laurie had sold him. The Hills testified for the prosecution and, to their deep satisfaction, Laurie lost.[245] Yet the Hills themselves were positively enthusiastic about the happy union of a Guarneri belly with a Montagnana back and ribs that Hippolyte Chrétien Silvestre, another Parisian maker, had recently offered them. "A fine violin for an artist,"[246] Arthur Hill called it.

The Bongartz case led to a third question: What happens when a dealer challenges an auction house? Dealers went to auctions for the same reason they read obituaries. Auction houses outsourced expertise to dealers to spare themselves the expense of salaried staff. Both played their games.

Dealers agreed not to challenge one another on lots of common interests, then settled among themselves after one of them placed the winning bid. Auctioneers looked heavenward when nothing was happening on the floor and took bids from the chandeliers. Still, each side was useful to the other and knew it.

The Lady Blunt sale was a watershed. Since 1971, the dealers and auction houses had become direct competitors. Expertise, which had always been the dealers' comparative advantage, was now their *force de frappe* as well. But whose expertise? Francais had been willing to sell the contested instrument as a Strad, Willem Bouman, the dean of Dutch dealers, declared as he deconstructed the Bongartz shootout for a visitor. But any live expert was likely to trump even a Hill, and some experts, like some Strads, were more equal than others.

And so in the end, all roads from Cologne led to Beare, the dealer's dealer and expert's expert. "Charles Beare's opinion is the only one apart from my own that I would seek," his onetime protégé, Peter Biddulph, told an interviewer as far back as 1991. Bein was good too, he conceded. But neither would consult the other, while both would defer to Beare.[247]

If Beare was born to the trade, Biddulph, the second of the late twentieth century's major dealers, could be said to have achieved it and thrust it on himself while still a schoolboy at Oundle, a public school—that is, a private school in the American sense—in northern England. The process began at fourteen, when he took up the cello to get himself out of boarding school as quickly as possible. Three years later, he was accepted at both the Royal Academy and the Royal College of Music. A major reason for attending the latter, he later explained, was that so many of his more talented youth orchestra peers opted for the Academy.

The first step to self-discovery was the sale of his own cello, an instrument his father had bought him at Beare's for £180. Down £30, at the time a month's living expenses, after a bad night at cards, he turned it into a £70 profit. The next step was the sale of its replacement, followed, he said, by seven more instruments in his last student year alone. By this time, he said he had learned a few basic truths about himself with the help of his increasingly exasperated teacher, Anthony Pini. The one area where stress caused him no problems was business.

A serendipitous contact led to six years at Beare's, where Biddulph learned from Beare as Beare had learned from Sacconi, while nominally working behind the counter. He then set out on his own, "roaming around," as he later described it, "buying things in other people's shops, and then selling them for what they were."[248]

As he soon proved, the new globalization taking shape around him would be as congenial to a violin dealer as the great nineteenth-century globalization that ended in 1914. London was still a hub. But this time the traffic flowed away from Britain, not toward it. Beginning in the 1970s, with the Japanese market a Klondike waiting to happen, Biddulph aimed for Asia for the same reason that Willy Sutton had famously claimed to rob banks: "Because that's where the money is." He also discovered America.

Looking back on the 1980s, Biddulph estimated that he had flown almost a hundred times on the supersonic Concorde. He thought nothing of zipping off to Singapore for the day. And after hearing Daniel Barenboim fantasize about conducting in London, New York, and Los Angeles between breakfast and bedtime, he both set and met the goal of doing same-day business himself in New York, Philadelphia, Chicago, and Los Angeles.[249]

He traveled so regularly and to such effect that he became known even to himself as "the Flying Fiddle." Where he landed didn't matter— he brought a package of comparative advantages few peers could match. Among them were a tolerance, and even an appetite, for risk, as well as a generous portion of what Alix Kirsta characterized as "whiz-kid energy and skittish charm" and eyes that spotted things his competitors overlooked in places where most might not even think to go. After some two hundred years of dragnet pursuit, undiscovered Strads were about as frequent as undiscovered Rembrandts, Gutenberg Bibles, or Shakespeare folios. Yet Biddulph not only managed to find old master needles, including undiscovered Strads,[250] among the global haystacks, he regularly turned what looked to others like sows' ears into silk purses.

Early in his career, he partnered with Peter Moes, the German-American maker-restorer, till both agreed to part ways. He then argued resourcefully that restoration was overrated. "Offering the best of its kind, but not necessarily in the finest condition," he explained disarmingly as he also accepted a consultancy at Sotheby's.

There was apparently no agreement on what each contracting party expected of the other. "I needed them for some sort of status, and they needed me because they wanted an expert," Biddulph acknowledged.[251] As might be expected, the potential conflict of interest between Biddulph as consultant and Biddulph as dealer was a sore spot with some of the staff, as well as many dealers. Yet remarkably it was tolerated by Sotheby's lawyers and management.

Not surprisingly, there was a lot of daylight between Biddulph's recollections and staff recollections of his time at Sotheby's. Consultant Biddulph blamed "the new aggressive Sotheby policy" for "pressure to say the very best about an old dog, whatever the instrument." Dealer Biddulph bristled at "rougher elements of the trade" who criticized how much he paid for what he bought. With respect to his consistently cautious attributions, he insisted that he was only exercising the independent judgment that Sotheby's had hired him for. With respect to the generous prices he paid, he was only anticipating and responding to an active market, he added.

For their part, the smaller dealers seemed to have resented him for breaking ranks and pushing prices beyond their reach. Staff members resented attributions and estimates that trumped their own, as well as a consultant who earned a good deal more than they did for what seemed to them a lot less work. It was bad enough, as they saw it, that dealer Biddulph so transparently stood to gain from the estimates and attributions of consultant Biddulph. But his estimates and attributions also earned him a share of the department's profits. "Eventually," he recalled, "whenever they got a big fiddle, I wasn't consulted."

In 1985, the projected sale of four Strads triggered a climactic blowup, and he retired to a shop of his own on the other side of St. George Street. There he again reversed course, engaging some of the best restorers in the business to work on the premises. In 1989, with the help of Eric Wen, a former editor of *The Strad*, he produced a boutique collection of historic performances on a house CD label. A decade later, like the Hills before him, he published a series of benchmark Strad and del Gesù monographs with production values to match the scholarship.

A growing Rolodex testified to his exemplary command of the dealer-client relationship known in the trade as retail. High-profile entries included Yehudi Menuhin, Pinchas Zukerman, and Nigel Kennedy. But low, and some no, profile entries like Gerald Segelman could be even more interesting. Born to Jewish immigrants from Habsburg, Austria, Segelman was tiny, frugal, increasingly reclusive, occasionally cantankerous, very rich, and enchanted by the violin from childhood. Between the 1920s, when he went into business with his brothers, and 1956, when he sold out to the Rank Organization, he made his fortune in the golden age of pre-TV moviegoing. Between 1942 and 1966, he meanwhile turned his money and passion into a collection that included some of the greatest Strads and del Gesù at prices that began at £10 and extended to £8,000. By the end of World War II, he had already collected thirty-seven important instruments, making him Hill's last major customer and probably Britain's last great private collector.[252]

At once mythic and unapproachable, he seemed to surface only at violin auctions, invariably dressed in black. "All of us knew Gerald Segelman had built up an important collection," a Sotheby's staffer later recalled.[253] But almost no one save his bookkeeper and common law wife seems to have known the half of it—with one exception. Both Biddulph and Segelman adored violins and adored making deals. Despite their forty-some-year age difference, they struck up an acquaintance in the 1970s. For the last twenty years of Segelman's life, Biddulph seems to have been as close as Segelman came to a genuine family friend.

Yet as good as he was at retail, Biddulph was arguably still better at the dealer-dealer relationship, known in the trade as wholesale. "For years I always shifted the bulk of my stock to the major dealers in America and Japan," he recalled, looking back years later from the shop on St. George Street. "If a good fiddle came along, I'd sell half . . . to a colleague in exchange for fixing it up," he added. They generally hated it, he told an interviewer. They nonetheless bought in.[254]

Like Duveen, the legendary early twentieth-century art dealer, who connected America's status-hungry millionaires with Europe's cash-hungry aristocrats, Biddulph connected supply and demand at the highest level.[255] A former Sotheby's employee recalled Biddulph telling him more than once that he regarded Duveen as a role model.[256] But he factored for a few late twentieth-century adjustments. An obvious one was inclusion of ever larger swathes of the Asian rim. A second was the rediscovery of the peculiar virtues and comparative advantage of the specialist-dealer. In the art trade, the superior resources and global reach of the auction houses had long since pushed dealers to the margins. But whether its price was in four or in eight digits, the violin remained an instrument, whose trade differed from the art trade in both scale and nature. Even as it turned up in institutions like Taiwan's Chi Mei Foundation and Japan's Nippon Music Foundation, banks like the Deutsche, Dresdner, and Österreichische Nationalbank, and museums like the Smithsonian and Ashmolean, it was meant to be played, and the skills needed to deal it were neither taught in art history departments nor acquired and cultivated in auction houses.

The selling process was another difference. Auction house employees were as willing as anybody to pursue sellers anywhere anytime. But even in an era of smartphones and the Internet, bidders were mostly confined by the spatial and temporal limits inherent in the auction process. The brave new world of Asian tigers, floating exchange rates, and supersonic air travel offered opportunities beyond anything known since Laurie. Knowledge of and passion for the instrument were basic equipment. But so were energy, imagination, patience, stamina, and nerve.

Connections and cash reserves were also essential—or at least a credit line healthy enough to target the level of opportunity that the new dealers perennially sought and often found. For dealers like Biddulph, who came to the trade as players, access to bench skills was as crucial as access to a major international airport. An Internet connection and cell phone came later.

But a third adjustment was needed if supply and demand were to meet in a larger world with a minimum of wasted motion. Duveen shuttled between supply and demand as fast as steam would carry him. He needed a support system, including bribable servants to tell him where best to bump into their employers, lawyers to buffer the unpleasant consequences of overly optimistic attributions, and the young Bernard Berenson, already the Alfred Hill of Renaissance art. But for the most part, his circle of clientele was very small as well as very rich, and easily reached in their New York brownstones and the summer palaces in Newport that they called cottages. Hill's had it still easier. For special customers, they sent a uniformed employee to deliver the goods in person. For very special customers, the brothers delivered the goods themselves. But most customers were happy to come to them.

A century later, one-stop shopping was more complicated. Supply was growing steadily tighter. Demand was global. Competition was stiff. Information moved at the speed of light. Seller, buyer, and instrument might be located anywhere. Six- and seven-figure transactions extended across two or more continents. Exchange rates rose and fell like soybean futures. Even dealers needed dealers. Flexibility, brokerage, even arbitrage, was at a premium beyond anything imaginable by Laurie or Duveen. The dealer who could make it to Tokyo tomorrow was already ahead of the distinguished competitor who couldn't make it till next week.

In 1974, Robert Bein crossed paths with Geoffrey Fushi, Old World met New World in ways Duveen might have savored, and the vapor trails began intersecting over Lake Michigan. Neither Bein nor Fushi was "an

American, Chicago-born," like Saul Bellow's Augie March. Bein was born in an Ohio college town to musician parents, Fushi in North Carolina, where his father was serving in World War II. But colleagues, clients, and even random visitors who watched them interact could easily imagine both of them as characters in a Bellow novel. Was this, in fact, a union made in heaven? "More a marriage made in hell," concluded one collector, who observed their relationship over decades. Yet even he considered it possible that they liked each other.

Either way, it worked. Like any long-term liaison, it seemed to draw its strength from a reservoir of affinities, complementarities, and mutual need. Both partners were still within hailing distance of their immigrant origins, unmistakable baby boomers, and college dropouts. Both were unmistakably American, perhaps especially in their approach to business. Both freely acknowledged, even advertised, a deep and practical commitment to the Church of Scientology.[257]

Seeing the two do what they did best revealed a fairly transparent division of labor, with the partners in odd couple mode as the fastidious Felix and the expansive Oscar. To watch Bein pin down the craftsmanly fingerprints of a second- or third-tier Cremonese maker was like watching Ranke, the father of modern historiography, examine a manuscript, or Virchow, the father of modern pathology, a diseased organ. To listen to Fushi report on his latest adventures with highest-fi sound technology, or with Linda Lampenius (Linda Brava), who both attended the Helsinki Conservatory and appeared on the cover of the April 1998 issue of *Playboy*,[258] or with the owners of Las Vegas's new Bellagio casino, was like listening to Cervantes read aloud from *Don Quixote* or Laurence Sterne from *Tristram Shandy*. Now and then, a Bein attribution was successfully challenged. Neither the Brava nor the Bellagio deal worked out. But it hardly mattered. The visitor was never in doubt about being in the company of a master.

Fushi's and Bein's biographies were as similar as their physical presences were different. The tall, genial, and dapper Bein had set out, like Biddulph, to be a cellist. Instead, he became fascinated with the instruments. The discovery of a Dominique Peccatte bow had been a moment of truth. In his early twenties, he went to work in a small violin shop in Cincinnati, where he had time to pore over the classic monographs and historic instrument catalogues and occasionally visit Chicago.

Built like the Buddha, the short, voluble Fushi was five years older than Bein and came from an Italian family in working-class Chicago Heights that had once spelled their name Fusci. As a schoolboy violinist at a University of Illinois orchestra camp, he found himself seated next to a violin made in 1694. No one had ever told him there were such things. The experience was for Fushi what the bow had been for Bein. Approaching age thirty, he found himself a salesman at William Lewis, the venerable Chicago firm whose immigrant English founder had taught America's first great homegrown player, Maud Powell, when she was nine.

But Lewis had long since been folded into far larger corporate successors. At possibly a half percent of the firm's annual turnover of $100 million, violins had become a niche item. As the firm phased itself out of the Loop, Chicago's historic business district, and moved to the suburbs, the equally historic and prominent Lyon & Healy was in transition, too. But in the wake of the latest Arab-Israeli war, so were large parts of the world.

As petrodollars flowed around the globe in search of new homes and in pursuit of new assets, a thrilled Fushi sold his first del Gesù to C. M. Sin, the Hong Kong collector, for $175,000. The same year, after a common friend introduced him to Bein, the two pooled resources, bought a Strad that had only recently come on the market, and set off for Japan, where they incidentally met Biddulph. Within the year, Biddulph would take Bein to Segelman's apartment to admire his collection. "It was a wonderful life," Bein told a Chicago reporter years later. "We ate in better restaurants, we drank more expensive wines, and we had wonderful colleagues."[259]

Establishing their beachhead in the shadow of Kaku, a local trading company that dealt in cigars, cactus, guitars, electric organs, and old violins, Bein and Fushi began by setting up shop in a Ginza department store. They were soon selling instruments in lots of five hundred to what Bein called "people without grandfathers," a clientele as crazy for violins as nineteenth-century Englishmen, but without equivalent reserves waiting to be recycled in the nation's closets and under its beds. "Back then, the Japanese would buy anything," Biddulph recalled.[260] From Japan, they moved on to Korea, where Bein noted with interest that some forty-nine of fifty instruments were bought for daughters of the middle class and up, and violin teachers were among the nation's highest-paid professionals.[261] They would continue returning to Korea eight or nine times a year.

Back in Chicago, they opened their own shop on April 1, 1976. Their chosen venue was the Fine Arts Building, the pioneer high-rise on South Michigan Avenue, where L. Frank Baum and illustrator William Wallace Denslow had once worked on *The Wonderful Wizard of Oz*. For a couple of young dealers with a passion for violins matched only by their passion for the violin business, it was a propitious time in a propitious place. Sullivan's and Adler's Chicago Auditorium, another landmark of modern architecture, was next door. Their Carson Pirie Scott building was practically around the corner. The Chicago Art Institute, one of the world's signature museums, was visible from Fushi's window. Orchestra Hall, full of string players waiting to turn their instruments into retirement condos in Fort Lauderdale, was just down the street.

The city itself might no longer be hog butcher for the world, as Carl Sandburg had famously described it in 1916. But it was still a city of the big shoulders, full as ever of latter-day Fricks, Huntingtons, and Mellons just waiting for their latter-day Duveen. In an expert's report submitted to England's High Court of Justice in 2001, Boston dealer Christopher Reuning presented a list of the world's six most active collectors in 1992. Three lived in or near Chicago. Five lived primarily in the United States. At least five were Bein & Fushi customers.[262] On the threshold of the twenty-first century, Beare, as a credible source, estimated that there might be thirty Strads left in the whole United Kingdom. Bein, equally credible, estimated that there were at least as many in a fifty-mile radius of Bein & Fushi.[263]

By the late 1980s, annual turnover had reached $15 million to $18 million. By the 1990s, it had passed $20 million, with average annual sales of Strads and del Gesùs at three to six a year. By 2007, the year of Bein's death at fifty-seven, the firm had reportedly sold more than a hundred Strads, with gross sales since 1976 of more than $300 million.[264] It maintained a staff of twenty and a representative in Amsterdam. Its spin-off Stradivari Society, a consortium of owners who loaned instruments to young players, even maintained a pied-à-terre in Paris. By 2012, the year of Fushi's death at sixty-eight, it had outlived virtually all its peers and competitors as an heir to the legacy of Vuillaume, Hill's, Herrmann, and Wurlitzer.

There was no Fortune 500 of dealers to confirm whether Bein & Fushi was the world's biggest violin firm. But Fushi was certain that its combined overhead—staff, telephone, rent, utilities, insurance, security, promotion, and public relations—made it the world's most expensive. Low-overhead competitors elsewhere might hold instruments back, delay their tax payments, and wait for the market. Bein & Fushi, he declared emphatically, preferred to compete, sell, and deliver. Competitors grumbled that Bein & Fushi sold violins as though they were used cars. The loan of a Bergonzi to Kristin Castillo, Miss Illinois for 2001, to take to the Miss America finals in Atlantic City, was a representative Bein & Fushi response.

During their time there, former employees complained of burnout, recalled reminders to keep the pressure on "opinion leaders," meaning teachers, and take part in games of "tag," in which a colleague would rush in while a customer was trying out an instrument and report with fire-alarm urgency that a caller on the line in the next room was deeply interested in the instrument the customer just happened to be holding. Still, where the best of the best was consistently in stock—and there was no better alternative west of Philadelphia—the customers kept coming.

The idea of the Stradivari Society occurred to Fushi in the mid-1980s. Its prehistory was a violin shop standard. Dylana Jensen, a protégée of Joseph Gingold and Nathan Milstein, and silver medalist in the Tchaikovsky competition, needed an instrument on short notice. Fushi called Mary Galvin, a customer who had played as a child. Long since the wife of Robert Galvin, now CEO of the Motorola Corporation, she had acquired the 1708 Ruby Strad when she resumed playing as an adult. It was now resting in a closet. She agreed to an ad hoc loan.

The breakthrough came in 1985. Mary Galvin had since acquired the 1735 David del Gesù and a grand pattern Amati to keep the Ruby company. This time the designated beneficiary was Midori Goto, at the time a protégée of Dorothy DeLay. Fushi took her out to the Galvin home, where she played a bit of Paganini and the Bach D Minor chaconne. Mary Galvin offered her the use of the David del Gesù on the spot, then huddled with Fushi.

What emerged from the huddle was a consortium of patrons with no obvious precedent except, in Bein's preferred metaphor, the relationship of owner, horse, and jockey. Members of the newly constituted Stradivari Society, who owned or acquired major instruments from Bein & Fushi, undertook to loan them to young players who knew what to do with them. The players agreed to cover the insurance of several thousand dollars a year at rates Fushi negotiated; to turn in the instruments to John Becker, the society's curator, three times annually for inspections; and to play three concerts annually for the owner-patron. Like the winners of the MacArthur Foundation's "genius" grants, Stradivari Society candidates could be nominated by anybody. But Bein and Fushi did the screening. If the first year worked out, the loan could be extended for up to five.

Inevitably, it was not all sunshine. The seller-buyer relationship that made the whole thing possible precluded any claim to nonprofit status. Owners regularly complained about arrogant kids who treated their instruments like entitlements or rental cars. Players regularly complained about patrons who treated them like kitchen help and threatened to yank their instrument on the eve of important concerts or recording dates. Flattering, propitiating, negotiating, and threatening, Fushi shuttled among them like a combination marriage counselor and Figaro, the barber of Seville.

But even without the tax write-off that nonprofit status conferred, the Stradivari Society, with some twenty-five instruments in circulation, approximated the heavenly city of the game theorists where everybody wins. Owners bought into a three-fer: possession of something storied, old, and fine; the groupie pleasure of presence at the creation of a career; and a capital gain in the making. For extended periods, players got their hands on good, and even great, instruments that few were ever likely to afford. Regularly and expertly maintained, the instrument did what it was made to do.

As broker, salon, and moneymaker, the shop also fulfilled its nature in ways that might have impressed a Vuillaume. In the late 1980s, the society helped Leila Josefowicz, a prodigious ten-year-old and later MacArthur Fellow, to a Guarneri. In a serendipitous spin-off, Josefowicz's physicist father helped Robert Galvin, the Motorola CEO and a member of the society's extended family, to a mutually beneficial relationship with his company, Hughes Aircraft.

Motorola was meanwhile deeply involved in the creation of China's mobile phone market,[265] while Fushi invested in the cultivation of future Chinese superstars. In September 2002, he toured China with his son, Alec, the prodigious Lu Siqing, the society's manager, Li Ling, three Strads, the 1742 Wieniawski del Gesù, a Nicolò Amati, and Mary Galvin. Their itinerary included Tianjin, Motorola's Chinese home, as well as a reception by Zhang Zemin, at the time the president of the People's Republic of China. In twenty years, a Chinese president had never received the CEO of Motorola China, Fushi noted happily. A month later, on a state visit to the United States, Chicago Mayor Richard Daley welcomed Zhang in the presence of Fushi, the Galvins, China's ambassador to the U.S., and the chair of Motorola China.[266]

While Fushi welcomed China to Chicago, Dietmar Machold, the most recent entrant into the ever smaller club of new dealers, was just beginning to have fun in at least six places. His Anglophone peers tended to see him as a gate-crasher, and it was true that his résumé was in some ways even less traditional than Biddulph's, Bein's, or Fushi's. Yet in others, like his tailoring, it was as conservative as Beare's, his father too had been a dealer, and a son was in training.

The business went back to Markneukirchen, where his father, Heinz Joachim, had trained before World War II. After surviving the Eastern Front, he then fled westward like countless thousands of Soviet Zone contemporaries. In 1951, he opened a familiarly artisanal German violin shop in the ruins of Bremen, a Hanseatic city-republic, where what would soon be called the economic miracle was beginning to take shape.

Arisen from the same devastated landscape as the Federal Republic itself, Machold's shop continued to serve the professionals and amateurs of a solidly middle-class German provincial capital. But its staff now came from as many as nine countries and had established a reputation for skillful repair and expert restoration, which they had gained through archival research and professional travel.[267] Many people associated repair and restoration skills with England, where much of Machold's staff had actually trained. Dietmar, on the other hand, associated them with the United States, where immigrant wizards like Sacconi, Hans Weisshaar, and Vahakn Nigogosian made their reputations, as he saw it, restoring neglected trophies their clients had bought not wisely but too well from British dealers.[268]

In a country where the sun was setting on Hamma & Co., its only claim to an international shop, the senior Machold also discovered auctions, and traded increasingly in good and better instruments. People who bought Strads for themselves bought good three-quarter-sized French instruments for their kids, his staff reminded him. He took the message to heart. But by this time, the shop was effectively becoming his son's.

Neither a player nor a maker,[269] Dietmar had instead studied law at his father's instigation. Dealers with college diplomas were rare enough. No one could recall a major dealer before Machold with a law degree, even if he had never actually practiced law.

Although the company files and photo archive went back to Hart, the Hills and Hammas, and Dietmar claimed to see slides pop up before his eyes when examining an instrument, his expertise was not widely respected by his peers.[270] But expertise could be outsourced, for example, to Biddulph. He even occasionally, if reluctantly, bought expertise from Beare. He had a feel, on the other hand, for money and people. In a college cohort, whose weakness for Angela Davis posters and Che Guevara T-shirts concealed a deep yearning for the well-cushioned tenure of public sector employment, his appetite for private enterprise was notable, too.

In 1993, eight German companies, including Daimler-Benz, Volkswagen, VEBA, Siemens, Thyssen, and all three sucessors to the IG-Farben, were among the world's biggest.[271] Yet none postdated the postwar economic miracle, and all had roots reaching back to at least the 1930s.

In a sense, this was also true of Geigenbau Machold GmbH. Yet even as the postwar economy reached a plateau, Machold's began to take off. In 1977, Dietmar began to take charge in Bremen. In 1987 he opened a second shop in Zurich. A few years later, he established a third in Vienna within walking distance of the Staatsoper. With Jacques Francais's retirement in view, he established a fourth in New York, on Broadway just across from Lincoln Center. In 2004, he established a Chicago beachhead downstairs from Bein & Fushi.With a West Coast presence in Seattle, he was meanwhile thinking about still more, including a presence in mainland Asia, as he told an interviewer for *Entrepreneurs and Innovators*, a TV series jointly sponsored by the University of Washington Business School, *The Seattle Times*, and Seattle Community Colleges.[272] In summer 2005, Machold Rare Violins Korea opened in Seoul. China was obviously meant to come next.

In their respective ways, the Chanots, the Hills, and Herrmann had also been international dealers. But there had never before been a genuinely global dealer like Machold. "Dietmar had the balls," an admiring associate recalled, even if this meant borrowing from one bank to cover a loan from another.

On the eve of 2003, the editors of the *Economist,* tongue firmly in cheek, updated their readers on the redoubtable Felicity Foresight, "a brilliant but little known" American investor who had consistently seen where money would be made since her birth in 1900. Her conscientious parents had welcomed her arrival by investing a dollar on her behalf in a basket of shares. But she soon realized that she could do far better. Avoiding tips as well as proposals from Henry Hindsight, an old flame who consistently got it wrong, she did respectably on U.S. stocks, which had approached an average annual gain of 10 percent over the past century. Treasury bonds, by comparison, had earned less than half of that, and gold less than a third. Over the most recent decade, she had also done well in London residential property, with an annual average of 16 percent, though art had been a bit of a loser lately.[273]

But violin prices escaped her periscopic view. In 1999, Kristin Suess, an MBA candidate at the University of Cincinnati, matched the performance of a basket of sixteenth-century to twentieth-century Italian violins against the Dow, the Standard & Poor's Index, and ten-year Treasury bonds since 1960. Of her forty-three-maker sample, extending from Amati, A., to Ventipane, L., only Maggini, with 8.51 percent annual gain, had failed to match the return on U.S. stocks, she reported. The rest had yielded an average of almost 12 percent.[274] The trade, understandably, grabbed Suess's figures and ran with them.

Seven years later, Suess's findings were subjected to a stiff critique by Philip E. Margolis, a Swiss-based American market watcher, whose website was the closest the world had yet come to a comprehensive database of the globe's collectible violins. Reaching back to the 1850s and the beginnings of the modern market, Margolis also factored for inflation, fluctuating exchange rates, transaction costs, and skewed sources. His result was significantly more modest than Suess's—a 2 percent real gain over 153 years, reaching 3.5 percent around 1970. It had since slipped to about 0.5 percent. Margolis was reluctant to say whether this had any connection to soaring buyer commissions at the auction houses. But he conceded that instrument investments had been less risky than most others and, unsurprisingly, that the usual suspects, Stradivari and Guarneri del Gesù, had appreciated faster than their lesser-known contemporaries and competitors.[275]

Meanwhile, Felicity Foresight's oversight was Machold's gain. "Willie reports badly of Vienna as regards to their fiddle possessions," Arthur Hill noted in September 1892 on his brother's return from the Austrian capital. "All the good ones have left the country."[276] A little short of a century later, the Austrian National Bank set out to make up for lost time with Machold's help. In 1989 it minted a Vienna Philharmonic gold coin of one troy ounce (31.003 g.) for sale to global collectors.[277] The proceeds went into instruments for loan to the Philharmonic's concertmasters, leading chamber players, and the nation's deserving young. The same year, Machold sold the bank its first Strad, the 1725 Chaconne, for 6 million Swiss francs, at the time about $1.3 million.[278] "Interestingly, he seems to be much better at selling things to banks or other institutions . . . than to musicians," another former employee observed.

A few years later, the collection had grown to twenty-seven instruments, and twenty of them, some $25 million worth, had come from Machold. In all of Austria, Machold estimated, there were nine Strads. The bank owned seven of them, as well as three del Gesùs. Knighthood was no longer an option. But a grateful republic made him a professor, still one of Central Europe's favorite titles. Leaving Bremen ever further behind him, Machold also acquired Schloss Eichbüchl, a little white castle in Lower Austria, raised its fourteenth-century foundations to twenty-first-century biothermal efficiency[279] and made it a permanent residence, as well as a venue for sponsored musicales. In 2005, the governor of the state awarded Machold its gold medal for public service and declared him a citizen of the world.[280]

In 2001, Machold scored again with a model discovered and tested some years earlier by Nigel Brown. A Cambridge investment counselor with a degree in medieval history and a soft spot for the archaic game of court tennis, Brown had cultivated his own passion for old Italian violins over lunch hours at Sotheby's after the sale of the Lady Blunt.[281] In 1986, private passion paid off unexpectedly when he was approached to help buy the young Nigel Kennedy a Strad. In the first of some twenty such transactions, Brown recruited a consortium of buyers, with the understanding that Kennedy would buy them out after a designated period, or they would share in the expected gain when the instrument was again put up for sale.[282]

But unlike Machold, Brown was primarily in it for the fun with a garnish of civic satisfaction. By day, he opened Cambridge to IT, and advised the government of Singapore. In fact, he conceded, even the fun had limits. Finding buyers was time-consuming. Collectors, willing to sink tens of millions in a painting, couldn't see the point of investing a fraction in an object Brown considered the equal of the Sistine Chapel ceiling. Even his business partners were a hard sell.[283]

In the late 1990s, Machold, whose primary motive was profit, not fun, saw his chance, too. Robert McDuffie, a protégé of Dorothy DeLay, wanted the 1735 Ladenburg del Gesù. It had reportedly been played by Paganini and his great German contemporary, Ludwig Spohr, been named for the Ladenburgs, a family of German-Jewish bankers, and owned by the Stettenheims, a family of South German-Jewish professionals and business people. In 1939, Henry Werro in Bern bought it from Hamma. There is no indication of when and how Hamma came by the instrument, or why the owner chose to sell it. But it was only a few months after the Kristallnacht pogrom of November 1938 led to de facto expropriation of what was left of Jewish property. In 1942, Werro sold it back to Hamma, a reliable supplier and occasional agent of the Propaganda Ministry's music department.[284] Soon afterward, Hamma sold it to the Goebbels Foundation,[285] the ministry's discretionary fund. From there, it made its way to Walter Stross, who was a professor of violin at the Munich Conservatory and first violinist in a quartet still active twenty years after the war.

Postwar owners included Bernhard Sprengel, the Hannover chocolate manufacturer, Emil Herrmann, and the Argentinian-born Ricardo Odnoposoff, concertmaster of the Vienna Philharmonic, who came in second to David Oistrakh at the legendary Queen Elisabeth competition in 1937. In 1989, Machold bought it from an unidentified owner for $1.2 million, and sold it to Herbert Axelrod, the New Jersey collector, philanthropist, and pet supply millionaire, for an undesignated price.[286] A few years later, with Axelrod on the threshold of retirement, it was again at Machold's and back on the market. But at $3.5 million what was even an established player in his early forties to do?

Despite a cordial family relationship to McDuffie's wife and assets in twelve digits, Sun Trust, a major Atlanta Bank, was uninterested. A 6 percent loan supported by eighteen partners, each paying $10,000 a year, was another nonstarter. McDuffie's next idea was an extended lease and a limited partnership. But this meant partners. In early 1999, he began recruiting them with Machold's help at a series of invitation-only soirées from Atlanta to Manhattan. Among the hosts was Paul Tagliabue, commissioner of the National Football League. Among the guests were former U.S. Senator Sam Nunn, Atlanta Falcons owner Taylor Smith, and Mike Mills, a childhood friend of McDuffie's and bass player in the rock band R.E.M.

The message at every venue was what Machold was concurrently telling audiences in Singapore: Great instruments were beyond the reach of needy young players—but they were a can't-miss opportunity for individual and corporate investors, who could buy them to loan. Since there could never be enough to satisfy demand, everyone was bound to win.

"Perhaps for investors tired of the volatility of the stock market, an investment like this might well be music to their ears," a Singapore reporter mused.[287] It certainly seemed to work that way in lower Manhattan. Between September 2000 and January 2001, the Nasdaq fell by almost 46 percent. On February 5, 2001, sixteen partners, including McDuffie, met in a Wall Street law office to sign on collectively as 1735 del Gesù Partners LP. Shares sold at $100,000 each. An anonymous friend of Tagliabue's chipped in $1 million. Machold himself bought three and a half of them.

Dated retroactively to 1998, the lease was to run twenty-five years.

McDuffie undertook to play, maintain, and insure the instrument at an
estimated annual $15,000 to $20,000. The partners would then reclaim
and sell their instrument at a price no one could imagine. But if history
was any guide, Machold assured them, the long-run outlook was a substantial capital gain. Till then, the partners could look forward to two
private concerts a year by McDuffie and an annual outing at Machold's
Lower Austrian château.[288]

Four years later, Foresight found a prospectus in her in-box from the
Long Term Capital Company of Westport, Connecticut, announcing the
creation of the Machold Rare Musical Instrument Fund, capitalized at
$100 million. Conceived to "buy, manage, and sell" old Italian stringed
instruments, the fund would "eventually" be available to the public as
a registered, closed-end mutual fund. Machold Rare Instruments would
not only advise the fund, but it had also agreed to let the organizers use
its name, because they "thought it would add credibility in the music
world and extend the concept's marketing reach."[289] The plan was to "benefit investors, musicians and the public" by loaning instruments to well-
recommended young competition winners, who would play them for their
owners, and so keep their investment in eyeshot and earshot.

The idea for the Rare Musical Instrument Fund had come to John
Vornle, the president of Long Term Capital, after reading the footnotes to
the annual report of the Austrian National Bank.[290] As fellow residents
of the town that gave the world such giant economists as Schumpeter,
Drucker, and Hayek, the bank's managers had learned a thing or two
about long-term value, he concluded. Their investment of upwards of €32
million ($38 million at current rates) in twenty-three violins, two violas,
and four cellos as "real moveable assets" testified to a basic confidence in
"the sustaining value" of rare stringed instruments, he informed readers of
his prospectus.[291]

With a century's experience behind her, Foresight politely said no for
three reasons. The first was liquidity. Great violins were worth far more
than their weight in gold.[292] But they were not easy to turn into quick
cash. The second was passion. A del Gesù in the hand was a work of art
and a bit of history. It could be felt, seen, and heard as a fractional share
could not. But it was also hard to price. The third problem was the price
of admission, where pay to play already meant at least $1 million up front.

At the 2005 annual meeting of the American College of Trust and
Estate Counsel (ACTEC) in Orlando, Florida, Fellows and friends were

invited to bid on a weekend at Machold's castle, including "a personal concert played on a Stradivarius violin," with all proceeds to benefit the ACTEC Foundation.[293] Foresight again decided to pass. But she looked on with interest as Claire Givens, Charles Avsharian, and Christopher Reuning went boldly where Machold, Vuillaume, and Hill had not gone before.

Save for her gender and a documented commitment to transparency, Givens seemed hardly an innovator at all. But both qualities were remarkable enough in a trade in which women dealers were as scarce as women makers and transparency could be as rare as Stradivari violas. Brought up in a musical lawyer's family in western Minnesota, Givens had taken up the cello like Biddulph and Bein and pursued its study all the way to Florence. The experience settled her on Italy and instruments as a career. On her return with seven instruments in 1977, she was struck that the Twin Cities, a metropolitan area with two major orchestras and a serious school music program, lacked both professional makers and a serious shop. Learning as she went, she persuaded her father to cosign a $50,000 loan. She then recruited a talented Mittenwald grad for her workshop and found an enviable location in downtown Minneapolis within a block of the city's new Orchestra Hall.

But even in downtown Minneapolis, her inventory and clientele, as well as her marriage, rather recalled the eighteenth century and the second-tier shop of a Widhalm or a Rugeri. The supply of instruments, including from local and modern Italian makers, was understood as well-made and carefully chosen, but still affordable. Demand was understood as players, advanced students, serious amateurs, and local professionals. Big instruments, which sold at upward of $100,000, showed up also, but perhaps one a year, since Givens preferred to sell only what she owned, another natural limit.[294] Where expertise was indicated, she bought it ad hoc from established dealers like Beare, or Kenneth Warren in Chicago.

In 1990, Givens married Andrew Dipper, who had taught in Cremona, translated Sacconi into English, and worked on instruments since he was twelve. With the accession of Dipper and his personal spin-off, Dipper Restorations, a bit of London also set up shop in downtown Minneapolis, where the inventory at any given moment might include a mid-eighteenth-century violino piccolo by Joseph Hill or a 1999 viola d'amore by Dipper himself. By this time, the staff, including the proprietors, had grown to six in sales and management, five in repair, two in restoration, plus Dipper's spaniel, Lupot, as "chief of security."[295]

An ever more sophisticated website extended the shop's reach. The website was now industry-wide, but the assurance that surfers would not be tracked by cookies was new. Still newer was Givens's challenge to the ancient practice that had long been the violin teacher's equivalent of the feudal *droit du seigneur*. It was not something people liked to talk about, and both the teacher and the maker associations avoided an official stand on it.[296] But the practice was probably as old as the trade. Teachers sent pupils. Pupils bought instruments. Dealers wrote a check to the teacher and added the commission to the buyer's bill as an unacknowledged surcharge. Those days were over, at least at Givens Violins, the proprietor declared up front. Though teachers who brought their students to her shop might qualify for transferable gift certificates of $25–$250, there would be no more undeclared commissions. A few other shops followed her example. But they were about as common as left-handed violinists.[297]

If Givens's business model adapted Cremona to the land of Honeywell and ice-fishing, Avsharian's adapted it to the land of Sears, Roebuck and L.L. Bean. A child of the Armenian diaspora, the violin world's most overlooked ethnicity, Charles Avsharian came to the instrument in Ann Arbor, home of the University of Michigan. "In America, if you don't have a PhD, you'd better have a better cheeseburger," he reflected.[298] His father, who had operated a garage and an auto parts business before introducing Ann Arbor to three-hour dry-cleaning, was an obvious example. So were his elder brother Michael, who took up the violin before him, and Elizabeth A. H. Green, the remarkable Ann Arbor violin teacher and protégée of the redoubtable Ivan Galamian, who had turned a local high school music program into a national role model.[299]

Perennially on the lookout for talent, Green discovered Charles as she had earlier discovered his brother. A few years later he found himself practicing five hours a day at Meadowmount in the Adirondacks, the iconic Ivan Galamian's boot camp for the string world's best and brightest. He returned to home and high school to play the snare drums. "I'm from Ann Arbor, I'm an American," he told himself.

A dead-end college intermezzo nonetheless led him back to Michael, now professor of violin at the University of Oklahoma. From there, a year and a half of intensive practice led back to Galamian and four years at Curtis, perhaps the most proudly exclusive of all American conservatories. Curtis led to the summer festival in Marlboro, Vermont, the violin world equivalent of clerking for a Supreme Court justice. By now he was good enough to teach at the University of Michigan, a job he took and enjoyed. He was even offered a concertmaster's job in Dallas. On the other hand, he reflected, he was not another Heifetz or Perlman. He also had no desire to spend his life as a New York freelancer or section player, he liked taking risks, and he still dreamed of being an American capitalist.

The solution was right there. In his Curtis days, he had bought strings wholesale from Wurlitzer in New York and resold them to Philadelphia Orchestra players. Moennig, the Philadelphia dealer, offered professional players a 20 percent discount. Avsharian offered 30 percent. His father, who had since sold the family laundry and was in town to visit, looked on with interest. It occurred to them that the senior Avsharian could do what Charles was doing from Ann Arbor.

Beginning in 1962, the senior Avsharian ordered strings direct from Austria, typed up a catalogue, added a line of printed music, and founded Shar Products. The catalogue would eventually include books, tapes, CDs, DVDs and videos, Suzuki teaching materials, entry-level instrument sets reminiscent of Sears, Roebuck, and accessories of every kind from peg lubricants and violin cases to music stands. In 1964, Michael, now a professor at the University of North Texas, joined the company. Charles followed in 1969, thereby becoming in all likelihood the most accomplished player ever to enter the trade as a full-time dealer. In 1975, the Interstate Commerce Commission made its own serendipitous contribution by allowing the United Parcel Service to compete with the U.S. Post Office.[300]

In 1967, U.S. mail-order and catalogue sales were estimated at $2.6 billion.[301] Within the first five years of the twenty-first century, they were estimated at some $130 billion. Where mail-order yachts, llamas, and gourmet cheeses went, Shar followed and even led the way, with a staff approaching a hundred, a yearly volume of more than $20 million, and customers in some sixty countries.

The trade's most notable late twentieth-century innovation might well have been Tarisio, created in 1999 as the violin world's answer to eBay. The name was chosen for its historical resonance. Yet the enterprise had something of the spontaneity of Bill Hewlett and Dave Packard in their proverbial garage or the early days of Microsoft. Of its three founding fathers, Chris Reuning, the Boston dealer, had started small, as the child of Suzuki teacher parents whose quest for a dependable reserve of respectable start-up instruments had caused them to set up shop in their Ithaca, New York, home. Another cellist manqué, Reuning began to play at seven, then discovered making at age twelve. After study with Primavera in Philadelphia and Virgilio Capellini in Cremona, he bought out his parents' shop in 1984. Ten years later, he moved to Boston.

Like most dealers, Reuning was an auction-goer. So was his school-mate Dmitry Gindin, a professional violin hunter and appraiser of growing expertise and international experience. Both noticed that Americans were scarce at London auctions and that auctions of any consequence in the United States were even scarcer.[302] The Internet seemed an obvious way to redress the balance. But with its inferior graphics, inherent expertise deficit, and common conveyor accessibility to the honest and larcenous alike,[303] eBay did not.

The solution was a marriage of comparative advantages. Reuning and Gindin, the dealers, solicited consignments and attended to credibility and quality. Responsibility for the rest went to the third partner, Jason Price, who had worked for Reuning as a fiddle-loving schoolboy. He then aston-ished his parents by squeezing in an apprenticeship in Parma between dropping out and dropping back into Williams College.[304]

Needing a job after graduation, Price attended to customer relations, production of the catalogue, and day-to-day management of the business. Capitalization began at $9,000, a third from each partner. Overhead was minimal, allowing for rates 7.5–17.5 percent below their London competitors'. A combination of exemplary graphics, unusually fastidious descriptions of condition, and pages of readable terms and stipulations spelled out what the bidder was getting—and getting into. But there were also opportunities to see and handle the instruments in person at pre-auction viewings that extended by summer 2011 to ten major cit-ies, including two in Europe and four in Asia.[305] Registration was open to anyone willing to pay a dollar for a password and provide such basic contact data as a passport, credit card, or driver's license number. The auction itself, extending over a week or more, was demonstratively user-friendly and accessible anywhere and anytime the bidder could log on, with provision for proxy bids and assurance that the reserve would never exceed the low estimate.[306]

To the founders' delight, it worked so well that Price bought out his partners at the end of the first decade. The first try in November 1999 rounded up about two hundred lots, including a classic eighteenth-century Neapolitan violin by Fernando Gagliano and a twentieth-century Turinese violin by Carlo Oddoni, whose auction prices had increased since the 1980s by a factor of ten.[307] The second try, a half year later, turned up a Brothers Amati viola that went again for half its upper estimate and a Guadagnini violin. By 2002, posted sales reached $4 million.[308]

In May 2003, Tarisio all but matched this in a week, when it offered 164 lots of instruments and memorabilia from the estate of Isaac Stern, who died at eighty-one in September 2001. Over the course of a long and remarkable professional life, Stern had happily owned, bought, sold, loaned, and traded some twenty Cremonese instruments.[309] Among the instruments that now came up for sale were the 1687 Kubelik Strad and Zygmuntowicz's copy of the 1737 Panette del Gesù. According to Price, there were more than 600 bidders from 28 countries. By the time the last virtual hammer fell on what turned out to be the second-biggest violin auction in history, 92 percent of the lots had sold and gross receipts had reached $3.35 million. The Kubelik alone brought $949,500, the highest price yet for a pre-1700 Strad; the Zygmuntowicz brought $130,000, the highest price ever for an instrument by a living maker. A Tourte bow with a tortoiseshell and gold-mounted frog by Henryk Kaston brought $102,500, which was another record.[310]

A year and a half passed before it became universally known and embarrassingly clear that what was good news for Tarisio had come as bad news to Stern's children. Michael, a conductor, had only learned of the auction from a member of the Philadelphia Orchestra, who called his attention to Tarisio's website. With his brother and sister, he then sued his father's executor for $2 million.

It was soon apparent that death, debt, and divorce—the auction house staples— all had played their role in the pending lawsuit. Five years before his death, Stern had divorced his wife of forty-five years and the mother of his children, to marry a third wife many years his junior. Despite protests from his children and contrary language in his will, he transferred a Manhattan apartment to his new wife a few weeks before his death.

The apartment was valued at $3.7 million. But the executor, William Moorhead III, a socially prominent Washington attorney and friend of Stern's third wife, had not included it and other personal property among the estate's assets. Instead, he used it as an office at $8,000 a month, charged to the estate, and paid to Stern's new wife. The plaintiffs charged that Moorhead's failure to count the apartment had caused him to declare the estate insolvent. The presumed shortfall had thereby led to Tarisio— a "glorified eBay garage sale," as Michael Stern called it—as a source of quick cash to cover outstanding debts, including a million dollars his father owed a close friend. In May 2005 the judge ordered Moorhead to refund $312,000 in fees he had paid himself, plus $250,000 paid out in unnecessary expenses. "A legacy was squandered," the children's lawyer said. The judge, noting an "incalculable personal loss," concurred.[311]

It was easy enough to understand the family's sense of hurt and violation as an executor close to their stepmother hawked and dispersed what they felt to be their patrimony. But there was no suggestion of invalidating the sales, nor did anyone attach any liability to Tarisio. "I have bought several instruments and bows from Tarisio and have always found them to be honest, honorable, and helpful," one satisfied customer reported. "Tarisio has changed a few things on the auction scene by making things very player-friendly," replied another. Measured by "man bites dog" standards, such testimonials fell short of newsworthy.[312] But measured against a violin world with a history of hanky-panky and even worse dating back to the sixteenth century, and an auction business, whose leading CEOs in New York and London had recently been fined €20.4 million and placed under house arrest for fixing prices,[313] they could at least be considered noteworthy.

"FIDDLE, *N.* A SWINDLE. ORIG. U.S."[314]

AS THE VIOLIN has followed money and power, so have the law, civil litigation, criminal prosecution, and occasional violence followed the violin. In 1579, Bolognese instrument maker Giovanni dai Liuti a was murdered by bandits. But the connection of murder and banditry only became publicly known when the bandits were tried for another offense they committed a few days later.[315]

Ironically, the most famous murder is probably the one that never happened. In search of the younger Giuseppe Guarneri, Rosengard and Chiesa, the discoverers of Stradivari's will, combed the archives of Cremona and Milan for traces of the gaudy legend that possibly went back to the Mantegazza brothers, who never knew him, before making its way to Tarisio, who supplied his Parisian clients with stories as well as violins.

In fact, a GG really had killed a man. But it was a different GG, and both killer and victim were Milanese. The perpetrator was Giovanni Battista Grancino, a respected Milanese maker, then seventy-one. In the fall of 1708, for reasons unknown but certainly worthy of curiosity, he had come to blows with Antonio Maria Lavazza, a neighbor and fellow maker forty-six years his junior. It appeared that Lavazza was the first to strike, and had seriously injured the older man with his sword. After evading capture for a few days, he then returned to Grancino's shop, where the quarrel resumed. This time Grancino stabbed Lavazza, who died soon after. Grancino managed briefly to evade capture. But his considerable family property was seized in his absence. He was eventually tried, then executed the following May.[316]

In 1713, the battered body of Carlo Rugeri, one of four sons of Francesco and the sole heir to his father's shop, was found just outside Cremona's city wall.[317] But a killer was never found—and Guarneri was just fifteen. Toward the end of the century, another Milanese maker was locked up after what was evidently a serious offense. But Guarneri, long dead, was obviously not involved in this one either.[318]

In 1989, Max Möller, a third-generation Amsterdam dealer, was killed by burglars who had been tipped off by a former handyman that Möller's house was worth robbing. Möller, who tried to resist, was shot dead. The police needed about ten days to catch up with the perpetrators, who were young men in their twenties and early thirties, several of whom had a serious drug habit. Their capture led incidentally to the solution of some 120 other robberies. The suspects confessed, and even expressed remorse. The killing was ruled manslaughter, with a maximum sentence of twelve years. About fifteen months after Möller's death, the actual killer, who had already been sentenced to five years for an earlier offense, was sentenced to seven more, plus detention in a medical facility until he was found ready for release. The onetime handyman got three years.[319]

In 1996, Maria Grevesmühl, 60, a professor of violin at the Bremen Conservatory, the president of the European String Teachers Association, and the owner of the 1694 Muir-McKenzie Strad, fell or was pushed down a flight of steps while leaving a suburban Bremen train station around 9:00 p.m. She died of a skull fracture within minutes. Police found her jewelry and purse, including cash, intact. But the violin was gone.[320]

Her death seems to have been a consequence of one of those good deeds, which, it is said, never go unpunished. Struck by the talent of Vasile Darnea, a seventeen-year-old street musician with a cheap imitation Amati, she not only took him on as a protégé, but also managed to enroll him, an illegal immigrant and candidate for asylum, at the conservatory.

Marin Boaca, a thirty-one-year-old Romanian with a record of robbery, learned of Grevesmühl's Strad from Darnea. The police caught up with him within two days. He seems to have acknowledged the robbery without resistance, but he claimed that Darnea put him up to it. He had offered the violin to a relative. Aware that Grevesmühl's insurance company had offered a reward of DM 60,000, which at the time was equal to about $40,000, the relative tipped off the police.[321]

In the end, Boaca was sentenced to thirteen years, though only after a successful jailbreak and extradition from Brussels. Darnea, jailed as a suspect for thirteen weeks without bail, was totally exonerated in November 1998.[322] Four years later, he was still in Bremen, playing tangos with a Palestinian, a Chilean, and a German.[323] By 2005, he had advanced to world music as a member of the Bremer Immigrant Orchestra, with colleagues from Mexico, Ghana, Turkey, Iran, Slovakia, China, and Chile. He was at least off the street.[324] Grevesmühl's Strad had meanwhile made its way to Machold.

With or without murder, upper-end violins have been perennially desirable, portable, and easy to hide, disguise, and turn into cash. The same qualities that have made them irresistible to thieves allowed Sonia Simmenauer's grandfather, a founder and patron of Hamburg's Philharmonic Society, to beat Nazi larceny with a quartet of Brothers Amati he bought before emigrating in 1938. Since they weren't new and customs officials are not violin experts, he was allowed to take them across the Belgian border. They were then stowed away with other Jewish property in the cellar of a Brussels museum, where they survived five years of German occupation and storage near a munitions depot.[325]

But the case was a notable exception. As early as November 1940, Ernst Doring's Chicago-based *Violins and Violinists* reported that en route to Paris the Germans had plundered the workshop and private collection of prominent Mirecourt maker Marc Laberte. They then auctioned the furniture and household effects of deportees, filled freight cars with plundered pianos and harps, as well as art of every kind, and recycled the watches, jewelry, clothing, prosthetics, hair, and musical instruments of millions of death camp victims.[326] As usual in Nazi Germany, parallel institutions competed for the plunder. Individuals, like an SS X-ray technician who somehow acquired a Strad that had been bequeathed to the Warsaw National Museum on the eve of the war by "a certain Mr. Grohmann in Lodz," joined in ad hoc.[327]

The saga of a pilfered Strad that might not have even been one is an equally German story. With the abdication of the country's ruling houses in the aftermath of World War I, an instrument belonging to a Princess Schwarzburg-Sonderhausen was declared public property. But it was recovered and bequeathed to the daughter of a former court official. Again expropriated after World War II and declared a gift from Communist Czechoslovakia's first president, Klement Gottwald, to Communist East Germany's first president, Wilhelm Pieck, it made its way to the wind band of the East German Ministry of Interior. There it remained till the Berlin Wall came down, and the West German Ministry of Interior found itself heir to a nationalized collection of twenty-two instruments, mostly acquired from retired concertmasters. Between 1997 and 2000, the previous owner sued for recovery of the ex-Sonderhausen and won. But won what? The instrument had no papers. Pending settlement of ownership, the West German government had not sought authentication of the contested property. Charles Beare distantly recalled an inquiry and photograph from the owner. But no one ever appeared to show him the instrument.[328]

In a post–Cold War world, where both European art theft and post-Soviet nuclear security were billion-dollar challenges,[329] the theft of a Grancino, a Testore, a couple of Amatis, and a Stainer from Prague's Museum of Musical Instruments in the fall of 1990 was a more conventional Central European story. But violin thieves are seldom violin experts. So it was not surprising either that a tip from a dealer, who had been offered them, should lead police to the missing instruments in a Munich hotel room about a half year after they were stolen.[330]

For obvious reasons, makers and dealers have been targets since the beginnings of the instrument. In 1695, Giovanni Tononi reported the loss of two new violins from a storeroom over his shop.[331] In April 2002, the morning after an orchestra player-client tried the 1714 Le Maurien Strad, Christophe Landon, the New York dealer-maker, reported its loss from his shop near Lincoln Center. Landon had found the instrument a few years before at a Paris auction and had brought it back to restore, effectively doubling its value. Its owner was now the Cremona Society, a Dallas-based philanthropic organization, whose creator, Barrett Wissmann, was a pianist turned venture capitalist with an economics degree from Yale, a Russian cellist wife, and a demonstratively low profile. After hypnosis, voluntary lie detector tests, and the promise of a $100,000 reward failed to reveal its whereabouts, the society sued for $3.5 million, charging neglect and breach of contract. A few months later, the parties settled, with the understanding that rights to the instrument would revert to the underwriter in the event of its recovery. As of 2012, it had not been recovered.[332]

Just as naturally, police and courts have called on makers and dealers as witnesses and experts. Two years after the senior Tononi was robbed, his son Carlo testified in connection with an instrument stolen elsewhere that he claimed to have repaired.[333]

More recent variations on the story would probably not have surprised either Tononi. In January 1994, a San Francisco Bay Area musician and teacher brought a student instrument to Joseph Grubaugh and Sigrun Seifert in Petaluma, California, for repair. An acknowledged expert, Grubaugh soon suspected that this Strad, unlike many brought to his shop, had not been made in Czechoslovakia. An aggregate of clues, including label, scroll, and purfling, led to a photo in Goodkind's standard iconography, and the American Federation of Violin and Bow Makers' registry of missing instruments.[334] The missing instrument list led to the University of California, Los Angeles, which had acquired the instrument in question from a donor in the early 1960s. Made in 1732 and known as the Duke of Alcantara, it had been missing for about a quarter century after being stolen from a faculty quartet player's car or lost when he inadvertently drove off with the case still on the roof.

If it took a serious expert to identify it, it also took a serious lawyer to recover it. Theft presumes a thief. Its current possessor, who came by the instrument in good faith as part of a divorce settlement, was not one. Her former spouse had gotten it from a deceased aunt, who claimed to have found it alongside an LA freeway. Carla Shapreau, the university's violin maker attorney, persuaded the court to order the instrument locked out of reach of both parties pending settlement. She then argued that the university had advertised its loss as California law required, while the defendant could neither prove that the instrument had been stolen elsewhere nor that her ex's aunt had tried to find the rightful owner. In December 1995, the case was settled out of court for $11,500, and the university recovered the instrument, whose current value was meanwhile assessed between $800,000 and $2 million.[335]

In 1999, Chip Averwater, a Memphis, Tennessee, dealer, was just as skeptical when two brothers appeared in his shop with an eighteenth-century instrument from Markneukirchen. One brother said the instrument had been in the family for generations. The other brother said they had bought it at a yard sale. Asked about the discrepancy, the first explained that they had it bought it at a yard sale, but generations back. Averwater notified the police while the resident expert nominally appraised it. Averwater then helped the brothers fill out a declaration of intent to sell. They vanished as the squad car arrived but called back later in the day, then got in touch with the police themselves.

The police allowed Averwater less than a day to find the owner needed to prove a theft. Calls to local players, teachers, schools, universities, and the musicians union led nowhere. But an Internet search for the maker produced a bulletin board exchange two years earlier with a grateful Vietnamese-American MD/PhD candidate in Nashville. Devastated by the loss of the gift from his parents that he had played through school and college, he had never expected to see his violin again, he told Averwater.[336]

But for serious thieves, high-profile players, including Ludwig Spohr, Eugène Ysaÿe, Bronislaw Huberman, Roman Totenberg, Erica Morini, and Vanessa-Mae, the Singapore crossover virtuosa, seem to have been the real El Dorado.

In 1804, a delighted Spohr acquired an unspecified Guarneri on his twentieth birthday while on tour in St. Petersburg. A few months later, he discovered that it had been snatched from the back of his hired, and unfortunately rear-windowless, coach on his early-evening approach to Göttingen.[337] In 1907, Ysaÿe's Hercules Strad was snatched from a double case in his St. Petersburg dressing room while he was on stage playing his del Gesù.[338] Shortly before her death at ninety-one in 1996, Erica Morini's 1727 Davidov Strad, valued at $3.5 million, was stolen by someone with a key to her New York apartment and the wardrobe where it was kept. A friend, who was sent to check, found an empty case but no sign of forced entry or exit.

Some instruments were recovered, some not. In a classic case in 1895, Flechter, the New York dealer, was charged with stealing the 1725 Duke of Cambridge Strad from an elderly immigrant, who had once been concertmaster of the famous court orchestra of the duchy of Saxe-Meiningen, then trying to sell it. Both defense and prosecution deployed battalions of violin makers and handwriting experts. Glassy-eyed with information overload, the jury deferred to the expertise of the eighty-one-year-old August Gemunder, the first major American maker. The jury then returned from an all-night deliberation with a guilty verdict. Protesting at every step, Flechter was sentenced to a year in jail but released on appeal after three weeks.

Five years after the trial, a former employee discovered the missing violin. The thief had pawned it within an hour of stealing it. The pawnbroker had sold it for $30 to a tailor's wife in Brooklyn, whose son took violin lessons. Flechter notified the police, the buyer in Brooklyn waived all claims, and the violin, which would eventually be acquired by the New York Philharmonic, was returned to the owner's widow.[339]

A still juicier story, the 1713 Gibson Strad was not only twice stolen from Bronislaw Huberman but also twice recovered. The first theft was police blotter generic. In 1919, a burglar broke into his Viennese hotel room. Huberman notified the police. A few hours later, the thief was caught offering the violin to a dealer. He was tried and sentenced to three years.

The second Huberman theft involving the Gibson had movie potential, with a colorful cast of characters and a plot part *Rashomon*, part *Treasure of Sierra Madre*. In February 1936, while performing at Carnegie Hall, Huberman had gone on stage with his del Gesù and a pickup chamber orchestra of forty-one. Like Ysaÿe's, his unattended Strad stayed behind in its double case. His secretary discovered the theft and notified him shortly after the intermission. The imperturbable Huberman told her to call the police and returned to the stage.

The detectives were there before the concert ended. A thief who left an expensive case and six expensive bows was obviously no musician, the artist told them. A review of the concert and news of the theft of the Gibson appeared on the same page in the next morning's *New York Times*.[340] In due time, Huberman filed a claim, and his insurer, Lloyd's of London, paid out £8,000, which at the time was about $30,000.

Itzhak Perlman experienced something similar at age eighteen when a backstage burglar stole the Guarneri he had just performed on while taking part in the Leventritt competition at Carnegie Hall. What made it worse was that the instrument belonged to Juilliard, where Perlman studied. Mercifully, it was found the next day at a pawnshop that had paid $5 to $10 for it, "and that," as Perlman added, "was only because it included the bows."[341]

The recovery of the Gibson in 1985, thirty-eight years after Huberman's death, was major news, too. Alerted by Rachel Goodkind, daughter of the Strad iconographer, and accompanied by lawyers for the interested parties, Charles Beare arranged to meet Marcelle M. Hall, the widow of Julian Altman, a New York and Washington job violinist who had recently died in prison, where he had been sent after Hall had him arrested for molesting one of her granddaughters.

They arrived to find a house party, including a news crew from NBC. Beare identified the violin, champagne corks popped, and the lawyers drew up an agreement. Thoroughly cleaned and restored, Huberman's violin made its public reappearance a few months later at the Strad bicentennial show in Cremona, where it was even visited by Hall.[342] In exchange for the violin, Hall collected a finder's fee of $263,475.75, which equaled 25 percent of its assessed value. In 1988, Norbert Brainin, first violinist of the Amadeus quartet, bought it for $1.2 million.

Still more years would pass before the rest of the story unfolded. In 1991, Sherry Altman Schoenwetter, Altman's daughter by an earlier mar-

riage, sued Hall in probate court. She charged her stepmother, who was
Altman's executrix, with holding back assets from his estate. The court
ruled in her favor. Not only were the violin and claim to the finder's fee
declared part of Altman's estate, Hall was also ordered to pay 10 percent
annual interest for the years she had held the finder's fee. In 1995 and
1996, the decision was upheld, first in Connecticut Superior Court, then
in a 4–1 ruling in the state supreme court.

What remained unresolved was Altman's role in the theft. Had he
bought Huberman's Strad from the thief for $100, as Hall told Lloyd's and
the media in 1987? Or had he stolen it himself, as she would then tell successive judges? Hall testified in the months before Altman's death that he
directed her to the violin, left for safekeeping with a friendly repairman,
alerted her to newspaper accounts of the theft under the canvas cover of his
violin case, acknowledged that the instrument in the case was the missing
Gibson, and confessed to the theft.

According to this version, the theft had been a joint venture with Altman's mother. The idea was to find a foreign violinist with two violins,
who could first be robbed of one, then relied on to lower the resulting
heat by leaving the country. Huberman met the description. The evening
of his concert, Altman took a break from his job in a gypsy orchestra at
The Russian Bear, a café around the corner from Carnegie Hall. Familiar
to the staff as a youth orchestra regular, he had no problem getting in the
backstage entrance. A fistful of cigars apparently sufficed to distract either
or both of two doormen and a watchman with a view of the stairs leading
to Huberman's dressing room. Altman then stole the Strad, waited for
Huberman and the orchestra to leave the stage, slipped out a side entrance,
caught a taxi home, turned the violin over to his mother, and returned to
work, all the while apparently dressed in the Russian costume that went
with his job.

More than half a century later, the story is still a puzzler. With or without cigars, it is hard to imagine how a teenage violinist in a Russian peasant costume could slip unnoticed past doormen who already knew him.
With a criminal investigation under way, risk of punishment a credible
stick, and reward a credible carrot, the unbroken silence is at least curious.

Hall's credibility is a puzzler, too. She had lived with Altman since
1970 but only married him in 1985, two days before he was sentenced and
just months before his death. She was now his wife and heir. Her testi-
mony was hardly disinterested. If he was a thief, his estate had no claim to

a finder's fee. So in negotiating with Lloyd's, she had reason to claim that she was heir to a legitimate owner. Defending herself against the claim from Altman's daughter, on the other hand, she seemed to believe it in her interest to argue that as heir to a thief, she was under no obligation to share the finder's fee with his daughter.

Judge after judge was unimpressed. Hall "could not cite one case in the whole world where the second thief had greater rights than the first thief," one judge declared, as he authorized Altman's heirs to sue her for recovery of the finder's fee. By 1997, Hall owed a half-million dollars in principal and interest, none of which the other heirs ever collected.[343] Meanwhile, the violin went its own way. A few months after Hall died in 2001, one of the young stars of a new generation, Joshua Bell, traded in his previous Strad for $2 million and bought the Gibson for a reported $4 million.[344]

The theft and recovery of Pierre Amoyal's 1717 Kochanski Strad in 1987 had movie potential, too. But this time the fusion scenario might have been an idiosyncratic mix of Jules Dassin's *Rififi* and the odd couple frolics of Dean Martin and Jerry Lewis.

Unlike Huberman, Amoyal at least recovered his instrument while still young enough to play it. Although he had been willing to negotiate with the thieves as one might with kidnappers, in the end even the law was a winner. Ironically, it was Amoyal's Porsche, not his Strad, that the thief had been after. A pro of international reputation, he had grabbed the keys while Amoyal was checking out of his northern Italian hotel and was gone in seconds. The car was recovered a short time later.

In the four years that followed, Amoyal mobilized police and media and fended off a startling variety of kooks and scams. He hired a Swiss detective, who hired a somewhat equivocal but knowledgeable Torinese associate. He consulted an exemplary Italian magistrate. He had an unpleasant experience with his insurance company, ran marathons, and squabbled with his wife.

Yet for most of the first two years, the violin remained in Turin. Strapped for cash, the thief then tried the drug trade as a freelancer and was gunned down by the local syndicate. He had meanwhile sold the Kochanski cheap to a local antiquary, who died soon after of natural causes. His heirs resold it to an underworld collector, who knew from Amoyal's ad in the local papers that there was a legitimate private buyer, prepared to pay real money for it. Other, losing bidders agreed to cooperate with the police. To Amoyal's despair, a sting went awry. But a second proposed meeting in a Turinese church worked better. The obligatory car chase ended with the putative buyers trapped between the police and a laundry truck. After a press conference and a trial, there were jail sentences.[345]

YET FOR ALL the shock waves set off by the occasional homicide and the persistent background noise of theft, violins and the law probably collided most often at the intersection of Caveat and Emptor. The paper trail reached back to at least 1685, when Tomaso Vitali, a violinist attached to the court of Modena, addressed a petition to the duke, after discovering an original label beneath the visible one inside his new instrument. It told him that the supposed Amati a local dealer had recently sold him for 12 pistoles was actually a Rugeri, then valued at 3.[346]

There would be lots more where that came from, as generation followed generation, and case followed gaudy case. In installments extending from May to September in 1890, *The Strad* reported in three and four double-columned pages how Laurie, the seller, had been ordered to reimburse James Johnstone, the buyer, then take back the composite he'd sold as a Strad and pay the considerable court costs.

The editorial torch then passed to Edward Heron-Allen, who found plenty to say not only about Laurie, as well as an analogous case in Bavaria, but also a suit brought by Henry Hodges, a freelance dealer, against the younger Georges Chanot.[347] At issue was a "speculative violin" with a Bergonzi label that Chanot had bought from a Paris art dealer for £18 and sold to Hodges for £55. At Hodges' request, he then wrote a receipt for £75, a sure hint that Hodges intended to collect the difference from the next buyer. Pleased with themselves and the deal, both men then split a bottle of champagne and went out for dinner.

It was only when Hodges resold the instrument for £150 and the new buyer showed it to the senior Hill that things turned sour. Hill had evidently told him that the Bergonzi wasn't one. The customer had evidently brought it back to Hodges, who then demanded his £75 back from Chanot. Declaring a deal a deal, Chanot told Hodges to sell it himself. He even demanded that Hodges return the 5 shillings Chanot had paid to insure the instrument when shipping it. Hodges sued and was upheld. He then proposed a settlement: return of his £55, with the costs of the trial divided between them. But Chanot refused this too, after George Hart gave him cause to believe that he might actually have a Bergonzi, if not from Carlo, then at least from one of his descendants.

When the case went to trial again, W. E. Hill declared the Bergonzi a Pressenda worth £25 to £30. "But what would you sell it for?" Chanot's attorney asked him. "Depends on the client," Hill answered guilelessly, as the courtroom exploded in mirth. Chanot admitted to the Bergonzi label, but denied selling it as a Bergonzi. Unimpressed, the jury ordered him to pay £55 plus £15 damages and court costs, a combined penalty of almost £215, about twice what Hill's charged for a Bergonzi and two and half times what a miner earned in a year.[348]

Newspaper stories the next day questioned the authenticity of anything French sold in Britain. "Is it really Pomméry?" a cartoon customer in *Fun* asked the waiter about a bottle of champagne. "Yes, sir," the waiter replied. "I put the label on the bottle myself." In the shadow of the trial, Chanot sold the incriminated instrument for £50 to his son Georges-Adolphe in Manchester, who put it up for auction at Puttick and Simpson as a very attractive violin attributed to Bergonzi. It was immediately snapped up at £55 by Charles Fowler of Torquay, who let it be known in the trade press that he was proud to add it to his collection.[349]

Laurie recovered too. Less than two years after his Glasgow defeat, he had resold the composite, now known as the Court Strad, for £500, £40 more than he got from Johnstone. Identified only as an aristocratic con-noisseur, the buyer turned out to be Knoop.[350] Hill knew that Laurie's need for cash had led to the sale of the King Joseph del Gesù, one of the world's most desirable violins. He also knew that the same buyer had bought the Court Strad. But he refused to believe it was Baron Knoop, because, as he told himself, "it is absurd to speak of [him] as a connois-seur." A few months later, Knoop explained how Laurie had made him take the composite as a condition for selling him the Guarneri.[351]

Arthur Hill confided to his diary after testifying at the trial: " . . . heard Laurie put through his cross-examination, lied and evaded all through in the most wonderful manner." "Verily Scotchmen are canny," he added the next day.[352] Learning of Chanot's death a few years later, Hill conceded that he knew a lot and did good work. But he "brought considerable disgrace on the trade," he added, and "showed in himself the traits which have made the dealer in secondhand articles so much mistrusted."[353]

Fresh from the victory over Laurie, Arthur Hill itemized the failings of a nominal Amati that had just arrived with a Joachim student from Berlin. Authenticity was still to be determined. Head and body failed to match. The label was a forgery. The dealer was coy about how he came by the instrument. Even if it were bona fide, Hill found its price extortionate.

A few days later, he loaned the owner a Rugeri and took her aside for "a long chat, pointing out the difficulties of obtaining a good violin and some of the pitfalls to be avoided." A week later she reported that a friend spoke highly of a dubious Amati, which had been put up for sale by John Kruse, another Joachim protégé and a professor at the Berlin Conservatory.[354] Hill helped friends find her an alternative in Paris. But he also urged her to settle quietly with her dealer in Berlin. "Germans being so powerful in musical circles already, . . . we cannot afford to make any more enemies amongst them," he confided to himself.[355]

While unsentimental about dealers, Heron-Allen was not dewy-eyed about collectors either. *Collector* was a synonym for *amateur dealer*, and Johnstone was a Scotsman, he added with no suggestion of a twinkle. In any case, all old instruments had been worked on, and Laurie had offered Johnstone a good deal. Heron-Allen thought that the judge should at least have split the costs.

His view of Hodges and Chanot too was impartially unblinking. Of course, Chanot had mislabeled the Bergonzi. But Hodges, who was hardly new to the business, only turned active when challenged by his own customer. Chanot's real mistake, as Heron-Allen saw it, was coming clean with the court on practices everybody knew about but didn't speak of.

In 1937, with no Stradivaris in Cremona to exhibit at the bicentennial exposition, the organizers appealed to owners everywhere and even the general public for specimens. Of 128 instruments accepted for examination, eight were found to be genuine.[356]

With time off for World War II, the story resumed in Switzerland in 1952. Giovanni Iviglia, 52, author of a monograph on Celeste Farotti, an early twentieth-century Milanese maker-copyist, as well as introductions to Cozio's notebooks and Vannes's handbook of violin makers, was now general secretary of the Italian Chamber of Commerce in Zurich. Henry Werro, 56, an internationally recognized dealer in Bern who had taken over his father's business in 1932, was briefly jailed and still under investigation on both civil and criminal charges of fraud and falsification of labels going back to at least 1947. Iviglia, who considered defending the honor of the Italian violin a part of his official mandate and denied any personal stake in the business, had declared the Italian Chamber of Commerce an alternative source of expertise.

Six more years would pass before the Werro case finally came to trial before a jury in Bern with Iviglia, who had begun as a collector and then started reading seriously, as a witness for the prosecution. According to Iviglia, Werro had offered to buy his collection in 1951 on condition that he destroy his files and stop writing about Werro's shady practices. Werro concurred that they had talked but insisted that the quid pro quo was Iviglia's idea.[357]

Something of an Ahab to the now sixty-two-year-old Werro's Moby Dick, Iviglia saw the root of counterfeit in the authorities' willingness to leave the dealers to themselves. He saw only two solutions: a data bank of publicly accessible photos and measurements compiled by a board of disinterested experts, and rigorous prosecution of offenders.[358]

Unlike those who shared his concerns, Iviglia had actually tried to do something. He first recruited a panel of Swiss violin makers as his public experts. He then co-opted Max Frei-Sülzer, head of the forensic science department of the Zurich police. Over the trial's four weeks, Werro mobilized such colleagues and lions of the trade as Emil Herrmann, Albert Phillips-Hill, and Fridolin Hamma, to come to his support. Iviglia for his part countered with Frei, three local makers, and the director of the paint and varnish department of the Swiss bureau of standards.

The trial was covered at length in the *Neue Zürcher Zeitung*, Switzerland's Swissest paper.[359] Neither side had reason to look back on it as their finest hour. For almost five weeks expert challenged expert and claim confronted claim in all possible permutations, while a trail of Werro customers appeared on the witness stand in various degrees of unhappiness. Almost everyone testified to practices evidently common in the trade but seldom acknowledged in open court. Till only recently, one witness recalled, Werro had ordered high-quality facsimile labels from Markneukirchen. He conceded that he neglected to mention them in his certificates on grounds that they had no importance. "They matter to the buyer," the judge observed.[360]

Werro's lions, no longer young, were also underwhelming. Daylight was to be expected between the contending experts. But depending on the instrument in question, there seemed to be quite a lot of daylight between Hill and Hamma, and still more between Hill and Herrmann. The prosecution had even charged Herrmann with perjury after the court promoted him from witness to expert.[361] In at least one case, where Werro was charged with turning a relatively midprice Cappa into a thoroughly upscale Andrea Guarneri, there was even a stretch of daylight between Hill and Werro himself.[362]

Yet the Swiss makers also split with Frei on a contested Strad and with an Italian consultant brought in by Iviglia.[363] Asked to explain their differences with Hill over another contested instrument, they forthrightly cited instruments certified by the Hills or Herrmann as their standard of comparison. One of them even appealed—with "shocking candor," the *Neue Zürcher* added—to the authority of material he had seen at Werro's. Given the current confusions, the reporter wondered whether reliable attribution was even possible.[364]

The court wisely confined itself to questions it was better qualified to handle. Since 1952, fourteen charges had lapsed under the statute of limitations. In his closing speech, the state prosecutor appealed for conviction on eighteen others. He also called for a two-year jail sentence; a 5,000-franc fine, a price equivalent to a good modern French cello; and suspension of Werro's civil rights for three years. Lawyers for the civil claimants asked for damages and court costs. The defense, unsurprisingly, asked for acquittal.[365]

The court split the difference, dismissing twenty fraud charges and upholding two—the sale of a modern French cello as a substantially more valuable Italian one, and the sale of the Cappa turned Guarneri. In twelve other cases, it found Werro guilty of falsifying labels. He was also found guilty of threatening to bring pressure on the advertisers of a trade journal if the journal refused to publish his reply to an unflattering piece that had recently appeared there. In the end, Werro was given a suspended one-year sentence with four years' probation, fined 5,000 francs, required to take back the misrepresented instruments, reimburse their owners with interest, and assume three-quarters of the court costs. It was hardly a one-way ticket to Devil's Island. But it was not a whitewash either, though the trade understandably preferred to recall it as one, and it was certainly not the last word.

In summer 2000, the appearance of a composite in California was occasion to revisit *Johnstone v. Laurie* among the redwoods. At issue this time was the sale of a Guadagnini by Raymond A. Russell, trustee for a family estate, and George Woodall, to Kristina Lee Anderson. Anderson agreed to pay $260,000 over two years, including a $50,000 down payment. When payment was delayed, the owners sued for damages. Anderson, who continued her payments despite deviation from the contract, stood pat.

The case turned interesting after Anderson discovered serendipitously that Beare had questioned the instrument's authenticity before she bought it. She filed a countersuit for damages. When the case came to trial in Santa Cruz County Superior Court, it quickly morphed into *Expert v. Expert*. Russell produced Harry Duffy, a twenty-year veteran of Wurlitzer's. Anderson produced Reuning, who cited Beare. Russell's lawyer objected that Beare's opinion was hearsay.

Judge Samuel L. Stevens sustained the objection. "The Court finds by a preponderance of the evidence that the violin is an original Guadagnini, although repaired and not of collector's quality," he ruled. Since Anderson had sustained no damages, she had no claim on any. But none were awarded to Russell either. In the end, as in the beginning, Russell got his money and Anderson her violin, just not quite the one she thought she was buying.[366] It was a recognizable facsimile of what Heron-Allen thought appropriate in Glasgow.

Moral indignation was always easy, and often justified. But the conflicts of interest specific to an elusive and nonfungible product and the fierce but wildly imperfect competition of a tiny oligopoly were risks and hazards inherent in the trade, irrespective, in Haweis's words, of the averagely honest man's troubled relationship to horses, umbrellas, and fiddles.

In practice, even the best expertise is subject to uncertainty unimagined by the great physicist Werner Heisenberg, who defined uncertainty as a principle. Violins are notoriously easy to alter, mislabel, and confuse. Legitimately and otherwise, they can be copied with uncanny precision. In principle, any serious professional can make an educated guess about the age and general provenance of a given instrument and recognize most copies and fakes. But this still falls short of the high-resolution, clear-focus expertise needed to distinguish, authenticate, and certify a Strad or del Gesù, let alone a hundred-odd contemporaries, after upward of three hundred years of multiple new owners, repairs, modifications, and often abuse.

Art experts acquire their skills in graduate schools and museums and tend to practice their craft as professors and curators. Violin experts acquire theirs in the handful of shops where a widest variety of instruments are likeliest to show up for repair, certification, or sale and have usually practiced their craft as dealers. The art market likewise is hardly fraud-proof. The Vollers don't come close to Han Van Meegeren, the Dutch con artist, who forged an identity as a national hero by forging Vermeer during World War II, or Wolfgang Beltracchi, CEO of a merry band of forgers in the Lower Rhenish town of Krefeld, who faked Expressionists with impressive success for a decade beginning in the 1990s.[367] On the other hand, art expertise has existed independent of the trade since at least the mid-nineteenth century. Beginning in 1968, Dutch taxpayers underwrote a Rembrandt Research Project with a staff of academic experts. Even as it shut down, a successor project launched a data base, funded by the Mellon Foundation in New York.[368] Nothing comparable existed, or was even imaginable, in the violin world. From the beginning to today, the violin dealer and authenticator have usually been the same person.

Prosecution and litigation over several centuries range across a wonderful diversity of keys and tempi. But most cases looped back to a relatively modest inventory of themes from "Would you buy a used violin from this man?" and "What can we sell it as?" to "How much will the traffic bear?"

Like a short course in constitutional law and the evolution of language, German unification after 1990 also delivered a lesson in violin history. Between 1961 and 1989, when only the most privileged and politically reliable were allowed to travel in the West, authentication of the East German state collection was entrusted to Willi Lindorfer, a Weimar maker with a special relationship to the East German Ministry of Interior and no known relationship to the world of Beare, Bein & Fushi, or Vatelot.

In the wake of unification, East German players and the West German Interior Ministry took their instruments to Ingeborg Behnke, a Mittenwald graduate who had worked for Beare and Vatelot before becoming repairer and restorer-in-chief to the Philharmonic in her native West Berlin. By conscious choice, she was not a dealer. But she regularly saw and worked on old Italian instruments. The old East German establishment protested the unavailability of the former state collection while its status was renegotiated. In October 1998, a new minister of interior was welcomed to the sound of nominal old masters.[369] But most of them turned out to be copies.[370]

In 2005, a combination of textual criticism, X-ray, pigment analysis, and dendrochronology convinced both Ernst van der Wetering of the Rembrandt Research Project and George Wachter of Sotheby's that a Rembrandt last catalogued as a Rembrandt in 1915, dropped from catalogues after 1931, then sold as a Rembrandt in 1971 really was a Rembrandt.[371] The implications for the violin trade were not hard to imagine.

The results were both promising and problematic. The good news was that the computer now allowed people to search and see relationships and patterns in hours that had once evaded them over months, years or whole careers. In 1988, Minneapolis radiologist Steven Sirr, out of curiosity of what would come of it, submitted his violin and others to a CAT scan. Two decades later, Bruno Frohlich, a research anthropologist at the National Museum of Natural History in Washington, began doing the same with the Smithsonian and Library of Congress collections. "What use is an infant?" the great physicist Michael Faraday asked famously, citing Benjamin Franklin.[372] Answers included discovery of ancient repairs, measurement of wood density and air volume, and the kind of profile that might be of use in a police lineup. But the expense of a million-dollar machine and $1,000 per scan was likely to confine the practice to special venues, instruments, and occasions.[373]

Then came the bad news. That the march of science could also advance the sum of human error was hardly news to anyone who remembered the Werro case. If hard to book that situation as a victory for Werro, it was no easier to book this one as a victory for Iviglia's Chamber of Experts, and especially for Frei, the police commissioner in the white lab coat. In 1972, a half generation after the trial, Frei estimated that his experts had examined over a thousand violins submitted for certification each year. Most appeared to come from neighboring, German-speaking countries.[374] Though fees ranged from 100 Swiss francs for a single-page letter to 750 francs for a booklet with color photos, all submissions underwent the same examination and tests. Frei estimated that up to 20 percent were not what they claimed to be.[375]

There were only two problems. The first was the unwillingness, particularly of the British and American dealers, who now controlled the sale of most Italian instruments, to accept the Swiss findings. The second was a list of errors that seemed not only to vindicate their skepticism, but also dispose even fellow Swiss to write off Frei and his maker colleagues as the violin world's Keystone Kops.

Everyone understood that authentication was slippery and that experts could disagree in good faith. But it was hard to explain how the Chamber could issue three certificates for the same Grancino, declaring it respectively authentic, a mix, and a fake; how a nominal Santo Serafino could have been produced while its maker was still in diapers; or how a nominal Tononi could be dated twenty to thirty years after its maker's death.[376]

Obviously under fire, Frei resigned on the eve of 1973. But the experts marched on unfazed. Beginning in 1978, the Swiss Violin Makers Association put its authority on record in an eight-volume series, including all major Italian and foreign schools, with annotated descriptions, measurements, and photos in both natural and ultraviolet light.[377]

Their certificates meanwhile went their own way. In 1999, a Japanese player who considered himself done in by his teacher twenty-five years earlier tried in vain to get a Japanese court to accept a Beare certificate on behalf of a woman he considered a fellow victim. A few years earlier she had paid a Tokyo dealer some $250,000 for a nominal Omobono Strad that had been certified by the Swiss experts. In Beare's view, the instrument was a composite, probably Tyrolean. He valued it at £4,500, at the time about $7,000. An ad hoc consortium of Japanese dealers supported their colleague's claim that the Swiss expertise outweighed Beare's. The court upheld their petition. "Now I know well that the VIOLIN itself does not cheat us but people cheat VIOLINS," Beare's correspondent reported sadly.[378]

The other bad news, as Dutch-based American Rembrandt scholar Gary Schwartz noted thoughtfully, was that the march of science raised questions no one had ever thought to ask. His colleague, Thomas Wessel, a resident art historian at AXA Art Insurance, underwriter of a number of major museums and private collections, agreed that the new technology was fascinating. But he was understandably skeptical that the auction houses would warm to something that "sharpens the consciousness of how many fakes they may have sold."[379]

VIOLIN CASES

IN CASE OF doubt, the oldest and most widely practiced tiebreaker was the disciplined observation and analytical comparison known as textual criticism. Perfected and practiced in German universities in the lifetime of Vuillaume and the Hills, it brought credible scientific rigor to what till now had been a world of legend, hearsay, and family gossip. What worked in Ranke's history seminar, it appeared, could work just as well in the violin shop. A century later, dealer-experts like Beare and Bein still swore by it.

Like the Hills, they also hired contract researchers to comb parish archives for family and business networks and lost or imagined makers, and generally to reconstruct Cremona's golden age in much the way that archaeologists reconstructed Pompeii's. The combined results produced by a handful of dedicated walk-ons might have impressed Theodor Mommsen, the great historian, or Sherlock Holmes, the great detective.

But while all of this was necessary, none of it was sufficient. Expertise is essentially a visual process that almost anyone can master with a bit of effort, time, and luck, says Hargrave, an inspired copyist with decades of experience. But anyone who wants to practice it for money as opposed to fun, he adds, should be aware of the "potential for anguish, grief, and ruination."[380] Even Ozzie Smith, the Beare, Wurlitzer, and Alfred Hill of shortstops, committed errors.

Between them, three contested instruments subsumed a couple of centuries of trade history while testing the utility and limits of art, science, and human nature. As might be expected, two were Strads, or claimed to be. The third, with the same qualification was—or wasn't—a del Gesù.

The first, the Balfour Strad, was the violin world's equivalent of Piltdown Man, the forged fossil hominid that was its fairly close contemporary.[381] Advertised as "a magnificent example of Antonio Stradivari's unrivaled workmanship," it made its debut in the June 1901 issue of the *Strad,* where Balfour's, a shipping firm in London's financial district, offered it for sale at £1,000 cash. In fact, it was a Voller family copy, legitimately identified as such when the makers sold it to Balfour's for £45. After a month went by without a taker, Balfour's offered it, again without success, for £2,000. Claiming certifications of authenticity from Beare & Sons, Chanots in both London and Manchester, and four Paris dealers, including Chardon, they then put it up for auction.

This time, remarkably, there was a private buyer, who even paid £2,500 before being persuaded to reconsider and take Balfour's to court. Balfour's protested. But the defense collapsed when the buyer produced a sworn statement from one of the Vollers, attesting that he was the maker. The sale was annulled in an out of court settlement, and Balfour's filed for bankruptcy a little more than a year after its supposed Strad first came on the market.[382]

The episode left a trail of open-ended questions. Why had the Vollers not piped up earlier? Why had an auction room full of bargain-hungry dealers failed to bid? Where did the declarations of authenticity come from? Yet the violin proved as hard to kill as Dracula. In the 1960s it resurfaced improbably with authentic Stradivari ribs. In 1964, an advanced generation of Hills acquired it for a thousand much-diminished pounds and withdrew it from circulation. But there it was again after 1992, when the last of the family split, liquidated its patrimony, and sold the Balfour to Biddulph. From there, both Beare and Bein assumed it had made its way to Japan.[383] The second instrument, known with or without suspicion as the Sainton, was a del Gesù, eventually proven to be real, despite Charles Beare's conviction that it was a Lott.[384]

After a century's experience, it was also general knowledge that blind tests of violin tone were about as reliable as wine tastings. In a memorable sixty-minute broadcast on the BBC in 1977, Manoug Parikian, concertmaster of the Philharmonia Orchestra in its golden years and a longtime professor at London's Royal Academy, repeated passages of Bruch and Bach from behind a screen on a Strad, a del Gesù, a Vuillaume, and a Ronald Praill that had left its British maker's shop only the year before. Challenged to hear which was which, Isaac Stern, Pinchas Zukerman, and Charles Beare could as well have flipped a coin. Stern and Beare did best, getting two of four correct. One or another of the panelists mistook the Praill for both a Strad and a del Gesù. All three expressed strong views on flaws in the testing procedure.[385]

The Global Instrument

Carnatic violinists, southern India, 2007.

Władysław Trebunia of Trebunie-Tutki, Poland, 2006.
Courtesy of Jan Mehlich.

Mariachi violinists, Spain, 2006.
Courtesy of Jose Luis Martinez Alvarez, Mieres, Spain.

Arvel Bird, Southern Paiute–Celtic violinist, Rankokus Reservation, New Jersey, 2009. *Photo by Margaret Mehl.*

National High School Orchestra on the steps of the State, War, and Navy (now Eisenhower Executive Office) building, Washington, DC, March 1, 1930. President Herbert Hoover and Vice President Charles Curtis on the sidewalk, lower right.
Library of Congress, Prints and Photographs Division, LC-DIG-npcc-18555.

Making It

Violin maker Frank Eickmeyer at work in Bosa, Sardinia, 2008.
Courtesy of Frank Eickmeyer.

Bow maker James Tubbs at work in London, ca. 1917.
From the collection of Andy Fein, Fein Violins, Ltd.

François Chanot, Paris, 1818.
*Smithsonian Institution Collections,
National Museum of American
History, Behring Center.*

Alemannic viola by Joseph
Meyer, Black Forest, ca. 1670.
Courtesy of Felix Schleiermacher.

William Sidney Mount, Stony
Brook, New York, 1852.
*Smithsonian Institution Collections,
National Museum of American
History, Behring Center.*

John M. A. Stroh, London, after 1904.
Smithsonian Institution Collections, National Museum of American History, Behring Center.

Selling It

Jean-Baptiste Vuillaume, maker and dealer,
Paris, mid-nineteenth century.

Robert Bein and Geoffrey Fushi, dealer and
dealer, Chicago, late twentieth century.
Courtesy of Bein & Fushi, Inc.

A Wurlitzer certificate by Jay Freeman.
Certificate image courtesy of Tarisio.

PASSING THE TORCH

Do it yourself, ca. 1854,
and still in print for seventy-five cents in 1878.
Library of Congress, Prints and Photographs Division, LC-USZ62-96513.

Joseph Joachim and a young Franz von Vecsey, Berlin, 1903.

Shinichi Suzuki at work in America, 1984.
Courtesy of the Suzuki Association of the Americas archives.

Niccolò Paganini,
by Jean-August-Dominique Ingres, 1819.

Niccolò Paganini,
by Eugène Delacroix, 1832.

Joseph Joachim, by Sir Leslie Matthew Ward
("Spy"), for *Vanity Fair*, January 5, 1905.

Maud Powell, ca. 1919.

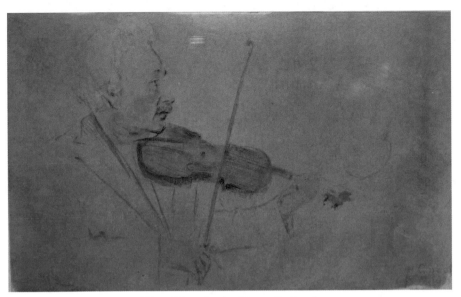

Albert Einstein, by Henry B. Goode.
Courtesy of Linda Goode Heath, granddaughter of Henry B. Goode.

Sherlock Holmes and the Alderney Street Mystery, chapter 74,
"Pipe and Violin," illustrated by Sidney Paget. *Courtesy of the
Sherlock Holmes Collections at the University of Minnesota Library.*

Jascha Heifetz at play with Fritz Kreisler, Efrem Zimbalist, and Alma Gluck, Connecticut, 1919. *Courtesy of the Constance Hope papers, Rare Book and Manuscript Library, Columbia University.*

Jascha Heifetz at work with the Meremblum Youth Orchestra, Hollywood, 1939. *Courtesy of the Constance Hope papers, Rare Book and Manuscript Library, Columbia University.*

The Joachim Quartet,
late nineteenth century.
*Courtesy of Brahmsgesellschaft
Baden-Baden.*

The Emerson Quartet,
late twentieth century.
*Courtesy of the Emerson Quartet
and Deutsche Grammophon.*

Bond, early twenty-first
century. *Uli Weber / Bond.*

Eddie South, mid-twentieth century.
Courtesy of the William P. Gottlieb/Ira and Lenore S. Gershwin
Fund Collection, Music Division, Library of Congress.

Regina Carter, early twenty-first century.
Photo by Ayano Hisa.

Imagining It

Jan Steen, *The World Turned Upside Down*, ca. 1660.

William Sidney Mount, *The Power of Music*, 1847.

William Michael Harnett, *The Old Violin*, 1886.
Courtesy of National Gallery of Art, Washington, DC.

Adolph-William Bouguereau,
Song of the Angels, 1881.

Arnold Böcklin,
*Self-portrait with Fiddler
Death*, 1872.

André Anisimov, *Beethoven Violin Concerto*, 1999.

The outcome was the same in a far more elaborate, double-blind test devised by Claudia Fritz, an acoustics physicist at the French National Center for Scientific Research, at the International Violin Competition of Indianapolis in 2010. In a darkened hotel room a platoon of mostly professional players, ranging in age from twenty to sixty-five, donned welder's goggles, then played their way through three distinguished, well-preserved, expensive, and emphatically anonymous old violins—two Stradivaris and a del Gesù—and three contemporary violins that neither they nor the audience could see or even smell. "Over the years, I have spent many thousands of dollars on research equipment—none of it quite so effective as a pair of $6 goggles," Joseph Curtin, one of the coauthors, reported. Though unaware of it, each had the opportunity to play them twice, a pair at a time, one old, one new. They were then asked to name their preference and judge them from worst to best according to their response, projection, tone, and ease of play. The results were practically random. Of seventeen participants willing to be asked whether they could identify the old Italian, seven didn't even try, seven got it wrong, and only three got it right, Curtin said.[386]

Norman Pickering, the polymath musician-recording engineer who had done as much as any contemporary to demystify the mechanics of the violin, made the same point in a paper delivered at the 1994 meeting of the Southern California Association of Violin Makers. He reported how Zukerman had played a number of violins that Pickering knew from lab measurements were different. But they didn't sound different. He then realized that a player as good as Zukerman could make different instruments sound alike by the way he played them.[387]

Ownership history was a little more promising. But there was too little of it, and it began too late. Unlike Stradivari, an icon in his lifetime, Guarneri was discovered a whole century after his death. Stradivari sold his product to the great and good. Guarneri sold his to the not so great and not so good. Documentation of surviving Strads could reach all the way back to Cremona. Documentation of del Gesùs had to await the era of Lott and Vuillaume. Stylistic comparison was only a little likelier to help. Guarneri's working life was short and his work uneven. As best anyone could tell, the Sainton was an anthology that resembled some del Gesùs and deviated from others.

Though the New York show was a unique opportunity to compare the contested Sainton with twenty-five authenticated specimens and an eye to what makes a del Gesù a del Gesù, the moment of truth was nearly a decade in coming. But it was worth the wait.

The tiebreaker, equally respected in violin shops and art history seminars, was dendrochronology. As much a technique as a science in itself,
it dated back to 1901, when it occurred to astronomer Andrew Ellicott
Douglass that there might be a correlation between tree rings and the sun-
spot cycle. Between 1914 and 1929, he also applied himself to dating pueb-
los in the American Southwest. Archaeology was dendrochronology's first
success. But many more, including climatology, fire and insect ecology,
hydrology, and geomorphology, would follow.[388] Architecture historians
learned to use it to date objects as diverse as Abraham Lincoln's birthplace,
the Bodleian library, and the cultural history of the ancient Middle East.
Beginning in 1958, instrument historians learned to use it, too.[389]

Software and statistical analysis of the data grew ever more sophisticated. But the principle remained essentially simple. Tree growth, variable
according to weather, is reflected in the amplitude of annular rings. Dated
backward from the most recent, or outer, ring, to the earliest, or inner,
ring, a given tree or series of trees allows construction of a data base. The
so-called reference chronology can be used as a standard of measurement
and matched to a violin.

In 2003, John Topham, a self-taught dendrochronologist with a science
degree from Britain's Open University, as well as a Mittenwald-trained
luthier and a former president of the British Violin Making Association,
was asked to examine the Sainton's two-part spruce belly. He not only
reported that its treble, or right, side dated to 1728, and its bass, or left, side
to 1731. He also discovered that the Sainton's bass side matched the treble
side of two uncontested del Gesùs. Though the Sainton had since moved
on to Biddulph, then Machold, Francais had finally earned his victory lap.

But by this time, all eyes were on the main event, the case of the Messiah Strad. Since the nineteenth century, Strads had been the gold standard
of violins, as intensively and comprehensively studied as the French Revolution. Since Vuillaume, the Messiah, also known as Le Messie, had been
the gold standard of Strads. "That unique example," the Hills called it.[390]
From its appearance at the Ashmolean Museum after World War II, visitors had stood in its presence as visitors to the Louvre stood in the presence
of Leonardo da Vinci's *Mona Lisa*. If the trade got Le Messie wrong, it had
presumably gotten many other things wrong too.

Documented skepticism reached back to Vuillaume. Why, for example,
did the Messiah look so suspiciously new? Who could even say for certain
that Vuillaume, a clearly interested party, was a credible source? Yet the

case for its authenticity was at least as powerful as the case against it. For most of its existence, it had only been seen, not heard. In effect, it looked new because it was new. "Were it but eight days, instead of one hundred and eighty six years old, it could not present a fresher appearance," the Hills exclaimed.[391] Beginning in the 1840s, even though it still belonged to Tarisio and years before Vuillaume laid eyes on it, the great Turinese maker Giuseppe Rocca seemed already to have used it as a model.[392] Then came the Hills, who had probably seen more Strads than anyone since Antonio and his elder sons. If the Hills didn't know a Strad when they saw one, who did?

In 1997, Stewart Pollens was invited by Biddulph and David Hill to photograph the Messiah for Rosengard's and Chiesa's monograph on Stradivari's newly discovered will. As conservator of musical instruments at New York's Metropolitan Museum, one of two such full-time professionals in the United States,[393] Pollens had photographed Stradivari materials since the Cremona show a decade earlier, and more recently published a book on Stradivari's templates.[394] He had especially impressed the violin world with his photos of the del Gesù on display at the Met in 1994. Hill and his brother Andrew were the last family members still active in the trade. As great-nephews of the donors, they were also the Messiah's gatekeepers, a detail of some relevance in the months that followed when the question of access to the instrument had become a matter of global interest.[395]

The photo session turned out to be interesting in ways neither Hill nor Pollens anticipated. A year later, Pollens delivered a paper at the annual meeting of the Violin Society of America. Its unassuming title, "Le Messie," barely hinted at what would follow. It was published a year later in the society's journal.[396]

Prepared to make the most of a once-in-a-lifetime opportunity, Pollens read everything he could get his hands on before packing his lighting equipment and 8x10 view camera and boarding the plane. But he also brought a dental mirror and miniature halogen lamps that would allow him to see the Messiah from the inside, Hill permitting. Hill agreed and Pollens looked. Cozio's voluminous but famously difficult notebooks described a 1716 Strad with two patches, one above the soundpost, the other added by Guadagnini to reinforce a crack. Neither was visible in the instrument in his hands. Hill conceded that he had not seen any patches either, nor had there been any when the instrument was X-rayed some years earlier.[397] Pollens noticed that Hill's great-uncles, when describing the instrument in 1891, had not mentioned patches either. He also noticed how they had been struck by details—f-holes, edges, corners—unlike any they had seen before in a Strad.[398]

Pollens kept looking. Cozio referred to a filled knot or rosin pocket on an instrument by Francesco. There was no such knot or pocket mentioned in any of his three references to a 1716 Antonio. Yet there was one on the instrument in Pollens's hands. Then there was the mysterious "G" in the peg box. Over his lifetime, Stradivari had developed seven templates or patterns. The Messiah corresponded to the pattern Stradivari called "PG."[399] The Hills, who had seen seven Strads with original necks, noted a "PG" inscribed in the peg box of six of them. But the Messiah bore no inscription at all, and there was still none when it was photographed around 1980. So how and when had the "G" gotten there, and who had gotten it wrong?

The stylistic discrepancies turned Pollens's thoughts to provenance. Cozio referred three times to a "most beautiful and large" 1716 Strad. He even measured it. But his descriptions could have covered up to nine 1716 Strads, while his measuring system was so idiosyncratic that no one could say for certain what he had measured. In any case, the instrument he measured was not among those Tarisio bought after Cozio's death, and neither he nor Cozio left any indication of a previous sale. Though both had been regarded as figures of awe and legend, it had been known since the 1930s that Cozio, too, was in business,[400] and that both he and Tarisio had been at least pragmatic in matters of labels, copies, and composites. It was also common knowledge that Stradivari's shop had survived him by some years, and that his tools, patterns, and even materials remained in use.

These thoughts led Pollens to Peter Klein, professor of tree biology at the University of Hamburg and an acknowledged master of dendrochronology. As a specialist in early panel paintings, Klein had dated violins for museums in Germany, Austria, and Belgium, as well as the del Gesù exhibited in 1994 at the Met. Without identifying the subject, Pollens sent him a full-size print, made from an 8x10-inch negative, of the Messiah's top and asked him to date it. Klein reported back that the last datable ring was 1738, a year after Stradivari's death. Asked to repeat the examination, he came up with the same result. Pollens then turned to Peter Ian Kuniholm, a professor of art history and archaeology at Cornell and another specialist in dendrochronology. Kuniholm's result was the same as Klein's.[401] The flutter set off by Pollens's paper soon turned into a giant flapping of wings.[402]

But both Klein and Kuniholm had worked from a photo. Beare and Andrew Hill responded by mobilizing Topham and Derek McCormick, a Belfast cancer researcher and amateur violin maker, to work from the Messiah itself. Topham and McCormick found no reference chronology that matched the Messiah. But they found two 1717 Strads that at least linked the Messiah to the Stradivari shop. The next step was to measure and match more contemporary instruments, in the end a total of thirty-three, including twenty Strads, and construct an undated sequence known as a floating chronology. They then matched this against an Alpine master chronology, wrote up their instrumentation, methodology, data, and findings, and sent them off to a peer-reviewed journal. The article appeared in 2000. "The youngest growth ring in the Messiah corresponded to 1682," they reported.[403]

Klein, who had already seen the Messiah data and discussed the details with Topham in Hamburg, had meanwhile notified Pollens that he could no longer support either Topham's findings or his own. He was nonetheless amenable to another try, this time on the Messiah itself. In November 1999, he joined Topham at the Ashmolean where, by Topham's account, everything that could go wrong did. Klein's concern that his instrument of choice, a jeweler's loupe, might damage the Messiah's varnish, required him to use Topham's equipment, plus software that Topham himself found difficult to use. Joint publication foundered on the question of who would be principal author. Separate publication was the alternative option. But Topham was fearful of being scooped, and unflattering website references by Pollens and his wife, violinist Stephanie Chase, made him dig in all the more in response to repeated requests from Klein to see his data.[404]

The story had long since appeared in papers read by people who might actually buy Strads. By the time Topham's article appeared,[405] players and spectators were begging for a rematch. Two years after Pollens's broadside, the opposition lined up to return his fire in the improbably named House of Tudor room of the Drawbridge Estate Inn in Fort Mitchell, Kentucky. The occasion was again the annual meeting of the Violin Society of America. "I think I'm going to charge admission," Albert Mell, the editor of the society's journal, announced in happy anticipation of the afternoon panel.

When the meeting resumed after lunch, Helen Hayes, the society's president, had replaced Mell in the chair. She recalled the great debate at the National Academy of Sciences, where the astronomers Herbert Curtis and Harlow Shapley fought to a draw over "The Scale of the Universe" in

1920. Four years later, Edwin Hubble settled the debate when he discovered that the universe really was expanding. "I'm sure the analogy is not lost on you," she told the audience as she opened the session.[406] There was little evidence that anybody's mind had been changed by such intrinsically contentious issues as the instrument's style and provenance, Cozio's hidden agenda, whether and how often the Hills had seen and described it, and the relevance of the mysterious "G."[407] But virtually everyone agreed that the dendrochronology shoot-out mattered.

The exchange had actually begun the day before with a session by Henri Grissino-Mayer, an assistant professor of geosciences at the University of Tennessee, whose listed title, "A Familiar Ring: An Introduction to Tree-Ring Dating," could as well have been "Everything You Always Wanted to Know About Dendrochronology, But Were Afraid to Ask." A day later, Pollens and Topham met face-to-face. "Have you read my paper?" Topham asked. "Yes, I have," Pollens said. "Do you understand it?" Topham continued. "No," Pollens replied.[408] Only one of the principals was conspicuously absent. Though invited and even announced in the society's newsletter, Klein sent regrets. "I hear nice things about Mr. Klein as a person, but he is very much, in my experience, like the Messie itself: often heralded but never arrives," Hayes explained to general hilarity.[409]

The solution was both obvious and effective. Hayes had invited Grissino-Mayer to the meeting. She now asked him to do a third examination. Accompanied by two colleagues, he took off for Oxford in summer 2001 with more than a hundred pounds of equipment, including a movable measuring stage, accurate to 0.001 mm., and a digital imaging system. Over a week in Oxford, each of them independently examined the Messiah. Like Topham before them, they then measured a sample of other contemporary instruments, including four Strads and a Rugeri. Again like Topham, they encountered problems matching the Messiah directly to a reference chronology for Alpine spruce. Yet cross-referencing Strads once more came to the rescue. The Messiah matched very well with two Strads that fit nicely in the standard reference chronology. To the delight of the three investigators, their results matched and concurred with Topham's.

On his return, Grissino-Mayer reported to the Violin Society of America, and the findings were published successively in *The Strad*, the *Journal of the Violin Society of America*, and the *Journal of Archaeological Science*,[410] and the final score was: two unpublished and almost unavailable dendrochronologists for 1738 versus five peer-reviewed and published dendrochronol-

ogists for 1682. Though Pollens was still unconvinced, Jon Whiteley, the
Ashmolean's curator, thought he had at least performed a public service by
making people think.[411]

But it was unclear where this left the Messiah. "Dendrochronology
can assign years to tree rings, but it cannot assign makers to violins,"[412]
Grissino-Mayer emphasized. Pollens's other red flags—the tangled provenance, the missing patches, the "G" that Dilworth delicately referred to
as "interesting but not necessarily fatal,"[413] the mystery of why an iconic
masterpiece should remain unsold for nearly sixty years—remained unanswered. In Philip Kass's educated opinion, the Messiah really was a Strad—
but an overrated one. Just possibly, he thought, it might also be the first
to show traces of Giovanni Battista, the first son by Stradivari's second
marriage, who died at twenty-three. A thirteen-year-old in 1716, when the
Messiah was presumably made, he would have been on the threshold of
serious work in his father's shop. If so, he might also have been the source
of its inconsistencies with the work of his father.[414]

Its celebrity could be traced almost entirely to historical circumstance.
The fact that it was kept off the market and then seen but not heard made
it uniquely well preserved. Assumed to come direct from the source via
Cozio, Tarisio, Vuillaume, and the Hills, it evolved successively into a link
in the trade's master narrative, an emblem of its patriarchal succession,
and a national icon. Attacked and doubted by continentals, skeptics, and
conspiracy theorists, it came to be defended with patriotic as well as professional passion by the Hills' successors and descendants.

What was reasonably clear was the legitimate antiquity of the wood
and its ties to the Stradivari shop. What was still clearer was the huge
advance in sophistication, if not transparency, in the half century since the
Werro trial, let alone the century-plus since *Johnstone v. Laurie.* If neither
side landed a knockout punch, the defense could at least claim a victory
on points. The Messiah was again in its glass case, and for all practical
purposes the case was closed.

But there were other cases. It was at once a testimonial to the globalization of the violin market and Japan's expanding economy that many of
them now involved Japan, where Yuko Kanda, a leading dealer, was buying midpriced instruments from A-list teachers, then marketing them as
upscale Italians with the teachers' A-list recommendations and counterfeit
certificates from Wurlitzer. The tip-off was Kanda's insurance claim on
five instruments stolen from a music school. Though he had cause to be

careful, Kanda had overlooked errors in the text of the certificates. In a country where English was widely taught but unevenly learned, it was also noteworthy that the police spotted them.

That the investigation led to Yoshio Unno, one of Japan's leading players, was less remarkable. Now in his forties, with an established international career and a 1698 Strad, Unno had been professor since 1972 at Tokyo's National University of Fine Arts, where he packed thirty students into a twenty-hour week. He then took on ten more as private pupils.[415]

The teacher-dealer relationship at the heart of the scandal was as ancient as the trade. Though complaining at every step, Hill's had paid commissions ranging from as little as 5 to as much as 25 percent. In this respect as most others, they presumably set the industry standard. In 1953, when a Guarneri filius Andreae could still be had for $5,000, William Lewis & Son of Chicago offered 20 percent on the first $1,000, 15 percent on next $2,500, and 10 percent on sales of greater than $3,500 in a catalogue prepared "For Professional Distribution Only."

Many in the trade averted their eyes or held their noses. But Fritz Reuter was not one of them. A Dutch-born Mittenwald graduate, Reuter had worked at Lewis before opening his own Chicago shop in 1964.[416] But he was better known, even globally renowned, for his views and website.[417] For some he was Don Quixote, improbably returned to life as a suburban Chicago violin dealer. For others, he was a man who took to heart the poet-philosopher Giacomo Leopardi's aphorism that the world is a league of scoundrels against people of goodwill[418] and made it his mission to fight back.

Like most of their peers, Bein and Fushi paid teachers commissions. In 1988, Reuter charged them with bribery. They responded by suing for libel. The suit wandered on for four years, costing up to $1.5 million in lost income, Fushi claimed, plus a disastrous ratio of legal costs to damages awarded. But the Cook County Circuit Court eventually declared Reuter's statements false and misleading and Reuter himself guilty of commercial defamation. It also ruled that commissions were not bribery and ordered Reuter to cease and desist.[419] But Japan was not Chicago. Unno was arrested, and in April of 1982 Kanda was charged with bribery, forgery, and fraud.[420]

But this was only half the story. As Geraldine Norman, the *London Times*'s redoubtable sales and auction correspondent, reported a month after Kanda's indictment, the saga had actually begun in London, where

Sotheby's had sold a set of wooden blocks that allowed their owner to print good facsimiles of famous Cremona labels. The Entente, the dealers' federation, had hoped to get them for £15 to £25. Instead, a couple of Japanese bidders made off with them for £700. By the time the embarrassed Sotheby's joined the Entente to buy them back, the labels had not only metastasized, but a second Tokyo dealer had also acquired the incriminating supply of blank certificates. The Interpol investigation led to Adolph Primavera, owner of two violin shops in one of Philadelphia's oldest and most elegant neighborhoods. Charged by a federal grand jury with perjury and obstruction of justice, he pleaded guilty and was sentenced to three years' probation plus two hundred hours of public service.[421]

By 2004, Primavera was gone. But the long shadow of the bogus certificates still fell improbably on the respondent property clerk of the New York Police Department. Ten years earlier, Sojiro Okada, a Japanese violin collector, consigned a real Rocca and a Strad with a Francais certificate for possible sale in New York. In July 1994, Francais informed Okada's dealer that the certificate was a forgery and the Strad a copy.[422] A day later, both instruments were stolen from the dealer's car. That November, the violins were offered to an undercover police officer. The seller was arrested, then he posted bail and vanished. Okada tried to reclaim his instruments so he could sell the Rocca and prosecute the vendor of the phony Strad. But the authorities insisted on holding the instruments as evidence, in case the fugitive suspect should return, another claimant should appear, or the dealer from whom they were stolen should file an insurance claim. In 1999, Okada died. Three years later, his son filed for return of his father's instruments. None of the anticipated or hypothesized scenarios had actually happened. The property clerk nonetheless continued to hold firm. With the rules and code of the City of New York seemingly at odds with law of New York state, the case was finally referred to the state supreme court, which published its decision in early 2004.[423]

Unlike the Strad, the Rocca was genuine, the justices ruled. Therefore there was no problem with a fraudulent insurance claim. Okada's son had also proven his ownership. He was therefore entitled to his father's Rocca. It was still uncertain what would happen to his father's phony Strad. But at least one thing was clear—Japan being Japan, an aggregation of bankers, consultants, advisers, silent partners, and ad hoc experts the size of a baseball team could well have been involved in the original sale to Okada. Thanks, ironically, to U.S. law, all of them were out of immediate danger.[424]

Supply side to demand side, America to Japan, the sad little story of Keith Bearden was a counterpoint to the wry little story of the Okadas. Grandson, son, and nephew of respected local dealers, Bearden learned the family business in the traditional way. At thirty-four he opened his first shop next to Powell Hall, the home of the St. Louis Symphony. Soon afterward, his sold his first Strad on consignment at 7 percent commission. The three-day transaction brought him $50,000, more than he had previously earned in a year. It was clearly a heady experience. By age forty-two, he was a nationally recognized bow maker and an officer of the American Federation of Violin and Bow Makers, with a clientele including local players, St. Louis Symphony members, and the estate of the orchestra's president. Witness after witness would later testify that everyone liked him. A few even advanced him money.

Then things fell apart. Like a gambler playing for ever higher stakes to recover his losses, he was soon in over his head. An affable conman who couldn't bear to say no or lay off staff, he was also a cocker spaniel among pit bulls. In early 1997, a copyright story in the *St. Louis Post-Dispatch* reported that he had fled to Japan a step ahead of the FBI and a federal grand jury investigation.[425] Over the next few months, he taught bow making and set up a small shop in Tokyo. By this time, sales tax and other bills accumulating since the previous summer had gone unpaid. A check advanced to bring a Cincinnati youth orchestra to St. Louis bounced.[426] One bill had already landed in small claims court.

Since nothing fails like failure, consigners became increasingly anxious about their instruments and money. In January 1997, a Los Angeles doctor, whose instrument had vanished with Bearden, won a $200,000 judgment.[427] The question was how to collect. Calls to his Tokyo number went unanswered. Six months later, he was under arrest on the eve of a flight to Korea and under indictment on fourteen counts of mail and wire fraud and awaiting extradition. Michael Becker, a former president of the federation of which Bearden had been secretary, was at a loss to recall a precedent. He had heard of fraud involving single instruments, he told a reporter. He had never heard of a case involving forty-five.

By the time Bearden returned to St. Louis, he faced up to seventy years in prison and a fine of $3.5 million. A guilty plea to the mail and wire fraud counts reduced the jail time to two years, the greater part of which would be spent at a minimum security institution with tennis courts, a weight room, and no bars. U.S. District Judge Carol E. Jackson was stern but realistic. "You can't steal your way out of debt," she told him as she pronounced sentence.[428]

Residual claims were assessed at up to $1.7 million.[429] Finding assets to cover them was obviously a challenge. A $250,000 reserve of pernambuco had already been seized by a claimant in a civil suit. Thanks to a federal statute requiring restitution for crimes committed on or after April 24, 1996, thirteen of the thirty-four fraud claimants, including the St. Louis Symphony's underwriter, were at least entitled to restitution. Laid end to end, the total came to $763,300, to be paid at $3,181 a month over twenty years after Bearden finished his sentence. In theory, the other twenty-one could file civil suits, though barring a bull market in bows, the odds were not in their favor.

Bearden insisted from jail that he would pay whatever he owed, however long it might take, as the *Post-Dispatch* published itemized FBI lists of his clients with the date and magnitude of their losses.[430] "I can't say I'm sorry enough," he told the newspaper's reporter. There was even talk of a book. Nothing more was heard of that.[431] But the long march to restitution began directly on his release when he took a job with Machold to work on bows. Not only was he again doing what he did best. It was widely assumed that he was paying off a major creditor.

YET EVEN AS the clock ran down on Bearden's fifteen minutes of fame, two far larger and gaudier cases showed promise of substantially longer runs. The first involved the estate of Gerald Segelman, who died in 1992 at ninety-three, leaving his executors to dispose of what was probably Britain's last great private collection. The second involved the collection of Herbert Axelrod, a New Jersey millionaire still vigorously active in his seventies and resolved to dispose of his collection himself.

The depth of plot and character of either case would have delighted the heart of Charles Reade. Each featured dealers with familiar names and instruments with ancient pedigrees. Each involved collectors, endlessly and equidistantly removed from the world of Lady Blunt. Each broke the eight-digit barrier in dollars, euros, and even sterling—a violin market first. Each would inspire platoons of lawyers on both sides of the Atlantic to strategies as convoluted as any violin scroll and test points of law[432] as remote from most people's experience as string theory. Though each was an intrinsically global story in an era of global media, it was notable again that both—eventually—came to public attention by way of a local angle.

Of course, the local angle was not entirely local. Gwen Freed, the arts reporter and music editor at the *Minneapolis Star-Tribune* and a conservatory product herself, was married to a Minnesota Orchestra player, whose worried colleagues feared that they might inadvertently have bought tainted goods from their dealers in London and Chicago. As things turned out, there was no cause for concern. There was therefore no cause for a follow-up story in Minneapolis, when the Segelman case came to trial in London a year later. But by that time, Freed's icebreaker story[433] had made it around the world.

Even the lead might have been a scene from Hitchcock. Biddulph, the only dealer Segelman trusted, was at Wimbledon watching the 1992 finals in the men's singles when he was called to the phone. The audibly distraught caller was Vera Farnsworth, 82, who had been Segelman's bookkeeper and partner of some sixty-five years. She reported that Segelman had just died and asked Biddulph to come to their apartment as soon as possible.

Three days later Biddulph appeared at the office of Timothy White, Segelman's lawyer, and presented a list of instruments that would eventually reach fifty-two, including three Strads, two del Gesùs, and assorted Amatis, Bergonzis, and Guadagninis.[434] He explained his relationship to Segelman and made himself available to executors, already aware of how little they knew about the violin world and its market.[435]

Yet even as Segelman's death set the affair in motion, it was his life that provided the story line. As representative of time and place as Abraham Cahan's David Levinsky and Scott Fitzgerald's Last Tycoon, Segelman had been hooked on the violin since childhood, when his mother bought him lessons at sixpence an hour on a product of Mittenwald or Markneukirchen. He was still in his twenties when he and his brothers bought the first of what would become a chain of fifteen provincial movie palaces. By the 1940s and 1950s, he had fortune enough to live out his fantasy life, and buy the best that Hill's could offer at austerity prices. Howard Reich and Williams Gaines of *The Chicago Tribune* cite $18,000– $19,000 for Strads in 1946–47 and, even more amazingly, $3,360 for the Mary Portman del Gesù in 1949.[436] Approaching retirement with television in irresistible ascent, he then sold his businesses and lived on his investments.

For the rest of his long life, his collection remained his major and only visible passion. So far as anyone knew, he neither played nor loaned, let alone exhibited, his trophies. The pleasure was in the pursuit and the possession. But he was also not getting any younger. As early as the mid-

1980s, he was liquidating his collection at what Bein considered realistic prices and, inevitably, huge capital gains.[437]

Violins aside, his tastes, habits, and apartment were demonstratively modest and his lifestyle reclusive to the point of eccentricity. He affected the name "Mr. Black" and dressed accordingly. It was believed that he had even hired his lawyer, Timothy White's uncle Jack, because he enjoyed the conjunction of Black and White, a reminiscence of a Black and White Café he had once owned. With Farnsworth on his arm, he enjoyed a frisson of recognition at auctions, where he was a familiar if mysterious presence. But only Biddulph, who had cultivated him since the 1970s and humored him from to time by buying things he didn't need or want at Segelman's price,[438] had any serious clue to what he had. On the threshold of both his own career and Bein's, he brought Bein to meet Segelman too. Anticipating what lay ahead, Bein spent the evening before reviewing Hamma's photos of the golden age Italians. On his arrival, Segelman challenged him to identify individual instruments from across the room. Unsurprisingly, Bein sailed through the exam summa cum laude. He was then allowed to see still more close up.

Yet almost twenty years would pass before even Biddulph realized how much Segelman actually owned. "I have now seen all his stock," he wrote a Japanese dealer in 1991, "but he keeps on surprising me with other violins."[439] In fact, there were still surprises to come. Practically to the end, Biddulph was learning of caches and instruments Segelman had never mentioned. "Anno domini, anno domini"—freely translated as "the end is nigh" —the old man told him only weeks before his death. He then asked Biddulph to expect a call from Farnsworth and see to the collection when the moment came. It was the last time he and Biddulph met.

Mr. Black to the end, Segelman had not mentioned the violins in his will. Yet even without them, both the disposition and extent of an estate estimated in 1998 "in excess of £12 million,"[440] were an eye-opener. Segelman had left £20,000 each to two nephews and £200,000 to Farnsworth. For the next twenty-one years, the rest was reserved for a charitable trust whose beneficiaries, as designated by the trustees, would be "poor and needy" Segelmans. Thereafter the payments would go to various Jewish charities.

"My uncle understood that Mr. Segelman was well-off, but not to the extent that emerged following his death," Timothy White recalled in a sworn statement submitted to the Chicago court seven years later. "My uncle also knew that Mr. Segelman had an interest in old violins, and had owned or did own a number of them, but had no idea of the full extent or value of the collection."[441] Biddulph was bowled over by what now came forth from under the bed, the safe in Segelman's apartment, and various bank vaults. The decorated 1722 Rode Strad was a practical example. Valued at probate at £2.54 million (about $4.78 million) in mid-1992, the collection would eventually be assessed at £11 million to £15 million (about $16.5 million to $22.5 million) in early 2001.

There had been nothing to match it since Gillott. But Biddulph was not Hart. This time the expert was not about to bow out. His argument, that the estate would "get much better prices selling the instruments individually through him than by placing the entire lot with one of the major auction houses,"[442] seemed too good to turn down. White was receptive, even grateful. He offered a 5 percent commission on the full collection and asked only for a suitably independent expert to submit a second opinion on Biddulph's proposed prices. Biddulph proposed, and White agreed to, James Warren of Kenneth Warren & Sons in Chicago. From there till the last hatchet was finally buried twelve years later, one of the few points the parties consistently agreed on was that the estate had engaged Biddulph to sell the collection *seriatim*.

According to White, the problems began soon afterward. With support from various Segelmans, Biddulph, and at least indirectly from Bein, Farnsworth laid claim to an increasing number of instruments, while disgruntled nephews and nieces challenged the will. There were collateral skirmishes with the family, which was resentful that the trust was reserved for charities, and with the authorities over inheritance tax. Almost every case was settled in favor of the estate. By this time some four years had passed, and Farnsworth, already declared incompetent, had died.

But Biddulph was White's primary concern, particularly after he learned in August 1996 that Biddulph had sold an instrument to Beare. As White understood their agreement, Biddulph was to sell directly to players and collectors at retail—that is, maximal—prices, unless otherwise authorized. Money was obviously of interest for itself. But there was also a legal dimension. White had a fiduciary responsibility to the trust as well as the estate.[443] That required an annual statement subject to public inspection. This, in turn, made him answerable in principle to the attorney general in the event that misappropriations were discovered.

What concerned White even more was Biddulph's murky and seemingly evasive record keeping. He found it hard to tell who had bought what for how much and found it still harder to tell where the money was. He also had the impression that payments had been withheld. In March 1997, he applied successfully for an Anton Piller order, a siege gun of an injunction, roughly analogous to pre-action discovery in the United States. Biddulph was now required to let White search his shop and records without prior notice, or risk being found in contempt of court.[444] Days later, his assets were frozen, what was left of the collection was impounded across the street at Sotheby's, and the investigators did what they came to do.

For White, the records seemed only to confirm his worst suspicions: Biddulph, whom he thought he had hired to work for the estate, had been collecting commissions at both ends; he had sold instruments to Warren, the nominally independent expert, at prices Warren himself helped ratify and legitimate; and he had already been dealing in Segelman instruments with Bein, Warren, and Howard Gottlieb, a Chicago collector and member of the Chicago Symphony board, since at least 1991.[445] It appeared that there were also instruments that Biddulph had not even mentioned and still more that he had sold as Farnsworth's, with the proceeds going to her, two Segelman nephews, and himself. In February 1998, White sued Biddulph in London. In March 1999 he filed suit against Bein & Fushi, Gottlieb, and Warren in Chicago.[446]

Biddulph acknowledged that he might have made errors of distraction and inadvertence. He had spent much of 1993 and 1994 planning the Guarneri show in New York. Over the same period, his parents had died, a long-standing relationship had come to an end, and he had had to move. He had generally been under personal stress. He also acknowledged that he had "never been very strong in terms of paperwork and accounts."[447] An incredulous White discovered that Biddulph had not even kept a stock book.[448]

What he denied—"hotly," according to Mr. Justice Hart, who took his lengthy affadavit[449]—was any intent to defraud. He found especially frustrating White's failure to understand "the delicate nature of the art of dealing in the narrow and highly specialised market for fine violins." It was a message he would stick to. Written contracts were uncommon, the handshake normal. Insurance valuations invariably exceeded market prices. Sale to another dealer was often the only way to reach the collectors who were his clients.

Called as an expert for Biddulph, Reuning spelled out the facts of violin market life in a statement of exceptional economy, clarity, and candor. There was only a handful of customers in the world for instruments like

Segelman's. A startling number of them were customers of Bein's. Be it in Chicago or Japan, Biddulph was better than anyone else at connecting the right instrument with the right dealer. It was true that the dealer then passed it on at a price Reuning called "super retail." But Biddulph's "relative premium," Reuning contended, still beat any price an auction house could offer.

Valuation, of course, was a moving target in a narrow market, where insider knowledge was trump, customers were idiosyncratic, and currencies and national fortunes sank or swam. Under the circumstances, price was a moving target too. The instrument—provenance, authenticity, condition—was only part of it. With four to six thousand square feet (360–540 square meters) of high-rent shop space, three to ten restorers at $50,000 to $200,000 each, sales staff who might earn as much as $200,000, tens of millions in capital tied up in slow-moving inventory, plus insurance, overhead was a major item in itself. Margins of 40–50 percent on owned instruments and commissions of 10–20 percent on consigned instruments were standard. Add certifications, insurance appraisals, repairs, strings, rosin, and rehairing bows, and the payoff might be 3 percent annual net profit.

For a court in need of one, Reuning's statement was a short course like none before or, very likely, since. But it was hardly proof that Biddulph's practice was common practice, let alone common law, when the litigants finally met in a London courtroom eight and a half years after Segelman's death. The trial was scheduled for a month. It was over within the week.

The plaintiffs opened with a blockbuster speech on Biddulph's dealings with the Chicagoans. In June 1991, Gottlieb, the Chicago collector, advanced Biddulph £1.2 million, or at the time about $2 million, to buy the Lord Coke and Mary Portman del Gesù from Segelman. Biddulph then sold them back to Gottlieb at the same price for on-site restoration at Bein & Fushi.[450] That fall, Bein & Fushi sold the first for $2.3 million to an anonymous sponsor to be played by the London-based, Japanese violinist Joji Hattori. Some months later, they sold the second for $2 million to Clement Arrison, a Buffalo, New York, investor and business executive, who loaned it via the Stradivari Society to Adele Anthony, the Tasmanian prodigy and wife of Gil Shaham, the Israeli-American virtuoso.[451] A little more than a year after Biddulph's acquisition, a $2 million investment had yielded a 115 percent return. The proceeds were divided among Gottlieb, Bein & Fushi, and Biddulph.[452]

Over three days, White's counsel set about to show how a very recent past was prologue. A successor case was close at hand. In December 1992, Gottlieb bought five Segelman instruments, including two Strads, for $2.7 million, Biddulph issued Gottlieb a $4.5 million insurance valuation, and Gottlieb paid him a $500,000 consultant's fee.[453] The clincher was a Maggini viola that Biddulph had valued in 1992, then sold to Warren, for £200,000. Warren thereupon valued it at $1 million and consigned it to Bein & Fushi, who sold it three months later for £750,000.

On the fourth day, under unceasing fire for what the plaintiffs charged were secret commissions, insider trading, and unacknowledged joint ventures, Biddulph consented to an £8 million settlement, although he still insisted years later that he would have fought on, but for the unsustainable cost in time and money. Yielding to his plea that the settlement threatened him with bankruptcy, the plaintiffs agreed to lower it to £3 million and take it in installments over two years with Biddulph's assets as security. The new settlement, made public at the plaintiffs' insistence,[454] forced him to sell his shop, although he remained in business and his landlord allowed him to remain on the premises. It was late 2005 before he returned to shared but regular premises, ironically on the second floor of a shop he had owned in the 1990s.[455] The Segelman relatives, codefendants in the case, settled too. Days passed before the settlement registered in the media, and almost a half year before the local story mechanism kicked into gear in Chicago.[456] But even without media amplification, the news circumnavigated Planet Violin at tsunami speed.

The main action then moved to Chicago, where, in contrast to England, civil cases are tried before juries. But what had begun with a bang in London trailed off in whimpers. Two years after being hit with the largest claim in violin history, Biddulph had met and completed the scheduled payments. By now, Gottlieb, then Bein, had settled out of court with ironclad confidentiality agreements. In December 2004, the imminent threat of a scheduled trial caused Warren to settle too. A few weeks later, the case was officially dismissed.[457]

With the settlements confidential and the instruments in custody, only the parties and estate could answer with any authority for what lessons were learned. But Herbert Axelrod came away with at least one. A New Jersey entrepreneur, philanthropist, and impassioned violin groupie, Axelrod had a collection of his own to dispose of. With the Segelman case as an example of what could happen if he didn't, Axelrod resolved to dispose of his collection himself.[458]

In fact, he had already been at it since at least 1997, when he sold TFH Publications, the pet care company he claimed to be the world's biggest, for $70 million in cash and a $10 million loan. Over two years, he made over the Strads he had loaned to the Smithsonian since 1987 as a donation. In 1986, they had been valued at $5 million, in mid-September 1997 at $25 million. Less than three months later, the figure had risen to $30 million. By the end of the year, Machold certified Axelrod's collection at nearly $50 million. Fushi called the figure preposterous. But preposterous or not, it made the donation one of the largest in the Smithsonian's history, even without factoring for at least thirteen more instruments he had donated, including quartets by Stainer and Vuillaume.[459]

The story, generic as Segelman's, began in Bayonne, New Jersey, a waterfront and oil-refining town of little romance, where Axelrod was born to Russian-Jewish immigrants in 1927. His mother worked in the U.S. Navy procurement office. His father, a high school math teacher who also worked as a private violin teacher at 25 cents a lesson, gathered his protégés to play quartets at night. "When I was a kid, we had two violins in our home," Axelrod recalled decades later. One, acquired for $10, was known as the Strad. The other, acquired for $12, was known as the Amati. He expected to play professionally when he got older. But that ended at thirteen, after his father took him to play for Efrem Zimbalist, director of the Curtis Institute and a onetime prodigy himself. A two-minute audition was enough. The Axelrods then went home to reconsider young Herbert's vocation.[460]

Four years later, he enlisted precociously in the Army, survived to serve in Korea, and eventually made his way to New York University on the GI Bill, where he enrolled as a twenty-five-year-old doctoral candidate in biometrics. An ad hoc job as lab assistant with a research project in tropical fish genetics led to the American Museum of Natural History, where he prepared a training manual that would appear in four editions over the next twenty years, earn $100,000 in royalties, and evolve into the company that made him rich.

The literal truth of this was arguable. But so were many things he said. "He seemed to be very proud of the things he had done in his life," the great American restorer Bruce Carlson reported after meeting him. "I guess what I'm trying to say is that he wasn't modest."[461]

This was surely true. But there was enough for a math teacher's kid from Bayonne to be immodest about. He had turned aquaria, fish farming, freeze-dried worms, and Nylabone, a synthetic dog chew acquired in

Britain, into gold. Over the lifespan of the company, his *Tropical Fish as a Hobby* spawned some four hundred coauthored titles, many in print years afterward. *Dr. Axelrod's Mini-Atlas of Freshwater Aquarium Fishes* alone went through ten editions between 1986 and 1995. The Federation of British Aquatic Societies honored him with a vice presidency. At least eleven and as many as forty newly discovered species were named after him.[462]

His passion for business supported his passion for violins and vice versa. According to Axelrod himself, he was struck by love at first sight when Moennig's showed him a Strad in 1970. When he couldn't bear to give it back a few weeks later, his wife pulled a diamond ring off her finger, and Axelrod wrote Moennig's a check for $90,000. Soon afterward, concluding that he now practiced so much that his business was suffering, he exchanged his Strad for another Strad plus $150,000. "Get me my diamond back," his wife reportedly told him. "Take what you have left, and play around buying and selling fiddles."

Known for a disposition to pay pennies on the dollar and a nose for the slow-moving heirloom, he aimed for the owner in need of short-term cash to pay inheritance taxes. "If someone wanted a hundred thousand, I'd offer them ten or twelve," he told an interviewer. "They would come back with twenty."[463] Though market watchers agreed that there was less than met the eye in much of what he bought, they conceded that there were good things too. Unlike Segelman, he also made them available to players, reveled in his patronage, and gloried in his philanthropy.

What no one doubted is that he loved the game. His enthusiasm even spun off an imprint called Paganiniana, which would generate a series of illustrated monographs, mostly translated from the Polish and Russian, on the lives and careers of classic players from Tartini to Enesco; a proudly unauthorized and intermittently useful scrapbook of Heifetz memorabilia that would go through three editions, despite its subject's threat to enjoin its publication;[464] and a fourteen-volume anthology of photos, interviews, annotated scores, and technical tips called *The Way They Play*, by Samuel Applebaum, who was another Auer pupil.

In the mid-1980s, it also produced *The Dr. Herbert Axelrod Stradivari Quartet*, a little monograph with a preface by Francais, full-page color photos of the decorated Strads, excerpted citations from the Hill monograph first published eighty-four years earlier, and full-page reproductions of the instruments' certificates. In 2002, there was a sequel called *The Evelyn and Herbert Axelrod Stringed Instrument Collection*. "There are some fine instruments in the catalogue, along with some good information," noted Stefan Hersh, at the time a Chicago orchestra player and buyer consultant, in his 1,754-word review. "But the errors, obvious omissions, inflated valuations, hyped provenances, and dubious attributions in the book are flagrant and too numerous to completely spell out here."[465]

Approaching his midseventies, he could still, in principle, consign his instruments piece by piece to the dealer of his choice. Instead, in midseason of 2001–02, a winter of discontent for both Biddulph and the New Jersey Symphony Orchestra, the Axelrods made the orchestra's president, Lawrence Tamburri, an offer his directors couldn't refuse. The four cellos, two violas, and twenty-four violins, including three del Gesù and eleven Strads, would come to be known as Axelrod's Golden Age Collection. It was valued at nearly $50 million, a figure supported and possibly even proposed by Machold.[466] But the orchestra could have it for half, he told Tamburri, if they came up with the money by June 30, 2002.

This was heady stuff for a middle-budget ensemble, squeezed between the New York Philharmonic and Philadelphia Orchestra and fully professional only since the 1960s.[467] For years, it commuted among eleven venues as urban New Jersey crumbled around it. In 1997, the clouds lifted briefly, when downtown Newark was awakened to new life and the orchestra took up primary residence in the city's shiny new Performing Arts Center while continuing to tour the state as its charter mandated. Then came the stock market crash of 2000, followed by the World Trade Center shock just across the Hudson a year later. "Here we are, presented with an opportunity for the holy grail,"[468] a board member would recall a year or two later. Yet as he and Tamburri knew ex officio, and Axelrod, a major patron, surely knew too, the orchestra was already $1 million in the hole. Its entire annual budget fell 40 percent short of Axelrod's nominal markdown.[469]

A post facto report would find that Tamburri had been less than forthright with his board. But it was also clear that he had met little resistance. He insisted that the instruments were an investment in the orchestra's future, catnip for potential players and conductors, donors, subscribers, and visitors to the state.[470]

It was Scott Kobler, a Newark lawyer, public finance specialist, and board member with years of experience in hospital and housing projects, who found the key to the money question. Put up the instruments as collateral, he persuaded his colleagues. His idea worked. But a few well-timed hints from Axelrod that the New York Philharmonic, Vienna Philharmonic, and Austrian central bankers were about to write $55 million checks are believed to have helped, too.[471]

It would nonetheless take over a year, some five hundred pro bono hours from up to twenty-five lawyers, multiple deadline extensions, and a couple of major concessions to secure the deal.[472] Five banks said no before the Prudential Foundation, a Newark nonprofit affiliated with Prudential Financial, the second biggest U.S. life insurer and one of the orchestra's patrons, came through with the first $5 million. Commerce Bank, the state's largest state-based financial institute, followed with $9 million. The orchestra then applied successfully to the state Economic Development Authority for tax-free bonds to refinance the loans at a lower rate. Four guarantors materialized, two of them board members. Board chair Victor Parsonnet, a cardiac surgeon and personal friend of Axelrod, pleaded with him to lower his price. There was even a direct call from New Jersey Governor James McGreevey, with an appeal to Axelrod to save the instruments for his native state.

In the end, Axelrod cut his asking price to $17 million by loaning the remaining $4 million himself and forgiving $1 million.[473] The sale was closed on Valentine's Day in 2003. A few days later, at a press conference in the Prudential Building, the acquisition was publicly announced along with music by five little Suzuki players from an orchestra-sponsored school program and a show-and-tell of the Axelrod instruments by members of the orchestra.[474] Two months later, some 250 guests assembled in evening dress at $2,500 a head for the Symphony Palace Ball. The venue was a recycled train station in Liberty State Park, which was a former waterfront industrial area with a ferry connection to the Statue of Liberty. It was done up in gauzy hangings and renaissance banners, with citrus and gardenia centerpieces on the tables, and what purported to be a fourteen-foot ice sculpture of Stradivari. The guests, including three former governors, the mayor of Cremona, and the Axelrods, were met at the entrance by a young man in a frilly blouse and brocaded vest who bowed artfully and greeted them with "Buona notte, signore e signori." Movements of Respighi, Mozart, and Tchaikovsky, clearly chosen to show off the instruments, were acknowledged with salvoes of applause. Gross proceeds for the evening were estimated at $700,000. The Axelrods' $32 million—Machold's estimate minus the orchestra's purchase price—placed thirty-first on the *Chronicle of Philanthropy*'s list of the year's sixty largest contributions.[475]

A year later, Axelrod was indicted on charges of federal tax fraud stemming from the sale of his business in 1997, severance payments to a former executive that found their way to a Swiss bank, and aiding and abetting a false tax return. But rather than appear for arraignment, he surfaced first in Cuba, where his yacht was spotted at the Marina Hemingway, a four-star resort. He was then taken into custody at Berlin's Tegel airport on arrival from Switzerland with an Austrian passport.[476]

Though the arrest was unconnected to his violin collection, the passport could only draw attention to it. A grateful republic had conferred it the previous December in recognition of Axelrod's gift of a Stainer quartet and permanent loan of two Strads and a Guarneri to Vienna's Museum of Art History.[477] Machold's close relationship with both Axelrod and the Austrian political establishment fueled further speculation about the source of Axelrod's handy second passport.

Meanwhile, in Washington, the donor-dependent Smithsonian was becoming seriously anxious about FBI and Senate Finance Committee interest in the figures Machold assigned to Axelrod's donations. The New Jersey Symphony was becoming anxious, too. Threshold panic that its ownership might be challenged was quickly resolved. The question of whether it got what it paid for was not. After approaching Charles Beare, then backing off, the directors hired three low-profile but respected New York consultants. They were at least as skeptical about Machold's attributions and barely in shouting distance of his figures. Their upper-end estimate of Axelrod's collection was $26.4 million, just over half Machold's figure. The negotiators were unwilling even to cite the $15.3 million that was their consultants' lower-end estimate. An exemplary eleven-thousand-word story by Mark Mueller of the Newark *Star-Ledger*[478] only confirmed that the counteroffers Axelrod cited had been a Potemkin village. By summer 2003, Zarin Mehta, the New York Philharmonic's manager, had already denied that Axelrod had even approached him. Wolfgang Schuster, the Vienna Philharmonic's public information officer, acknowledged that Axelrod had approached the Austrian National Bank. But it was agreed that his asking price was prohibitive with no payoff in the orchestra's already legendary sound.[479]

Seven months after Axelrod's flight to Cuba, the Germans and the Justice Department settled on extradition terms, and he returned to the United States. German law protected him against extradition on charges non-extant in German law—for example, conspiracy to defraud the Internal Revenue Service. But that still left the lesser charge, aiding and abetting a false tax return. Appearing for arraignment in November, he winked, waved at friends, pretended to smoke a Cuban cigar, and pleaded not guilty. At his trial three weeks later, he was considerably subdued. This time, appearing in shackles and jumpsuit, he reversed his plea. The following March he was sentenced to eighteen months with credit for time in German detention. "It was always my goal to be remembered as an outstanding philanthropist," he told the judge. "Instead I will be remembered as someone who disrespected the law and this court."[480]

For those interested in the theory and practice of the violin market, Axelrod's trial, like Warren's settlement, was an opportunity lost. It would have been a service to see Warren defend himself against White's charges before a Chicago jury. It would have been an education to see Machold defend in open court the Smithsonian and New Jersey valuations that he continued to uphold against all comers. Legal scholars regretted that there would be no test of unjust enrichment, a concept in civil law describing a situation where one party gains a windfall at another party's expense, and the unjustly enriched party can be sued for restitution.[481] But, according to Axelrod's attorney, the Smithsonian Strads were also covered by the plea bargain; the New Jersey sale was not at issue, since he had not filed a tax return for 2003.[482]

The *Star-Ledger*'s tenacity at least shone some light on what the orchestra had actually bought. In a post facto report, even the orchestra acknowledged that there might be some truth to the newspaper's claim that as many as five of its acquisitions were ringers, a purported del Gesù was largely the work of the maker's father and that several of the Strads were composites. But there had been no intent to defraud on the part of its management, it found, and both management and players still believed that the orchestra had gotten its money's worth, if not the pot of gold at the end of the rainbow.[483]

Remarkably, even a budget crisis that showed every promise of becoming the worst of times turned out for the best. Aglow with euphoria in 2002, the orchestra had seen Axelrod's instruments as a comparative advantage bordering on divine intervention. Faced with a $14 million deficit in 2007, including some $10 million still owed to Axelrod, it now saw them as its last best hope. By a convenient coincidence, after thirty years at the Metropolitan Museum, Stewart Pollens had recently opted for the private sector at Violin Advisor, a one-man corporation. The orchestra engaged him to sell its collection.

Pollens set to work with a prospectus addressed to all imaginable orchestras, all possible foundations, and in principle, as he explained later, "anyplace with a pipeline running through it."[484] There was a show of interest in individual instruments. But only two bidders expressed interest in the whole collection. A nine-month courtship, including a few lessons with Stephanie Chase, Pollens's violinist wife, paid off. For an announced price of $20 million plus an unspecified share of the proceeds on eventual resale, the instruments went to an unspecified "group of investors" led by thirty-seven-year-old identical twins and amateur violinists Brook and Seth Taube. They had Harvard degrees and were authorities on distressed investments. It was also agreed that the orchestra could continue to play them for at least the next five years. "This is the best we could get, and we're pleased with it," the orchestra's CEO was heard to say.[485]

He had every reason to be. So did the Taube brothers. Only a few months later, a hugely inflated American housing bubble popped, taking much of Wall Street and the global economy with it. Yet even to the surprise of Jason Price, now Tarisio's CEO, the violin market rolled on like "Ol' Man River." While Tarisio's New York receipts of about $9 million in 2007 fell to a little less than $7.5 million in 2009, a drop of about 17 percent, London receipts actually rose by a quarter over the same period, from about £1.2 million to a little more than £1.5 million.[486] By comparison, American family net worth, an estimated $64.4 trillion in the second quarter of 2007, had plunged by more than a quarter by November 2008, home equity by a third, and the Standard & Poor's Index by 45 percent.[487]

In a landscape filled with distressed investments, a few emblematic transactions also confirmed what they usually did—that investments in Strads and del Gesùs were not distressed. Even in a relatively tiny prewar market, rendered still tinier by the Great Depression of the 1930s, they had held or soon recovered their value. In the genuinely global market of the late twentieth and early twenty-first century, they only went up. Almost unnoticed, the ceiling price had nearly doubled over the decade since David Fulton had bought the 1742 Lord Wilton del Gèsu from Yehudi Menuhin's estate for a reported $6 million. In 1971, still in living memory, Robin Loh had transfixed the violin world when he paid $200,000, a little over a million in 2009 dollars, for the Lady Blunt. In 2007, its reported resale to the Nippon Foundation brought a figure believed to approach $10 million. Between 2004 and 2009, Sotheby's sold nine Strads and five del Gesùs by what it called private treaty, meaning for prices well above anything available at auction.

In late 2009, an unnamed Russian billionaire bought the 1714 General
Kyd Strad for a reported $8 million from the Taiwanese owner, who had
bought it for $5.5 million only a year or two earlier. A week later he paid
a reported $10 million for the 1741 Kochanski del Gesù, named for the
distinguished Polish player who headed the Juilliard Conservatory's violin
department from the mid-1920s to his death in 1934. It had once belonged
to Richard Bennett, then the Hills, who sold it to Kochanski. His widow,
reluctant to sell, left it at Wurlitzer's for the next quarter century. At current prices, troy ounce for troy ounce, it was now valued at about six times
the price of gold.

Even in deep recession, the price might not have set a record. But buyer,
seller, broker, and the transaction itself, were of equal interest, virtually
irrespective of price. The seller, Aaron Rosand, was well past retirement
age. A veteran concert player and longtime member of the violin faculty
at Philadelphia's Curtis Institute, he had bought the Kochanski in 1958
when the postwar dollar was still almighty and upper-tier instruments
were still, if only just, affordable to players. Even so, it took him ten years
to pay off the loans. Parting from it after more than half a century was
like losing a body part, Rosand told an interviewer. But he was now over
eighty—it was time to stop and to take an opportunity to steer $1.5 mil-
lion of the proceeds to Curtis. "Where the violin market will go is anyone's
guess," he said, "but I think this is where collectors are headed because
they can't trust the banks and they can't trust the market."[488]

The buyer, whoever he might be, appeared to be one of an estimated
thirty-five post-Soviet billionaires to survive a global meltdown of commodity prices. Only a year earlier, there had been as many as 101, enough
to move Gridskipper, a frolicsome international travel blog, to compile a
conspicuous consumer's guide to London.[489] For the most part, they had
become fabulously rich in oil, gas, and minerals. Some bought art, others
French vineyards, London townhouses, yachts with sixty-five-man crews,
Lear jets, and English soccer clubs. That newly monied buyers from anywhere should look to violins was itself unremarkable. They had been steady
customers since the Amatis, not to mention the Hills. What made newly
monied Russians remarkable was their extended absence from the market between the coming of World I and their country's reemergence from
the terminally distressed investment in human capital that had been the
Soviet Union. Even Tim Ingles, the head of Sotheby's instrument department, acknowledged that the new price scale was exciting.[490] Yet seen
against the great geopolitical panorama extending from the assassination

of the Grand Duke Franz Ferdinand in Sarajevo to the fall of the Berlin Wall, the Kochanski sale could also be viewed as a return to normality.

Arguably most interesting of the three was the matchmaker who brought buyer and seller together. In 2001, Peter Biddulph seemed irreparably damaged by his courtroom collision with the Segelman estate. But he had never stopped doing business, nor was it in anybody's interest that he should be given the immense burden of obligations the court had imposed on him. He was now relocated on the edge of London's garment district, some social as well as physical distance from the shop he'd been forced to give up across the street from Sotheby's. "Open Monday through Friday by appointment only," was posted on the website.

Did it matter? The prudent answer was probably yes, but—. Since the birth of the modern trade, generations of dealers had succeeded and even flourished in Paris, Stuttgart, Berlin, Vienna, Amsterdam, New York, Boston, Philadelphia, and Chicago. Dan Daley, a largely self-taught expert on baroque instruments and the Amati family, had even made a good thing of it in the tiny crossroads of DeWitt, Iowa. The world's great collections had already migrated to East Asia. Later if not sooner, the majority of the world's violinists would presumably live there, too. Yet well into a second and even third century it was still hard to beat London as a place to deal in violins.

On the other hand, Biddulph's success had always been largely independent of location. His enterprise, expertise, and world-class knack for connecting supply with demand not only traveled well. They were often his stock in trade. Soaring prices and the downsized overhead that came with his new location seemed only to favor another advantage that set him off from his peers. In court in 2001, his claim that he could not maintain his shop on a 5 percent commission was a major part of his defense. In 2009, with the General Kyd at $8 million, the Kochanski at $10 million, a downsized shop on the far side of both Oxford and Regent Streets open by appointment only, and a reported rate of 2.5 percent that none of his competitors could apparently match, he was evidently just fine.

Like the sale of the Axelrod collection, the sale of the Kochanski on the heels of the General Kyd was game theory heaven. It was a win not only for everyone involved but even for some who weren't. Rosand could console himself with a record sale. A money-strapped Curtis was ahead by $1.5 million. The buyer had two trophies to show when he returned to post-Soviet Oligarchistan. In case anyone still doubted it, Biddulph was back from violin dealer Siberia. Even the competition had reason to be grateful for two blockbuster sales that lifted the whole market.

"In this market, numbers move pretty fast," Ingles noted without overstatement in the wake of the Kochanski sale. Even as Biddulph was connecting Rosand and his billionaire buyer, Ian Stoutzker, a retired London investment banker, arts patron, and contemporary of Rosand's, was consigning the 1741 Vieuxtemps del Gesù he had owned and loved for decades to Bein & Fushi with a reported asking price of $18 million. "Can you believe that in ten years, we'll be talking about violins worth $40 million?" Ingles asked.[491]

Sooner or later, the answer would probably be yes. As undeflected by global recession as the violin market, China's growth rates also continued skyward, and 1.3 billion mainland Chinese had still to discover the joys of Strad ownership. Years before his death, Robert Bein already predicted an endgame as prices soared beyond the reach of the wealthiest private collector, and the iconic instruments that had served the trade as lodestone for at least three hundred years vanished for who knew how long in bank vaults and glass cases.

Prediction was no easier than ever. But it was clear that *a* future, if not *the* future, had begun. Each in their way, Tarisio and Biddulph demonstrated how business could be done without a shop. Like the downtown department store and the family-owned newspaper, the flagship violin shop—a fixture of the trade since Vuillaume—had been in retreat for years. The Internet only advanced the process. Even as dollar-denominated del Gesù prices achieved their eighth digit, still another grand old seller vanished when Moennig's, a Philadelphia institution since 1909, went the way of Hill's, Wurlitzer, and Hamma.[492]

Only a year after his Seoul office opened, Machold's New York shop closed, too, a victim, he claimed, of prohibitive rent. It was not long before Chicago, his new North American capital,[493] also shut down, and the walls began to close in. As consigners reported instruments gone missing and collectors said no when approached for loans, other outposts of the empire followed, until all that was left was Bremen.

In late 2007, Carsten Holm, a staff writer at *Der Spiegel,* reported how Renata Koeckert, a Munich dealer and one of the few women in the trade, had acquired a del Gesù consigned to Bein & Fushi. She then sold it to Machold, who had a buyer. But Machold, clearly short on liquidity, was painfully slow to pay. Face-to-face with a lawsuit from Fushi, Koeckert found herself on the brink of insolvency before the deal was finally set right.[494] "Since then, I don't do business with Machold," Fushi told Holm. "I won't take chances like that with Machold again," Koeckert added. It was not the first known case of reach exceeding grasp. In November 2010, Machold filed for bankruptcy in Vienna.[495] Months later, extradited from Switzerland, he was again in Austria, where he faced bankruptcy claims in the tens of millions of euros, and charges of fraud, misappropriation of property, and concealment of assets. "It's a very sad story for the whole business," said Biddulph. "He deserves it," said Axelrod.[496]

Where giants once stood, there was now a whole family of new business models. Investment counselors like Pollens, Philip Kass (formerly of Moennig's) in Philadelphia, and Staffan Borseman (formerly of the Royal Swedish Chamber Orchestra) in Copenhagen guided aspiring collectors through the trade's mysterious landscape. Emigrant Bank Fine Art Finance in New York happily accepted string instruments as collateral.

For the first time in a profession historically dominated by makers, experienced player-dealers in shops like Sean Bishop's in London and Bruno Price's and Ziv Arazi's in New York offered player-customers a practitioner's feel for their requirements as well as idiosyncrasies. Surrounded by such complementary musical enterprises as a recital hall, teaching studios, and an instrument rental on the top floor of a historic Chicago high-rise, players and brothers Julian and Stefan Hersh joined maker Michael Darnton in a joint venture, horizontally integrated to offer the student, amateur, and professional player one-stop shopping.

Housed comfortably in a leafy residential neighborhood well to the north of central London, even Florian Leonhard's shop, the closest approximation of the traditional model, could be called neoconservative. In contrast to the usual well-worn Persian carpets and nineteenth-century autographs, the shop was hung with real art, including some by Leonhardt's father. Shop and living quarters shared common space in ways that recalled the parish of S. Domenico—or might, at least, had the Cremonese patriarchs furnished their houses in the blondest Scandinavian modern, with a mini-bar off the dining room, and conducted regular seminars on as yet undiscovered masters around a table any corporate board might envy.

For nearly two hundred years, bellwether shops like Hill's and Wurlitzer had served as the graduate schools of the violin trade, where generations of aspiring makers learned to identify, compare, and distinguish the great Italian makers from the stream of old and not-so-old instruments that passed across their workspace. Where would their successors learn to do the same, and where would the future experts come from, if the big city shop went the way of the typewriter and print journalism? While still a kid, he began memorizing photos from old Lyon & Healy catalogues, said Julian Hersh. There were wonderful digital photos, said Jason Price.[497]

BOOK 3

Playing It

*F*OR ALL THE incentives to make, sell, collect, and even steal them, and the satisfaction to be gained by owning, displaying, donating, and investing in them, violins existed to be played. It would take a couple of centuries for them to sweep away the rebec, vihuela, lira da braccia, and gamba. But long before the eighteenth century it was remarkable how many people found cause to play them—in palaces, settlement houses, log cabins, lumber camps, farmsteads, frontier parlors, and city parks, and on street corners, roadsides, and ocean liners—sometimes well or sometimes badly, for love or for money, solo or in groups.

The number and variety of people attracted to the instrument was itself a wonder to behold. By the early eighteenth century, the accademia, where local gentlemen met local pros, was a fixture not only in Bologna, Mantua, and Cremona but in any self-respecting Italian town.[1] In England, where professional playing was looked down on as a trade but amateur playing was looked up to as a social accomplishment, gentlemen, including members of the royal family, imported Italians to "trot about from house to house every morning to give lessons for 2 guineas a dozen, while the winter lasts."[2] By the turn of the nineteenth century, the wave had reached Vienna, where a few thousand amateurs were happy to stay close to home, play whatever composers and publishers threw their way, and generally keep out of trouble with the authorities.

As early as 1766, Stephen Philpot, a relatively uncommon London pro, endorsed violin lessons as "an advantage to youth" and a wholesome alternative to "gaming, drinking, or other expensive diversions." Eighty years later, J. F. Hanks made the same case in a manual for Americans. "By industry and perseverance in the 'shreds and patches' of time, which other young men spend at the grog shop, gambling table or foolishly waste in dissipation and idleness, you may cultivate a neat and agreeable style of performance on the violin in all the major and some of the minor keys, and in three or four positions of the hand."[3] By the turn of the twentieth century, amateur performance in general and the string quartet in particular were as typical of middle-class life as Sunday church and McGuffey's Readers.

If the celestial civic orchestra picked section principals and concert-masters by seniority, painter Thomas Gainsborough (b. 1727), astronomer William Henry Herschel (b. 1738), and the third president of the United States, Thomas Jefferson (b. 1743), had solid claims to a front desk, while the perennial Austrian chancellor Prince Klemens von Metternich (b. 1773) was a strong candidate to succeed them. A passionate groupie and enthusiastic collector, Gainsborough could "accompany a slow movement on the harpsichord, both on the fiddle and the flute, with good taste and feeling," according to Harry Angelo, the society fencing master and a credible witness.[4] Herschel, son of a Hanoverian military bandsman, was concertmaster and soloist in Newcastle before his interest in astronomy led to the discovery of the planet Uranus. Like many Virginia gentlemen, Jefferson was a serious amateur player. He brought Corelli, Vivaldi, and Geminiani sonatas home from Paris, made sure that his nephew got violin lessons, and saw to it that his daughters and granddaughters got music lessons, too.[5] While still a junior diplomat, Metternich took his violin to Rastatt, where he arranged a concert, conducted the orchestra, and played quartets when not negotiating the claims of the Westphalian aristocracy with Napoleon. As chancellor, he took it along again on a visit to Rome two decades later, where it was conveniently available for Paganini to perform on when he was invited to drop by and get acquainted.[6]

More artists, scientists, and public figures lined up behind them. So dedicated an amateur that "le violon d'Ingres" became a synonym for any serious hobby, the artist Jean-Auguste-Dominique Ingres still held up his end of a Haydn quartet just weeks before he died at eighty in 1867. Paul Klee, the son of a music teacher and a singer, played well enough to join the Bern orchestra while still in school, then support himself as an orchestra player while an art student.[7] Henri Matisse, who played as a child, resumed in earnest as he approached fifty, at least in part for fear that he might lose his sight and have to support his family by playing on the street.[8]

Where artists led, doctors followed. Salomon (or possibly Samuel) Severin Kreisler, a Viennese physician and serious amateur, launched his son Fritz on what would be one of the violin's great careers at age four.[9] Theodor Billroth, the first surgeon to excise a rectal cancer, re-section an esophagus, and perform a laryngectomy, was also the first violinist to see and play the A major sonata by his great friend Johannes Brahms.[10] William Sunderman of Philadelpia, who pioneered the use of insulin to bring a patient out of a diabetic coma and invented a method for measuring blood glucose, not only played from age five to his death at 104 but also raised a doctor-violinist son in his image.[11] Looking back on four decades as a major league concertmaster, soloist, and chamber player, Henri Temianka acknowledged the dedication, enthusiasm, and even occasional skill of the seventy or so string players—from every specialty, including veterinary medicine—he conducted on Tuesday nights in postwar Los Angeles.[12]

Then came the scientists. Simon Ramo, a leader in microwave research who helped develop both the electron microscope and Atlas intercontinental missile, practiced bowing and fingering as methodically as he did business. Martin Kamen, discoverer of radioactive carbon-14, was good enough to play for fun with his friend Isaac Stern and hold his own in a Bartók quartet.[13] Albert Einstein—the greatest of them all—who started lessons at five and discovered the Mozart sonatas at thirteen, went on to play with colleagues at Cal Tech, and with Queen Elisabeth of Belgium and even the Juilliard Quartet when it came to visit him in Princeton in 1952.[14]

The public figures were inevitably a cut or two down from Thomas Jefferson. But they were hardly colorless. The fiddler contingent alone included the longest-serving member of the U.S. Senate, Robert Byrd of West Virginia, who recorded an album for the Library of Congress in 1977,[15] and the emblematic industrialist Henry Ford, who indulged his passion for hours at a time on one of the Stradivaris he later left to his Dearborn museum.[16] Among the violinist contingent were a Speaker of the House, an associate justice of the Supreme Court, even the thirty-seventh president, seen with violin, bow tie, and watch-the-birdie smile in a studio photo at the Nixon Presidential Library.[17] Nicholas Longworth, a Cincinnati patrician and Ohio Republican who served twenty-eight years in the House of Representatives, six of them as Speaker, played well enough to impress violinist Paul Kochanski and conductor Leopold Stokowski.[18] A generation later, Abe Fortas, a Washington insider, presidential confidant, and Supreme Court justice as Democratic as Longworth was Republican, played Sunday-night quartets with friends including Isaac Stern, Alexander Schneider, and the violist Walter Trampler.[19]

Meanwhile, the instrument found its way into very different public hands. Eugenio Pacelli, later Pope Pius XII, was an enthusiastic amateur player. Mikhail Nikolayevich Tukhachevsky—who joined the Bolsheviks in 1918, distinguished himself in the Civil War of 1919–20, became Red Army chief of staff in 1921, was elevated to marshal of the Soviet Union in 1935, and was liquidated in the Stalinist purges of 1937—

was a hobby luthier as well as a serious player and a friend of Dimitri Shostakovich.[20]

While still a young naval officer, Reinhard Heydrich, the SS general who presided at the Wannsee conference, the interagency meeting in January 1942 that produced the guidelines for the murder of Europe's Jews, was regularly invited to quartet evenings by the wife of his superior, Admiral Wilhelm Canaris, who later became head of German military intelligence. It was later reported that Heydrich even showed signs of humanity when playing.[21]

E. Millicent Sowerby, a rare-books expert at Sotheby's, recalled Hitler's foreign minister Joachim von Ribbentrop as "a keen and gifted" sixteen-year-old. He insisted that Sowerby rent a cello so that she could play trios with him and his brother.[22] "My violin went with me everywhere, throughout my life," Ribbentrop would later write while awaiting execution in 1946. "It never let me down, as so many people did."[23]

Benito Mussolini—"His Excellency, Head of Government, Duce of Fascism, Founder of the Empire," as he was known after 1936—was a violinist, too. "I wasn't an ace, but I didn't do too badly for a mediocre amateur," he said of himself.[24] Flattered when Kreisler's wife recognized the telltale abrasion beneath his jaw, he saluted her as a detective. An interviewer asked Kreisler in 1931 who the better violinist was—Mussolini or Einstein? Laughing merrily, Kreisler dodged an answer.[25]

Entertainers also got into the act. Charlie Chaplin, who played left-handed and claimed to practice four to six hours a day (though he couldn't read music), made his farewell from film in a hilariously anarchic scene with two violins and Buster Keaton at the piano.[26] Jack Benny, who was forced to change his name from Kubelsky while still a vaudeville performer to avoid confusion with the great Czech violinist Jan Kubelik, was a respectable player in real life.[27] Henny Youngman made his "Stradivari-cose" a regular prop over a six-decade career as "king of the one-liners."[28] Marlene Dietrich played until a wrist injury in late adolescence forced her to give up the violin for the musical saw.[29]

There were still more violinists in the world of letters. Honoré Balzac fiddled enthusiastically as a child, although his family wasn't quite sure what he was playing.[30] It was natural that Thomas Mann, the good bourgeois son, also learned to play. So did Arnold Gingrich, the founder and longtime editor of *Esquire*. By his own description, the great American literary critic Alfred Kazin remained a "poor but determined violinist" throughout his eighty-three-year life.[31] Frank Kermode, the great British literary critic, who took up the violin while serving in the Royal Navy, came away at least with "an increased respect for the technique of people who could really play."[32] Thomas Hardy, who came from a musical family, started young, played regularly, and bought a violin at Hill's that "became his constant companion throughout his long life."[33] Dorothy L. Sayers, the mystery novelist, who at six began with her father, considered a career as a professional.[34] Laurie Lee, whose first memoir, *Cider with Rosie*,[35] would sell six million copies, would busk his way from the Cotswolds to London and fiddle his way through Spain on the eve of civil war. This was all thanks to his mother, who invested sixpence—2.5 percent of the weekly £1/0/0 remittance from her husband—to buy him violin lessons.

While most amateurs tended to agree with G. K. Chesterton that "if a thing is worth doing, it is worth doing badly," a collateral literature and a collective memory reaching back to the nineteenth century made a credible case that people didn't have to play badly to have fun. Born Victorian middle-class in 1870, Edmund Fellowes was taking three violin lessons a week by age six. In an era when £25 would buy a hundred-acre homestead in Australia,[36] his family borrowed £100 to buy him a Nicolò Amati at Hill's. At Oxford, he played occasionally with pros, found time to rehearse between boat races, and toured with a college chorus. "I had acquired a technique sufficient for the needs of an amateur violinist," he noted carefully. It was evidently enough. In 1900 he helped organize the Oxford & Cambridge Musical Club in London, which limited membership "to university men" and survived until 1940. He estimated in his memoirs that since 1880 he had played in "five or six hundred" concerts, the majority of which were before 1920.[37]

A generation later, Catherine Drinker Bowen, a kind of Main Line Philadelphia Fellowes, took up the violin at seven so she could play Beethoven's Kreutzer Sonata with an older brother. Her father even allowed her to attend Baltimore's Peabody Conservatory and the Institute of Musical Art, which would later become the Juilliard School. She should just remember, he cautioned, "that with us music is an accomplishment, not a profession."

It comes as no surprise that her first book, an amateur's memoir, is precociously, even uniquely, sensitive to the interaction of amateur art and real life at the intersection of Main Line WASPs and immigrant Jews. Uncomfortable with "the pale black-haired youths about me," Bowen appreciated that they, unlike herself, were playing for their lives. She squabbled with a friend who worried that her daughter might take her lessons as seriously as Izzy, her teacher. Bowen's understanding aunt consoled her: Rich people, "rich women especially," don't get it, she explained. "That's why they can't respect the Izzies."[38]

Respectful to a fault, Bowen herself learned to practice while the cake was baking and the baby was napping, and even in the presence of an unmade bed. She recommended the viola with its spirit "of sturdy, self-respecting subordination" as "an excellent instrument for wives."[39] But she also pointed to "the sincerely musical wife," whose marriage, like her own, ended in divorce. "Let me show my true colors," she declared preemptively. "I would hang fifty wives, sixty husbands on a tree as against two lines of Beethoven's op. 132."[40]

Wayne Booth, as emblematic a literary critic as Frank Kermode over a thirty-year career at the University of Chicago, could only agree. As a private in World War II, he lost his original, Mormon faith. A Ford grant that paid for adult cello lessons helped him find a new one, as well as a wife who was an accomplished fiddler. They had even played with Bowen. The connection led to Bowen's brother, Henry Drinker, who invited the young couple to musicales in his vast family music room. Hundreds of lessons, summer institutes, coaching sessions, and ad hoc quartet evenings later, Booth reported in a lovably idiosyncratic memoir: "The history of cultures shows that the lives of all but the literally starving can be at least partly redeemed by the song of the amateur."[41]

By 1947, after too many evenings alone with his violin in a hotel room, Leonard Strauss, an Indianapolis incinerator manufacturer, music patron, and frequent business traveler, had reached the same conclusion. In collaboration with a kindred spirit, Helen Rice, who taught at the Brearley School on Manhattan's Upper East Side, he conceived the Amateur Chamber Music Players (ACMP), which anyone was welcome to join. From its conception until her death in 1980, Rice managed the directory and even a newsletter from her apartment.

For everyone else, the yoke was easy and the burden was light. Registrants ranked themselves by instrument and level of skill according to a tolerant honors system. On his death in 1992, Clinton B. Ford, who was both an amateur astronomer and an amateur violinist while proving that he was a very professional investor, left substantial bequests to the American Institute of Physics, the American Association of Variable Star Observers, and the ACMP, which had accepted him as its youngest member sixty-four years earlier. Ten years later, the ACMP bequest supported $2.2 million worth of grants to community music schools and youth orchestras.[42] By now, there was concern for the future. But membership figures—some six thousand in fifty states and sixty-one countries in 1965, and some five thousand in fifty states and fifty-eight countries in 2008— did not, at least, point to a precipitous decline.[43] Amateurs of all ages and venues were likely to recognize themselves in the pages of *Das stillvergnügte Streichquartett,* a winsome how-to manual produced in Munich in 1936 by local broadcaster Bruno Aulich and home publisher Ernst Heimeran.[44] By 1938, when the English-language version, *The Well-Tempered String Quartet* appeared, the original had already sold twelve thousand copies. In 2006, a twenty-first edition was still available from Amazon.

The Ill-Tempered String Quartet, Lester Chafetz's American sequel, picked up where Aulich and Heimeran had left off.[45] Chafetz, a professor of pharmacy retired from many years in private-sector research and development, looked back to a self-taught violinist father, a large, extended family that couldn't afford a piano, a Bohemian Strad recovered from a relative's attic, and school orchestra experience as "second sour note from the right." Like many of his peers, he resumed playing as an adult. In fact, he conceded, his quartet consisted of himself plus any three players available on short notice from a list of twenty. "One of the characteristics distinguishing an amateur from a professional in any field is that the amateur is inconsistent in a much wider range," he observed, with the credibility of a man who has known both sides. *"Never let a professional hear you play unless he or she is being paid by you!"* he added, italics his. "Violation of this principle may lead to severe damage to the ego."

But no one said it better than Walter Willson Cobbett, whose ninety years between 1847 and 1937 spanned two productive lives and nearly a century of eventful music history. In his first life, as cofounder of Scandinavia Belting, he made his fortune marketing a superior material for brake linings and conveyor belts.[46] In the second, he put his fortune where his passion was, with prizes for chamber music composition and performance, a collection of upper-end instruments that he loaned out to deserving players, a Free Library of Chamber Music, and a wonderfully entertaining two-volume *Cyclopedic Survey of Chamber Music.*[47]

The contributors included some of the era's best and brightest. But he reserved the article on the violin for himself. While pianists, with their huge, self-contained literature, could go it alone, "I hug to my heart an

instrument whose incompleteness is that of the human voice." Cobbett
reflected on what could well be the amateur's credo: "It has made of me
a gregarious musician, finding satisfaction in the company of my fellows,
than which no better fate can befall any man, who is not a born cynic, during the brief term of his terrestrial existence."[48]

Carl Flesch, a great teacher, a good writer, and no stranger to irony,
considered amateurs the most enviable of all players and fully deserving of
respect from professionals, not least because the concert business would go
broke without them. He asked only that they understand their limits and
be discouraged from any thought of turning pro.[49]

That still left room for respectful interaction. Even Flesch and Joachim
showed up from time to time for an evening with amateurs. "Professional
musicians will come to a musical party if there is abundance of good food
and drink, if they know they are to meet their friends, or if they are to
take an unofficial part in the program," Bowen reported from the field
in the mid-1930s.[50] "So what's in it for you?" a curious amateur asked
David Juritz, concertmaster of the London Mozart players, some sixty years
later. He liked talking to grown-ups who weren't musicians, Juritz replied.
He enjoyed playing music he didn't ordinarily get to play. He especially
enjoyed just turning the pages. Things only turned uncomfortable when
the amateurs wanted to rehearse. "If I want to rehearse," he said, "it won't
be with you."

LEARNING HOW

⌒

THERE IS NO known monument to the first violin teacher. But documentary evidence of formal teaching reaches back at least to the sixteenth century. As early as 1558, an indenture drawn up for John Hogg, a Colchester bandsman, stipulates that his new apprentice will be "enstructed, enformed, and taught" in "the vial & viallyn." A few years later, violins showed up in aristocratic household accounts and inventories with indications that the pros, employed to play them, were also expected to teach the master's kids.[51] The gentrification of civic job titles around the same time points to purposeful teaching across the Channel. Since the fourteenth century, almost any working musician between the North Sea and the Upper Rhine had been known generically as Spielmann, literally someone who played. But so had itinerant jugglers and magicians. Now, on the threshold of the seventeenth century, official usage distinguished increasingly between the Spielmann, who played by ear at weddings, taverns, and dances, and the professional, who played from notes at church, court, and civic occasions. The former, real and present as ever, was understood to be itinerant, downmarket, and more or less disreputable, despite imperial laws in 1548 and 1566 that declared him eligible for guild membership. The latter, variously known as Musicant, Instrumentist, and even Kunstgeiger (art violinist), was regularly employed, often a guild member, with all that implied, including certified attainment and a six-year apprenticeship, and regarded as a solid citizen.[52]

For many professionals, the family was the school of choice, even if the choice was often a parent's or relative's. A civic equivalent of butchers, bakers, and candlestick makers, orchestra players often learned their trade from orchestra player fathers, brothers, and uncles, who were their first, and often only, teachers.[53] Jobs passed from generation to generation.

In London, members of the Lupo family played in the court consort from 1540 until at least the English Civil War a century later.[54] In Germany, J. S. Bach, from a multigenerational musical family that was at once unique and representative, presumably learned the ABCs of string-playing from his father, a string-player, town piper, and court trumpeter, who died when his son was ten. It seems likely that Antonio Vivaldi also learned from his father, a onetime barber turned orchestra player at St. Mark's in Venice who would later be his son's colleague, traveling companion, and copyist.[55]

There were options for young talents from less remarkable families, too. Masters of the guild, known as "Honorable artisans," were qualified to teach by definition. So were clergymen like the Faenza priest in the 1650s who was presumably the young Arcangelo Corelli's first teacher, and the resident professionals who advanced his education between 1666 and 1670 at the cavernous San Petronio basilica, which was at the center of Bologna's celebrated violin culture. Church schools like San Salvator, the Jesuit gymnasium in Augsburg, existed primarily to generate priests. But they could also turn out a Leopold Mozart.[56]

While neither Corelli nor Mozart came from a musical family, both would go on to emblematic teaching careers in their own right. Corelli's method was never codified. But it was at least passed on by a brigade of protégés, both foreign and domestic, who would dominate the Italian scene for the next generation and make their way as far as Britain and could be inferred from a collection of solo sonatas still in print three hundred years later. Thanks to music publishing, the Enlightenment version of streaming video, Mozart's method, in contrast, could be bought, read, even practiced, from 1756 on.

The printing press had, in fact, connected musical supply with amateur demand since the early sixteenth century, when Venetian madrigalists discovered its possibilities.[57] By the mid-seventeenth century, German and English publishers extended its potential across a European market. As always, aspiring pros bought face-to-face instruction from masters disposed to keep their secrets in the studio. On the other hand, amateurs, who needed and wanted all the help they could get, were happy to buy their lessons over the counter.

Though at least one early manual leaves it up to the player to decide how to hold the instrument and bow, early titles like *Compendium Musicae Instrumentalis Chelicae, The Self-Instructor on the Violin,* and, best of all, *Nolens Volens or You shall learn to Play on the Violin whether you will or no* at least showed him and the occasional her how to to play a few simple tunes with variations and ornamentations and even shift positions. They had their lessons for posterity, too, confirming by their existence that the violin was on the march while also confirming the growing distance between amateurs and professionals.[58]

Yet even as those who played for love diverged from those who played for money, both pros and amateurs needed and wanted to be taught. As demand proliferated, supply followed in hot pursuit. By the middle of the eighteenth century, what began as a speculative trickle was already a stream.

The icebreaker, Francesco Geminiani's *The Art of Playing on the Violin*, appeared in London in 1751. The author, an Italian expatriate, who was possibly taught and certainly influenced by Corelli, had already lived nearly four decades in Britain as performer, composer, impresario, music publisher, and even art dealer. The first title of its kind to address the aspiring professional at nearly every level of performance, it was published at the author's expense. But it was soon cited, imitated, translated into French and German, though not Italian, and reprinted as far away as Boston, where a publisher produced *Abstract of Geminiani's Art of Playing on the Violin*, with subtitles where he thought they might be helpful, but minus the graphics and musical examples.[59]

Though even the most dedicated do-it-yourselfer was likely to need the help of an on-site teacher, the book's conception is as practical as it is high-minded. Almost fifty of the seventy-one pages are reserved for drills and practice pieces, which presumably were lesson-tested and designed to get the contemporary reader from the sea level of basic theory to the High Sierra—arpeggios, ornamentations, higher positions, and double stops—of contemporary technique.[60]

Five years later, Leopold Mozart's *Versuch einer gründlichen Violinschule*, translated as *Treatise on the Fundamental Principles of Violin-Playing*, appeared in Salzburg. Like Geminiani, he published it himself. But it had already gone through second and third editions before the author's death in 1787, and there was a posthumous edition in 1800. Two centuries later, new editions were still appearing. Meanwhile, it was translated into Dutch, possibly into unauthorized French and Russian, and acknowledged by contemporaries, including Goethe's friend Carl Friedrich Zelter, as a classic.

The many reproduced engravings, contrasting a player doing things right with a player doing things wrong, already constitute a selling point. But the text—intelligent, articulate, and relentlessly practical—is the

book's real comparative advantage. "Here are the practice pieces," a characteristic passage announces. "The less appealing, the more I like it: and so
I thought I'd make them that way."[61]

Successive chapters—on reading notes, rests, and tempo signatures;
how to bow and finger one, two, and three notes at time; when and how
to shift positions; the right and wrong way of dealing with ornamentations—leave no doubt that the author knows his way around the trees and
leaves. But 12 chapters and some 275 pages of text make it just as clear
that his main concern is a forest where too few people enter together and in
tune, observe key signatures and tempo indications, respect the composer's
intentions, and play, so far as possible, the way a singer sings.

A third addition to the canon, this one French, appeared in Paris in
1761 from an author familiar with both Geminiani and Mozart.[62] Though
born Joseph-Barnabé Saint-Sevin, he was known as M^r l'Abbé le fils, the
son, because his father and uncle, distinguished cellists who performed
in clerical collars as church musicians, were known respectively as l'Abbé
l'aîné and l'Abbé le cadet, the elder and the younger.

Ironically, his career and lifestyle could hardly have been less clerical.
Yet another prodigy who studied with his father, he began to play professionally at eleven, when his audition for the orchestra of the Comédie
Française made such an impression that the great Jean-Marie Leclair took
him on as student and protégé. Two years later, the pubescent Abbé performed a Leclair duet with his fellow virtuoso in training, Pierre Gaviniès,
at the Concert Spirituel, pre-Revolutionary Paris's Carnegie Hall. Soon
afterward, he cracked his father's wardrobe, took his savings, and headed
for Bordeaux on the next stagecoach. Understandably upset, his father had
him chased down and locked up by order of the Comte de Maurepas, secretary of state for the royal household. But he soon had second thoughts and
appealed to Cardinal de Fleury, prime minister in all but name, to have
the young man released so that he "could continue his exercises."

One can only imagine the family conversation on the son's return to
Paris. But at sixteen, the young Abbé auditioned successfully for a place
in the orchestra of the Opéra and his career took off. For the next decade,
he appeared at the Concert Spirituel as a frequent soloist in contemporary
pieces, including *Spring* from Vivaldi's *Four Seasons*. Meanwhile, he produced a steady stream of his own music that was dedicated to cultivated
amateurs and patrons.[63]

He was still in his midthirties, with more than twenty years of professional playing behind him, when his book appeared. Apart from the obligatory dedication, the text reads like the user's manual it is: "The violin should rest on the clavicle in such a way that the chin is to the side of the fourth string." But the reader then realizes that it just happens to be the first instruction on record of how the violin has been held ever since. The description of the bow hold, the use of ten positions and what are now known as half-positions, as well as the discussion of harmonics, both natural and artificial, are new frontiers, too.[64] Contemporaries considered it a classic. Looking back across two centuries, Boyden considered it a watershed twice over, not only between the old and the modern bow, but also the Italian past and the Franco-global future.[65]

The mystery of why there was nothing Italian to match it was all the more curious, given the breadth and depth of Italian influence, the ubiquitousness and celebrity of Italian players and instruments, and the long shadow of Giuseppe Tartini, a musician of such celebrity that he was practically a stop on the Grand Tour.[66] Virtuoso, composer, and teacher, he also wrote a lot, including a book-length manuscript, whose French title, *Traité des Agrémens*, a treatise on ornamentations, is not exactly wrong. But the Italian title, *Regole per ben suonar il Violino*, or "principles for playing the violin well," comes considerably closer to what the author had in mind. By Boyden's estimate, it might have been written anytime between 1728 and 1754.[67] The questions were what became of it and why had he never published it.

Boyden surmised that at least part of the failure reflected a reluctance to spill professional beans in a culture that privileged the relationship of teacher and pupil as it did the relationship of priest and communicant and considered teaching methods the equivalent of trade secrets. But changing fashion also played its part. By the turn of the nineteenth century, the Tourte bow was in and Tartini was out. If no one had found his manuscripts, it was very likely because no one was looking for them. Yet contemporaries, who wanted to know them, did. By 1756, Leopold Mozart, with a bow to "a great Italian master," had already incorporated a piece of Tartini in his own book. A full French edition, presumably translated from a manuscript brought back to Paris by a French pupil, appeared in 1771, the year after Tartini's death.[68]

Eight years later, another Tartini manuscript, "A Letter from the late Signor Tartini to Signora Maddalena Lombardini (now Signora Sirmen), published as an important Lesson to Performers on the Violin," appeared in London in a bilingual edition.[69] It was only a few pages long. The translator, Charles Burney, was Georgian England's favorite commentator on things musical. Dated 1760 and nominally addressed to a readership of one, the text must already have been in the public domain for some time.

How it got there is again anybody's guess. But it seems to have originated as Tartini's reply to a query about how and what to practice from a gifted fifteen-year-old who was eager to study with the sixty-eight-year-old master as soon as the governors and principal of her Venetian boarding school would let her leave—escorted, of course—to attend another institution in Padua. An inquiry about how to approach the study of physics, addressed to Albert Einstein at the Institute for Advanced Study in Princeton by a gifted undergraduate in New Brunswick, would be an approximate parallel. Classic in the nicest way, Tartini's reply is still instructive in what it says and exemplary for how he says it. Teachers then and since have made a priority of mastering the bow. But few have done it with such graciousness, precision, and economy, or with an apology for not having answered earlier and an invitation to write back with any further questions.

By the end of the nineteenth century, a pedagogical literature that had begun as a creek approximated the mighty Volga. A selected list of schools, methods, studies, études, guides, exercises, and caprices included thirty landmark titles, which had been variously published between 1751 and 1895 in London, Augsburg, Paris, Rome, Vienna, Berlin, Milan, Leipzig, and Prague.[70] Pirate editions, plagiarisms, and eclectically customized knockoffs added 166 more.[71] Between 1769 and 1905, their authors and editors included Anon.; Elias Howe, a self-taught fiddler, music publisher, supplier of drums to the Union Army and proprietor of Boston's flagship music store; and the engagingly named Septimus Winner, son of a Philadelphia violin maker and music publisher, as well as composer of the wildly popular "Ten Little Injuns." Ureli Corelli Hill, the first president of the New York Philharmonic Society, also got into the act.

By 1986, the pas de deux of supply and demand had led to at least sixteen more original methods, with publishers in Paris, Berlin, London, as well as Englewood Cliffs and Princeton, New Jersey. By the beginning of the twenty-first century, classes and masses, amateurs from entry-level to advanced, the rich and needy, the secular and godly, beginners as young as three, and aspiring middle-class Asians from South Korea to Singapore could choose from a buffet of print, disk, tape, film, YouTube clips, and streaming video.

PRACTICALLY ANYWHERE, POPULAR music education tended to be a trade-off between utility and civic improvement. But serious experimentation began, as so often, in France. The basic issue—whether music was an art, a science, or a language, and if so whose—went back to the Reformation, if not to the Greeks.[72] But as in so many areas of national life, the Revolution turned theory to practice. As thrashed out among philosophers, litterateurs, mathematicians, essayists and polemicists, the original question was something only an encyclopédiste could love.[73] The policy arguments, on the other hand, were as simple as "Allons, enfants de la patrie": a great nation accustomed to imports and outsourcing needed its own national style, music, and musicians. The capital of revolutionary France needed an opera that wasn't Italian. A program of national festivals, understood as religion by other means, needed tunes the newly minted Citoyen could sing, ideally *con amore*, and a musical militia to play them. Like the festivals, plans for a nationwide music ed program, including eight designated music schools, soon lost their glow. So did designs on the Opéra. But long after all else had vanished, the capstone reform, the one-of-a-kind Conservatoire, was still standing with quasi-papal authority for the education of composers and performers,[74] including violinists as young as nine. A little less than two hundred years later, China's Cultural Revolution would resume where France stopped and end with a somewhat similar outcome.

The British, as usual, did it their way. As early as 1839, a mix of commerce, self-improvement, and high-minded paternalism in a form of group instruction made in Leipzig found a home at the Birkbeck Mechanics Institute. By the 1880s, in Birmingham alone some two hundred adult registrants were reported to show up for violin classes with forty violins among them. The project was so successful that private teachers felt threatened.

In 1897, the J. G. Murdoch Company, a London-based music publisher and instrument maker, heard opportunity knock and saw its chance to do well by doing good.[75] On a tip from T. Mee Pattison, its music adviser, it organized the Maidstone School Orchestra Association, which they named for the town in Kent whose All Saints National School was the first of some three thousand to sign up. Equipped with Murdoch teaching materials, taught by Murdoch-recruited teachers, outfitted with Murdoch instruments they could buy in installments at a shilling a week for thirty weeks, they were eligible for Murdoch festivals, certificates, medals, and even scholarships if they worked long and well enough. Some 400,000 schoolchildren, 10 percent of Britain's entire state, or public, school enrollment, had signed up for classes at the program's peak.[76] The program lasted until 1939, when the schools were dispersed and the teachers drafted. In 1943, the company itself went belly-up. But classes resumed when the war was over, though the Ministry of Education was now in charge.

Yet it was the United States where Maidstone left lasting foot and fingerprints. In fact, ad hoc string classes went back to the 1840s, when Lewis Benjamin, an enterprising New York singing teacher, and his son added instrument teaching to their repertory in countless academies and violin schools as far west as Pittsburgh, while making their money on books and instruments. A half century later, Benjamin organized or inspired so-called Children's Carnivals. With orchestras in the hundreds and choruses in the thousands, they drew large audiences in Brooklyn, Philadelphia, and other large cities. By the turn of the twentieth century, school orchestras had shown up in school districts as far west as Los Angeles.

But it was 1908 before Charles H. Farnsworth, a professor of music education at Columbia Teachers College, discovered Maidstone while touring Europe, and the future began in earnest. Immediately on his return, Farnsworth reported his discovery to the annual meeting of the Music Teachers National Association. Albert G. Mitchell, assistant director of music for the Boston public schools, was so inspired by what he heard that he took off to see the British scene for himself. On his return in 1911, the school board let him offer classes before and after school. Three years later, Mitchell's classes had made it into the regular curriculum, and from there to schools around the country. In 1918, Joseph Maddy, the city's first supervisor for instrumental music, persuaded George Eastman, who did for cameras what Henry Ford did for cars, to donate $10,000 worth of instruments to the Rochester, New York, schools.[77] By the early 1930s, Dorothy DeLay's hometown of Medicine Lodge, Kansas, with 4,000 people, 400 high school students, and 5 violin teachers, was so proud of its high school orchestra that the community baked cakes, washed cars, and mowed lawns to bus it to Philip Greeley Clapp's annual summer clinic at the University of Iowa.[78]

Meanwhile, a very different music education program was taking shape in what claimed to be the worker's fatherland. An unanticipated by-product of a revolution that considered itself in every way heir to the French, it was as elitary, meritocratic, and inherently conservative as anything devised in Napoleonic Paris, let alone imperial St. Petersburg. In 1932, on the initiative of the piano professor, Alexander Goldenweiser, fifteen gifted children were allowed to take their lessons at the Moscow conservatory. With support from the violin professors, Lev Zeitlin and Abram Yampolsky, the program had evolved within a few years from a "special children's group" to a Central Music School; and it would eventually serve as a model for twenty-three more around the country. By 1962, enrollment had stabilized at 390, some 200 from Moscow itself. Its alumni not only included many of the Soviet Union's, but the world's, best and brightest. Children of alumni were prominent among the current registrants.[79] But the same could be said of any Oxford college, Juilliard, Yale, or Harvard.

While the institution was new, there was nothing particularly new about the curriculum or pedagogy. The goal was neither more nor less than highest-level professionalism. Prodigies were rare, but prodigiousness was not the point. Admission, by audition only, began at age seven, with instruction in general courses as well as music in classes no larger than twenty to twenty-five. It was estimated that one applicant in five was actually admitted. The dropout ratio over the school's eleven-year course appeared to be about the same. Those who made it through qualifying exams after the first, fourth, and eighth years would presumably go on to conservatories. As music's equivalent of Olympic athletes, they would then emerge from the tunnel as world-class professionals and People's Artists, ready to take their chances in regional, national, and international competitions. Any graduate looked forward in principle to regular employment and adequate income. But winners looked forward to state-managed concert and recording careers, possible foreign travel, and the expectation that the next generation of teachers would be themselves.[80]

Deeply impressed by what he saw in Moscow, Yehudi Menuhin, one of the twentieth century's supreme prodigies, returned to England to create his own special school in Surrey with private funding for about sixty, ages eight to eighteen.[81] The scepter'd isle had not exactly been known as a demi-paradise for early childhood music educators. But it had plenty of experience with elite educational institutions. A generation later, a cohort of players directly or indirectly associated with the Menuhin School— Nigel Kennedy, Daniel Hope, Tasmin Little, Nicola Benedetti—made the first strong case for a British violin school as competitive internationally as British soccer teams and rock bands, though two of the four, like Menuhin himself, were either immigrants or from immigrant families.

Decades passed before it occurred to anyone that there might be alternative ways to get violinists past entry-level and up to speed. But innovation once more began with a national revolution. This time, it was Japan, and went back to the 1860s, when a critical mass of foreign challenge and domestic response set off a chain reaction of modernizing reforms that would make themselves felt around the world.

Among the immediate casualties was Masaharu Suzuki, one of nearly two million hereditary warrior-bureaucrats, called samurai, unexpectedly faced with extinction. His strategy was at once modern, traditional, and ingenious. He learned to make samisen, a kind of indigenous banjo. He then passed on the business to his son, Masakichi, who learned English, switched production to violins, fathered seven sons and five daughters, and got rich. In 1908, Masakichi was elected to the National Assembly. In 1910, he spent five months in Britain and Europe, where he may or may not have heard of Maidstone and possibly saw less of Markneukirchen than he wished.[82] In 1917, the emperor honored him with the Order of the Rising Sun.

Meanwhile, his third son, Shinichi, born in 1898, pitched for his high school baseball team, internalized Tolstoy, studied Zen, and discovered, while listening to Mischa Elman play Schubert's "Ave Maria" on the family Victrola, that what he had assumed were money-making toys could also make music.[83] The experience was life-changing, he reported in a memoir decades later.[84] He first tried teaching himself to play. A fortunate connection to Nobu Kohda, who played the Japanese premiere of the Mendelssohn concerto in 1896, then led to lessons with her sister, Ko Ando, the first Japanese violinist to study in Berlin.[85]

In 1920, an invitation to join a family friend and patron on a world tour led Shinichi too to Berlin, where he talked himself into private lessons with Karl Klingler, a pupil of Joachim's and a professor at the Berlin Conservatory. As a man who would show uncommon character in the Nazi years, he was obviously no racist. The challenge of a seventeen-year-old beginner from the other end of the world may well have struck his fancy. In country whose currency was already in free fall and en route to record inflation, payment in real money may also have had its appeal.

What was in it for Suzuki was clear enough. For the next four years, he seems to have played scales and études.[86] In the spring of 1923, he applied for admission to the conservatory. Of forty-four candidates, twelve were accepted, including a young Jewish woman from Tblisi. But while Suzuki came close, the not-so-young man from Nagoya wasn't among them.[87] He nonetheless continued with Klingler till 1928, when he returned home with a German wife and a Vuillaume violin he had to sell a year later after his father fell victim to the Wall Street crash.

The next fifteen years were devoted about equally to survival and gestation of what would become a new school of pedagogy. He played recitals. He joined his brothers in a string quartet, possibly the country's first to broadcast on the radio. He took students. He accepted an invitation to teach at the Imperial Music School in Tokyo. There was also the war to cope with, and his brother's request to help the family factory make seaplane pontoons. But what mattered most were thoughts on early childhood education, going back to his years in Berlin.

What Suzuki himself called "talent education," and the rest of the world would soon call the Suzuki method, was a clever improvisation on language acquisition. Children would learn the violin early just as they learned to speak early and play from memory in graded classes. A parent would be involved in their lessons and practice. The teaching process was essentially imitative. Children would learn to read music only after they first learned to play it. Then came a sequence of exercises that eventually grew to ten books, beginning with tunes, many of them familiar to any German three-year-old, targeted at specific points of technique. "Talent education merely applies the method of learning one's native language to education in music or some other subject," he told the International Society for Music Education in 1963.[88]

In 1955, a Suzuki concert in Tokyo was duly noted by the national media, members of the royal family, and various embassy personnel. By the early 1960s, Suzuki recitals were taken to heart by such A-list visitors as the great Spanish cellist Pablo Casals and the Belgian virtuoso Arthur Grumiaux. Finally, in March of 1964, a ripple of what had begun between Tokyo and Kyoto a century earlier reached the Grand Ballroom of the Sheraton Hotel in Philadelphia. A show-and-tell demonstration by Suzuki and a cadre of ten students, ages six to thirteen, at the Music Educators National Conference created a sensation. "Playing without a conductor and using no score, the youngsters were a living testimonial to the validity of Suzuki's unorthodox teaching method," *Newsweek* reported. "This is amazing," pronounced Ivan Galamian of the Juilliard School, the closest the church of violin teachers came to a pope.[89] "A new phenomenon in teaching has emerged in recent years," Henri Temianka noted a few years later in his memoirs. "Rumor has it that Suzuki will next enroll pregnant housewives, so that not a moment need be wasted when a baby is born."[90]

It was ironic that countries that once exported musical infrastructure now imported it from Japan just as they imported Japanese cars and consumer electronics. But it was just as ironic that it was the American breakthrough that finally brought the prophet honor in his own country. In the mid-1950s, there were some thousand little Suzuki violinists in Japan. In 1960, there were about 3,000. By the early 1990s, as the bubble economy began to lose air, there were 15,000, ages three to fifteen, plus some 15,000 Suzuki pianists, 600 cellists, and 200 flutists, according to Akio Mizuno, the director of Suzuki's Tokyo office.[91] A color photo on Mizuno's office wall showed the master and his wife with the emperor, the empress, and the former board chair of the Sony Corporation.

By the time Suzuki died in 1998, his life and career were themselves a lesson. He had been awarded the highest decoration of the Federal Republic of Germany, declared a national treasure by the emperor of Japan, and named with ten other Japanese, including filmmaker Akira Kurosawa, industrialist Eiji Toyoda, General Hideki Tojo, and Admiral Isoroku Yamamoto, on a list of a thousand "Makers of the Twentieth Century." An estimated eight thousand Suzuki-trained teachers were teaching Suzuki pupils in as many as forty countries.[92]

There was no shortage of poster-child graduates, beginning with the very first, Takako Nishizaki (born in 1944), who started in Nagoya at three. At eighteen, she talked herself into New York's Juilliard School, where she competed for prizes with classmates Itzhak Perlman and Pinchas Zukerman. She then moved on to a career that inspired her spouse, Klaus Heymann, to create Naxos Records, one of the late twentieth century's most successful enterprises.[93] In Iowa City, Iowa, William Preucil Jr. started at five with his mother, herself an Eastman Conservatory graduate and at least a third-generation violin teacher as well as a Suzuki pioneer. He grew up to be first violinist of the Cleveland Quartet and concertmaster of the Cleveland Orchestra.

But Suzuki's goals always extended far beyond music. Donald Becker, director of the Suzuki Institute of Boston, who spent three years with Suzuki in the 1980s, recalled that he had only twice seen Suzuki angry.

Once, in a country where tipping is uncommon, was when Becker failed to tip a cabdriver. The other was when describing how war damaged children and families.[94] "Without good people, you cannot have good nations," he wrote in a 1973 essay.[95] Mizuno, the director of the Tokyo office, took dutiful pride in the battalions of Suzuki alumni who now populated and often led major orchestras. But good people was what it was really about, he emphasized.

Good people is not the easiest demographic to track. In Tokyo it seemed to mean children, about 70 percent of whom were girls of upwardly mobile, salaried employees, a third of whom worked for large companies. In Boston, on the other hand, where Becker began teaching in 1977, it meant Roxbury, a neighborhood with an African-American majority and a growing Hispanic minority. On his return from Japan, he resumed where he had left off, working eight hours a week as a security guard, while collaterally teaching private students like Martin Himmelfarb, a Boston attorney, his eight-year-old son, and his eighty-two-year-old father.[96] By 2008, his constituency had extended to 120 kids from Boston's Haitian community and Stephen Jay Gould, the Harvard paleontologist and baseball nut, and his alumni included an opera singer, a Juilliard School student, a basketball coach, and a defendant facing a life sentence on federal drug charges.[97]

Roberta Guaspari, a divorced mother of two and a blue-collar kid from Rome, New York, had never had a private teacher herself until she matriculated on scholarship at Syracuse University. In 1981, she created a Suzuki program for first and second graders at three East Harlem magnet schools. Admission was by lottery, with three times more applicants than places. Within a few years, the program's success had turned Guaspari into a beacon. Adversity then turned her into a hero. In 1991, New York's Board of Education cut funding. Guaspari persuaded the board to let her continue with her own financing. Her appeal for support attracted media attention a presidential candidate might envy. "Roberta is not teaching children to play the violin," said Itzhak Perlman, who volunteered to help after watching Guaspari on TV. "She's teaching them how to be doctors and lawyers, and how to have dreams."

Two years later, much of the New York fiddle community—Perlman, Isaac Stern, Midori, the Kavafian sisters, Arnold Steinhardt and Michael Tree of the Guarneri Quartet, the jazz players Diane Monroe and Karen Briggs, the fiddler Mark O'Connor—turned up for Fiddlefest, a $1,000-a-plate concert-dinner-reception benefit for Guaspari's project at

Carnegie Hall.[98] "The graying of our present audience is on everybody's mind," said Steinhardt, "so there wasn't a musician who didn't say 'yes.'"

Guaspari meanwhile turned her program into Opus 118 Harlem School of Education with help from the Petra Foundation, established only a few years earlier in memory of a German-American civil rights activist to honor unsung heroes. In 1996, Opus 118 survived adversity when a rainstorm ruined its instrument collection. But in 2009, it also knew triumph, when it was invited to play at the Children's Inaugural Ball in Washington.[99]

In October 2010, the John D. and Catherine T. MacArthur Foundation awarded Sebastian Ruth, founder of Community MusicWorks of Providence, Rhode Island, one of its five-year "genius" grants. Weeks later, his project made it to the White House after being declared winner of a National Arts and Humanities Youth Award. Like Guaspari's project, Ruth's offered stringed instrument instruction to kids who couldn't afford it in a town where the school system had long abandoned it. But unlike Guaspari's project, Ruth's quartet, his associates, and their students also performed for a community almost untouched by the music they played, with a supplementary menu of blues, hip-hop, Friday night discussions, occasional field trips to area concerts, and spaghetti dinners. "We're not searching for genius," Ruth told the New Yorker's Alex Ross. "We're relating music-making to the community."[100]

The idea came to Ruth in his undergraduate days as a music and education student at Brown University. By his early thirties, he had leveraged a $10,000 grant into an annual budget of $750,000, a staff of thirteen, and two storefronts—one for office use, the other as rehearsal space. En route to the White House, his constituency of 115 was 51 percent Latino, 16 percent African-American, ages seven to eighteen, with a waiting list slightly larger.[101] He worried that the neighborhood might be on the threshold of gentrification. But he savored the paradox inadvertently proposed by a colleague's mother. She loved his program, she told an interviewer, because the classical music he played was "for people who have class." Class was the very thing he wanted to avoid, Ruth mused. "But we're both moving in the same direction," he added hopefully. "We are both moving toward Violin."[102]

Rosemary Nalden, a London violist with an established career, proved that what worked in Boston worked even in Soweto. In 1992, she learned from the BBC of a struggling string school in Johannesburg's heavily black satellite. She first mobilized 120 colleagues to play and pass the hat—*busk* in British English—at sixteen London rail stations. Then she took off for South Africa to hand over £6,000 in proceeds. That should have been that. But the scene on arrival caused her to reconsider. "After years of sitting in a viola section, there was something in me that needed to be the boss," she said.[103]

After a few years of commuting between London and Johannesburg, she moved to South Africa full time. The Buskaid Soweto String Project was launched in 1997. The idea was in part to teach Western classical music with a bracing admixture of the local idiom. But in a corner of the world where nearly every child had experienced or witnessed AIDS or violence, and Nalden herself was mugged twice, it was also to keep a cadre of about eighty enthusiastic, gifted, endangered, hungry kids between age four and their early twenties off some of the world's meanest streets. "I think there are some youngsters who, I would risk saying, are alive now, who might not be alive if it weren't for Buskaid," Nalden told an interviewer in 2010.[104] Older kids tutored younger kids. Staff teachers tutored trainee teachers. Countless applicants were turned away for lack of money and staff.

By the end of its first decade, Buskaid was a registered charity in South Africa and Britain, with corporate sponsors including De Beers, the international diamond companies, and private sponsors including the actress Gillian Anderson. It was en route to an endowment that would make it self-sufficient. It enjoyed international media attention.[105] By this time, Nalden and her young players had performed for Queen Elizabeth II and their own former president, Nelson Mandela. They had played under Nalden's old boss, the conductor John Eliot Gardiner, at the London Proms. They had toured the United States from New York to Los Angeles, where Nalden batted down accusations of Eurocentrism. "Are people saying that blacks shouldn't play classical?" she demanded. "If that's the case, maybe they shouldn't play cricket, talk on cell phones, or wear suits."[106] Their project had spun off and supported a variety of other township music projects. It had even sent two members to study at the Royal Northern Conservatory in Manchester.

Most remarkable of all was Venezuela, a country of 26 million, with a conflicted history and huge oil reserves. A major drug entrepôt, according to the United Nations Office of Drugs and Crime,[107] its income inequity and political instability were remarkable even by Latin American standards. The homicide rate in its capital, Caracas, matched and even challenged the rates of Mogadishu and Ciudad Juárez. Yet somehow, the country was home to the Fundacíon del Estado para el Sistema Nacional de las Orquestas Juveniles y Infantiles de Venezuela, a nationwide music education program universally referred to as El Sistema. The music pedagogical equivalent of a health delivery system, with multiple agencies, services, and providers, its scale and quality moved visitors to tears, served as a role model to much of Latin America, and inspired much of the world.

Suzuki was decentralized private enterprise. Opus 118, Buskaid, and Community MusicWorks, where the schools had either thrown music education overboard as ballast or ignored it altogether, were islands of private enterprise in a sea of public sector default. El Sistema, born in 1975, began in a Caracas parking garage. By 2010, an ad hoc ensemble of 11 had grown into a nationwide program with a national children's orchestra of 337, a network of 184 so-called nuclei, a staff of nearly 1,000, an army of teachers and 368,000 participants. Only two years earlier, it had been a mere 265,000. In fact, its creator told Spain's second-largest daily paper, it aspired to a million.[108]

"The most important thing happening in music anywhere in the world," declared Sir Simon Rattle, conductor of the Berlin Philharmonic, who had himself played in Britain's National Youth Orchestra as a teenager.[109] Foreign players from the Baltimore Symphony, the Berlin Philharmonic, and the Leipzig Gewandhaus came to see and coach. But proposals for a permanent institutional presence were politely declined. On the contrary, El Sistema proposed to export its own message.

In 2009, a national center for an El Sistema USA was established at the New England Conservatory in Boston, with a one-year program, whose fellows were to study El Sistema both at home and in its natural habitat, then return and practice at home what they learned in Venezuela. Within two years, programs were up and running throughout the United States in Atlanta, Georgia; Philadelphia, Pennsylvania; Durham, North Carolina; and Juneau, Alaska, though the New England Conservatory, fearing mission and above all budget creep at the expense of its own priorities, canceled further affiliation with the national center.[110]

Enveloped in aphorisms of almost Zen-like elusiveness and ambiguity like "*tocar y luchar*" (perform and struggle) and "*ser no ser todavía*" (to be and not yet to be), El Sistema was not easy to explain to an outsider. Comparison with Suzuki, Opus 118, Buskaid, and Community Music-Works helped, but only to a point. For all of them, music was essentially

added value, a means to an end. Like Suzuki, El Sistema echoed with
reminiscences of the Enlightenment, of Friedrich Schiller, Wilhelm von
Humboldt, Mozart's Temple of Sarastro, and even Plato's Republic, where
arts education was civic education and the link between great music and
good people was a truth held to be self-evident. Like Opus 118, Buskaid,
and Community MusicWorks, El Sistema targeted the marginalized and
underserved. Like Suzuki and Buskaid, it owed much of its legitimacy and
success at home to the validation of patrons and audiences abroad, high-
profile attention from global media like the *Times* of London, the *Financial
Times*, the *New York Times*, the BBC, and CBS, and the success of alumni
like Edicson Ruiz, a bass player who auditioned successfully for the Berlin
Philharmonic at nineteen, and Gustavo Dudamel, a onetime violinist who
was named conductor of the Los Angeles Philharmonic at twenty-six. The
earthly payoffs were familiar, too. Nobody needed a Sherlock Holmes to
find Suzuki grads in a class of Harvard freshmen. The claim that El Sistema
grads were likelier than others to finish school and go to college—even that
they comprised 75 percent of Venezuelan medical students—was believ-
able. The Inter-American Development Bank calculated that for every dollar it invested in El Sistema, it got back $1.68 in social dividends.[111]

What was never in doubt was who made El Sistema happen. Born
in 1939, José Antonio Abreu—pronounced in three syllables—earned his
PhD in petroleum economics at twenty-two. Three years later, he graduated from the national conservatory as a keyboard player. For several years
he served as a member of the Venezuelan Congress before returning to
the academy to teach economics and planning. In 1983, he served briefly
as minister of culture. El Sistema was clearly his life's work. Austere as
an El Greco, he assured his earliest players that they would change the
world. A generation later, an acorn of recognition had turned into a mighty
oak of honors from Sweden, Japan, Canada, Italy, the United States, the
United Kingdom, Germany, and the Venezuelan Jewish community, as
well as from UNESCO, the World Economic Forum, and TED (Technology, Entertainment, Design), an international conference series, whose
eighteen-minute presentations by selected visionaries, Abreu's included,
were an Internet favorite.

A fortuitous conjunction of artist and material seemed an essential part
of his success. While nationalism, high culture, oil wealth, and endemic
poverty could be found in many countries, there were relatively few where
all four converged as they did in Venezuela. It was Abreu's genius to see

opportunity where others not only failed to see it, but also probably never thought to look for it. Within days, the legendary eleven, who were present at the creation in 1975, had reportedly doubled and tripled. Abreu was showing them off to dignitaries within a month and taking them on tour within a year. It is hard to imagine that his parliamentary career had any larger purpose than winning friends and support for El Sistema. In an interview with a Russian musicologist decades later, he pointed to statutory, even constitutional, guarantees of a musical education for the nation's young.[112] Within two years of its creation, his youth orchestra returned triumphantly from a competition in Scotland. From there on, El Sistema would enjoy full public funding.

That the money came not from the Ministry of Culture, where Abreu himself served briefly as minister, but from the Ministry of Social Welfare, was further evidence of his political virtuosity. But so was a 1982 UNESCO grant, ingeniously invested in seven trainee violin makers. Five years later, they were ready to train more themselves. By 1998, when Hugo Chávez, a former paratroop officer, acceded to the presidency of a new, "Fifth Republic," El Sistema had not only survived, but also flourished under multiple regimes from right to left. In 2007, after Abreu's orchestra returned from ecstatic receptions at London's Royal Albert Hall, Chávez let it be known that Venezuela was entering a golden age of arts and culture and increased support to $29 million, something over a hundred dollars per participant, in an oil-rich country where a third of the population was living below the poverty line.[113]

According to the American arts educator Eric Booth, who observed El Sistema with informed fascination, participants begin to sing and play as young as toddlers in ensembles that meet four hours each day, five to seven days a week for full rehearsals, sectionals, and private lessons. The programs are cost-free for everyone, and advanced students are even paid small stipends to help with family expenses. Like anywhere, there are dropouts. But no one who wants in is turned away, and motivated players move on and up in a network that includes sixty children's orchestras, two hundred youth orchestras, thirty adult orchestras, and peaks in the Simón Bolívar Youth Orchestra.

Received in Los Angeles like a rock star, Dudamel assumed responsibility for three orchestras, including the Bolívar and YOLA (Youth Orchestra of Los Angeles), as well as a Mahler series. His image and LA Phil could be seen and heard on high-definition theater screens across the country.

Would they love it in 80 percent Hispanic, 20 percent African-American South LA as they loved it in Caracas? If they could make it there, could they make it anywhere? If not, it would certainly not be for deficient commitment, and Watch This Space was a prudent answer.

IT WAS ONE of history's little ironies that the conservatory, the classic institution of musical higher learning, also began as a marriage of utility and civic improvement. It was ironic too that the primordial Latin mission statement said nothing about music.

The institution dated back to the sixteenth century, when a whole new class of charitable foundations was created in Naples as well as Venice. Known as conservatories because they took in orphans and foundlings, they made it a part of their mission to train the children of needy families in reading, religion, and useful trades. For the most part, useful was understood as manual. But it was clear from early on that music was a useful accessory to religious services and, in at least one documented case, to institutional fund-raising.[114]

In a culture where church holidays could number in the dozens and civic holidays in the hundreds, the conservatories found their seawall against a rising tide of operating expenses in the demand for musicians from oratories, confraternities, private academies, and the opera. From there on, the teaching of music acquired a life of its own. By the middle of the seventeenth century, four Neapolitan foundations had transformed themselves from shelters for foundlings and orphans into music schools.

The Venetian institutions were similar in many ways but radically different in others. A confluence of Rome, Byzantium, and classical antiquity, Venice was also a republic, with a powerful sense of identity and a well-developed civil society. In one way or another, the *ospedali*, as they were officially known, were a representation of all of these. Centrally located, built to be noticed, governed by citizen boards, and elaborately organized, they were also generously financed from a variety of sources, including lotteries, banking, even gondola revenues. As in Naples, music and Catholicism met in the *ospedali*, too. But in Venice the chorus was made up of girls, and they performed on site rather than in other people's churches. With twenty to forty memorial masses a day plus almost daily concerts, there was demand enough to keep them busy.[115]

As Naples became a brand, the *ospedali* of Venice became an A-list tourist destination. In 1703, the Pietà, which took instrumental music especially seriously, hired the twenty-five-year-old Antonio Vivaldi as violin teacher, with collateral responsibility for instrument acquisition and maintenance. By 1716, when he was appointed music director, he was a European celebrity, and the Pietà was on the map. Decades later, with the sun sinking rapidly on six hundred years of glorious civic history, it continued to field an orchestra of fifty-six, including sixteen violinists. With six violinists, three violists, thirteen violin students, and six cellists, it was downsized but still recognizable in 1807, a decade after the sun had set.[116]

First created as a diocesan home for lepers and beggars, the Mendicanti went back to 1182. But it was privatized in the fifteenth century and reconstructed in the sixteenth century to accommodate four hundred adults and a hundred children, including orphans, widows, and the elderly, as well as the previous medical cases and beggars. On the threshold of the seventeenth century, a chorus of four grew to twelve and eventually to sixty. It was a decision in 1740 to increase it to seventy that opened the door to young Maddalena Lombardini.

Born in 1745 to a middle- or lower-middle–class Venetian family, she auditioned at seven before a committee of thirty-three. Of thirty candidates, they admitted Lombardini as fourth of four by a vote of 18–15. Over the next eight years, she learned to sight-sing and play the instruments in the school's collection, took lessons in ear training, performance practice, and composition from several of the city's most respected musicians, and studied Greek, Latin, French, grammar, logic, poetry, and history with a resident clerical faculty. Like her classmates, she was issued a uniform and a lace collar to wear at performances. Before concerts there was an extra ration of meat and fish. Parents were allowed one visit a month, of course under supervision. Once a year, the girls were taken out to an island for a picnic.

By 1760, the governors considered it in everyone's interest to let Lombardini study for two months with Tartini in Padua, where she could live with an aunt and uncle. They even covered her tutor's expenses as chaperone en route. In 1764, she was allowed to go again, though it took three meetings to reach a decision, and it was unclear who paid for the trip. A year later, en route to a career that would carry her as far as London and Dresden and to a long and interesting life as a singer, composer, and violinist, she was mentioned in a local diary as the institution's best violinist and a protégée of Tartini.[117]

Memorable for its practicality, Tartini's famous letter was also noteworthy for its greetings to Lombardini's teacher and the Mendicanti's director.
Look, it said almost casually, what until now has been private, deferential,
a service occupation like tutor or nanny, has become institutional. We're
now professionals.

Tartini's institution was, in fact, himself. As president, provost, and
faculty rolled into one, he was still in his midthirties when he returned
from four years in Prague as employee of one of the Habsburg Empire's
oldest princely families to establish the school that would be his main
source of income until his death in 1770. For more than forty years, he
would teach up to ten hours a day, ten months a year. Until Tartini, teachers went to their pupils. As many as ten at a time, the pupils now came to
him, some from considerable distances, for a two-year course of violin and
composition lessons. Thanks to matriculees from much of Italy, Germany,
and France—who would go on to active and distinguished careers as far
away as Sweden and Russia—his academy was known unofficially as the
School of the Nations. But there were also players from the local Basilica
of San Antonio, where he had served for many years as concertmaster, as
well as gentlemen, ambassadors' pages, and Lombardini, the addressee of
his famous letter.[118]

Within a generation of Tartini's death, the conservatory, like so many
Italian ideas, was on its way across the Alps, where it was transformed into
public policy. As so often, the boom began in Paris. It then made itself seen
and felt in every aspiring metropolis between St. Petersburg and San Francisco. But no other conservatory owed its creation so directly to a revolution.
Founded in 1792, the year of the Battle of Valmy and "La Marseillaise" by
Bernard Sarrette, who was a captain in the National Guard, it was intended
as an institute for the civic education as well as the musical training of the
new republic's military bandsmen.

Two years later, Sarrette's institute had morphed into *the* Conservatory,
though the name, according to Emanuel Hondré, was chosen rather by
default than by design.[119] With an eye to multipurpose use, it was now
meant to supply domestic talent to a music scene dependent on Italian
singers, German players, and British and German instrument makers.

In 1797, with restoration, foreign intervention, and renewed terror
equally unlikely, and peace at least a theoretical possibility, the first violin
teacher was hired. Six years later, the Prix de Rome was introduced to
allow the best and brightest French talents to study the arts, so to speak,

in their now French-dominated homeland. In 1812, the year of the Russian campaign, the great violinist Pierre Baillot revised the mission statement again to include the theaters of Paris, the orchestras of the new départements, the armies, wherever they might be, and music education around the empire. A few years later, the empire had vanished and the monarchy had returned, and the Conservatory introduced church music, orchestra music, and a famously rigorous entrance exam. By this time, a faculty of distinguished player-teachers was already turning it into the gold standard of advanced violin study that it would remain until well into the nineteenth century, and creating a teaching literature, canonic as the Code Napoléon, that was still in use two centuries later.

A very different by-product of the revolutionary times, the Vienna Conservatory was first proposed in 1808, a year before Vienna was occupied by the French. But it wasn't until 1817, in what was arguably the most musical city in the world, before the proposal was finally acted on, and the conservatory was created as a private foundation with a fragile financial base and fourteen registrants for a four-year course. It took two more years to hire its first violin teacher, Joseph Böhm, who would go on to play Beethoven and Schubert premieres. It was 1827 before the original four-year course was extended two years for students with soloist potential. In November 1848, with the local revolution barely under control and Hungary in open rebellion, teaching stopped altogether. It was 1851 before Böhm's successor, Joseph Hellmesberger, introduced a new era of professionalization; 1854 before the school admitted its first women violin students; 1896 before teacher education was added to the curriculum; and 1909 before the conservatory finally went public as the Royal and Imperial Academy of Music and Performing Art.[120]

Yet Britain made Vienna look almost purposeful by comparison. In 1728, Daniel Defoe, the novelist, proposed adding a music school to Christ's Hospital, a London foundation roughly equivalent in function and antiquity to the *ospedaletto* in Venice or the Pietà in Naples. In 1774, Burney and composer Guardini, with an eye to native players to replace foreign imports, proposed something similar at the Foundling Hospital, a relatively recent foundation for "the education and maintenance of exposed and deserted young children."

Some forty years later, it occurred to the Earl of Westmorland, an enthusiastic amateur violinist, "in Sicily, while serving as adjutant-general" to found the Royal Academy of Music on his return to London.[121] As in

Vienna, the academy was to be funded with private donations and subscriptions. There were to be forty boys and forty girls in residence. When
the doors opened in 1823, twenty-one students from ten to fifteen years old
showed up. Four years later, money was so short that the academy almost
had to close again. In 1829, François-Joseph Fétis, reviewing the scene with
Parisian eyes, noted coolly that the existing violin faculty was "incapable
of forming good pupils." After more than forty years of operation, there
were only three violin students, and academy alumni made up only 20
percent or less of London's major theater orchestras, and even there they
tended to be outnumbered by foreign players.[122]

Yet everything had turned around within a generation. By 1890, one
of the era's reigning concert performers, the French-born Emile Sauret, was
the academy's senior professor, as well as a regular customer at Hill's. Academy students were regular customers, too. Thanks to its patron, John Rutson, the academy itself owned instruments. When the insurance premium
came due, they hired Arthur Hill to appraise them. From time to time,
the academy's secretary even dropped by Old Bond Street for tips on fund-
raising. The Guildhall School, created in 1880 as the first school of its kind
under municipal management, was meanwhile transforming itself from a
part-time academy for middle-class girl amateurs to a second conservatory.

In 1883, a third conservatory, the Royal College of Music, opened its
doors, and more good things began to happen. Eight years later, George
Bernard Shaw, 35, recalled that in his childhood "the sight of a fiddlecase
in a drawing room filled me with terror," until Paganini's protégé Sivori
convinced him that the instrument could actually be played. Yet "a guild
of young fiddlers" from the college now regularly astonished him with
their "vigor and skill." In fact, Joseph Joachim's brother told Arthur Hill
in 1894 that the Prince of Wales himself had approached Joachim about
a job at the college, but the offer came two weeks late.[123] Instead, it went
to Henry Holmes, a native Londoner, who had studied with his father and
made his debut at the Haymarket Theater at eight. If anyone was responsible for Shaw's astonishing young fiddlers, it was presumably Holmes.
But his career at the college ended abruptly in 1894, when he was fired for
sexual harassment.

Yet even as Holmes decamped for San Francisco, the college moved
into splendiferous new quarters in the shadow of the Royal Albert Hall.
The Prince of Wales, much of the royal family, the U.S. ambassador, and
"nearly all the members of the cabinet and the diplomatic corps" appeared

for the dedication. The story was even reported in the *New York Times*.[124] Soon afterward, the Spanish-born Enrique Fernández Arbós, a former concertmaster of the Berlin Philharmonic and Boston Symphony and a Joachim protégé, arrived as Holmes's successor. Joachim recommended him highly, as did Arbós's Spanish compatriot, Pablo de Sarasate. Arthur Hill, who welcomed Arbós's business, lobbied energetically on his behalf. Joachim and the equally iconic Eugène Ysaÿe agreed to serve as examiners.

While music-loving Britain still dithered over the creation and survival of the Royal Academy, the idea of the conservatory was already undergoing renovation in Leipzig, where the key figure was Felix Mendelssohn, who ironically would have been as happy to establish a conservatory in his hometown of Berlin. But while the minister of culture and even the king of Prussia were eager to have him, neither could agree on what he was to do.

Instead, Mendelssohn accepted a job conducting the Gewandhaus Orchestra in Leipzig. In 1842, when local demand and a windfall donation coalesced in plans for a new music school, he saw his chance and zipped off to Dresden to confer with the king of Saxony. The idea was a place that not only provided advanced training for people who already played, but also conferred a diploma to confirm that they had learned what they came for. The special relationship of conservatory and orchestra was written into the bylaws. Mendelssohn was to be the president. Ferdinand David, the orchestra's concertmaster, was to be professor of violin, with responsibility for advanced and intermediate students. Orchestra board members were to be conservatory board members. In principle, orchestra players were to teach their instruments. But for the moment, the violin was the only orchestral instrument in the teaching program, followed by the viola in 1848 and the cello in 1853. Despite the Gewandhaus link, which included access to the hall and library, orchestra was secondary to chamber music.

Neither a trade school nor a training camp for aspiring virtuosi, the school's nearest analogue was the gymnasium, the rigorously academic secondary school, whose curriculum was designed to deliver liberal education as Gewandhaus concerts delivered music education. Half a century later nearly half the conservatory's students were foreign, and over half were women.[125]

Like Mendelssohn, Anton Rubinstein was born Jewish and assimilated with fifty-some members of his family,[126] prodigious at an early age, and shown off in the usual Western capitals to the usual celebrities, including

Mendelssohn himself. He was even received by Queen Victoria. Like Mendelssohn, he aspired to build a conservatory. But it was not an easy sell.

What came naturally to Leipzig, with its old university, ancient trade fair, and centuries of civic music making, did not come naturally to St. Petersburg. Russia was another country, even another world, where the aristocracy consumed Western music and Western singers and players were imported to perform it, and there was no middle class.

Like the country's new, demonstratively Western capital and its resident middle class, Western music was essentially a political statement. From the creation of St. Petersburg in 1703, art mattered. By the 1720s, a secular theater and Italian singers had surfaced. Domenico Dall'Oglio, a native of Padua, followed a decade later, the first in a succession of Italian, then French, then Central European violinists, who would eventually turn Russian-trained violinists, like Russian chess players and mathematicians, into a global gold standard. Catherine the Great, German-born, French-educated, and empress from 1762, made in-house concert attendance compulsory for courtiers. By midcentury, there were public concerts. By the eve of the nineteenth century, Russia's first authentic violin virtuoso, Ivan Yevstafyavich Khandoshkin, descended from serfs and taught by the obligatory Italian court violinist, had already come and gone, and the city, with its own orchestra, concert life, musical societies, salons, and patrons, was on the European circuit.[127]

The musical energies unleashed in the new capital were just as transformative in Moscow. Italian opera arrived via the Polish court by 1731. A foundling hospital staged opera and taught music. The Kerzelli family, a clan of Czech composers, conductors, teachers, and impresarios, opened a music college with a special department for "the highborn nobility, the bourgeoisie, and serfs" and followed with a school specifically dedicated to the training of serf musicians. The Bolshoi Theater opened in 1825. By the mid-nineteenth-century, Moscow too was on the international circuit.[128]

Full of promise and still younger than twenty, Rubinstein returned from eight years abroad to a St. Petersburg palace, where his patron, the Grand Duchess Yelena Pavlovna of Russia, née Princess Friederike Charlotte Marie of Württemberg, was the czar's sister-in-law. The relationship was respectful and productive, but hardly equal in a society where the most gifted pianist the country had yet produced had no legal status but "son of a merchant of the second guild," and his patron had every expectation of getting her own way. As artist-in-residence, quasi-employee, and a bit of a house pet, Rubinstein was engaged to play at her parties, often in the presence of the imperial family.

Approaching twenty-five, he toured Europe again, where the one-time prodigy was now received as a star. But in the winter of 1856–57, he rejoined the grand duchess at her home on the Mediterranean, where patron and protégé talked seriously and at length about a basic reform of music education, with the goal of developing a homegrown profession acknowledged in law, in a country where the state was indifferent, and some of the country's most gifted musicians saw an idea conceived in Nice by an assimilated Jewish pianist and an assimilated German princess as a threat to their native creativity and originality.[129]

The creation in 1859 of the Russian Musical Society with the approval of Yelena Pavlovna's nephew, Czar Alexander II, was an important first step. At once initiator, propagator, and lobby for an institution and profession, the society proposed to introduce local concert audiences to Western as well as local masters. If necessary, it was also prepared to teach all interested comers in Yelena Pavlovna's Petersburg palace and the Moscow home of Rubinstein's equally gifted brother, Nikolai. The emancipation of the serfs in 1861, in a country whose professional musicians had heretofore been serfs or foreigners, was an important second step. A year later, the St. Petersburg conservatory opened for business with Anton Rubinstein, still in his early thirties, as founding director and his sometime concert partner, great Polish violinist Henryk Wieniawski, still in his midtwenties, as professor of violin. In 1866, Nikolai, 31, opened the new conservatory in Moscow with Peter Ilich Tchaikovsky, still in his midtwenties, as professor of theory and harmony. Entrance requirements were modest, with five- to nine-year curricula. After decades of bureaucratic trench warfare, it was agreed that graduates would not only earn a diploma—allowing for preferential hiring, superior civil service status, and a pension—but they could also look forward to a "free artist" certificate, conferring the legal status of "honored citizen" that exempted its owner from poll tax and military service, and allowed Jews to live outside the Pale of Settlement. Admission, in principle, was open to anyone older than fourteen. With no state support to buffer them, tuition fees could approach a few months' income. But it was not long before the Moscow municipality and merchant community pitched in to help, and there were scholarships for candidates in rarer specialties like the wind instruments.

As elsewhere, there was considerable social distance between the aspir-

ing pros and the art-loving amateurs, and it was understood that student pianists, violinists, and opera singers were more equal than others.
Non-Russian diversity consisted for the most part of the empire's national
minorities, Jews prominent among them. But women were a 60 percent
majority when the conservatory opened, though it was unclear whether
the cause was discriminatory university admissions, a social consensus that
young ladies belonged at pianos, or an institutional interest in fathers rich
enough to buy their daughters pianos and pay for their tuition.

Whatever the reason, there was no question that by 1900 the new
conservatories met Western standards. More conservatories had meanwhile
popped up as far away as the Caucasus, violin teaching was in full bloom
in Odessa, and Moscow alone employed a faculty of one hundred to teach
two thousand students. By this time, orchestra jobs had become so attractive that many students dropped out before finishing diplomas. But substantial numbers at least got themselves certified as "free artists."[130]

Thanks to an established virtuoso and a Prussian minister's wife, Berlin
would finally have its state conservatory too. But by now it was 1869, a
generation after Mendelssohn had given up in frustration. On the eve of a
transformative decade, Berlin was still a provincial capital of under a half
million, with a music scene that generated about as many concerts in a
year, by Moser's estimate, as it would in two weeks in 1910.[131] Until then,
the private sector filled the space and met demand.

In 1848, as in much of continental Europe, German liberals headed for
the barricades. Their demands included public support for the arts and a
conservatory. As in most places, the revolution's reach exceeded its grasp.
But there was at least the Stern Conservatory to show for the effort. Located
in a discreetly neo-baroque building around the corner from the Anhalter
rail station and within walking distance of what would become Cold War
Berlin's famous Checkpoint Charlie, the Stern was a private foundation
created in 1850. The Stern came to life through the combined effort of
Adolf Bernhard Marx, the university music director and Beethoven biographer, Theodor Kullak, the piano teacher to the Prussian princes and
princesses, and Julius Stern, the son of a lottery collector in Breslau, whose
talent had taken him to Paris in the mid-1840s, where he met composers
Hector Berlioz and Giacomo Meyerbeer. Within three years, the school
offered an orchestra class in a city still years away from a major orchestra.
Hans von Bülow and Ferdinand Laub, both still in their early twenties,
joined the faculty two years later, en route to the Berlin Philharmonic

and the Moscow conservatory, respectively. Some sixty years later, Bruno Walter, who matriculated there when he was nine, still remembered it for holding its own at a relatively affordable price in a city that by now was full of serious music teaching.[132] On the eve of World War I, enrollment had grown to 1,334, about 30 percent local, 30 percent foreign, with half of the foreigners from Russia.[133]

Both directly and indirectly, the Berlin Conservatory was a spin-off of 1864 and 1866. Great capitals like London, Paris, Vienna, and St. Petersburg, even second-tier capitals like Munich and Dresden, had great conservatories. Victory over Austria and confederation with Prussia's North German allies turned Berlin into a great capital. "Founded in 1869 and generously expanded in the years that followed," as Dietmar Schenk would elegantly express it, "the Hochschule was a consequence in the form of a school that the Prussian government drew from its military and political gains."[134]

Berlin's success was also a function of Hanover's misfortune. Since his appointment in 1862, Heinrich von Mühler, the Prussian minister of culture, had been brooding ex officio about the deficit in musical infrastructure that not only made Berlin uncompetitive with Munich and Dresden, but even the tiny Thuringian principality of Schwarzburg-Sondershausen. In April 1869, it occurred to him that the death of the venerable Wilhelm August Bach, a pillar of the local music establishment as director of the Royal Institute of Church Music, might be an opportunity for an initiative already long overdue. It had meanwhile occurred to his wife that Joseph Joachim, the era's reigning virtuoso, was living in Berlin.

Now on the concert circuit, Joachim had resigned demonstratively as music director at the Hanoverian court a few years earlier to protest a discriminatory statute that barred Jacob Grün, a young Jewish colleague and later professor at the Vienna Conservatory, from tenure in the court orchestra. In time, the affair was settled with a face-saving compromise. Then came the war of 1866. Hanover supported Austria. Prussia annexed Hanover. Even had Joachim wanted to return, there was no longer a court to return to. But this was no problem anyway. His concert career was booming, his Berlin connections went back to the early 1850s, and though born Jewish in Hungary as a subject of the Austrian crown, he was already a certified Lutheran, well on the way to becoming a cheerleader for Otto von Bismarck, the German chancellor and Prussian prime minister. "A blessing to have someone like Bismarck in charge of our government," Joachim

would write his wife the following year. "I consider myself a German, not
an Austrian," he added. "I'm not worried how this will come out; justice
and faith in Germany's mission to extend its culture keep me going."[135]

Linked to a growing conservatism, anti-Wagner as well as pro-
Bismarck, his faith in the German mission can only have enhanced the
minister's interest. Another job as music director was not enough, he told
von Mühler's wife when she approached him tentatively with a concert
project. He wanted "to awaken and sharpen a sense of the highest art in
some number of young souls," so that they would go out and spread the
word to the people by their teaching and example. The possibility of royal
patronage appealed to him because it would allow him to think about art
without having to worry about money.[136] Von Mühler's wife went home
and reported the conversation.

The minister's reply, the first item in what would soon be Joachim's
conservatory personnel file, is a bureaucratic classic. "It is desirable that
this project not be postponed or delayed too long, if proposals and sug-
gestions from the opposition are to be avoided, with all the complications
they involve," he warned. "With the death of Director Bach, a member of
the Music Section, we have an opportunity that needs to be recognized
and made use of."[137] If Joachim needed time off for travel or other projects,
well, they could work something out.

The minister's offer was one a man already sick of concertizing could
hardly refuse. It included three months off in winter, a month and a half
in summer, plus a guaranteed lifetime income, even in the event of disabil-
ity. The concert tour couldn't begin to match it, he happily informed his
brother in England. Von Mühler briefed his cabinet colleagues with strategic references to the abortive negotiations with Mendelssohn a generation
earlier and "the glorification of God," though that part was absent from
the draft charter that appeared sometime afterward. In June, Joachim
dropped by the minister's home for an evening of Mozart and Beethoven
sonatas with the von Mühler daughter. She was talented but clueless about
Beethoven, Joachim reported to his wife.[138]

That fall the conservatory opened with a faculty of 3—a pianist, a cellist, and Joachim. Of 19 registrants, 14 came to study violin. Three were
women, one of whom was a Schumann daughter who had come to study
her mother's instrument, the piano. But there was exponential growth over
the next few years as new courses and instruments were added. By 1876,
the 3 had grown to 38, the 19 to 249.[139]

There were still innumerable institutional and administrative loose ends. But only one was likely to engage the imagination of later generations with a very different sense of what conservatories were good for and what they could do. The issue was who appointed faculty. The question was of obvious interest to both Joachim and the minister, but for very different reasons. When the inevitable moment of truth arrived and von Mühler vetoed Joachim's choice of a pianist, Joachim resorted to his battle-tested attention-getter. He submitted his resignation to the king, effective January 1, 1871. Since Joachim and von Mühler weren't speaking, mediation was necessarily indirect. Since it was also unsuccessful, the matter was referred to the king, although he was neither in Berlin nor Potsdam, but Versailles, where German troops were besieging Paris in Bismarck's third war of German unification. The king dutifully heard the arguments, and ruled in Joachim's favor.

A year later, the royal family was conspicuously present when Joachim conducted the conservatory's debut orchestra concert, as was Field Marshal Helmuth von Moltke, the hero of the war with France. In 1872, the local papers published extra editions, and Joachim was cheered at an evening concert, when von Mühler was forced to resign. Thirty years later, the now globally celebrated conservatory moved into neo-Renaissance quarters with a 1,044-seat concert hall on a prime tract of downtown real estate. The royal family was again present, as were senior officials of the Prussian and imperial governments, deputations from the universities, and representatives from domestic and foreign conservatories.[140] The building was destroyed in World War II, but its successor was built on the same site.

By the end of the nineteenth century, conservatories were established in the United States, too, at least east of the Mississippi and north of the Ohio. Though actual operation began only a decade later, the Peabody Institute, founded in Baltimore in 1857, technically predated both St. Petersburg and Berlin. Founded in 1865, the Oberlin Conservatory, the oldest in the United States in continuous operation, affiliated with Oberlin College two years later. Two conservatories in high-minded Boston, and a third in Cincinnati, a kind of Ohio River Düsseldorf, opened the same year.

As so often, the American scene was both more of the same and entirely different. The Berlin logic—that great cities needed great conservatories—worked in America, too. But grand duchesses, entrepreneurial virtuosi, let alone ministries of culture, were nowhere in sight. A few years after the Civil War, Jeannette Meyers Thurber, the daughter of an immigrant Danish violinist, returned from violin study in Paris inspired to create a Conservatoire à l'américaine. With the support and wholesale grocery fortune of her spouse[141] and a cadre of the city's business and financial aristocracy, including Andrew Carnegie, on her board, she took the first step in 1885 with the creation of a National Conservatory of Music of America, open to all qualified comers, irrespective of gender and race, on East Seventeenth Street. When Jean Sibelius, her first candidate for director, was unavailable, she settled for Antonín Dvořák at $15,000 a year, in an era when the average manufacturing worker earned a little over $400.[142] But the prime mover was herself.[143]

In 1888, she petitioned Congress to underwrite a new institute. Congress was to put up $200,000. Every member could then nominate a candidate from his state or district for tuition-free admission, subject to the Conservatory board and an appropriately rigorous entrance exam.[144] In a bitterly contested presidential year, there were no takers. But three years later, Congress agreed to charter an unfunded "national conservatory of music within the District of Columbia." Reaffirmed in 1921, the project then vanished from view.

Yet private initiative too could be taught to cultivate what Thurber referred to as a "national musical spirit." In time, others would do likewise, even as Thurber's conservatory faded along with her fortune and her energy. Between 1918 and his death in 1932, George Eastman invested $20 million in the University of Rochester's Eastman School of Music. Between 1917 and 1928, Mary Louise Curtis Bok, whose father published the hugely popular *Saturday Evening Post* and whose husband edited the equally popular *Ladies' Home Journal*, invested at least $12.5 million in Philadelphia's Curtis Institute of Music. Inspired by John Grolle, a Dutch immigrant and former Philadelphia Orchestra violinist, the next step was a full-scholarship conservatory for a rigorously selected class of 203, with a demonstratively well-paid faculty, including Josef Hofmann at $72,500 a year, and the soprano Marcella Sembrich at $40,000. Carl Flesch, imported on Grolle's recommendation as the era's emblematic violin teacher, earned $25,000 a year for three and a half months' work.[145] Assuming a fifty-week year, unionized New York plumbers at the time earned about $3,000. Again assuming a fifty-week year, manufacturing jobs paid about $1,200.[146]

Yet it was two very different American foundations that increasingly set the global pace. Juilliard, conceived as a Manhattan-based teachers college in the year of the first Russian revolution, would morph over the new century into the Harvard of conservatories with 810 students and a 1998 budget of $39 million. Indiana, a university-based little house on the prairie, fifty miles from Indianapolis in the state's seventh largest city, would evolve over the same century into an inland empire with over 1,700 degree candidates, nearly half of them grad students, and an annual budget of over $30 million.[147]

Named, ironically, for a man who never knew nor set foot in it, Juilliard presumably enjoyed the comparative advantage of New York, New York. With some 3.5 million people by 1900, an established public school music program and private teachers of every musical art yet devised, the five newly consolidated boroughs alone were a reserve of demand and talent just waiting to be developed. Yet Thurber's National Conservatory was evidence enough that making it in New York took more than location, location, location.

Frank Damrosch and James Loeb, on the other hand, were serious comparative advantages. Damrosch, a Sunday organist at Felix Adler's Society for Ethical Culture, a socially conscious choral conductor at Cooper Union, and supervisor of music for the New York public schools since 1897, wanted a school that not only taught players and singers, but also produced all-around musicians and music teachers. Loeb, a classicist and cellist as well as a pillar of New York's German Jewish establishment and reluctant partner in the family bank, was happy to help.

With a half-million-dollar endowment from Loeb and friends, Damrosch hired a faculty and applied for a charter from the New York Board of Regents. His Institute of Musical Art, accessible by subway, opened to 281 students, few of them high school graduates, in October 1905. Woodrow Wilson, then president of Princeton, spoke at the opening ceremony. Respected for its solid curriculum, thoroughly professional faculty and good connections to the public concert scene, Damrosch's institute was still there twenty years later, with enrollments of around a thousand, about two-thirds women, a quarter Jews, a few African Americans.

Yet there was also competition, increasingly real and present, for faculty, students, buildings, and resources. This was where Augustus D. Juilliard, a childless New York textile millionaire, came in. His will, filed for probate two months after his death in 1919, left an estimated $12.5 to $13.5 million to a Juilliard Musical Foundation, with a mandate to advance the education of qualified students, underwrite public performances, and support the Metropolitan Opera.[148] His nephew Frederic, an admirer of President Warren G. Harding, hired Eugene A. Noble, a Methodist minister and former college president, as the foundation's director. A man of nativist disposition, deeply conservative leanings, no known musical attainments, and an oracular administrative style, Noble let the money draw interest for several years, then turned a former Vanderbilt guest house in midtown Manhattan into his own home as well as the foundation's.

Finally, in 1924, he selected a hundred white, native-born candidates for advanced instruction, approached a dozen high-profile teacher-performers, including the violinists César Thomson, Paul Kochanski, and Georges Enesco, and announced the creation of a so-called Juilliard Graduate School, though few of the student-candidates had graduated from anything, and there were no apparent plans for a certificate or even curriculum. By now, his board was in open rebellion. But Damrosch's, too, had reached a few conclusions, among them that Juilliard money talked, even if Noble didn't. By 15–5, they voted to join what they couldn't beat, turn over their assets to the Juilliard Foundation, and merge their Institute of Musical Art in a new, combined school.

It was not quite a hostile takeover. But it was also not Cinderella and the prince. What might have been the Damrosch-Loeb School of Music was now the Juilliard School of Music, a de facto confederation, joined lovelessly under a common roof. Neither Damrosch nor Loeb was invited to join the new board. But neither was Frederic Juilliard, and Noble's contract was not renewed.[149]

The new team was a model of respectable credibility. Though white, male, and Episcopalian, the dean and later president, Ernest Hutcheson, had studied with Liszt as a child, taught at the Stern Conservatory, played three Beethoven concerti in one concert with the New York Symphony, produced a roster of distinguished pupils, and even sheltered George Gershwin from admirers while he was composing the Concerto in F. The president, John Erskine, was not only a Columbia PhD and a popular professor of English, but a pianist and author of a novel, filmed in 1927, and still accessible online from Australia some eighty years later.[150]

Unlike Thurber's model, this one worked. A new professor of conducting introduced, and a new building accommodated, a widely admired orchestra and opera program. The new management looked after the money, inspired media attention, and maintained the necessary social network. New faculty, like Louis Persinger, who had taught the prodigious Yehudi Menuhin and

Ruggiero Ricci in San Francisco, now attracted the best and brightest young violinists to Morningside Heights. A growing list of distinguished alumni attracted more and more talented applicants. In darkest 1935, an onsite placement bureau got 2,500 unsolicited requests for teachers and performers. In darkest 1938, 489 graduates and students found jobs teaching and performing. There was even money left for an eighteenth-century violin, viola, and cello that would eventually grow to a collection of some thirty bows and a hundred more collector-quality instruments by the beginning of the twenty-first century, among them one Amati, two Testore, two Vuillaume, two Stradivari, three Bergonzi, four Gagliano, five Guarneri, four of them del Gèsus, and six Guadagnini violins.[151]

Returning veterans, postwar prosperity, the United States' ascent to world power, and New York's ascent to world capital were all that was needed to lift Juilliard to world class. Under William Schuman, a first Jewish, first native-born president, the antique separation of Damrosch and Juilliard was leveled. The institutional mission was refocused on performance. Ivan Galamian and Dorothy DeLay established themselves as the world's go-to violin teachers for the next six decades. The Juilliard String Quartet showed the school colors around the world. By 1962, when Schuman descended from Morningside Heights to wake up president of the new Lincoln Center in the city that didn't sleep, there seemed be no question who was king of the hill, top of the heap.

Yet there was Indiana, a public university music school with a faculty of Juilliard size and quality, teaching Juilliard-dimensional classes of Juilliard diversity in a town of 30,000, including students. In a state of under 5 million, it maintained five orchestras and produced seven to nine operas, a season matched only by the Met. It also awarded at least four different bachelor's degrees, four different master's degrees, three different doctorates, and an Artist Diploma.

In fact, it had been around since 1910. There was a giant step in 1919, when the department was declared a school with a direct line to the president, and a new dean, who had studied in Berlin with Joachim and Moser, declared that music was "a business proposition in the state and in every city of Indiana."[152] There was another giant step thirty years later, when a new president and new dean set out to demonstrate that this was true.

The new president, Herman B Wells—with the B, like the S in Harry S Truman, untethered to name or place—was an Indiana native, Indiana graduate, and trained economist, who played the French and baritone horns, and had experimented with the cello. He had worked as cashier in a local bank, traveled the state for the state bankers association, and advised the legislature before he was thirty. At thirty-five, he was named president of the university, a job he held till 1962. It was only clear afterward how his musical enthusiasms would work like catnip on a Music School with zero appeal to the state's best and brightest high school violinists and in desperate need of a "distinguished teacher of violin."[153]

In 1947, an unanticipated vacancy in the dean's office turned a Cinderella music school into a national princess. Wells, who led the search, returned with Wilfred Bain, a Canadian-born, thirty-nine-year-old son of a Methodist minister, who had already transformed an ugly duckling music school at North Texas State Teachers College into a regional swan.

If Bain was appalled by a local scene that found his wife recruiting orchestra players at the checkout counter of the neighborhood A&P, it helped that he enjoyed an ease of access to the president's office matched only by the sexologist Alfred Kinsey.[154] With Wells behind him, he set about creating virtuous circles. A first-rate conductor and opera director attracted first-rate performers, who in turn attracted first-rate students to the orchestra needed for a first-rate opera. Opera attracted both audience and media attention. Meanwhile, Indiana ensembles toured as far away as Brussels, Japan, Korea, and the New York World's Fair, and Bain continued to bring back trophies like Janos Starker, principal cellist of the Chicago Symphony, and Joseph Gingold, concertmaster of the Cleveland Orchestra, despite relatively modest salaries. Starker was grateful to be freed from the constraints of an orchestra calendar. Gingold, who loved to teach, agreed to come for what he was paid in Cleveland. In effect, everyone who could perform was allowed to perform, with the understanding that lessons would be made up later. There were the psychic rewards of good colleagues, good students, and association with an A-team. In a profession not known for steady employment and job security, there was the comfort of regular income, at least while it lasted.

In the end, Bain like Schuman did what he came to do. Where he had once hoped to attract 500 students, he now advised a ceiling of 1,500. He left behind a trademark reputation, even a new home, but above all a faculty of global visibility,[155] beginning with the violin professors, who had personified their institutions since the creation of the Paris Conservatoire and whose appointment was considered news fit to print all the way up to the modern era.

Their story began, as such stories usually did, in Paris, where the eighteen-year-old Pierre Rode made his sensational debut on the threshold of the Reign of Terror. From there on, he would be considered one of the top-tier violinists in Paris, "which is saying something," his biographer added, "for excellent violinists abounded there as never before in such numbers and such magnificence."[156] Three years later, he was nominated for a professorship at the newly created Conservatoire. In 1803, with his colleague and contemporary Pierre Baillot, he took off for St. Petersburg, where there was money to be made. In their absence, the slightly older Rudolphe Kreutzer compiled and edited the official Méthode.

In 1812, Rode and Baillot returned to Paris, where the Prince de Chimay, a Napoleonic adjutant and amateur violinist, co-opted them for an "elite orchestra where the most celebrated artists came to take part, like a salon, on the same day each week."[157] They otherwise resumed their normal routine as performers and teachers. Shelves of concerti and occasional pieces that they composed for themselves were already obsolescent in their lifetimes. But of six classic étude collections published beween 1796 and 1835 and still in print a couple of centuries later, four were by Paris conservatory professors, including Kreutzer, Baillot, and Rode.

Most durable of the three, Baillot continued to play chamber music with amateur friends as well as professional colleagues. Through 154 subscription concerts between 1814 and 1840, he introduced Paris audiences to the quartets of Boccherini, Haydn, Mozart, and Beethoven. At sixty-two he was still good for a farewell tour of Italy and Switzerland.

His *L'Art du Violon*, at once a how-to book, a progress report, a memoir, and a testament, appeared in 1834. When he and his colleagues began, he recalled, there was little to go by. Over some years they had figured out a few of "those processes known as secrets of the art" by trial and error. Looking back, he was impressed by how all great players since Corelli had adapted the violin to their needs. That included "Mr. Paganini," whose approach had turned it into an instrument unique like the artist himself. His own twenty-four études, published as a supplement, were themselves a measure of how far things had come in thirty years. The Conservatory was there to establish a foundation, not set limits, said Baillot.[158]

Without even realizing it, little Charles Dancla set out to prove him right, beginning around 1823. At six, he was ready for the local theater orchestra. At eight, he played a benefit, including concerti by Rode and Kreutzer and a trio by Baillot, for the poor of his little hometown on the edge of the Pyrenees. His father then took him to Bordeaux to audition for Rode, who recommended him to Baillot. At nine, he was admitted to the Conservatory. A year later, he had learned to play in public "without trembling," he noted in his memoirs.[159] At eighteen he was solo violinist at the Opéra.

From small-town beginnings to his death at ninety, his career mirrored an era extending from the Restoration to the Dreyfus affair. Some sixty years after hearing them, he was still digesting the uncanny precision of Paganini's tenths and fingered octaves. Though Beethoven was still "too advanced," he played Haydn and Mozart quartets with his brothers and survived the great cholera epidemic of 1832. In 1848 he was offered a job as assistant conductor at the Opéra Comique. He declined politely, preferring to wait out the revolution as postmaster in Cholet, a little town about as far west of Paris as one could get without a boat.[160] On his return to Paris, a draft notice ordered him to report to the militia with a clarinet. With an assist from Adolphe Adam, a military bandmaster and composer of ballets, he managed instead to master the tonic "oom" and dominant "pah-pah" required by the part and transfer to second horn.

His Conservatory experience had operetta potential. In 1842, when Baillot's professorship at the Conservatory became vacant and the Belgian virtuoso Charles de Bériot declined, Habeneck, conductor of the Conservatory orchestra, proposed his student Jean-Delphin Alard and Dancla. Then Jean-Baptiste Teste, the minister of public works, weighed in with a third candidate, the Belgian virtuoso Lambert Joseph Massart, a student of Kreutzer's. Alard and Massart, each with heavyweight patrons, were short-listed. "As for me," Dancla reported, "I had only the glorious title of Baillot pupil, and that was not enough." It should be added, in fairness, that Massart, who got the job, became the most famous teacher of his time after teaching Kreisler, Ysaÿe, and Wieniawski.

The second act began fourteen years later at a social occasion at which the host, Achille Fould, perennial minister of finance in the government of Napoleon III, asked Dancla whether he had any good students in his class. "But Minister," Dancla replied, "I'm not a professor at the Conservatory." Fould went straight to Camille Doucet, the director of state theaters. A few days later, Dancla was offered a job at the Conservatory, though five more years would pass before he was appointed professor. In 1892, after thirty-four years, he was forced to retire at age seventy-five. Massart was allowed to stay forty-seven years, till he was seventy-nine, Dancla protested. But it didn't help.[161]

Successor generations recalled the Conservatory with a mix of irony,

qualified respect, and affection. The tricolor élan of the founding fathers
had clearly faded decades earlier. Carl Flesch, who arrived from Vienna in
1890, remembered a faculty whose average age was seventy-five.[162] Henri
Temianka, who arrived via Rotterdam and Berlin in the 1920s, remembered that "one of the most famous musical institutions in the world" was
also "one of the shabbiest."[163] John Sidgwick, who arrived from England
after World War II, remembered a place where people were taught to play
the violin as they might be taught to upholster a chair but could still learn
to play an authentic détaché and martelé bow stroke,[164] thanks to Lucien Capet, whose classic *La technique supérieure de l'archet* appeared in the
middle of World War I.

By this time, the action had long since moved on to other places, among
them St. Petersburg, Moscow, and New York, but above all Berlin "For the
travelling virtuoso, Berlin is now what Paris was," Heinrich Ehrlich noted
in 1895.[165] In 1909, it occurred to Richard Stern, a local piano dealer, that
a directory of the city's musical resources had serious moneymaking potential. Its success could only have made him wish he had started earlier. The
directory appeared annually till July 1914, when other priorities took over.

Its volume alone, 178 pages in the first edition, had almost doubled six
years later. Fifty pages of display ads led to directories of virtually everything musical, from private teachers of lute, breathing, opera conducting,
and rhythmic gymnastics, the Conservatory and twelve private conservatories, to the musicologists at the university, military bands, and organ-
ists at dozens of churches and five synagogues. There were a full corps of
music teachers from the city's seventy-nine secondary schools, seventy-two
music writers at thirty-three newspapers from Conservative to Socialist,
twenty concert halls, twelve concert presenters, seventeen music publishers, even forensic experts prepared to testify to the authenticity of instruments or violation of copyrights. Rooming and boardinghouses advertised
their amenities, languages, and permissible practice hours. Violin teachers alone, among them Joachim's successor, Henri Marteau, his protégé
Andreas Moser, the great Fritz Kreisler, and Carl Flesch, the next generation's emblematic teacher, filled nine pages, including their methods, languages, and hourly rates in increments descending from 25 marks, twice
the price of a box seat at the Royal Opera, to 6 marks. Flesch was already
booked out for 1914–15.[166]

Though Joachim himself was not listed, his long shadow still fell on
virtually everyone and everything. Inevitably, his spiritual presence was

most palpable at the Conservatory, where a department created in his image had grown from three to eight over his thirty-eight-year tenure and a marble bust looked down on posterity from an elaborate monument dedicated in 1913. His legacy extended in principle to wherever people wanted to hear or play Bach and Beethoven on violins.

The veneration was real, as was the affection. Generous in his paternalism, sincere in his collegiality, unchallengeable on his merits, and genuinely concerned to do the right thing for the right reason, he personified much of what really was good about the good old days. Flesch, among the brightest inhabitants of Planet Violin ever, had his reservations about the way Joachim played and taught, but none about his significance or character. From early on, Joachim had educated, even elevated, his audience, he noted respectfully. He could only thank him for relegating virtuosity from an end in itself to the subordinate role it deserved, and instead emphasizing music.[167]

Leopold Auer, the next pedagogical superstar, who studied with him in Hanover while Joachim was still court violinist to the king, recalled a teacher who not only shared an occasional gig but arranged for a court official to slip him an occasional envelope of supplementary cash. Waldemar Meyer was accepted into Joachim's first class in Berlin on full scholarship. Theodore Spiering, a German American from St. Louis who would later be Gustav Mahler's concertmaster of the New York Philharmonic, recalled a teacher who helped his students with jobs and recommendations long after they'd left his studio.[168] Arthur Hill's diary frequently notes him shopping for one or another of his students.

Moser, his protégé and biographer, cites pedagogical ironies most colleges of education would frown on. "No need to apologize for coming from the city of Pure Reason, but you don't have to make it so obvious when you play," Joachim told a boringly earnest student from Königsberg, hometown of the philosopher Immanuel Kant. "That's supposed to represent a wreath with flowers on it, not potatoes," he told another student, who overdid a trill.[169] Yet even after a domestic crack-up that dismayed his closest friends, in a profession crowded with large egos and a culture where envy could hold its own against all six of the other mortal sins, he seems unfailingly to have inspired good feelings.

Moser himself conceded that he was an unconventional teacher who sat on a small podium in the middle of the room and taught by example. Auer, who venerated Joachim as everyone else did, recalled, "This is how you need to play it," accompanied by an encouraging smile, was as close

as he usually came to an explanation.[170] Neither a theoretician nor an analyst, Flesch observed, Joachim demonstrated what he couldn't analyze or
convey in any other way. There was no question that he took teaching seriously. With a respectable salary and a flourishing concert career in the era's
musical capital, he could also recruit as he wished, which tended to mean
five or six advanced students a year over a five-decade teaching career. In
1898–99, the master's sixtieth anniversary as a concert performer, Moser
organized an alumni orchestra in his honor. With forty-four first violins,
forty-four second violins, thirty-two violas, twenty-four cellos, and twenty
basses, seated alphabetically, so many former students turned up that seating in the hall had to be reduced by eight rows, and the Conservatory
bought a supplementary three-day insurance policy to cover their instruments. Regiments and brigades of former students now played in leading
ensembles, served as concertmasters of leading orchestras, taught at leading conservatories, even made solo careers. But it was widely noted and
generally agreed that over forty years none had become world-class players
in the sense that their teacher had.[171]

There was no clear explanation for this, though Flesch had serious reservations about Joachim's successors. In his opinion, they had first turned
the master's idiosyncratic bow arm into a school. Then they turned pupils
into "violinistic cripples." But that was hardly Joachim's fault. Was the
problem the absence of a school? Unlikely, according to Enzo Porta, a former concertmaster of Bologna's Teatro Comunale with a scholarly passion
for the history of violin teaching.[172] Contrary to the traditional view of
Joachim, the master of show-and-tell, Porta was impressed with how his
three-volume method, coauthored with Moser, linked technique to music
from the bottom up till finally arriving at startlingly articulate, essay-
length instructions on how to play the Mendelssohn or Brahms concerto.[173]
Like Hillel challenged to explain the Torah while standing on one foot,
Joachim could even reduce his method to 135 words in a letter to the nine-
year-old Franz von Vecsey in 1904. Teach yourself, he told the boy. Shift
positions so the violin doesn't scream or weep. Play in tune. Don't overdo
the vibrato. Playing fast may impress the dummies, but it's not enough.[174]

On the other hand, Flesch noted, great individuals, turned teacher,
are often vampires who suck up their students' individuality. He regarded
Joachim and Ysaÿe, like the pianist Feruccio Busoni, as giants—and
cautionary examples for just this reason.[175] This seemed as plausible an
explanation as any for students who were accomplished, respected, and for-

gettable. Paganini taught only one, the six-year-old Camillo Sivori, whom he regularly reduced to tears.[176] Heifetz the violinist left Flesch awestruck; but even the formidable Flesch might have had second thoughts about Heifetz the teacher, of whom it was said on the occasion of his eightieth birthday, "He plans to continue teaching, but students are few because he is so intimidating."[177]

Yet a test case, already well under way to the east, suggested that other factors, including luck, might influence outcomes as much as any method. Like Joachim, Leopold Auer was born Jewish on the Hungarian side of the Austro-Hungarian divide, started his professional life as a prodigy, and was shipped to Vienna for his musical higher education. Again like Joachim, he launched his adult career as a concertmaster and concert artist before moving on to a newly founded conservatory—while maintaining active concert schedules. Both led quartets with loyal establishmentarian constituencies. Both had even been dedicatees of classic concertos, though Auer, unconsulted during the Tchaikovsky's gestation and convinced that it still needed work, turned down the dedication and famously let it go to Adolf Brodsky by default.[178]

In 1868, Auer, 23, was invited to London to play Beethoven's "Archduke" trio with Anton Rubinstein and Alfredo Piatti, the era's reigning cellist. He then left for a Black Forest vacation, where a Cologne newspaper clipping, forwarded by a Brussels colleague, informed him of a message waiting for him at a music shop in Bad Kreuznach, a little town in the Palatinate. On arrival he found a contract. Henryk Wieniawski, an authentic superstar and the first professor at the newly founded St. Petersburg Conservatory, had resigned to resume full-time concert playing. Rubinstein proposed Auer for the job. Uncertain whether he'd like it, Auer signed for three years; he stayed for forty-nine. By that time, as the world's most famous violin teacher at seventy-two, he would presumably have returned for more had World War I not caused him to relocate to Norway, and successive revolutions in St. Petersburg not demolished the ancien régime that had been his support system. Instead, as he wrote in his memoirs, he packed two steamer trunks and his Strad[179] and followed a vanguard of his most brilliant students to America, where he recorded, played at Carnegie Hall, and picked and chose from private applicants, exhilarated by the opportunity to go through life as "Auer students." Though he was by then over eighty, both Damrosch's Institute and Mrs. Bok's Curtis were happy to engage him for a late pedagogical Indian summer.

Student memories published decades later are a colorful but highly selective record of what his classes were like. Mischa Elman, who spent six-teen months with him in his early teens, recalled a teacher who left "much to the individuality of his pupils" and taught by force of personality.[180] Heifetz, who spent six years with him, remembered playing concert reper-tory in class but never any technical study, and he was at a loss to iden-tify anything that could be specifically called an Auer method.[181] Nathan Milstein, who came to Auer fairly late, recalled how, unlike Joachim, he rarely demonstrated; when he did, he was no longer at the top of his form. Calculated tantrums were an effective deterrent to goof-offs or laziness, he added.[182] Efrem Zimbalist remembered two two-hour master classes a week, Auer's imperfect Russian, a debut lesson, where Auer pitched a music stand into the corridor, and a session where Auer was so bowled over by what he'd just heard from little Mischa Elman that he bounded out of his chair and knocked the boy over. The class resumed after a quick check of Elman's borrowed Amati.[183]

Both Schwarz and Porta make a strong case that his intelligence, empiricism, common sense, and discipline would have made him out-standing anywhere. A very good player himself, he expected the same of his students but without a party line. Not dogmatic about such tech-nicalities as high elbow, low elbow, and which digit went where on the bow, he even resigned himself to coexistence with the newly fashionable continuous vibrato, although he abhorred it.[184] Talent, of course, was a nec-essary condition, but not a sufficient one. Students were expected to attend class regularly and punctually, dress for the occasion, and produce. Classes were always given in the presence of peers and often of distinguished visi-tors, and they were as demanding as concert performances.[185] Yet for all of this, he too would have been remembered for well-trained, profession-ally accomplished, and generally forgettable students had his career ended around 1900.

The difference in outcome, which distinguished him not only from Joachim but from virtually all other Western contemporaries was existen-tially linked to a repertory of skills that had little to do with the violin and virtually everything to do with the uniqueness of Russia. Remark-able enough, given his own origins, Auer seems to have discovered and developed them almost by chance. Over a century later, his version of the turning point is still remarkable. On tour in Ukraine, he had encountered a familiar occupational hazard, the self-proclaimed father of an eleven-year-old genius. In this case the genius was not only real but pointed to a reservoir of potentially world-class talent where no one had yet thought to look for it. If Auer's achievement as a teacher was to be judged objectively, Flesch observed decades later, one had to factor for the quality of his raw material. Of any forty applicants to the Berlin Conservatory, he estimated that 10 percent were above average. In St. Petersburg, the figure approached 95 percent.[186]

Too bored and tired to hear the boy himself, Auer outsourced the audition to a former pupil, who confirmed that the boy's father had not exaggerated. From there, things moved quickly. Auer telegraphed his colleague, Alexander Glazunov, in St. Petersburg, to arrange a scholarship. As required by law, he then proceeded to negotiations with Vyacheslav von Plehve, the deeply anti-Semitic minister of interior, for permission to bring the boy's father to St. Petersburg. Indignant about foreign news coverage of the recent Kishinev pogrom, Plehve initially stonewalled. The tiebreaker was a private audition not only for Plehve but for the entire cabinet, and a nominal butler's job at the home of a sympathetic music patron for Mischa Elman's father.[187]

As more and more such talents appeared, Auer's tenacity and negotiating skills sharpened, and the professional challenges grew. In effect, Auer had become the world's leading, even its first, full-service violin teacher. Beginning with Elman, he introduced his mostly impoverished, deeply provincial, and brilliantly talented protégés to the right people. He saw to it that they were equipped with good instruments. He made sure that they acquired social skills, table manners, and languages. He made sure that they were properly prepared and dressed for their debuts in Berlin and London. As newspapers picked up the story, his own international career was launched as well as Elman's. From 1906 to 1911 he kept a summer studio in London that he later moved to a suburb of Dresden, and began taking foreign students. The message was hard to miss. Great teachers produce great students. It also worked the other way around.

In many ways, Flesch, yet another German-speaking Jew from the Hungarian side of the Austro-Hungarian border, was the counterpoint to Auer's theme. Both mentored troops of distinguished Jewish students. Both trained in Vienna and Paris. Both were orchestra players turned freelance concertizers en route to distinguished conservatory careers on two continents.

Children and beneficiaries of a liberal age, both also saw the *Titanic* sink, at least metaphorically. With a raftful of prospering students to throw

him a line, Auer, at least, made it to Lifeboat America and a private studio
on New York's West Side where lessons that began at $30 an hour had
reached a princely $100 by the late 1920s.[188] Flesch, whose formidable IQ
cohabited with miserable luck and disastrous political judgment, lost his
savings twice in a decade, first to the firestorm German inflation of 1923,
then to the Wall Street crash of 1929, where his losses were compounded
by supersized loans invested in failed stocks. His interest in money, prominent not only in his memoirs but in student recollections, is unique in the
literature. At once a Dow Jones of the profession and a useful social metric,
it tells where violin teachers stood both with respect to those in other professions and to one another. But it also reflects real concern about making
a living and supporting a family in trying times.[189] After the first crash,
Flesch was hauled back from the edge by Mrs. Bok's dollar-denominated
largesse in much the way that postwar Germany was bailed out by short-
term credits from American banks. But the only solution after the second
crash was to sell his Strad to Franz von Mendelssohn, his friend, banker,
and living room quartet buddy.

As though losing his money weren't enough, Flesch also did his best
to lose his life. As very possibly the best-paid violin teacher of his time, he
left Philadelphia for Berlin as the Weimar Republic began its irreversible
plunge into the abyss. Safe again as a refugee in Britain, he lost his chance
at a first asylum by leaving safe, if unremunerative, private teaching in
London for a conservatory job in Amsterdam on the eve of the German
invasion. Stateless in German-occupied Holland, he lost another chance at
asylum by waving off an inquiry from an American university on grounds
that it was trying to get him cheap.[190] In the end, it was the intervention
of colleagues, among them the composer Ernst von Dohnányi and the conductor Wilhelm Furtwängler, that allowed him, still a Hungarian citizen,
the visa needed to transit Germany en route to a final job at a new conservatory in Lucerne, where he died in 1944.[191]

By his own account, his professional moment of truth was the discovery that the essence of practice was how, not how much. He liked to call
himself a doctor of violin playing, his protégé and assistant, Max Rostal,
noted. Ida Haendel, too young at five to appreciate his originality, recalled
his lessons as similar to concerts, just more intimidating. Students and
family reported unanimously and credibly that he could be generous,
approachable, charming, even funny. He just put these qualities on hold
during working hours. His teaching presumed a kind of social contract.

Students were to do what he told them. In return, they would get what they came for.

It was hard to quarrel with the results. In 1935, Poland organized an international competition, the first of many, to honor the centenary of Wieniawski's birth. Ginette Neveu, the first-place winner; Temianka, the third-place winner; Haendel, still a child, who won a special prize for Polish entrants—all were Flesch students. In 1937, Ricardo Odnoposoff, a Flesch student, became the only non-Soviet laureate when he finished second at the famous 1937 Queen Elisabeth competition in Brussels.

In the 1920s, like so many before him, Flesch packed his experience, observations, reflections, and bracingly emphatic opinions into a book, *The Art of Violin Playing*, still available in English eighty years later. His discussion of technique in general and its particular applications was already a salutary kick. But the third part, with its field-tested proposals for coping with perspiration, concert dress, and misanthropic conductors, its thoughts on ethnicity, particularly Jewish, and clear-eyed overview of Planet Violin from Artist to Amateur, was a new departure altogether. "The teacher, this musical pastor, who bears the responsibility like no other for his art's unbroken line, is the most indispensable member of the violin hierarchy,"[192] he wrote of his guild. The proposition could still be posted with profit on the door of every studio.

For those disposed to look for them, there was no shortage of role models. Within a generation, America alone offered three. Their students would people the world's major orchestras and concert platforms for the next half century. That two of them were immigrants, aware from an early age of their place in their art's unbroken line, and impelled and driven to distant shores by very large historical forces, would not have come as a surprise to Flesch.

The first, Ivan Galamian, was Armenian, though fellow Armenians only barely considered him one of their own. Born in 1903 in Tabriz in the East Azerbaijani province of what was still called Persia, he was raised and educated in Moscow from age two. His longtime associate Dorothy DeLay understandably thought of him as Russian. Mercifully underage for military service in 1916, he entered the class of Konstantin Mostras, a student of Auer's, and himself still only thirty. In time, Mostras would make his mark as father of an indigenous Soviet school of violin teaching. On graduation in 1919, Galamian played a couple of public recitals, then joined the orchestra of the Bolshoi Theater. For anyone, Armenian or otherwise, it was not a good time to be a young bourgeois in Moscow. It was bad enough that the Bolsheviks confiscated the family estate. It would apparently have been still worse but for the timely intervention of Anatoly Lunacharsky, responsible at the time as Commissar of Enlightenment for the newly Sovietized theaters. In 1922, Galamian left for Paris, reportedly with a del Gesù he had bought for $2,000 and was allowed to take along, nominally as a tool of his trade, in fact as start-up capital. How he did any of this is a mystery.

The story from here on is better documented. There were two years with Lucien Capet, the master of bow technique. There were concerts in Germany, France, and Holland. Above all, there were early teaching successes. The pilot model was Paul Makanowitzky, who, like Galamian himself, would go on to teach at Juilliard, Curtis, and Meadowmount, Galamian's eight-week summer studio in the Adirondacks. In 1930, still in his twenties, Galamian opted for full-time teaching at the Russian Conservatory in Paris. There America began to discover him, beginning with Roland Gundry, 11, and Veda Reynolds, 9, both prodigiously gifted children of Franco-American parents. Gundry would go on to an American concert career; Reynolds became the first female member of the Philadelphia Orchestra and a professor at the University of Washington. For a few years, Galamian commuted between Paris and New York in half-year increments. In 1937, with World War II just over the horizon, he packed up for good and moved to New York, where he quickly became an item. In 1944, Auer's protégé Efrem Zimbalist, now director of Curtis as well as Mrs. Bok's spouse, made him an offer he couldn't refuse. The same year he opened Meadowmount. In part, the idea was to make himself available to advanced players from anywhere. He also dreamed of a talent factory of his own, on the order of Piotr Stolyarsky's in Odessa, where brigades of brilliantly gifted children would be taught to "practice, practice, practice" by a man who might have qualified for an orchestra job in Oberhausen, according to a former pupil, and had a weakness for metaphors—like a note that should sound like fat borscht or playing that should sound like a bellyful of melon.[193]

By the time of Galamian's death in 1981, Meadowmount had grown from an ad hoc summer course with an enrollment of thirty to an institution in its own right, with a core of distinguished assistants like DeLay and Sally Thomas and a corps of distinguished studio pianists. Distinguished friends and colleagues like Joseph Gingold and Isaac Stern showed up for master classes and chamber music. Distinguished performers like Zino Francescatti and Joseph Szigeti showed up for one-night stands.

Students were rigorously screened. The day began at 7:00 with break-fast, and work started at 8:00. There was time off for lunch and an hour of recreation before dinner. Even the practice routine allowed for fifty-minute hours, with ten-minute breaks for recuperation and natural functions. Four to five hours of daily practice was the rule. An example to the rest, the master himself worked eight to ten hours with no break at all, while also patrolling the grounds between lessons, listening for suspicious sounds of silence. In principle, bedtime was 10:00 p.m., though the auda-cious might sneak out to such modest nightspots as the neighborhood offered. Even readers of *Time* knew that to be caught "in the bushes," to use Galamian's preferred expression, was tempting fate.[194] "Like a prison camp in a national park," said Arnold Steinhardt,[195] who would move on to a long and distinguished career as multiple prizewinner, concertmaster of the Cleveland Orchestra, and first violinist of the Guarneri Quartet. Visi-tors loved it as they might love a summer weekend at the lake.

Save for the venue, the rest of the year was more of the same. There were no weekends in Galamian's calendar, and the workday ended ten hours after it began. Over the course of a given week or month, up to a hundred students, most from Curtis and Juilliard, where he had also taught since 1946, trooped to his Upper West Side apartment for lessons of legendary rigor and punctuality. Occasionally, one or another of them even lived there. Recalled for his dedication to his dogs, Galamian was also a whiz at ping-pong, fond of detective stories, and good at chess problems. Personal problems, on the other hand, were not his field, not least, his stu-dent Robert Zimansky speculated, because they would interfere with his schedule.[196] The world as he knew it was real and earnest, a fiercely com-petitive and basically unforgiving place. Supply was engaged in an uneven match with Demand. His job, as he saw it, was teaching professional sur-vival skills to the wise student who would come to learn them by doing what he said. "I cannot promise a great concert career to every student, but I can guarantee that each one will be able to make a decent living with his instrument," he said, and there was really something to this.[197]

From time to time, individual students spotted a Galamian not usually visible to their peers. There was the ingenious Galamian, who got an Israeli student to raise his violin and keep it at the indicated height by holding a lit cigarette lighter three inches below the student's left elbow. There was the generous Galamian, who saw enough redeeming talent in the thirteen-year-old Margaret Batjer, later concertmistress of the Los Angeles Chamber Orchestra, to disregard her technical deficiencies, make her a personal project, and send her to Curtis rather than tell her to go home, as she had expected. There was even a funny Galamian, who advised the student who showed up at a Carnegie Hall concert with a bald boyfriend that her beau needed rehairing.

Virtually all his students recalled—though probably exaggerated[198]—a one-size-fits-all approach to basic technique; the regimen of progressively more challenging exercises he prescribed to acquire it; his parsimony with words, compliments, even smiles; and, above all, the Look—a stare that made the Gorgon seem kindly—when he thought someone was unserious or slacking off.[199] "Football is like life—it requires perserverance, self-denial, hard work, sacrifice, dedication and respect for authority," said Vince Lombardi, the Ivan Galamian of football coaches, with a conviction and emphasis that would surely have sounded familiar to Galamian students. "Winning isn't everything, it's the only thing," Lombardi added famously. "Twenty-seven of my students won prizes at fifteen major international competitions, including the Leventritt, Tchaikovsky, Queen Elisabeth, Wieniawski, Paganini, and Indianapolis," Galamian, the Lombardi of violin teachers, could have replied.[200]

Yet all the while two of his closest associates were proving that nice guys could finish first. It might be assumed that Joseph Gingold's formative experiences, like Galamian's, were not conducive to a sunny view of human nature. Gingold seemed born with a gene for turning vinegar to wine.

To be born Jewish in the Russian-Polish borderlands was already an inauspicious start. With the outbreak of war in 1914, his family found itself between the German and Russian lines. When the war ended four years later, they found themselves in a newly independent, robustly anti-Semitic Poland. At this point, it seemed a good idea to the Gingolds to leave for other parts.

The first year of emigration meant poverty in Paris. The second meant poverty in New York, and public school in the land of the free, where a history teacher failed the young Joseph Gingold despite a perfect test score, a principal told his classmates to stop applauding him for his performance in the school assembly, and an art teacher acknowledged his success in the assembly with a vicious whack across his left palm that might have ended his career before it began.[201] Even silver linings like study with Vladimir

Graffman, an assistant of Auer's, and three years with Eugène Ysaÿe came packed in clouds. The Depression was waiting on his return to New York in October 1929. The aspiring soloist settled for a job at the Ritz-Carlton Hotel, playing with the A&P Gypsies, before lucking into steady employment as concertmaster in a series of Broadway pit orchestras. In 1937, things brightened when he auditioned successfully for the all-star orchestra the National Broadcasting Company was organizing for Arturo Toscanini. He was invited to join a remarkable quartet with his colleagues Oscar Shumsky, William Primrose, and Harvey Shapiro. In 1944 he left to be concertmaster in Detroit. In 1947, he moved to Cleveland, where George Szell wanted Gingold's help to make the local orchestra one of the world's great ones, and he began teaching in a Cleveland settlement house. With personal experience of at least two generations of great players, and careers of his own as job player, orchestra player, chamber player, and major league concertmaster to draw from, he clearly had plenty to teach and a breadth and depth of professional credibility few teachers could match. In 1954, Galamian hired him to teach chamber music at Meadowmount. There were plenty of reasons to say yes, among them, as Gingold confided to an interviewer decades later, the chance to watch Galamian work his magic at close range. In 1959, when Bain offered him a job at Indiana, there were plenty of reasons to say yes to that too, among them tenure and the comparative advantage of an academic pension. "I felt at home right away," he acknowledged when asked. "I had more artistic freedom than ever before in my life."[202]

"It's a mitzvah to be a teacher," he told an interviewer, and clearly meant it. He continued to do what he liked best with as many as forty students at a time till his death thirty-five years later. Master class and seminar and jury invitations took him around the world. In 1982, resolved that America should have an Olympic-quality competition like those he judged in Europe, he fathered the International Violin Competition of Indianapolis, whose respective Romanian, Japanese, Russian, Canadian, Icelandic, Hungarian, and German winners would come from virtually everywhere but the competition's home country.[203]

Like Galamian's, Gingold's students grew up to be prizewinners and concertmasters. But it took no more than a visit to Gingold's studio to see that there were alternative ways to go about it. All Galamian students were likely to take to heart the story of the student who regularly showed up underprepared. Galamian first let the student play his entire lesson in icy silence, then picked up his chair and threw it at the wall.[204] In the Gingold variation, as reported by Mary Budd Horozaniecki, the studio pianist was excused with a polite "Thank you for coming in today; please give my best regards to your teacher." With an avuncular chuckle, Gingold then congratulated the terrified student on her sight-reading. "From then on, I practiced five hours a day," she remembered.[205]

Like Galamian and Gingold, Dorothy DeLay, the third titan, lived to teach violin, and into advanced age maintained a work schedule that would turn a union secretary pale. A partial roster of students who made it professionally included 231 names, including entire companies of active soloists, chamber players, and concertmasters of the world's major orchestras. The resemblance to her peers was not entirely coincidental. Her association with Galamian went back to 1946, when a get-acquainted interview led to a half dozen violin lessons and a regular Monday night dinner. The same year, Juilliard asked her to join the staff of its Pre-College Division. In 1948, Galamian invited her to assist him at Meadowmount. For the next twenty-two years, summers at Meadowmount alternated with shared committee assignments and increasingly strained collegiality at Juilliard. She then declared her independence.

In 1970, DeLay called Galamian to tell him that she had accepted a summer invitation from the Aspen Music School in Colorado. Galamian hung up without a word, demanded that she be fired, and never spoke to her again. He then called in the dozen or so students who studied with both of them and told them to make their choice. Most went with DeLay.

DeLay's relationship with Gingold presumably went back to Meadowmount, where Gingold had been active almost as long as she had been and countless students had studied with both. Affinities of temperament and the guildish nature of the profession would have made them aware of one another irrespective of Meadowmount. Had there been a Nobel Prize for Positive Reinforcement, both would have been strong candidates.

It was the dissimilarities that made DeLay unique. As far back as anyone could remember, the profession had been European and male. Now for the first time ever, an A-list violin teacher was not only American and female but literally a Dorothy from Kansas. She had scored 180 on a childhood IQ test. She drove with the zest of a NASCAR driver into her eighties. Sovereign even in her disregard for punctuality and fondness for Chinese take-out, she was at once lowercase republican and imperial, a large presence in every sense.

It was Galamian's example that turned her thoughts to teaching. Invitations from Manhattan's Henry Street Settlement School and Sarah Lawrence College then allowed her to try it. Descended from generations of teachers and preachers, she discovered, to her surprise, that she was good at teaching and that she liked it.

To watch her at work was an education in itself. She occasionally demonstrated with her elegantly manicured right hand, though not with her elegantly manicured left, Anastasia Khitruk recalled. She was terrific at explaining things. The principle was essentially simple. The violin and bow each constituted an axis. If things didn't sound as they ought to, it meant that one or the other axis needed attention.[206]

It was hard to tag along for a day without realizing how many things she really knew—for example, about motivation, the politics and economics of concert management, the psychology of adolescents, the care and management of parents, the dynamics of the job market, the decline of public virtues, who looks good in red, and where to find an assertiveness coach for young female Koreans, as well as music theory, musical form, and the Heifetz versus Perlman style of shifting position on the fingerboard. "Tell me what you'd like to do with this piece?" she asked brightly of a young Russian with a history of intonation problems. "What sins do you have in mind?" she asked mildly of a young and clearly anxious Chinese student who wanted to know where she stood on the position that "Jesus had died for our sins." Her lessons were a mix of Socratic dialogue and John Dewey, the early twentieth-century American educational reformer, a visitor observed admiringly. It was very possibly the first time that anyone had ever noticed. DeLay was clearly pleased. Dewey had been one of her father's heroes, she told him.[207]

If DeLay was normal—and American—as blueberry pie, Zakhar Bron was as Soviet as the Special School, whose graduates, like their mathematician and basketball player peers, were among the Soviet Union's few competitive export products. Born in Kazakhstan, he trained in Odessa at the famous school for young talents still named for its founding father, Piotr Stolyarsky. The next step was Moscow, where Boris Goldstein and Igor Oistrakh, superachievers in their own right, buffed him to an international prizewinning sheen. At this point, the normal course led to a state-managed concert career. Instead, he took a job at the Special Music School for Children in Novosibirsk, a minimally charming industrial city of a million-plus, nearly four time zones east of Moscow.

Over the next fourteen years, in what even Russians would consider one of the world's least propitious cultural centers, he established himself as a latter-day Leopold Auer. By forty, he had seen a lot of the world without even leaving the Soviet Union. The frequent flying then began in earnest. He was first carried west by the winds of Soviet reform and an invitation from Justus Frantz, the entrepreneurial pianist, whose Schleswig-Holstein festival was fast becoming a north German institution. His teaching language, an idiosyncratic mix of native Russian, quaint German, and minimal English, seemed not to be a problem.[208] Within a few years, he was DeLay's antipode, and in many ways Galamian's, too, first in Lübeck, then Cologne, Rotterdam, and Madrid, with cameo appearances, one-night stands, and jury duty virtually anyplace that could afford him.

Like DeLay's, his lessons were as much an education for the spectator as the student. But the logic behind them, with its basic menu of scales, Kreutzer, Rode, and à la carte concert repertory, was as classic as it got.[209] The basic raw materials were discipline and talent, both his own and, ideally, the student's. The ten-hour teaching day was standard. If asked, he would explain that he taught professionalism.

What was uncommon was the directness, even urgency, of the message delivered by this fuzzy-haired, roly-poly force of nature. He might stamp, dance, conduct, or play a piece himself to make his point. "He seemed to inspire us in very different ways—either through demonstrating or through screaming at you—and each of us received a really individualized treatment," the Soviet-Israeli Vadim Gluzman told an interviewer cheerfully.[210] Bron seemed never to forget a student's name, and wielded his violin, and also occasionally his cell phone, as though it were just another extremity. "You know how to vibrate. That's a good thing. But when you do it all the time, that's a bad thing," he might caution the child of a German-Japanese couple, as he struggled to impose a bit of structure on a movement of Lalo. "You've been lazy. Really, honestly, you can't do that," he might admonish the post-Soviet teenager in best "more in sorrow than in anger" mode, when the boy's Wieniawski sounded rather the way a teenager's room might look. A Korean girl looked on in earnest bafflement as he compared the variations of Paganini's Caprice No. 24 with labyrinths and kaleidoscopes.

Yet she, and anyone watching, was as likely to remember how he got her to play fingered octaves, very possibly for the first time in her life. By the threshold of another new century, reaching a culture-shocked Korean had, in fact, become a credible measure of any good late twentieth-century, let alone any twenty-first century, violin teacher. Since 1983, Kurt Sassmannshaus, a DeLay protégé, had been aiming at just that while quietly turning his Cincinnati studio into a hatchery as productive as Bloomington, Indiana, and Novosibirsk.

His own hatchery lay more or less between them. German-born and German-trained, he had gone into the family business. His father, Egon, a postwar autodidact, had parlayed unorthodox beginnings into a respectable and respected career as an orchestra violist, private teacher, head of the public music school in Würzburg, and creator of an innovative method of teaching four- to six-year-olds. As heir to more normal circumstances, his son studied with Igor Ozim, an international prizewinner, now settled comfortably in a Cologne professorship. Save for the year and destination, he could as well have been leaving to study with Flesch, or even Joachim.

Then came a sequence of windfalls unknown in Berlin's golden age. A Fulbright grant brought Kurt to Juilliard and DeLay, a figure rare enough in America and scarcely imaginable in Germany. Impressed in Aspen by a standard of playing also unknown at the time in Germany, he decided to stay on as a degree candidate with the hope and expectation of returning to a conventionally respectable German concertmastership.[211]

On the eve of his departure, a call from DeLay led instead to an entry-level teaching job at Sarah Lawrence College and changed his life. A few years later, he took a job at the University of Cincinnati's College Conservatory of Music, a merger of two nineteenth-century foundations that allowed him to be enterprising in ways unthinkable in a counterpart German conservatory.

A further bit of local serendipity was all that was needed to start making wheels turn. In 1919, Dorothy Richard Starling graduated from the Cincinnati Conservatory with a teacher's certificate and the warm regard of the professor of violin. In 1920 she added a diploma cum laude. In 1969, her widower, Frank M. Starling, established a small memorial foundation in Houston, Texas, to fund violin teaching. In 1987, Sassmannshaus parlayed a Starling grant into a visiting professorship for DeLay and a weekend chamber orchestra for high-achieving teenagers from as far away as St. Louis, Missouri, Chattanooga, Tennessee, and Portland, Oregon.[212]

Meanwhile, the DeLay connection yielded its own great leap forward. In 1972, President Richard Nixon and Secretary of State Henry Kissinger had rediscovered mainland China after twenty-three years of nonrecognition. In 1979, the Carter administration normalized relations with the People's Republic. The same year, Isaac Stern, an experienced cultural ice-breaker, toured China with a film crew in tow.[213] Soon afterward, a widening stream of young mainland Chinese talent began converging, first in DeLay's studio, then Sassmannshaus's.

By 2009, the Starling project had grown into a network of major orchestra players and other professionally active alumni extending from London to Taipei. The China connection had spun off a Great Wall Academy, where Sassmannshaus brought some of China's best and brightest for summer lessons and master classes with himself and colleagues from Cincinnati, Beijing, and Shanghai. A weekend feeder program called the Sassmannshaus Tradition extended the services of his studio to beginners age four and up. A website, www.violinmasterclass.com, extended it gratis around the world. "Toto," as Judy Garland said famously in the movie version of Frank Baum's iconic novel, "I've a feeling we're not in Kansas anymore." Nor Padua, Paris, Vienna, Berlin, St. Petersburg, or even Juilliard, Sassmannshaus might have added.

PLAYERS IN GENERAL

BUT THEN WHAT? For the Duke of Edinburgh, the von Mendelssohn brothers, Walter Willson Cobbett, or Catherine Drinker Bowen, it was a largely theoretical question. But for generations of less favored and more gifted players, it had been real and earnest since at least the sixteenth century.

Heinrich Ehrlich had lived in Berlin since 1862 as a professional pianist, composer, and teacher. He had personally experienced seven epoch-making decades of Central European music history, four of them as political and music correspondent for respectable papers as far away as St. Petersburg.[214] Within a generation, he had watched an ugly duckling hometown turn swan on its way to becoming the most musical city in the world's most musical country. But he was not entirely happy with what he saw.

There were some 112 music schools in Berlin alone, he estimated in 1895. There were 60 more in Vienna, and 125 more in other German cities. Without even counting schools in Budapest, Prague, and the rest of the Austrian Empire, this already meant some 15,000 music students. From Aachen to Königsberg and Czernowitz, virtually every town with a train station had a theater, an opera, and an orchestra. Living composers like Mahler and Richard Strauss were celebrities on a scale unimaginable a century later. Demand for musicians soared as did demand for coal, iron, and steel. Yet it was not imaginable that demand could continue to outpace supply. Starting in 1890, factoring in three years of conservatory, and assuming that only 30 percent of graduates aspired to play for a living, Ehrlich estimated that there were 18,000 entry-level professionals in Germany alone. Parents could at least make sure that their sons, let alone their daughters, knew what they were getting into when they decided to be musicians, he noted soberly.[215]

A century later, his warning seemed to have gained in urgency. London's four conservatories alone turned out 90–100 fully qualified young string players each year, Norman Lebrecht reported in 2007.[216] In 2005, it occurred to Daniel Wakin, a reporter at the *New York Times*, to ask what had become of the still young professionals from its class of 1994. The results were Ehrlich revisited. Of forty-four instrumentalists, eight had vanished from alumni files altogether. Of the remaining thirty-six, three considered themselves soloists, four were freelancers whose principal income came from teaching, five were full-time freelancers, and eleven held orchestra jobs from Radio Nederland to Singapore. That left twelve in work as different as tax preparation and the diamond trade.[217]

For those with a taste for adventure and a tolerance for risk, there were certainly role models. On the threshold of the nineteenth century, the great G. B. Viotti opted for a second career as theatrical entrepreneur before moving on to a third in the wine trade and a fourth as director of the Paris Opéra. In the middle of the twentieth century, Joseph Wechsberg made his way to the *New Yorker* staff, via a Czech law degree, the Paris Conservatory, ad hoc gigs in seedy Paris nightclubs and aboard French liners, freelance journalism, a staff job with a Czech parliamentarian, a commission in the Czech army, and the latrine detail as an American GI.[218] It was not the easiest itinerary. But it eventually brought him a "middle-class" Strad from Emil Herrmann. Yeou-Cheng Ma, a violinist and the elder sister of Yo-Yo Ma, opted for medical school, a four-day week as a developmental pediatrician at Yeshiva University's Albert Einstein College of Medicine, coupled with a seven-day week as executive director of the Children's Orchestra Society in New York.[219] George Lang (b. György Deutsch) made his way to a Strad via the Franz Liszt Academy, a wartime Jewish labor camp, and a postwar People's Court in his native Hungary, followed by a career in *New York* that would carry him from ad hoc gypsy primás, Carnegie Hall page-turner, and NBC Symphony substitute to celebrity owner of the Café des Artistes in midtown Manhattan.[220]

Historically, for those who hung on, neither supply nor demand were congenial to long-term forecast. The parameters of boom and bust shone through successive editions of a London directory over a single working lifetime. From 255 in 1890, the cadre of registered violinists/violists rose to 929 in 1900. More slowly, but still impressively, it rose again to 1017 in 1910. In 1920, it climbed to 1319, possibly buoyed by a short-lived postwar boom. With national income down more than 13 percent since 1929, it then fell over 60 percent, to 529 in 1931.[221]

Technical mastery, including sight-reading skills, was a prerequisite, but provided only starting capital. The player most likely to succeed would look for any opportunity—churches, restaurants, tea dances, amateur entertainments, private parties—to play. In a city famed for its lavish employment of substitutes, the ambitious newcomer would network wherever possible and cultivate the fixers who booked their colleagues on the side. It was a plus to live in a place and time where live music was still unchallenged by anything more threatening than the music box, more and more people wanted more and more Beethoven, and orchestras, refitted for Wagner, Mahler, and Richard Strauss, needed more and more string players.

Gender was still professional destiny. Entry-level players who were female were up against it, no matter how well prepared or connected. "There should at least be some concern for the future, if our orchestras aren't to be made up of men and women,"[222] Ernst Rudorff, piano professor at the Berlin Conservatory, complained to his colleague Joseph Joachim in 1881.

There were distant indications that this might change. In 1883, 185 young women applied for piano scholarships at the Royal College of Music. Only sixteen applied for violin scholarships. Only one made it.[223] By 1910, women comprised 16 percent of the violinists listed in the professional directory. Three years later, Sir Henry Wood, originator of the Prom Concerts, hired six women for the Queen's Hall orchestra.

Women of extraordinary talent like Wilma Neruda and Marie Hall could make it as soloists. There were even a few all-women quartets. The conductor Sir Thomas Beecham was nonetheless assured a laugh whenever he quoted the orchestra player who told him, "If she is attractive, I can't play with her; if she is not, then I won't." The 1921 directory confirmed the default alternative. Of 21,000 music teachers in England and 2,000 in Scotland, 76 percent were women.[224]

Race, ethnicity, and nationality could dictate job-market destiny, too. In America, black string bands might make it on what the industry called "race records."[225] In Hungary, Romania, and Russia, Gypsy fiddlers might make it in restaurants and as hired entertainers.[226] In Central and Eastern Europe, where many orchestras were public-sector and some, like the Berlin and Vienna Philharmonics, were co-ops, native players defended their turf. Jobs for Jews like Jacob Grün in Hanover reflected the current state of Jewish emancipation.[227] Asia was still behind the moon. Japan's first permanent orchestra, now the NHK, formed in 1927, was at least a job opportunity for Japanese instrumentalists.[228] The same year, the heavily

Russian and Jewish Shanghai Municipal Orchestra allowed Tan Shu-zhen, 20, to become its first Chinese player, though "of course," its Italian conductor told him, he wouldn't be paid.[229]

In Britain, such things only mattered at the margins. A staple of British musical life since the sixteenth century, foreign players still comprised a quarter to half of several major London orchestras as late as 1866. As might be imagined, German players, "and their number was legion," left in 1914 "to the great delight of many British artists, who found themselves with increased work and considerably improved chances of livelihood," Eugene Goossens remembered decades later.[230] Normally tolerant native players reportedly gave even Italians and Jews a hard time. Though union rules barred Americans from the British musical labor market, the postwar taste for jazz seems to have inspired a panic about race. But the flourishing interwar careers of the Dutch-born David de Groot, the Rome-born Alfredo Campoli, the Magenta-born Emilio Colombo, the Venice-born Annunzio Mantovani, and the Mauritian-born Jean Pougnet in London's fanciest restaurants, tearooms, and palm courts suggest that what President Harding called "normalcy" kicked in again when the war was over.[231]

Technology had consequences, too. In Britain alone, the coming of silent films created an estimated 12,000 jobs in movie theaters, enough to employ 75 to 80 percent of the nation's musicians in a workplace where the music director put their sight-reading skills to the test after screening the weekly feature. In 1926, American movie houses employed 22,000. Three years later, 19,000 were still there, earning up to $60 weekly, twice the real earnings of a skilled industrial worker.[232] Then came sound, and orchestras that couldn't get theater players to look at them three years earlier had twenty applications for every vacancy.[233] The coming of talking pictures also created studio jobs in Hollywood paying up to $500 a week, but there were only a few hundred of them.[234] Invited to Hollywood by Ernst Lubitsch for MGM's *Merry Widow* in 1934, violinist Louis Kaufmann earned $275 a day, twice union scale, and $1,500 a week in the very trough of the Great Depression. The concertmaster of the Chicago Symphony was meanwhile earning $250 a week at Orchestra Hall. Twenty years later, Hollywood's seven major studios employed 303 musicians full-time, while another 4,000 part-timers earned an average of $300 a year, a little more than the average monthly wage.[235]

From modest beginnings in local studios, radio, too, had its possibilities, including the creation of company-sponsored orchestras in New York, London, Manchester, Glasgow, Cardiff, Paris, Rome, Turin, Milan, and Naples. With all possible fanfare, NBC created a studio orchestra in 1937. With the enthusiastic support and participation of the occupation authorities, postwar West Germany launched eight radio orchestras within months of the Nazi surrender.[236] With the coming of TV and the passing of its larger-than-life conductor, Arturo Toscanini, NBC allowed its orchestra to die in 1954. But with public money for the most part assured, the European orchestras played on.

In the aftermath of World War II, Walter Legge, a producer of genius, created the Philharmonia orchestra for EMI, proprietor of the famous Abbey Road studios. Like most orchestras, the Philharmonia went on to play public concerts. But from its conception, its primary mission was to record under a succession of virtuoso conductors.[237] Between the early 1950s and the end of the twentieth century, successive innovations in the recording industry, including the long-playing record and the CD, were bonanzas for other major orchestras, like the Philadelphia, whose discography under Eugene Ormandy alone came to nearly four hundred,[238] and perhaps, most conspicuously the Berlin Philharmonic under Herbert von Karajan, which asked for and got up to £65,000 for a single recording[239]

But the coming of the Internet once again marked the end as well as the beginning of an era. As the CD, too, approached the slippery slope to Lethe, the audience showed signs of moving in the same direction. There were wistful hopes for boutique and even artist-led production and online sale for direct download from Internet to iPod. But this was no longer an era when a collection of Caruso, Kreisler, Rachmaninov, and Powell was as much a part of a middle-class household as a Sears catalogue, and whole opera productions could now be downloaded from YouTube without charge.[240]

Occasionally, the supply side managed to get a leg up. From the sixteenth century on, the union of violin and Western music was a job creator. Paris needed violins for dances, Venice for operas and oratorios, and Munich, Dresden, Mannheim, not to mention the occasional landed melophile like Haydn's patron Prince Nikolaus Esterházy, needed violins for orchestras.

Demography, economic development, discretionary income increases, urban growth, social diversity, developing tastes, civic vanity, conspicuous consumption, entrepreneurial zip, and musical genius did their part, too. A *tour d'horizon* published in the *British Bandsman* in 1887 confirmed how the profession had come to extend over an ever broader social landscape. There were the serious players of concerts, opera, and oratorio who taught on the side. There were the well-connected purveyors of musical yard goods for balls and private receptions, especially those willing to play in Hungarian costume, which was the current rage. There were the worker bees who made their living in the theater, playing drama, opera bouffe, and burlesque. At the low end of the scale, there was the engine room crew who played four hours a night at the music hall. Though it might take a long workweek to do it, by 1925 fair numbers of musicians were in reach of outearning the mail carrier. By the mid-1960s, Joseph Szigeti, the most thoughtful and perceptive concert artist of his time, had the impression that there were more orchestra jobs in the United States, Britain, France, and Germany than there were qualified players to fill them.[241]

Still, it was a fact of professional life that demand could never be taken entirely for granted, nor were all jobs created equal. Like sight-reading, multitasking and self-invention often became critical survival skills. In 1779, it was reported in London that a certain Signora Rossi performed "most surprising Feats on the stiff Rope, also Capers and Elevations with great Dexterity, Decency and Elegance," among them violin pieces "in six different positions, quite new and agreeable."[242] In 2004, five Princeton undergraduates with a common weakness for Davie Bowie and Bela Bartók, and respectively armed with a mandolin, a bass, a cello, a violin, and drums, set off in space suits acquired from eBay to introduce the world to what they called orchestral space pop.[243] In 2008, it was reported in New York that Caleb Burhans, who had studied violin at the Eastman School of Music, sang countertenor in the Trinity Church choir, both sang and played in a pop theater piece, performed with several new music ensembles, and concertized with "itsnotyouitsme," his ambient rock duo. At the same time, he was working on a piece called "oh ye of little faith . . . (do you know where your children are?)" for a group called Sound the Alarm, in which he also played.[244] For the authors of titles like *Making Your Living as a String Player* and *Beyond Talent: Creating a Successful Career in Music*,[245] his career could reasonably be regarded both as a cautionary tale and as a success story.

While the violin allowed its players, concurrently or seriatim, to be more things to more people than any instrument save the human voice, the history of the profession ran more or less parallel to the history of the orchestra. Both began small. Musical clerics often enjoyed fast-track careers; musicians seldom did. Bards, troubadours, and trumpeters enjoyed some respect. Violinists, on the other hand, were well to the lower end of the social totem pole, and trumpeters, who earned twice as much as lute players at a wedding in Frankfurt, earned four times as much as fiddlers and bagpipers.

In a corporate society that conferred legal status, however restrictive, on virtually everyone, musicians had little or none. The itinerant musician was ineligible for military service, disqualified as a witness, barred from carrying a sword and wearing armor, and considered fair game for bandits. In Goslar, in Lower Saxony, now Germany, his children were excluded from inheritance. The provisional solution, for those skillful or fortunate enough to pull it off, was to gain a patron-protector who might show his appreciation by offering a ring, a horse, room and board, clothing (though not used clothing), or even real property. Cash payment for the job musician was generally understood as an expression of disdain.[246]

Things got worse before they got better. In the Romanian and Hungarian provinces of the Ottoman Empire, Gypsy musicians were among the most respected slaves, or vice versa: Gypsy slaves were among the most popular musicians, traded, loaned, or rented out to taverns, mills, and inns by Turkish pashas, Hungarian aristocrats, and Romanian monastic clergy. In early nineteenth-century Russia, upscale music lovers met the player deficit by co-opting the serf population. This initiative reached its peak in the years before 1812, when, according to one estimate, there were as many as 310 serf orchestras of all sizes, from three up. Some were awful. Others were surprisingly good, and certainly good enough to be bought, sold, and shown off to neighbors while bankrupt owners hired foreign coaches and conductors to train them. At least one eighteenth-century magnate played along with his serfs under their serf conductor.[247] Another sent his serf to the Paris Conservatory.[248]

As early as the 1690s, colonial Virginia valued its slave musicians, too, with the violin as the preferred instrument. While their amateur owners made recreational music in the parlor, "slave musicianers," as they called themselves, were de facto pros, as essential to a successful party or dance as the punch bowl. Hired out to resorts during the season, they were also deployed at ordinary inns to entertain the guests after a hard day on the road, and their work was generally appreciated as a source of supplementary cash. Occasionally, an owner would even add value to his human resource pool by buying instruments and hiring teachers, as did his Russian counterparts.[249]

Municipal employment, established in Germany as far back as the fourteenth century, was a first step to both job security and social respectability. In 1685, a local court in Flensburg heard a complaint from the wife of a local businessman who was indignant that the town musician's wife had presumed to enter the church ahead of her.[250] But until the position finally disappeared with the general post-Napoleonic abolition of estates and guilds, the town musician's job was worth the occasional speed bump. It generally came with an honorific title as well as a regular salary. For the first time, it conferred civil status as artisan and citizen, and with it legal recourse, even the right to bear arms. It opened the possibility of court employment, which tended to pay better, though there was some risk of layoff when times were hard. It also left room for freelance employment at parties and weddings, while assuring protection, at least to a point, against the foreigners and job players, who were the era's equivalent of non-union laborers.

Leipzig, a town of about twenty thousand, where church, town, and university intersected, was a good place to watch the new world take shape. Beginning in the sixteenth century, the city had hired four wind players, known as pipers, for two daily fanfares from the city hall tower, as well as for processions and fancy public occasions. The city then added three string players, known as art violinists because they played from written music, to perform at dances and indoor concerts. Their wages, equivalent to a carpenter's or secondary school teacher's, were modest. But each was given a house, an instrument, lifetime tenure, a pension of sorts, and a monopoly claim to such occasional gigs as weddings, civic banquets, and university ceremonies.[251]

On Sundays and holidays, the players joined forces at the two principal churches. In 1653, they also formed a guild. Within a decade, the string players were appealing for official help against encroachments on the wedding trade, not only by the wind players but by some twenty-eight moonlight session fiddlers, including a butcher and a shoemaker. The solution, a thirteen-point agreement that took two years to negotiate, was already in ruins by the end of the next decade. It was agreed that pipers should get five thalers for a wedding to the violinists' three. It was also clear that the status quo was on its last legs in a town whose population was about to increase by half over the next thirty years.[252] In 1698, an entrepreneurial job fiddler named Christoph Stephan Scheinhardt and his band of violins, oboes, trumpets, timpani, and French shawms (predecessors of the oboe) got the bid to play at a lunch for the visiting Russian czar. In 1712, the city council legitimized his band as the city's third official musical organization. By 1750, the year Bach died, any thought of a monopoly by local players was history.

Pragmatic where flexibility was indicated, a few violinists joined what they couldn't beat and were promoted to pipers. Others added violin making to their repertory with such success that some apparently made violins good enough to impress Bach. For those who were exceptionally good performers or well-connected enough to get one, a court job, particularly a royal job, was not only better than any municipal job but potentially the best position possible. By the sixteenth century, bands of some sort, employed to play at court, civic, or even private entertainments and ceremonies, had become the rage in much of Western and Central Europe. Most mixed consorts of instruments and singers were essentially similar from place to place and court to court, but the corps of string players attached to the French court was recognized early on as the best there was.[253]

This expert group began during the reign of François I as a cadre of six musical multitaskers on the payroll of the royal stables. But with the coming of the dance-loving Bourbons in 1589, the royal string players were promoted to the king's immediate staff. It was sunshine from there. By 1609 there were twenty-two of them. Five years later, there were twenty-four, known as Les Vingt-quatre Violons du Roi, a corporate brand that would assure them institutional survival till 1761, despite the arrival of a conductor as the twenty-fifth member, and footnote immortality ever after.

Despite their name, they were actually a consort of six violins and six cellos, with four violas as middle voices. Their mandate included playing for court balls, major receptions, state banquets and religious processions. Their specialty was the court ballet, where they marched into the hall playing their instruments, and took their place on a bandstand reserved for their use. At the same time, players maintained independent identities as members of the Confrérie de St-Julien, the Paris guild that allowed individual players to take part in public concerts and the whole group to hire itself out for occasional private engagements.

With the coming of the Italian-born Jean-François Lully and the comic dramatist Molière in the mid-seventeenth century, the mandate expanded to include theater and opera, and the middle voices thinned out in favor of more violins and cellos. The working conditions remained consistently good. In effect salaried civil servants, royal players were entitled to allowances for food and transportation and could look forward to occasional supplementary payments in kind. They were paid substantially less than their singer, keyboard player, and lutenist colleagues for the limited season at court, but when not at Versailles, they could live, freelance, and teach in Paris. They also received intangible rewards like regular contact with the king and court, honorific titles like "honorable homme" and "bourgeois de Paris," and the right to wear a sword.[254]

Since this was the ancien régime, where offices could be bought and sold, freelance opportunities were of more than casual interest. The official salary was 365 livres a year. The basic price for a position was two to three thousand, but there were also the supplemental expenses like a little something for the seller's wife, fees for the notary and the official who approved the sale, and a fancy dinner for the buyer's twenty-three new colleagues. Together these extras could cost half again the price of the position.

Quality control is an obvious question: how talented were these players? While the court retained a veto, no one seems to have exercised it, very possibly because most newcomers came from player families or were already familiar to their colleagues as substitutes or supernumeraries. Lully, tirelessly active as a dancer, composer, and personal favorite of the king since entering royal service in 1651, was "infuriated by their ignorance and routine playing."[255] For some years a second group, apparently created for the personal use of Louis XIV and known as Les Petits Violons, existed in the shadow of the first. What was "little" about it is unclear, since it eventually comprised twenty-five players. But unlike the group of twenty-four, it lived on-site, traveled with the king, and included a small complement of winds. Its members earned 600 livres a year to the Vingt-quatre's 350, a clear hint that they were strong players. They became Lully's ensemble of choice.

On special occasions ensembles were combined for maximal effect. The second day of a multiday entertainment called Les Plaisirs de l'Isle enchantée featured thirty-four strings, twenty from the Vingt-quatre, fourteen from the Petits, in addition to elephants and camels. The water ballet on the third day raised the string total to thirty-nine. By 1681, a ballet called Le Triomphe de l'Amour mobilized seventy-six, including forty-six strings, apparently the full membership of both ensembles.

In 1669, the poet Pierre Perrin and the composer Robert Cambert negotiated a royal charter assuring exclusive rights to singers, actors, staging, and costumes and established an Académie Royale de Musique to produce French opera as well as Italian. But Lully, Master of the King's Music since 1661, remained in charge of the court orchestras. Three years later, Lully saw his chance to buy out the previous owners, acquire their prerogatives, and add the court orchestras. As de facto director of the Opéra, the only institution in France authorized to "employ more than six violins or other instrumentalists,"[256] he then organized Europe's first large, integrated standing orchestra, with an auditioned string section of twenty-five. He expected them to rehearse. While known to smash violins over players who failed to meet his expectations and fine them for missing rehearsals, he nonetheless paid well, mended fences after quarrels, looked out for his players' interests, and even got them extra gigs, provided that they didn't work for the competition.[257]

By 1687 when Lully died, things had undeniably improved. In Leipzig, Italian innovation arrived secondhand with Johann Georg Pisendel, a Bavarian law student who had studied with expatriate Italians.[258] In Rome, Corelli organized and directed orchestras for every purpose drawn from a network of the city's best and brightest, including recruits from household payrolls and local churches.[259]

The Vingt-quatre were, meanwhile, down to eight or nine court services a year. Many of the players earned multiple incomes from multiple offices. Others, who owned only a piece of their position, could freelance most of the year. By the middle of the eighteenth century, the vast expense of the royal establishment compounded by the vast expense of the Seven Years' War did the rest to finish off what was now approaching a two-hundred-year run. It was decided that the court orchestras would be downsized and their tenured players bought out.

By this time, it hardly mattered. The theaters, the Opéra and its Lenten spin-off, the Concert Spirituel, were happy to have them. So were any number of princes, dukes, and counts. The Concert Spirituel paid court violinists a respectably middle-class 1,000 to 1,500 livres a year, equivalent to the annual earnings of a college teacher or royal librarian.[260] Alexandre Riche de La Pouplinière, the royal tax farmer and a celebrated patron, alone engaged a household orchestra of fifteen; only a third of the players were young French up-and-comers, imported from the provinces, while the rest were German and Italian professionals.

In London, a catch-up capital in 1600 but destined for great things,

court musicians show up on court payrolls by the beginning of the Tudor
era. Like so many things British, hiring policy seems to have been based
on a combination of pragmatism and precedent. Direct petition was possible. So was recommendation by a courtier, a serving musician, or a diplomat. In a marrying mood once more in 1539 and eager to recruit the best
available talent, Henry VIII outsourced the search to Edmund Harvel,
England's man in Venice. Rising to the occasion, Harvel located not only
four well-recommended Bassano brothers happy to accept the offer but six
more a year later. "And because thes me(n) are pore," and couldn't afford
the trip, he reported of the first group, he advanced them "cix crownes of
gold and providid beside(s) livre(s) of credit" to get them to their destination.[261] Four generations of Lupos, even more of Bassanos, would show that
connections helped and arriving in Britain as an immigrant Italian Jew
didn't hurt. Beginning in 1545, official documents also confirm that the
newly recruited royal consort had something to do with violins.

Contrary to appearances, engagement of a violinist to fill what was officially understood as a bagpiper or lutenist position was only a bureaucratic
convenience. The job description was nominal. The violinist was real.
While court wages seemed unattractive, they not only compared favorably
with noncourt wages but included such fringe benefits as livery, the title
of "gentleman," multiple budget lines for a single player, free board, tax
exemptions, exemption from some kinds of arrest, and payments in kind
from lute strings to real estate leases.[262]

Assigned to dinner but especially to dance music, the band played on
through successive reigns, while the violin encroached progressively on
territory occupied till now by viols. By the 1560s, violins showed up in
aristocratic household inventories. By the 1580s, the violin had even made
its way to school curricula in places where little English boys, like little
Venetian girls, were trained to be professionals.

At this point, English as well as French names showed up increasingly
on court rosters. The violinists were seen with their court musician colleagues in Queen Elizabeth's funeral procession. They appeared more and
more often as accessories to masques, the stylized entertainments hugely
popular at the court of her successor, James I. When the monarchy was
restored in 1660, the violinists were also restored, this time identified, for
fairly transparent reasons, as the Twenty-four Violins, though the number
seems not to have been taken literally. Most were paid from the king's
personal funds. Others, following no apparent system, were paid from the

Royal Exchequer. There are hints that the intervening Puritan years had not been easy. But neither were the Restoration years with Parliament now in control of the royal budget. In November 1666, twenty-two of the royal violinists petitioned the king for wages already almost five years in arrears. A number of them had lost their homes to the Great Fire the previous July.[263] In 1673, a few more would lose their jobs to the Test Act, which excluded Catholics from court employment.[264]

Yet the masque economy flourished, and Restoration-era theater, a personal favorite of the king, created job opportunities unimagined before the Civil War. In 1661, the Twenty-four Violins played at the coronation of Charles II, whose tastes in dance and dinner music kept them fully employed and whose taste in church music created new jobs in the Chapel Royal. By the end of his reign, there were thirty-four places for the Twenty-four Violins. In 1685, they played at the coronation of James II, but less auspiciously. Three years later, when he was allowed to escape to French exile, the whole ensemble was still owed back wages.[265]

William and Mary, the new king and queen, brought austerity as well as a preference for wind bands. The group now known as the King's Band of Musick was limited to twenty-four players paid £40 a year for a shrinking schedule of yearly services. They were also entirely English, since a law of 1701 reserved civil service jobs for the native-born. (Though budget lines survived till World War I, the band gradually faded into footnotes as court ceremony and British musical life wandered off in other directions.)

However, shrinking opportunities to play at court hardly mattered as London morphed into the capital of a global empire, with a population of over 600,000, a flowering private sector, and a court whose schedule left plenty of opportunity to moonlight. In 1672, John Banister, a former court violinist, became the first to buy newspaper space to advertise a public concert.[266] Six years later, Thomas Britton, "the musical small coal man," turned the upper story of his house and place of business into a performance space accessible by ladder from the courtyard for concerts every Thursday.[267]

As "the numerous traine of young travellers of the best quallity and estates, went over into Itally and resided at Rome and Venice," where they "heard the best musick and learned of the best masters," Roger North saw a future that seemed to work. Player, listener, and amateur composer, as well as an occasional publisher, theoretician, groupie, and autobiographer, North noted how "the violin is so universally courted, and sought after to

be had of the best sort, that some say England hath dispeopled Itally of
violins."[268] Returning home from Italy, high on Corelli, the "Young Nobil-
lity and Gentry" then regarded the preferred instrument of "common fiddlers" as "the best utensill of Apollo."[269]

North watched as resident music teachers like the two his father had
employed yielded to the kind who "trot about from house to house every
morning, to give lessons for two guineas a dozen, while the winter lasts."[270]
He reported that domestic consorts gave way to public concerts by virtuoso performers like the Neapolitan Nicola Matteis, who "could hold an
audience by the ear longer than ordinary, and a whisper not to be heard
monst them."[271]

By 1734 when North died, a subculture of London gentleman amateurs
happily paid two guineas a year to get together at the Castle Tavern to play
with professionals or to gather in public rooms to hear "the best masters,"
recruited from the theater orchestras, play in series of twelve to twenty
concerts. A generation later, Carl Friedrich Abel together with J. S. Bach's
son Johann Christian drew five to six hundred well-heeled and socially
exclusive listeners to orchestra concerts in the Hanover Square Rooms, a
prototype of the dedicated concert hall. By the end of the century, London
was awash in orchestras, and Johann Peter Salomon, yet another German
walk-on and a respected violinist, trumped the competition by recruiting
orchestras of up to forty players, including sixteen violinists, to premiere
twelve symphonies composed for the occasion by Franz Joseph Haydn, the
father of the form.[272] A single concert performed two months after Haydn's
arrival brought in £350, double Salomon's original guarantee.[273]

By 1730, concert life was also in full bloom across the Channel. Paris's
version of the London impresario was the sort of patron whose name began
with Prince or Duc. But the English ambassador could also do the job, as
could Jeanne Agnès Berthelot de Pleneuf, mistress to the Duc de Bourbon,
the king's principal minister, whose short-lived but fashionable Concert
Italie drew sixty subscribers at half to two-thirds what a qualified artisan
earned in a year for a twice-weekly series at the Louvre.

Ironically, the era's winner was at best highborn by association. Named
for his godfather, the Duc Anne de Noailles, Anne Danican-Philidor was
actually male, and was an oboist in the Chapelle royale, a member of the
Petits Violons, and music librarian to the king.[274] It was Philidor's inspiration and claim to a place in music history to circumvent the Lenten
prohibition against concerts and opera with a series called Concert Spiri-

tuel. The court made the Salle des Cent Suisses, adorned with gold leaf and twelve enormous chandeliers, available rent free for as many as sixty players and singers. The orchestra, which eventually employed twenty-four violinists, included a heavy contingent of Opéra players who were happy to be employed on what would otherwise have been unpaid days off.

Philidor died three years later. But his series continued until 1790, becoming less spiritual and more popular as time passed.[275] Contemporaries were consistently impressed by the size, repertory, and professionalism of the orchestra. But the real novelty was the appearance of soloists, and lots of them, with a particular emphasis on singers and violinists like Jean-Marie Leclair, who performed at the Concert Spirituel as early as 1729.[276]

The Concert Spirituel, in turn, spun off additional orchestras and series, among them François-Joseph Gossec's Concert des Amateurs and the Concert de la Loge Olympique. At Gossec's, the city's best gentleman amateurs, carefully screened by the impresario himself, paid not only to hear but to play weekly concerts with the city's best professionals from December to March. At the Olympic, one of the city's more exclusive Masonic lodges, 363 subscribers paid 120 livres a year to hear 12 concerts performed by a 65-member ensemble, considered one of Europe's best, whose 40 violinists appeared in embroidered concert dress and lace cuffs, wearing swords at their sides. In 1785, it even commissioned 6 symphonies from Haydn.[277]

Though well on his way to international celebrity, Haydn remained at Eszterháza, the Versailles-dimensioned palace where he had resided for nearly thirty years. As composer, conductor, music director, and orchestra manager to Prince Nikolaus Esterházy, he was responsible for a large music establishment, parallel in stature to the kitchen, stable, and groundskeepers on the household flowchart. His contract stipulated that he was to be "considered and treated as a member of the household . . . an honorable official of a princely house."[278] In return for a respectable salary, plus fringe benefits and supplementary payments in kind, he was expected to eat with his peers and discharge his official duties in a handsome blue uniform.

During Haydn's tenure, the orchestra, which grew from fourteen to twenty-four, enjoyed official status, with salaries on a par with those of minor government officials. Players ate and lived together and received furnishings, linens, firewood, candles, and maid service, as well as instruments, uniforms, medical coverage, and pensions. In return, they were expected to play whenever asked and were required to live apart from their families for extended periods. They were heavily fined for being absent without permission and, in at least one case, denied permission to marry—on grounds that the married quarters were all occupied.

Eszterháza's music establishment was unusually large and uniquely linked to a resident genius. There were many more of lesser scope and of lesser brilliance in a Germany of some three hundred more or less sovereign territories. As much a part of the princely household as the cooks and gardeners (whose jobs they sometimes shared), musicians were seen and saw themselves as craftsmen who produced music much as their peers produced bread or horseshoes. Most musicians were local, often related, and were basically conservative and modestly educated.[279] Demand for their services, like demand for most things, was limited only by available resources, princely vanity, and, at least at the margins, proximity to France.

Stuttgart, the capital of the duchy of Württemberg, was a museum-quality example of how far princely vanity could go. First traces of a court orchestra date back to 1683, when a French-style string band was hired to play for the seven-year-old Duke Eberhard Ludwig's dancing lessons. On reaching sixteen, he transformed it into an ensemble of about twenty, with doubled violins and violas and a female trumpeter. At the same time, he turned his Ludwigsburg hunting lodge into another mini-Versailles, with staff, entourage, and deficits to match. Between 1693 and 1718, family allowances rose 63 percent, court salaries 71 percent, stable and hunt expenses 136 percent, musicians' salaries 576 percent. Meanwhile, the duchy's deficit soared by almost 30 percent between 1716 and 1717 alone and reached millions of gulden a year later. By 1731, there were nonetheless thirty musicians on the payroll, in part because composers called for larger ensembles and in part because the neighbors had a large music staff. The next duke, Carl Alexander, shut down the building projects, the Italian opera, and the French theater and threatened to cut the orchestra, although nothing apparently came of this threat. Dazzled by the courts of Louis XV and Frederick the Great, Carl Alexander's successor, Carl Eugen, reversed course again and returned to Stuttgart, where he distinguished himself equally as an ironfisted autocrat and as a patron of the arts. He hired a French architect, acquired a theater and a ballet, built an Italian opera house to accommodate four thousand, and hired superstar Italian violinists much as later autocrats might hire star quarterbacks or shortstops. By 1764, the orchestra numbered forty-one, and salaries had increased by a factor of five.

As creative as he was desperate, the duke sold offices. He invented a lottery and forced people to buy tickets. He made court officials lend him money and mortgaged properties to anyone, including Voltaire, who was willing to take them. He levied taxes on property, inheritances, Jews, and transit and imposed fines on all possible transgressions and tolls on all possible services. He created an efficient revenue service to make sure these loans, taxes, fines, and tolls were collected. For an appropriate subsidy, he transferred three thousand troops to Louis XV, a generally happy arrangement till Carl Eugen was forced to join the Seven Years' War on the Franco-Austrian side and put the money in the war effort. The war required a few short-lived economies, and by 1776 the orchestra was down to fourteen. But by 1780 it was back to what it had been before.[280]

If Stuttgart was a well-tended white elephant, Mannheim was a beacon and bellwether, renowned for discipline, flexibility, and uniform bowing. In 1720, Carl Philipp, the Elector of the Palatinate, made Mannheim his seat of government. Within three years, he had hired fifty-two musicians, twelve of them violinists. By 1778, when his nephew and successor Carl Theodor moved to Munich as the new Elector of Bavaria, the orchestra had grown to seventy-two musicians, including twenty-five violinists, thus putting little Mannheim in a class with far larger capitals like Paris and Naples. In return for premium salaries and even pensions, Carl Theodor's players performed for meals, chapel, the opera, theater and ballet, masked balls, chamber music with the elector himself, and twice-weekly concerts that seem to have done double duty as tea and card parties.[281] Many of his players owned their own homes. Unlike Carl Eugen and Prince Nikolaus Esterházy, Carl Theodor also paid on time and allowed his players to travel, believing correctly that their out-of-town performances were good for public relations.

Carl Philipp might even have hired Mozart, who showed up in Mannheim in October 1777 in search of a job after leaving Salzburg. At first, things looked promising. Mozart was invited to teach the elector's children. Their governess put in a good word for him. The elector, who sat in on a lesson in December, seemed to like what he heard.[282] But nothing came of it. A few months later, Carl Philipp had relocated to Munich, Mozart had moved on to Paris, and Mannheim's orchestra was left to dissipate, beginning with the principal players.

Yet even as musical chairs were moved, in Leipzig, where city, church, and student musicians played unusually well together, the future was taking shape almost imperceptibly. In 1743, fifteen local establishments hired sixteen selected players for a series of home concerts in 1743. Their discovery of Johann Adam Hiller in 1762 was a first stroke of luck. An inspired organizer, Hiller multitasked as orchestra trainer, founder of a school for young singers, music director at several of the city's churches, and problem solver. A second stroke of luck in 1780 led to renovation of the Gewandhaus, a fifteenth-century guildhall, as the orchestra's home, with the city as the orchestra's patron.

As conductor of what was now the Gewandhaus Orchestra, Hiller negotiated a contract that transformed his players—about half from the university, a quarter from the guild, a quarter self-employed—into the closest approximation yet of a self-sustaining professional orchestra, structured as a cooperative. With a median age of thirty-two, players were not only able to live on their earnings, they also were able to buy timpani using funds from fines levied on delinquent colleagues, raise a pension fund from member contributions plus the proceeds from benefit concerts, and invest these funds at 3 percent interest.[283]

The nineteenth century brought Mendelssohn and his Violin Concerto in E Minor, his concertmaster and the concerto's dedicatee, Ferdinand David, the founding of a conservatory and a new home in a New Gewandhaus. The twentieth century brought two world wars, the Nazis, and an air raid that destroyed much of the inner city as well as the New Gewandhaus in 1944. The Communist regime that followed replaced it with a new, New Gewandhaus in 1981. Eight years later, the intervention of the orchestra's conductor, Kurt Masur, with Party officials, helped avert a potential massacre as thousands of demonstrators approached its main entrance as participants in the first peaceful, democratic, and successful revolution in German history.

It was a lot of history in a relatively small space. But the orchestra, now grown to 185 members, not only survived it; in 2009, with Tesa, Germany's version of Scotch tape, Tempo, its preferred pocket tissue, and Nivea, the hand cream, Gewandhaus was even declared a Trademark of the Century by the German Market Association.

Decades would pass before anything like the Gewandhaus Orchestra was seen again. In 1813, a cadre of London's most respected professionals constituted themselves as the Philharmonic Society, with the general intention of performing serious orchestral and instrumental music at the highest level. Declared the Royal Philharmonic Society a century later, it continued playing through two world wars and was still going strong on the threshold of its third century. But by now, it had phased itself into a private charity and sponsor of scholarships, lectures, and concerts, leaving the playing to others.

While patrons were a necessary condition, it was assumed from the beginning that the players, among them some of the city's best freelancers, would run the show. The signatories of the statement of intent included some of musical London's biggest names. Three hundred subscribers recruited one another to pay 4 guineas each, half a skilled artisan's monthly wages, to underwrite the first season of eight concerts. Seven of the city's stars, including five violinists, even agreed to play for free. But that only happened once. In 1818, the violinist Felicks Yaniewicz was turned down when he appealed for a two-concert guarantee to cover return to London from an engagement in Edinburgh.[284]

The beginnings of the Philharmonic Society provided a template for a London orchestra culture that would survive into the twentieth century. In time, the Society was superseded by very different orchestras: the London Symphony, formed in 1904 as Britain's answer to the continental player co-op; the Royal and London Philharmonic orchestras, invented by and for their conductor, Sir Thomas Beecham, heir to a pharmaceutical fortune, and an amateur genius; the BBC Symphony, first to guarantee a fifty-two-week season, four weeks of vacation, sick leave, and three-year contracts for principals;[285] and the Philharmonia, created after World War II to record for EMI. But the Society's legacy could be seen and heard in all of them.

Demonstrated in its first season, the Society's history was a saga of high aspirations, upper-end patronage, occasional excellence, shaky quality control, unceasing personnel turnover, and endless crisis management. In 1817, the Society tried and failed to commission a pair of Beethoven symphonies. Eventually A-list conductors from Mendelssohn, Berlioz, Wagner, and Tchaikovsky to Richter and Nikisch were invited and came, as did A-list violinists including Viotti, Spohr, Ernst, "a Boy of the name Joachim,"[286] Sarasate, Ysaÿe, Kreisler, and Zimbalist. In 1845, the Society managed to recruit the child prodigies known as the little Milanollo sisters. In 1876–77 Wilma Neruda was reportedly the only violin soloist of the season to succeed "in rousing an apathetic conductor and evoking some show of satisfaction and enthusiasm." In 1893, Gabrielle Wietrowitz, a protégée of the venerated Joachim, played the Brahms concerto, already an acknowledged mountain of the repertory, a generation before women won the right to vote.

While concert demand increased, so, from the 1860s, did both orchestral supply and the player pool. The result was fierce competition for players at lower wages. Rehearsal time was often cut to save money. In 1879, Brahms's German Requiem was introduced almost unrehearsed in a program that also included a Mendelssohn overture, two violin concertos, and Beethoven's Second Symphony. Joachim, who regularly appeared with the orchestra, warned Brahms himself off a Philharmonic engagement. Invited to play something comfortably familiar to both the orchestra and herself in order to spare a rehearsal, Clara Wieck Schumann politely declined.

With money perennially short, string sections with strong principals often fell off alarmingly from first to last chair. The so-called deputy system, part of the local landscape as late as the 1920s, hardly helped. "A, whom you want, signs," the standard joke began. "He sends B, whom you don't mind, to the first rehearsal; B, without your knowledge or consent, sends C to the second rehearsal, who, not being able to play at the concert, sends D, whom you would have paid five shillings to stay away."[287] Unsurprisingly, "promptitude in reading novelties at first sight" was highly valued.[288]

What nineteenth-century Paris was like can be inferred, at least in part, from Berlioz's *Soirées avec l'Orchestre*, one of the funniest books ever written about music, in which the author and various members of the Opéra orchestra swap stories during catatonically routine performances of paralyzingly mediocre repertory while a dutiful bass drummer maintains the beat. Carl Flesch, who signed up for private lessons with the great Martin Marsick at 20 francs an hour about a half century later, paid for them with the 25 francs he earned each week for three to four rehearsals and a Sunday concert with the Lamoureux Orchestra. "In my experience," he recalled, "French conductors did not extend the 1789 Declaration of the Rights of Man to the orchestra players."[289]

By the end of the nineteenth century, the orchestra had nonetheless become as significant a part of the cityscape as the Louvre and Notre Dame. The Conservatory, an institution London could not pretend to match, turned out class after class of solid professionals. There and after, successive generations of energetic entrepreneurs then marshaled them into quasi-proprietary orchestras that made France safe for Beethoven.

The succession began in 1828 with François-Antoine Habeneck, whose Orchestre de la Société des Concerts du Conservatoire of seventy-six strings and twenty-six winds survived till 1967, when it morphed into the Orchestre de Paris, with a push from André Malraux, France's all-purpose intellectual and minister of culture. From Habeneck, the torch passed to Jules-Etienne Pasdeloup, a former Conservatory professor turned semi-official impresario to the Emperor Napoleon III, whose orchestra of 110 played genuinely popular concerts even during the Prussian siege of Paris. From there it passed to Charles Lamoureux, who married a fortune and was named to the Légion d'Honneur, and Edouard Colonne, a former Opéra concertmaster. With direct and indirect subsidies, both drew audiences of two and three thousand to hear orchestras that still performed and bore their names in the twenty-first century.

In Vienna, where concerts by foreign and domestic, as well as professional and amateur, players were well established, orchestras were not. As late as 1841, the Friends of Music, the city's most exclusive sponsor, was advertising for an ensemble to play Beethoven's Fifth. A year later, the critic and musicologist Alfred Julius Becher, and August Schmidt, the editor of the Wiener Allgemeine Musik-Zeitung, proposed that Otto Nicolai, music director of the court opera, conduct a series of Philharmonic concerts to showcase the city's great composers, while incidentally steering a little extra income to his orchestra. Extra players from the city's other theaters were recruited to double the string section. Eight rehearsals, instead of the usual one or two, were needed to prepare a heavy-duty program that included Beethoven's Seventh, the second *Leonore* overture, and the aria "Ah! Perfido," as well as two Mozart concert arias and a duet from Cherubini's *Médée*. The orchestra then elected a board and standing committees and rented a hall. Antonio Bazzini and Henri Vieuxtemps, two of the era's top-of-the-line virtuosos, were among the early soloists.

Though ticket receipts fell short of receipts from performances of such crowd-pleasers as the Milanollo sisters and the dancer Fanny Elssler, the audience was gratifyingly large, and there were funds available for the often underpaid extras recruited from outside the opera orchestra. There was even talk of an elected conductor and an orchestra that governed itself.[290] However, things ended badly. In late 1848, Becher, 45, was executed for revolutionary activity. In spring 1849, Nicolai, 38, died of a stroke.

But like so many of the causes of 1848, the orchestra only seemed lost. Subscription concerts began in 1860, bylaws were drafted, and it took only two years more for it to constitute itself as the Vienna Philharmonic, a self-governing, private spin-off of the Opera orchestra, with an elected steering committee. Its members, all Opera players, recruited and co-opted one another, arranged their own concerts, invited conductors and soloists, contracted with record companies, managed festivals and organized tours, when these became options, and added a supplementary season to what was already a busy work schedule.[291]

Mid-nineteenth-century Berlin, with its own court, court opera, and court opera orchestra, might have gone the same route. Instead, it acquired a Philharmonic as assertively self-reliant as Vienna's, but born of serendipity. A gifted violinist and entrepreneur in the style of Pasdeloup, Colonne, or Lamoureux, its founder, Benjamin Bilse, began to play as a public employee in his Silesian hometown, studied in Vienna, and played with the senior Johann Strauss before returning home to establish a proprietary orchestra that toured as far afield as St. Petersburg and Riga. After a squabble with his hometown council in the mid-1860s, he relocated to Berlin, where his concerts became a valued institution: the young Eugène Ysaÿe signed on as concertmaster, and Richard Wagner appeared as guest conductor.

A fortuitous sequence of events in 1882 led to his greatest achievement. An appearance by Hans von Bülow's Meiningen court orchestra reminded Berlin music lovers of the orchestra they wanted but did not yet have. A scheduled engagement in Warsaw a few months later reminded Bilse's players of the wages and working conditions they wanted and did not yet have. The fourth-class rail tickets they were issued were often cited as a cause of what followed, but unhappiness with rail tickets was probably incidental. The real issue was Bilse's contract, which required his players, most of them under thirty, to support their families in Berlin while supporting themselves over an extended tour in Warsaw, where the exchange rate put them at a serious disadvantage. Given twenty-four hours to take it or leave it, five players, including Bilse's brother, took it. But fifty-four of seventy not only left it. They quit altogether.

Bilse canceled the engagement and set about to hire a new orchestra.[292] A cadre of the secessionists marched off to a notary, registered a new orchestra, elected a three-man board, recruited colleagues, and aimed for the local niche market. Within months they were working with the city's best choral societies. By summer, they were touring northern Germany. As the Philharmonic Orchestra, they played their first three-hour concert in October. By early 1883, they had established meaningful relationships with Joseph Joachim—the city's closest approximation of a musical pope—and the thirty-seven-year-old Hermann Wolff, whose concert agency would dominate much of Europe's concert life for the next half century.

The infant orchestra's early years were marked by a series of near-death experiences. Wolff found and recycled a roller skating rink that would serve as the orchestra's home till the bombs fell in 1944. Meanwhile, Joachim persuaded the ministry of culture to subsidize the orchestra as an accessory to the Hochschule, the city's newly founded conservatory, and, when that subsidy ended, he persuaded the new Dutch beach resort at Scheveningen to hire the orchestra for the summer. A fire in 1886 would cost the orchestra most of its instruments. The Dutch connection would last till 1911. Reaching ever deeper into its pockets, the Mendelssohn family even talked the city into providing free tram rides for ticketed subscribers.

In 1887, the charismatic Hans von Bülow took over, and things turned for the better. Over the next 120 years, he would have only six successors. By the turn of the twentieth century, the orchestra toured the continent from Portugal to Russia, while making itself both an indispensable addition to the musical landscape and available for hire to aspiring soloists at home. In 1903, its players were incorporated as shareholders at 600 marks each. New members got their shares advanced like a loan or mortgage to be paid off at the going rate of interest. The Wolff agency paid their salaries and distributed the dividends. From its birth as a tiny republic in a constitutional monarchy, the orchestra had grown into a corporation, with Wolff's widow as its queenly CEO. In 1912, the little republic dodged another bullet when the Berlin City Council agreed to a laboriously negotiated agreement to replace the Scheveningen engagement with six gratis school concerts and forty neighborhood concerts for low-income audiences at reduced prices.[293]

The war and postwar years were as difficult for the orchestra as they were for everyone in Germany. Inflation shriveled the value of gate receipts, but raising ticket prices was risky. Management was obliged to pay soloists even when "war, epidemic or illness" caused cancellations.[294] Municipal subsidy was at least compatible with the little republic's dignity and bylaws. The Great Depression, the implosion of the Weimar Republic, and the coming of the Nazis subjected it to stresses the orchestra was as little prepared for as the country. Over twelve years of Nazi domination, it lost its independence to the propaganda ministry and its hall to bombs; it surrendered its few Jewish players and even its conductor's secretary to its new masters[295] and watched its basically well-intentioned conductor,

Wilhelm Furtwängler, let himself be used in a variety of compromising ways.[296] Yet within three weeks of Germany's capitulation, the little republic had returned to work, beginning with a performance of Mendelssohn's Overture to *A Midsummer Night's Dream*, unheard in Germany since 1933. A decade later it toured the United States with Herbert von Karajan, the orchestra's choice as Furtwängler's successor.

Imperious, entrepreneurial, and charismatic, Karajan was not easy to work with or for.[297] But in the dowdy, downsized Western half of a once-was metropolis, he seemed born to take over a rare surviving claimant to world-class status. By the 1960s, the orchestra had settled into a busy, artistically productive, and remunerative twelve-month routine that would come to include concerts, festivals, tours, TV specials, and recordings in each successive medium from LP on. Hans Scharoun's Philharmonie, the innovative new hall built in a wasteland bordering the Berlin Wall and inaugurated in 1963, inspired architects around the world. Reconfigured to accommodate nonprofit public ownership, highly profitable corporate free enterprise, and fully participatory player democracy, the orchestra's revised governance system captured the imagination of industrial engineers and systems analysts. In 2000, Harvard's Center for European Studies, housed in a neo-Teutonic Wilhelmine heap originally named for Adolphus Busch of the St. Louis brewery family, invited the Vorstand, the orchestra's two-player executive board, and the Fünferrat, its five-member player committee, for a business school–style, case history–based discussion with grad students in music, business, and public policy. It was not the first time that Boston had looked to Greater Teutonia for inspiration. But it was certainly the first time it had looked to Berlin—or anywhere—for a model of orchestral self-government.

There were ironies enough to go around. In 1882, fifty-four orchestra players had created a republic in Prussia's capital in the land of blood and iron, where a Hohenzollern king had only recently become emperor of a united Germany and where the installation of a parliamentary government was still almost forty years away. A year earlier, Henry Lee Higginson, a Boston investment banker, impassioned abolitionist, Civil War veteran, enlightened philanthropist, and paternalistic autocrat, had created an absolute musical monarchy in the cradle of the American Revolution and the land of the free.

Since 1900, Higginson's creation, composed almost entirely of European players, made its home in a Bostonian version of Leipzig's Gewandhaus designed to Higginson's specifications by the architectural firm McKim, Mead and White.[298] As late as 1918, barely half of the orchestra's hundred members were American citizens. Of these, only seventeen were native-born.[299] The orchestra did not name its first American music director until 2001.

In 1912, Higginson negotiated with William II, the German emperor, to allow Karl Muck, music director of Berlin's Royal Opera, to conduct the 1906–7 season in Boston. Wilhelm agreed on the condition that Muck return at the end of the year. Higginson, keen for an extension before the first year was over, offered the German conductor what was meant to be a permanent appointment, and Muck accepted.[300]

Unlike Berlin, where Philharmonic players were shareholders, Higginson's players were employees. A front desk first violinist might earn $5,000–$10,000 a year, at least equivalent to the six-digit contracts his successors would earn a century later, and worth still more in the visibility that conferred an additional payoff in private students.[301] But, like a member of the Red Sox, an orchestra musician signed a short-term contract individually negotiated with the owner. In Berlin, players elected their conductor, auditioned their colleagues as a committee of the whole, and made tenure decisions. In Boston, personnel decisions were reserved for Higginson, who also covered the orchestra's considerable deficits and leased Symphony Hall from a private corporation.[302] On his death in 1919 ownership was vested in a nine-member board, and in 1934 a private grant enabled the orchestra to acquire Symphony Hall.

Over a century of American orchestra building that began in 1842 with the New York Philharmonic, the autocratic model prevailed. An exception, the conductorless Orpheus Chamber Orchestra, was founded in 1972. Governed and managed by its thirty-plus players, it not only survived, flourished, recorded, and toured, but was named a Most Democratic Workplace in 2007 by Worldblu Inc., an Austin, Texas–based NGO. With about eighteen concerts a year spaced out over twelve months, it was only a part-time employer for elite players with Boston and New York area day jobs. The nonprofit corporate capitalist framework remained the normal American business model.[303] Self-governing orchestras, where they did exist, as in Denver, New Orleans, and Tulsa, Oklahoma, emerged from the ruins of conventional ensembles that had gone broke or faced extinction for other reasons.[304]

WHETHER IN LONDON or Leipzig, Vienna or Bologna, orchestra operations were essentially similar,[305] although the parameters of professional experience extended across considerable expanses of local and cultural diversity. Modern free enterprise competed and coexisted with remants of feudalism and long-forgotten royal initiatives. In London as at Esterháza, orchestras played Haydn symphonies. But the players at Esterháza were still virtually indentured to an enlightened lord of the manor, while the players in London, many of them immigrants, were musical free agents in the age of Adam Smith. Players in the Emilia-Romagna tried with mixed success to function as a guild. Instrumentalists in Leipzig, working for a third to a sixth of what their colleagues earned at Esterháza, clung to their exclusive but anachronistic rights to play at weddings, christenings, banquets, university ceremonies, and spring trade fair theatricals. Despite protests, Bach nonetheless hired students at market rates for his Leipzig church orchestras.

Players at Esterháza were on call at all hours because their employer demanded it. Players in London, Vienna, Leipzig, and the Emilia-Romagna were on call at all hours because they worked multiple jobs to support their families and wanted to stay on good terms with their fixer, who might be a senior family member. Vienna's iconic Burgtheater paid wages equivalent to those at Esterháza for less work and fewer benefits but offered more discretionary time. Cities made no provision for their players' concert dress or room and board, and furnished no candles or firewood, let alone the in-kind benefits such as medical attention, pension, and survivor benefits provided at Esterháza. On the other hand, they allowed their players to go after whatever supplementary gigs, dances, and church occasions they could find, an option entirely foreclosed to Esterháza's players by the eighteenth-century equivalent of a reserve clause.

For many players, the risks of debtor's prison, forced emigration, and a destitute old age were real and well documented. Even a local success like Giacomo Conti, a Burgtheater concertmaster in the 1790s, left an estate valued at somewhat less than a year's wages. Though wages at Vienna's second-tier theaters began at 150 gulden a year and reached as high as 400, two-thirds of the instrumentalists surveyed by Julia Moore in a University of Illinois dissertation[306] left estates of 100 gulden or less, much of it in furniture and clothing that was probably job-related. The relative frequency of clocks and watches suggests a world where time already mattered. On other hand, the absence of instruments from two-thirds of the sample estates suggests at least that their owners had already sold them.

Yet the profession could also provide an eighteenth-century version of a middle-class lifestyle. In London, a player in Salomon's orchestra could not only earn three times more in a night than a typesetter earned in a day, he could parlay his savings into additional businesses such as real estate and investments.[307] Different as local standards might be, players everywhere fell into a category approximating the local version of a skilled artisan, teacher, or government clerk.

For the player with the appropriate skills, location, connections, and energy, social mobility was a possibility. Virtually anywhere north of the Alps and west of the Carpathians, demand for qualified players chased supply. In Italy, where the ancien régime was in retreat and the modern world would be a long time in coming, local openings were limited, leaving orchestra players to ride a regional circuit or take their chances abroad. But the Italian market was not the same as the market for Italians. Felice Giardini, who left Turin for London, was invited to join the Noblemen's and Gentlemen's Catch Club and play informal house concerts, known as "bread and butter parties," at the homes of gentlemen amateurs. Native-born players, too, might socialize with their patrons like golf pros or personal trainers a couple of centuries later.[308] Even in Vienna, where pay scales were significantly lower and players from very modest families lived modest lives, brothers Johann and Anton Stadler, both clarinetists, fraternized with the great and good in the city's Masonic lodges.

Italy remained an outlier, where centrifugal politics, discovery of the New World, a static economy, and other people's wars had long since turned a cultural pacesetter into a baroque Disneyland and European caboose. Yet even without steam power, the Italian opera scene looked something like the early stages of the Industrial Revolution.

Impresarios rushed new scores into production the way Hollywood would later produce movies and TV sitcoms. Orchestra players, like everyone else, scrambled for comparative advantage and regular employment. Likely as not, Rosselli reports, this meant working in one town while litigating back pay in a second, negotiating the coming season in a third, and speculating on future seasons in a fourth and fifth. Scores could be works in progress just minutes before curtain time, and a good job might also require sight-reading till 3:00 a.m. in an unheated theater, then playing four or five performances a week from parts that might or might not match the score. Management necessarily lived close to the edge. Labor understandably did all it could to defend its market value.[309]

North of the Alps, the new conservatories were transforming a craft into a profession; demography, social change, the telegraph, and railroads were doing their bit to turn the profession into a business. Respectable mid-

nineteenth-century Britons maintained two views about the music profession, despite the occasional knighthood given to a musician like Sir Arthur
Sullivan, who composed symphonies as well as *The Mikado*, or Charles
Hallé (Karl Halle), who created Britain's first permanent fully professional
orchestra in 1858. On one hand, a musician might be "an itinerant fiddler
and of the lowest grade of society," according to William Henry Byerly
Thomson, a lawyer, whose manual of vocational options for the up-and-
coming young male appeared a year earlier. On the other hand, Thompson
conceded, a musician could also be "a man of the highest attainments,
moving in the most exclusive circles."[310] The Census Report saw it this
way, too, bracketing musicians with "literary men, artists, actors, teachers
and scientific men."

"Except for a large number of very low-class foreigners, with foreign
habits and very foreign morals, [who] have unhappily taken up their abode
in England," most musicians personified virtue, the Rev. H. R. Haweis
added a generation later. Even Herbert Spencer, the prophet of survival
of the fittest, let it be known that musicians "exalt the emotions, and so
increase life."[311]

Was this enough to pay the rent and feed the kids? "Musicians are at
the crossroads of the proletariat and the liberal professions," wrote William Martin, a Swiss journalist turned director of studies at the newly
founded International Labor Organization, in 1923, in what might have
been the earliest cross-border survey of the profession. He considered café
and theater musicians comparable to artisans. Orchestra musicians, on the
other hand, were like skilled labor with instruments for machines. Nationality complicated things again: French musicians, who were significantly
better paid than their German colleagues, thought of themselves as artists.
German musicians, who worked under proletarian conditions, regarded
themselves as laborers.[312]

Seen from the pit of the monumental new Court Opera in Vienna,
its orchestra's reinvention of itself as the Philharmonic was above all a
giant advance in labor relations. In the 1862–63 season, nineteen members of the newly constituted Philharmonic, including entry-level Opera
principals, second violins, violists, and the last desk of bass players, were
paid on a par with the stage and lighting crews. Between 1860 and 1869,
when the new house opened in the presence of the Emperor Franz-Josef
and the Empress Elisabeth, revenue increased by 60 percent, and the new
bylaws provided for sick pay. Even factoring for the conductor's triple and

the concertmaster's double share, Philharmonic concerts brought the average player a welcome 30 percent supplement to his opera salary.[313] On the threshold of the twentieth century, there was a revealing flap when Gustav Mahler, the Opera's music director, promised Philharmonic membership to eight new brass players he wanted for productions of Wagner. Furious that their music director had, in effect, issued eight new meal tickets at their expense, the Philharmonic players rose in protest. The crisis was resolved by amending the orchestra's bylaws. Philharmonic membership would remain at 108. New players would be phased in as current members retired or resigned.[314]

In Berlin, where the Philharmonic lived entirely from concerts, the solution from early on was an extended schedule that anticipated the twelve-month season. Thanks to Joachim, there was a summer season in Scheveningen to follow the regular season in Berlin. Thanks to the wonders of modern rail travel, there were also trains and fourth-class tickets to deliver the orchestra to any engagement Wolff could book to fill remaining dates. In return for a fifty-concert tour of twenty-eight towns in forty-seven days, or Germany, France, Spain, Portugal, and Switzerland in thirty days, including five in transit and only two days off, players earned enough to buy homes in the leafy southwest, where the new subway system reached out toward the city's new boroughs.

With the creation of its indoor Pops and outdoor Esplanade concerts in 1885, the Boston Symphony offered a similar trade-off. Higginson and his successors kept their players on short leashes, but they also made sure that they were well paid, with access to affordable mortgages and charge accounts at Filene's department store.[315]

Cyril Ehrlich cites many cases like the theater violinist in the London borough of Walthamstow who learned to play from his brother. Married and the father of two, he brought home a gross income about the national average for semiskilled labor. Up to half of it appeared to go for rent and transportation. Teaching was not an option in his working-class neighborhood, where it would pay next to nothing and would have to be done at night.

Another theater violinist with three years of training at the Royal Academy made more money and climbed a few rungs higher. He still trailed the entry-level lawyer or dentist, despite matinee supplements, promotion to section principal, teaching fees, and a half-dozen oratorio gigs. But he earned nearly as much as a skilled laborer and enjoyed the psychic

payoff that accompanied white-collar employment in an elaborately stratified society.

Still another rung up the ladder was Eugene Goossens, fresh out of
the Royal College and delighted to join the first violin section of Henry
Wood's Queen's Hall Orchestra. His £3-a-week wage was not only three
times the weekly earnings of a carriage washer and 40 percent more than
the earnings of a delivery courier, it was also enough to support his stand
partner's large family.[316]

Some players did better than others, and ever-growing numbers of
new conservatory graduates might wonder what would become of them as
their numbers kept growing. Even in Britain, the proverbial "land without
music," census data reported a sevenfold increase in the number of active
musicians between 1840 and 1930, while the population barely doubled.
Over the half century between 1861 and 1911, the number of music teachers tripled. In 1896, British Musician reported, fifty domestic applicants
showed up for a job in the opera orchestra, where a half century earlier
management had scrambled to recruit foreign candidates.[317]

Not even a calamity like World War I and its aftermath seemed to
decrease the demand for musicians appreciably. In America, the war's clear
winner, new orchestras like Cleveland's, founded in 1918, and the Los
Angeles Philharmonic, created in 1919, kept coming, despite occasional
setbacks where titanic aspirations collided with local icebergs. In Germany, the war's big loser, where defeat nearly led to civil war and inflated
the mark from 4.2 to 4.2 trillion to the dollar, instruments and musicians
left the country if they could. Yet Weimar Berlin remained the world's
music capital, and the era would be remembered decades later as a benchmark of innovative performance and creativity.

In Italy where even victory had led to the threshold of civil war, the
domestic scene was bleak and the foreign scene still bleaker. Historically,
the Italian player could try his luck abroad. But postwar recession and the
Bolshevik Revolution foreclosed that option. Still, Rome's Augusteo, the
country's only permanent symphony orchestra, managed to arrange a South
American tour. In Milan, the great and famously demanding Arturo Toscanini kept La Scala's orchestra of 103 busy on three-year contracts for an eight-
month opera season, followed by a supplementary concert series in June. Two
rehearsals, or a rehearsal and performance a day, extended uninterrupted
over seven days. Players made a bit of supplementary income from recording.[318] They also gained a degree of job security, as their contracts ran for
three years.

In francophone Belgium, home to an internationally recognized violin culture, conservatory professors nominally earned twice what they had before the war, but purchasing power had declined by half. The same inflationary process caused orchestra players to strike, bringing concert life in Brussels to a stop. If they could, orchestra players took theater and movie house jobs and looked for substitutes when called to play a concert. It was practically taken for given that many of the thirty-six who graduated annually in Liège or the six hundred who matriculated in Brussels would not have been admitted before the war. But they paid tuition.[319]

In Paris, the city's four orchestras played on as before but as more or less interchangeable co-ops, drawn from a pool of up to three or four hundred players who played a first shift with the Colonne, the Conservatory, or the Lamoureux Orchestra in the afternoon, a second shift at the Opéra, the Opéra Comique, or one of the larger movie theaters in the evening, and moved on to a café, cabaret, or nightclub for a third shift before retiring for the night. On the one hand, three to four thousand regular concertgoers let an intrinsically conservative music establishment make Paris a center of new music. On the other, as Martin noted, nothing could keep a player from a private gig, if he could just find one.[320]

Among the ashes of an abortive postwar boom, the devastation wrought by the Wall Street crash, and the complicated opportunities and challenges of network radio and the recording industry, the musical landscape was at once bleak, not quite hopeless, and still recognizable. In Philadelphia wages were reluctantly cut by 10 percent. In San Francisco a voter-sanctioned half-cent tax helped avert disaster.[321] In Boston, the young Harry Ellis Dickson happily traded his position as founder and conductor of a federally funded orchestra for unemployed musicians for a regular job in the violin section of the Boston Symphony. At $70 a week for a forty-week season, it paid nearly half again as much as the average U.S. wage in 1938.[322] In Berlin, housing and cost of living supplements brought Philharmonic base pay to nearly 2.5 times the earnings of a skilled metalworker. But the workload was heavy: three services (that is, rehearsals), concerts, or both, of up to eight and a half hours a day, up to forty a month, and five to six hundred a year, as well as sixteen seventeen-day concert tours, requiring up to a hundred hours of travel in third-class train compartments.[323]

Anticipated for decades, Boston's musical ancien régime finally imploded in an America again at war. As far back as 1917, several unions were competing to represent players in most American orchestras, with the exception of the Boston Symphony. As elsewhere in the labor movement, the competitors fought it out with one another as well as with employers in a Darwinian scramble that included beatings, bombs, holdups, body-guards, and bulletproof cars. The winner was the American Federation of Musicians (AFM). Elected president in 1940, James Caesar Petrillo aimed above all at the recording industry, whose product allowed radio broad-casters to phase out live musicians. But he first had to dispatch two other adversaries who stood in his way.

The first, the American Guild of Musical Artists (AGMA), aspired to organize solo instrumentalists and their accompanists and conductors. It lost steam as the courts declined to challenge AFM's claim to jurisdiction, and AFM threatened to stop AGMA artists from performing with AFM-affiliated orchestras. By February 1942, AGMA had agreed to a dignified surrender.[324]

The Boston Symphony, the last nonunion orchestra, had employed for-eign players since its creation. Since Higginson's death in 1920, the orches-tra had leaned more and more on tours, radio broadcasts, and records to generate income. Managements, broadcasters, record companies had arms. Petrillo knew how to twist them. Peace terms were finally negotiated at a summit in the Berkshires, where the orchestra's conductor, Serge Kous-sevitzky, had his summer home. From a player's perspective, the case for unionization could hardly have been more clear-cut. Players in union orchestras were better paid and got a better deal on records.[325] The board had yet to be persuaded, but it came around. Petrillo was "a very able man in his line," Koussevitzky told a *New York Times* stringer in Rochester, New York, where the orchestra was on tour. The orchestra was composed of very intelligent men whose active interest would also be good for the union, the conductor added.[326]

If so, it was barely apparent in an overview published in 1955 in the *Juilliard Review,* house organ of an institution with every reason to take the subject seriously.[327] The writer, S. Stephenson Smith, had recently served for five years as AFM's research director. History, at least American history, was repeating itself, he reported. This was not meant as good news. Though movies, radio, and foreseeably television consumed enormous quantities of music, each medium had wiped out thousands of jobs and replaced them at best with hundreds. Records might theoretically have made up the dif-ference, but copyright was nonstatutory, and a federal court ruled in 1940 that common law copyright ended when a record was sold, meaning that it could be played on the air without obligation to the performer. The ruling was appealed, but the Supreme Court declined to hear the case.[328]

"Nowadays the only serious music heard over the major radio network stations is played by the graveyard shifts of erudite, highly literate musicological announcers who officiate from midnight until six or seven o'clock in the morning," Smith noted presciently. Half a century later this was still true. Possibly 1,500 musicians continued to work in what Americans called legitimate theater for about half of what the Bureau of Labor Statistics defined as poverty line income. A thousand, some possibly violinists, continued to work for somewhat less in what remained of vaudeville. Another 145, few of them presumably violinists, continued to work in what was left of burlesque.

Though ballet and record sales boomed, and the Metropolitan Opera's spring tours sold out, only the Met traveled with a full orchestra; other companies recruited, often with difficulty, in the towns they played. According to the Bureau of the Census, the average family income for 1955 was $4,400.[329] A Boston Symphony player now earned at least $5,000 for a forty-eight-week season. A New York Philharmonic player, like a plumber, might earn $6,000.[330] Twenty-four major orchestras employed 3,200 men for average seasons of twenty-two weeks, paying on average less than $2,000. This was less than half the contemporary poverty-line income for a family of four. In fact, it meant still less, since four of the twenty-four orchestras, including Boston's with its longer season, inflated the average by paying significantly more. According to 1960 census data, musicians and music teachers were paid 30 percent less than all other professionals. Counting everyone and everything, it appeared that music provided slightly more than 13,000 full-time jobs, whereas movie theaters alone had employed 22,000 musicians a generation earlier.

Then, as after, Americans were as likely to embrace European-style public support for the arts as they were to embrace European-style health insurance or gun control. But there were alternatives. In 1962, twenty years after Boston unionized, a cadre of Chicago Symphony players voted Petrillo out of the local presidency he had held like a fiefdom for forty years. They then called a meeting to discuss contracts, wages, and working conditions. A few months later at a follow-up meeting in Cleveland, where Daniel Majeske, a Cleveland Orchestra concertmaster, sold Fuller brushes door-to-door during the off-season,[331] representatives of twelve major orchestras created the International Conference of Symphony and Orchestra Musicians (ICSOM), with a mandate to represent the interests of orchestra players in negotiating such basics as legal counsel, meaningful representation, collective bargaining, a reliable pension plan, and regular hours.

There were *Götterdämmerung*-like noises from the AFM, which feared secession, and from the McCarthyite right, which speculated darkly about a communist takeover.[332] What came, instead, was a new era. Three years later, after an eight-year gestation, the Ford Foundation announced a grant so vast that the story appeared as front-page news, as commentary, and also as a profile of the project's initiator in a single issue of the *New York Times*. It was the largest arts grant in the history of American philanthropy: $80 million plus $77 million in matching funds, the equivalent of $800 million when adjusted for inflation forty years later.

Intended to do the greatest good for some sixty orchestras across the country by extending their seasons and increasing player income, the money came in two parts. About a quarter was to be paid out directly. The rest, to be distributed over ten years, was held back as an endowment and was invested in a trust fund, contingent on matching funds from the beneficiaries. For ten years annual income from the trust fund would go to the participating orchestras. The fund itself would then be liquidated and the capital distributed.[333]

It worked. In 1960, a full-time, twelve-month orchestra job was unknown even in Boston, Philadelphia, New York, or Chicago, America's so-called Big Four orchestras. A decade later, there were six fifty-two-week orchestras, with another five on forty-five-week contracts or better. Between 1962 and 1972, players' salaries, adjusted for inflation, grew by 60 percent in Chicago, 75 percent in Cleveland, 88 percent in Detroit, 103 percent in Minneapolis, 147 percent in San Francisco.[334]

By the threshold years of the twenty-first century, there were eighteen orchestras with fifty-two-week seasons. Even factoring for inflation at about 4.5 percent a year, budgets had risen dramatically, from $2 million to $34 million in New York and from $2 million to $55 million in Boston. For the first time, at least in music's major leagues, players could anticipate the salary, job security, and lifestyle of middle- and upper-middle-class professionals. In 2003, the median American household income was a little over $40,000. Cleveland, an unchallenged addition to the Big Four, trailed the others with a base pay of $100,620, compared to the New York Philharmonic's $113,360. But paying double premiums or better for principals and triple premiums for concertmasters was standard practice everywhere.[335]

For those who knew where to seek work, good money could also be made in Europe. In a divided Germany, with seventy-six orchestras in the East and eighty-nine in the West, members of the Berlin Symphony, East Berlin's best and brightest, earned a quarter of the wages of their colleagues in West Berlin's world-class Philharmonic. At the same time, a minor league East German earned 40 percent of the wage of a West German counterpart. But with seventy-seven professional orchestras for a population of 16 million, only thirteen fewer than West Germany provided for its population of 62 million, East Germany at least offered the consolation of full employment, in addition to job security, medical care, and a modest pension. Like its dinosaur industries, East Germany's redundant orchestras were natural candidates for attrition after unification in 1990. But a unified country still invested half again as much of its GNP in the arts as did Britain and ten times as much as the United States; 1,700 musicians played on in 26 radio orchestras, while 133 publicly supported orchestras continued to employ some 10,000 competitively recruited players with the equivalent of civil service status.[336]

An El Dorado of musical free enterprise since at least the seventeenth century, London remained a shining city on a hill on the threshold of the twenty-first. For at least a few, a hundred-day-per-year salaried job plus eight or nine months of intensive freelancing could add up to a pretax gross nearly triple the nation's median household income, according to David Juritz, concertmaster of the London Mozart Players. Colleagues willing, as Juritz wasn't, to take any gig that came their way could almost double that figure. Yet even at London's orchestral summit, where a twenty-one-year veteran was likely to earn less than the average value of his/her instrument, and an estimated 86 percent held second jobs, pay for rank-and-file players was likely to lead to "a near-dead musician who hates music," according to Roger Chase, a respected veteran of the London scene, who had picked up and moved to the United States.[337]

In many ways, the odds of making it in major league music were equivalent to making it in major league baseball, Britain's Premier League, or Germany's Bundesliga. Juritz estimated that of seventy applicants for one of the London Mozart Players' fourteen violin jobs, five would be invited to audition.[338] Bernd Gellermann, a longtime member of the Berlin Philharmonic, recalled how he and his colleagues had winnowed applications for an available violin position from sixty résumés to forty invitations. Twenty asked for auditions, but only ten showed up, and three were short-listed. In the end no one was hired.[339]

In 1990, it occurred to Jutta Allmendinger, a music-loving German sociologist with a professional interest in careers, and J. Richard Hackman, a music-loving Harvard social psychologist with a professional interest in leadership, that the lab animal of their dreams was no further away than Boston's Symphony Hall. Whether in Boston, Berlin, or Beijing, orchestras were roughly the same size. They existed for the same purpose and played roughly the same repertory. They employed roughly the same mix of similarly trained and socialized players. Where everything else was so similar, they reasoned, differences of national culture, management style, and especially gender should stand out like palm trees in a cornfield.[340] Harvard Business School and the Max Planck Institute for Human Development obliged with funding for the project.

Over the next five years, Allmendinger and Hackman approached eighty-one orchestras and made contact with seventy-eight of them; talked with board members, managers, and, occasionally, conductors in Britain and the United States, as well as the recently united Germanys, and polled and interviewed players. They pored over histories, rosters, financial and attendance figures. Wherever possible, they sat in on rehearsals and concerts with an eye to learning how players were recruited and retained, and how managers, conductors, and player representatives interacted.

In time, their findings made their way into Hackman's award-winning essay on the theory and practice of teamwork.[341] For anyone interested in music as a business and vocation, the findings were their own reward. Remarkably, all players seemed happy, although the East Germans, counterintuitively, seemed happier than others, despite constraints and frustrations that would have caused Western colleagues to take union action or Valium.

When unhappy, each orchestra family tended to be unhappy in its own way. British orchestras were almost as unhappy about funding as their East German colleagues; and members of regional orchestras outside of London and beyond the security blanket of BBC support were even more unhappy than their East German colleagues. No players anywhere were very happy about opportunities for player involvement in their orchestras. But BBC players, with steady income and benefits, were significantly less happy than their peers, while East German contentment, despite a top-down bureaucracy that ran East German orchestras the way it ran everything else, was exceeded only by the Thameside contentment of the player-owned London Symphony, London Philharmonic, Royal Philharmonic, and Philharmonia.

When asked if they felt good when they played well and bad when they didn't, players in all orchestras answered in thundering unanimity. Scoring 6.2 out of a possible seven, their marks for internal motivation were much higher than those of twelve other, wildly different, occupational groups, from mental health treatment teams to amateur theater companies. There was also consensus on general job satisfaction. Scoring a towering 6.5, professional string quartets and airline cockpit crews led the pack. With 5.4, orchestra players came in seventh. When asked whether their work led to personal growth and development, quartet players still scored in first place, but orchestra players fell to ninth, ahead of operating room nurses, but behind federal prison guards. Almost all the musicians polled agreed that merit was honored in their line of work, but affirmation was strongest at the London co-op orchestras, followed by the East Germans, whose principals earned little more than the rest of the players.[342] Almost everyone agreed that their orchestras would benefit from more money. Americans were more satisfied than most, and Britain's regional players were more dissatisfied than their East German colleagues.

Happiness was incidental to success, Hackman concluded, but money was not. Good orchestras were those whose boards and managing directors let their music directors set goals and standards and let players do their jobs.[343] "Someone has to run things, and that someone has to have the attention of musicians," Robert Levine, principal violist of the Milwaukee Symphony, acknowledged. But effectiveness didn't come without a price. The last of Herbert von Karajan's thirty-four years with the Berlin Philharmonic, for example, offered an extreme but instructive tutorial in the trade-offs spelled out in chapter 17 of Machiavelli's *The Prince*. It was better to be feared than loved, Machiavelli concluded, provided you weren't hated. Brilliant, imperious, and entrepreneurial to the end when he died while chatting on the phone with Sony executives, Karajan made his orchestra rich while driving it into open rebellion. Orchestra players could be ungrateful, but the Berlin Philharmonic was the champion, he declared in a press release, "They want it all, ideally my head."[344]

The authority of the conductor derived from the myth that he knew more than the orchestra, Levine explained in an article coauthored with his father, a distinguished neuroendocrinologist. Given the collective experience, aggregate skill, and physical as well as psychic fragility of a hundred highly trained professionals who had seen many conductors over their working lives and inevitably had views of their own, the trade-offs included "chronic stress, job dissatisfaction, and infantilization."[345]

Stage fright was a widely reported occupational hazard, not at all confined to soloists, and it often increased with age. If principals were haunted by anxiety that they might muff the occasional solo, section players balanced the oppression of anonymity against the subliminal anxiety that they might come in too soon or too late. Regardless of where they sat in the section's hierarchy, violinists and violists especially were vulnerable to neck and shoulder problems.[346]

Coping strategies included alcohol and beta blockers. Hobbies were another possibility, with cooking, gardening, writing, and home improvement projects among the favorites. Guerrilla warfare was a third option, with conductors the adversaries of choice. Barbara Fraser, for many years a violinist with the Chicago Symphony, recalled how its conductor, Sir George Solti, appeared one day with Sir Edward Heath, a former British prime minister and church organist. Heath had a passion for Elgar's concert overture *Cockaigne*. Like good children, the orchestra let Heath conduct until he blamed them for an abortive entrance, then took their cues from the concertmaster as though Heath weren't there. Hellmut Stern, for many years a violinist with the Berlin Philharmonic, recalled how the string principals gathered around the podium, like manager and infielders around the pitcher's mound, and persuaded a young guest conductor to cease and desist at the famously difficult first violin entrance—presto, *alla breve*, beginning on an offbeat—to the coda of Beethoven's third *Leonore* overture. The orchestra then negotiated the entrance without him.

Union action was a fourth option. String players occasionally claimed that their instruments, which are much more expensive than brass or woodwinds, entitled them to extra consideration. In 2004, much of the music world laughed out loud when sixteen violinists of Bonn's Beethovenhalle Orchestra threatened to sue after management rejected their demand for a salary supplement based on the claim that they played more notes.[347]

In 1966, on the threshold of the Ford Foundation's new deal for orchestra players, the Philadelphia Orchestra, already among the world's most recorded, opened the new season with a fifty-eight-day strike, its fourth since 1954.[348] Thirty years later, by unanimous vote, it struck again after losing its record contract with EMI.[349] This time it was out for sixty-four days. The same year, the Atlanta, Oregon, and San Francisco symphonies struck, the last for nine weeks. Two years later, the Montreal Symphony walked out for three.

In 1992, patrons arriving at Bologna's Teatro Comunale for the evening's performance of *Götterdämmerung* were met at the door by orchestra musicians and choristers carrying spears and wearing horned helmets. They explained their position on impending budget cuts. In January 2005, salary blues in St. Louis led to a forty-five-day work stoppage that the orchestra called a lockout and the local office of the National Labor Relations Board called illegal before the parties agreed on terms well above those in the original package with the help of a federal mediator, the mayor, and the president of the Greater St. Louis Labor Council.[350] A few months later, Montreal's players exited to the tune of "When the Saints Go Marching In," demanding parity with colleagues in Toronto. Five months passed before they returned, it was generally agreed, as losers.

On the eve of 2010, with the U.S. and global economy entering the second year of the severest recession since the 1930s, Chicago's Lyric Opera averted a strike with a last-minute agreement to accept $91,624 as base pay for twenty-seven weeks of twenty hours each. The Cleveland Orchestra was hauled back from the brink with an agreed-upon freeze at the current mean of $140,200, including ten weeks of paid vacation and twenty-six days of paid sick leave. Members of the Seattle Symphony agreed to a cutback of 5 percent from its base of $78,750. "Thankfully," a senior violinist added privately, referring discreetly to colleagues who had come to think of their salaries as entitlements in a town where official unemployment of 10 percent made public support unlikely.[351] In 2011, the mighty Philadelphia Orchestra filed for bankruptcy protection.[352]

WAS IT THE best of times or the worst of times? For orchestras and their musicians, it was arguably both. Like blue jeans, Coca-Cola, and basketball, Western orchestra music had become one of the Western world's most successful exports. Where there had been no orchestras at all on the threshold of the twentieth century, there were good, even great ones on the threshold of the twenty-first. Kuala Lumpur wanted and got an orchestra, in part to keep up with Singapore and Hong Kong, in part for the 885-seat concert hall built to accessorize the Petronas Towers, which were the world's tallest buildings from 1998 to 2004.[353] In 2008, an international panel listed Japan's Saito Kinen Orchestra among the world's top twenty.[354]

Like Olympic athletes, audition candidates were now held to standards unimaginable generations earlier. At a concert in 1941, a little over a century after Paganini's death, the whole first violin section of the New York

Philharmonic played a movement only Paganini could play in his lifetime.[355] Impracticable if not impossible to play, Leopold Auer told Tchaikovsky in 1878, on his first encounter with the concerto the composer
wanted to dedicate to him. "If you can't stand up in front of an orchestra
and play the Tchaikovsky concerto, forget it," Willem Blokbergen, the
Dutch-born, Curtis-trained concertmaster of Bologna's Teatro Comunale
told a friend in 1997 when asked the minimal entrance requirement for a
decent orchestra job.[356]

The case for best and worst was especially powerful in the United
States, where federal arts spending was about as popular as foreign aid,
yet a critical mass of tax breaks and local initiative both created and supported music machines of remarkable flexibility and virtuosity. Among the
twenty orchestras listed in 2008 as the world's greatest were one Czech,
one Dutch, one British, one Hungarian, one Austrian, one Japanese, three
Russian, four German, and seven American.

Years of prosperity had meanwhile made them rich, and their players
richer. But the new prosperity was hardly confined to the United States.
As helpfully interpreted by Joseph in chapter 41 of the Book of Genesis,
Pharaoh dreamed of seven years of plenty. With only intermittent down
years from the 1960s to the Wall Street meltdown of 2008, both American and Western European players had lucked into nearly fifty of them.
Plenty stopped, of course, at the Iron Curtain, and there were some rough
years after 1989 as support systems crumbled across Central and Eastern Europe. But even under Communism, Russians, East Germans, and
Czechs showed how official favor, the inherent appeal of a meritocratic and
mostly unpolitical profession, plus the heady incentive of foreign travel,
could pay off in professional excellence and personal fulfillment.

Top-tier orchestra players could now afford to live down the street and
around the corner from doctors, lawyers, and retired diplomats. From a
subservience not all that different from that experienced in Carl Philipp's
Mannheim or Archbishop Colloredo's Salzburg, they now enjoyed a job
security comparable to a university professor's or German civil servant's.
They could also try their luck as free agents. Openings were publicly
advertised. The imperial conductor, board chairman, and managing director had gone the way of the imperial baseball owner. Employment was
subject to the orchestral equivalent of peer review.

Even among winners, of course, some individuals are likely to win
more than others. For the season ending June 30, 2008, Cleveland's con-

ductor, Franz Welser-Möst, earned $1,316,120, putting his earnings about halfway between those of the Cleveland Indians' starting pitcher, Fausto Carmona, and those of its veteran catcher, Mike Redmond. Concertmaster William Preucil's earnings, $414,159 plus $19,658 in benefits, matched the earnings of relief pitcher Rafael Perez, who was thirteenth on the Indians' salary schedule. Mean compensation for the orchestra, $140,200, was 35 percent of what the Indians paid baseball's equivalent of section players for a six-month season.[357] But unlike the athletes, the musicians could play on into their sixties. They enjoyed tenure. They didn't play half their season on the road. Compared to the Indians' pay scale, where the top earner was at a 30:1 advantage over his journeyman teammates, the 10:1 advantage of the conductor over the base pay of the entry-level player looked good, too. Measured against the 419:1 CEO to average worker ratio the Cornell University economist Robert Frank pointed to in 1999, it practically looked egalitarian.[358]

Among the most remarkable breakthroughs was the coming of the equal opportunity orchestra. The discovery that even pregnant women could play as well as men was comparable in its way to major league baseball's discovery of Jackie Robinson in 1947 or Balliol College's election of all-male Oxford's first female Fellow in 1973. Faced with loss of players to the military draft in 1942, first-tier orchestras like Philadelphia and Chicago took their cues from J. Howard Miller's iconic "We Can Do It!" figure for the duration of the war. But then the war ended. Three years later, most of the women had either gone home or reverted to their traditional default position among the amateurs and semi-pros.

And yet, as usual, it moved. Generational benchmarks reflected changing times. In 1948, only 109 women appeared on America's full-time professional orchestra rosters. In 1970, an enterprising *Milwaukee Journal* reporter noted that women already comprised a third or more of players in low-budget major orchestras like Atlanta's and Milwaukee's, although they still comprised fewer than 20 percent of the St. Louis Symphony and the Cincinnati Symphony, and next to zero in the Big Four orchestras, Chicago, Philadelphia, Boston, and New York. These figures, too, would shift in twenty years, predicted Barbara Fraser, who had recently joined the Milwaukee Symphony after tours with the Houston Symphony and Amsterdam's Concertgebouw, and would live to see her prediction come true.[359]

In 1980, women comprised nearly 30 percent of ICSOM's forty-four-member orchestras, and Fraser, who had moved on to the Chicago Symphony in 1974, proudly showed a visitor Orchestra Hall's first-ever women's dressing room. In 1976, it was estimated that women comprised 10 percent of the players at America's orchestral summit; by 1999 that figure had grown to 25 percent. In 1977, ten of the Metropolitan Opera's ninety-seven players were women; in 1999 there were thirty-six women among ninety-five instrumentalists.[360]

In 1979, the manager of the Berlin Philharmonic explained how a statutory provision intended to protect expectant mothers from playing night shifts made it impossible for the orchestra to hire women. In 1983, the orchestra approached the brink of war when its imperious conductor hired the gifted clarinetist Sabine Meyer, 23. Yet virtually unnoticed, a twenty-six-year-old Swiss woman, Madeleine Carruzzo, had become the orchestra's icebreaker a year earlier, beating out twelve male candidates for an opening in the violin section.[361] By the 2009–10 season, there were 16 women among the orchestra's 128 members, 12 of them violinists, including Carruzzo, who was still active. At Amsterdam's Concertgebouw, 11 of 20 first violins, 11 of 17 second violins, and 4 of 15 violas were women; at the London Symphony the equivalent figures were 7 of 18 first violins, 5 of 15 seconds, 4 of 12 violas, and 6 of 11 cellos.

Always mindful of tradition, Vienna lagged behind. Women don't play worse but differently, Rainer Küchl, the Philharmonic's concertmaster, insisted as late as 1997. Given the problems of staffing both the State Opera and the Philharmonic orchestra, he was also grateful for colleagues who didn't get pregnant.[362] But by 2009, even Vienna had begun to hire women. Among 120-plus members of the Philharmonic, there were only two in addition to the obligatory female harpist.[363] But there were seven women among the 149 members of the parent State Opera orchestra, and the Bulgarian violinist Albena Danailova had been awarded a tenured contract as one of its four concertmasters.

The treatment of women orchestra members varied over time. Yet Hackman and Allmendinger were struck by the consistency of response from otherwise dissimilar orchestras over multiple national borders. Female icebreakers consistently reported how they were met with a collegial, even cordial, reception.[364] Things then turned worse as the number of women increased. It was only as the gender ratio approached parity that relations improved.

Nicolai Biro-Hubert, a veteran of many orchestras in many countries, considered gender war practically inevitable. Women tolerated, even welcomed, the domination of masterful conductors, he insisted, in a memoir of orchestra life extending from the 1920s to the 1960s. They accepted overwork. They expected to be underpaid. Feelings of impotence were inherent in the job, Biro-Hubert insisted. Acquiescent women only made their male colleagues more aware of it.[365] Yet even he acknowledged that it would not be long before women, too, found their place on player committees like Delacroix's Liberty on the barricades.

Hackman and Allmendinger noted that American regional orchestras had already reached the tipping point of gender equality by the end of the twentieth century. Only a few years after this work appeared, the economists Claudia Goldin and Cecilia Rouse confirmed that the new, gender-neutral audition model, with its screen and heel-muffling carpets, worked to counter gender biases in hiring.[366] In 1990, like most new employees, women literally played second fiddle.[367] Twenty years later, in the Chicago Symphony's second violin section of seventeen, thirteen women still did. But women occupied eleven of sixteen first violin positions in Boston and Cleveland and twelve of eighteen in the New York Philharmonic. In Philadelphia, Cleveland, and New York, women occupied the front of the section. Both Seattle concertmasters were women. In 2005, an aggrieved violinist brought discrimination charges against the New York Philharmonic, claiming that at least seven women had been promoted while he was passed over for tenure. Two years later, the suit ended with an undisclosed settlement.[368]

Yet even as wages and working conditions improved, orchestras and those who cherished them worried increasingly about metrics that read like the handwriting on the wall. Since the days of Haydn and Mozart, the symphony orchestra had relied on a regular supply of skilled and motivated players, an ever-expanding repertory, a steadily growing population of middle-class concertgoers, and a reservoir of patrons, both public and private. Of the four, only the first was still reasonably solid.

Ironically, the huge Ford grant and the gifts of deep-pocketed patrons led to unprecedented expenses. Twelve-month seasons, million-dollar conductors, and six-figure salaries required extensive cash flow. Extensive cash flow required extensive infrastructure, including squadrons of vice presidents for planning, finance, and educational outreach; expanded personnel departments, teams of audio, media, IT, and marketing specialists; and a corps of professional fund-raisers. Infrastructure increasingly needed cash flow.

"The ground beneath us is shifting—has already shifted—in fundamental ways," Lowell Noteboom, chairman of the League of American
Orchestras' strategic planning committee, reported without exaggeration
in 2006. Forty years after the "near miracle" of the Ford grant, America's major orchestras had become big businesses. Programmed for almost
two generations to supply "bigger, bigger, bigger, more, more, more,"
they now faced a public that preferred smaller, smaller, smaller, less, less,
less.[369]

It was not only tempting but plausible to look for the roots of the challenge in global shocks and tectonic changes far from the world of music.
The long shadow of September 11, 2001, the Tuesday from hell when
the twin towers of New York's World Trade Center and the Pentagon in
Washington were struck by hijacked airliners, fell on America's concert
halls as it did on much of the world. A little masterpiece, even by *New
Yorker* standards, George Booth's cartoon two weeks later showed Mrs.
Ritterhouse, the normally indomitable anchor of her neighborhood orchestra, desolate on a piano stool, her back to her music stand, her violin silent
on the carpet. Her dog, every bit as desolate, is stretched out on the floor
with its paws over its eyes.[370]

"In the first months after that tragic event, attendance at all public
events fell off sharply, and philanthropic priorities shifted dramatically,"
Noteboom observed. But "looking back, we can now see that the 2001
phenomenon was really just a major dip in a downward trend." Seven years
later, the Wall Street meltdown caused hard times beyond any since 1929
for nearly everyone, with no end in sight.

But the problem lay deeper. The grounds Noteboom rightly pointed
to were shifting. The orchestra was historically a city dweller. Yet the city
had been declining for nearly half a century. Between the middle of the
twentieth and first decade of the twenty-first century, St. Louis, Cleveland, Pittsburgh, and Detroit, once proud and flourishing communities
with proud and flourishing orchestras, had lost half their populations to
suburbs ever more removed from the concert halls and city centers. Their
neighborhoods had meanwhile changed or even vanished. "If you approach
Severance Hall from downtown, you drive through several miles of urban
dilapidation and patchy renewal," Charles Michener wrote of rustbelt
Cleveland. "The challenge is how to maintain a world-class orchestra in
what, at best, is a third-tier economy," its orchestra's board president told

him.[371] Five of ten top corporate sponsors, happy till now to underwrite the orchestra, had left the city.

In rustbelt Detroit, where the collective memory already reached back to 1987, when the orchestra had struck for twelve weeks, management proposed—and players rejected—not only a 30 percent salary cut for the 2010–11 season but a job description that included school concerts, teaching assignments, even office work.[372]

THE PROBLEM WAS not exclusively American. In 2005, seven years after National Insurance rules were changed, eight British orchestras, with annual budgets of about £10 million, found themselves with a tax bill of at least £33 million, not counting interest arising from back payments to freelancers. After unification West Germans, with their own corps of orchestras to support, discovered that they had inherited yet another behind the Wall, where their East German counterparts had overbuilt orchestras the way Japan had overbuilt hotels and office space. Heavily dependent on handouts since the end of World War II, Berlin, with a combined population of about 3.5 million, now found itself with three operas and at least four orchestras to support on a public payroll already billions underwater.

With music education and the school orchestra, the future of the string pool could be numbered among the half-empty glasses. They had been a matter of concern since at least the 1950s. But concern had long since become a sustained wail, especially in America's old core cities.[373] The good news for a historically European art form and patron reservoir was immigration, for which America, as always, had a particular feel. By the 2009–10 season, Asians or Asian Americans occupied six of the Boston Symphony's sixteen first violin positions, seven of the Cleveland Orchestra's sixteen, seven of the Chicago Symphony's sixteen, and seven of the New York Philharmonic's eighteen. Two of the Philadelphia's concertmasters, its principal violist and principal cellist, were Asians or Asian Americans. A glass at least half full for the orchestras of the West, ten million young violinists reportedly aspired to professional careers in China alone.[374]

For those with the chops and stamina to make it to the top, there were also incubators like the New World Symphony in Miami Beach, where Michael Tilson Thomas, music director of the San Francisco Symphony, presided over a training orchestra created by Ted Arison, an Israeli-American billionaire who had once dreamed of being a pianist. An admissions rate of 3 percent made Harvard look practically permissive by comparison. For three to four years, players, known as Fellows, lived rent-free on modest stipends, played nearly seventy concerts a season, enjoyed coaching by some of the world's great professionals, and learned to cope with real-life vicissitudes at mock auditions that combined elements of major league baseball tryout camp and Marine basic training.[375]

Yet the greater danger, as every indicator confirmed, was less a shortage of players than an impending shortage of audience. Between 1982 and 2008, the number of Americans attending classical concerts fell by 29 percent. The decline between 2002 and 2008 alone was 20 percent. As late as the 1990s, unsold tickets were a rarity at season concerts of the Chicago Symphony. By 2005, nearly 20 percent of these seats went unsold, and the Philadelphia Orchestra reported that its summer sales were declining by 5 percent a year. Suburbanites everywhere were increasingly hesitant to drive to the city for concert tickets that could cost as much as an anniversary dinner or a night on the town with an out-of-town visitor. The older demographic was also uneasy about parking at night in the vicinity of St. Louis's Powell Hall or Cincinnati's picturesquely named "Over the Rhine."

Since the days of Haydn and Mozart, the appeal of the concert hall was actually enhanced by living room–friendly piano reductions of orchestra repertory, phonograph records, radio broadcasts, even television. Well into the twentieth century, people came to hear new music. These expectations too were fading. Conductors still programmed new pieces. But they seldom played them twice, and they prudently sandwiched them between "greatest hits" and a high-profile soloist to discourage people from leaving early. Classical records, which had been a cash cow and career-maker through the second two-thirds of the twentieth century, comprised only about 3 percent of total sales by the early years of the twenty-first century, according to the general manager of Sony Masterworks, heir to once proud Columbia.[376]

Though 26 percent of America's adult population claimed to like classical and chamber music, only 18 percent actually listened to broadcasts or records, and only 9 percent attended concerts, down 3 percent since 2002. Attendance averaged three performances. Concertgoers were more likely to be over than under forty-five, and 20 percent were sixty-five and older. A bleak 15 percent of respondents listened "often" to classical music, though the outlook for jazz was still bleaker. Fifty percent of those surveyed listened "hardly ever" or "never."[377] Among respondents age sixty-five and older, 23 percent reported that they listened "often" to classical music; among those age fifty to sixty-four, 15 percent "often" listened to classical music; and people in the cohort ages thirty to forty-nine, 12 percent "often" listened to classical music. Respondents in the age range of sixteen to twenty-nine reported a 14 percent rate of frequent listening to classical music.[378]

Most alarming of all, the concertgoing population was not replacing itself. Its median age, forty in 1982, had risen to forty-nine by 2008. Over the same period, the median age of the general population had risen from thirty-nine to forty-five. This phenomenon could be seen in Europe as well. The French concert audience, for example, was aging even faster, with a median age of 55, compared to a national median age of 39.4.[379]

Swimming resolutely against the current, Allan Kozinn of the *New York Times* insisted that obituaries announcing the death of classical music were premature. There was plenty to hear on the Internet. Listeners were downloading classical music, even if they were no longer buying CDs. The performance season was now year-round as it had never been in that purported golden age when the NBC broadcast Toscanini on Saturday evenings and CBS broadcast the New York Philharmonic on Sunday afternoons. Things were no worse at New York's Metropolitan Opera than they had been in the years between the Wall Street crash and World War II. In Nashville, Los Angeles, Toronto, Miami, and Kansas City, standard repertory was now marketed in much the same way that the neighborhood multiplex marketed movies and Ben & Jerry's marketed ice cream. The New York menu extended from Machaut to minimalism.

"What about the whole big world outside New York?" the critic Greg Sandow added plausibly.[380] There too there were at least signs of fire in the ashes. In 2005–6, 1,800 American orchestras, 350 of them professional, played 36,000 concerts, according to the American Symphony Orchestra League; this figure was up 30 percent from 1994. In 2005, there were 1.4 million downloads of the Beethoven symphonies, 50,000 of them in Holland and 17,000 in Vietnam, when the BBC made them available for free.[381] Recession notwithstanding, concert attendance at London's Barbican Centre rose 4 percent and ticket sales increased

11.2 percent from 2008 to 2009. In 2009, the International Federation of the Phonographic Industry reported that one of every six nonpirated recordings sold in China was Western classical music. The same ratio was reported from South Korea.[382]

Most heartening was the rediscovery of what had been clear to the pub and coffee house crowd by the eighteenth century. The cellist Matt Haimovitz took his art to Schubas, a popular Northside Chicago tavern, and Sam Bond's Garage, a vegan coffee house in Eugene, Oregon.[383] The violinist-composer David Handler and cellist Justin Kantor played new music at Le Poisson Rouge, a recycled jazz club in New York's Greenwich Village.[384] In 2005, a committee of Milwaukee Symphony players discovered the iPod and made nearly three decades of broadcast tapes available on Apple's iTunes. There were five thousand downloads the first year. While 40 percent of the revenue was reserved for the players, the real payoff was the enhanced visibility—and audibility—of a good local orchestra, founded a century after the Boston Symphony in a postindustrial city that once proclaimed that it fed and supplied the world.[385]

Additional musicians were moving their performances out of the concert hall to reach nontraditional audience members. The Cleveland Orchestra, for example, extended their playing space to include outlying towns and a metropolitan school district with a 70 percent African American enrollment. It also established homes away from home in New York, Lucerne, Vienna, and Miami, where a fourteen-member consortium underwrote concerts for an estimated 20,000 adults and 3,500 fifth graders.

WAS TRADITIONAL CONCERT dress too close for contemporary comfort to the Congress of Berlin or the Viennese Opera Ball? Nigel Kennedy, a protégé of Yehudi Menuhin, repackaged himself as Kennedy and played the Beethoven concerto at the Berlin Philharmonie in customized grunge, accessorized with a movement of solo Bach as encore, and ad lib jokes only he understood.

During the first decade of the twenty-first century, efforts were accelerating nationwide to increase the diversity both of classical music's leadership and its audiences. Were the traditional ensemble and its aging audience distressingly white and European? Not to worry, the Audience Demographic Research Review of the League of American Orchestras, previously the American Symphony Orchestra League, reported in 2009 in its response to gloomy numbers from the National Endowment for the Arts. Already 15 percent of the U.S. population, Hispanics were expected to comprise 17 percent by 2020. But their share of the concert audience was expected to reach 20 percent by 2018. Bellwethers had already been spotted. In New Orleans, the Mexican Carlos Miguel Prieto, who had agreed to be music director of the Louisiana Philharmonic Orchestra before Hurricane Katrina devastated the city, made good on his commitment. In 2009, the Venezuelan Dudamel, still under thirty, became the first Latino to take charge of a major American orchestra when he took over the Philharmonic in Los Angeles, where Hispanics already comprised a third of the population.

Meanwhile, in Detroit, with an estimated African-American population of 80 percent, the Sphinx Organization worked to increase the African-American and Hispanic orchestra presence from 2 percent or less. The program originated with Aaron Dworkin, a graduate of the Interlochen Arts Academy, an arts-based prep school, and the University of Michigan with degrees in music and violin performance. An African-American raised in a family of white professionals, he was enchanted at an early age by his adoptive mother's violin. But he soon noticed that there were few other young violinists who looked like him. Nor were there many on stage when visiting orchestras played in Ann Arbor.

In 1996, still in his midtwenties, Dworkin set out to do something about this. With a few years of sales, marketing, and nonprofit administrative jobs behind him, he proposed a training program for young African-American and Latino string players to James Wolfensohn, then president of the World Bank. Wolfensohn replied with a personal check for $10,000. With $70,000 more gathered from corporate sponsors including Texaco, Sphinx organized its first competition, offering scholarship money, coaching, a loan instrument, and even orchestra appearances for the winners. In 2005, the John D. and Catherine T. MacArthur Foundation designated Dworkin one of its annual "geniuses" and awarded him a grant. By 2010, Sphinx's budget approached $2.5 million, with 59 percent of its income in corporate and foundation grants and private contributions. Guided by its vision of "a world in which classical music reflects cultural diversity and plays a role in the everyday lives of youth," the organization sponsored orchestra internships, summer scholarships, financial aid, instrument acquisition, school visits, a recital series at Borders bookstores, a show-and-tell string quartet, and a chamber orchestra.[386]

This entrepreneurial approach was shared by Marin Alsop, a Juilliard graduate in violin performance, music director of the Baltimore Symphony and herself named a MacArthur "genius" in 2005. "We have to forget about blaming the education system for the lack of music in the public schools," she told an interviewer in 2007. "We have to be the leaders on this."[387] She spoke not only as a woman conductor, one of music's most exotic minorities, but as a student of Leonard Bernstein, whose fifty-three Young People's Concerts, staged and broadcast between 1958 and 1972 and reissued on DVD in 2004, were still regarded with awe. The *New Yorker*'s Alex Ross reported admiringly how David Robertson, the newly arrived music director of the St. Louis Symphony, engaged 1,800 school-children at a Tuesday morning Young People's Concert. From there, Robertson took off for an inner-city elementary school to read and sing along with another fourteen students while many of his players doubled as public school music teachers in a city where 35 percent of all children lived below the poverty line.[388]

In New York, Clive Gillinson, a cellist turned orchestra manager and director of Carnegie Hall, and Joseph Polisi, a bassoonist turned president of Juilliard, created the Academy, a two-year fellowship program for up to twenty of the year's best and brightest recent conservatory graduates, intended to develop "good musical citizens" capable of connecting and interacting with teachers, composers, concert presenters, the media, the New York Public Schools, and one another.[389]

From New York to Beijing, Berlin Philharmonic players performed and coached wherever they traveled.[390] A joint venture created by the redoubtable Midori when she was twenty-two, Midori & Friends, has been dispatching player-teachers to New York elementary schools since 1992. In her forties, Midori had added a professorship at the University of Southern California to an active concert schedule. Yet she could also be found twice a year coaching, performing, and brainstorming with local orchestras and their associated youth orchestras in Anchorage, Alaska, Great Falls, Montana, Winston-Salem, North Carolina, Albuquerque, New Mexico, or wherever she was wanted and needed.[391]

Did the indicators point forward to the past? In 2010, the Moscow State Radio Symphony Orchestra gamely toured small-town America by bus, shopping for groceries at Walmart and doubling up in motels at $40 a day, with only a day off every two weeks. "I am strong man, and I am Russian," said a stoic bass player. Their American peers, understandably, looked on in horror. "I can't imagine why a band like that would sell better than a decent American orchestra," said Rachel Goldstein, a twenty-year veteran of the Chicago Symphony. "Then again, I don't want to buy clothes made in sweatshops, and boy, does that cut down where I can shop." Assembled by Google in 2008, with an assist from Michael Tilson Thomas, who conducted it, the YouTube Symphony Orchestra was an alternative form of interactivity. London Symphony and Berlin Philharmonic players reviewed some three thousand video auditions; the violinist Gil Shaham coached the strings; and the composer Tan Dun wrote a four-minute piece for the occasion. Parts were distributed via the Internet, a cadre of London musicians offered online instruction, and there were even videos of Tan conducting auditioners section by section. Ninety-six players from thirty countries eventually made it to New York for the performance at Carnegie Hall, an exhilarating weekend of media attention and what impressed several observers as cascades of self-congratulation. All had a wonderful time, according to Michal Shein, a young cellist from the New England Conservatory. While YouTube and Google were pleased by the opportunity to show how they could find talent, nurture online communities, and possibly even sponsor an online orchestra, as NBC had once supported Toscanini's, reviews were mixed.[392]

A third, digital option pointed to still another future that flesh-and-blood musicians regarded with understandable horror. Not only could computer programs already in reach assemble anything, including Beethoven symphonies, from millions of individually recorded notes on all possible instruments. They could enable these digital fragments to respond to an electronic baton. Aspiring composers could try out new work without having to pay live performers. Small towns that could no longer support a local philharmonic could replace it with a philharmonic computer program. In 2003, New York musicians went on strike when Broadway producers threatened to replace them with virtual orchestras. Their strike was successful, but some players lost their jobs when London theaters and American road companies discovered that digital orchestras were gratifyingly cheap and convenient.[393]

Reassuringly human, Hiroyuki Ito's photo in the *New York Times* on

July 23, 2005, pointed to an entirely nondigital future already well under way. Since its very beginning, the violin had been consistently male and European. Since the end of the nineteenth century, Eastern European Jewish males had played it as though they owned it. Heir to a century of Jewish male violin virtuosity now approaching its sunset, Pinchas Zukerman had taken up conducting with the St. Paul Chamber Orchestra in 1980. He still enjoyed sitting in with orchestras he performed with as soloist. Ito's photo showed him at the back of the New York Philharmonic violin section, surrounded by four young Asian women. The message could hardly have been clearer if he were passing them a torch or a baton.

Unlikely to change were the intangible rewards of a profession that went back to Monteverdi's *Orfeo*. Like Italians and New Yorkers, musicians lost few opportunities to commiserate with themselves and one another before agreeing that they couldn't imagine doing anything else. Asked his views on job satisfaction, Simon James, an assistant concertmaster of the Seattle Symphony and a freelance fixer, pointed to those rare and resonant moments when players, conductor, and audience connect like Keats on first looking into Chapman's Homer. He savored the glow of a student's "aha" moment, and the high that came with nailing down a TV commercial, video game, or movie deal.[394] Asked what they would do if they were not musicians, several young members of the New World Symphony had to stop and think. "Work in a bakery," said one young violinist. "Chef, lawyer, or wine-maker," said a second. "No idea," said a third.

FOR A MINORITY of dedicated players with a passion for some of the greatest music ever composed, armor-plated psyches, and a preference for life without a conductor, chamber music could not only be an alternate career. It could be a professional Promised Land intended for small ensembles in small rooms. It already had a long and established history by the time Bach died and Mozart was born. But no previous combination of instruments could match the open-ended possibilities of two violins, a viola, and a cello, discovered almost serendipitously by Haydn, Mozart, Beethoven, and Schubert within little more than a generation.

Not surprisingly, professional as well as amateur players wanted to play quartets, and audiences wanted to hear them. Paganini played Paganini in public, but he played quartets with colleagues in private and even knew the late Beethoven quartets.[395] By the mid-nineteenth century, professional quartets had emerged from private chambers and made their appearance in concert halls. Touring lions like Baillot, Ernst, and Vieuxtemps joined local colleagues where and when they could find them. In 1844, Joseph Joachim, 13, played Mozart and Beethoven with local talent on his first visit to London. His own quartet, launched the same year as the Berlin Conservatory in 1869, survived till his death in 1907. The season of four programs, each repeated twice, began in October and ended in December. Meanwhile, the quartet's members, all professors at the conservatory, maintained their day jobs. It was 1891 when four students in Prague, among them Dvořák's future son-in-law, Josef Suk, formed the first full-time professional quartet. By 1902, it had played its thousandth concert. It survived till 1933.[396]

It was not, of course, a way to get rich. "How do you become a millionaire by playing quartets?" was the mother of all quartet jokes. "Start out as a billionaire," was the answer. For some, "Find a billionaire" was the next best option. By the end of the nineteenth century, the ensemble was as well established and as ubiquitous as the opera and symphony orchestra. Those who could supplemented their income with recitals, teaching, and freelance and orchestra jobs.

"Wealth is only useful for two things, a yacht and a string quartette," Robert Louis Stevenson remarked.[397] Fortunately, a number of notable philanthropists agreed. In Boston, Henry Higginson, the father of the Boston Symphony, underwrote his concertmaster's quartet, the Kneisel. In New York, E. J. De Coppet underwrote the Flonzaley Quartet, which played an occasional charity concert but otherwise, as the *New York Times* reported in 1905, "plays exclusively for Mr. De Coppet at his home in New York in Winter and at his villa, Le Flonzaley, in Switzerland in Summer."[398] Reportedly, De Coppet's players were required to remain single for the first ten years they were under contract.[399]

In Philadelphia, Mary Louise Curtis Bok underwrote a Curtis Quartet to serve and represent her conservatory. In Washington, Elizabeth Sprague Coolidge, who had already founded the Berkeley Quartet while living in Pittsfield, Massachusetts, endowed the Coolidge Quartet to play in the dedicated five-hundred-seat concert hall she had also endowed at the Library of Congress, and where the four Russian Jews of the Budapest Quartet, outfitted with Mrs. Whittall's Strads, would serve from 1939 till 1962 as the Library's resident ensemble.[400]

In 1940, a bad year to be a Belgian, a new era began for string quartets when the University of Wisconsin offered the touring Pro Arte Quartet a new home and established them as America's first campus artists in residence. Then came postwar prosperity, a bull market in higher education, and a sea change in support for the arts that extended into the heady 1970s. By the late 1940s, there were three or four active string quartets in the United States. A generation later, resident quartets graced campuses across the country, and college and university concert series accounted for half of the Guarneri Quartet's hundred-plus annual concerts. For the first time, musicians could make a living by playing in a quartet. Arnold Steinhardt, the Guarneri's first violinist, left steady work and an upscale job with the Cleveland Orchestra to play quartets. "If you could leave a steady job to meditate at the feet of a guru in India, why not trade an orchestra position for the intimate, personal expression of a chamber-music group?" he would later write of his decision.[401] A half-generation later, Phil Setzer of the Emerson Quartet reflected on college contemporaries who had aimed at solo careers, wrestled day and night with the Tchaikovsky concerto, and were now selling insurance. Setzer, too, had no regrets that he'd taken up string quartets.[402]

A third of a century after their 1976 debut, the Emerson still played as many concerts as they wished. They taught at the State University of New York at Stony Brook and were among the last quartets with a steady relationship to a major record company. But the golden age had long since turned yellow as audiences turned gray. "String quartet music is clearly not for young people," Sonia Simmenauer reported in an endearing memoir of her life as manager of at least three major ensembles whose members could have been her uncles or older brothers. "If the median age is 50, you've encountered an amazingly youthful crowd."[403] Yet people seemed to like the music, Anne Midgette noted in the *New York Times*. Would it help to find another word for "chamber"?[404]

Cash flow remained a perennial problem. Still relatively unknown in 1938, the Budapest split $300 of an evening while Efrem Zimbalist and his pianist divided $650. Nationally known seven years later, they split $600 while Nathan Milstein, playing solo, earned at least $1,000.[405] A medley of early twenty-first-century fees—$15,000, €12,000, £8,000— only confirmed the iron law of quartet economics: at best, four for the price of one.[406]

Attrition, both physical and psychological, was another challenge. People of often uncommon individuality, quartet players spent several hours a day in intensive interaction and weeks and months away from home, as dependent on one another as mountain climbers. Come domestic and physical rain or come shine, they were expected, like all performers, to arrive cheerful and well pressed and play great music well. Wherever they went, Goethe's famous letter to the Berlin composer-conductor-music teacher Carl Friedrich Zelter was sure to follow. "You hear four sensible people talk, and believe you profit from the conversation,"[407] he told his friend Zelter. This wasn't entirely wrong. But anyone who heard, watched or met a professional string quartet en route or in action soon realized that quartets, like families, converse in many ways, not all of them sensible.

Happy quartets were all alike. Each unhappy quartet was unhappy in its own way. A photo of the Budapest Quartet in the files of Sony Classical, heir to Columbia Masterworks, shows the four in shirtsleeves at a recording session, bright-eyed as schoolkids on the first day of vacation. Someone has obviously just said something very funny. A photo by Gjon Mili in the files of *Life* magazine shows the four in hat and coat at the Seattle airport, two at opposite ends of a bench, two seated back-to-back behind them, with all four staring straight ahead. Valentin Erben, cellist of the Alban Berg Quartet, recalled how a rehearsal discussion in Toronto had once reached a point where one member stomped out. Since nothing better occurred to them, the other three decided for lunch at a favorite restaurant, where, of course, they found him.[408]

Only a little less ubiquitous than Goethe's letter to Zelter, a cartoon by James Stevenson shows four players among the wreckage of their music stands and instruments. "As far as I'm concerned, gentlemen," says one, "this marks the end of the Schwarzwälder String Quartet."[409] From time to time, life actually imitated art. In 2000, three members of the Audubon Quartet, for some years the resident ensemble at Virginia Tech in Blacksburg, Virginia, threw out their first violinist. He sued and won a $611,000 judgment. Six years later, the case was still unresolved, the violinist had burned up life savings of more than half a million dollars in legal fees, and bankruptcy trustees demanded the assets of his former colleagues, including their instruments.[410] The suit was finally resolved by a freelance French horn player, who bought the contested instruments for $200,000 and loaned them back to their original owners for the next ten years.[411]

Some quartets just retired. Together for nineteen years, Germany's Cherubini Quartet called it quits in 1997 when its members, now living in four different places, decided that it had become just too hard to stay together.[412] After twenty-six years and three personnel changes, America's Cleveland Quartet bowed out in 1995, the year its first violinist, William Preucil Jr., took a job as concertmaster of the Cleveland Orchestra. In 1987, Britain's Amadeus Quartet, together for forty years, stopped when its violist died and his colleagues couldn't bring themselves to replace him. In 2005, Vienna's Alban Berg Quartet, together for twenty-five years, stopped for a similar reason.[413]

Other quartets renewed themselves like deciduous trees. Founded almost simultaneously after World War II, New York's Juilliard Quartet and Moscow's Borodin Quartet were still active after a biblical lifetime. Their personnel at all positions had meanwhile turned over multiple times. The Pro Arte Quartet, survivor of any number of near-death experiences before and after coming to rest in Madison on the eve of World War II, dated back to at least World War I, when a Belgian cavalry general with a passion for music recruited qualified players and let them rehearse when the regiment was pulled back for rest and recuperation.[414]

Though the profession remained as precarious as ever, "never in my lifetime have there been so many outstanding quartets," Norman Lebrecht, born in 1948, reported in 2010.[415] In 2011, Chamber Music America reported some seventy-five professional string quartets among its membership alone. But even for the United States, the list was far from complete. It was anybody's guess how many more quartets were spread around the world, many presumably sighing like so many New Yorkers and Italians that their situation was hopeless, but how could anyone do anything else?

For believers, a population that presumably included most past, present, and future quartets, the answer was self-evident. "There is simply nothing better than playing string quartets and performing them in public," Steinhardt declared as he looked back on the quartet he helped found in 1964 and saw to its sunset forty-five years later.[416] "I never thought you four would make it as a quartet," he quoted Charles Avsharian, the Ann Arbor dealer, fellow violinist, and Curtis alumnus, who had been present at the creation.[417] People often said the same of old married couples.

PLAYERS IN PARTICULAR

FOR PLAYERS WHO wanted to shine in solitary splendor, there were options too. There were no soloists in view in 1556, when Philibert Jambe de Fer famously reported that the instrument was only of use for dancing, and of interest to "those who make a living from it with their labour."[418] Yet half a century later, it seemed self-evident, at least in Italy and Germany, that the instrument could not only be played well enough to hold people's attention, but raise the bar to levels that even the brave new world of virtuoso singers might aspire to.[419]

Carlo Farina, born in Mantua around 1604, was already a second-generation string player when he was hired at the age of twenty as concert-master to the Saxon court, where his Capriccio Stravagante, a crowd-pleasing buffet of instrumental music and animal imitations, was soon among the era's greatest hits.[420] By the mid-seventeenth century, a generation of Italians had inspired a generation of Germans to go and do likewise. At twenty-two, Thomas Baltzar was employed at the Swedish court. Three years later, he was received like a rock star in London before anticipating countless late twentieth-century successors and drinking himself to death in his early thirties.

Young players in search of a role model were better advised to look to the Bohemian-born Heinrich Biber, who arrived in Salzburg at twenty-six via court positions in Graz and Kremsier, today's Kroměříž, where he began as the valet de chambre to the archbishop at the entry level wage of 10 florins a month. Twenty years later, as Heinrich Biber von Bibern, whose virtuosity as a composer as well as a player had carried him to knighthood, he earned six times his starting salary plus board, lodging, and bread, wine, and firewood supplements, and was known and admired as far away as France.[421] To judge by the diarist John Evelyn, who was his contemporary, the Italian-born Nicola Matteis, who surfaced in London only a few years later, was at least as remarkable. "I heard that stupendious Violin Signor Nicolao, whom certainly never mortal man Exceeded on that instrument," Evelyn reported.[422]

"The Italians call painters, sculptors, as well as scholars and poets, but especially honest musicians, virtuosi, that is, excellent, noble and famous people," Johann Kuhnau, Bach's predecessor as cantor of Leipzig's St. Thomas Church, reported helpfully in 1700.[423] By midcentury, not least because of Arcangelo Corelli, "the new Orpheus of our days," as one contemporary called him,[424] the concept was well on its way to its modern meaning.

From his arrival in Rome, Corelli proved that he could make himself known as a player, composer, conductor, and teacher. He first connected with the art-collecting, music-playing, libretto-writing Cardinal Benedetto Pamphili, one of the city's leading patrons, then went to work for Christina, the redoubtable former queen of Sweden, who was an intermittent resident of Rome for almost a quarter of a century and a major patron of the arts. A third super-patron, Cardinal Pietro Ottoboni, the twenty-two-year-old nephew of Pope Alexander VIII, took over after her death. For the next twenty-three years, Corelli lived like a family friend in the Cardinal's palace, where he took charge of the Monday night concerts, directed opera productions, and composed twelve violin sonatas for yet another well-placed patron, Sophie-Charlotte, the electress of Brandenburg, first queen of Prussia, and a friend of the sciences as well as the arts. Like Cardinal Pietro Ottoboni a few years earlier, and Goethe more than a century afterward, he was inducted into Rome's Accademia degli Arcadi, a creation of Christina's, and the city's most exclusive literary society. On his death a few weeks short of sixty, he left a substantial estate and art collection and was buried in the Pantheon in the company of the painter Raphael.

Over the next three centuries, virtuosi including Paganini, Joachim, Vieuxtemps, Ysaÿe, a squadron of various Auer protégés, and Oistrakh would experience their own variety of royal favor from a Bonaparte princess, a Prussian king, a brigade of Russian grand dukes and duchesses, and two Belgian monarchs.

By his death in 1931, Eugene Ysaÿe was not only a Grand Officer of the Orders of Leopold, Wasa, the Nile, and Dannebrog, and a Commander of the Orders of Christ of Portugal, Isabella the Catholic, and the Crowns of Italy and Romania, but a knight of the Russian Legion of Honor and the Oak Crown of Holland. Menuhin, Vladimir Spivakov, Anne-Sophie Mut-

ter, and Isaac Stern were knights of France's Legion of Honor. As Baron
Menuhin of Stoke d'Abernon, Menuhin was also named a life peer. At
thirty-four, James Ehnes was named a member of the Order of Canada,
created in 1967 to honor lifetime accomplishment. Stern and Milstein
were awarded the Kennedy Center award, America's equivalent. Heifetz,
of course, would have been so honored too, but turned it down in a fit of
petulance on grounds that the U.S. government had failed years earlier
to acknowledge his services in World War II.[425] Yet even after three centuries, Corelli's social and professional achievement remained exemplary.
Meanwhile, his protégés and influence effectively redefined the standards
of virtuosity.

By the middle of the eighteenth century, it was clear that talent was a
necessary, but not a sufficient, condition for the aspiring virtuoso. German
competition was coming up fast. French competition was just over the horizon. But the greatest stars were still Italian. Now and then, one of them
might even be a woman like Tartini's protégée Maddalena Lombardini
Sirmen or Regina Strinasacchi, the dedicatee of Mozart's wonderful B-flat
major sonata, K. 454. But it obviously helped to be a male. A healthy sense
of self-regard didn't hurt, either. "There is but one God, and one Veracini," said Francesco Maria Veracini, a third-generation professional violinist, whose career extended over seven decades and who performed from
Florence all the way to London, Düsseldorf, and Prague. "With a violin
in my hand, I am Caesar," said Gaetano Pugnani.[426] At ten, he joined the
Turin court orchestra. At twenty-three, he inspired the *Mercure de France* to
report that "the connoisseurs insist that they have never heard a violinist
superior to this virtuoso." At thirty,[427] he was hired by Johann Christian
Bach as concertmaster at London's King's Theater. At fifty, he performed
for Catherine the Great in St. Petersburg.

Appreciative and accommodating employers were career enhancers,
too. The directors of the Ospedale della Pietà terminated Vivaldi's teaching job in 1716, possibly for reasons of economy or redundancy. But they
almost immediately promoted him to music director and allowed him
to tour much of Italy, on the condition that he deliver two new concerti a month, if necessary by mail, and show up for rehearsals when in
Venice.[428]

As reconstructed by the violinist-musicologist Simon McVeigh, the
long and varied career of Felice Giardini is a model career in the era's closest approximation of a musical capital. Born in 1716 in Turin, the up-and-

coming capital of the kingdom of Savoy, Giardini studied with Giovanni
Battista Somis, a protégé of Corelli's, and music director of the court opera.
He took his first job at twelve as an opera player in Rome. He soon moved
to Naples, where he quickly worked his way to the front of the section and,
as he later told music historian Charles Burney, was cured of his habit of
showing off when he received a resounding slap from the composer Niccolò
Jommelli.

Giardini was thirty-five when he finally arrived in London. The occasion was a benefit for the aging soprano, Francesca Cuzzoni, who had once
earned £2,000, vastly more than most people saw in a lifetime, for performing a season of Handel at the King's Theater, London's opera house.[429]
The evening was a modest success for Cuzzoni, but it was a launching pad
for Giardini.

Thirty-three years later, he returned to Naples for what may have been
intended as retirement, and moved into the house of Sir William Hamilton, the newly named British ambassador to the Kingdom of Sicily, husband of the famous and beautiful Lady Hamilton, and a onetime pupil.
Gifted with wit, charm, and entrepreneurial zip in a place receptive to all
three, he was, again according to Burney, "engaged and caressed at most of
the private concerts of the principal nobility, gentry and foreign ministers."

Through much of his career, Giardini was handsomely paid for performing at benefits, among others, for the "Fund established for the Support of Decay'd Musicians and their Families" or for "Sufferers by the Late,
Dreadful Hurricane in Jamaica and Barbadoes," where people paid what
a civil servant might earn in one month and a miner in three to hear him
play. He also played public concerts in the provinces as well as in London
and was regularly engaged as concertmaster at subscription concerts and
at the Italian opera, where he was active for thirty years. When he was
not performing, Giardini taught singing to ladies and violin to gentlemen and organized a morning accademia at his house, where his pupils
could perform. Like any self-respecting virtuoso from the seventeenth to
the twentieth century, he composed, primarily for his own use. But he also
composed for others on request, for example for Selina Shirley, Countess
of Huntingdon, a leading Anglican evangelical who wanted a tune for the
anonymous "Hymn to the Trinity."[430] For a few years he even operated
an "Italian Musick Warehouse" in the Haymarket, then and since prime
commercial real estate, with a cellist partner, where customers could buy
printed music, as well as instruments, and could also have instruments

repaired. At his peak, he earned an estimated £700 a year, enough to put him in a bracket with the lesser gentry. Though well short of the going rate for singers, his income was surprisingly little, in Dr. Samuel Johnson's opinion, for a man of his accomplishments.

Adoring patrons such as the Baroness Bingley and the Dukes of Gloucester and Cumberland, both brothers of King George III, not only settled annuities on him but practically treated him as an equal. On social terms with the Earl of Pembroke, Giardini lived like a family member at Blenheim, home of another of his pupils, Caroline Russell, the Duchess of Marlborough. In 1763, he was one of nine "privileg'd"—that is, nonaristocratic—members admitted to the Noblemen's and Gentlemen's Catch Club, a singing group.

Not everything worked out as hoped or planned. He was not skilled at money management. His career as opera impresario ended with imposing deficits. Nothing came of his joint venture with Burney, to turn London's Foundling Hospital into an English version of a Venetian *ospedale*. As he aged, the wine increasingly turned to vinegar and the roses wilted. The relationship at Blenheim ended when he was accused of overcharging for lessons. The Prince of Wales turned his back on Giardini after what seems to have been a slippery violin deal. In his midseventies, Giardini attempted a comeback in England, but it flopped. He died in Moscow a few years later, poor and nearly forgotten.[431] Till well into the next century, foreign violinists tended to see Russia as a last best hope, where Italians were paid better than anywhere else.[432] But few were prepared like Giardini to tour in stagecoaches at eighty.

He left two traces in the adoptive country where he spent so many of his best years. The first appears in the second stanza of a four-part "Ode to the Memory of Italian Virtuosi" by Henry Harrington, a Bath physician and amateur composer, much admired as a master of the glee. In a text consisting entirely of names, Giardini rhymes with Nicolini, the alto castrato who premiered the title role in Handel's "Rinaldo." The second could still be found on page 365 of the 1982 edition of the Episcopalian hymnal in a popular hymn beginning "Come, thou almighty king." Given the composer's melancholy end, the title, "Moscow," is ironic. But the irony is almost certainly unintended.[433]

FOUNDING FATHERS

THE FUTURE BEGAN again with an Italian in Paris. Giovanni Battista Viotti was the son of a workingman from the Piedmont with a musical avocation. Introduced to music at eight, he impressed the local bishop when he was eleven. The bishop recommended the young Viotti to the Marchesa di Voghera, who wanted a study companion for her son, the young Prince dal Pozzo della Cisterna. Viotti's poise and talent soon persuaded the Marchesa that he was adequate to the assignment. "Charmed by such natural talent, I decided to do all that was necessary to make sure it bore fruit," dal Pozzo explained to Fétis, the Belgian musicologist, some sixty years later. Only eighteen himself, the young prince settled the boy in the family house in Turin and hired Pugnani, recently back from London and music director at the Savoy court, to be his violin teacher. Viotti's education would eventually cost him 20,000 francs, he told Fétis, but he considered it worth every penny, "because such a talent can never be paid for too highly."[434] Seven years later, Viotti was hired as a probationary member of the Savoian court orchestra. He received tenure at twenty-one, presumably with plenty of opportunity to play private concerts. He had already begun to compose.

In 1780, Viotti left with Pugnani on a two-year tour that took them to Geneva, Bern, the Prussian and Saxon courts, Poland, and Russia. Pugnani then returned to Turin, while Viotti proceeded to Paris with its hyperactive concert life. As convention prescribed, he first performed at an exclusive private concert in an exclusive private home. The host and probable patron was Carl Ernst von Bagge, a Baltic baron of considerable wealth and celebrated eccentricity. A Paris resident since 1750, von Bagge was a composer of modest talent as well as a violinist who so liked to teach that he paid his pupils on a sliding scale, with their wages rising as they progressed. Among his nominal protégés were some of the era's most distinguished players, including Viotti and Kreutzer, who evidently managed to keep a straight face while being instructed, and welcomed a bit of extra cash.[435]

Armed with a Stradivari and an approximation of a modern bow, Viotti made his obligatory public debut on short notice at the Concert Spirituel on March 17, 1782. Decades later, his pupil Pierrre Baillot recalled "this fine genius whose accents were so true, natural and at the same time so lofty that they gave the most agreeable and noble character to all his inspi-rations."[436] The local papers declared the occasion a benchmark like none since Jean-Baptiste Lully's debut in the mid-seventeenth century. There would be twelve more such concerts before the year was over, and all of Paris wanted a piece of him.[437]

But Viotti did not fully appreciate popular acclaim, as Fétis noted, a blind spot that would have serious consequences.[438] In September 1783, he dropped out of public concertizing in favor of a salaried job at court as "accompanist to the queen." With its assured income and minimal obliga-tions, the new position allowed him to compose as many as eight of what would eventually be twenty-nine violin concerti. Most interesting and con-sequential was a network of connections that allowed him to think about a new career, only distantly related to the first.[439]

In 1788, Viotti returned to public life as a theater director and impre-sario. His partner was Léonard Autié, the queen's coiffeur and thus an art-ist in his own right. Though known informally as the Théâtre Italien, the theater was registered as Théâtre de Monsieur, a reference to its patron, the king's younger brother and later Louis XVIII.[440] Over the next decade, its name would change five times, as "Monsieur" and even "Italien" lost their brand appeal.

The theater proposed to engage three different companies to produce Italian opera, lirica, buffa, and seria, as well as French opera, comedy, and vaudeville. The producers faced the perennial challenges of space, cash flow, artistic temperament, and seats in need of filling. Yet the project might have worked save for two problems, one more daunting than the other. The first was the French Revolution. The second was that virtually every habit Viotti had acquired since he was eight and every connection he had made since coming to Paris was fast becoming a serious liability.

Moderately liberal by disposition, he welcomed the revolution in its early phase, joined the National Guard, and performed at a well-attended private concert in the fifth-floor apartment of a parliamentary deputy and member of the first revolutionary government. He was soon accused of anti-royalist sympathies by a right-wing pamphleteer.[441] On the first anniversary of the storming of the Bastille, his singers and orchestra performed in the celebratory Te Deum at Nôtre Dame. But the Théâtre de Monsieur had prudently morphed into the Théâtre Français et Italien before the year was over, and the next year Autié left abruptly for England.

Viotti hung on for another year till it became dangerously clear that Paris was no longer a safe place for an "accompanist to the queen." Since March 1792, he had been in contact with Johann Salomon about concerts in London. A comedian from his French company, now Jacobin first commissioner for the district of St. Germain, owed Viotti a favor for his help with the actor's marriage to a member of the theater's Italian company. An exit visa from his former employee allowed Viotti to follow Autié to England.[442]

In 1798, the British government, fearful enough of French invasion to suspend habeas corpus, suspected Viotti, the unlikeliest of candidates, of Jacobin sympathies, forcing him to leave under protest for a two-year stay in Germany. It was 1811 before the Duke of Cambridge helped him return to England, where he would live and even flourish for most of the next twenty-five years.

Like his Paris debut a decade earlier, his London debut was such a success that Salomon had to buy newspaper ads, politely but firmly cautioning nonsubscribers that the five-hundred-seat hall had limits. He was back the next year to play with Salomon and Haydn. The distinguished castrato Venanzio Rauzzini, now retired to a rewarding second career as an impresario in Bath, engaged him to play for his winter, Easter, and especially fashionable fall season. In 1795, Viotti was hired to manage the concert series at the King's Theatre, the capital's biggest hall.

All the while, Viotti was a regular at private concerts hosted by William Bassett Chinnery, chief clerk at the Treasury and an enthusiastic amateur cellist, whose rich, loyal, and well-educated wife, Margaret Tresilian, was a gifted amateur pianist. Wednesday was "bread and butter concert" night, when the guest list might include the French and Spanish ambassadors, the Prince of Wales (later George IV), and his brother, Prince Adolphus, Duke of Cambridge, who was a well-regarded amateur violinist. A "substantial supper" was served at midnight.

As he had been taken in at eleven as an adjunct family member in Turin, Viotti was now taken in again as an adjunct family member in London. But this time, known to the family as Amico, it was he who was charged with

the musical and even moral education of the young, in this case the Chinnery son and daughter.[443] With the help of a £2,600 loan from Margaret,
he also invested heavily in the wine trade in partnership with a Chinnery
family friend. Meanwhile, he continued to teach and compose. But a visit
to Paris in 1802, when the Treaty of Amiens allowed him to return for the
first time in ten years, left no doubt that business was his new priority. In
partnership with Rode, Kreutzer, and the composers Méhul, Boieldieu, and
Isouard, his old friend and colleague Luigi Cherubini had recently gone
into publishing. They paid in cash for concerti and trios at more than three
times the previous going rate. The cash went straight into Viotti's new wine
enterprise.

In the spring of 1812, the party ended abruptly when Chinnery, the
longtime beneficiary of a remarkably tolerant auditing system, was accused
of embezzling £88,000 from the Treasury over twelve years. The equivalent of more than £4 million in 2007, the figure was all the more remarkable when measured against his annual salary of £100 a year when he was
hired in 1783.[444]

Chinnery first took off for Sweden and then relocated to Calais when
the Bourbons returned in 1814, and to Le Havre a year later. There he
acted as an agent for Viotti and his partner. Both his wife and Viotti regularly showed up to visit. Cheerful accessory to what seems to have been a
mutually consensual and fully functional ménage à trois, William never
returned to England.

Viotti helped Margaret auction the family estate, inherited from her
father, but considered under English law to be William's property. She
then resumed entertainment at a large town house in Portman Square,
where she hosted the once and future elite of the French Restoration and a
selected cadre of musicians. Viotti, always patient with amateurs, appeared
at countless musical soirées. He even traveled to Richmond, far up the
Thames from Margaret's summer place in Fulham, to teach Albertine, the
daughter of the formidable Mme. de Staël, a fellow exile and old friend
from Paris. With at least thirty ex-Chinnery guests, he also helped found
the Philharmonic Society, where he played in the orchestra, appeared occasionally as soloist, and served on the board for an annual compensation of
two subscription tickets.

In 1818, the wine shop failed when a major customer defaulted so spectacularly that the authorities froze the shop's assets. In need of regular
income and resolved to repay the loan from Margaret, Viotti applied, as

he had on the eve of the Revolution, for the directorship of the Opéra and Théâtre Italien in Paris. This time he was offered a two-year contract at 12,000 francs plus a 3,000-franc housing supplement at a time when even the director of the Conservatoire earned only 8,000 and faculty salaries ranged from 700 to 3,000.[445] But Viotti was now sixty-four, not thirty-four, and an untenured public functionary without a financial safety net, facing the usual challenges of claqueurs, a partisan as well as a frequently venal press, and a contentious bureaucracy.

The job might still have worked out but for another of the era's collisions of art and life. In February 1820, the Duc de Berry, the king's nephew and the royal family's last best hope for an heir, was assassinated by an anti-monarchist as the Duc escorted his wife to her coach at the Opéra entrance. The government shut down all theaters for ten days and, at the request of the archbishop of Paris, the Opéra building itself was razed. Pending construction of a new one, space and stage capacity were hard to come by. Meanwhile, budget cuts required layoffs and salary reductions, morale and discipline sank, and audiences found the new productions underwhelming.

Viotti was the inevitable target. "What is the use of the finest army commanded by an unskillful general?" an anonymous newspaper critic asked on October 31, 1820. The next day Viotti was relieved as director of the Opéra. Whether he resigned or was fired is unknown.[446] But his pension at half-salary was further reduced by half, and there were tangles of litigation. Habeneck, his successor, did his best to explain tactfully that Viotti's box had been reassigned to a hereditary prince of Denmark but that Viotti would at least be allowed to keep his complimentary tickets. Appointment to the Legion of Honor was apparently a consolation prize. He spent his remaining years composing, worrying about money, and playing the French stock market on Margaret's behalf with advances from William. He died in London in 1824 and was buried in Paddington Street Gardens. In 1886, the area was officially rededicated as a recreational ground.[447]

Though Viotti spent fewer than ten of his sixty-nine years as a professional concert player, he was still alive when the Conservatoire began turning his legacy into a curriculum. His concerti fathered one of the century's standard genres. Posterity recognized him as the most influential player of his time. Even his instrument, declared "among the five most beautiful Strads" by Fétis in 1856 and "one of the most perfect Strads" by Vuillaume in 1862, had become as iconic as the *Messiah* by the time it reached London's Royal Academy in 2005.[448]

Though they never met, Paganini could be considered part of Viotti's legacy, too:[449] well into the 1820s, Paganini played Viotti concertos, just as he played Rode and Kreutzer, and echoes of Viotti could be heard in his compositions. "I have seen Paganini, who has never ceased to ask me in every way about the first and greatest of violinist-composers," Viotti's chorusmaster, Ferdinand Hérold, reported from Naples in spring 1821. "He also wishes to come to Paris, above all when he will be able to meet there the man he most admires."[450]

By 1831, when Paganini finally reached Paris, Viotti was gone. Paganini was now first and greatest of violinist-composers. Within days of his arrival on February 24, he'd heard Malibran sing Desdemona in Rossini's *Otello* and Habeneck conduct Beethoven's Fifth, signed a contract for ten concerts, visited dozens of old friends and acquaintances, and taken to his hotel bed with a psychosomatic coughing fit that caused him to cancel a performance for the new King Louis Philippe, which his composition teacher Ferdinand Paer had arranged for him in order to consult Francesco Bennati, a pioneer laryngologist. On March 6, he played his first concert. "His bow gleams like a steel blade, his face is pale as crime itself, his smile is lovely as Dante's hell, his violin weeps like a woman," the journal *L'Entr'acte* reported. His performance of the "Campanella" movement from his second violin concerto moved an orchestra cellist to write couplets in the part on his music stand.

> Nature wanted us to see
> Her power in our century.
> To dazzle the world, two men made she,
> Bonaparte and Paganini.[451]

Separation of Paganini the man from Paganini the myth, much assisted by the historian Arturo Codignola's annotated publication, in 1935, of 287 letters extending from 1814 to 1840, took more than a century. But even demystified, the story was remarkable enough. Musical phenomenon and legendary crowd-pleaser, gambler, cheapskate, and social climber, tireless but conflicted womanizer, devoted father, serial litigant, and medical mess, he began life as the third child of a working-class family in Genoa. His musical education began at five and a half, when his father put a mandolin in his hand. A violin followed two years later.

Many myths about Paginini circulated within his lifetime. A Faustian pact with the devil was a particular favorite. The legend of the solitary prisoner, behind bars for strangling his wife, was not far behind, as the great German violinist Ludwig Spohr noted in his diary.[452] Stendhal recycled it in his *Life of Rossini*. Paganini was indignant.[453]

In fact, he did a bit of time in prison, in 1815, when, in the first of countless romantic caprices, he eloped to Parma with the underage Angelina Cavanna. She returned to Genoa pregnant and unmarried. Her father sued for damages. Paganini countersued, charging that she was of age, had joined him voluntarily, and had previously worked at the oldest profession. He was sentenced to jail and fined but was soon released without paying the fine. Nine years later, he entered into a relationship with the singer Antonia Bianchi, the only one of its kind. It was short-lived and surely dysfunctional, but not homicidal. There was no divorce, most probably because there was no marriage. She left the relationship with a settlement. He left with custody of their son. Many more affairs followed. In 1830, Helène von Feuerbach, whose father reformed the Bavarian penal code, went so far as to leave her marriage for him. But he didn't marry her.[454] As often with prodigies, he was two years older than a widely published birthdate claimed. But in this case, as he confirmed in a letter to his long-suffering friend and attorney Luigi Guglielmo Germi, the fictitious date originated with himself. His claims of childhood poverty seem to have been largely self-invented, too.

Like many prodigies, he was sensitive about his educational shortcomings. But like his father and siblings, he was literate, no small attainment in a city where many of their social superiors were not. Remarkably, his musical education, compared with that of his peers from Corelli on, is among the least documented of all great players.[455] As a young customs official posted to Livorno, Jacques Boucher occasionally played quartets with Paganini. A credible witness, he reported how Paganini had told him he was self-taught. But this was also mythmaking. Paganini's father had turned him over early to Giacomo Costa, a local orchestra player, possibly hoping that little Niccolò, too, might one day join the orchestra. A local paper even reported that "an extraordinarily able 11-year-old, Sig. Niccolò Paganini, was received with universal admiration." Two years later, his father took him to Parma, "the Athens of Italy," to study violin with

Alessandro Rolla, the court concertmaster and later music director of La Scala in Milan, and to learn composition from Ferdinando Paer, later music director at the Saxon court in Dresden. Dazzled by the prodigious talent on his doorstep, Paer then passed him on to his own teacher, Gasparo Ghiretti.[456]

Over the next few years, Paganini may have composed some of the twenty-four caprices that were eventually published in 1820. But he never played them in public. Again by his own account, he took up the guitar and learned to play it, too, with supreme virtuosity. When Napoleon turned the old oligarchical Genoese republic into a satellite Ligurian Republic, the Genoese National Guard began drafting seventeen-year-olds, and Paganini left for the countryside. In an area the invading French turned into a war zone, he played his variations on "La Carmagnole," the revolutionary era's equivalent of a football fight song, as well as bird songs and the usual movements from concertos by Rode, Viotti, Kreutzer, and Pleyel, at ad hoc concerts from Livorno to Modena.

At eighteen, he discovered that there were games as well as instruments to play, but also that they could cost him more in one evening than he could earn from many concerts. Where he contracted syphilis is a matter of speculation. But mention of the diagnosis already appears in an 1822 letter to Germi. The prescribed treatment, as it had been for centuries, was heavy doses of mercury. As so often in Paganini's life, his doctors and their prescribed treatments were as devastating as the diseases they treated.[457] In 1801, the French revived La Musica, a famous and traditionally well-paying music festival in Lucca, a diminutive Tuscan protectorate near the Mediterranean coast. Paganini played a successful audition and was invited to perform after the opening "Kyrie" at a solemn pontifical mass there. Everyone admired his virtuosity, a local priest reported afterward, but his bird, flute, trumpet, and horn imitations moved the audience to unchurchly titters.[458]

He would remain in Lucca for most of the next eight years. For the first four, he was concertmaster of the little republic's Capella Nazionale. The job allowed him to travel sometime between 1802 and 1804 to nearby Livorno, where a French businessman named Livron loaned him a violin so he "could play a concerto of Viotti's"[459] and declined to take it back. The instrument was in all likelihood the Cannon, the 1742 del Gesù that would ever after be associated with Paganini.

For the next four years he was court violinist to Napoleon's eldest sister, the art-loving and hyperactive Elisa Bonaparte Baciocchi, installed

by her brother as Duchess of Lucca and Princess of Piombino. His duties
included three performances a week, conducting the opera, and providing
lessons and quartet practice to Félix Baciocchi, the fiddle-loving duke and
prince. By his own account, Paganini also conducted a brief fling with the
duchess-princess.

He now enjoyed the rank of a captain in her honor guard and was paid
nearly twice what he had earned on arrival. But he still lagged behind the
resident Latin professor, the court chef, and the court physician and was
passed over for promotion when Elisa, with her eye on a bigger, better
court in Florence, downsized the Luccan orchestra to a string quartet.

In late 1809, the Luccan chapter of Paganini's life ended in an inglori-
ous squabble with his employer. At last appointed Grand Duchess of Tuscany, Elisa was in Florence, trying with minimal success to win friends and
influence the local gentry by awarding prestigious positions in her honor
guard. Paganini, still on her payroll, arrived in the prince's entourage to
perform at a gala laid on for the occasion. As a hired musician, with the
status of a professional entertainer, he was expected to perform in subservi-
ent court black. Instead, according to an early biographer, he insisted on
the uniform he was entitled to as a member of her honor guard.[460]

His Carmagnole days long past, Paganini now played in principle for
anyone wealthy and powerful enough to pay him. His audience extended
from the Bonapartes to Metternich, the Austrian chancellor, who was their
implacable adversary. In 1827, Leo XII, a pope with "little insight into the
hopes and visions of those who were then pioneers of the greater liberty
that had become inevitable," according to the *Catholic Encyclopedia*,[461] presented him with the Order of the Golden Spur. It was an honor previously
conferred on Gluck and Mozart. In December 1832, Paganini accepted
the Grand Cross of the Order of St. Stanislaus from the Prince of Salm
Kyrburg, whose little principality had lost its sovereignty in 1810, and
with it, the right to confer such honors. The broker was the con-turned-
cop, Eugène François Vidocq, literally a character in Hugo and Balzac,
who charged up to 8,000 francs for his services. A few weeks later, the
Moniteur Universel, France's newspaper of record, announced that Paganini
was now the Baron Paganini, an honorific title that went with his trophy
decoration.

His political manifesto could be found in a letter, posted from Warsaw
in 1829, to a cellist protégé in Parma. "It is necessary to be fully active,
objective, timely about recommendations, to surmount obstacles, to accept

reverses gracefully so far as this is compatible with self-respect, avoid trip-wires, and be on the lookout for trapdoors set by many so-called gentle-men, with whom one is always in contact," he advised, "In two words, it's not enough to know how to play," he concluded. "You also need to know how to present yourself in the world, which is the same as saying how to live." Or, better still, survive, his biographer, Pietro Berri, added in a parenthentical Italian pun.[462]

In late 1834, Paganini again played the Bonaparte card. Anxious to legitimate the son officially born "to unknown parents," he played a benefit in Parma in the presence of the Duchess of Parma, Napoleon's widow. A year later, to the chagrin of Fétis, who was distressed to see "the king of artists descend to the level of the courtiers,"[463] he accepted her invitation to turn her resident orchestra of thirty-four underachievers into a serious ensemble. With direct access to the duchess, it might have worked. With-out it, his project, like Viotti's, stalled in the ministerial bureaucracy. He resigned barely half a year after his arrival.

But the Bonaparte years were bookends. It was the years between them, and the fortuitous connection of supply and demand, that turned Paganini the man into Paganini the legend. " . . . if only he could stop trying to be the grand buffoon of the violin, he could be its grand duke, even emperor, and declare himself a real virtuoso as in 'I'd rather be the emperor of the violin than the violinist of the emperor,'" Boucher de Perthes wrote, as his onetime quartet partner set off to seek—and find—his fortune. Demand was no problem. It was true that his workplace was located in a dystopia of banditry, wretched roads, and pre-industrial infrastructure, only recently transformed from a war zone to a jungle of restorationist mini-sovereignties with smothering bureaucracies, whose interior ministries were reflexively suspicious of his Jacobin past. But it was also true that singers were trump, and instrumentalists were favorite accessories to an evening of opera or ballet.

None of this was a problem for Paganini. If people wanted entertain-ment and were prepared to pay for it, he was happy to entertain them. Art was not an issue.[464] In 1816, Paganini crossed paths in Venice with Spohr, an artist in what was already approaching the modern sense from a con-cert culture still years from reaching Italy. Spohr understandably expressed interest in hearing him. Paganini begged off.[465] Some years would pass before Spohr finally heard him in concert. He admired Paganini's tech-nique. "But there was an odd mix of absolutely brilliant and childishly tasteless in his compositions and performance style," he noted in his memoirs.[466] As a rule, people got what they came for. "I've heard him interpellate donkey, dog and rooster noises as organ point in a Viotti concerto," Boucher de Pertes wrote his father in early 1810. He'd also heard Paganini break a string, continue on three strings, and finish up on one. But Italians liked that kind of thing, applauded like mad, and when he left the theater, three hundred people escorted him home.[467]

On occasion, people got more than they came for. Now and then, it was reported credibly, he liked to show up foreign show-offs, especially from north of the Alps. On one such occasion, a French visitor did a creditable job on a difficult German piece, then ruined the effect by declaring "This is how they play in Paris." Without a word, Paganini took the score, which he was reading at sight, turned it upside down and played it backward with such uncanny virtuosity that the Frenchman's jaw dropped, and the audience went wild. "This is how they play in heaven," he said.[468]

In 1816, he consented to a joint appearance at Milan's La Scala. But this one was not a setup. The Frenchman was Charles Philippe Lafont, a protégé of Kreutzer and Rode, and a favorite of the French king and Russian czar. Both played a group of solo pieces, then joined for a double concerto by Kreutzer. Though many declared the performance a contest and mythologized it as a Paganini victory, it was neither. Paganini found Lafont good, if unsurprising. Lafont denied that either of them was a winner, but defended the excellence of the French school.

Two years later, Paganini agreed to appear with the somewhat younger Polish virtuoso, Karol Lipinski, again to play Kreutzer, in Piacenza. This time the occasion was entirely amicable and Lipinski came away impressed. It might have stayed that way had Paganini's appearance in Warsaw in 1829 not coincided with the coronation of Russia's Czar Nicholas I as king of Poland. Polish nationalists simmered that another foreigner, Paganini, was also allowed first billing, while Lipinski, the hometown hero, was relegated to accessory status as concertmaster of the orchestra. His friendship with Paganini was among the collateral damage.

On occasion, Paganini also gave his audience what he thought they deserved. In Ferrara in 1812, where he shared the bill with a singer friend and hired prima donna, the friend's ballerina flame agreed to pinch-hit when the scheduled prima donna left. Paganini accompanied her on the guitar. When the audience whistled her off the stage, Paganini picked up his violin, and gallantly replied with donkey noises addressed to the protesters. The local police encouraged him to leave town as quickly as possible.[469]

By 1828, he had played every Italian city of note, most of them multiple times. He was painted, sketched and sculpted, reported, reviewed, and analyzed. Critics associated him with Michelangelo, Raphael, Dante, Tasso, and Virgil and hailed him as the Genoese Orpheus, and the Apollo and angel of paradise. To them, he could perform wonders and miracles.

No one associated him with Ehlers-Danlos syndrome, an inherited connective tissue disorder identified only around 1900. But at least two contemporary reports suggest that Paganini's astonishing dexterity may have had something to do with it.[470] Matteo Ghetaldi, the last doge of the Republic of Ragusa, now Dubrovnik, reported after a concert in Venice that Paganini could move the joints of his left fingers laterally, and bend his thumb back till it touched his little finger, as though he had neither muscles nor bones. Carl Guhr, who observed Paganini in Frankfurt, noted a hand of moderate size. It could play three octaves at the same time, a phenomenon Joseph Gingold had read about but was to observe only once, many years later, in the thirteen-year-old Itzhak Perlman.[471]

Contemporaries noted with deepest interest how, like none before him, Paganini played everything from memory, how his left hand did things on the G string that had never before been seen or heard, as well as single and double harmonics, left-hand pizzicati with and without the bow, even double trills in octaves.[472] Local correspondents spread the word across the Alps to the musical press of Leipzig, London, and Paris. Honorific academies elected Paganini a member.

His apotheosis still lay ahead. In March 1828, he set out with Bianchi for Vienna. It was the first time in his forty-six years that he had left Italy. More than six eventful years would pass before he returned. What followed was all the more remarkable in an era when social media consisted of introductory letters to bankers, theater managers, and local patrons, and mass media of handbills, wall posters, and press runs of maximally a few thousand. Add a local manager, who spoke the local language, contracts negotiated on arrival, and an advance team hired on site. Yet the effect was remarkable even by Rolling Stones standards. Vienna would lead to Prague and Warsaw, to much of Germany, of course to Paris, and from there to London, a half-day journey by steamboat. There was even a barnstorming tour of Ireland and Scotland.

Though modest, the audience for the first concert in Vienna included all the important violinists in town. From there on, filling seats was no problem, even at prices five times the usual local price. A contingent of the royal family including the empress was there for the second concert. By the end of July, when Paganini left Vienna, Bianchi left Paganini. He had not only played fourteen concerts, including one for the imperial court that turned out for the occasion in full uniform, but the box office had taken in an estimated four times what Schubert had earned in twelve years.[473] For the serious fan, there were Paganini lithographs, miniatures, rings, pendants, cameos, necklaces, hats, tiepins, neckerchiefs, buttons, walking stick knobs, and cookies and confections of marzipan and spun sugar. There were even Paganini stories, like the one about the customer, furious with the fiacre driver who demands five florins, a "Paganinerl," for a short ride. "But Paganini plays on one string," the driver replies. "Are you going to drive on one wheel?" the customer replies.[474]

In Paris, where ticket prices were doubled and he played seven concerts in six weeks, the audience included the writers Gautier and de Musset, as well as George Sand in suit and tie in the company of the cool young men de Vigny, Heine, and Börne, the artist Delacroix, whose portrait of Paganini would one day hang in Washington's Phillips Gallery, the violinists Baillot and de Bériot, the singer Malibran, and the composers Rossini, Auber, Donizetti, and the twenty-year-old Liszt. Castil-Blaze, the city's star critic, encouraged mothers of newborns to bring their babies, too, so they could later boast of having been there. In London, where Paganini played fourteen concerts and seven benefits between June 3 and July 25, a *Times* editorial writer steamed with indignation about doubled ticket prices. Yet hundreds had to be turned away on one evening, Paganini wrote Germi, while Paganini arranged for two hundred more to sit on the stage among the orchestra players so the usual orchestra seats could be sold for a little less than a Manchester carpenter, and a little more than a Manchester tailor, earned in a week.[475]

Along the way, Paganini met the Austrian emperor, the Russian czar, the Prussian, Saxon, French and English kings, and the future Queen Victoria.[476] The artistic aristocracy was naturally eager to meet him, too. In Vienna, he played quartets with Beethoven's violinist, Ignaz Schuppanzigh, and was moved to tears by a performance of Beethoven's Seventh conducted by Schuppanzigh. In Berlin, he was invited to dinner by Mendelssohn's parents and asked to play at the wedding of the crown prince, who would become Kaiser Wilhelm I. In Weimar, he made a courtesy call on Goethe. In Kassel, he was invited to lunch by Spohr. In Leipzig, Friedrich Wieck brought his prodigious daughter Clara, 10, to play for him; Paganini fed her English pudding and delighted her by writing in her autograph album. In Paris he heard Baillot play a Mozart quartet. In London, where he had recently bought his famous Stradivari viola, he invited the cellist Robert Lindley and the young Felix Mendelssohn to join him for a trio he composed to show it off.[477]

Meanwhile, there was a steady counterpoint of lawsuits, abortive love affairs, public relations clunkers, and occasional near riots. Paganini coped for the most part with tired resignation but hated the murder and prison myth. In Vienna, he enlisted friends to protest its latest iteration in the *Theaterzeitung* and even raised the price of tickets to his concerts to show the local public what he thought of it. In Prague, he agreed to Schottky's pioneer biography as a way to set the record straight but neglected to mention the Cavanna affair. When the legend resurfaced in a Paris lithograph, he fired off a letter to the *Revue Musicale*. Yet the myth remained as hard to shake as a summer cold.

In Leipzig, he walked out on a scheduled engagement when the orchestra demanded a pay supplement. In Breslau, now Wrocław, where he thought he'd agreed to play with a student orchestra, he arrived an hour late, found a nonpaying audience of 1,500, and refused to play till his indignant hosts threatened to throw him down the stairs. In Paris, where he refused a request to play for a National Guard benefit, public hostility forced him to back down and donate some of the receipts from the next concert to the Paris poor and a local orphanage. In Cheltenham, where two concerts sold out, he was again forced to back down after demanding his fee in advance on the chance that a scheduled third concert didn't sell out. In Scotland, where he threatened to cancel over disagreements with the management, indignant ticket holders in Dundee threatened to riot. In Boulogne, where local amateurs asked only for free tickets for themselves and the supplementary professionals they hired to play for the occasion, there was another commotion when Paganini offered instead to pay the players at the prevailing rate, so he could sell the requested tickets at the usual markup. In London he successfully sued the pianist Moscheles and his publisher for selling unauthorized piano transcriptions of his music.

In the end, the paths of glory trailed off in soap opera. In 1832, Paganini hired a new manager, John Watson, a singing teacher, pianist, arranger,
composer, and father of six, including Charlotte, a soprano with aspirations
of her own. Accompanied by Watson, Charlotte, and a second soprano,
a Watson protégée, he then went off to play some sixty-five concerts in
thirteen weeks, while a previous manager sued unsuccessfully for unpaid
wages. In March 1834, he even took his entourage to Belgium, where they
were not warmly received.

Two months later, when Watson was arrested for debts, a concert
had to be canceled. Paganini bailed him out, returned to London for
a farewell concert advertised as a benefit for Charlotte, and crossed the
Channel for Boulogne, where Charlotte was to meet him. Her father got
there first, mobilized the British consul and local authorities, and hauled
her back to Britain on the next boat in full view of the local British community. From there, father and daughter took off for America. With the
help of his first media manager, Paganini published an open letter to a
local paper, explaining that he only wanted to develop Charlotte's talent
and liberate her from a tyrannical father. He volunteered to join her in
New York and marry her. The same year, P. T. Barnum arrived in New
York. It is hard not to think of them meeting there as one of history's
lost opportunities.

Though Paganini spoke about a music school, nothing came of that
either. Investments in silk-weaving and juice-extraction machines were
another bust. Sick, aging, and increasingly misanthropic, he complained
of rheumatism, orchitis, fever, hemorrhage, tenesmus, and grippe. The
state of his health was not entirely surprising after years of syphilitic
and tubercular infection, compounded by dysfunction of the vocal
cords, possibly caused by Marfan's syndrome, a connective tissue disorder, leading to an aortic aneurysm that compressed and damaged the
laryngeal nerves. Everywhere he went he underwent horrendous medical
treatments by doctors, certified and self-made. Massive doses of LeRoy's
Vomito-Purgative Elixir, a hugely popular patent emetic and laxative,
were his own idea.[478]

A last initiative, the Casino Paganini in Paris, was planned as a kind
of nightclub, with a ballroom, concert hall, billiards, gaming and reading rooms, as well as "a retiring room, or boudoir, padded in flannel for
the soloists and a special armchair on the stage for the soloists."[479] But by

now Paganini wouldn't or couldn't appear in person, his partners declared bankruptcy, and the police shut it down. In the tsunami of damage suits that followed, the court ruled against Paganini. Damages were set at 50,000 francs. His legal expenses were estimated at 100,000 francs. The 1722 Rode Strad changed hands around the same time for 4,000 francs.[480]

Even his death and burial seemed subject to Murphy's Law. The French vice consul in Nice pursued him on behalf of the Casino attorneys. A local priest pursued him, intent on a deathbed confession. Church officials at first refused interment in a church cemetery. Four years passed before a friend prevailed on authorities in Genoa to allow his body to be transferred there. Meanwhile, it was provisionally stored in a cellar, a leper house, and an abandoned vat in an olive oil factory. It was 1845 before the Archbishop of Parma acceded to Achille's request to move his father's body to the grounds of his estate. Over thirty years passed before it was finally moved to a Catholic cemetery, and another twenty passed before it finally reached the monumental tomb in Parma, where it has since remained. His will provided for Achille as universal legatee, with trust funds for two sisters and small annuities for Antonia Bianchi, another former lady friend, and a maternal cousin. His preferred concert instrument, the del Gesù known as the Cannon, went to his hometown, Genoa, as a perpetual bequest. Capuchin priests were supposed to say one hundred masses in his memory.

But his mystique was already a downpayment on immortality. His legacy went on indefinitely. The variations, designed to shock and awe, still do. At least one big piece, the first violin concerto, is still in the standard repertory. Five successors, which he guarded like state secrets, have since been discovered. The caprices, of course, are classics. By the end of the twentieth century, nobody made it to the second round of a major competition without mastering at least two or three of them. By 2012, the 24th had inspired as many as twenty-six composers to variations of their own, as well as arrangements for everything from piano left hand to solo balalaika.[481]

His technical invention alone qualified him for a place in violin heaven. In 1829, after weeks of intensive observation, Guhr, the Frankfurt violinist, conductor, and theater manager, managed to a point to demystify Paganini in a biography that explained with practical examples what he did and how he did it. "If you can't play a hundred clear notes a second, you're out of luck, because you won't be able to make use of the revolution I've achieved in the field of music," Paganini told him. Even for a man with a weakness for the words "magic" and "secret," this was some-thing of an overstatement.[482] But in 1832, a Paris orchestra player with a nondigital watch clocked Paganini playing his *Sonata Movimento Perpetuo* on gut strings at 2,272 notes in three minutes and twenty seconds—or 11.36 notes per second. It would be 176 years before the German-American David Garrett, digitally timed and playing on modern strings, established a Guinness record by zipping off Rimsky-Korsakov's "Flight of the Bumblebee" at something over 13 notes per second on the BBC's children's show *Blue Peter*.[483]

With the strictly qualified exception of little Camillo Sivori, a diminutive hometown prodigy, born in 1815, he had no students in the usual sense. Sivori aside, his aversion to students was practically unique among the great players before and after. "Tear this up, and don't let anyone see you do it, or they'll steal the secret," he wrote Germi in a memo on harmonics that would later end up in the Library of Congress.[484] In Frankfurt, he slipped his manuscript under the bedcovers when the young Heinrich Wilhelm Ernst came to visit him while he was composing. But it was clear that he already taught by example in his lifetime. Allowed to audition for the master, Ernst effectively out-Paganinied Paganini by misunderstanding the flautato indication in the 9th Caprice and playing the double stops in double harmonics. Paganini was so impressed that, when Ernst booked adjacent hotels rooms so he could hear Paganini practice, he let it happen.

Within a generation of Paganini's death, a cohort of young players from Spain to Poland extended the range and repertory of the instrument across most of the Old World and much of the New World, leaving a legacy of knuckle-busters that matched and exceeded Paganini's own. A century and a half later, they were still the violin equivalent of the four-minute mile. But they were now played by adolescent Asians. Technique was one thing, personality another. A decade after Paganini's death, Sivori told his family how the French imperial couple had declared that Paganini lived on in him.[485] It's questionable whether Sivori or anyone else took this entirely seriously. Ernst, whose technique was no less awesome, was universally remembered as likable, generous, and funny, qualities not usually associated with Paganini, and characterized himself as an artist, an idea that would probably not have occurred to Paganini either.[486] When Vieuxtemps's fans in New Orleans presented him with a medal inscribed to "The premier violinist of his epoch," it was Vieuxtemps they meant. The closest approximation of a Paginini heir apparent, gaudy even by mid-nineteenth-century standards, was Ole Bull, big, handsome, charismatic, and improvident, whose larger-than-life personality and formidable talent turned him into an international superstar and national icon. He started at five in Bergen, Norway's second city, where he trained with local students of Viotti and Baillot and made his local debut at nine. At fourteen, he discovered and mastered the Paganini caprices. He then built a repertory around Ernst, Lipinski, and Paganini's greatest hits, adding his own contributions to the ever-growing inventory of opera fantasies and acrobatic genre pieces.

At nineteen, he applied to study with Spohr, who declined to take him on as a student. At twenty-one, he relocated to Paris, where he arrived in time to hear Paganini, share an apartment with Ernst, survive the famous cholera epidemic, and burn up his allowance at such an alarming rate that his parents cut him off. His luck turned when he was invited to breakfast with Ernst and Chopin at the home of the young Duc de Montebello, who would go on to a career in diplomacy and politics. Breakfast led to a joint concert that succeeded so well that Bull's share of the proceeds set him afloat again. A second stroke of luck led to his landlady's daughter, who would become his wife after a five-year courtship, and a tour of France and Italy. In Bologna, luck struck again when he was called on to pinch-hit for the scheduled violinist, Charles de Bériot, and performed so triumphantly that Maria Malibran, the legendary soprano and de Bériot's partner, took him in tow and introduced him to still more influential patrons.

Over the next five decades, he would crisscross Europe from Spain to Russia and Scandinavia to Algiers with the stamina of a triathlon contender. In Prague, he played twelve concerts in one month. On a single tour of Britain, he played 280 engagements over sixteen months.[487] He also discovered America, and vice versa. Trumpeted by his manager as "the world's greatest violinist," Bull kicked off the tour with triumphs in New York and Boston. Fifteen concerts between New York and Richmond netted him the equivalent of 40,000 francs. He played his way south to Alabama and added ten concerts in Havana before returning via Charleston for five concerts in Boston that drew audiences as large as two thousand, and an invitation from the poet Henry Wadsworth Longfellow. After two years, two hundred concerts that covered one hundred thousand miles and took him as far west as St. Louis, and earnings estimated at $100,000, a figure approaching $3 million in early twenty-first-century dollars, Bull returned to Europe.[488]

A second American tour in 1852 lasted for five years. It began with a request from thirty-seven members of Congress including Henry Clay, as well as ten foreign diplomats, for a concert in Washington. Bull then performed for an audience of three thousand in New York and another concert in Washington for President Franklin Pierce. Although Washington was billed as a farewell appearance, he had barely begun. Next came a seven-month tour with the ten-year-old singer Adelina Patti, and a western swing via the infant metropolis of Chicago, where she sang Donizetti and Bellini and he played Paganini.[489] The hall sold out. He went on to San Francisco, spent two months in California, and took a detour to Panama. In 1854, he played Milwaukee, in 1856 Janesville and Madison, barely a half decade after Wisconsin became a state. Eventually, his seventeen-year-old son had to be dispatched to Albany, New York, to bring him home.

A last American tour after his wife's death was as colorful as its predecessors. Accompanied by his son, he once again made his way from New York to Wisconsin. A shipboard fire on the Ohio River that required a hasty swim to shore cost him money and valuables, but he saved his violin. At a Boston Peace Jubilee in the summer of 1869, he served as concertmaster of an orchestra of 1,094. Just a year after completion of the transcontinental railroad, he took the train to San Francisco. On his return, he stopped off again in Madison, where Joseph Thorp, a pioneer and state senator, had built a home overlooking Lake Mendota. A few months later, after a brief trip to Norway, Bull, 60, and Thorp's daughter Sara, 19, were quietly married by a local pastor. The caterer arrived from Chicago with $30,000 worth of solid silver flatware and serving dishes. There were two gorgeous cakes in Norwegian and American colors. Over a thousand guests, over 10 percent of the city's population, were invited to the reception. The couple's first child was born six months later in West Lebanon, Maine.[490]

The opinion makers were ambivalent about Bull's talent. Jules Janin, France's star critic, referred to him as "ce jeune sauvage," and meant it as a compliment. Eduard Hanslick, Central Europe's star critic, called him "Paganinic," and didn't.[491] Unlike Paganini, Bull played the classics occasionally and by request, among them Beethoven's Kreutzer sonata with Liszt in London and with Mendelssohn in Leipzig, Mozart's G Minor quintet with Mendelssohn's concertmaster, Ferdinand David, as well as recreational quartets with Spohr. But these were neither his personal favorites nor a usual part of his repertory. His idea of a quartet, it was noted, was a little orchestra with a soloist. A reprise of the Kreutzer with Liszt when both men were in their seventies ended with Liszt smashing a chair in rage and frustration.[492] Joseph Joachim, the gold standard of classical performance, who had no illusions about Bull's limits, was nonetheless full of admiration for his virtuosity and intonation at a time when their young contemporary Sarasate could dazzle the still younger Eugène Ysaÿe by playing in tune.[493]

Audiences couldn't get enough of Bull's music—and his drama. His sense of the theatrical was good to the end. As a young man he improvised solo at night in the Colosseum. As an old man he climbed the pyramid of Cheops, followed by a hired violin-bearer, turned to the north, and played his Norwegian mountain hymn. Even his funeral in 1880 was an occasion. A flotilla escorted his body to Bergen's harbor. Cannon sounded, church bells tolled, choruses sang, and an orchestra played Chopin's funeral march.[494]

Bull's legacy, ironically, was almost entirely extramusical. There were no pupils, no repertory currently known and played beyond his native Norway. But there was a lifetime of civic, entrepreneurial, even nation-building activity on a scale few of his peers or successors could match. Success was admittedly uneven. His plans for a Norwegian farm colony in Pennsylvania began with a bang when he turned the required citizenship application into a media event at Independence Hall in Philadelphia. The project, known as Oleana, soon became a source of international hilarity.[495] Plans for a Norwegian national theater also fizzled, as did plans for a New York opera theater. Investment in a new, improved piano, with an assist from Bull's friend John Ericsson, inventor of the Civil War's ironclad *Monitor*, was a loser, too.

One of his American projects, sculptor Anne Whitney's statue of the Viking discoverer Leif Ericson, still stands on Boston's Commonwealth Avenue, while a second copy adorns Milwaukee's Juneau Park, in both cases looking west. A living legacy, his propagation of the Hardanger fiddle and his cultivation of Hardanger fiddlers helped make this traditional eight- or nine-stringed instrument as basic to Norwegian identity as lutefisk, and for many more appealing. Another living legacy, his island home would become a popular tourist destination and house an annual international music festival. But Bull himself had long become an ambassador from another era.

MORE THAN ANY other performer, Joseph Joachim typified the new era, in which Great Music was understood as religion by other means, the composer as prophet, and the interpreter as priest. Like Viotti and Paganini, he accepted royal employment in his twenties, but on his own terms, under a contract that allowed him five months a year to pursue free enterprise. Thanks in large part to Joachim, titled employers who had patronized artists in both senses were now glad to be seen in their company and showed up ex officio at the inauguration of the new conservatories where the religion of Great Music was taught and practiced.

Joachim's appearance in Vienna in 1861 was a convenient measure of how far and how fast things had moved since Bull had appeared there only three years earlier. It was no coincidence that he played the Beethoven concerto, introduced in 1806 at a benefit for the soloist Franz Clement. A generation later, it was still so rarely played that its occasional performances are documented.[496] It was 1844 before the concerto finally experienced its Sleeping Beauty moment when Felix Mendelssohn, 35, invited the precocious Joachim, 13, to perform it in London. John Callcott Horsley, who had invented the Christmas card the year before, commemorated the scene in a famous cartoon of a small boy with a large violin atop the globe, feet firmly planted in Britain. Allegorical figures representing Europe, Asia, America, and Africa look down indulgently on the prodigy. A watercolor by Carl Johann Arnold a decade or so later shows Joachim with his back to the viewer playing a Beethoven quartet in the salon of the venerable Bettina Brentano von Arnim while the hostess looks on contemplatively from her armchair and a demonstratively highlighted bust of Goethe looks down from above.[497] It could hardly get more metaphorical than that.

From the time of Joachim's performance, the Beethoven concerto, like the Bach solo sonatas and partitas, would be understood as the bedrock of the violin repertory. Playing it had become basic to the violinist's very job description, and Joachim's identification with the piece would last to the end of his life, even though he retired from the concert stage at thirty-seven. From here on, he played what he wanted to, when he wanted to, which effectively meant almost forty seasons of chamber concerts with a quartet named for himself, which inspired Charles Gounod, the French composer, to observe that Joachim had one-upped the Christian deity by making four into one.[498] Sixty years after his London debut, at a diamond jubilee concert before an audience of three thousand, it was inevitable that Joachim would again play what had come to be known as his concerto at Queen's Hall.

Joachim's life coincided almost perfectly with the reign of Queen Victoria, an epoch extending from the afterglow of Napoleon to the eve of World War I. Thanks to Mendelssohn, he was a witness to the rediscovery

of Bach after almost a century of oblivion. His experience of Beethoven
was vicarious, too, but in this case was informed by people who had known
Beethoven personally. His experience of Beethoven's successors—Mendelssohn, both Robert and Clara Schumann, and Brahms, who would dedicate
his own violin concerto to Joachim—was immediate and personal. Not
only was his position as high priest of high art sufficient to protect him
when critics eventually pointed both coldly and credibly to the deteriora-
tion of his once mighty technique, it sufficed to see him through one of
the era's more spectacular domestic meltdowns when he accused his wife of
twenty years and the mother of his six children of an affair with Simrock,
the music publisher. The litigation consumed four years. In the end, custody was split, three boys going to him, three girls to her. But his charges
were quickly dismissed. The real problem, as the Hamburg musicologist
Beatrix Borchard spelled out in an exemplary biography, was the incom-
patibility of his patriarchal ego with the lieder-singing career she resumed
with impressive success after sacrificing a promising opera career as a condition for their marriage.[499]

Yet even as friendships fractured along the his/her fault line, his public image stood firm. People still stood in awe of him. But they also liked
him, and both friends and intimates referred to him without irony as
Uncle Jo. Joachim quartet subscriptions were still treated like heirlooms.
From London to St. Petersburg, audiences as reverent as church congre-
gations still flocked to hear him play Beethoven. A performance of solo
Bach in 1890 inspired one of the funniest reviews ever produced. Yet
even George Bernard Shaw, who wrote it, acknowledged that everyone,
including himself, had "applauded like anything" and saluted Joachim's
"dignified artistic career."[500]

By this time, British universities lined up to award him honorary
degrees. In 1888, the fiftieth anniversary of his concert debut, local admirers presented him with 100,000 marks as a gesture of appreciation, and a
Berlin choir presented him with an elaborately carved, hand-tooled, and
fulsomely embossed commemorative chair that would eventually make
its way to the University of Edinburgh. In 1904, British admirers got
their chance when Joachim arrived in Britain for a valedictory concert after
sixty years of visits. Arthur James Balfour, then prime minister, headed up
the festival committee. Local fans took up a collection to present Joachim
with a Stradivari. John Singer Sargent, the Joachim of society painters, was
commissioned to do a portrait that eventually made its way to Toronto.

Even by the standards of an eventful century, his career was remarkable several times over. As the kid from the sticks—Austrian Kittsee, Hungarian Köpcsény, Croatian Gieca, Slovak Kopčany—who made it big in the coming country's big city, he practically personified one of the era's favorite story lines. As artist, professor, and Prussian civil servant, he was a walking trifecta of the society's most cherished values.

Even his death in 1907 was an occasion. His obituary appeared in the *New York Times* within hours of his death, accompanied by a thoughtful editorial acknowledging that, while he had inevitably lost some of his zip and had never been any great shakes as a composer, he was gladly heard and still "worth hearing" even in his seventies.[501] In Berlin, a hearse drawn by six horses and escorted by students in formal dress brought his body to the cemetery of Berlin's Kaiser Wilhelm Memorial church. Five wagons of floral tributes followed the hearse. Carriages as far as the eye could see followed the wagons. The ceremony, with the crown prince, Admiral Tirpitz, the physicist Max Planck, and the director of the Berlin Zoo in attendance, approximated a state funeral. The music included works by Bach, Beethoven, and Brahms.

The Mendelssohn brothers organized a committee to commission a memorial sculpture including an arrangement of nymphs, lutes, and lyres, from Adolf von Hildebrand, a kind of John Singer Sargent of sculptors. In 1913, it was dedicated in the presence of the emperor's fourth son in the foyer of the Berlin Conservatory. In 1931, with money tight and memory fading, the conservatory, the house that Joachim built, dutifully commemorated its founder's centennial. In part, though only in part, for political reasons, it was downhill from there. A tiny green sliver of Joachimplatz in postwar Berlin-Wilmersdorf, in walking distance of the Furtwänglerstrasse, the Richard-Strauss-Strasse, and even the Bismarckstrasse, was essentially a pitstop for pigeons. His bust stood again in the foyer of the conservatory. But, as Borchard noted, it was likely to be mistaken for Brahms.[502]

For all that, Joachim's legacy, like Paganini's, was profound and lasting. The conservatory, the quartet, the Berlin Philharmonic, and the Wolff Agency, the mother of modern artist management, all model institutions that turned Berlin, a minor league franchise, into the era's Big Apfel, are hard to imagine without him. From Mendelssohn, who was a friend in his pre-adolescence, to Brahms, a friend for nearly forty years, his friendships and the company he kept left a repertory and performance tradition still intact and recognizable a century later. Thanks to Joachim, dozens and hundreds of young quartets came to play as colleagues, even a single instrument of sixteen strings, rather than as little orchestras with violin soloists. No one avoids the Brahms concerto as Sarasate did because the big tune in the second movement goes first to the oboe.[503] Joachim's transcriptions of Brahms's *Hungarian Dances* are as familiar even to listeners who don't know what they're hearing as Rossini's Overture to *William Tell* and Strauss's *Blue Danube Waltz*. While there are countless alternative cadenzas to the Beethoven concerto, Joachim's remains as familiar as pumpkin pie at Thanksgiving.

In 2007, with the centennial of his death just over the horizon, Joachim's legacy was even on view at the White House. The occasion was a visit by Queen Elizabeth II of England. Official photos show the great Israeli-American violinist, Itzhak Perlman, looking out at an audience including President George W. Bush and Mrs. Bush, Vice President Dick Cheney and Mrs. Lynne Cheney, and Chief Justice John Roberts and Mrs. Jane Roberts, as well as the queen and her consort, the Duke of Edinburgh. That none dared chat during the music, and Perlman was on the list of dinner guests, was part of Joachim's legacy, too.

HOW TO GET TO CARNEGIE HALL

⟋

EACH IN HIS way, Paganini and Joachim had both seen the future and made it. Thanks in large part to Paganini, audiences and composers could now expect a level of technical achievement undreamed of before Paganini led the way. But Beethoven was the game-changer. "Centuries of skillful artisanship would, in one blow, become *art*," Alessandro Barrico observed in 1993.[504] That the name of Beethoven, as Alex Ross noted,[505] was now to concert halls what a crucifix was to churches was thanks in large part to Joachim. As both Paganini and Joachim showed, there was also money to be made in the process. Even in the relatively simple days before and after World War I, when concerts were a growth industry, their successors enjoyed celebrity treatment, and a career might go on for decades. But the slope was increasingly steep and most beginnings were a scramble. Where the Concert Spirituel had once been the aspiring player's launching pad, it was now the Berlin or New York debut where the young and hopeful paid their own, their parents', their patrons', or their managers' money and took their chances. Armed with a prize from the conservatory, letters of introduction, and a few provincial reviews, they rented a hall, hired an orchestra (or at least a pianist), posted ads and posters where they might be noticed, and did what they could to attract a bit of media attention, hoping that a few impresarios or conductors would show up for the concert. After that they waited for the early editions of the morning papers.

For those who made it up the slope, the view was better at the top. Discovered in 1888 by Edmund C. Stanton, the manager of the Metropolitan Opera, the thirteen-year-old Fritz Kreisler signed on for his first American tour at $50 for each of fifty concerts. This was real money in an era when an American blacksmith, bricklayer, or carpenter might earn $750 to $1,000 a year and his European peers substantially less. But as was often the case, much of it was consumed in expenses. In 1910, the Boston Symphony signed Kreisler for a tour at $600 per concert, plus $800 for two recitals. On the eve of World War I, he reportedly grossed $1,000 a night, with the purchasing power of the dollar essentially unchanged since 1888. His near contemporary Mischa Elman, still in his early twenties, was meanwhile bringing in $100,000 a year for a hundred concerts, record sales, and collections and études he edited for the music publishers Schirmer and Fischer.

In 1930, when the annual white-collar salary averaged a little under $1,400, Kreisler's concert fee reportedly averaged $3,000 per concert.[506] Jascha Heifetz, coming up fast, was already setting the pace. In 1919, when a Chicago plumber earned $33 for a forty-four-hour week, the New York Philharmonic paid Kreisler $2,000 and Heifetz $2,250 for two concerts. Between December 1949 and March 1950, the New York Philharmonic engaged seven violinists. Heifetz was paid $9,500 for three performances of the concerto he had commissioned from William Walton for £300, then the equivalent of $1,500, in 1936. None of the others—Nathan Milstein at $3,800, Zino Francescatti at $3,600, Isaac Stern and Joseph Szigeti at $2,800 each for three concerts, Szymon Goldberg at $1,350 for two concerts, and Miriam Solovieff at $250 for one concert—even came close.[507] With average annual household income around $4,200,[508] it was nice work, even for Solovieff. A couple of generations later, when home run hitters were becoming millionaires and junk bond impresarios were becoming billionaires, Stern reportedly received a concert fee of $45,000, about twice the U.S. per capita personal income for a year.[509]

In principle, the necessary conditions for a solo career—talent, temperament, stamina, patience, and emotional resilience—were unchanged since the time of Corelli. "The artist who has these qualities," Franz von Vecsey's biographer quoted a prominent conductor, "can excel at a dozen other trades, including artist management, while I've never met an impresario who could play a decent C major scale, or assemble a tour for me without scrambling schedules, getting things wrong, and long nocturnal layovers in cold, inhospitable stations."[510]

Adventures and encounters with the great, good, and colorful are a favorite thread in a biography and memoir literature reaching back to the nineteenth century. But tedium and other vicissitudes—bad roads, miserable ocean crossings, inedible food, and dubious hotels—are the unmistakable common denominator. Travel, an inevitable part of the job, took its predictable toll on marriages and family life. Stable, even happy marriages like Joseph Szigeti's, Albert Spalding's, Nathan Milstein's, and Itzhak Perlman's were not entirely unknown. But personal histories back to Viotti, Paganini, and Joachim are reminders that conventional family life and domestic stability do not come easily.

An essayist of uncommon gifts, as well as one of the most interesting violinists of his generation, Gidon Kremer describes a Day in the Life beginning at 6:38 a.m., when he tumbles out of bed to review his checklist, and leaves for the airport, where the ambient music, "as in hell," never reaches a final coda. On arrival, he needs to find his hotel and rehearse. He then sits for an interview; breaks for lunch, is interrupted by a phone call, and attempts to nap with mixed success.

"It's the most snobifying, humiliating business there is," Joachim wrote his brother in the middle of the nineteenth century. "No dog would live the way we do," Christoph von Dohnányi, the longtime conductor of the Cleveland Orchestra, told Kremer, only half in fun, on the threshold of the twenty-first.[511] Similar thoughts surely occurred to Sarah Chang a few years later. A onetime prodigy now approaching thirty, she had been scheduled to play in Detroit, a city even more battered than Cleveland. The Detroit Symphony had just struck to protest proposed salary cuts of over 30 percent. She agreed to substitute a recital sponsored by the orchestra's management, with proceeds to go to the musicians' pension fund. A barrage of protests not only from the local players but from their colleagues in Los Angeles and San Francisco caused her to reconsider. "I have been unwillingly drawn into an inner dispute that does not appropriately involve me," she said as she fled Detroit for the West Coast.[512]

Maintaining a solo career was certainly not a profession for the fainthearted; nor was it just idiosyncratic crankiness that caused Heifetz to keep a copy of Kipling's "If" in his violin case.[513] On occasion, the stresses could prove tragic. Christian Ferras, with a global career, an A-list discography, two Strads, and a Thunderbird, was an established star at thirty. Trapped in a circle of anxiety, depression, alcoholism, and gambling debt, he killed himself at forty-nine.[514] Gerhard Taschner, named concertmaster of Furtwängler's Berlin Philharmonic at the astonishing age of nineteen, made a flourishing career in wartime Europe. But a precocious career in Nazi Germany was not a winning ticket after 1945. His postwar career was hardly a failure, but he was not invited to Britain or the United States. Teaching, which he did neither gladly nor particularly well, was no substitute for concertizing. Two marriages failed. By his early forties, back problems brought his performing days to an end. Brilliantly promising at nineteen, he died at fifty-four from cirrhosis of the liver.[515]

The demands of travel were a constant reminder that not everyone was made to play a hundred concerts a year (let alone upward of two hundred like Adolf Busch).[516] Getting there itself could be an existential challenge. Traveling from St. Petersburg to Moscow, 488 miles and a favorite itinerary of Italian violinists, took thirteen days in a good carriage, an English traveler reported in 1781. It was best done in winter, he added, when snow offered a relatively smooth surface.[517] Touring Britain by stage and hired coach between September 1 and October 31, 1833, Paganini played thirty-two concerts in twenty-five cities. Touring Britain in the 1870s, the Belgian virtuoso Ovide Musin played sixty concerts in ten weeks. But a few years later, on tour in the United States, he missed a concert in Des Moines when his train stalled in a snowdrift.[518] Traveling by coal-powered ocean liner in 1888, en route to his first American tour, Fritz Kreisler, 13, spent three weeks being seasick between Germany's North Sea coast and New York.[519] Von Vecsey's del Gésu came unglued while he was crossing the Andes.[520]

In late 1917, traveling by the seat of his pants and whatever else would put some distance between his family and the cascading Revolution in Russia, Jascha Heifetz, 16, made it to his benchmark Carnegie Hall debut via Siberia, Japan, Hawaii, and San Francisco. Compared to that, a three-month, forty-concert tour in 1940, extending from Puerto Rico to Argentina and back via Chile and Costa Rica, might have seemed like an easy commute. On the other hand, successive USO tours to North Africa and Italy while the big guns were still firing within earshot and England, France, and Germany were in the last months of the war was genuinely dangerous.[521] A decade later, in the sunset of American passenger rail service, Heifetz made it from San Antonio to Chicago in time for a historic recording of the Brahms concerto despite a weather system that grounded much of the nation's air traffic in Kansas City. He was, as usual, imperturbable. Schuyler Chapin, his tour manager, was a nervous wreck.[522]

A generation later, Takako Nishizaki looked back on a recording schedule that included odd airlines, bizarre airports, and Nigerian auto parts buyers en route from Taiwan. Film profiles showed violinist Hilary Hahn, still in her twenties, and violinist Ida Haendel, well into her seventies, trudging through airports where no one came to meet them.[523]

They could at least remind themselves that, unlike Jacques Thibaud and Ginette Neveu, who died in plane crashes, and Ossy Renardy (born Oskar Reiss), who died in an auto accident, en route to concert engagements, the Polish Jewish Bronislaw Huberman survived a plane crash that killed four other passengers.

If talent and stamina were necessary conditions for success, the good fortune to be in the right place at the right time was not far behind. The village priest connected the twelve-year-old Viotti with the Turinese gentry. A succession of Budapest patrons and well-married Viennese relatives made sure that little Pepi Joachim was properly attended to in Vienna and passed on to Mendelssohn in Leipzig. In 1872, Eugène Ysaÿe, 14, just happened to be practicing Vieuxtemps in a cellar in Liège when the composer himself passed by and knocked on the door.[524] Váša Příhoda, 19, who was discovered fiddling in a Milan café on Christmas day in 1919, so impressed a local newsman that he mentioned the young man to the conductor Arturo Toscanini. The great pianist Artur Rubinstein rediscovered the Warsaw-born, Berlin- and Paris-trained Henryk Szeryng in Mexico, where the virtuoso had been reduced to recording Coca-Cola spots and moonlighting in piano bars after his family, country, and promising career were swept away by World War II.[525]

Fed up with apartheid in the mid-1970s, Christopher Hope left South Africa for England, where his wife took a job as Yehudi Menuhin's secretary. Their son Daniel, who accompanied her to work, decided at four to be a violinist. By the age of eleven, he was playing duets onstage with Menuhin. A major career as soloist and chamber player followed.

Midori's moment arrived while she was playing with the Boston Symphony at fourteen. When a string broke, she immediately borrowed the concertmaster's violin and continued playing. When another string broke, she borrowed the associate concertmaster's violin and continued playing. The next morning, a Sunday, the *New York Times* spread the story across four front-page columns. A 690-word interview followed the next day.[526]

For the violinists Itzhak Perlman, Pinchas Zukerman, Jaime Laredo, and Midori, as well as the cellist Yo-Yo Ma and the conductor Zubin Mehta, a postwar cohort known vernacularly as the Stern Gang and Kosher Nostra, the practical support and interest of the persuasive and well-connected Isaac Stern was a gift that kept on giving.

Luck, of course, could also run backward. Like the oldest kid upstaged by a younger brother, Mischa Elman, triumphantly ascendant since he was thirteen and still active at seventy, spent the last six decades of his long career in the shadow cast by Heifetz on his arrival in 1917. "Very warm in here," Elman reportedly complained to the pianist Leopold Godowsky at Heifetz's legendary Carnegie Hall debut. "Not for pianists," Godowsky reportedly replied.[527]

The story is a classic for good reason. But it would not have the same resonance if the scene were Salt Lake City. Location was another of the priority career variables. It was all right to be born in Fusignano, Genoa, Fontanetto, or the Austro-Hungarian border town of Kittsee (also known as Kopčany and Köpcsény), just as it would later be all right to be born in Talnyone in Ukraine, Vilna in then-Russian Lithuania, Osaka, or Seoul. But for the young violinist who aspired to make it, the breakthrough had to be done in Vienna, St. Petersburg, and, later, Moscow, Paris, London, Berlin, or New York if it was to be done at all.

For a whole cohort of whiz kids born after World War I, it would matter existentially whether they were born on the Polish or Soviet side of the border drawn by the Treaty of Riga in 1921. If born on the western side, like Max Rostal or Ida Haendel, they would aim to study with Carl Flesch in Berlin. The unanticipated outcome for both was the wartime asylum in Britain that saved their lives, but it also cut them off for the duration of World War II from the far larger U.S. market, where the Auer protégés had already had a generation to establish their hegemony. If born on the eastern side, like Oistrakh or Leonid Kogan, they were likely to spend their careers in the Soviet bloc, a market that extended in principle from Central Europe to the Black Sea and Pacific. It also locked them into Gosconcert, the state management monopoly, or its regional equivalents, which, for better or worse, would arrange their careers for them.

Though his hometown Riga was hardly a village, Kremer realized at fifteen that he, too, would have to leave for the big city. For the moment, he leaned toward Leningrad, the former and future St. Petersburg, where he could study with Mikhail Vaiman. "Pro," he wrote, in an earnest dialogue with himself: "Vaiman is an excellent player. I need to leave no matter what. Life in Leningrad is less stressful. Move from home to a dormitory. Con: Vaiman is often on tour. What about his assistants? Probably won't get to play concerts. I'm worried about the hand position they teach there. Dormitory life can be tough, new friends, difficult learning conditions." In the end he settled for Moscow and studied with Oistrakh.[528]

Being a prodigy, though not necessary for success, often helped. But the costs could be considerable, extending from loss of school and playtime to serious psychological damage. By the dawn of the modern era, Neapolitan and Venetian *ospedali* recognized that their child prodigies were potential moneymakers. Leopold Mozart set the bar as high as it has ever been when he toured Europe with his young daughter Nannerl and still younger son Wolfgang in the 1760s and 1770s. "Miss Mozart of eleven and Master Mozart of seven Years of Age, Prodigious of Nature; taking the opportunity of representing to the Public the greatest Prodigy that Europe or that Human Nature has to boast of,"[529] declared a British prospectus. The language was giddy but not exaggerated.

The coming of the modern concert business did much to turn the prodigy into a product. Between 1805 and 1884, Vienna alone heard eleven soloists ages seven to thirteen. Half a century later, Charles Dancla remembered how Paris had gone wild over Teresa Milanollo, 14, in 1843. Even Berlioz was impressed.[530]

There would be lots more where that came from. In 1903 Franz von Vecsey, 10, appeared onstage in Berlin wearing a white sailor suit and carrying a big violin. Declaring him a miracle, Joachim embraced him in public while the audience stood on their seats and applauded, waving handkerchiefs and throwing flowers. A year later, the American-born Florizel von Reuter made his London debut in a lace collar and Lord Fauntleroy suit at a relatively ripe fourteen, though the audience was told he was twelve. Apostrophized by Romania's Queen Elisabeth as "my golden-haired angel" and proclaimed by Ysaÿe as "the most marvelous genius I have ever known," he had already played at the White House on the recommendation of his patron, Lyman Gage, President McKinley's Secretary of the Treasury. A few days after their London debuts, both von Reuter and von Vecsey played at Buckingham Palace for the slightly deaf Queen Alexandra, who thought it would be interesting to invite them together.[531]

Wherever there were hopes and aspirations, parents, for obvious reasons, were never far behind. Saul Elman and Moshe Menuhin even published memoirs on their careers as fathers.[532] "Look at a prodigy, what you see is frustrated parents," Ruggiero Ricci reminded an interviewer, recalling his father's discovery that Menuhin, Ricci's San Francisco contemporary, was a moneymaker.[533]

There were also cases where the child took the initiative. Menuhin decided his future for himself after his parents took him to a concert at age four.[534] "I wanted to go on stage and work with conductors," Sarah

Chang remembered of herself at eight.[535] Gil Shaham and his pianist sister recalled how they practically had to demand instruments of their scientist parents.[536] A musician's child who wanted to be a violinist by age eight, Christiane Edinger recalled her childhood as outright happy.[537]

But happiness was hardly the default position. Max Rostal, born in 1905, was at least ambivalent about a father who dressed him in wunder-kind style and carried a pocketful of newspaper reviews. He even let his little son rejoice in a new hobby horse while the audience cheered, before returning it because he couldn't afford it. Pushed into unwanted competi-tion by their respective fathers, Rostal and his little contemporary, Erica Morini, would happily have played together. But her father said no. In a mini-memoir that reads like a therapy session, Gidon Kremer reports how he came to see the violin as a vocational option like firefighting, chimney sweeping, or waiting on tables. His joyless mother and father, whose fam-ily had lost thirty-five members to Nazi genocide, meanwhile reminded him that he needed to be ten times better than anyone else if he wanted to succeed.[538]

As "Roger Rich," appearing in a Buster Brown–style suit and haircut, Ruggiero Ricci made his debut at seven, beating out a twelve-year-old and a thirteen-year-old for first prize in a competition sponsored by the Columbia Park Boys' Club of San Francisco. Four years later, his concert fee of $2,500 was more than most Americans earned in a year. In 1930 at age twelve, he was listed with Menuhin, Britain's Princess Elizabeth, and Christopher Milne (Christopher Robin) among the world's "six most famous children."[539]

The same year, his parents went to court to regain custody from Beth Lackey, assistant to his teacher, Louis Persinger. For five years, with their parents' consent, she had served as Ruggiero's and his brother's guardian. Replete with dueling writs of habeas corpus, speculations on the boys' pref-erence for ice cream at their parents' house over bread pudding at their guardian's, and even a short-lived intervention by New York's Mayor Jimmy Walker, the case extended over forty-one hearings and half a year before a state supreme court justice ruled in favor of the parents, while commending Lackey for "her unselfish and unerring devotion to these children."[540]

As was usual when marketing and reporting on prodigies, ages were understated. In another draft chapter of his unpublished memoir, Max Rostal recalled how, by 1919, his birth date had crept upward by three years.[541] Until he was twenty, Menuhin's age was reduced by nine months and his birthday celebrated accordingly.[542] "I was called fourteen until I was eighteen," Joshua Bell reported years later.[543] Von Vecsey's father reportedly preferred to keep his Franky's age secret, claiming, presumably with a straight face, "We want to show the audience an artist and not a child prodigy."[544]

When necessary, the game could also be played in reverse. In 1905, Narciso Vert of London's leading concert management was hauled before a magistrate and fined £25 and £5 in costs for presenting Vivien Chartres, 9, a prodigy violinist, at a Queen's Hall concert in violation of the Prevention of Cruelty to Children Act. In 1936, with a breakthrough concert at stake, Ida Haendel's age was raised to accommodate a London County Council statute prohibiting players fourteen and under from performing.[545]

While there was invariably a moment of truth as prodigies morphed into young adults, disaster was not inevitable. Many prodigies, including Menuhin, led productive lives, established families, transitioned gracefully to teaching and elder statesmanship, and attained a relatively serene old age. Huberman, who enraptured Vienna at fourteen, took four years off before resuming a career as an artist and public citizen that countinued until his death at sixty-five. Von Vecsey made it uneventfully to adulthood, married well and comfortably, assembled an impressive violin collection, and toured the world till his premature death at forty-two. Von Reuter, a dedicated and voluble spiritualist, remained active into his nineties.

But even for survivors, there were cautionary tales. Coping with the meltdowns of her own and her brother's first marriages, Hepzibah Menuhin pointed to "that lack of contact with life as it is generally lived amongst those who were not absolutely sheltered."[546] On the threshold of forty, after a lifetime of success, Menuhin realized that he had played the violin since childhood without really understanding how he did it.[547] "He had no practical knowledge of human relations," his son, Jeremy, told the writer Norman Lebrecht after his father's death.[548]

"Heifetz's childhood as a prodigy and the responsibilities that went with it made almost everything understandable and forgiveable," said Ayke Agus, who was his student and studio pianist, as well as chauffeur, cook, housekeeper, social secretary, and general factotum during his final years. "I was eager to see how much more I could learn from him without breaking down emotionally." Both passionately loyal and dispassionately objective, she recalled a man who "had built an impenetrable barrier around himself as protection for the innermost uncertainties about his worth as a human being." Students, who experienced him from time to time as discreetly generous and acidly funny, were worshipful, fascinated, and terrified.[549]

For a few, the route passed literally through the valley of the shadow of death. Miriam Solovieff, another San Francisco prodigy and Persinger protégée, made her local debut at ten and performed with major orchestras soon after. At fifteen, she made her New York debut at Town Hall. " . . . a truly talented musician, more than ordinarily rich in promise," said Noel Straus in the *New York Times*. Resettled in New York at eighteen after a family breakup, she fled to safety in a neighbor's apartment when her father, cantor to a prominent San Francisco congregation, reappeared to appeal for reunion with the family. Rejected, he shot her mother and sister and killed himself.[550]

Midori's story, spelled out with uncommon forthrightness in a memoir unaccountably published only in a German translation,[551] was an almost eerie remake of Solovieff's. Born in Osaka in 1971 as the only child of an intensely purposeful violinist mother and a father who seems by her account to have been as extraneous as a male bee, she was already playing at preschool age and practicing unsupervised while her mother worked. A fortuitous family connection then brought her at age ten to the attention of Dorothy DeLay. She was swept off to New York, where her life was effectively governed by strict rules: sink or swim, and practice, practice, practice. In 1982, on the eve of her first appearance with the New York Philharmonic, her father came to visit. He was clearly resolved to take his family back home, but he was rejected out of hand. That night, Midori awoke to find her father leaning over herself and her mother with a large kitchen knife. Mercifully, this episode ended without violence. "I look back on my childhood with great fondness," she told the critic Tim Page over ice cream and cake nine years later.[552] But this was not the message that would appear in her memoir.

"Midori is fast approaching the crucible all prodigies must face: the moment when they become ex-prodigies," Page observed presciently. What was not immediately apparent to those who watched her at twenty-one playing up to ninety-five concerts a year while practicing "only" four or five hours a day was that she was plunging ever deeper into rebellion, anorexia, and suicidal depression.

It was only after five hospitalizations that she finally pulled out of her descending spiral. She was now approaching thirty. Declaring her independence of Juilliard and DeLay, she matriculated at New York University, where she earned degrees in psychology and gender studies. She then took on a formidable regimen of concerts and recitals that took her as far afield as Mongolia. She began playing contemporary music, conducted master classes, appeared with regional orchestras, accepted a professorship at the University of Southern California, and created Midori & Friends, a charitable foundation, to teach music in the New York public schools and in Japan.[553]

The fact remains that not every child prodigy made the cut. A famous case and a secular talent, the Polish-born Joseph Hassid was snatched from the path of impending German devastation at age fifteen by a timely British visa that brought him to London in 1938 to study with Flesch. But three years later he was diagnosed with schizophrenia, subjected to insulin-induced coma and electroconvulsive therapy, and finally, in 1950, to pre-frontal lobotomy. The operation led to fatal meningitis. The coroner's report certified "Death by misadventure."[554]

By this time, Michael Rabin was just taking off. The son of a New York Philharmonic violinist and a Juilliard-trained pianist mother who had lost a previous gifted child at seven, he took up the violin with his father at the same age. A year later, he was studying with Galamian. From there on, he practiced six to eight hours daily under his mother's relentless supervision. Promotional material sang the praises of "Mike," the prodigy next door, and his everyday enthusiasms for cars, photography, stamp collecting, and his bike. But playtime, his biographer, the psychiatrist Anthony Feinstein, notes, essentially meant chamber music with the other kids at Meadowmount. With his mother as manager, he played his first public concert at eleven, and his Carnegie Hall debut at thirteen; with a Menuhin-sized talent and a rock-solid, Galamian-based, technique, he succeeded, at least professionally. He recorded regularly on EMI, a major label, toured the United States, Australia, Europe, and Israel, became an offscreen favorite in Hollywood, showed up on living-room TV screens in the golden age of family-friendly programming, bought himself a Corvette, and even found a girlfriend.

Dealing with stress and loneliness, on the other hand, was challenging in ways that dealing with conductors, managers, and record producers was not. No longer prodigiously cute and progressively addicted to tranquilizers, he missed notes and concerts, and was even hospitalized for detoxification. Contrary to posthumous legend, he neither stopped playing, nor committed suicide. Instead, he died at thirty-five of a skull fracture and brain hemorrhage after losing his balance under the influence of medication and slipping on a freshly waxed apartment floor. In its way, loss of balance, always an occupational hazard, was a metaphor for his final years.[555]

THE ALTERNATE ROUTE to success, one that seemed to grow and flourish even as the prodigy market declined, was international competition. In 1959, Galamian dispatched Jaime Laredo, 17, to compete in Brussels. If nothing else, Laredo recalled over forty years later, preparing for the competition provided an excuse to practice as he never had before or since. He fully expected to lose to players ten years his senior. Instead, he came home winner of Belgium's Queen Elisabeth competition, music's World Series. He had already signed a contract with Arthur Judson, the era's emblematic manager and an intimidating figure. Victory in Brussels brought him a contract with RCA Victor, the company that had once recorded Elman and Kreisler and for decades recorded Heifetz.[556]

Practically unnoticed before the 1930s, the competition became positively newsworthy in the years after World War II. But its roots reached well back into the nineteenth century. The meritocratic single-mindedness of postrevolutionary France, the intramural competitions of the Paris conservatory, and the Prix de Rome, the Olympic gold of aspiring composers, served as its models and inspiration. As early as 1904, Ysaÿe, a product of the Franco-Belgian school, who could barely imagine life without competitions, was already giving thought to a kind of Olympic pentathlon for the best of the best, the first-prize instrumentalists and vocalists who, unlike aspiring composers, were ineligible for the emblematic Prix de Rome. The candidates would be put up for eight to ten days with a concerto score,[557] charged with producing an interpretation not already predigested by their teachers. They were also expected to present a repertory of twenty pieces ready to play for the jury, sight-read a passage in sonata form, execute a transposition, and undergo a short exam on aesthetics and music history.

In 1926, America, too, got into the act when Walter Naumburg, a retired merchant banker, enthusiastic amateur cellist, and second-generation music patron, endowed a foundation to help America's young and talented compete for the Town Hall debut then considered indispensable to a serious concert career. Evidence alike of his intentions and connections, he engaged Persinger to schedule auditions, hire the jurors and pianists, and manage the recitals. Of 37 first year applicants, 22 reached the finals. Three violinists, two of them women and most of them long forgotten, made it to the promised land of Town Hall. Four years later, the applicant pool had grown to a benchmark 223, though there were no violinists among the eventual winners. But there were also good years for violinists, for example 1941, when the prize went to Robert Mann, who was for the next half-century the flagship member of the Juilliard Quartet, and 1981, when all six violin semi-finalists left for distinguished careers as teachers, concert and chamber players.[558]

In 1961, with Mann on the board, and an unanticipated windfall from the founder's estate, the winner's pot was restocked with a two-year management contract, a solo recording, and an appearance with the New York Philharmonic. But the largesse lasted barely a decade before it was downsized to two recitals at Lincoln Center's Alice Tully Hall. These then morphed into a gala concert and a recording on a niche label. By the 1980s, with U.S. median family income a little over $22,000, the cash awards for win, place, and show in the Naumberg competition were fixed at $5,000, $2,500, and $1,000.[559] With the traditional recital rapidly going the way of the typewriter, the prize changed yet again on the threshold of the competition's ninth decade. Winners now received management services for two seasons, or until they were taken on by a commercial management group.

But Naumburg, at least, was still in operation, unlike the Leventritt Competition, created in 1939 as a memorial to Edgar Leventritt, a lawyer with a Broad Street office and a well-connected amateur player, whose Park Avenue apartment was New York's most exclusive private chamber music venue. The most elite of competitions, the Leventritt was essentially family-run, with no official application form and no regular schedule. The rules specified only that candidates play a concerto by Mozart, Beethoven, or Brahms. Candidates submitted written applications. Of these, slightly fewer than a hundred made the cut, qualifying them for a twenty-minute audition before an unpaid jury that in any given year might include George Szell, Leonard Bernstein, Rudolf Serkin, or Isaac Stern, and a few invited guests.

Winners included Steinhardt, Perlman, Zukerman, and Kyung-wha Chung. As a rule, there was no cash prize, but there was a virtually assured entry to the promised land of major orchestra appearances, listing by a major agency, and access to a major record label. It was discreet, elite, ruthless, but impressively efficient, at least till 1976, when the competition shut down after an ambivalent and unpersuasive effort to attract the kind of popular attention it had always disdained.[560]

Though scarcely noticed in the United States, the real fun and action in the years before World War II were well to the east, where indigenous fiddlemania, broad international participation, and World Cup enthusiasm first intersected in Warsaw in 1927 when a freshly reconstituted Poland built a piano competition to commemorate its first world-class musical icon, Frédéric Chopin. In 1935, Poland created a violin competition to commemorate the centennial of its second, Henryk Wieniawski. Fifty-five competitors from sixteen countries came, including a Soviet contingent for the first time since the Revolution. Equally gifted for playing the violin exceedingly well and being funny, the British-born Henri Temianka learned of the competition only by chance well after the official application date. But he was admitted with three days to spare, just time enough to learn a few of the devilishly challenging Wieniawski études required of all entrants. He was bemused to find himself on arrival as accessory to a scene, part war, part carnival, where the natives bet on the contestants as they might bet on horses, and the immigration authorities quizzed him on his Polish-Jewish antecedents.

As would soon enough become a familiar part of the competition scene, there was speculation on the impartiality and credibility of judges with an obvious interest in getting their own students into the winner's circle, or at least keeping their colleagues' students out. Yet seen through the historical telescope, the outcome is hard to fault. Throughout his life, the second-place winner David Oistrakh, then twenty-seven, was reportedly convinced that he had lost points because he was both Russian and a Jew. But even he acknowledged that Ginette Neveu, 15, French and a woman, deserved to win. Other winners included Temianka, already twenty-eight, Boris Goldstein, 13, Ida Haendel, possibly seven, although she might have been ten, and recovering from scarlet fever, as well as Bronislaw Gimpel, a stately twenty-four. "Five Jews Prizewinners," a Polish correspondent reported.[561]

Two years later, Ysaÿe's grand design at last reached fulfillment in an international competition originally named for him but later renamed for Elisabeth (his friend and protégée), the Bavarian princess, now queen of the Belgians, who had made the competition her mission. Of 120 successful applicants, 68 showed up, including 6 from the Soviet Union. Recruited, coached, proven fittest by a Darwinian series of domestic competitions and outfitted with Strads and del Gesùs from the state collection, the Soviet contingent arrived with a transparent mandate to display what would later be known as "soft power." But there was nothing soft about it.

The local papers acknowledged and amplified the fantastic achievements of "the magic five" in what they also acknowledged was "murderous competition." Belgians placed bets as Poles had two years earlier, and program directors in the sunrise of broadcasting rewrote their prime-time schedules to accommodate the action. Oistrakh, who wrote home that he had slept badly and even experienced nausea, complained of tension, shortness of breath, and shaky hands. But it all paid off. In what was arguably the greatest victory for the Soviet Union between the October Revolution in 1917 and victory in World War II, Oistrakh finished first, and Team USSR, with Gilels third and Goldstein fourth, won five of the top six prizes.[562]

Scheduled in multiyear cycles, the competitions vanished for the duration of World War II. They roared back as Europe recovered, and Cold War competition added to the excitement. Since the first postwar Wieniawski in 1952 was confined almost entirely to the Soviet bloc, no one had to guess where the winner was likely to come from. But his name could hardly help but make an impression. As though an admission of remorse for his father's second-place finish in 1935, first prize went to Igor Oistrakh, David's son. Only then came Wanda Wilkomirska of Poland in a tie with Julian Sitkovetsky of the Soviet Union. "If I finish second to Igor, I must be good," Wilkomirska told herself, and it was true.[563] Things had already changed by 1957, when second place went to Sidney Harth, an American from Cleveland. In 1962, first place went to Charles Treger, an American from Iowa.[564]

In 1958, the Soviet Union launched its own, the International Tchaikovsky Competition. Four years later, Shmuel Ashkenasi, an Israeli from Zimbalist's class at Curtis, shared first place. But it would be 1974, a year without a winner, before Eugene Fodor became the first American violinist to share second place, and 1978, the era of détente, before Elmar Oliveira, already a Naumburg winner, became the first and so far the only American violinist to share first. Like all foreign competitors, Oliveira recalled that it was easier to play the Tchaikovsky concerto than to get the hotel staff to open the dining room, that there was neither laundry service nor reliable information about what would happen when, and that he lived on cold eggs and potatoes for the duration of his stay. On the other hand, it was worth a few weeks of misery to jump-start a career in a way that even the Naumburg didn't.[565]

The dissolution of the Soviet Union was inevitably a challenge. In 2002, a new judging system and a significant cash transfusion, some from a Japanese TV network, rescued the Tchaikovsky Competition from intensive care. But the days were long past when results from Moscow provided reason to celebrate. A seventeen-year-old Chinese violinist who would go on to win the silver medal was even beaten up by Moscow soccer fans who were furious that Japan had knocked Russia out of the World Cup.[566]

The Queen Elisabeth competition also receded from front-page news to a single wire service paragraph. Violin standards, tested on solo Bach and Paganini, an unpublished concerto, an Ysaÿe sonata, remained essentially where Ysaÿe wanted them. Juries were prestigious, but neither infallible nor clairvoyant.[567] Winners—from Japan, Taiwan, Armenia, Latvia, Polish-Israeli from Denmark, Taiwanese-born from Australia—were ever more global.

On the threshold of the twenty-first century, violin competitions had become truly global. A World Federation of International Music Competitions based in Geneva identified thirty-one competitions as major. Their venues—Genoa, Prague, Hanover, Montreal, Indianapolis, Auckland, Sendai, and Seoul, among others—reached across the globe.

It seemed only appropriate that there should be a competition somewhere to commemorate Joachim, just as the Genoa competition commemorated Paganini. The improbable initiators were a Polish-American odd couple in a middle-sized north German town. Born in Gdansk, the former Danzig, in 1953, Krzysztof Wegrzyn studied in Warsaw where he became one of three young Poles to enter the 1974 Tchaikovsky competition with their own modest instruments and no official support. He brought home the consolation of a fortuitous handshake from Oistrakh, as well as ideas for a new kind of competition, in which entrants would stay with local families, get two chances to play the first two rounds, and winners would receive professional management, a professional CD, and thirty to fifty concerts, as well as a cash prize. His partner, Linda Anne Engelhardt, a onetime southern California cheerleader, had meanwhile taken a management job at the Lower Saxony Foundation, a state agency created in 1986 to funnel private sector funding and state lottery revenue into educational and cultural projects. With an assist from Wegrzyn and Engelhardt,

Joachim once more made himself useful to the town where he had served as royal concertmaster. Among the best-funded of the new foundations, the competition was launched in 1991.

As more and more international competitions showed up in more and more unlikely places, it was salutary to remember that they were a relatively recent invention and that generations of great violinists had never competed in one. Heifetz forbade his students to enter them. "Studying with Heifetz was like playing at an international contest every week," said his student, Pierre Amoyal.[568] "Competitions are for horses, not musicians," said Szigeti, who was nonetheless a regular juror.[569] Ricci, resigned and pragmatic, weighed the secondary virtues—an excuse to practice and learn repertory—against the risk of being dumped in the first round "by an idiot set of judges." A veteran judge himself, he told his students to go for the experience and not expect to win.

Dmitri Sitkovetsky's father, Julian, died tragically early after finishing second at the Queen Elisabeth competition in 1955. A product of the Soviet system, Dimitri understood that a competition was needed to launch himself in the West. In 1979, he won the newly created Kreisler competition, in part, he suspected, because Menuhin, the presiding judge, felt guilty for supporting the American, Berl Senofsky, over Julian in Brussels twenty-four years earlier. But once established in the West, he took a different view. He now refused even to judge competitions, he told an interviewer in 1997. Ten years later, he joined Ida Haendel and Tatiana Grindenko, a Wieniawski winner, on the jury of the new competition, created in 2003 by Maxim Viktorov[570] and named for Paganini, whose cosponsors included Nestlé, Sotheby's, and the Russian Ministry of Culture.[571]

Organizers, unsurprisingly, liked competitions fine. Engelhardt, for one, was delighted with a project that connected the world with Hanover, promoted the arts, and spun off concerts.[572] Many teachers welcomed them as potential advertising.

Was one competition victory still as valuable as ten years on the road? In precompetition days when there were many newspapers, there were many reviewers at many recitals. In the postwar decades, as the Cold War played out in Brussels, Poznań, and Moscow, the bellwether competitions drew media, managements, and record producers. By the late twentieth century, recitals, newspapers, and recording, let alone the Cold War, were going and gone. That left the competitions. But there were now so many of them that, save for the very top tier, even first place had little impact.

"When I was young and you won a competition, at least it was good for a year," said Wilkomirska, now a veteran judge.[573] The consensus, such as there was one, was that competitions were unavoidable; that they tended, like standardized school testing, to discourage individuality; that objective judging was both desirable and unattainable; that a win, while no guarantee of future success, couldn't hurt; and that even place or show could be useful in a résumé.

RACE, CLASS, AND GENDER

⌒

OTHER INDICATORS—RACE, CLASS, nationality, ethnicity, gender—
were beyond the volition and control of even the most prodigious. But
they were at least as determinative. Race and gender were usually hard to
mistake. People were rarely in doubt about their nationality and, where the
distinction mattered, their ethnicity. Class, a moving target on a sliding
scale, was the hardest to pin down.

Among the ranks of the profession, it was still possible to make out
the occasional rich kid, like Joji Hattori, a Menuhin competition winner
and member of the Seiko family, and Nicola Benedetti, the BBC's Young
Musician of the Year in 2004, whose Italian immigrant father had turned
a Scotch dry cleaning shop into a fortune and a place on the Queen's Honors List. There were occasional hints of gentrification, like von Vecsey, son
of a Hungarian countess and a colonel in the Austrian emperor's army, or
von Reuter, who acquired the von, though no one seemed to know where,
after being born without it to a family of immigrant musicians in Dav-
enport, Iowa. Albert Spalding, whose parents were a singer-pianist and
the cofounder of a sporting goods fortune, and whose uncle was a very
early Chicago Cub, was at least gentry American-style. So, in a different
way, was Maud Powell, whose father served successively as school super-
intendent of Aurora, Illinois, and the District of Columbia, and whose
uncle, John Wesley Powell, was the pioneer explorer of the Grand Canyon,
before moving on to direct the U.S. Geological Survey, help found the
National Geographic Society, and establish Washington's Cosmos Club,
whose membership would eventually include three presidents, two vice
presidents, and a dozen Supreme Court justices.

But it would not occur to anyone to think of violin playing as a patrician profession. Well into the era of Ysaÿe and Sarasate, New York's Wal-

dorf Hotel told Martin Marsick, freshly arrived from Paris for a first U.S. tour, that it took no guests who played the violin or piano.[574] Well into the era of Elman and Heifetz, Catherine Drinker Bowen's father only allowed her to study at Baltimore's Peabody Conservatory on the condition that she not turn pro. On the other side of the Atlantic, Ruth Railton, an Anglican vicar's daughter, public (that is, private) school alumna, and Royal Academy graduate, resolved to fight British amateurishness as her country had recently fought the Axis.

Her National Youth Orchestra hatched a respectable flock of professional performers, including, some sixty years later, the conductor of the Berlin Philharmonic, Sir Simon Rattle. It also employed a director of communications who pointed with pride to a nonwhite, non-British contingent of 13.1 percent, compared to 3.6 percent whose parents could afford to send them to private prep schools like Railton's without financial aid. But this was long after 1947, when Railton, hard put for a desk and a typewriter, set out to recruit Britain's musically best and brightest from a pool of two thousand applicants extending across most of the British Isles and across both of what Benjamin Disraeli, a novelist before he became prime minister, called its "Two Nations." The response was stonewalling resistance and literal death threats from the music establishment of Britain's state schools, the institutions known in America as public schools.[575] A year later, her orchestra was nonetheless up and running, thanks in part to a disciplinary code that might have impressed a Marine drill instructor, but also to her readiness to take young Etonians aside for a quiet word about the need for them to interact with players who hadn't enjoyed the same advantages they had.[576]

Accommodating real-life violins and bows to real-life hammers and sickles was no easier than persuading Britain's two nations to play well and easily together. While Corelli came from the peasant scene that Vivaldi presumably had in mind when he composed the suite of concertos published in 1725 as *The Four Seasons*, Corelli's father was a landowner. Joachim, Auer, and Flesch all came from the same rustic corner of Hungary bordering on Austria, but none was either peasant or gentry. Elman's father, from a Ukrainian village near Kiev, sold hay by the bushel and supplemented his income by teaching Hebrew.[577] On the cusp of the twenty-first century, Edmund Savage, a sometime short-order cook and laser printer operator, entertained an appreciative audience and earned a living many conservatory grads might envy by playing reels at the foot of the

escalators at King's Cross St. Pancras, the London Underground's largest
interchange station. The physical distance from Wigmore Hall, London's
premier recital venue, was five stations and a short walk, but the cultural
distance could as well have been intercontinental. In 2007, Joshua Bell, an
accomplished concert performer, struck out playing the Strad known both
as Gibson and the ex-Huberman to indifferent passersby at Washington's
L'Enfant Plaza Metro station on a Monday morning.[578]

What was left was an amorphous middle class, extending over two
hundred years from Paganini's father, ambiguously settled between the
longshoremen and the provisioners in the harbor of Genoa, to Joshua Bell's
father, a full professor of psychology at Indiana University with a theology
degree and a specialty in sexology. From the seventeenth-century patriarchs to the frequent fliers of the early twenty-first, generations of notable
violinists descended from professional musicians. Children of lawyers, pas-
tors, doctors, and engineers were not far behind. There was the occasional
businessman like Christian Ferras's father, the hotelier, and the occasional
colorful outlier like Tasmin Little's father, the actor. More recently, there
was a growing contingent of parents who were scientists and academics.

Admired and cultivated like Daniel Mendoza, the boxing champion, or
Harry Angelo, the society fencing master, the eighteenth-century virtuoso
passed his, and very occasionally her, professional life playing to audiences usually considered to be his/her social superiors. In Russia, where
Auer regularly presented his adolescent protégés to the autocratic capital's
grand and good, the eighteenth century prevailed into the twentieth. But
in Western and Central Europe, and even in U.S. cities such as Boston or
Philadelphia, where the middle class grew in parallel with social esteem
for the artist, the distance between performer and audience narrowed. In
the American West and South, where Vieuxtemps and Wieniawski went
to make money, and Bull went to marry it, the traveling virtuoso for the
first time met an audience he could, if he wished, look down on.

But no one in Berlin or anywhere else patronized Joachim or his protégé, Waldemar Meyer, a school dropout at fourteen who parlayed native
enterprise and Joachim's seal of approval into a very good living in London. As a society favorite who played up to five after-dinner musicales an
evening, Meyer was confident enough of his market value to require that
hostesses tell their guests to stop chatting while he played. In time, he was
even invited to dinner. "Much as I disliked eating before I performed, I
accepted, because the invitation testified to a high regard for the artistic

profession, which many of the upper class still regarded as a trade," he reported in his memoir.[579]

By the first quarter of the twentieth century, everyone happily passed around a joke that S. J. Perelman might have scripted for Groucho Marx and Margaret Dumont. "That will be a thousand dollars," the virtuoso tells the hostess. "Very well, but please understand that you're not to mingle with the guests," the hostess replies. "In that case, it's seven hundred fifty dollars," says the virtuoso. Meanwhile, Efrem Zimbalist, director of Mrs. Bok's Curtis Institute and now an Episcopalian, was accepted as a member in good standing of Philadelphia's Main Line society. Other new immigrants, who might have been Zimbalist's cousins, adopted Auer's protégés and their descendants as role models and culture heroes. They passed on their affection for Elman, Heifetz, Milstein, Stern, even the young Perlman and Zukerman, like the family candlesticks. But the curve had peaked by the time it reached the next generation. With the celebrity and popular fascination mostly gone, the early twenty-first-century virtuoso was more likely to be a woman, a major conservatory product, and to think of herself as a professional rather than an artist. She was also more likely to play for audiences that looked more and more like her parents, grandparents, and her parents' friends and colleagues.

Nationality or, more accurately, geographical origin was at least easier to define and recognize than class. No one in the baroque era was in any doubt about where to look for a concertmaster or soloist. It was only in the eighteenth century that France began to develop a domestic product. It would be at least another century before Russia and, still longer, before Britain did the same.

Till well into the nineteenth century, Paris was not just France's but Europe's conservatory. Then came Joachim's victory over Prussian inertia, and Prussia's over France. By 1890, the Berlin conservatory was music's answer to the Berlin university. For Central Europeans in the interwar years, Flesch's class in Berlin was to the violin what Göttingen was to physics. Seven weeks into what would be World War II, Hitler ordered lists of the most qualified artists who needed to be preserved at all cost.[580] But at least a generation was lost in the global disaster and national suicide attempt that followed.

While West Germany's postwar "economic miracle" had lost much of its energy by 1980, a West German violinist miracle was still blooming in the threshold years of the twenty-first century. Only the eldest, Ulf Hoelscher and Christiane Edinger, were born during World War II, and were still not sixty when the youngest, already a third generation, were barely past their teens. The gender ratio was about equal. A few had Asian mothers. But their common origin was professional middle class.

What accounted for them, in Christoph Poppen's opinion, was world-class teaching.[581] But as with the sciences, social sciences, and much else, the teaching had found a new home in America. "In Germany, many students are too lazy, and even recognized teachers haven't a clue what's required and accomplished at American conservatories," Hoelscher told an interviewer on his return from Indiana and Curtis in the 1960s.[582] An exception, Anne-Sophie Mutter stayed close to home, where she channeled Flesch with the aid of teachers who had studied with him. Discovered by Karajan in her early teens as one of her cohort's few prodigies, she was already one of its senior statespeople in her forties.[583] Children of the competition era and gold medal winners, the youngest cohort, Isabelle Faust, Julia Fischer, Augustin Hadelich, were born, educated, and for the most part trained in Germany. But unlike their predecessors, they neither considered themselves a German school nor aspired to create one. They were just good violinists.

Britain, as usual, remained an offshore island, where a world-class violinist was scarcely imaginable till deep into the twentieth century. Marie Hall, who could easily have stepped out of a late Victorian novel, had a remarkable career and was very close to a unique exception. Born in 1884 to a father who played the harp at Newcastle's Empire Music Hall, she joined a family ensemble on the street, where she was discovered at an early age by a succession of patrons who might have stepped out of a novel by Horatio Alger. Her family needed her earnings too much for her to accept a scholarship at the Royal Academy at thirteen. It was only the interventions of another fairy godmother and the Czech virtuoso Jan Kubelik that finally allowed her to study gratis first with John Kruse, a protégé of Joachim's, and then for three years in Prague with the redoubtable Otakar Ševčik. In 1903, she made her London debut "amid a scene of enthusiasm rarely witnessed in a concert-room," according to the London *Times* reviewer. Two years later, she left for a sixty-concert tour of the United States, followed by tours of South Africa, India, Australia, New Zealand, and even Fiji, where she played in a tent for an audience of a thousand while an electric fan cooled her hands.[584]

Albert Sammons, Marie Hall's almost immediate contemporary and

Britain's other likeliest contender for an international career, was essentially self-taught. Like her, he was playing professionally at thirteen to help support his family. He was still in his twenties when the conductor Sir Thomas Beecham discovered him leading the orchestra at London's Waldorf Hotel. Beecham hired him practically on the spot. A year or two later, Sammons was appreciated as a local soloist. But he declined to tour the United States. "They'd compare me with Heifetz and Elman," he said.[585]

A Londoner since age six, when his father emigrated from Rome, Alfred Campoli could at least claim a foreign name. But his London accent, plus a Depression-era day job as a Palm Garden violinist at London's Dorchester Hotel, put him at a disadvantage not only against Menuhin but Max Rostal and Ida Haendel, recent immigrants whose first-rate talent coexisted with the foreign accents British audiences expected of serious violinists.[586]

In Russia and Japan, musical catch-up was just another dimension of social, political, and economic modernization. Well into the nineteenth century, Russians imported Italians, then French, then Central Europeans. Some were on tour. Others remained as residents at court for years at a time. In the last years of the eighteenth century, the native-born Ivan Yevstafyevich Khandoshkin actually held his own with the visiting Italians, although he was paid less than half of what they received, and never went abroad.[587] He even left a modest collection of respectable compositions, including several sets of variations on Russian folksongs. But two centuries would pass before his compositions were appreciated, and his achievement rediscovered.

By this time, the legacy of another wave of imports had changed the course of violin history. In 1862, the year after Alexander II emancipated the serfs, Wieniawski, the youthful Paris prizewinner from Polish Lublin, agreed to do his bit to advance Anton Rubinstein's national mission and establish a violin department at the shiny new St. Petersburg conservatory. Six years later, the even more youthful Auer from Hungarian Veszprém agreed to succeed him. By the first decade of the twentieth century, Russia had become a net exporter of world-class violinists, and Piotr Solomonovich Stolyarsky, an inconspicuous section player in the Odessa Opera orchestra, launched a career in early childhood teaching and talent scouting that would produce four of the top six prizewinners at the benchmark 1937 Queen Elisabeth competition. As a serious student of audiences, Menuhin admired the discipline and good manners of Japanese and Germans, the open-mindedness of Americans, the sincerity of the British and the "unrepentant individualism" of Israelis. But it was "only in Odessa that local fans crowded backstage, demanding to know how I fingered this or that passage."[588]

The idea that there might be more Odessas waiting in East Asia struck Westerners as odd well into the twentieth century. Yet this future, too, was already under way in 1868, when Japanese reformers added Western music to the curriculum of a universal school system that was itself subsumed in a modernization program that extended to industry, agriculture, the military, and law. Within a generation, there were affordable domestic violins in Japan, an expansive collection of user's manuals full of adapted native pieces, and street musicians wearing derby hats and Western shoes who accompanied themselves on violins while singing from a large repertory of satirical and political ballads. Within a decade, an Office of Music Studies with a mandate to produce teachers and teaching material had morphed into a Tokyo conservatory.[589] In 1890, Nobu Koda, a conservatory graduate, left for advanced study in Boston and Vienna. On her return to Japan five years later, she taught her younger sister, Ko, who then studied in Berlin as well, before returning to join Nobu on the Tokyo conservatory faculty. Eventually, both sisters were allowed and even encouraged to drift into obscurity.[590]

The Bolshevik Revolution produced a cadre of fugitive musicians happy to show the Japanese what serious professionals could do. From the 1920s on, Japan was on the international concert circuit. In 1926, the Japan Symphony, known as the Japan Broadcasting Corporation (NHK) Orchestra since World War II, was established as Japan's first permanent ensemble. In October 1943, just days before Allied bombs leveled the Berlin Philharmonie, the very young Nejiko Suwa played the Brahms concerto with the Philharmonic under Hans Knappertsbusch. In Vienna, on D Day, June 6, 1944, Joseph Goebbels, Hitler's minister of propaganda, presented her with what was claimed to be a Strad.[591]

That millions of the war's survivors would live to see prodigious little girls from Asia replace prodigious little boys from Russia seemed about as likely as the coming of a Toyota plant to Huntsville, Alabama, or a pin-striped Japanese center fielder to Yankee Stadium. Yet music would be no less a growth industry than automobiles, shipbuilding, and consumer electronics as Japan rose from the ashes. Music school enrollments—1,402 in 1952; 7,139 in 1965; and 18,605 in 1980—soared like Japan's GNP. So did employment opportunities. In 1950, there were 3.32 musicians per 10,000 employed in a population of 83.2 million. In 1980, there were 16.88 per 10,000 in a population of 117 million.[592] Barely a generation after the war, Takako Nishizaki, 23, runner-up to Perlman, 19, in the 1964 Leventritt competition, was en route to a Carnegie Hall recital and an improbable career as China's favorite violinist. By 2007, Nishizaki's recording of Vivaldi's *Four Seasons* had sold more than a million copies worldwide.[593] Midori, the onetime prodigy, occupied the Heifetz Chair at the University of Southern California's Thornton School of Music. Daishin Kashimoto, still in his twenties, had become the Berlin Philharmonic's second Japanese concertmaster.

If Osaka, Tokyo, or Matsumoto seemed unlikely successors to Odessa, Seoul, not to mention Pyongyang, seemed even more unlikely. Reduced in the seventeenth and eighteenth centuries to a playing field for its neighbors' imperial games, Korea, too, was reluctantly hauled into the modern world in the last decades of the nineteenth century. For the moment, Korean reformers looked to Japan as a role model. But that ended in 1910, when Japan effectively annexed Korea. Western music was one dimension of Japanese modernization. Brutalization was another.

The arrival in Korea of young Protestant missionaries and a German bandmaster, on the other hand, were an unqualified success. By the 1920s, mission school graduates made their way to advanced study in Japan, Europe, and the United States. Between 1923 and 1937, violin recitals were a particular crowd-pleaser in a dedicated concert hall where Japanese and Koreans alike filled the seats.[594] In the years before World War II, international players added Seoul to their itineraries.

Yet even as international conflict and civil war divided the country, Kyung-wha Chung, 6, and her equally musical siblings took up the instruments that would bring the family to America, and Kyung-wha herself, at the age of thirteen, to Juilliard, where her flautist sister, Myung-soh, was already enrolled. A generation later, it was estimated that one in four Juilliard students was Asian or Asian American.[595] But they were still novelties in 1961. Depressed after five years with Galamian, Chung thought seriously about dropping out. Instead, her family persuaded her to enter the Leventritt as Nishizaki had three years before.[596] The result was a first-place tie with Zukerman and a symbolic victory for Korea. Twenty years later, with South Korea's economy growing at an annual rate of 8 percent, and three national and eleven regional orchestras where there had formerly been just one, Sarah Chang, 6, a Menuhin rediviva in white party dress, white stockings and white patent shoes, entered DeLay's class accompanied by her violinist father, Min Soo, himself a former DeLay student.[597]

In many ways, the Chinese experience recapitulated Japan's and Korea's. But the evolution from imperial entertainment to modernization strategy to export of finished players also recapitulated Chinese history. A first exposure to Western music could be traced to the Italian Jesuit and pioneer Sinologist Matteo Ricci who left his clavichord to Chinese posterity. A Jesuit successor reportedly liked it so well that he hired Western teachers to train an ensemble of eighteen eunuchs to perform contemporary Italian music, possibly even opera, wearing Western-style suits, shoes, and wigs.

If the first appearance of Western music in China stopped at the walls of the Forbidden City, the second reached well into the future. By the end of the nineteenth century, all major powers but Austria had encroached on Chinese sovereignty, and even Japan had set out to turn Taiwan into a model colony. Enter Western music once more, this time as a colonial import. As elsewhere, military reforms included bands, and missionary schools brought Western instruments. Western music courses were introduced in Taiwan's teacher training schools, a proliferation of refugee players from Russia and Central Europe arrived, and an all-Western, Western-style orchestra was established in Shanghai.[598]

Tan Shu-zhen personified Chinese experience with the violin and violinists. Born in 1907, he attended a mission school and took up the violin, as had his father. At fifteen, he moved to Beijing in search of a violin teacher. At eighteen, he moved to Shanghai, where he attended orchestra concerts, taught elementary violin, and resolved at twenty to approach the orchestra's Italian conductor to ask about joining it as a violinist. Success at the first rehearsal and concert made him the orchestra's first Chinese member. Of course, he was not paid. On the eve of war, the orchestra plus church and theater jobs kept the family afloat. But an invitation to play for a Japanese general in 1940, with the city under occupation, was a compromise too far, and Tan resigned from the orchestra.

One world war and one civil war later, there were two Chinas, one on the mainland and one on Taiwan, where the island economy evolved into the region's bellwether little tiger and Lee Shu-te became its Dorothy DeLay. From there, her star pupil, Lin Cho-liang, set off at fifteen for New York with $300 taped to an inside pocket, and an introduction to John Oakes, then editorial page editor of the *New York Times*, who put him up while he studied with DeLay. At nineteen, he made his New York debut. At twenty-one, Lin was playing over a hundred concerts a year. At twenty-three, he bought his first Strad.[599] In 1985, another of Lee's protégés, Hu Nai-yuan, who had gone on to study with Gingold, won the Queen Elisabeth competition.

Meanwhile, in the mainland caves of Yan'an, where China's Communists took refuge from the Japanese and the Nationalist government, musical Stakhanovites stamped out a new canon of revolutionary songs, cantatas and operas, while a Yan'an Central Orchestra played waltzes, two-steps, and "Old Black Joe" at Saturday night dances, enthusiastically attended by the party leadership. In 1947, Tan listened with cautious optimism to speeches by Zhou En-lai, the People's Republic's first premier, and General Chen Yi, the city's first Communist mayor. In 1949, the violinist Ma Si-cong, the first Chinese player accepted at the Paris Conservatory, was appointed first president of the newly founded National Conservatory. With a chauffeur, two chefs and a salary approaching Chairman Mao's, his appointment looked promising.[600] More promising still, a reluctant Tan agreed to serve as vice president, taught sixteen students and was allowed to set up a violin shop. By 1961, the teaching staff had grown to five hundred with three thousand students, including seven hundred at the advanced level. In the interest of art, some two thousand Chinese students were sent to study in the Soviet Union. Others were posted under trees as part of the Four Pests campaign, where they contributed to the Great Leap Forward by playing their instruments till exhausted sparrows, afraid to land, dropped dead from the skies.[601]

Then came the Cultural Revolution, and the skies darkened for Tan. "It's night," Tan told himself, "but the sun will come out eventually." This was true, but it would be a while in coming. In 1963, a friend's son, a violin student, denounced Tan for his Western suit. Soon he was beaten with sticks, publicly attacked, locked in a closet, and assigned to maintain and repair the conservatory's 122 toilets. In 1966, violins were declared "accursed symbols of imperialism."

Six years would pass before it was decided that violins were needed for the performance of revolutionary operas. A year later, they were practically unavailable in Guangzhou.[602] In 1978, a reinstated Tan returned to a conservatory that would soon take off like a new leadership's new economy. But before the sun again came out, seventeen members of the conservatory family—professors, spouses, students, including at least two of Tan's fellow violinists—had killed themselves. Three of his four children were now professional musicians, but two of them had emigrated to the United States. In 2002, when Tan died at ninety-five, the Shanghai Symphony Orchestra dedicated a concert to his memory, playing Barber's Adagio for Strings as a final salute. By this time, a former son-in-law was a violin dealer in New York, and a great-grandson studied with Sassmannshaus.

In 1987, Qian Zhou, a Shanghai alumna via the Peabody Conservatory in Baltimore, finished first in France's Marguerite Long–Jacques Thibaud competition. By the mid-1990s, Zhang Shi-xiang, a professor at the Shanghai conservatory, had stopped teaching students who couldn't manage Paganini and Wieniawski by the time they were sixteen. Even before Tan's death, foreign visitors noted with interest that violins could be bought over the counter at Taoist temples for the equivalent of $30. A few years later, it was estimated that private music teachers in Shanghai earned five times the local average per capita monthly income. There were an estimated ten million Chinese violin students, large numbers of them eager to get to the Western conservatories that recruited and were delighted to have them. Annual conservatory applications, a few thousand a year in the 1980s, now approached two hundred thousand, and Western music enjoyed a status, part icon and part social escalator, reminiscent of the position it had held in the West a century earlier.[603]

IF TWENTIETH-CENTURY ASIA confirmed that the international date line was permeable beyond the Koda sisters' or Tan Shu-zhen's fondest hopes, Western, and especially American, experience made a strong case that the color line was not. Still, there were exceptions, including the remarkable George Bridgetower, who made his debut at the Concert Spirituel on April 13, 1789, at age nine, and the still more remarkable Chevalier de Saint-George.

Whether Bridgewater really was black was a matter of cultural definition. But as the child of a possibly Central European mother and a father of African descent, he was at least nonwhite. Before his debut year was over, "the very best of company" paid up to five guineas to hear "this wonderful child . . . the grandson, it is said, of an African prince" at his sold-out concert in Bath. The princely connection may well have been the inspiration of Bridgetower senior, a polyglot charmer who favored Turkish dress.[604] Betty Matthews's educated guess that the family name derived from Bridgetown, Barbados, and that his father was a former slave, freed on arrival in England by a law of 1772, seems more accurate.[605] Prince or not, Bridgetower junior was taken in tow by the Prince of Wales. He was on cordial terms with Viotti and performed with Haydn. But for "a silly quarrel about a girl," to go by a second-hand report some decades later, he might have been the dedicatee of Beethoven's Kreutzer sonata.

Joseph Bologne, George's senior by a generation, led a life that might have been invented by Alexandre Dumas. Born in 1745 to a French sugar and coffee planter and his slave mistress, he was whisked away from his native Guadalupe at an early age after a family brawl and a dubious court proceeding caused his father to leave in a hurry for Paris, where a 20,000 livre loan to the cash-strapped crown bought his father a title. The title eased the young Bologne's way into Le Boëssière's Royal Academy of Fencing and Riding, where his spectacular aptitude for fencing so impressed the king that the young man was named to the royal life guard. The military appointment, in turn, qualified him for the title of Chevalier de Saint-George and a network of A-list contacts.

Meanwhile, his spectacular aptitude for the violin led to a second network and an entry-level place in the Concert des Amateurs, where he set off on a flagship career as a soloist, composer, and conductor before near shipwreck in the turbulent seas of the Revolution, and death in near obscurity at fifty-four.[606] But he was flagship in a fleet of two. In 1762, a registration list, born of anxiety about an African peril to Caucasian France, peaked at 159 black and mixed race residents of Paris, a city of over half a million. In all of France there were an estimated 4,000 nonwhites, none of them slaves.

In 1790, the year after Bridgetower's debuts in Paris and London, the black population of the United States was estimated at 750,000, over 90 percent of them slaves. By 1860, it had grown to about 4.5 million. But the free-to-slave ratio was virtually unchanged. In fact, like the Jeffersons and Randolphs, many of America's African-descended population played the violin. It was possible that there was a potential Bridgetower or Bologne among them. What was missing was the infrastructure—for example, the entrepreneurial father, the network of well-placed patrons, the academy, the schools and tutors, let alone, the royal intervention—that transformed potential to actuality.

Instead, while their owners played for themselves and their peers in drawing rooms, black fiddlers from Virginia to the Gulf played both the white folks' dances and the black folks' frolics. Ubiquitous in diaries, plantation records, and newspapers,[607] the so-called musicianers were envied before 1865 for the travel opportunities and cash income that could come with the job, and respected afterward as teachers, entertainers, and role-models. In time, they were superseded by jazz, blues and gospel players. But the rural string bands continued to sell on so-called race labels as late as World War II.

As keen as any other aspiring middle class to make it in the mainstream culture, the tiny black middle class also had its fling with the middle-class violin. The iconic Frederick Douglass, pioneer abolitionist, writer, lecturer, public official in the District of Columbia and U.S. Minister to Haiti, was an amateur violinist. His son was another. His grandson Joseph, a professional, even went on to tour black churches and colleges and teach at Howard University before his death in 1935.

A professional of a different sort, born in 1933 to Caribbean immigrant parents in the Bronx, Louis Eugene Walcott took up the violin as a Boston schoolboy. At nine he heard Heifetz play with the Boston Symphony. The experience left lasting marks. At thirteen, he played Vittorio Monti's indestructible *Csárdás* on *The Original Amateur Hour*, a hardy perennial of network radio and early television. He might have gone on to Juilliard. Instead, he opted for a track scholarship at a historically black college in North Carolina.[608]

In a world and an era when orchestras were no more accommodating on race than they were on gender, it was not an irrational choice. Instead, he tried his luck as a calypso singer. He next reinvented himself as Minister Louis Farrakhan of the Nation of Islam, a black nationalist sect.[609] For the next forty years, he put the violin on hold. Resolved to play the Mendelssohn concerto, he then approached Elaine Skorodin Fohrman, a respected Chicago player, for intensive coaching. Two years later, the *New York Times* was on hand for his debut performance before a small, carefully screened audience in Winston-Salem, North Carolina. "Can Louis Farrakhan play the violin?" its reviewer, Bernard Holland, asked cautiously. The answer was a ringing affirmative. "Mr. Farrakhan's sound is that of the authentic player,"[610] Holland reported.

But even for Fohrman, Farrakhan's decision to move on to the Beethoven was a challenge too far. This time a bit of serendipity came to his aid. Farrakhan's assistant had taken his Gagliano to Bein & Fushi in Chicago for its annual check-up. Fushi handed her a copy of Ayke Agus's recent memoir of her years with Heifetz as student, studio pianist, chauffeur, social secretary, short-order cook, and general factotum. Then he introduced Farrakhan directly to the author.[611] Agus not only agreed to coach Farrakhan as Fohrman had. She rented the Cerritos Performing Arts Center in southern Los Angeles County, and recruited an orchestra for the next Nation of Islam conference. At Sweet Strings, a neighborhood project in south central Los Angeles, Farrakhan encouraged children to take up the violin to combat the prejudice that it was something only white people could do.[612]

In 1996, a Perlman performance in St. Louis provided a similar epiphany for Gareth Johnson, a ten-year-old in tiny Festus, Missouri. Resolved to play, he squirreled away lunch money until his awestruck parents bought him an $80 violin and took him to St. Louis for lessons. A year later, his teacher took him to play Mendelssohn for DeLay. The connection first led him to Sassmannshaus in Cincinnati and to Elmar Oliveira, America's first Tchaikovsky violin competition winner at Florida's Lynn University Conservatory.[613] After that, he moved on as coach, teacher, and role model to Aaron Dworkin's Sphinx Organization, which might have been conceived with him in mind.

Though often neglected or forgotten, jazz could also be played to spectacular effect on violins, and jazz players didn't need conservatories. Some of the greatest players were white, like the durable Joe Venuti, who was probably born in Philadelphia, and the indestructible Stéphane Grappelli, who was certainly born in Paris. But in a society where conventional orchestra careers were as inaccessible to African Americans as they were to women Americans, other pacesetters—Eddie South, Stuff Smith, Ray Nance, and Claude "Fiddler" Williams—made jazz the African-American violinist's Plan B.

South, whose formidable technique left little doubt of classical training, went straight from school to vaudeville and a forty-year career in jazz that included a memorable set of studio recordings in prewar Paris with Grappelli and the great guitarist Django Reinhardt. Nance, impressed by Smith but clearly inspired by South, was the only violinist ever engaged to solo with Duke Ellington, whose status in the jazz world was roughly equivalent to Toscanini's in the world of opera and concert music.

There was even room, if barely, for a woman instrumentalist. Ginger Smock, who was biracial and began life as Emma, was a Smith protégée. At ten, she played Kreisler at the Hollywood Bowl. Surrounded by strictly Caucasian peers, she also played in the Los Angeles Junior Philharmonic

under Otto Klemperer. But her career, like her male peers', led inexorably to jazz as well as to an early initiation in the indignities common at
the time to both women and African Americans. At thirteen, she played
her first professional engagement at a cocktail lounge in Glendale. RCA
executives liked her demo record, but they abruptly lost interest when
their talent scout identified the player as "a colored girl up there in San
Francisco."[614] Her talent would nonetheless take "The Sweetheart of the
Strings," also known as "The Bronze Gypsy and her Violin," from Las
Vegas to Hawaii before her death at seventy-five in 1995.[615]

By this time, jazz was an option, not a last resort. Regina Carter's
mother, an elementary school teacher in aspiring, blue-collar Detroit, sent
her daughter to Suzuki violin lessons and dreamed that she would grow up
to be a well-paid orchestra player with health insurance. Carter dreamed of
a solo career and even matriculated at the New England Conservatory. She
then discovered Grappelli and experienced her moment of truth. In 1987,
she returned to Detroit and joined an all-woman band. In 1991, she moved
to New York and her career took off. In 2002, she became the first jazz
player ever invited to play Paganini's Cannon. In 2006, she was awarded a
MacArthur Foundation "genius" grant.[616]

By now, ironically, African-American and Latino players, both men and
women, were actually in demand to play the music of dead white European
men. But demand began, inevitably, at a baseline close to zero. In 2008,
the League of American Orchestras estimated the African Americans and
Latinos made up no more than 1.8 percent of U.S. professional orchestras.
In a postimperial world where people moved from, not to, the colonies and
some 12 percent of the British population was Asian or black, Manchester's
venerable Hallé Orchestra employed one black player from the Caribbean
and one Chinese player. The Ulster Orchestra employed sixty-two whites
to one Asian player. In the BBC Scottish Orchestra there were no black or
Asian players at all. "Why are our orchestras so white?" they asked.[617] The
answer, it was agreed, had less to do with racism than an applicant deficit.

In 2010, five years after winning a MacArthur grant, Dworkin estimated that American youth orchestras were 75 percent white and 17
percent Asian, with the rest of the musicians split about evenly between
Latinos and African Americans.[618] Four, even eight, percent was still a tiny
increment. On the other hand, that was more than double the current
representation in professional orchestras. There were also indications that
growth of the African American player pool was a work in progress. In

Baltimore, network cameras showed a truckful of instruments pulling up at a West Baltimore elementary school. They were intended for Orchkids, a privately funded project initiated by the Baltimore Symphony's conductor, Marin Alsop, an exceptional presence herself as one of the relatively few women in a historically male profession. On America's opposite coast, the Los Angeles Philharmonic struggled mightily to build Youth Orchestra Los Angeles (YOLA), a local version of Venezuela's Sistema, in South, formerly South Central, Los Angeles's not so green and pleasant land. A brigade of institutional stakeholders and corporate patrons assured their support, and the orchestra's young and charismatic conductor, Gustavo Dudamel, could be depended on for media attention.

WOULD IT WORK? It had certainly worked for Jews, Armenians, Asians, and women, to mention only a few of the area's wonderfully diverse groups. Before the twentieth century, classically trained violinists were as common to the area as ivory-billed woodpeckers. By the end of the twentieth century, the greatest of them all, the Russian-Jewish Heifetz, had made his home in Los Angeles from the 1930s to his death in 1987; the Armenian Movses Pogossian, a rare non-Russian winner of the Tchaikovsky Competition, was in charge of the violin department at the University of California at Los Angeles; and two women, Eudice Shapiro, Jewish and born in 1914, and Midori Goto, Japanese and born in 1971, were respectful colleagues at the University of Southern California's Thornton School of Music.[619]

Although not widely noticed, Armenians too were a notable presence in the violin world, though they themselves were puzzled, even defensive, when asked how such numbers of them happened to take up the instrument. Inferences helped, but only to a point. Like many small nations with large neighbors, Armenia has not had it easy. As many as 1.5 million Armenians were lost to Ottoman massacres in World War I. Christians since the fourth century in a part of the world where the majority of their neighbors were not Christian, they had identified with Europe and the West as early as the crusades. Stringed instruments, both plucked and bowed, had always been part of their musical culture. A taste for European music, much of it acquired in St. Petersburg, dated back to the middle of the nineteenth century.

Whatever their motive, it was curious how easily their collective presence went unnoticed when the presence of highly gifted individuals was so visible. Maybe management hadn't pushed them, Charles Avsharian, a former president of the American String Players Association, speculated in 1998.[620] Maybe it was because there were many Jewish, but no Armenian, managers to promote their careers, or that there had not yet been an Armenian Heifetz. Maybe it was because no Armenian had yet won a major prize. That argument at least took a beating in 2000, when Sergey Khachatryan, 15, an Armenian from Armenia, became the youngest-ever winner of the Sibelius competition.[621] Five years later he came in first at the Queen Elisabeth in Brussels.

Meanwhile, another Avsharian brother, Michael, who was also a Galamian student, attended Meadowmount and graduated from Juilliard as Charles would graduate from Curtis, before joining Charles to grow the family business from kitchen-table dimensions to string, instrument, case, accessory, sheet music, learning aid, and violin beach towel merchant to the world, with a staff of seventy-five. There was Galamian himself, the era's emblematic teacher, though his pupil, Ani Kavafian, recalled that he was indifferent to his heritage and spoke next to no Armenian. There were, of course, Kavafian and her sister Ida, high-powered soloists and chamber players, who began to play as toddlers in Detroit, Ida explained, because their parents were musicians, and it never occurred to them to do otherwise.[622] There was Kim Kashkasian, remarkable for making a career as a solo violist. There was Manoug Parikian, not only a role-model concert-master in the golden age of London's elite Philharmonia Orchestra but also a teacher of Peter Oundjian, first violinist of the Tokyo Quartet, and Parikian's nephew, Levon Chilingirian, founder at twenty-three of the blue-ribbon quartet that bore his name.

Eastern and Central European Jewish players were products of a milieu, historical experience, and cultural dynamic that would have felt familiar to most Armenians. Yet their affinity for the violin could hardly have been more conspicuous from the mid-nineteenth century on, and well into the twentieth century seemed practically a genetic disposition. "The violin has always been a Jewish instrument," the Russian-Israeli Vadim Gluzman declared. "I hope I'm not perceived as chauvinistic, but it's a fact of life."[623]

To say that the violin had always been a Jewish instrument was a stretch. But there was certainly an affinity, to judge by experience in parts of Europe in the nineteenth century and in a Western world that would extend from Israel to Los Angeles by the third quarter of the twentieth century. "It was clear to me from an early age that I could get anything I wanted from my parents or their friends if I were Jascha Heifetz or Leon Trotsky," Ronald Al Robboy, a cellist in the San Diego Symphony, recalled.[624] He was being only half-ironic.

It was also true that music had been a Jewish occupation in Spain and Portugal, that refugee Jews, among them musicians, settled in Italy after the expulsions of 1492 and 1496, and that some of them made it to Cremona.[625] Among the Italian violinists migrating north in the mid-sixteenth century, there may well have been Jews escaping persecution by Pope Paul IV, inventor of Rome's Ghetto, and a ferociously Counter-Reformationist pope (later saint), Pius V.[626] In an England nominally without Jews since 1290, and where Jewish settlement remained prohibited till 1655, there is solid evidence of Spanish and Italian Jewish string players at the court of Henry VIII from as early as the 1520s.[627]

Demand for imported players continued, and a shadowy descendant of Henry's band played on through the seventeenth century. Until the Austrian occupation of 1630 and the heavy hand of the Counter-Reformation stopped the music, Jews continued to sing, play, even dance in the ghettos of Mantova, then Venice. As late as the eighteenth century, a Jewish father and son would still take off from Verona to work as court musicians in England.[628] But as Europe's center of gravity moved ever further from Italy and the Iberian Peninsula, and the Jewish center of gravity moved with it from the Sephardic south to the Ashkenazic north, supply migrated in directions no one, and certainly no English king, could have foreseen.

Orthodoxy, strictly understood, had frowned on instrumental music since the destruction of the Second Temple. But it was allowed, even expected, at weddings and Purim, the one genuinely frolicsome holiday in the Jewish calendar. Central and East European practice accommodated *klezmorim*, semiprofessionals who made their living playing for and even with non-Jews.

Instrumentation was flexible. A popular subject of photos in the pioneer years of ethnomusicological research, *klezmorim* can be seen holding clarinets, a bass, or a cello, occasionally a flute or piccolo, a drum, tiny cymbals, and a tambourine. But there are always violins. Practically by definition, *klezmorim* played what people wanted to hear. Repertory extended from waltzes, polkas, and polonaises to jazz and the Romanian doinas that were a particular favorite of the players, many of them non-Jewish, who would revive *klezmer* in a late twentieth-century Europe, where Jews had vanished between 1939 and 1945.[629]

Where Gluzman's violin came from and where it went could be traced across successive branches of the Mendelssohn family tree. Moses Mendelssohn was a prophet of Haskalah (a Jewish version of the Enlightenment), which would lead German Jews to secular culture. Over the lives of his children, grandchildren, and great-grandchildren, it would set off a chain reaction across Eastern Europe. His grandson Felix, no longer a Jew, met Goethe, venerated Beethoven, rediscovered Bach, and composed one of the most beloved of all violin concertos. His great-grandsons Franz and Robert bought Strads from Hill's, commissioned the Berlin Conservatory's Joachim monument, and played recreational quartets with Carl Flesch. His great-great-granddaughter Lili, another family violinist, married the violist-conductor-composer Emil Bohnke, an adjunct professor at the Berlin Conservatory.

The evolution of the Jewish violin could also be seen in the metrics of a population virtually polarized between a precarious handful of very rich and a mass of disenfranchised poor, inclined to follow where Moses Mendelssohn led. By 1848, some 30 percent, and by 1871, some 60 to 80 percent of German Jews were taxed as middle class or upper-middle class. While over half earned their living and supported their families in business, manufacturing, trade, and finance, they or their sons (rarely daughters) leaned increasingly to the professions.[630]

Education obviously figured in the equation. In Vienna, where secular education for Jews went back to Emperor Joseph II, Jews comprised 8 percent of the city's population but 30 percent of the enrollment at the city's *gymnasien*, the secondary schools that prepared their students for university study. By the early twentieth century, Jewish enrollment in the German-language *gymnasien* of Prague was 46 percent and, in the German-language *gymnasia* of then-Polish Lvóv, 50 percent. The principle was the same in the Polish-language *gymnasia* of Lvóv, where Jewish enrollment was 21 percent; in the *gymnasia* of Budapest, where Jewish enrollment was 35.8 percent; and the *realschulen* of Budapest, which gave modern languages priority over Latin and Greek, and where nearly half the students were Jewish.

The ripples could be seen and felt all the way to Czernowitz and Odessa, where large Jewish populations who aspired to the modern world understood Western culture as German culture.[631] Provided that he, or theoretically she, played the violin well enough, a Jew could conquer Vienna without a word of German. Born in Austrian Poland in 1882, Bronislaw Huberman took up the violin at six. He was presented to the emperor at nine. He played sold-out concerts for the next two years.[632] According to Leon Botstein, himself a living echo of Central Europe's Jewish past as president of Bard College, editor of *Musical Quarterly,* and conductor of orchestras in New York and Jerusalem a century later, Jews made up a third of the Viennese concert audience. As early as the 1840s, a Jewish music teacher was reportedly doing fine in Odessa. By the 1860s, Jews reportedly filled the local opera house, main floor seats included.[633] In 1892, Sophie Jaffe from Odessa beat out Carl Flesch from the Hungarian border town of Moson for first prize in the annual competition at the Paris Conservatory.[634]

Conservatory enrollment was another signpost metric. On the threshold of the twentieth century, 80 percent of the students who matriculated at the Vienna Conservatory came from the Habsburg monarchy and 57 percent from Vienna, with its Jewish population of 8–10 percent. Of the total conservatory enrollment, 27 percent were Jews. They comprised about a third of the matriculees who came to study violin, one of the most popular majors, along with piano and voice. At the St. Petersburg Conservatory, an improbable island of philo-Semitism in an ocean of anti-Semitism, Jewish enrollment had meanwhile grown from about 12 percent of 584 matriculees in 1888–89 to 34 percent of over 1,000 in 1907. On the eve of World War I, Jewish enrollment comprised 50 percent of a total now approaching 2,000. Over half of the Jewish students were women, who outnumbered their male classmates in piano and voice by a ratio of three to one.[635] This implies that a substantial contingent of Jewish males were aspiring violinists.

The careers of Elman, Zimbalist, Heifetz, and Milstein, who left the conservatory at St. Petersburg and went forth to conquer the world, would soon be a matter of great interest from Odessa to New York. "At home, there was no talk save of Mischa Elman, exempted by the Tsar himself from military service," Isaac Babel's narrator reports in the story of an Odessa childhood that might have been the author's. "Zimbalist, his father would have us know, had been presented to the King of England."[636]

In 1922, the Gershwins put it in a song they sang "at the slightest provocation," Ira recalled.[637]

MISCHA, JASCHA, TOSCHA, SASCHA

We really think you ought to know
That we were born right in the middle
Of Darkest Russia.
When we were three years old or so,
We all began to play the fiddle
In Darkest Russia.
When we began,
Our notes were sour—
Until a man
(Professor Auer)
Set out to show us, one and all,
How we could pack them in,
In Carnegie Hall.

Temp'ramental Oriental Gentlemen are we:
Mischa, Jascha, Toscha, Sascha—
Fiddle-lee, diddle-lee, dee.
Shakespeare says, "What's in a name?"
With him we disagree.
Names like Sammy, Max or Moe
Never bring the heavy dough
Like Mischa, Jascha, Toscha, Sascha—
Fiddle-lee, diddle-lee, dee.

Though born in Russia, sure enough,
We're glad that we became relations
Of Uncle Sammy.
For though we play the high-brow stuff,
We also like the syncopations
Of Uncle Sammy.
Our magic bow
Plays Liszt and Schumann;
But then you know
We're only human
And like to shake a leg to jazz.
(Don't think we've not the feelings
Everyone has.)

Temp'ramental Oriental Gentlemen are we:
Mischa, Jascha, Toscha, Sascha—
Fiddle-lee, diddle-lee, dee.
High-brow He-brow may play low-brow
In his privacy.
But when concert halls are packed,
Watch us stiffen up and act
Like Mischa, Jascha, Toscha, Sascha—
Fiddle-lee, diddle-lee, dee.

You find our pictures ev'rywhere.
They show you we're artistic persons
Who play the fiddle.
When critics hear us, they declare
The rest are all so many worse 'uns
Who play the fiddle.
We're from the best;
The critics said it—
But to the rest
We still give credit.
And so we want it understood
We think that Paganini also was good.

Temp'ramental Oriental Gentlemen are we:
Mischa, Jascha, Toscha, Sascha—
Fiddle-lee, diddle-lee, dee.
We give credit when it's due—
But then you must agree
That outside of dear old Fritz,
All the fiddle-concert hits
Are Mischa, Jascha, Toscha, Sascha—
Fiddle-lee, diddle-lee, dee.[638]

The matriarchal Zipporah, a stand-in for her author, the novelist
Hortense Calisher, locates Jewish identity by default between "Those
united still, if only by a Talmud they have never read," and those united
with "dozens of New York City Lower East Side kids in the kinship of having been forced to play the violin."[639]
For most of the twentieth century, Central and Eastern Europe would

supply an ever-larger area of the world with Jewish violinists. Swept mostly westward, the emigrants found a world of multipliers—concert managements, record companies, movie studios, broadcast media, orchestras and conservatories—beyond anything known or imagined by Joachim, let alone Paganini, as well as a devoted audience of people who might have been their cousins. Like their predecessors in the land of the white czars, even those who remained in the land of the red czars enjoyed prizes, patronage, and the local version of meritocracy. From generation to generation, Jewish violinists begat Jewish violinists—Auer and Heifetz, Stolyarsky and Oistrakh, Blinder and Menuhin, Flesch and Szeryng, Gingold and Bell—until their grandchildren lost interest and the torch passed to young Asians, who, till only recently, had been as underrepresented, even exotic, as those little Jewish boys in sailor suits a century earlier.

"SIR, A WOMAN'S preaching is like a dog's walking on his hind legs," Dr. Johnson famously replied, when his biographer, Boswell, reported a recent experience at a Quaker meeting. "It is not done well; but you are surprised to find it done at all." This had also been the default position for women fiddlers. Yet there they were on the threshold of the twentieth century, women not only from Asia but from England, Canada, Germany, Georgia, and Iceland. "If you ask me, concern that a woman can't hold her own is totally invalid," the Viennese critic Eduard Hanslick wrote in 1897.[640] Both the juries and the prizewinners at any competition from Moscow to Indianapolis a century later confirmed that the world had finally learned to cultivate and appreciate women violinists.

Though women arrived well ahead of Jews, a couple of centuries would pass before their presence would be remembered. Henry C. Lahee's *Famous Violinists of To-Day and Yesterday*, first published in 1899 and still going strong in 1916, can be seen as an index of women's relative importance. Only one of its eleven chapters, comprising about 12 percent of the book's 384 pages, is dedicated to women. Yet, as an early reviewer noted approvingly, "Perhaps the most useful section of his book is that on women as violinists."[641]

Try as he might, the author could locate only twenty women who performed in public between 1610 and 1810, and three of them were gambists. But from the mid-nineteenth century on, he added encouragingly, "the violin has become a fashionable instrument for ladies, and has become correspondingly popular as a profession for those who are obliged to earn a living."[642]

Yet even in the eighteenth century, distinguished female players were seen, heard, and appreciated in places that mattered. In 1767, Maddalena Lombardini, Tartini's Venetian protégée and the addressee of his famous letter, married her way out of the Ospedale dei Mendicanti, where she had passed her youth and learned her craft. She then took off with her new spouse, concertmaster at the Basilica of S. Maria Maggiore in Bergamo, as well as a clerical *cavaliere serviente,* a kind of socially sanctioned male companion, for a colorful and independent career that would carry her from London to St. Petersburg.[643] In 1784, Regina Strinasacchi, a product of the same school and also a friend of Haydn's, joined the composer Mozart in the presence of Joseph II for the premiere of the sonata, K. 454, which he composed with her in mind.[644] After what seems a period of hibernation, the gender returned in the mid-nineteenth century in the persons of the Milanollo sisters, to the documented enthusiasm of contemporary audiences. From there till the last quarter of the twentieth century, when a conjunction of emancipatory feminism and deep décolletés brought an odd but arguable version of equal opportunity, women would remain a small but regular and increasingly interesting presence.

The talent came from multiple directions. Born in France in 1842 to a Sicilian-Portuguese musician couple, Camilla Urso began playing at six. She was admitted to the Paris Conservatory at seven as its first-ever girl candidate. She left at ten, first in her class. By the time her family decamped for America three years later, her twofold appeal as a girl and as a prodigy was already irresistible. The fact that she had helped support her family since conservatory days was by now familiar, too. "A face so solemn and unchanging in its expression that it seemed as if a smile had never visited it,"[645] one contemporary noted. "Most of the women violinists, the best ones, hate their instruments,"[646] the great Maud Powell declared in a blast at the Boston critic Philip Hale. It was unlikely that she included herself. But given the unequal work for unequal pay that went with the job, she wanted it known that if others hated their violins, it was not without good cause.

After three years that took her as far as St. Louis, Urso vanished from public view. At twenty-one, she returned in 1863 to play with the day's major orchestras, including the infant New York Philharmonic, the Philadelphia Philharmonic Society, and the Pasdeloup orchestra in Paris. She

played a wide repertory. In 1869, her performance of the Beethoven concerto with the Harvard Musical Association may not only have been the
first performance of the piece in the United States but the first time she
had actually heard herself. Between December 16, 1873, and January 1,
1874, she played eight concerts, holidays included. In the 1878–79 season,
she reportedly played over two hundred concerts from Massachusetts to
Denver, on an itinerary that included fifteen states, two territories, and
Canada. She then took off on a strenuous tour of California, Australia, and
New Zealand, before retiring in her midforties to assume a teaching career
in Boston and New York, where she was a colleague of Dvořák's at Mrs.
Thurber's National Conservatory. In the absence of an adequate pension,
this was still not enough to spare her an occasional postretirement vaudeville gig. " . . . I should say to young girls who are thinking of becoming
professional violinists, 'Don't,'" was her bleak advice at fifty-one. Three
years later, she came out of retirement to tour South Africa, doing concerts,
as Lahee notes, "in such out-of-the-way places as Bloemfontein."[647] She died
after an appendectomy at age sixty.[648]

But for her sex, Teresina Tua might have been just one more notable
Italian player. But the fact that she was a woman made all the difference.
Born in 1872, she was performing at age six with her guitarist mother in
local cafés to such effect that her father, himself an amateur violinist, left
his day job as a mason to take the family to Switzerland and France. Her
Horatio Alger moment came four years later, when an aristocratic patron
arranged an audition with Lambert Massart, teacher of Wieniawski, Kreisler, and Ysaÿe. A few years later, as a winner of the Paris Conservatory's
highest prize, Tua was ready for the road.

Over thirty-five active years, her path would lead to republican America and imperial Russia, a handsome collection of instruments, a startling
collection of jewelry from admirers including the Prince and Princess of
Wales, the queens of Spain and Italy, and the Russian Empress,[649] and two
titled spouses. She also experienced more than her share of personal tragedy, including her mother's suicide and the loss of two children. Whatever
her limits as a player of the violin, contemporaries from Maud Powell and
Carl Flesch to the young Sergei Rachmaninov testified to her virtuosity as
a player of audiences. At a farewell concert in still-Austrian Trieste in 1915,
it wasn't even necessary for her to put bow to strings to please her audience.
Her appearance "in a red Empire style gown, with green sleeves and sash,
and the décolleté veiled in white: the three colors of the Italian flag" was
already a triumph.[650] "She has a face that will be music to the unmusical,

and an unfailing knowledge of the value of her delightful smiles, which she rained down on the front rows in a manner calculated to diminish whatever soundness of judgment the young men in that neighborhood possessed when they entered the hall," the *New York Times* reported.[651] She died in a convent at the age of ninety.

Gender enhanced the Moravian-born Wilma Neruda's visibility, too. Surrounded from birth in 1840 by a professional musician father and a houseful of musical siblings, she reportedly discovered the violin by herself while still a toddler. Her astonished father took over from there. She made her Vienna debut at six, impressed Hanslick by the time she was eight, and appeared with the Philharmonic Society in London at nine.[652]

Twenty years would pass before she returned to London, by then honored with a title from the Swedish crown and highly regarded by Joachim. Coming from Germany, where women violinists were already "quite common," she told a British interviewer some forty years later, she was startled to find herself in a country where the species was regarded as "almost improper, certainly unladylike." It would be no problem for her. Fall and spring, she was invited back biennially from 1869 to 1898. In 1876, the Duke of Edinburgh and the Earls of Dudley and Hardwicke expressed their regard by presenting her with a 1709 Strad.

A testimonial to her stature as a role model, an 1880 article in *The Girl's Own Paper* declared her nothing less than a "musical St. George."[653] Powell, an avatar of tough-mindedness, recalled her as "a cross old patch" and conceded that "she was not a Vieuxtemps." But she was just as emphatic that Neruda "played better than any local man in London when I lived there."[654]

Johannes Brahms's testimonial to the twenty-two-year-old Marie Soldat only raised the bar. "Isn't little Soldat terrific? Can't she take on 10 men? Who'll do it better?" he asked in 1885,[655] after she became the second player to perform his violin concerto six years after Joachim's premiere. Three years later, she played it at her London debut, where a reviewer acknowledged her "magnificent technique" while also calling attention to her "surprisingly vigorous and masculine" bowing and attack.[656] Between a performance in Leipzig the same year and a reprise in 1905, the piece was performed only seven times by six performers, including Joachim.[657] Like Soldat, two of the six, Gabrielle Wietrowitz and Leonora Jackson, were women, a fact forgotten by the late 1930s, when the English cellist Felix Salmond assured Dorothy DeLay and her Juilliard classmates that the concerto's reach exceeded the female grasp.

A natural talent from the Austrian provinces whose organist-choirmaster father died when she was twelve, Soldat learned early on to play for her mother's supper as well as her own. Her Lana Turner moment came two years later at a summer spa, when Brahms was so taken by her playing that he recruited a singer to join him in an ad hoc recital for her benefit, then bought her a train ticket to meet Joachim. When strings on her own violin broke, it was later reported, Joachim offered her his Strad, a new experience twice over, since it was also the first time she had played a full-sized instrument. The audition was so successful that he invited her to Berlin, taught her for free, and arranged for friends to make sure that the penniless Soldat and her mother got regular meals.

Over a career that extended into her seventies, she would form two all-women quartets, a novelty at the time, marry, record, and teach. All the while, the Joachim connection remained a gift that kept on giving: the Wittgensteins of Vienna loaned her a del Gesù for life. A network of English fans, friends, and groupies continued to invite her back. She once spent an evening in Oxford playing Mozart and Haydn quartets with an enthusiastic amateur named Albert Einstein as second violin and established professionals as viola and cello. A last surviving link to a world that reached back to Mendelssohn, she died at ninety-two, honored but forgotten.

Different as they were in style and temperament, the European founding mothers emerged from a shared landscape. There was no such precedent for the Americans Leonora Jackson, Arma Senkrah, Leonora von Stosch and, the mother of them all, Maud Powell. One or another might have been taken for European, especially von Stosch, a count's daughter and baronet's wife, who sat for a 1907 portrait by John Singer Sargent. All four were at least a half generation ahead of patrician Albert Spalding as America's first notable concert violinists; at least two were as middle-class American as McGuffey Readers and *The Joy of Cooking*; and only an American could have said, as Powell did, "[O]ur wonderful but intensely practical country will never develop the arts except on a sound business-like basis."[658]

The eldest, Brooklyn-born as Anna Levretta Harkness in 1864, was hauled off to Europe at an early age, where she studied with superstars including Massart, Wieniawski, and, possibly, Vieuxtemps. At seventeen she finished first in her class at the Paris Conservatory. A year later, she made her debut at London's Crystal Palace. She then toured the continent as Arma Senkrah. According to Amy Fay, the Boston pianist, who met her in the aging Franz Liszt's circle in Weimar, the faux Indian inversion of her family name originated with the manager Hermann Wolff, who thought Harkness might be a hard sell, especially in Anglophone countries. Times had changed since then, Fay noted gratefully. A much-reproduced photo, dedicated "To the distinguished violin virtuoso" by "her most devoted accompanist," showed Senkrah with Liszt, Liszt's piano, and the score of Beethoven's op. 24 "Spring" sonata in prominent view. Fay recalled "a beautiful and fascinating young woman, and an artist of the first rank." Unfortunately, she added, the dedicatee of the photo "had the misfortune to fall in love with a dissipated German lawyer," marry him, and retire.[659] The marriage didn't work out. In 1900, Senkrah shot herself at thirty-six, leaving a ten-year-old son. She was buried in the Weimar municipal cemetery beneath a black marble tombstone with the undated inscription "Arma Senkrah Hoffmann."[660]

Stosch was born in Washington, D.C., to an American singer and the former Count Ferdinand von Stosch, a German immigrant who had served in the Union army. She kept equally distinguished company, but over eighty-three years, two marriages, work in two countries and two careers, and at least two violins, she enjoyed more luck with less collateral damage than Senkrah. On her return from study in Brussels and Leipzig, she made her debut with the Boston Symphony at eighteen and later played with the New York Philharmonic. In 1893, a young admirer unexpectedly bought a 1710 Strad, once owned by Vieuxtemps, for her to use. Resulting litigation called attention to "the well-known violinist," as well as the dealer who brokered the sale and had to sue for his commission. That she was "young and beautiful" was news that the *New York Times* also saw fit to print.[661]

"The chief charm of her playing is its finish and refined expression, and these attributes will probably secure her widespread favour in this country," the *Musical Times* reported in 1901.[662] It certainly secured favor with Sir Edgar Speyer, the New York–born CEO of the British branch of a German-American investment bank. A major investor in what would become the London Underground, he was also a friend of the composers Sir Edward Elgar, Richard Strauss, and Claude Debussy. "I love London, and should like to settle here," von Stosch told a *Strad* interviewer in 1901.[663] In 1902, she married Speyer and did. Then came World War I. In 1915, anti-German zeal caused the couple to make use of her U.S. passport and return to New York, where neuritis caused her to give up playing professionally in favor of writing. As Leonora Speyer, she then won the Pulitzer Prize for poetry in 1927.

Leonora Jackson, descended from a veteran of the battles of Lexington and Bunker Hill, was the youngest of the founding mothers. Born in Boston, she made a lasting impression on Amy Fay as a ten-year-old in Chicago. In September 1893, the *New York Times* reported that "Miss Leonora Jackson, the phenomenal violinist, who is only 14 years old" was already "in great demand for musicales" in Bar Harbor, Maine.[664] By her midteens, she had so impressed George Pullman, the inventor of the sleeping car, George Vanderbilt, grandson of Cornelius, the shipping and railroad king, and Frances Folsom Cleveland, wife of the President, that they organized a fund to send her to Paris and then Berlin, where she studied with Joachim. In 1897, the *New York Times* found it newsworthy that she had become the first American to win the Mendelssohn Prize, Berlin's equivalent of a first prize in Paris.[665]

She was also the first American to appear with the Gewandhaus Orchestra and was engaged by the Philharmonic Society and Concerts Colonne. In the style of the era, she performed for Queen Victoria as well as the kings of Sweden and Norway. In January 1900, Jackson's friends and patrons showed up in force at a public rehearsal of the New York Philharmonic. She could have made it easy for herself by playing Mendelssohn or Bruch. That "she elected to play the serious and difficult music of Brahms spoke volumes for her courage," the *New York Times* noted.[666] That summer, her decision to cancel a European tour and sign up, instead, to tour the United States was again considered news fit to print. Before the season was over, Jackson had played 160 concerts.

She continued to perform into her thirties and entered a first, short-lived marriage. In 1913, Robert Todd Lincoln, the president's son, and his wife engaged her to perform at a dinner party in honor of former President Taft at their home in Manchester, Vermont.[667] But her career as artist morphed into a career as patron after her marriage, in 1915, to Dr. William Duncan McKim, twenty-four years her senior and an advocate of eugenic euthanasia, whose three manual, thirty-five-stop organ was the largest in any Washington, D.C. private residence.[668] On her death at ninety, she left an art collection and twenty-one linear feet of papers and memorabilia now in the Library of Congress.[669]

Of the four, only Powell, who married her manager but remained childless, continued to perform to the end of her life. From early on, she looked to Urso as a role model. She was still in her midtwenties when it occurred to her that she had already become one herself after organizing a three-day Women's Musical Congress at the Columbian Exposition in Chicago, and performing for an audience of 1,500.

The role, as usual, came early. She was practicing three and four hours daily by the time she was in school, and was playing both with and for grown-ups at nine. At fourteen, she was off to Leipzig, where Henry Lewis, her Chicago teacher, thought she should be. At fifteen, she was among eighty-four candidates for six places at the Paris Conservatory. Six months later, her teachers, Dancla and the Belgian Hubert Léonard, told her to go play concerts in England.

She opened London like an oyster. On tour with singers, in the fashion of the era, she also became a favorite on the after-dinner circuit, performing twice for the Prince and Princess of Wales. There was a concert before three thousand in Glasgow and a solo appearance with the Hallé orchestra. With an introduction from a patron and an invitation from Joachim, she then set off for the obligatory master class in Berlin, and a performance of the Beethoven concerto with Joachim and the Philharmonic.

Four years after leaving, she returned to Aurora for a hometown recital and auditioned in New York for Theodore Thomas, the pioneer conductor and founder of the Chicago Symphony. He signed her on the spot for a summer concert in Chicago. "I want the honor of paying you the first fee you've earned as an artist," he told her as he greeted her with a bundle of cash after the concert. He then offered her a two-year retainer as soloist with his orchestra at $150 a concert. It was about what a Pennsylvania carpenter might earn in sixty ten-hour days, and three to six times what a cowboy in Texas or Wyoming might earn in a month.

From there to her death at fifty-two, presumably of heart disease, she led a life that even Theodore Roosevelt, her contemporary, might have found strenuous. Over the course of her career, she would premiere fourteen concertos. She was the first American to perform the Tchaikovsky concerto that Leopold Auer turned down and made Eduard Hanslick, the great Viennese critic, want to hold his nose. In the presence of the composer, she auditioned the Dvořák concerto that Joachim had once considered too difficult for a woman. She became the first American to perform it publicly. She was the first American to perform the Sibelius at a time when audiences regarded it as daring. In 1891, she played seventy-five concerts in two months with Patrick Gilmore's band. In 1893, she formed a quartet with three male colleagues; they performed every night for five weeks. In 1903, she played two concerts a day while touring Europe with the John Philip Sousa band. In 1904, she was the first instrumentalist to record on Victor's Red Label, with gratifying results for both herself and the company.

Beginning in 1907, she also toured the American West, playing in halls like the Dreamland Rink in Seattle and in communities like Ogden, Utah, where no one had ever heard anyone like her. While trying to limit herself to three concerts a week, she wrote her own program notes, transcribed the work of squadrons of living American composers, and endured entry-level orchestras like the one in Bellingham, Washington, where no one had ever heard of the viola. Born in an age when American concerts were often organized as variety shows, she helped pioneer the solo recital, shut up front-row conversationalists by suggesting that they ask for a refund at the box office, and once stopped midpiece to point out to the mother of a squalling baby, "The concert hall is not a nursery."[670]

"Maud believed that it was possible to make a good living with the violin provided that ambitions squared with talent and circumstances," her biographers note.[671] She certainly earned enough to live in comfort. She aquired a respectable collection of instruments, an Upper West Side apartment, a car when it still meant something, a Long Island summer house, a sailing yacht she called "Cremona," and a New Hampshire summer house, where she golfed, gardened, and practiced.

She also left a paper trail of unblinking tough-mindedness. If men had it tough, women had it tougher, she told her readers. The trade-offs included lost childhoods, school years, social life, "the hours of practice, the careful diet, the keeping in physical trim, the constant self-denial in the matter of social pleasures, late hours, shopping expeditions." Concert playing "is one of the most disheartening professions a girl can possibly enter," she declared, ticking off the intimidating odds, psychic costs, and practical expenses that even extended, in an era of extravagant upholstery, to "the discomfort of our clothes, the time and trouble that it takes to keep oneself looking respectable, etc., etc., etc." "I verily believe I am the only woman who, having stuck to her fiddle unflinchingly, has preserved the remnants of a sweet sanity," she concluded briskly.

Her legacy included her favorite violin, bought in 1907 as a 1775 Guadagnini. Four years later, when burglars tried and failed to steal it in an era when most telephone operators earned less than $500 a year, she estimated its value at around $10,000.[672] Many decades later, James Warren, the Chicago dealer, declared it a copy by the German-born George Gemunder, the first notable American maker.[673]

The equivocal violin became an equivocal metaphor after her death. In 1921, the *New York Times* reported that her widower and manager, H. Godfrey Turner, also known as Sunny, had decided to pass it on to the young Erica Morini after her sensational debut at Carnegie Hall.[674] Morini's agent, very possibly acting without her knowledge, appears to have been the source of the story. Four years later, the *Times* reported that the French violinist Renée Chemet was to play it on WEAF, a pioneer New York radio station, presumably on loan from Turner, who denied ever having given or sold it.[675] Sometime afterward, it was sold to a New York collector, who sold it to Henry Ford in 1926.[676]

Like the ownership of Powell's presumed Guadagnini, Morini's birth-date was also a moving target, as so often in a profession where it was practically impossible to be too young. But unlike Chemet, who surfaced in Japan in the early 1930s and was then lost from view, Morini was not really mysterious. Prodigious from age three (or four), the youngest candidate ever accepted by the Vienna Conservatory at eight (or nine), she made her debut with the Gewandhaus Orchestra and Berlin Philharmonic in her midteens. She would play fifty-six times with the New York Philharmonic.

She was certainly respected by her peers and adored by her fans. In 1951, she was invited to play with the boys, including Isaac Stern and the violist William Primrose, at the great cellist Pablo Casals's festival in Perpignan, France. She was invited in 1962 to play with Stern, Zino Francescatti, and Nathan Milstein at a memorial concert for her fellow Viennese Fritz Kreisler. On her last visit to Israel, a year after the 1967 Six-Day War, she was received to such acclaim that the management laid on two extra concerts and sold out the three thousand seats in Tel Aviv's Mann Auditorium within two hours.

She was still performing as well as ever in her midseventies. "Probably the greatest female violinist who ever lived," noted Harold C. Schonberg of the *New York Times*. Though meant as a compliment, it was not taken as one. "A violinist is a violinist and I am to be judged as one—not as a female musician," Morini replied.[677] Over more than five decades, more than three in the United States, where she settled permanently in 1938, she virtually owned the niche reserved, like it or not, for women players.

Jelly d'Arányi and her sister, Adila, natives of Budapest, a half generation older than Morini, got themselves to England, where native wit and charm, Joachim family connections, and real talent paid off socially and professionally in careers that extended over thirty years from the country house weekend circuit to the Prom Concerts, local premieres of the Bartók sonatas, and the dedication of Ravel's popular "Tzigane" to Jelly.[678]

Gioconda de Vito, née Martina Franca, who was Morini's contemporary and almost as durable, was celebrated in Europe. Reluctant by temperament, and limited by her teaching contract at Rome's Accademia di Santa Cecilia and wartime contingency, she traveled relatively little, never appeared in the United States, despite urgings from major conductors, and retired early. Guila Bustabo, born in Manitowoc, Wisconsin, in 1916 to a stage mother from hell, was prodigious at five, studied with Persinger at Juilliard, where classmates noticed that she sometimes arrived with bruises, then toured Europe with her mother in the mid-1930s. Her mother's disastrous decision that she continue playing in occupied Europe destroyed the promise of a brilliant career by making her daughter poison in the postwar United States. "Menuhin was lucky, he got away from his parents" she said later. "I never got away from mine." She married an American military bandmaster, made a small career in postwar Europe, and returned to America as concertmaster of the Alabama Symphony after retirement in 1970. She died at eighty-six, ten years after her mother, in 2002.[679]

Ginette Neveu, victor over David Oistrakh at the memorable Wieniawski competition in 1935, died in an air crash at thirty. Her younger contemporary and Flesch classmate Ida Haendel, a child of the usual indeterminate age when she won a prize at the same competition, was still active and formidable in her seventies, after a long and distinguished, but far from easy, career in Europe and beyond. She had never had a problem getting concerts, she told an interviewer in the 1980s. The problem was equal pay for equal work. "They thought a woman is not worth as much as a man," she said. "And that really made me angry."[680]

Yfrah Neaman, Britain's Galamian as professor at the Guildhall School, was convinced that her management had set her up to fail when she tried to break into the U.S. market after World War II. In Britain, where the family had been fortunate enough to settle before disaster struck their native Poland, Haendel was a teenage celebrity. In America, her management booked recitals in Marinette, Wisconsin, and Hannibal, Missouri, before bringing her back for an anticlimactic recital in New York. "I must tell you that it's not easy to procure concerts for women violinists even if they play like goddesses," the manager Sol Hurok told her. Meanwhile, Neveu made her debut with the Boston Symphony.[681] It seemed self-evident to Neaman that access to the women's niche was a zero-sum game, where Haendel had been designated to lose and Neveu to win.[682]

Between 1952 and 1955, Community Concerts, an agency that supplied much of Middle America with affordable talent, listed four women among its fifteen violinists. Among them were Camilla Wicks, whose recording of the Sibelius concerto would become a classic, and Carroll Glenn, the first American since Maud Powell to dominate "the distaff side of the violin field," as the agency described her. All four dropped out while young. Neaman recalled a lesson from the mega-manager Arthur Judson. "You're no good to me if you're not marketable," Judson said. As Haendel still confirmed decades later, the numbers alone were an education. Of eleven men invited to play with the New York Philharmonic between 1945 and 1950, only two were paid less than $1,500. Of the six women, only one—Morini—was paid as much as $1,500. Six of the men appeared with the orchestra at least twice. None of the women appeared more than once.[683]

There were alternative careers. In early 1933, Alma Rosé, 27, whose father, Arnold, had been concertmaster of the Vienna Philharmonic since the early 1880s, introduced her *Wiener Walzermädeln*, the Viennese Waltz Girls, to a local audience with a repertory of waltzes, polkas, and greatest hits from the still flourishing world of Central European operetta. They were soon on the road, where they shared the bill ad hoc with Yvette Guilbert, the French cabaret singer, Vera Schwarz, the Croatian soprano, Joseph Schmidt, the Romanian tenor, trapeze artists, stunt cyclists, and cowboys. Hopes for a solo career had not worked out. Neither had a marriage to the Czech virtuoso Váša Příhoda, whose own career was in full bloom. Save for Munich, where the newly ascendant Nazis shut down the theater on their arrival, the ten or so *Walzermädeln*, with their frilly dresses, décolleté tops, coordinated smiles, and hummable repertory, soon became a Central European favorite. They might have remained one but for the tidal wave of disaster that rolled over Europe, the world, and themselves soon after. Rosé continued as best she could to look after her elderly father in London while remaining professionally active in occupied Holland. She ended her career as conductor of the women's orchestra at Auschwitz, where she died, possibly of botulism, in 1944.[684]

In 1934, Phil Spitalny, a onetime clarinet prodigy from Odessa turned conductor and band leader in Cleveland and Boston, introduced his All-Girl, also known as his Hour of Charm, Orchestra, featuring Evelyn Kaye Klein (Evelyn and Her Magic Violin) to a national radio audience. It would survive over twenty years, many with corporate sponsorship, an eternity even by all-male standards. Klein, who had studied at Juilliard's antecedent Institute of Musical Art, actually played a Carnegie Hall recital in 1937. A promotional photo shows her flanked by twenty-four players, including seven violinists, arranged in rows like the little girls in the Venetian *ospedali*. In $500 gowns over seven layers of taffeta skirts, they are all looking straight ahead.

The show was intended to look and sound as easy as singing around the parlor piano, and as unthreatening as the high school orchestra. Of course it wasn't. As many as 1,500 candidates had reportedly auditioned for the original 32 places.[685] Klein would eventually marry Spitalny. Remembered by many players as a conscientious employer, though also for auditioning candidates in his shorts, he paid $75–$100 a week, with a supplement for soloists that might reach $350, at a time when most women musicians were grateful to be employed at all, and $40 sufficed to rent a house for a month.[686]

A third option, Eudice Shapiro's solution, was to go to California. A Curtis graduate from a Jewish immigrant family in Buffalo, New York, she had been admitted as the only woman in her class and studied with Zimbalist. Told that Shapiro played like a man, the standard compliment, Mary Louise Curtis Bok, the Institute's founding mother, replied firmly, "She plays like a woman." Either way, it was no help the morning after graduation, when Shapiro found herself with a small prize and a few ad hoc concerts leading to nowhere.

Managers assured her that women's clubs were the likeliest bookers. But they preferred men, and singers at that. An appeal to the pianist Josef Hofmann, the institute's former director, brought a sympathetic but bleak reply of classical economy. "The only remedy is success," Hofmann wrote. "But success without a manager is difficult to bring about, and managers aren't interested unless an artist has had success." This side of a sensation, the prescribed New York recital was unlikely to bring anything but bills.[687]

Marriage to Victor Gottlieb, a former Philadelphia Orchestra cellist, led to his hometown, Los Angeles, where union rules made jobs at the movie studios conditional on a year's residence. It was equal opportunity from there on, and Shapiro made the most of it. Her appointment as concertmaster at RKO and Paramount was a win for everyone: for the studios, who neither had to film her nor identify her in the credits; for her, because she cashed in at union scale in the golden age of the Hollywood studios; even for the cohort of gifted film composers who wrote expansive solos into their scores for her.

Meanwhile, in the diaspora landscape that was midcentury Los Ange-

les, there was discretionary time to play Mozart with the conductor Bruno
Walter, play quartets with the cellist Gregor Piatigorsky and the host
himself at Heifetz's house on New Year's Eve, and make friends with the
composer Igor Stravinsky.[688] A living bridge linking the age of Heifetz and
the little Jewish boy with the age of Midori and the little Asian girl, Shapiro was still teaching at the University of Southern California's Thornton
School of Music in her nineties. She died in 2007.[689]

Neither for nor against women's suffrage although she was both daughter and niece of active suffragettes,[690] Powell might have registered with
wonder at least four notable gains since her involuntary exit from the
world just months before ratification of the Nineteenth Amendment. "Her
playing is virile with a virility that is of the masculine, and not of the
feminine type." "Her style was full of masculine power." "There is never
a hint of feminine lack of vigor." "She has an extraordinary masculinity
of touch." " . . . a firmness of attack astonishing for a woman."[691] All of
them were presumed to be compliments, and they were once as common as
woman driver jokes. They had virtually disappeared from a world in which
women now served as chancellor of the Federal Republic of Germany, Her
Majesty's prime minister, U.S. secretary of state, and president of Harvard.

The Armenian-American Ani Kavafian, reflecting on her Juilliard
years with Galamian in the 1960s, couldn't recall that the gender subtext
had ever come up. Better still, she had the impression that women might
actually have become an easier sale than men for the first time since violinists began playing concerts for a living. As she approached fifty, her solo fee
was toward the lower end of a scale that extended from $6,000 to $60,000.
She played about ninety concerts a year. If disadvantaged, she reflected, it
was only for being constrained like most of her peers to play what the presenter asked them to play rather than make the choice themselves.

A third significant gain that Powell could hardly have overlooked was
a freedom of choice that the world she grew up in would have found as
remote as the suffrage. Ida Kavafian, Ani's sister, would have liked more
solo appearances, she told an interviewer. But that would require more
aggressive management, and she liked it where she was, traveling half the
year, playing chamber music and festivals, including her own, and raising show dogs with her spouse and colleague. Given the choice between
"Get the money" and "Get a life," she opted for the latter. It was her
choice. Christiane Edinger noted prudently that a performer is never too
old to remain in contact with conductors and managers. She also welcomed

the conservatory professorship that both allowed her to play forty to fifty concerts a year and turn down a request from the German foreign ministry's soft power and cultural diplomacy section to pinch-hit in Calcutta on short notice.

The last gain—greater freedom than ever before to play *and*, not *or*, have children—followed from the third. In a blog post, Lara St. John tut-tutted like Morini decades earlier about the undesirability, even impossibility, of raising a child while on tour ten months a year. She was then reminded of Leila Josefowicz, a Chanel model and MacArthur Fellow, who was doing just that while remaining professionally active and even enrolling in a kick-boxing course.[692] "What's the point in having children if you never see them?" asked Tasmin Little, who cheerfully continued playing concerts till two weeks before giving birth, then took her two preschoolers along on tour. "The experience of children gives you more to say," she told an interviewer from the *Daily Telegraph*.[693] "What would be the biggest tragedy for me?" Anne-Sophie Mutter, mother of two, replied to a question from James Oestreich of the *New York Times*. "To be a bad mother."[694]

While a preoccupation with looks would have struck Powell as being as self-evident as the sunrise, the new emphasis on the young, swinging, and sexy could hardly have been further from the Gibson Girl of her own era. Powell's late-twentieth-century successors were quick, even defensively quick, to point out that the preoccupation extended across the sexes. They had a point. A glance at websites and CD covers confirmed that managements also worked hard to package young males like Gil Shaham, Maxim Vengerov, and Joshua Bell in jeans, leather jackets, and boyish smiles.

There was no question who got the most attention. Startling décolletés on Anne-Sophie Mutter and Anne Akiko Meyers were meant to attract attention and did. A 1996 cover that seemed to show Lara St. John dressed only in her violin sold over thirty thousand copies, not usual for solo Bach.[695] "Good violinists draw a crowd," Elmar Weingarten, the Berlin Philharmonic's manager, acknowledged. The average fee for soloists in the sunset years of the deutschmark was 10,000, and 3,000–5,000 for beginners. Gidon Kremer commanded 40,000, Anne-Sophie Mutter 80,000–100,000. How was it, he was asked, that Mutter commanded eight to ten times what the orchestra usually paid? It wasn't just music, Weingarten said.[696]

It was widely noted that few careers now extended past the performer's fiftieth birthday. This came at the cost, for example, of an Ida Haendel, who still played like a major artist in her seventies. Haendel, who spent much of her career swimming upstream, was both resigned and understandably bitter about being upstaged by fresh young faces and plunging necklines. "I am not an entertainer," she told the critic Norman Lebrecht.[697]

Her Polish colleague and contemporary Wanda Wilkomirska was more flexible. She recalled her son asking her to bring back Nigel Kennedy's runaway best seller of Vivaldi's *Four Seasons* as well as Steppenwolf from a trip to London in the 1980s. She did, and fondly recalled hearing her green-haired teenager whistling, "Ta ta-ta-ta tata TAH!" soon afterward. Was there more like this, he wanted to know? For all she cared, Powell's great-granddaughters could wear anything or nothing, Wilkomirska said, if it got people to come and listen to the music.[698] The victories of organized feminism, the globalization of the Asian Rim, the recovery of at least the German West from the self-inflicted ravages of the Nazi years, the windows of meritocratic opportunity before and after the end of the Soviet Empire, had peopled the supply side of the violin world with talent unimaginable as recently as the mid-twentieth century. The challenge, now on the demand side, was getting people to come listen to them, and it was not gender-specific.

BUSINESS AND POLITICS

⌒

A SELF-TAUGHT VIRTUOSO in his field, Sol Hurok discovered his managerial vocation almost serendipitously, while trying to attract fellow immigrants to Socialist campaign rallies and political benefit concerts in early twentieth-century New York. He realized early on that the way to their hearts was not food, let alone drink, but music. On Sundays, he peddled silverware to get himself to concerts, where he could scout performers he could book from the Wolfsohn Musical Bureau, the city's leading agency. His moment came when he approached the young Efrem Zimbalist, newly arrived and in stiff competition with the equally young Elman, Kreisler, and Ysaÿe. To his manager's surprise, Zimbalist said yes. At least according to Hurok, they settled on Zimbalist's normal fee of $750 but agreed that the artist would write over a third of that amount to the party afterward. The concert cleared $1,600, and Hurok was on his way. A year or two later, an impressed Zimbalist let Hurok book him at Carnegie Hall, where ticket buyers turned up in such numbers that 250 had to be seated on stage. By 1915, Elman and Ysaÿe were also among his clients, in an era when up to thirty-nine violinists performed in Manhattan over the course of a season. Of the $6,000 budgeted per concert, $1,800 went into ads in the ethnic press with detailed instructions on how to get to midtown Manhattan. Tickets sold for 50 cents to $2 at drug stores, at a jewelry store, and at Jewish-owned music stores. There was a 50 percent discount for block sales to unions. "A manager does not make an artist," Hurok would say later, with the authority of one who'd been there and done that, "What he makes is an audience."[699]

This insight was as old as the public concert business. As far back as the holiday season of 1672, the violinist-composer John Banister—"old Banister," as Roger North referred to him—had signed up "a set of gentlemen . . . most violinists" and "spoke of about towne . . . opened an obscure room in a publik house in White Fryars; filled it with tables and seats, and made a side box with curtaines for the musick." Then he bought what might be the world's earliest concert ad in the *London Gazette*. "1s [one shilling] a peice [sic]," it read. "Call for what you please, pay the reckoning, and *Welcome Gentlemen*."[700] It worked in late seventeenth-century London. It worked again in early twenty-first-century New York, where Old Banister's heirs, a couple of Manhattan School of Music grads, opened Le Poisson Rouge, a multimedia cabaret in Greenwich village with a full bar, happy hour, and performers, including the Dutch violinist Janine Jansen.

Between Old Banister and Le Poisson Rouge lay over three centuries of concert life, private and public, exclusive and affordable, with and without a full bar and happy hour. The patron, promoter, or presenter might be a prince, a bishop, a court, an upscale host or hostess, a bourgeois gentilhomme, teacher, orchestra or individual player, even "shopkeepers and Jew speculators," to quote a sniffy, mid-nineteenth-century appreciation by the London *Musical Union*.[701] The presenter might also be a walk-on genius like P. T. Barnum, with a nose for anything likely to draw a crowd, or a charitable organization. The audience might be a court, a salon, dinner guests, men, women, the monied and the professional middle-class, the subscribers, or a group of friends—in principle, anyone who wanted to see or be seen and could afford a ticket.

Up to the threshold of the railroad age, Paganini could still toot his own horn and connect with local patrons, relying on local help to find a place to play, negotiate ticket prices, hang posters, initiate a buzz, do what was needed to draw a crowd, assure that he got paid, and get himself to the next town or country. But a new era was already in view in 1841, when the twenty-year-old Franz Liszt hired Gaetano Belloni, a music copyist, as his nominal servant and friend, with the real mission of acting as his advance man. Four years later, a support group of sixty-one, including two duchesses, four viscountesses, five marchionesses, and ten countesses, rounded up several hundred untitled friends to hear Liszt play a benefit. But Belloni got there first. In his own way, Barnum did the same thing when he invited the Swedish soprano Jenny Lind to America in 1850. The terms—150 concerts at $1,000 each (tax-free), the equivalent in 2010 dollars of nearly $22,000 a night—might have made even Paganini stand at attention. These terms still made Barnum a fortune.[702]

In London, where social connections still sufficed, the future was slower to arrive. Everywhere else, professional management soon advanced from cutting-edge practice to a practical necessity.[703] Liszt could look after himself without Belloni, the German critic Heinrich Ehrlich reflected. The aging Sivori couldn't, and what Belloni did for him in Berlin and north Germany was magic.[704] A century later, even Heifetz had a publicist.[705]

The new management had many fathers. The railroad and telegraph were among the most prominent. Ehrlich, who had personally experienced both Before and After, was struck by the way the railroad, Pullman car included, had even increased productivity. He noted how Liszt, not yet twenty, complained in 1838 that he was expected to play three or four pieces in an evening. A couple of decades later, Anton Rubinstein, whose adult career took off in the mid 1850s, was expected to play eight to ten pieces. Liszt had meanwhile gone on to play whole concerts by himself. Ehrlich worried that more concerts and longer tours might favor athleticism over art.[706]

He also looked on with interest as servants turned master, and what began as a subordinate, even a gofer, job developed into independent concert promotion, and from there to artistic management with a global reach. By the turn of the twentieth century, every self-respecting musical capital had its agency. "My gang of thieves," Ysaÿe called them. Thanks, at least in part, to their efforts, a hundred concerts a season brought him an annual income that would convert to several million early twenty-first-century dollars.[707]

As emblematic a patriarch as Werner von Siemens or Henry Ford, Hermann Wolff effectively created an industry and profession in his image. Unlike most of his peers, he had actually studied piano and theory. To supplement his earnings as a stock trader, he also wrote for the *Neue Berliner Musik-Zeitung* whose editor, the music publisher Hugo Bock, offered him a job. When Rubinstein looked to Bock for a manager to arrange a tour of Spain, Bock looked to Wolff. On his return, Wolff found his calling. Charming, conciliatory, as fond of food and drink as he was of music, he was also well connected, apparently unflappable, polyglot, resourceful, and tough, as well as imaginative. Flesch, presumably looking for management in 1896 at the age of twenty-three, found a kindly looking man in his middle years who received him with cordial reserve. "In almost every case, his personal recommendation paid off in the desired engagement," Flesch recalled. He also recalled a photo on Wolff's desk of a certain soprano in what he delicately called décolleté, with a reminder that she had neglected to pay Wolff for his services.[708]

Strategically located in what was about to become the era's city that didn't sleep, he seemed born to the new profession. From 1880 till his death in 1902, he managed and presented artists all the way to San Francisco. He saved the infant Berlin Philharmonic from imminent shipwreck, then turned it into a going concern. He built Berlin's first dedicated recital hall and generally helped transform a minor league town into one of the world's music capitals. In 1879, his icy review of Brahms's new violin concerto produced indignant letters to the editor (Bock) from Brahms, Brahms's publisher, Simrock, and Joachim. Fourteen years later, Joachim had become a longtime Wolff client, and Brahms and Wolff were the best of friends.[709] The mature Kreisler would be a Wolff artist, and the precocious Menuhin another. When Wolff died, the Berlin Philharmonic played a concert in his honor. His wife, whose instincts and toughness matched his own, continued where he left off. For at least two generations, her Sunday lunch would be among the city's most desirable invitations, coveted by those who wanted to network or to just be seen in her company. The coming of the Nazis was the end of all that. She died a few weeks later.

If Wolff was the overture to a heroic age, Hurok was its coda. " . . . the last of a species which is fast fading from the American scene," a *Life* magazine profile called him in 1944, when Hurok was reportedly fifty-six.[710] If Wolff was almost certainly unique as dedicatee of a memorial concert, Hurok, very much alive and kicking, was the subject of a full-scale Hollywood movie with Isaac Stern as Ysaÿe.[711] Stalin's death the same year, and the Cold War thaw that followed, cleared the way for Russian artists Hurok had wanted to bring to the United States since at least 1930. Violinists had practically been lost from view in the middle of his career. The best and brightest, among them three generations of Russian-Jewish violinists from Russia, America, and Israel, returned in battalion strength for the finale. Well into his seventies, Hurok was still active: sixty Hurok artists and ensembles performed in two thousand concerts for five million audience members. Even his death at eighty-five had its showmanly flair after he was struck down by a heart attack between lunch with the great guitarist Andrés Segovia and a meeting with David Rockefeller, CEO of the Chase National Bank. Carnegie Hall was nearly filled for his memorial service. Isaac Stern played solo Bach.[712]

In a world where impresarios had long since become CEOs, there was no real successor. As Hurok's biographer noted, his constituency was vanishing, too. The immigrant audience of his own generation not only aspired to the art and artists he brought them; they understood them as popular, even glamorous entertainers, available at popular prices. But this was becoming ever less true for their Americanized, increasingly suburban children, who went to the movies, wanted to see Broadway musicals, and watched TV, as elite and popular entertainment drifted apart.

A number of factors soon shrank profit margins and transformed the economics of concertgoing: unionization, the cost of continental and intercontinental air travel, the rental fees that supported the shiny new performing arts centers, and the attendant expenses of an evening in town all played a part. As Hurok's lower-middle-class audience gave way to an upper-middle-class audience, campus performing arts centers became surrogates for the big city concert hall, where resourceful managers like Wallace Chappell balanced gourmet tastes for orchestras, ballet companies, and string quartets with reliable crowd-pleasers like road show productions of *Grease* and *Cats*.[713]

Major structural changes went back to the Depression years, when retrenchment, the potential synergies of radio and records, and the potential economies of scale of a nationwide network of local audiences gave birth to two corporate giants. NBC Artists Bureau and Columbia Concerts Corporation seemed as similar as eggs to all but those who worked for them. But they were as different from Wolff and Hurok as Alfred Sloan's many-headed General Motors was different from Henry Ford's family-held Ford Motors. Between them, they controlled 80 percent of the concert trade. Hurok was a real person with his own brand identity: "S. HUROK PRESENTS" was understood to mean color, fun, and flair. It would not have occurred to anyone to associate Columbia's Arthur Judson or his successor, Ronald Wilford, with flair or fun.

A native of southern Ohio with a remarkable résumé, Judson had studied violin in New York, edited *Musical America*, a premier trade journal, and managed orchestras in Philadelphia, New York, and Cincinnati. Over half a century, he parlayed his experience into a major concert agency associated with a major record producer. He was present at both the creation of the Columbia Broadcasting System and the acquisition of Civic Concerts, the musical equivalent of a restaurant chain. At its peak, Civic Concerts split a market of as many as two thousand towns with its competitor-twin at the National Broadcasting Company. Artists' frustration with restrictive programs, compounded by concern about restrictive practices at the Department of Justice and Federal Communications Commission, led to separation of the networks from their concert agencies in the 1940s. The principle remained. Judson conductors of Judson orchestras hired Judson soloists to record for Columbia Records, and between them, the two concert agencies still dominated the market.

Wilford, the Salt Lake City native who was his chosen successor, neither played nor even read music. But, as one commentator noted, he "plays the classical music business like a Stradivarius."[714] At the dawn of the twenty-first century, his company listed as many as eight hundred singers, three hundred instrumentalists, nine stage directors, four choreographers, and three composers in an empire that also included the Ballet Folklórico de Mexico, the Pipes, Drums and Band of the Scots Guards, the National Acrobats of the People's Republic of China, the Sound of Christmas, and thirty-four orchestras.[715] But a collection of at least a hundred jet-propelled conductors whose job prerogatives and multiple guest appearances conferred godlike authority over soloists' careers was widely regarded as the source of his comparative advantage.

There was meaningful competition from the classical music division of International Creative Management (ICM), a hypertrophically diversified agency with offices in Los Angeles, London, and New York, a large presence in Hollywood, plus a major stake in publishing, television, and popular music. Sheldon Gold, the division's creator and the closest thing to an indirect Hurok heir, was Stern's close friend as well as his manager. His successor, Lee Lamont, who had been Stern's secretary, inherited Perlman and acquired Midori. The first challenge was followed by a second from International Management Group (IMG). The corporate giant was created by Mark McCormack, a Chicago-born lawyer and accomplished amateur golfer, to represent golfers, tennis players, skiers, and motor racers. A golf-course meeting with the soprano Kiri Te Kanawa in 1978 then led McCormack to music. "I decided that there was a tremendous parallel," he told Norman Lebrecht, the British music writer. Both artists and athletes performed without concern for language. Both had cause to think about taxes and money as they progressed from country to country.[716] McCormack conceded that music left him unmoved, but he found its impact compellingly interesting. Two years later, he signed Perlman, and IMG Artists was en route to a global presence in all respects but profit. Unlike McCormack, who died in 2003, his successor, Barrett Wissman, both liked and knew something about music. He was a serious amateur pianist, married to a Russian cellist. He was a board member of the Dallas Symphony, cofounder of music festivals in California, Italy, and Singapore.

As a Dallas hedge fund manager, he also had money. Within months of McCormack's death, he acquired IMG Artists.[717] Three years later, he was reported to be within handshake distance of acquiring the concert division of ICM. The deal failed, but Wissman's company flourished without it, as did its clients, whose soaring fees pushed all other costs upward.[718]

By 2008, Wissman was producing an arts festival in Abu Dhabi and considering moving into offices there and in Dubai. "If we can connect a corporate sponsor with a great art event, why shouldn't we make money by doing so?" he told an interviewer.[719] A year later, when he pleaded guilty to securities fraud and agreed to $12 million in penalties and forfeitures, it appeared that he had connected a corporate sponsor to an art event. The corporate sponsor was an investment firm he co-owned with the very, very rich Hunt brothers, and the art event was "Chooch," a low-budget comic film involving Mexican prostitutes and a nine-pound dachshund. Its producer was the brother of the chief investment officer of the New York state comptroller's office. The International Arts Managers Association expressed "sadness and concern" for IMG, while pointing out that Wissman had acted as an investor and executive, not as an agent or artist manager. Wissman resigned his board chairmanship.[720] Perlman and fourteen fellow violinists, among them Joshua Bell, Hilary Hahn, and Sarah Chang, nonetheless stayed with IMG.

Given the nature of the relationship, both performers and managers were likely to have their repertory of stories. Joseph Szigeti remembered Norbert Dunkl, who looked after Jan Kubelik, the early twentieth-century virtuoso, and Alexander Gross, who looked after the prodigious von Vecsey, for their common habit of getting themselves photographed with their young clients, looking both reverent and proprietary. There was also the manager who peddled jewelry in coffeehouses when not producing Central European summer concerts. Henri Temianka recalled the Columbia Artists Management, Inc. (CAMI) executive who left to sell Reddi-Wip.[721]

On occasion, a manager could work wonders or at least try. Walter Homburger, a German-Jewish emigrant to Canada, was so good that you practically felt guilty when you said no, Elmar Weingarten, manager of the Berlin Philharmonic, told a visitor admiringly. There were also cases in which a young player was grateful for a manager who did anything at all. William Primrose, who began as a violinist in the 1920s before becoming the era's premier violist, recalled how the fewest of British agents considered promoting their clients part of their job.[722] Instead, the aspiring performer bought space among the next week's concert ads in the weekend paper, hoping that a reader out there might be interested enough to approach his or her agent.

A decade or so later, the young Ida Haendel had it good by comparison. Still a Polish citizen a year after she won a prize at the first Wieniawski competition, she played a five-minute audition for Harold Holt, at the time Britain's best-connected and most influential manager. It was all she needed. Holt offered a three-year contract committing her to "fulfill all the engagements which I offer" and saw to a good-sized audience for her debut. When Haendel and her family moved to Britain, a move that would save their lives, and the Polish government canceled the grant the family lived on, Holt pitched in with a monthly subsidy of £50. But true to the terms of the contract, he also booked his little whiz kid wherever possible, including a music hall in which she shared a bill with "conjurors, crooners, acrobats and funny-men." Haendel was still indignant some thirty years later. When her father protested, Holt rewrote the contract, stipulating a commission of 15 rather than the usual 10 percent, to cover his previous advances. He also negotiated her first record contract and arranged three appearances at London's summer Prom Concerts.[723]

Though few conservatory grads were likely to read Paul Samuelson, let alone Adam Smith, their real-life MBA program—Music Business Administration—inevitably introduced them to two basic concepts. The first—that it's a buyer's market, with the manager as buyer and themselves as sellers—was a challenge almost all of them faced. In theory, of course, they could try managing themselves; but that was easier said than done. "An artist without a manager has the status of an unwed mother,"[724] Temianka noted, in an era when traditional prejudices about single parenthood still prevailed. The second concept was comparative advantage, the indeterminate something needed to distinguish a soloist from a crowd of similarly gifted peers in the winner-take-all market he or she increasingly shared with actors, athletes, academics, entertainers, executives, columnists, novelists, and celebrity chefs.

Writing in the mid-1950s, an era recalled a half century later as a golden age of American concertgoing, Artur Holde, a German-Jewish immigrant, began with the good news. As music faculties grew, jobs opened up. As campus concert series flourished, chamber music boomed and programming got more serious. For the successful soloist, a strenuous life paid off with a decent living. But travel expenses and managerial commissions weighed like an anvil on players the next tier down. The threshold of success was an annual gross of $12,000–$15,000, which required thirty concerts or more at $400–$500 each. This, in turn, presupposed a successful concert in New York where the hall alone cost $1,200–$2,400, a full-page ad in *Musical America* cost $600, and success stood or fell on the next morning's review in one or more of the city's six surviving papers. The young player might then be picked up by one of the two national mega-managements and packaged in a series marketed annually to some 1,500 community subscribers.[725]

An assured season's work for the performer, the series was also a meal ticket for the manager and a good deal for subscribers, who enjoyed a potential world-class product at minimal expense. But it was the performer—who paid a commission to the series management, a second commission to the parent company, and the pianist's fee, plus travel expenses for both of them—who played the weakest hand. What was left before taxes could be as little as 30 percent of the nominal concert fee. With lots of available talent, management had little incentive to skip the second commission by finding local talent in Chicago or New York. Unsurprisingly, the dropout rate was considerable. The socialist alternative was hardly more attractive. Under capitalism, went the standard East German joke, man exploits man. Under socialism, it's the other way around. In fact, this was true. One of the few East German stars allowed to perform in West Germany, the Tchaikovsky Prize–winning pianist Peter Rösel, was paid in West German hard currency. But 12.5 percent of his earnings went directly to the East German state agency, and 50 percent was paid out in East German soft currency, an effective depreciation of 75 percent.[726]

Yet even as the Soviet bloc sank, Community Concerts, with a history reaching back to 1927, was also headed for the rocks. In 2003, artists sued, e-mailed, and looked hopefully to the Manhattan district attorney's office for help with an estimated $1.5 million in back fees. Subscribers declared their independence. Where once an imperial Arthur Judson looked out on a continental empire, a former interior designer, daughter of a Florida real estate developer, did her best to explain a stack of bouncing checks. As Wilford was quick to point out, she even owed money to CAMI.[727]

Where Community Concerts went, recording followed. By coincidence, Edison's pioneer phonograph was an almost direct contemporary of the Wolff agency. Progress remained incremental for about a generation. But a quick sequence of breakthroughs at the beginning of the twentieth century made the crucial difference between an office machine and a home entertainment machine. Founded in 1901, the Victor Talking Machine Company replaced Edison's cylinders with discs that allowed recordings of first three, then five minutes. Five years later, Victrola turned the machine into a respectable piece of furniture, its brand name into a synonym for the phonograph, and the middle-class living room into a little concert hall.[728] Sarasate, Joachim, and Ysaÿe, persuaded to play into a conical horn at the ages of sixty, seventy-three, and a relatively youthful fifty-four, respectively, were now on record for the ages. In 1904, Powell joined Victor, where her sales were second only to the great tenor Enrico Caruso's. In 1907, Kreisler and the thirteen-year-old Elman joined the party.[729]

Powell fans regularly asked her for live performance of pieces they had first heard on record, her manager-spouse reported happily. In 1917, she went so far as to play seventeen of her greatest hits at Carnegie Hall, after asking members of the public to choose from a menu of forty-five.[730] Kreisler conceded that he had worried that records would cut into his concert audience, but his wife had got it right, he added, and while authoritative figures were unavailable, one source estimated that a Kreisler record had at least once outsold a Caruso.

Within two weeks of his legendary New York debut, Heifetz, too, was in Victor's studio, where he remained for most of his career. By 1972, when he played his last public performance, Heifetz had recorded enough music to fill sixty-five CDs, the only technological advance he missed over a career extending from acoustical recording to the stereo LP. A final contract, signed in 1953, guaranteed royalties beginning at $22,500 and rising by $5,000 increments annually for the next ten years. By the end of the decade, he had earned a guaranteed total of $495,000 against sales of $308,694 from a company willing to accept the losses just to keep him under exclusive contract. The company then bought him out.[731]

With the coming of the CD a generation later, the latest in a series of technological breakthroughs reaching back to Edison, a burst of corporate enterprise and a generation of new recordings lifted sales of classical titles to a 10 percent market share. But the CD wave had already crested by 1994, when the Heifetz Collection came on the market. For the baby boom generation and younger, the age of the LP, let alone the Victrola, was already as remote as tail fins and Prohibition.

By 2002, the industry-wide sale of classical records was down to about

3 percent and stayed that way. There were unlikely exceptions, such as Nigel Kennedy's *Four Seasons*, which sold over two million copies, and Takako Nishizaki's *Four Seasons*, which sold at least a million and a half.[732] A phenomenon unto itself, Nishizaki's recording of Chen Gang's and He Zhanhao's co-composed *Butterfly Lover's Concerto* sold over three million copies. In comparison, the Emerson Quartet was delighted when its recording of Bach's *Art of the Fugue* sold sixty thousand copies. Yet even with the wind in her sails from a recent appearance on a popular late-night TV show, sale of a thousand CDs was enough to carry Hilary Hahn to the top of *Billboard* magazine's weekly classical chart; sales of two to three hundred was the more usual chart topper.[733]

The crossover market, which had a history going back to Elman's parlor favorites and even Paganini's animal noises, was now relocated in albums that brought the Singapore-born, Anglo-Chinese Vanessa-Mae Nicholson a fortune estimated at £32 million in 2006.[734] Speculating on the niche market the same year, Ruth Palmer, a graduate of London's Royal College and Royal Academy, approached an investment bank, a hedge fund, and private patrons for the £30,000 she needed to hire the Philharmonia Orchestra, recruit a classmate to conduct, rent a hall, and record Shostakovich's first violin concerto on a do-it-yourself label. Over-the-counter sales of around six hundred in Britain were conventionally considered modest. But her recording beat seven competitors for media attention, brought her a Philharmonia engagement, and led to an Asian tour.[735]

Klaus Heymann, the very model of a postmodern record executive, was an expatriate German college dropout based in Hong Kong and New Zealand. His Japanese wife, Nishizaki, was China's favorite violinist. In the 1960s, he took a job selling ads and writing ad copy for *Overseas Weekly*, a tabloid beloved of American enlisted men for its pinups and stories that were not publishable in the semiofficial magazine *Stars and Stripes*. From there, he proceeded to Hong Kong, where he sold watches, cameras, and audio equipment locally and by mail order to U.S. troops in Vietnam and Thailand. He also tried his hand at concert management and pioneered what would become the Hong Kong Philharmonic. When visiting artists regretted that their records were locally unavailable, he took care of that too. Nishizaki's engagement with the Hong Kong Orchestra led to a performance of Wieniawski's second violin concerto and her marriage with Heymann. Their son's name, Henryk, memorialized the meeting.

Launched to maintain and advance his wife's career from her new home in a remotely located British crown colony, Heymann's first record label, Marco Polo, soon made her one of the most widely recorded violinists. Five years later, as big-spending companies in Europe and America inflated a CD bubble, he created a second company, Naxos. A budget label aimed at first-time listeners and second-time collectors disposed to replace their LPs with affordable CDs, it employed East Europeans who were hungry for hard currency and minimized overhead by paying performers a onetime fee with no provision for royalties. Naxos also maximized its repertory and sold globally.

"I didn't think it was a long-term business," Heymann told an interviewer twenty years later.[736] But Naxos succeeded; it spun off a catalogue of accomplished performances of steadily improving quality, many by young players willing and even happy to sacrifice royalties and accept Heymann's fee for the opportunity to record commercially and make themselves known globally. Unsurprisingly, the violin repertory was a particular favorite, extending from the long-forgotten concertos of the Chevalier de Saint-George for Nishizaki and the long-neglected concerto of Samuel Barber to circus pieces by the Spohr protégé Léon de Saint-Lubin and the Russian serf virtuoso Ivan Khandoshkin. As copyrights lapsed, Naxos offered a historical series with expertly remastered performances by Powell, the young Heifetz, the young Menuhin, Kreisler, and Huberman, all available at prices the original owners were unwilling or unable to match. The twentieth century began with expensive records and cheap concert tickets, Heymann noted with understandable satisfaction. It ended with the reverse.[737]

Much changed in the music business in the years following the CD revolution. The full-page ad in *Musical America* was now a website with videos and even free downloads. Nipper, RCA Victor's mascot, could watch his master, as well as hear his master's voice, on YouTube. From Jaime Laredo, who had moved on to conduct, play chamber music, teach, and manage the Indianapolis competition, to Sebastian Ruth, who played blues, hiphop, and string quartets while reaching out to neighborhood kids in Providence, Rhode Island, there were role models for many types of careers.

As aspiring supply grew and traditional demand declined, the race was probably more competitive than ever. It was still great to come in first. But neither players nor managers were likely to get rich on the 5,000-deutschmark jobs awaiting the second-, third-, and certainly fourth- and nth-place winners in Germany's decentralized version of Community Concerts, where nominally local concert presenters survived in much the same way that nominally local breweries and newspapers did. The minor leagues now extended to Kazakhstan and Taiwan. Yet they were still the minor leagues.

For those in search of management there was a new generation of managers, too, a majority of them women, as well as a new group of boutique agencies no one could confuse with CAMI. For IMG, diversification meant adding a short list of musicians to a roster of athletes. For Kirshbaum Demler, an Upper West Side boutique agency launched as a home industry in 1980, it meant adding a short list of singers to a short list of instrumentalists. Musicians themselves, energized as much by love as by money, the new managers delivered customized service to clients including Zukerman and the Emerson Quartet and a constituency of presenters all the way to Arizona, whose calls they always took.[738]

Daniela Wiehen, a conservatory-trained clarinetist, learned the management business at the innovative Schleswig-Holstein Festival. She then partnered with a slightly older colleague and looked for a small clientele she could get to know personally and whom she could book a year to eighteen months in advance. A half generation later, she was still in business, with clients that included one conductor, two violinists, a clarinetist, and a Dutch-Flemish tango ensemble. For advice she warmly recommended *What They Don't Teach You at Harvard Business School*, by Mark McCormack, the founder of IMG.[739]

Cornelia Schmid, who had studied at Harvard, limited her artists' list to a football squad of conductors, a basketball squad of pianists, a short list of chamber ensembles, and a handful of instrumentalists. Her six violinists included Christian Tetzlaff, one of the great players of his generation, the Latvian Queen Elisabeth winner Baiba Skride, and the Italian-German Indianapolis winner Augustin Hadelich. Summer cash flow could be a problem, as were aging superstars accustomed to super fees. She considered it part of her job to talk a promising player out from under the long shadow of a larger-than-life teacher. She was reasonably confident that people over forty, a demographic with considerable growth potential in all developed countries, would continue to go to concerts.[740]

For those in search of concerts, there was a new species of impresario, too. Neither Martijn Sanders, manager of Amsterdam's Concertgebouw, nor Clive Gillinson of New York's Carnegie Hall could be easily mistaken for the other. But they were equally representative of this emerging group.

A Rotterdam business grad with an MBA from the University of Michigan and a soft spot for jazz, Sanders had first managed a chain of movie theaters. The Concertgebouw opening turned up just as he was considering a new job. As the interview turned from music to capital improvements, it was clear to both sides that the building, home to Amsterdam's emblematic orchestra since 1888, needed to be used more effectively. Why, for example, had the likes of Isaac Stern never been heard in recital there? The answer was disarmingly simple. No one had ever invited them.

The solution was just as simple. An ad hoc committee invited Stern and others for the anniversary season. It then created a nonprofit foundation, part public, part private, to promote and manage more concerts. Stern even recycled a part of his honorarium to help the project on its way. A decade later, the foundation produced 250 concerts, about 40 percent of the hall's annual total. The problem, Sanders explained, was keeping sponsors happy, because concerts had to be booked years in advance, while tickets went on sale only weeks in advance of the concerts. A subsidy of about 33 percent was needed to cover the deficit. He estimated that about 10 percent of his job consisted of managing the hall and 90 percent was devoted to managing the foundation while keeping the sponsors happy. He was also in regular contact with some fifteen other halls—in Paris and Cologne, as well as New York's Carnegie Hall—that had embarked on a similar course.[741]

In a metropolitan area with a population up to 20 percent larger than the entire population of Holland, Carnegie Hall faced similar challenges. Only three years younger than the Concertgebouw, it survived a near-death experience in 1960 when its resident orchestra, the New York Philharmonic, migrated to the shiny new Lincoln Center. Isaac Stern, whose intervention became a civic legend, barely saved it from becoming a parking lot. Instead, like the Concertgebouw, it became what Sanders liked to call a garage, with no other purpose than to rent its space. In 1986, wholesale renovation led to acquisition of the building by the city of New York and the creation of a nonprofit Carnegie Hall Corporation, with a mandate to present concerts as well as accommodate them. By 2003, the building had acquired two smaller halls of 293 and 599 seats, respectively, to supplement the original auditorium seating of 2,804. By 2005, the foundation had built up an impressive endowment, a third of it dedicated to family-friendly, budget-priced concerts.

Unlike Sanders, Gillinson really was a musician. A longtime cellist in the player-governed London Symphony, he had saved the orchestra with a resourceful combination of consciousness raising, belt tightening, fundraising, innovative programming, and in-house recording. In 2005, Carnegie Hall invited him to repeat the magic. Of 250 concerts in the big hall in 2005, a third were house-booked, a ratio approaching Sanders's. Four years later, 200 of the 800 performances in all three halls were house-booked.[742]

For $15,600 on a Friday or Saturday night, less than a star pianist might take home in an evening, out-of-town orchestras and ensembles from around the country and the world could perform in a reconstructed hall named for the politically astute and civic-minded Stern. Younger audiences came to hear local start-ups and young, hopeful performers in affordable spaces at a historic address. An ongoing series of festivals celebrated everything from China to Leonard Bernstein. A partnership agreement with Ariama, an online affiliate of Sony Music Entertainment, offered Carnegie Hall audiences discounts and special deals, recorded performances, and conducted interviews with Carnegie Hall performers.[743] The Academy, a Juilliard–Carnegie Hall joint venture, generated its first batches of role model–teacher-performers like Nathan Schram, 23, an Indiana-trained violist, dispatched to help with a violin program at an inner city public school in Brooklyn, while polishing his performing skills three days a week at Juilliard.[744]

BUT EVEN AS the future of the violinist's art depended more than ever on faith, philanthropy, and an effective business model, politics also mattered, as it always had. Still haunted by childhood memories, the German publicist Klaus Harpprecht recalled a time when even Haydn and Beethoven were fitted out in Nazi brown. "Let no one say that music and politics are worlds apart," he warned, just in case anyone was still—or again—inclined to view them that way.[745]

Over much of the fearful decade from 1966 to 1976, China's educated middle class, violinists included, were harassed, persecuted, and literally humiliated to death. But there was still a market for musicians to help the country "sing and dance down the voluntarist road to revolution." A kind of Chinese Soldier Švejk, born in 1949, Xiao Tiquin made his way from the Guangzhou Conservatory middle school to the Red Guard. As early as 1968, the demand for violinists had reached such a point that Xiao's bourgeois talent connected him to a musical propaganda team of thirty that toured Hainan prefecture for four years, playing Chinafied folk music on Western instruments. He returned illegally to Guangzhou as a private teacher with a clientele that included both the children of intellectuals and of ranking party officials.[746] In 2008, a generation after Chinese tanks cleared Tiananmen Square in full view of the world, the *New Yorker*'s Alex Ross visited a very different People's Republic, where the conservatories, like the economy, were booming. While toleration for dissidence was minimal as ever, Ross reported, musicians were now encouraged to win prizes, make good, and make money. They were also encouraged, like generations before them, to practice self-censorship as well as to practice, practice, practice.[747]

From its conception as a string quartet in 1939 in the ancient capital of a fortuitous post-Ottoman colonial protectorate, the Iraqi National Orchestra was a metaphor for much of the Middle East. Its emergence as a full orchestra coincided with a nationalist military coup in 1958, bloody even by regional standards, With its Sunni and Shi'ite Muslims, Christians and Kurds, the orchestra was as close as Iraq came to a spontaneous national body, with members working together and playing both standard repertory and local music in harmony. In 1966, it was disbanded for two years by a populist anti-Western government. Over its first half century, its wages and numbers rose and fell like the tides in the Bay of Fundy as war and international sanctions battered the economy and a medley of war, civil war, Islamist fervor, and anarchy caused players to run for cover or foreign asylum. In 2003, when an American invasion gave birth to a paternalistic and incompetent occupation regime, the U.S. State Department brought the orchestra to Washington to perform at the Kennedy Center with President George W. Bush and top administration officials in attendance. Five years later, as Iraq emerged from bloody chaos, the orchestra appeared in Sulaimaniya in Iraq's Kurdish north with scheduled concerts in the Shi'ite clerical hot spots Karbala and Najaf. "There's no indecent music," its conductor explained hopefully.[748]

Was this true? Robert Fisk, the Beirut-based old Middle East hand and a correspondent for the *Independent*, recalled how Ayatollah Khomeini, the father of Iran's Islamic Republic, had banned Haydn and Mozart. A onetime violinist himself, Fisk wondered how the traditional ensemble of violinist and drummer he subsidized with a few rials on a Tehran street in 2009 was viewed by the Revolutionary Guard. Assiduous Saudi students were known to beat up music-fan classmates, and there were reportedly sheikhs who encouraged their followers to burn instruments, Fisk noted. In Lebanon, the ex officio music monitor was the Ministry of Defense. Of the issues raised by Muslim Brotherhood parliamentarians in the Egyptian Assembly between 2000 and 2005, 80 percent addressed media and culture. By 2006, it was estimated that 80 percent of Iraq's professional singers had left. The same year, National Orchestra membership fell to forty-three, and as few as seventeen players showed up for rehearsals. At first, Fisk's young men dodged the question. They made a living, they told him. But as they went their separate ways, they conceded that the Revolutionary Guards sometimes stopped them and broke their instruments.[749]

Little of this was unique. Every epoch had its style. Direct or indirect, supportive or oppressive, the link between the violinist and politics was virtually as old as the instrument. Church and state bought instruments and hired players; careers depended on their support. What seemed sensible career moves in the last years of the ancien régime cost Viotti his livelihood and nearly cost him his life a few years later. The Paris conservatory was music's answer to the new Napoleonic military academies, Saint-Cyr and the Polytechnique. Paganini discovered and pioneered the private sector only after decades of playing to and for the titled great and good. As concertmaster in Weimar and Hanover and tenured professor in Berlin, Joachim spent most of his working life employed in the public sector. By the time he died, conservatory buildings were as emblematic of time and place as train stations and parliament buildings, and royalty showed up at their dedications. Even private foundations like the Concerts Lamoureux and the Berlin Philharmonic ended up becoming public charges.

Yet even as national identity displaced dynastic loyalty, the Prussian bureaucracy displayed a liberality unexpected in Germany and unimaginable in France when it hired Henri Marteau, 34, son of a French industrialist and a Paris Conservatory graduate, to succeed Joachim.[750] Local papers groused discreetly about hiring a Frenchman but awarded him benefit-of-the-doubt points for his German mother.

All this changed in 1914 when the Austrian Kreisler and French Thibaud were called up as reserve officers by their respective armies and the Belgian Ysaÿe took off for London. "Musicians may well doubt the sanity of a world in which Kreisler is in arms against Ysaÿe and Thibaud," the English critic Ernest Newman noted sadly in the *Musical Times*.[751] With a German wife, a German job, but also a French reserve commission and French passport, Marteau was immediately interned as an enemy alien.

Hermann Kretzschmar, the conservatory's director, managed to get him released so he could at least teach privately at home. But his colleagues not only rebelled at the idea of further collegiality; they were incensed that an enemy alien remained at his job in Berlin rather than meeting his obligations as a French reserve officer. In March 1915, there was a settlement: Marteau's contract was allowed to lapse a half year later, and he was allowed to leave for neutral Sweden.[752]

Kreisler, who met his obligations as an Austrian reserve officer, was wounded on the Eastern Front, hospitalized, reported dead, and demobilized, all between August and December 1914. He returned to the United States, dedicated a little book on his war experience "to my dear wife," an American,[753] and resumed normal life with benefit remittances arriving at his home till April 1917, when America entered the war.

In November, he again came under fire, but this time in Pittsburgh, where the city's director of public safety found cause to cancel his scheduled concert after demonstrators, including the local chapter of the Daughters of the American Revolution, accused him of aiding and supporting an Austrian enemy with which the United States was not yet at war. The *New York Times* published Kreisler's reply with an editorial declaration of support. Two days later, a Brooklyn minister charged in his Sunday sermon that Kreisler had traded U.S. concert fees for discharge from active service, then rerouted the money to the Austrian war effort. Kreisler demanded retraction or that the minister allow him "the opportunity to confront him as man to man." He canceled the rest of his tour. Despite a bit of fuss from the American Legion, by late 1919 Kreisler resumed playing benefit concerts.[754]

Few performers spelled out the distance between prewar and postwar routine as colorfully and comprehensively as did Eduard Soermus. An Estonian Bolshevik whose career began in his student days around 1900, he would eventually tour Europe under Comintern and local party management, and live for some years in Germany and England, where the police were among his most reliable audience. In 1928, he reportedly played an estimated two hundred benefit concerts and lecture-recitals. In Leningrad, where he reportedly played at the Conservatory when it was awash in revolutionary fervor,[755] local music lovers acknowledged his performances with what his biographer calls "delicate reserve." In the early thirties, with revolutionary fervor past and traditional musical values again ascendant, he was not invited to play at the Conservatory in Moscow.

Even his biographer seemed at a loss to explain where and how he had learned to play. His first teacher was apparently an itinerant tailor. There were hints that he had talked Auer into a few lessons pro bono while a student in St. Petersburg. When he was in his thirties, grateful Dutch workers supposedly took up a collection so he could study with Marteau and Capet in Paris. But even V. A. Lunacharsky, the infant Soviet Union's first Commissar of Enlightenment, an educated man who took his job seriously, noted that Soermus played like an autodidact.

Though Soermus took on heavy-duty repertory and reportedly played the Mendelssohn concerto, a police report of a performance in 1926 at a working-class bar in Rudolstadt, a little town in central Germany, is probably a reliable review of Soermus in action. The program included Bach, Handel, Beethoven, and Paganini. But first there was an introduction. Bach was a role model who would guide the working class to victory, Soermus explained. Handel's Largo represented longing for the peace that mankind had waited two thousand years for, but only work could bring it about. Beethoven, he claimed, a guiding star and the greatest man who ever lived, died in abject poverty. After a Russian song dedicated to fallen comrades, there was an appeal for contributions to a charitable fund for children. Schubert's setting of Goethe's "Heidenröslein" was an encore.

If his musical training was vague, his political development was clear enough. What began as nationalism soon morphed into class consciousness. He discovered Marxism while still a schoolboy, was at least a spectator and possibly an accessory to the Russian Revolution of 1905, and reportedly met Lenin in London. "What should I do, Comrade Lenin?" his biographer quotes him. "I'm a Bolshevik, but I love the violin." It was all right to be a violinist, Lenin replied, provided he was a Bolshevik violinist. After years in Britain, Soermus returned to the Soviet Union in time for the Stalinist purges. He was evicted from the Metropol Hotel, now a precarious home for Soviet party officials and frequently terrified nomenklatura-in-exile, and died of leukemia soon after the Soviet Union annexed his native Estonia. His fellow Estonians named a school, a conservatory scholarship, and a fishing trawler after him. A half century later, a few streets named in his memory still survived in what was once East Germany.[756]

Save for Google entries[757] and a substantial paper trail, there are no known monuments to Gustav Havemann. But his career, extending over nearly sixty years and three German regimes, was every bit as emblematic of time and place. A Joachim protégé born in 1882, he was concertmaster in Thomas Mann's hometown, Lübeck, at nineteen, and in Hamburg before he was thirty. When war came, he volunteered, but, at the request of the King of Saxony, he was discharged as a corporal to serve as concertmaster of the State Opera in Dresden.

Twenty years after leaving Joachim's studio, he returned to Berlin, now capital of an unloved postwar republic, to join the faculty of a conservatory with a large Jewish constituency, a gravitational pull felt all the way to Japan, and a firm determination to reinvent itself as the postwar world's most progressive music academy. Years later, it was recalled, and not in his favor, that Havemann was affiliated with the November Group, an association of artists the Nazis loved to hate. As conservatory faculty pitched into repertory that the Nazis would happily declare degenerate a decade later, Havemann played Arnold Schoenberg and Paul Hindemith. Both were among the most modern of modern composers. They were also colleagues. He even signed on for an experiment in quarter tones.

With unemployment approaching 25 percent and the Nazi vote close behind, his career took an unanticipated turn. In November 1931, his colleague Carl Flesch sent him some recently published thoughts on the technical challenges of violin tone production. With twenty years of teaching experience in Berlin and Bucharest and at Curtis, Flesch speculated that the characteristically big tone associated with East European Jewish players might be linked to cultural reminiscences of the synagogue. Havemann acknowledged receipt with an open letter in the *Allgemeine Musikzeitschrift*. To let his colleague's celebration of Jewish violin tone go unanswered, he declared, was to compromise the virtues of German violin tone.

Flesch tried hard to be both rational and civil toward a man who had the stuff, as he later recalled in his memoirs, to be a significant violinist.[758] Tone was only a means to an end, he insisted. The teacher's job was to make sure it matched the composer's intentions. East Europeans were known to overdo vibrato, but there was nothing particularly "Jewish" about it. As Havemann should know firsthand, he added, there was nothing "Jewish" about Joachim's tone. A few weeks of shadowboxing ended with a figleaf statement declaring that Flesch and Havemann saw eye to eye on art and pedagogy, that they would continue to devote their entire energies to the service of German art and youth, and that their personal relationship was as cordial as ever.[759]

Barely a year later, in January 1933, Hitler was appointed chancellor. In

February, civil liberties were suspended. In March, the questionable results of a dubious election were declared a mandate. In April, a government that now ruled by executive order issued a Law for the Restoration of the Professional Civil Service that cost an estimated 2,500 Jews their public sector jobs, including positions in orchestras and conservatories.

A few months later, a new directive invited foreign artists to perform in Germany, regardless of race or nationality. Eager to put it to use and to bring back "one of few soloists, who could fill the Philharmonie with a solo recital several times in the course of a season,"[760] Furtwängler fired off a newspaper clipping to Huberman in Vienna, begging him to appear with the Philharmonic as he had for decades. Huberman, who characterized himself as "[a] Pole, a Jew, an independent artist and a pan-European," said no. So long as no one had been reinstated and Jewish performers were defined as pariahs incapable of understanding "pure German music," his appearance could only serve as an argument that everything was fine, when it obviously wasn't.[761]

Three years later, Huberman had raised enough money in Europe and America to audition and recruit a Palestine Symphony Orchestra of seventy-one refugee players, which would later become the Israel Philharmonic. He persuaded Arturo Toscanini, a non-Jewish Italian and outspoken antifascist, to conduct its first concerts, and Adolf Busch, a non-Jewish German and outspoken anti-Nazi, to play the Brahms concerto as the orchestra's first soloist.[762]

Havemann had meanwhile "realized as early as 1929 that successive republican governments were leading Germany over the cliff, and that Jewish influence was ruining German culture." In 1930, he informed Georg Schünemann, the deputy and de facto director of the conservatory, that he intended to vote Nazi. Remarkably, just months after his skirmish with Flesch, he turned over a portrait etching of Joachim to the conservatory, with the request that it be hung in his studio. He also recruited a Nazi musicians' guild, organized its members into an orchestra, and paid them out of his own pocket. In 1933, with the Nazis in charge of the country, he met no resistance as he took charge of the conservatory and purged the faculty after the composer Franz Schreker and the resourceful and long-suffering Schünemann were fired.

The new director expressed discreet concern about the time Havemann spent away from the studio on party business. Ironically, the problem was resolved in 1935 when Havemann's support for Hindemith got him in trouble with Goebbels, and cost him his party offices. Apart from damaged vanity, there were no further consequences. For the remainder of the war, he toured occupied Europe, performing for the troops.

There were inevitably a few uncomfortable years after the war, when he apparently lived from private lessons. Fortune smiled again as he approached the age of seventy. In need of a high-profile professor for their new conservatory in East Berlin, the freshly installed Communist regime not only hired him, they threw in a comfortable salary in hard currency, a generous benefit package, plenty of leave time, a supplement for guest lecturers, and a car and driver.[763]

"Intermission chat with Furtwängler," Goebbels noted in his diary in July 1937, still giddy from a Bayreuth performance of *Siegfried*. Furtwängler wanted more serious music on the radio. No problem, Goebbels assured him.[764] A few months later, in the presence of Hitler, senior party officials, members of the diplomatic corps, and selected luminaries from the arts and sciences, Goebbels pointed with pride to the disappearance of nearly three thousand Jews from German stages and concert halls since 1933.[765]

The occasion, the fourth annual meeting of the Reich Chamber of Culture, the arts division of the propaganda ministry, was also notable for the premiere performance of Robert Schumann's violin concerto eighty-four years after its composition. Though a lapdog press hailed its "glorious romanticism," the piece would soon settle into sleeping princess mode, awaiting the occasional Henryk Szeryng or Gidon Kremer to wake it briefly to life.

But the story was only incidentally about music. The concerto's nominal rediscovery attracted media attention reminiscent of the world championship bout between the African-American heavyweight Joe Louis and the German Max Schmeling. In fact, as Olin Downes was at pains to spell out in the *New York Times*, its existence had never been a secret.[766] Schumann composed it for the young Joachim and referred to it in his diary. Joachim referred to it in his correspondence. Moser referred to it in his Joachim biography. Arthur Abell, longtime Berlin correspondent for *Musical America*, recalled talking about it with Brahms and the composer Max Bruch. But for Schumann's breakdown, he and Joachim would presumably have revised it together. With the composer beyond reach, his widow and Joachim found it best to leave it on the shelf. After Joachim's death, it was sold to the Prussian State Library with a stipulation that it not be published or performed till the centennial of the composer's death in 1956. In the early 1920s, Busch, the greatest German player of the era, looked up the score at the request of Schumann's daughter, Eugenie, and concluded that Joachim was right.[767]

That might have been the end of the story, but for the composer's reported intervention from the beyond. In 1933, Jelly d'Arányi reported after a London séance also attended by her sister that the composer's spirit had told her—in curiously bad German, Downes was quick to point out—to locate and perform his forgotten concerto. From there, according to Baron Erik Palmstierna, the Swedish minister to London and another enthusiastic spiritualist,[768] one spirit message led to another till the search ended up at the Prussian State Library, where Schünemann, once the conservatory's de facto CEO, was in quasi-exile as music librarian.

Schünemann showed the material to Wilhelm Strecker, a director at Schott, the Mainz music publisher. Strecker sent Menuhin a photocopy and asked for his opinion. Menuhin was aglow with enthusiasm. Declaring it the "missing link" between the Beethoven and Brahms concertos,[769] he wanted to premiere it. Strecker persuaded the heirs to abrogate the will, and a date was set. Upset at being ignored, d'Arányi appealed to Prime Minister Neville Chamberlain, who dutifully replied that the Foreign Office would approach the authorities in Berlin.[770] Meanwhile, she consulted Schumann's spirit on the appropriate performance practice and played through the score with Sir Donald Tovey, a friend of her great-uncle, as well as the era's star musicologist.[771]

But there could be little doubt who would win the race. The copyright was firmly in German hands and much of the music scene was firmly in Goebbels's hands. Nazi hopes for a suitably German alternative to Mendelssohn were in full bloom. The alternative contenders were Menuhin, a Jewish violinist, Pierre Monteux, a Jewish conductor, and d'Arányi, a Joachim descendant as the alternative contenders. The Berlin Philharmonic was Goebbels's orchestra. The Reich Chamber of Culture was his baby. Its annual meeting was his party. Georg Kulenkampff, the last internationally significant player still living and working in Germany, was already the designated soloist, the Berlin Philharmonic the designated orchestra, and Karl Böhm the designated conductor. What was not announced publicly was Kulenkampff's collaboration with Hindemith on revisions to the score or his ongoing contact with Flesch, another conservatory colleague, now in London exile. "How happy Schumann would have been with the changes for which he had vainly asked Joachim several times," Kulenkampff wrote Flesch.[772]

Happy or otherwise, Schumann got his premiere on November 26. It was broadcast internationally on shortwave. Menuhin got up early to tune in. In December, he performed the unedited score at Carnegie Hall in piano reduction and later that month with orchestra in St. Louis. There is not a word about any of this in the final version of Menuhin's memoirs. It was February 1938 before d'Arányi got her turn.

Between them, Havemann, Busch, and Kulenkampff personified the German scene. Havemann, a sincere and forthright Nazi, was a clear case. Busch, a sincere and forthright anti-Nazi who laid one of the era's most distinguished careers on the line as early as March 1933 and who declined to play again in his native country until the Nazis were gone and even refused to accept letters signed "Heil Hitler!," was a clear case too. He nonetheless conceded Havemann a few points for standing up for his sympathies before they seemed likely to pay off, unlike the armies of opportunists who discovered their inner Nazi only after 1933.[773]

Kulenkampff was neither a Nazi nor an anti-Nazi. The same was true of Gerhard Taschner, Furtwängler's concertmaster. But the differences mattered too. Like Kulenkampff's, Taschner's career flourished during the war years. Like Furtwängler, he was on the propaganda ministry's "Grace of God" list, which shielded high-profile artists from the draft. He was also a thoroughly unpolitical foreign national, a Sudeten German, barely out of school, and only sixteen in 1938, when his mother hauled him back from Boston, where his teacher, Adolf Bak, had presciently returned from Vienna to be concertmaster. He was only seventeen when Germany annexed Bohemia-Moravia, where he was concertmaster of the orchestra in Brünn (Brno); only nineteen when appointed concertmaster of the Berlin Philharmonic. He was not known to have joined anything. He never spoke ill of a succession of Jewish teachers, including Hubay, Huberman, and Bak. He continued to play Kreisler's cadenzas to the Beethoven and Brahms concertos, although they were on the propaganda ministry's no-play index.[774]

Kulenkampff, on the other hand, born in 1898, was an established artist by the time the Nazis came to power. Conservatory administrators in Berlin had already begun turning cartwheels to accommodate his salary and teaching load to his concert schedule when they engaged him as an adjunct in 1923, a year when his salary, 640,000 marks in July, had risen to 1,280,000 in October before reversion to 192 marks after the introduction of the new currency in December.[775]

Why only twelve hours of teaching, the ministry asked in early 1932? The negotiations were hard enough as it was, Schünemann replied. Kulenkampff was among the most popular artists on the current scene, at home or abroad. A year later, with Flesch, Kreisler, Busch, Morini, Huberman, and Goldberg gone and the country off-limits to the likes of Elman, Hei-fetz, Milstein, Menuhin, Szigeti, and Thibaud, he could effectively write his own ticket. He continued to play Joachim's cadenzas. In 1935, he played the Mendelssohn concerto in Berlin and threatened to emigrate when the propaganda ministry disapproved.[776] Like everyone, including Hindemith, he signed the obligatory oath to Hitler in January 1937. A few months later, he served on the jury in Brussels that awarded five of the Queen Elisabeth competition's six prizes to Soviet violinists, four of them Jews. As a gesture of appreciation, the Belgians awarded him the Officer's Cross of the Royal Order of King Leopold. This time the foreign ministry expressed concern. In 1935, the journalist Carl von Ossietzky had not been allowed to leave a concentration camp to accept the 1935 Nobel Peace Prize. Ossietzky was almost certainly, and Brussels very possibly, on the ministry's mind when it inquired of the conservatory whether the award was compatible with Kulenkampff's status. The conservatory dodged the question. Meanwhile, in a letter to the *Völkischer Beobachter*, the semi-official party paper, an indignant reader hammered Kulenkampff for being a fan of Carl Flesch, who also served on the Brussels jury, and for telling a questioner that he'd given up piano trios because the great Jewish cellist Emanuel Feuermann was no longer available.

One question, at least, was answerable. It arose a year later in connection with Kulenkampff's nomination for a professorship. The ministry of education wanted to know whether he was worth 1,250 marks a month. He rarely accepted an engagement for under 1,000 marks an evening, the conservatory replied. Concert demand had, in fact, reached such a point that Kulenkampff submitted his resignation. In the event, Hitler allowed him to accept the Belgian medal and confirmed the professorship. The new contract stipulated that he would teach ten hours a week with six months of unpaid leave in each of the next two years, which happened to be the last year of peace and the first of World War II.

By March 1943, a month after Goebbels's famous declaration of "total war," Kulenkampff was in such demand for both civilian and military purposes, he informed his employers, that there was hardly any time left to teach. Given the length of the war and the recent intensification of the war effort, there was also no one left to teach, he added.

Actually, this was not quite true. In April 1938, the ministry of education informed Kulenkampff that Karl-Heinz Lapp, 15, from a family with three children and a monthly income a fifth what Kulenkampff earned in an evening, had been awarded a propaganda ministry scholarship of 150 marks a month. In May, the conservatory administration informed him that his charge had got entangled with an older girl on a recent orchestra tour of Italy and regularly cut classes. Kulenkampff filed an official report. In September, the scholarship was evidently suspended and Kulenkampff was asked to contact the young man's anxious father. Kulenkampff explained that he hadn't meant to stop the scholarship; he only warned to ensure that the young man worked harder.

A month later, Lapp signed on with what appears to have been a student quartet, dispatched to entertain the troops in occupied France and Norway. He needed the money, his father explained. In early May 1941, his son's conservatory career was declared over. A week later, a slightly mysterious letter from a major's wife in Königsberg (Kaliningrad) announced that Lapp was engaged to her daughter. The baby arrived in February 1942.

When last heard from, the new family was living on a propaganda ministry retainer. Amazingly, Lapp still managed to get a draft exemption as late as the summer of 1944. Though a request for a concert furlough between September and January 1945 was turned down, he was also granted a study leave from August to October. By this time, overwork and deteriorating health had taken Kulenkampff to Switzerland, where the Lucerne conservatory offered him the job left vacant by Flesch's death. There is no trace of Lapp in postwar directories.

An acknowledged authority on the Nazi era, Fred Prieberg, noted that all revolutionary regimes bore a family resemblance, including a common desire to put music to political use. But only the Soviet regime left a clear and lasting impact, and its political organization was neither as totalitarian as it could have been nor as totalitarian as Goebbels's Chamber of Music in Germany.[777]

That Soviet musical life managed to be terrifying, exploitative, deeply serious, and liberal, at least by Nazi standards, was an obvious paradox. The paradox had its logic in a regime that regarded its artists as an owner might regard a winning racehorse and viewed its citizens with fear, suspicion, and indifference. A society already socialized by centuries of autocracy was accustomed to living very different public and private lives. "Keeping our mouths shut was just part of life," Kremer noted in his childhood memoir. "Without anybody telling us, I knew and all kids in those days very well knew what you can only say to friends or in the family, and what you were never supposed to talk about at school."[778] Like friendship, music could matter in ways practically unimaginable in the West. Not only was it inherently meritocratic, like athletics or chess, but it was implicitly liberating. Even in the land of party infallibility and Stalinist omniscience, there was no politically correct way to play Beethoven.

In 1977, with help from friends, Dmitri Sitkovetsky pulled off a different kind of artistic success by faking mental illness so persuasively that the Soviet authorities let him leave the country.[779] Yet he was also grateful to a conservatory where there was no instant anything, and people learned to pay their dues and look to the grown-ups, know their place and work hard. Giants like the cellist Mstislav Rostropovich and the pianist Sviatoslav Richter were right down the hall. His teacher, Yuri Yankelevich, produced prizewinners with Stakhanovite consistency. Sitkovetsky recalled him as an autocrat but with the qualities of a great Mafia don who did the kind of favors that people reciprocated, put people up when they needed a place to stay, and intervened with the authorities when boys got girls in trouble. For Sitkovetsky even Moscow was exciting, a place where everyone he knew went to the theater and Shostakovich premieres and talked about them afterward. In New York, where everything was in reach, including freedom, it struck him that most of his Juilliard classmates carried on as though the city weren't there.[780]

"For us, music was the only window onto the sun," Rostropovich told an interviewer.[781] In the Soviet Union, everything was backward, his wife, the singer Galina Vishnevskaya, added in their joint memoir. "We were actors in life and human beings on stage."[782] The regime could control everything, Rostislav Dubinsky mused years later from his new home in Bloomington, Indiana. But they couldn't control the performing style of his Borodin Quartet, which played Tchaikovsky and especially Shostakovich with such intensity that it might have got them tried as anti-Soviet propagandists if performers had been supervised as closely as other artists.[783]

The paradox went back to the revolution itself, with its tangle of hope and apprehension. The conservatories and theaters were nationalized, but they remained open. There was a serious talent drain, but that still left more talent than most countries enjoyed at full strength. There was no end of disorder, violence, and chaos. But only one violinist, Karol (Carl, Charles) Gregorowicz (Grigorovich, Gregorowitsch), a superstar who had studied with Wieniawski, taught Huberman, and played first violin in the

St. Petersburg Court Quartet, was known to have come to actual harm under uncertain circumstances.[784]

Modernism, variously understood as futurism, atonalism, and all the other innovations of an experiment-happy era, fought it out with proletarianism, understood as "laboratory brigades," which were examined and graded collectively. Bach and Beethoven were declared "alien to the proletariat." Soloists, individual by definition, were abolished. Bolshevik-style affirmative action was another challenge. Of 1,751 matriculants at the former St. Petersburg, now Leningrad, Conservatory in 1922–23, thirty-three were listed as being from the working class, 333 from the peasant class, and 1,114 from bourgeois families. By 1925, 172 of 836 were working-class, and 128 were peasants. Five years later, faculty morale and traditional standards were in free fall, approaching sea level or below, and protest was a one-way ticket to dismissal. At the 1932 Warsaw piano competition, the three Soviet entrants didn't even make the final round.[785] Then came new guidelines and Stalin. Yet even then, Juri Jelagin would recall in a postwar memoir, he couldn't think of a single Moscow Conservatory professor who had been fired or arrested.

A violinist and postwar defector to the United States, Jelagin was still impressed with the professionalism of the institution where he matriculated in 1934. He was also struck by the change in the cultural weather. The coming of Stalin included the coming of technocracy. The coming of the Nazis was a reminder that traditional forms of international acceptance might still be of use to the workers' fatherland. In 1933, the Soviet Union introduced national competitions. Four years later, they had already paid off internationally in Soviet triumphs at the Wieniawski and Queen Elisabeth competitions. Success in Warsaw then paid off at home, where Oistrakh, who finished second, and Boris Goldstein, who finished fourth, returned to a medal, an apartment, and a car. The diminutive Goldstein, not yet fourteen, even had his picture taken with Stalin. Rosa Fain, an Odessan like Oistrakh, and later his assistant, remembered how the afterglow from Brussels reached all the way to their storied hometown, where the legendary Stolyarsky, who taught four of the prizewinners as well as Fain herself, was rewarded with a car, a professorship, and a medal.[786] Oistrakh's first prize in Brussels seems to have brought him a dacha.

Neighbors interviewed by the filmmaker Bruno Monsaingeon after Oistrakh's death, squabbled cheerfully over whether he owed the dacha to Queen Elisabeth or to Stalin. But there was consensus that it was right around the corner from another that had once belonged to Karl Radek, the most prominent of the seventeen Old Bolsheviks famously tried in 1937 for crimes they hadn't committed.[787] Eight years and a second world war would pass before Oistrakh was dispatched westward as far as Vienna and allowed to play abroad again in the wake of the victorious Red Army. Some of the darkest years of the Cold War would pass before he was again allowed to play in the West.

By the late 1930s, Jelagin remembered, exam standards were rigorous, objective, and intimidating. By now musicians had overtaken teachers, doctors, and even engineers as the most equal of animals, though they were still outranked by secret police, senior party officials, and the Red Army general who had not been purged. A cleaning lady might earn 100 rubles a month; a worker or teacher, 300; a good engineer, 700; an A-list orchestra player, 700–1,200; and a conservatory professor, 1,500 rubles a month.

In 1937, twenty years after the October Revolution, hundreds of thousands of people, including seventeen Old Bolsheviks and Marshal Tukhashevsky, were arrested and shot. The same year, Soviet aviators became the first to fly to North America over the North Pole, and Soviet violinists returned from Brussels with every prize but one. That November their achievements were duly noted at the annual parade in Red Square, where a first column of Moscow schoolchildren marched past with a huge blue banner reading, "We want to be aviators," followed by a second with a yellow banner reading, "We want to be violinists."[788]

Even in wartime, violinists qualified as a national resource. In 1940, the Soviets reversed Russia's defeat in 1878 and cashed in on their 1939 pact with the Germans by annexing much of eastern Romania. Not only were Stolyarsky's little charges from Odessa deployed there, Oistrakh himself was dispatched to display the sunny side of Soviet power.[789] When war came a year later, Lev Schinder, a professor at the St. Petersburg Conservatory, recalled how he and his classmates were packed into boxcars and shipped to Tashkent, where even practice rooms were rationed: from 5:00 a.m. to 9:00 a.m. for the youngest kids, from midnight to 5:00 a.m. for the bigger ones. Evacuated by ship, Fain also ended up in Uzbekistan, where she got a daily violin lesson as well as a daily bowl of soup and often fell asleep while playing past bedtime in the pit orchestra of an evacuated Jewish theater.[790]

For Jews, the return to Moscow and the first postwar competition was no victory lap. Some twenty were swept out after the first round. Dubinsky, a founding member of what would become the Borodin Quartet, was

among them. An unexpected protest from the Moscow Conservatory led to
his reinstatement, but it was clear that neither the reprieve nor the protest
would survive the second round, and a girl who joined the protest disappeared in the gulag a few years later, Dubinsky reported in his memoirs.[791]
Leonid Kogan, a first-place winner in Brussels six years later, was also a
casualty of the second round. Only Julian Sitkovetsky made it to the finals.

As the Cold War began and thousands of Russian Jews turned out to
cheer Golda Meir, the first Israeli ambassador, Stalin showed promise of
resuming where he had stopped in 1939. Dubinsky noticed that Mendelssohn's portrait vanished from the conservatory's main hall. Soon Jewish
violinists were selected to stay home when a student orchestra was selected
to play at the biennial, Communist-sponsored World Festival of Youth
and Students. Two Jewish quartets, including Dubinsky's, were left behind
when a quartet of young Russian women and a Georgian quartet were
selected to take part in an international competition in Prague. The Russian girls' victory was no surprise. The Georgians hadn't even auditioned.
"The trouble with us is that we have lost ourselves," Dubinsky's second
violinist protested. "We aren't Jews anymore, but they wouldn't allow us
to become Russians, and they never will."[792]

In 1953, Dubinsky's quartet, reconstituted with one less Jew, was told
to appear in tails and black tie and play Tchaikovsky, while Stalin's body
lay in state and crowds filed past. The quartet was understood to be filler
between one or another of at least three orchestras. Oistrakh, whose piano
trio was also summoned for the occasion, had prudently brought a pocket
chess set that he tucked unobtrusively into a score he was nominally studying, while Dubinsky called his moves in a whisper. Uncertain as to when
they were needed and apparently expected to stay, performers overnighted
as best they could. A buffet was apparently consumed early on and not
restocked. The evening of the second day, a colleague appeared with a
bottle of wine and paper cups. The evening of the third day, they were
finally allowed to go home.

Again reconstituted, the quartet would establish itself as one of the era's
emblematic ensembles, famed for its close relationship to Shostakovich. It
was even allowed to travel—first to East Germany in the mid-1950s, then
to Scandinavia and the United States in 1964, where it contended with
anti-Soviet demonstrators, and to West Germany where it was invited to
stay but didn't. Protean in its capacity to reconstitute itself, it was still
in operation sixty-five years after it was founded. By this time, thirteen

players had joined or passed through, from Rostropovich, present at the creation, who left after a few weeks, to his successor, Valentin Berlinsky, who remained with the quartet till 2007. After thirty years of bureaucratic harassment, overt exploitation, and the miseries of the domestic concert circuit, Dubinsky, the founding father, decided he'd had enough. Like Rudolf Barshai, the quartet's original violist, he emigrated in 1976. Rostropovich had left the Soviet Union two years earlier.

Oistrakh, who didn't leave, was often asked why. In the presence of strangers, reporters, and the KGB detail that typically followed him abroad, the answer was likely to be boilerplate.[793] But he could be candid with friends. "Whatever its faults, I owe this regime my life," Menuhin quoted him. "They gave me my musical upbringing and that's where I am."[794] For better or worse, this was true. It also explained how an exemplary career could at once be a role model, a cautionary tale, and a tragedy.

It was no less true that his stupendous talent would have marked him for greatness had he been born in Tasmania or Tierra del Fuego. But the odds for both success and co-optation were significantly better in Odessa. The charismatic Stolyarsky was available, affordable, and supportive, and a new regime was about to reconfigure the artist's life as a form of public employment.

The beginnings were slow—local performances; invitations to Kiev and Leningrad, where the orchestra was less than welcoming; resistance from the Moscow violin establishment to a walk-on from the provinces; on tour with itinerant concert brigades, the Soviet version of Civic Concerts; an accessory role in *Petersburg Night*, the film director Grigori Roshal's adaptation of a Dostoevsky story with music by Dmitry Kabalevsky. But a victory in the regional competition in Ukraine in 1930 and a victory in the national competition in Leningrad in 1935 resonated as they were meant to, and the Leningrad victory led to the breakthrough in Warsaw.

From then till his death in 1974, there was no question about who was the king of violinists, his friend and colleague Rostropovich told Monsaingeon. Had the Politburo mandated a commission to design an ideal Soviet violinist as it might design an aircraft, it would have been hard put to beat the real model of Oistrakh. Not only a brilliant player, he was a man one would like to have as an uncle, Sitkovetsky said.[795] For those in charge, he was a show-and-tell exhibit of how the Soviet Union pampered its artists. Even his Jewishness was a plus, intended as proof positive that the Soviet Union had overcome official anti-Semitism.[796] Arguably most remarkable of all in an economy whose only competitive manufactured export was high-tech weaponry, he was a world-class hard-currency earner.

If there was an award—People's Artist, Honored Art Worker, Stalin Order, Lenin Prize, Badge of Honor—he won it. Film or photos of him performing in white tie and tails, covered with medals like a Red Army marshal, were as representative of the society he lived in as was the line at the Lenin mausoleum. Beginning in 1953, he was also allowed to travel to the West, among the rarest of Soviet privileges, to play in London and Paris. In 1955, he made the first of eight visits to the United States, playing two Carnegie Hall concerts in three days and participating in a recording session with the Philadelphia Orchestra. In 1955, he visited Japan and wrote about the experience. In 1959, as the first Soviet artist since the Civil War to visit Spain, he wrote about that, too, remembering to mention the gratitude of Civil War orphans, who had found asylum in the Soviet Union and since returned to Spain. In 1966, he was even allowed to tour Israel. But he made no further mention of that.

That none of this came free was a fact of life that he was always aware of—and was meant to be. In 1942, he joined the party. The same year he was co-opted with some of the Soviet Union's most prominent artists and intellectuals as a member of the Jewish Anti-Fascist Committee, a kind of Bolshevik assimilationist cheering section and public relations agency.

A decade later, the philosopher Isaiah Berlin invited the Oistrakhs, father and son, to dinner in Oxford, where a minder stood behind them as they ate. "Who's your friend?" Berlin inquired. It was their secretary-tour manager, he was told. "Shouldn't we ask him to sit down?" Berlin asked. "Oh, no," Oistrakh replied. "He's much happier standing." Elman, who negotiated a bureaucratic steeplechase to invite Oistrakh to dinner in New York, looked on as his guest arrived with a KGB agent who checked behind the curtains for hidden microphones. Milstein, a classmate from their Stolyarsky days, recalled a dinner conversation in Vienna where Oistrakh explained, almost certainly with a seasoning of self-irony, that his appetite was better than Milstein's because he didn't need to make decisions about where to go next.[797]

There was nothing particularly new or unique about the political itinerary. As far back as World War I, the Berlin Philharmonic followed the flag to Allied and neutral countries. America, Britain, and Germany, as well as the Soviet Union, mobilized artists and ensembles in World War II. Historically averse to public support for the arts at home, Cold War

America deployed Louis Armstrong to Africa, the Juilliard Quartet to Frankfurt, and Isaac Stern to Iceland, the Soviet Union, and China. Like Oistrakh's in New York, debut appearances by the Boston Symphony in Moscow, the Philadelphia Orchestra in Beijing, and the New York Philharmonic in Pyongyang were both meant and understood to be elements of public policy. But they were invited to go, not ordered.

Oistrakh went where and when he was told. Even an entry-level Sovietologist could decode deployments like his performance in Vienna in 1961 coincident with the Kennedy-Khrushchev summit. An appearance at the Leipzig Fair in 1965 was a ritual celebration of Soviet–East German friendship. The parameters of what was allowed and not allowed were consistently arbitrary, inherently conflicted, and frequently disingenuous. "Did you not know, David Feodorovich, that he is a well-known Zionist?" Yekaterina Furtseva, the formidable minister of culture, demanded of Oistrakh, when the famously anti-Zionist Menuhin invited him to his festival in Switzerland.[798]

How did you qualify for a Western tour? It helped to be famous, his student Gidon Kremer explained to an interviewer from the German newsmagazine *Der Spiegel*. Your calendar had to be compatible with official Moscow's priorities. If possible, you should play a lot of Russian music, just not by living composers who were non grata at home. And, of course, you had to agree to terms that might have made a robber baron blush. Contracts stipulated that half to 90 percent of foreign earnings go to Gosconcert, the state—and only—artists' management. On return, after no more than ninety days abroad on a modest per diem, the artist was paid in rubles at the going Soviet rate per concert. The more distinguished the player, the worse the terms. While a beginner might earn the equivalent of 500 marks on a fee of 1,000 marks, a performer in Oistrakh's category would earn the same on a fee of 10,000 marks.[799]

Intrinsically decent and likable, Oistrakh pushed back as best he could. In fearful 1948, when the party cast Shostakovich and Prokofiev into musical outer darkness, he evaded the obligatory signature on the denunciation letter with a strategy that might have impressed Joseph Heller's Yossarian. He had played both composers so often with such conviction, he argued. What would people outside Russia say, where both composers were so popular?[800] In 1950, aware before Dubinsky himself that the *apparatchiki* had turned thumbs down on the Borodin Quartet, he approached Rudolf Barshai, another future star and the quartet's violist, to propose that they play Ernest Chausson's concerto for quartet and soloists with himself and the pianist Lev Oborin. "Right now, I just want your names to appear on my posters," he explained.[801]

In 1951, there were rumors at the Conservatory that Queen Elisabeth's invitation to the first postwar Brussels competition had made its way to Stalin himself. "First prize must be ensured," Stalin reportedly demanded. The problem was naturally referred to Oistrakh. He proposed the Jewish Leonid Kogan as the only sure solution. It worked. Insecure, widely disliked for his obsequiousness and deference to power,[802] but as distinguished a player as Oistrakh himself, Kogan came back with first prize.[803] Mikhail Vaiman, another Soviet Jew, came in second.

In 1967, Oistrakh created a small sensation when he refused to sign an anti-Israel resolution unless non-Jews like Shostakovich, Khachaturian, and Khrennikov, the perennial secretary of the Composers Union, also signed. A daylight break-in, unmentioned in the Soviet media but reported on Voice of America, was a reminder, gentle by Soviet standards, of what it cost to be a dissident. The burglars left his instruments but took his records, tapes, art books, a symbolic key to the city of Jerusalem, letters from Einstein, and a print of *City Lights* that was a gift from Charlie Chaplin. Some weeks afterward, everything was mysteriously returned. Months later, after the Soviet invasion of Czechoslovakia, Oistrakh appeared in Prague and played Prokofiev, now safely dead, rather than the perennially embattled Shostakovich.[804]

The 1960s were not the fearful 1930s or the terrifying early 1950s, when Jewish intellectuals, artists, and professionals of any prominence were made to appeal to Stalin, in a letter intended for publication in the official party paper, *Pravda*, to deport them to Siberia to shield them from the righteous anger of the Soviet people.[805] But it was still the Soviet Union. Fain, whose grief at Oistrakh's death was exceeded only by her grief at the death of her mother, recalled a man eternally aware of himself as a mannequin in a Soviet show window, alert to the threat of persecution, and terrified that he might die poor. At least theoretically, this was possible. Apart from his instruments, he owned only a dacha. His pension was thin. He had no insurance. Most of his fees and all of his royalties went to Gosconcert.[806]

In 1970, Rostropovich became an unperson by publicly speaking up for Alexander Solzhenitsyn, the year's Nobel Prize winner in literature and a devastating critic of the Soviet regime. Not long before Oistrakh's death, he happened to be in Paris at the same time as Rostropovich and proposed that they go for a walk. Oistrakh was full of admiration for his friend's courage and character. Then he warned Rostropovich that he'd find Oistrakh's denunciation of him in the next day's edition of *Pravda*. In 1936 or 1937, Oistrakh recalled, all the men in his apartment building had been arrested save for himself and a neighbor across the hall. His wife had even packed a little bag of necessaries, just in case. When the police finally came at 4:00 a.m., as it was clear they would and as was the custom, Oistrakh and his wife listened to the footsteps on the stairs. Then—long pause—the footsteps went to the other door. He had lived in the shadow of that experience ever since.[807]

In an essay published nearly a generation later, Kremer remembered an interview with Isaac Stern, who wanted to know why Oistrakh agreed to thirty-nine concerts in two months on his first trip to America. "If I stopped playing, I'd start thinking," Oistrakh reportedly replied, "and if I start thinking, I'll die."[808] In 1974, the year Oistrakh died, the Soviet Union deported Rostropovich. Five years later, Kremer, too, would leave, though under very different circumstances. Ever more fearful of defections, the authorities had allowed him two full years abroad with the understanding that he would then return. As the two years ended, Kremer made clear that he was perfectly willing to meet his obligations, but he wanted to settle in West Germany, close to his aging parents. In an odd and indirect way, the Soviet invasion of Afghanistan in late 1979 settled the matter. The United States showed its disapproval by boycotting the 1980 Olympics in Moscow. The Soviet authorities countered by forcing Soviet artists to cancel American engagements. A conspicuous exception, Kremer was allowed to play in America as scheduled. But he was barred from his scheduled engagements in the Soviet Union, where it was assumed with good reason that others might want to do what he did. Put to the test, the proposition was self-fulfilling. While denying he was a dissident, Kremer decided to stay in the West. "I just felt I had to do my duty, and defend composers and compositions I believed in," he said.[809]

In September 1981, Solidarity, the first independent trade union in Communist Europe, challenged the status quo in Poland. In December, Wanda Wilkomirska, Poland's premier violinist, returned from Paris as the army proclaimed martial law and thousands were arrested. Two months later, she appeared in West Germany and declared her intention to stay. Over a thirty-two-year career, she estimated that she had played more than 2,500 concerts for the equivalent of a salary and per diem. At

80 to 163 concerts a year, it was like meeting a production quota, she said. In the mid-1970s, she had joined KOR, an independent support group for political detainees. Her then-spouse, second in the Polish nomenklatura, warned her what "they" could do. "Why do you say 'they'?" she asked. She recalled it as the hardest decision of her life. But this time she'd had enough, she told the *Frankfurter Allgemeine*, and registered a final protest by turning around and leaving.[810]

A year later, Viktoria Mullova went missing. Kremer, the Tchaikovsky competition winner of 1970, defected because he wasn't allowed to come home. Mullova, the Tchaikovsky competition winner of 1982, defected because she wasn't allowed to leave. There was one unlikely exception. Thanks to an invitation from Imelda, the shoe-loving wife of then-President Ferdinand Marcos, she had been allowed to appear in the Philippines.

Thoughts of defection had already been in the works for at least two years. Invitations to play in Helsinki and Kuusamo, a little town in northern Finland, then opened a window, as well as an opportunity to bring along another international prizewinner, her conductor and partner Vakhtang Jordania, as pianist. For years, Jordania had programmed the works of Khrennikov, the perennial head of the Composers Union. His cultivation paid off in a helpful intervention with the KGB that allowed Jordania to leave the country. Even so-so reviews in Helsinki worked in their favor as an excuse for Mullova to stick to the hotel and mope. When their Gosconcert keeper proposed a bit of tourism, they persuaded her to go alone. When she returned, Mullova's Strad, on loan from the state collection, was still on the hotel bed, reportedly costing KGB investigators several hours while they doubted that Mullova was gone. Meanwhile, Jyrkie Koulumies, a friend and longtime Moscow correspondent for Finnish media who arrived with a photographer, whisked them across the Swedish border in a rental car. They arrived in Stockholm on a weekend. The American Embassy was closed for the Fourth of July. They applied for asylum the next day, the story appeared in a Finnish tabloid without reference to their helpers, and another graduate of the Russian Violin School was in the West.[811]

A few years later, Gosconcert had gone the way of the Warsaw Pact, the Russian School had opened new studios in Lübeck and Baltimore, and another generation of great Russian players had settled in New York and London. Meanwhile, cash-starved orchestras from St. Petersburg to Leipzig were off to the West at the drop of a mark, pound, or dollar. Left to sink or swim without the patronage of czars or commissars, Russian conservatories and ensembles rolled their eyes, swallowed their pride, looked hopefully to the private sector and took in foreign students whose parents could pay.[812]

On September 11, 2001, the politics of a new century cast its shadow out of a literally clear blue sky. Nineteen young Arabs associated with al-Qaeda, a radically anti-Western, Afghanistan-based, Sunni Muslim paramilitary, crashed hijacked airliners into the twin towers of New York's World Trade Center and the Pentagon in Washington. The following Sunday, William Harvey, a newly arrived grad student in violin at Juilliard, joined a couple of classmates at the 69th Regiment Armory, where National Guard came and went, and families of the missing sat, still waiting for news. The three sight-read quartets till 7:00 p.m., when two of them left. From then till nearly midnight, Harvey carried on by himself, playing everything he knew, from the Bach B Minor solo partita and Paganini caprices to "Amazing Grace" and a valedictory National Anthem. "I've never understood so fully what it means to communicate music to other people," he wrote afterward. "Words only go so far, and even music can only go a little further." In 2005, he founded Cultures in Harmony, a modest NGO that launched projects in Papua New Guinea, the Philippines, Cameroon, Egypt, and Tunisia, where his arrival coincided with terrorist attacks in London that killed fifty-two. In 2010, he took a job teaching violin and viola to thirteen young people, including girls, at the Afghanistan National Institute of Music in Kabul.[813]

BOOK 4

Imagining It

"$\mathcal{M}$USIC I HEARD with you was more than music," the American Conrad Aiken declared in a poem first published in 1917.[1] To the artists, novelists, poets, playwrights, stage directors, filmmakers, songwriters, photographers, cartoonists, even ad writers whose cumulative images, impressions, and reflections reach back about as far as the instrument itself, it would be just as clear that violins they heard, saw, or played were more than violins. For Gottfried Keller, the renegade "black fiddler" of his classic novella *Romeo und Julia auf dem Dorfe* (*A Village Romeo and Juliet*) personifies an entire transgressive order of society.[2] For Proust, the recurring "little phrase" in an invented violin sonata by the invented composer Vinteuil is a representation of "the supra-terrestrial, extra-temporal, eternal essence of things,"[3] as indispensable to his seven-volume *À la Recherche du Temps Perdu* (*Remembrance of Things Past*) as the celebrated madeleine dunked in tea.

The "Méditation," a four-minute entr'acte between the second act of Massenet's *Thaïs*, when the title figure retires for the night as Alexandria's favorite call girl, and the third, when she awakes as a candidate for sainthood, is familiar to thousands, even millions, who have never heard of Keller or Proust, let alone the opera itself. But the trope—the violin as heaven's instrument of choice—has been a cultural perennial since Monteverdi.

The final movement of Gustav Mahler's Fourth Symphony, allusively paired with a very different trope in the second movement scherzo, is an unmistakable member of the same iconic family. As is the case so often in Mahler, its source is Arnim and Brentano's classic collection of folksongs, *Des Knaben Wunderhorn* (*The Youth's Magic Horn*). The very simplicity of the title *Der Himmel hängt voller Geigen* is elusive in translation. But whether translated as "Violins hang all over heaven" or "Heaven is full of violins," it says all that need be said about the link between the instrument and the cosmos.

The text, in fact, makes no direct reference to the violin. Instead, it revels for four stanzas in a demotic vision of paradise, where lambs volunteer their lamb chops, angels bake bread, and the wine is on the house. Then, in the fifth stanza, the music deepens. A hymn to heaven's menu turns unexpectedly into a hymn to music itself. "No music on earth compares with ours," says the text, and for a moment it's true.

Yet the heavenly trope is only half the story. The dark end of the cosmogony has been just as irresistible, and the violin becomes as natural a companion to death, damnation, and the creatures of the underworld as it is to the angels. In his *Dance of Death* series of 1538, the younger Hans Holbein, a contemporary of Andrea Amati, shows a cadaver fiddling at the foot of the bed while a skeleton, presumably Death, prepares to haul away a startled princess.[4] In 1817, Schubert turned Matthias Claudius's poem "Tod und das Mädchen" ("Death and the Maiden") into a song. In 1828, four years short of his own premature death, he turned the song into variations for string quartet that are as terrifying as anything ever composed.

In 1858, the scene lightened briefly when Offenbach's two-act *Orphée aux Enfers* (*Orpheus in the Underworld*) opened at Paris's Théâtre des Bouffes-Parisiens, featuring an Orpheus who really played the violin, a Euridice who couldn't stand the violin, and an underworld where the traditional minuet became a cancan. In 1874, Saint-Saëns's version of the medieval *Danse Macabre* made its debut before an audience rather more uneasy than was Offenbach's. The solo violin, with its E string tuned down to E-flat, is obviously cast as Death.

Where death went, the devil was sure to follow. But it took one of those strokes of chance only a historian could love to preserve the cloven hoof-prints. In 1765, Joseph Jérôme de Lalande, professor of astronomy at the Collège de France, took two years off from what was to be a lifetime post for the obligatory grand tour of Italy. The home stretch included a short stop in Padua, where he looked up Giuseppe Tartini, for many years music director at the Basilica of St. Antony[5] and acknowledged by no less a figure than Leopold Mozart as "one of the most famous violinists of our time." The result was a serendipitous bit of violin history that would presumably have vanished forever had Lalande not included it in the eight-volume travel memoir he published on his return.

Determined to leave nothing out, Lalande checks every box—Tartini's distinction as a performer, his modesty, his good manners and piety, his international reputation as a teacher, Rousseau's regard for him, and a handful of additional biographical particulars. "No one has invested his compositions with more spirit and fire," he continues, citing the famous story "told to me by Tartini" to make his point. Published only thirty years after Tartini's death, the sonata known as *The Devil's Trill* would anchor his fame and become respected, even feared, by violinists ever after for its technical challenges. Lalande's is the only known source on how it came to be composed.

One night in 1713, according to Lalande, Tartini dreamed that he had made a pact with the devil, who anticipated all his wishes and surpassed all his desires. He then handed the devil his violin to see what he could do with it. The devil responded with a sonata of such singular beauty that Tartini, who had never heard anything like it, woke up, reached for his violin, and tried in vain to reproduce what he had just heard. He regarded the result as the best piece he ever composed. But it fell so far short of what the devil played, he added, that he would have smashed his instrument and given up music were it not such a consolation to him.[7]

For a generation that was weaned on *Faust* and cut its teeth on Byron and E. T. A. Hoffmann, the devil trope was catnip. Johann-Friedrich Lyser, the Hamburg cartoonist, happily caricatured a dancing Paganini fiddling for a sextet of dancing skeletons. Ignace-Isidore Grandville, another contemporary, shows him drawing a broomstick over what appears to be an enormous rubber band, while a grinning demon seated behind him pumps a bellows.[8] A whole cohort of violinist-composers—Ernst with his transcription of Schubert's *Erlkönig* for solo violin, Bazzini with his *Dance of the Goblins*, Wieniawski with his variations on *God Save the King*—continued where the violinist-composer of the variations on *The Witches* stopped. Contingent on mood and circumstance, they may or may not have looked to demons for their inspiration. But for all but the most formidable violinists, what they wrote to play themselves has been devilish enough.

In 1849, with Napoleonic law and order reestablished, and the Paris Opéra again in flower, the devil reappeared, but this time in six scenes, including a divertissement finale. The vehicle was a ballet called *Le Violon du Diable*, based on a Hoffmannesque story about a violinist who eventually gets the girl in white tutu and wings with the aid of two magic violins, one of them the devil's. The piece had previously been known as *Tartini il Violinista*. A year later, it was revived at the Paris Opéra. It remained in the repertory of various European companies through the 1850s.[9]

In the hellish aftermath of World War I, Igor Stravinsky and the Swiss writer C. R. Ramuz took a Russian folktale about a soldier who sells his violin to the devil with the usual results and turned it into *L'Histoire du Soldat* (*The Soldier's Story*), a masterpiece of irony, a twentieth-century classic, and a spectacular workout for the solo violinist. A half century later, the American composer George Crumb's *Black Angels*, for amplified string quartet, became an overnight classic. "Finished on Friday the Thirteenth, March 1970 (*in tempore belli*)," it was replete with references to "Death and the Maiden," "The Devil's Trill," and "Danse Macabre," and it had intervals representative of the mystical numbers three, seven, and thirteen. "Good versus evil was part of my thinking," the composer explained.[10] In the mid-1980s, the trope came to rest, at least for the moment, in the country classic "The Devil Went Down to Georgia." In multiple stanzas with instrumental bridges, the title figure challenges Johnny, the local champ, to a fiddle contest and loses in straight sets. With an assist from Mark O'Connor and Johnny Cash, Charlie Daniels's version sold a lot of records and even a few books, after Daniels turned his song into a short story.[11]

STILL PICTURES WORTH A
THOUSAND WORDS

PICTURES GO BACK to the beginnings of the instrument. Among the earliest, Gaudenzio Ferrari's imperturbable angels, fiddling for the greater glory of God in the cupola of Saronno cathedral, or Plato, Hippocrates, Galen, and Aristotle united in Champier's woodcut[12] as the first amateur string quartet, even predate the violin. From there on, images of the violin would line the walls of churches, palaces, and museums, grace the pages of pamphlets, brochures, magazines, books, and newspapers, and sell products as different as computer software and special purpose steels.[13] At least one violinist, Ysaÿe, made it to a postage stamp. In paintings, watercolors, and pencil portraits, twenty-three violinists made it by 2006 to the walls of Britain's National Portrait Gallery.

On the eve of the sixteenth century, Italian artists already found the great blue yonder unimaginable without bowed stringed instruments, ideally resting on angelic or cherubic shoulders or clavicles.[14] By the eve of the seventeenth century, the fiddle family had overtaken the lute as the favorite instrument of artists from Anon. to Zampieri.[15]

Saints, church fathers, and the gods and heroes of classical antiquity were equally responsive to its magic. As early as 1511, Raphael's Apollo, pictured on the wall of the Vatican Palace's Stanza della Segnatura, has traded his lyre for a *lira da braccio*.[16] Some sixty-five years later, Titian's Apollo has done the same in *The Flaying of Marsyas*, in the gallery named for the artist in the archbishop's palace of Kromeriz, now in the Czech Republic. The message was simple: satyrs play flutes and lose; gods play stringed instruments and win.[17]

Not even a god, Roelandt Savery's Orpheus plays his violin to an attentive audience of lions, flamingos, elephants, mixed ruminants, mixed waterfowl, a rooster, and a parrot in London's National Gallery.[18] Caravaggio's Amor, looking pleased with himself in Berlin's Dahlem Museum, poses with a fistful of arrows in his right hand. Astolfo Petrazzi's Amor, in Rome's Galleria di Palazzo Barberini, grasps a bow with the slightly disingenuous look of a kid explaining that the dog ate his homework. Rutilio Manetti's Amor looks cherubic in the National Gallery of Ireland as he averts his eyes from a drawn bow. A violin or possibly viola is in easy reach on the floor behind all three of them.[19] Bartolemeo Cavarozzi's St. Cecilia, c. 1620, gazes heavenward with a violin and score laid out on a table in front of her. Both are presumably hers. A St. Cecilia attributed to Guido Reni is actually seen playing the instrument while she, too, looks heavenward.[20] Even Mattia Preti's blind Homer of 1613 in Venice's Gallerie dell'Accademia is a violinist. Who knew?

Unsurprisingly, the imagery of angels is replicated on earth as it is in heaven. If the Dutch artist Pieter Lastmann (1583–1633) shows a more or less conventional King David performing a harp concerto, the orchestra behind him includes a tambourine, trombone, gamba, bombard, and violin.[21] In the midst of an unmistakably Italian landscape, Caravaggio, the tumultuous baroque master who "put the *oscuro* into *chiaroscuro*,"[22] shows a very tall female angel playing what is unmistakably a violin from a score held up to her by Joseph. A clearly exhausted Mary with baby Jesus in her arms is meanwhile resting after the flight into Egypt.

In 1553, Veronese included a whole ensemble of bowed stringed instruments in a wedding at Cana; the picture is now hanging in the Louvre. In 1575, the gambas reappear at a representation of another mystic marriage, this one St. Catherine's, now hanging in the Gallerie dell'Accademia in Venice. A third ensemble, deployed front and center in Veronese's *Parable of the Rich Man*, c. 1530–40, is entirely earthly. With the principal player's back to the mendicant Lazarus, the scene reminds the viewer that conspicuous consumption at the expense of the poor in this world exposes the host to hefty transaction costs in the next.

The Parable of the Prodigal Son, as envisaged by Jean Le Clerc in 1621–22, is a natural candidate for similar cautionary treatment. Eight people, selectively lighted, are seated around a table in a darkened room. On the left, an older woman peers into space. On the right, a violinist peers at what might be a crumpled sheet of music, but might also be a handkerchief, in the hand of an older man seated at the table. A well-dressed young man behind the table is making out with a willing partner. The man to their right would like to do the same but is meeting serious resistance from a younger woman with a sheet of music in her hands. At the head of the table, another young man reads intently from a score while a lutenist in the foreground with his back to the viewer seems to be reading from a sheet of music in the hands of a still younger man whose expression suggests distress, even anguish.[23]

The affinity of the professional fiddler and the wages of sin was an inexhaustible favorite north of the Alps but especially beloved in Calvinist Holland. A variation on the theme of wine, women, and song, the genre tended to be a medley of booze, fiddle, and fun, such as Cornelis Dusart's *Village Festival*, dated 1684, in the Hals Museum in Haarlem. Adriaen van Ostade's weathered village fiddler of 1672, in the collection of the Mauritshuis in The Hague, does what he hopes to be paid for before a basically friendly, if not overly attentive, audience of children, adults, and a dog.

Closer to the slippery slope where virtue is no more, Georges de La Tour's squabbling street musicians, c. 1620–25, have at one another, armed respectively with a knife and what appear to be well-aimed squirts of lemon juice. A disconcerted wife and a leering violinist look out at the viewer from behind the combatants. Well past the edge, a sodden crowd of peasants squabble, gamble, smoke, and above all drink in Benjamin Cuyp's mid-seventeenth-century watering hole, while a bleary piper toots into his recorder and a fiddler with a formidable beer belly and a W. C. Fields expression peeps out at the viewer.[24]

Jan Steen's *The World Turned Upside Down* of 1663 is the masterpiece of the genre. Amid a pictorial medley of such Dutch proverbs as "The young ones chirp as the elders sing," "Opportunity makes the thief," and "Pearls before swine," the artist shows the mistress of the house snoozing, a dog picking through the leftovers on the table, a monkey playing with a counterweight of the clock on the wall, a pig poking a rose on the floor, the maid stealing the silver, and a little boy smoking a pipe. A prostitute in yellow silk with a jug in one hand and a glass in the other looks out at the viewer. Her unbuttoned customer, who might be auditioning for Hogarth's *Rake's Progress*, rests his leg on her knee. A man of indeterminate age in Dutch Master mode with a duck on his shoulder appears to be reading or singing from a book. A similarly dressed woman of indeterminate age with an extended forefinger leans forward as though correcting him or beating time. A representation of voluptuous idleness, an adolescent fiddler stands in the middle of the scene, exchanging a meaningful wink with the maid.[25]

It was no long step from there to the bleak world of the allegory and still life, devoted to the ineluctable vanity of things. In Leonaert Bramer's *Allegory of Vanity*, c. 1640, a black-cloaked lutenist stares out at the viewer while a shadowy woman contemplates herself in a mirror. A table is strewn with disordered gold and silver. From an adjacent table, instruments, including violins, are spilling over onto the floor.

Successive still lifes by Evaristo Baschenis, now hanging in Vienna, Brussels, Milan, Venice, Brera, and the artist's native Bergamo, dutifully make room for such conventional representations of vanity as globes, astrolabes, bound books, and printed music. Ecclesiastes to the contrary, each of these was, in fact, quite new under the sun and was already changing the world. In the spirit of the genre, Baschenis even tosses in an occasional piece of fruit or broken string. The main attraction in a series extending from his professional beginnings in 1645 to his death at sixty in 1677 is a tableful of instruments, with a lovingly rendered violin, another relative novelty, prominent in each. Both a priest and a plague survivor, he surely needed no encouragement to paint intimations of mortality. He was also an amateur musician, in an era of modest economic recovery, who clearly liked instruments and enjoyed the challenges of painting them in perspective, just as he enjoyed painting kitchens.[26]

There are hints of sensuality in Terbrugghen's *Concert* (1629), in the National Gallery of Rome's Palazzo Barberini; but there is no apparent censoriousness. An artfully semidressed young woman with an enigmatic smile reclines on a lute, her eyes turned to the light. An artfully and fully dressed young man with an enigmatic smile leans toward her, playing his violin. His gaze is turned the other way. The most obvious message is that the painter has spent some years in Italy and seen a lot of Italian painting.

Painterly virtuosity aside, the message of Gerrit van Honthorst's *Happy Violinist with Glass* of a few years earlier, now in Amsterdam's Rijksmuseum, is equally neutral. The subject, in eye contact with the viewer, is elaborately turned out in Renaissance mode. With a violin and bow in his left hand, a glass of wine in his right, and a twinkle in his eye, he could be toasting the viewer. "What the subject is intended to suggest is unclear," the art historian Stefania Macioce concedes, citing a fistful of inferences and authoritative speculations.[27] But he is clearly not urging the viewer to repent.

A comparative overview of three works by Jan Miense Molenaer (c. 1610–58) is a short course on the domestication of the violin by Europe's most middle-class society. The first, in London's National Gallery, is the work of a startlingly talented nineteen-year-old with the genes of an Old Master magazine illustrator. It shows two boys of ten or eleven and a little girl of six or seven. The boy on the left, barefoot like Huck Finn, is stirring a jug. The little girl in the center, decked out in an armored carapace designed to protect an adult's neck and shoulders but in her case reaching to her middle, is whacking the helmet with two spoons and a bashful smile. The boy on the left, in an adult's battered hat with a clay pipe stuck through the crown, is pretending to play a violin. They are nominally making music. They are unmistakably having a good time.

The second, a privately owned depiction of a rural wedding painted around 1662,[28] shows a barn full of modestly dressed but clearly well-fed people gathered around tables. Four couples stand out in the foreground, mugging as though for a vacation snapshot or the high school yearbook. They, too, are having a good time. Another couple to the rear is whooping it up on the dance floor. A figure in the shadows has had a little too much to drink. The bride and groom are indistinguishable among the celebrants, but it hardly matters. The fiddler at the back is doing what he was hired to do.

The third (1668), now hanging in the Frans Hals Museum in Haarlem, is a counterpoint to the second, as respectably sober as the rustic wedding is not. Dressed to the seventeenth-century nines in black set off by ruffs and lace collars, the artist and respective family members are arranged from left to right as though posing for a class photo. Most clutch a plucked or bowed stringed instrument, among them a violin and cello, while a younger sister sings from the pages in her hand. The master, presumably the artist himself, stands slightly to the side with his eyes on the viewer, as though introducing his family. To his side stands a younger son, swinging a hand bell. The floor is checkered black-and-white tile. The cabinets behind them are seriously expensive and professionally crafted. The walls are hung with family portraits. The family dog snoozes at the mistress's feet.

The scene is full of conventional symbolism, but disdain for the earthly is clearly in retreat. In the pictorial language of the time, the small boy with the bell represents the fragility of human existence. The family dog, on the other hand, represents fidelity; and music, far from a stand-in for dissipation and abandon, represents domestic harmony. Violin included, the family ensemble is a tableau of togetherness. Music—at any rate this music—has gone respectable and the violin with it.[29]

As late as the 1750s, generic peasants reappear in a tableau by Janu-arius Zick, a respected Bavarian professional. Now in Munich's Alte Pina-kothek, it shows a bass fiddle duo hard at it outside a village tavern, while a man behind them hoists his glass and another smokes his pipe. One couple is engaged in conversation. Another is dancing to the music, the man perhaps a little more enthusiastically than his partner. But the scene is nonjudgmental.[30] Still less is there any intimation of morality twenty years later in a family scene now at the German National Museum in Nurem-berg. Siblings or cousins are engaged in an impromptu musicale, including three violins. The singer, gazing pensively at the viewer while waiting for her entrance,[31] might be thinking about any number of things, including dinner. It is unlikely that she is thinking about eternity.

Each after his fashion, Carl Spitzweg (1808–1885), Adolph Menzel (1815–1905), and Adolphe-William Bouguereau (1825–1905) pick up where Zick leaves off. Their portraits and village scenes have been resized to fit the very different sensibilities and markets of an altogether new era, con-currently hooked on classical antiquity, gothic arches, demonstrative piety, and romantic sentiment. Charm and even humor make their debut too. Contrary to conventional expectation, these works appear east of the Rhine.

Charm, let alone humor, was neither Bouguereau's priority nor his strength. But no one could deny the extraordinary technique, welded seamlessly to the spirit of the age, that he practiced with inexhaustible energy and spectacular success over a long and happy life. American mil-lionaires wanted all that they could get of these motifs. Reproductions of *Alone in the World* (1867) and *Virgin of the Angels* (1881) graced middle-class and wannabe middle-class living rooms around much of the world. In a city, culture, and era in which the violin reigned supreme, violins fit naturally into his repertory. The peasant girl, alone in the world standing in front of Notre Dame looking out with a pre-Raphaelite gaze, is also clutching a violin and bow. Two of the three life-size angels watching over Mary and child in the Los Angeles Getty Museum clutch a mandolin and a violin. There's no question which is playing the celestial tune.[32]

In Menzel's 1861 reconstruction of daily life at Schloss Rheinsberg a century earlier, Franz Benda, the court composer-violinist, is playing the tune, in the foreground, right. The artist Antoine Pesne is goofing off com-panionably with his Rubensesque model on a scaffold in the background left. A wooden mannequin is sprawled in the left foreground, headfirst. An assistant, scrubbing a palette, is facing forward. Looking in, up, and discreetly amused, the prince regent, Frederick, not yet the Great, is coming up behind them, followed by staff wearing dubious expressions.[33]

If charm was among Menzel's options, it was Spitzweg's stock in trade, just as it had been the priority and strength of Munich, where he was born and spent most of his life as a confirmed bachelor, self-taught artist, and exemplary self-promoter. Like Bouguereau, he lived to see his product on domestic walls around the world.[34] But his landscape of choice was as un-French as only pre-industrial Germany could be. Already vanishing under the impact of blood and iron, its violinists, invariably amateurs, cluster beneath Rosina's window in a scene from Rossini. They serenade themselves in hermit retreats and climb ladders, roofs, and garden walls by moonlight to serenade their lady loves. Neither angelic nor demonic, they remain as familiar to generations of Central Europeans as their Aunt Elsa and Uncle Emil.

Well into the nineteenth century, America, too, had its nostalgia masters, among them William Sidney Mount, the Long Island genre painter who not only played the violin but, like Chanot, the French naval officer, had a crack at reinventing it. A rustic scene from about 1830 now in Boston's Museum of Fine Arts shows a roomful of middle-class white merrymakers dancing to the fiddle of a cheerful black teenager following a sleigh ride, while an equally cheerful black boy tends the fireplace. About as licentious as Currier & Ives, the ambience is a harmonious microcosm, where white and black each have and accept their place.

In his incomparably more accomplished *Power of Music* (1847), now hanging in the Cleveland Museum of Art, Mount shows a man in cap and shirtsleeves fiddling for a couple of respectably dressed friends inside his barn. Leaning against the barn door where only the viewer can see him, a black man in work clothes listens, transfixed. Remarkable for the period, the man is realistically drawn, not a caricature. The title alludes to a Wordsworth poem about a blind street fiddler entrancing an audience of baker's boys and barrow girls. A sensation from the start, the canvas would soon be publicly exhibited in New York and London and then marketed in lithograph and postcard copies for decades afterward.

It was not, however, an abolitionist poster. On the contrary, Mount was an impassioned conservative Democrat with a soft spot for paternalism who had literally lived at New York's Tammany Hotel. His passion for the violin went back to a slave player owned by his mother's family in an era when the black fiddler was a fixture on every Southern plantation.

The Power of Music was the sum of the parts: a young white man holding his audience as Wordsworth's blind fiddler held his and an older, otherwise subordinate, black man listening approvingly as his white pupil showed his stuff.[35]

Nostalgia also animates George Caleb Bingham's Missouri River boatmen in Düsseldorf-inspired landscapes that look back to sixteenth- and seventeenth-century Italian models. In an 1846 version, now in the Manoogian collection of Taylor, Michigan, a Dionysian archetype at the apex of a pyramid dances for his friends on the cabin of a flatboat in mid-river. In an 1857 version, now in the St. Louis Art Museum, the archetype dances for the viewer at the apex of a larger pyramid as his flatboat docks in what might be St. Louis or Kansas City.[36] Once again, Puritan disapproval is totally missing, but so is any Whitmanesque celebration of America singing. In fact, like Bingham himself, his boatman-fiddlers are on a nostalgia trip in an era when flatboats, already superseded by steamboats, are also being overtaken by railroads.

Like the Düsseldorf-Italian landscape, the still life as memento mori enjoyed an improbable reprise in the virtuoso trompe d'oeil work of William Michael Harnett. An Irish immigrant who died in 1892 at the age of forty-four, he left a trail of acolytes and a minimum of documentation. Of his 170 known works, 48 feature musical themes. Among them, dated 1876, is the earliest, *Mortality and Immortality*, now in the Wichita Art Museum. The title alone leaves little to the imagination. The various elements in the composition—books, skull, blush rose, and a violin resting on its bow—might be taken from a checklist for a seventeenth-century Dutch *vanitas*.

Its successors could hardly be more different. Created ten and twelve years later, they testify in part to the artist's earlier career as an engraver, in part to four years' study in Philadelphia and New York and five years' study in Europe. The first, *The Old Violin*, now in Washington's National Gallery, created such a sensation on its first appearance at the Cincinnati Industrial Exposition of 1886 that extra security was needed to keep viewers from grabbing at the canvas to see if the objects within the frame were real. The second, *Music and Good Luck*, is now at New York's Metropolitan Museum. Dated 1888, it only emerged from decades of private obscurity on the eve of World War II, when a shrewd New York dealer rediscovered the artist as a kind of pioneer surrealist.

Common to both paintings was a medley of odds and ends—an easily readable page or two of music, rather the worse for wear, from the early years of the century, the artist's calling card, an envelope with a Paris postmark addressed to himself in New York, a hasp, and a horseshoe—hanging on or from the outer side of a door. Above all, both paintings included a violin, authentic or otherwise, that the artist had bought as a Guarneri del Gesù in Paris. In *Music and Good Luck*, there is also a straight, so-called transitional bow. Was the artist, like his Dutch antecedents a couple of hundred years earlier, pointing to the transience of earthly things? Or was he just testing viewers, as did Frank Tuchfarber, the amateur player, violin maker, cofounder of what would become the Cincinnati Symphony, and professional lithographer, who bought *The Old Violin* straight from its public debut and began marketing a seventeen-stone chromo reproduction at $12, complete with "elegant 3-inch hardwood frame," a year later?

Looking back on the era of Vuillaume and Laurie, an American commentator was equally struck by Harnett's feel for an object Americans, Harnett included, had just begun to collect and a style of painting they were likely to turn into a collectible. A British commentator was equally puzzled by his ambiguous perspectives, a bow that had vanished from use nearly a century earlier, and a violin, even if it weren't a del Gesù, hung on the outside of a door.[37]

So what was the message? Was it that the violin worked as well as ever as an intimation of mortality? Was it that even in an increasingly secular world it was of sufficient intrinsic interest to hold an artist's attention? In the absence of any clue from the artist, either explanation was plausible, and there was no reason why they couldn't coexist.

ACCOMPLISHED, PROLIFIC, AND long-lived, Francesco Guardi (1712–1793) was a working model of an artist as comfortable on earth as he was in the heavens. In time, his work would fill eighteenth-century Venetian churches with saints and miracles and twentieth-century museums with postcard views of Venice in the last decades of the republic. But he was also the man to turn to in January 1782, when the Russian grand duke Paul Petrovich and his wife were taken to see the girls of the *ospedali*.

Guardi's *Ladies' Concert at the Philharmonic*, now in Munich's Alte Pinakothek, is significant both as art and document. Along the left margin of the canvas, the players are strung out in three tiers like so many birds on a telephone wire. The floor below is crowded with tiny figures, includ-

ing two lines of women dancers surrounded by elegantly dressed spectators, also predominantly women. Only one figure stands out clearly in the
foreground, facing the viewer, as though under a spotlight. It is a liveried
waiter carrying a tray.

James Jacques-Joseph Tissot's *Hush!* (1875), now in the Manchester
Art Gallery, is a Victorian reprise by a Beaux Arts contemporary of Bouguereau who fled his native France for London after the Franco-Prussian
War. Endowed like Guardi with a shrewd sense of the market, he has obviously found what he came for in a high-ceilinged and brilliantly lighted
English salon. The beautiful people who fill the space are clearly at home
in it. In the front row there are even a couple of Indian gentlemen, leaning
forward a little uncertainly. Although Wilma Neruda, both a celebrated
professional and the future Lady Hallé, is about to play, center rear, a
crowd of guests is still coming down the stairs. The most visible figures
are still in animated conversation in the left foreground.[38]

But by this time, any number of revolutions had swept away the Venetian republic, an ancient French monarchy and its successor, two French
empires, much of Paris as it had existed since the Middle Ages, and any
number of artistic conventions reaching back at least as far. Their collective impact can be seen in *The Old Musician* (1862) in Washington's
National Gallery, one of the earliest masterpieces of the thirty-year-old
Edouard Manet. As distant from Bouguereau's marzipan sentimentality
and Spitzweg's anticipations of Norman Rockwell as they are from Tissot's
Manchester and Guardi's Venice, a very young girl with a baby, two small
boys, a young man, and an elderly man stand side by side in an open field
like an intergenerational frieze. All are refugees from Baron Haussmann's
colossal urban renewal. None is looking at any other, nor anything else
apparent to the viewer. The sky above them shades ambivalently from
bright to threateningly black. A gray-bearded man clothed in a well-worn
cloak and a loser's dignity is seated between them with a violin under his
arm and a bow in his hand. Believed to be Jean Lagrène, a sometime organ
grinder, artist's model, and Gypsy bandleader, he looks out at the viewer
without expression.[39]

A real person with a credible identity, the Old Musician testifies to
another relatively new departure in violin imagery. Five generations of
Amatis, three of Guarneris, and the magisterial Stradivari left real estate,
paper trails, iconic instruments, and names with global resonance, but not
a single image. Biber, Veracini, Nardini, Tartini, Geminiani, and Leopold

Mozart all qualified for portraits, if only because their publishers wanted cover art.[40]

Save as a likeness of record, John Smith's 1704 copy of Hugh Howard's much-copied portrait of Corelli[41] in Britain's National Gallery is unremarkable. But the portrait of the artist is itself noteworthy in a world where Jonathan Swift grouped virtuosos with "gibers, censurers, backbiters, pickpockets, highwaymen, housebreakers, attorneys, bawds, buffoons, gamesters, politicians, wits, splenetics, tedious talkers, controvertists, ravishers, murderers [and] robbers," and fiddlers with "lords . . . judges and dancing masters."[42] The violin hanging behind a magnificently uniformed and mustachioed János Bihari in János Donát's 1820 portrait in the Hungarian National Museum may resemble a muskrat pelt. But for the first time, the Gypsy music personified by the self-taught Bihari is recognized as a national institution.[43]

Jean-Baptiste Chardin's portrait of the young Charles Godefroy, now in the Louvre, has its message too. Partial to the striving bourgeois a half century before the Revolution, the artist portrayed a society jeweler's son improving himself with his violin—to make a point as well as to make art.[44] The unsigned portrait of a cold-eyed, all-business Leopold Mozart in Salzburg, attributed to Pietro Antonio Lorenzoni in the mid-1760s, is equally good. Gainsborough's elegant portrait of the composer and oboe virtuoso Johann Christian Fischer, now in the Royal Collection at Windsor Castle, shows its subject standing at the piano, slim and handsomely tailored, with pen in hand. An oboe, his instrument of choice, is in easy reach. His first instrument, a violin as handsome as its owner, stands on a chair behind him.[45]

With photography still over the horizon, the coming of Paganini was a bonanza like none before or after. Painters, sculptors, illustrators, cartoonists, even porcelain designers[46] could hardly get enough of him. Yet multiple portraits and limitless caricatures only confirmed that the inimitable cuvée of talent, charisma, self-promotion, and progressive physical decrepitude that made him irresistible was as elusive and challenging for artists as it was for everyone else.

The famous pencil portrait of 1819 by Jean-Auguste-Dominique Ingres (1780–1867), now in the Louvre, is an accomplished amateur player's homage to the pro of pros. It also honors the classical virtues the artist acquired as a student and would retain to the end of an eighty-seven-year life. Done in Rome, where the artist was supporting himself with pencil portraits and his subject was between concerts,[47] Ingres's masterly Paganini is a pleasantly self-assured, sharp-featured, still young man, dressed well and almost tangibly in the style of the period,[48] with a violin under his right arm. But the only man alive who could play his twenty-four caprices, and who had already driven women and audiences wild from Bergamo to Lucca and would soon do the same from Rome to Palermo, is nowhere in view.

Fourteen years would pass before he appeared in a very different portrait by Eugène Delacroix (1798–1863), as much the avatar of the romantic as Ingres was of the classic. Delacroix had only recently returned to Paris from exotic Algeria. Superstar, living legend, and impending medical disaster, Paganini had only recently returned to Paris from exhausting and remunerative England, Ireland, and Scotland. Epidemic-prone, as nineteenth-century cities tended to be, Paris was meanwhile in the grip of cholera. Ingres's irenic Paganini is essentially similar to his irenic Baillot a decade later. Delacroix's Paganini, on the other hand, is a portrait of the era as well as the artist.

In contrast to his dramatically highlighted Chopin of 1838, with its pale and painfully expressive face, Delacroix shows Paganini in full figure, essentially black on black, lit only indirectly by the unseen footlights of a concert stage. It is clear that all of him counts. The face, turned to the instrument, is painfully gaunt, the expression inward; he seems impervious to the world around him. The violin effectively merges with the body. The sum of the parts, the suffering artist in the midst of death, is unlike any violinist portrait before or since.[49]

Another great artist's impression of art in progress, Menzel's much-reproduced drawing of 1854 could hardly be more different. Very young, very handsome, very serious, and with a startling high right wrist, Joseph Joachim is seen in recital with an equally serious but no longer so young Clara Wieck Schumann. Neither Faust nor Mephistopheles is anywhere in sight.

Joseph Kriehuber's much-reproduced lithograph *Matinée at Liszt's* (1846) is kitsch of genius, with the composer Hector Berlioz, the pianist Carl Czerny, and the artist himself posed reverently around Liszt's piano. Decked out in velvet jacket and Prince Valiant haircut, the master himself is shown with his pre-Raphaelite profile turned to the viewer. As impeccably drawn as any Ingres, the violinist Heinrich Wilhelm Ernst is seated on the right with his eyes on Liszt's fingers and his violin turned back to front. But Kriehuber's Ernst, the best-known portrait of an artist whom

Joachim considered the best violinist he'd ever heard,[50] is only an accessory to a celebration of Liszt.

While both the instrument and a certain sort of player continued to hold the interest of painters, their images diverged as the photographer and photograph took over. Regularly photographed solo, at work, and en famille, and occasionally honored with a cartoon,[51] Joachim continued to be painted by artists including Menzel, a fellow national monument and lifetime subscriber to the Joachim Quartet; by Philip de László, a Hungarian immigrant, who became a wildly fashionable British society painter; and by the American John Singer Sargent, portraitist of choice to the Anglo-American establishment. In 1903, the young and dazzling Jan Kubelik, a gardener's son en route to an estate of his own in Silesia, rated a de László portrait too. So did the artist's fellow Hungarian, the well-connected Jelly d'Arányi, a quarter century later. Even American amateurs who could afford it donned white ties, picked up their violins, and posed for a local artist of equivalent talent like William J. McCloskey of southern California.[52]

Other artists, like Juan Gris and Pablo Picasso on the eve of World War I, deconstructed the instrument, turning its baroque parabolas into cubist angularities. Still others, like Henri Matisse and Raoul Dufy, members of a school known as Fauves—wild ones—turned it into a domestic object at once so familiarly decorative that, in 1965, the French post office turned Dufy's celebrated *Red Violin* into a one-franc postage stamp.

Influenced by both schools but associated with neither, Marc Chagall (1887–1985) mixed the perennially impoverished, essentially defenseless East European shtetl with the stuff of dreams that was its principal export. He then transfigured it as a world of people, animals, and a fiddler on the roof who challenged himself to play without falling off. "Don't let that horse / eat that violin / cried Chagall's mother," in an endearing poem by Beat poet Lawrence Ferlinghetti, the founding father of San Francisco's iconic City Lights bookstore. "But he / kept right on / painting / And became famous."[53]

In 1964, the composer Jerry Bock and the librettist Joseph Stein took a scenario from the great Yiddish writer Sholom Aleichem and helped Chagall's fiddler to near-global recognition, including a version for middle and elementary schools. In 1999, the British screenwriter Richard Curtis took another Chagall, *La Mariée* of 1950, and wrote it into a scene in *Notting Hill*, a romantic comedy featuring Julia Roberts and Hugh Grant. In the embrace of a lover suspended in space, a bride in red is escorted by a violin-playing goat beneath a deep blue sky. Grant, who owns a print, asks Roberts whether she likes Chagall. "Happiness isn't happiness without a violin-playing goat," she replies. Between 1999 and 2004, *La Mariée* was the website Artcyclopedia's third best-selling art poster, outpaced only by Klimt's *Kiss* and Van Gogh's *Starry Night*.[54]

Meanwhile, the initiative for portraits of the artist passed increasingly to the players, their parents, managers, and impresarios, while the art and craft passed from painters to photographers, photo editors, art directors, and ad agencies. From the threshold of the twentieth century, the collective family album with its folk fiddlers by artists as great as André Kertész and Ben Shahn,[55] its mariachis, maypole processions, lumber camps, Guatemalan Indians, school orchestras, Gypsy funerals, Busby Berkeley production numbers, military bands in frontier outposts, and brigades of little Suzuki players, only confirmed what had been clear to Rousseau by 1768. Always portable, now cheap and accessible as never before, the violin really was the instrument of varied and universal choice.

An 1880 photo by the Rev. Charles Dodgson, also known as Lewis Carroll, shows the sixteen-year-old Xie Kitchin somewhat tentatively playing a violin.[56] An undated photo by Marconi Gaudenzi (1841–1885) shows a model clothed only in a violin and a pained expression.[57] Arthur Hughes's 1882–83 portrait of an angelic Mrs. Vernon Lushington shows her at the family piano, flanked by two equally angelic violinist daughters and their angelic cellist sister, as light floods in through the parlor's leaded windows.[58] The Lushingtons seem, at least, to have a pretty good idea of what their instruments are for.

Successive photos over five decades show Joachim gaining weight, adding a beard, and growing monumental, just as he did on canvas. Toward the end of his life, a slightly more tolerant technology allowed him to take the wheel of an effigy auto in a visored student cap while his colleagues Moser and Riedel sit in back in their fedoras. Even as they sat there, a generation of prodigies in sailor suits and lace collars posed, unsmiling, before other cameras. Reflecting in retirement on the Lord Fauntleroy costumes and haircut inflicted on him in childhood, Max Rostal gratefully remembered how Carl Flesch had won his heart forever on their first meeting in 1919 by ordering the fourteen-year-old Rostal to get himself to the barber before his first lesson.[59]

Equally fearless of the camera as prodigy and patriarch, public and family man, Menuhin could be seen over the full trajectory of a twentieth-century life, progressing from shorts to knickers to Norfolk jacket, rubbing shoulders with Elgar, Bartók, Britten, and Einstein, displaying solidarity with recently liberated Holocaust survivors and the not-yet de-Nazified Wilhelm Furtwängler, as comfortable with the sitar virtuoso Ravi Shankar as he was with the jazz virtuoso Stéphane Grappelli and the virtuoso's virtuoso David Oistrakh. "The most embarrassing thing he ever did to me—I was only 10—was appear on the front of *Life* magazine with his tongue hanging out to his navel," his daughter Zamira told the journalist Norman Lebrecht. "I didn't go to school for three days after that."[60] Over the same decades, Heifetz could be seen in classical profile, tennis togs, and a motor launch, with Charlie Chaplin, Irving Berlin, Jack Benny, an infant son, a mustache, an accordion, and a battery-driven Renault. Now and then, he could even be seen with a smile.

As audiences aged, players grew younger, and cameras turned digital at the beginning of a new century; angels and demons grew ever more remote, while blogs and homepages proliferated. At least in CD liner notes, the most brilliantly accomplished players of the Brahms concerto and solo Bach now appeared professionally in jeans and ever-deeper décolletés. Photographed some thirty years before as a cute little English boy in shorts and school tie, Nigel Kennedy now showed up before the camera as a midlife adolescent in Jimi Hendrix mode, bouncing on a Paris hotel bed with a violin in his hand. In 2007, Vanessa-Mae Nicholson, the Singapore-born, Thai-Chinese Londoner and global crossover star, turned the hotel motif from fun to profit in a full-page display ad for the Mandarin Oriental Group. Toothsome in jeans and a plaid shirt, with no bow in sight but a violin under her arm, and an expression that says, "I've made it, how about you?" the artist looks straight out at the viewer. "She's a fan," says the ad copy.[61]

String quartets were a particular challenge. Once seen bearded, portly, and unfailingly sober in profile, they were now young, trim, and often enough of mixed gender. Press kits and websites showed them lively as puppies, bright-eyed and cute, at work and at play, with no tie in sight.

In 2001, Bond, an Anglo-Australian crossover quartet, literally sat for the photographer with only a couple of electric instruments for cover. The four young women, all with conservatory diplomas, had been brought together by Mel Bush, who also managed Vanessa-Mae. With a hint of reluctance, Decca, their record company, said no to the photo.[62] But it covered the world via the Internet within hours. Meanwhile, the quartet sold over a million copies of their first album,[63] topped the classical charts in ten countries, and played for Wall Street traders on their first New York appearance.

A few years later, Deutsche Grammophon hired the British photographer Mitch Jenkins to do the Emerson Quartet, an all-male American ensemble that had not crossed over to anything. Together since 1976–77, they had already recorded the complete quartets of Bartók and Beethoven. A complete Mendelssohn was in production. A Haydn sampler was in the works. Jenkins's pitch-perfect cover art[64] showed how and why the four very bright, frequently funny, occasionally playful, and no longer quite young men, with their hands in their pockets, and varied and universal expressions, were the era's most interesting string quartet. Erect, fully clothed, and without their—needless to say acoustical—instruments, they are as far from Joachim as they are from Bond. If Bond's debut CD was worth a quarter of a million copies, Jenkins's photos of the Emerson were worth at least a thousand words on how art can be turned to image, but image can also be turned to art.

POETRY

THERE ARE ONLY two ways to make a point, the philosophy tutor explains to Molière's title figure, Jourdain, in *Le Bourgeois Gentilhomme*.[65] One is poetry, the other is prose. The violin has left its marks on both.

As early as the 1530s, a couplet ("In the meantime, felowes, pype up your fiddles, I say take them / And let your frendes here such mirth as ye can make them") shows up in the anonymous *Gammer Gurton's Needle*, one of the earliest English stage's greatest hits.[66] Whether the fiddles referred to are violins is, admittedly, a musicological guess.[67]

In any case, the question has been answered by 1708, when mirth resurfaces after an intervening Puritan ice age:

> Hark how the chearful Violin
> Its Silver Sounds sends forth,
> Whose sprightly Notes our Hearts incoine
> to Musick and to Mirth.[68]

A century later, mirth and fiddles reappear in cognate poems by William Wordsworth. In the first, Benjamin, the long-suffering title figure of Wordsworth's "The Waggoner," lets a retired sailor talk him into a couple of hours at "The CHERRY TREE," where not only " . . . a welcome greeting he can hear, it is a fiddle in its glee," but "The fiddle's 'squeak'—that call to bliss, [is] ever followed by a kiss."[69] Two hours and a toast to Lord Nelson later, the fiddle is there again, but mirth is in short supply. This time the scene is London's Oxford Street where "dusky-browed Jack," "the pale-visaged Baker," "the errand-bound Prentice," "the Newsman," "the half-breathless Lamplighter," "the Porter," "The Lass with Her Barrow,"

"The one-pennied Boy," "that Tall Man," "that Cripple, who leans on his crutch," and "that Mother, whose spirit in Fetters is bound," testify to "The Power of Music" as they crowd around a blind fiddler, while "coaches and chariots" roll imperviously by.[70]

By now, the street fiddler, a demotic Orpheus who peddled the consolations of art a penny at a time, was already a favorite of very different poets, whose very different poems would extend to the threshold of another new century. Translated from a poem by Hans Christian Andersen, Adalbert Chamisso's "Fiddler" preemptively defends himself against the disdain of the guests while doing his professional thing at the wedding of a lover he jilted. Joseph von Eichendorff's "Wandering Fiddler" hugs the violin that remains his friend, despite howling cats, barking dogs, and irate neighbors. Anton Wilhelm Florentin Zuccalmaglio's "Hunchback Fiddler" plays so well for partying witches on Walpurgisnacht that they send him home without a hump, thus inspiring a buddy to try to do the same. But he plays so badly that they send him home with a new hump in front as well as the old one on his back. Thomas Hardy's boy fiddler consoles a man in handcuffs being led to a train by a constable. William Butler Yeats's "Fiddler of Dooney" looks forward to entering heaven ahead of his two priest brothers:

> For the good are always the merry,
> Save by an evil chance,
> And the merry love the fiddle
> And the merry love to dance.[71]

Sooner or later, Robert Schumann, Reinhard Schwarz-Schilling, Johannes Brahms, Benjamin Britten, and Ivor Gurney would enshrine the respective fiddlers in art songs.

At the beginning of the twentieth century, Archibald Lampman, posthumously regarded as English Canada's finest nineteenth-century poet, also took up the fiddler trope in eighteen Tennysonian stanzas:

> In Dresden in the square one day,
> His face of parchment, seamed and gray,
> With wheezy bow and proffered hat,
> An old blind violinist sat.

And so it goes in penniless silence until an unidentified violinist happens by and takes charge to such effect that

> Throughout the great and silent crowd
> The music fell on human ears,
> And many kindly heads were bowed,
> And many eyes were warm with tears.

The crowd responds by filling the old fiddler's hat as the stranger slips away. As the last line reveals, the player is Ludwig Spohr.[72]

Beginning in the 1920s, the coming of radio and the recording industry turned successful fiddlers into national, even international, figures, and fiddling itself into a business sturdy enough to survive without Spohrs and to withstand the coming of rock 'n' roll.[73] In 1974, with help from Henry John Deutschendorf Jr., aka John Denver, John Martin Sommers's "Thank God I'm a Country Boy," with his daddy's injunction to "live a good life and play my fiddle with pride," became an instant classic.

To go by the career of Robert C. Byrd, the country boy from Stotesbury, West Virginia, who lived a good life and played his fiddle with respectable skill as well as pride en route to the longest-ever career in the U.S. Senate, the injunction could even be seen to work in real life. It all began with the school music teacher, who not only taught him from seventh to twelfth grade but sat him at the head of the school orchestra, Byrd explained to an interviewer from National Public Radio thirty years after Denver's bluegrass dithyramb made it to the top of the charts. But his future father-in-law and a left-handed contemporary who played a wicked "Old Joe Clark" also played a crucial role. So did Byrd's foster daddy, Titus, who laid out $20–30 for violin, bow, and case. It was more than most miners earned in a week. But it was also enough to carry young Bobby to the garden clubs, Odd Fellows Lodges, and Congress, where he was to remain from 1952 till his death in 2010.[74]

Other poets let a thousand tropes and paradigms bloom in images and languages as global as the instrument that inspired them.

> Violin seahorse and siren . . .
> Violin pride of light hands . . .
> Violin morganatic wife . . .
> Violin alcohol of the soul in pain . . .
> Violin knight of silence . . .

So wrote Louise de Vilmorin, poet, novelist, heiress to a seed fortune, penpal of Jean Cocteau, and companion of André Malraux, in verses that would be set to music by Francis Poulenc.

"Exulting violins," whose "streams of cries, sobs and kisses are unceasing and unrestrained," whose bows, "red hot irons, strip shreds of living flesh from our bodies."[75] So wrote Anne de Noailles, hostess to the likes of Claudel, Colette, and Valéry, painted by Laszlo and sculpted by Rodin, and commander of the Legion of Honor, in verses that would be set to music by Saint-Saëns.

"A violin is the voice of a fountain / Blown by rough, sweet puffs of wind," said the Colombian-born Carmen Conde, the first woman elected to the Royal Spanish Academy.

> Strange violin, do you follow me
> In how many distant cities did
> Your lonely night speak to mine?
> Do hundreds play you? Does one man play you?[76]

asked Rainer Maria Rilke, among the greatest of twentieth-century German poets.

> Violin was torn to pieces begging,
> And then broke out in tears
> So childishly,
> That Drum couldn't handle it any longer . . .
> The orchestra looked strangely, as
> Violin cried herself out—
> Wordless—
> Without tempo—
> And only somewhere
> Foolish Cymbals
> Were banging out:
> "What is it?"
> "How is it?" . . .
> I got up,
> Shaking, crawled over the notes,
> Bending low under the horror of the pupitre,
> For some reason cried out,

"Oh, God!"
Threw myself at her wooden neck,
"Violin, you know?
We are so alike:
I do also
Shout—
But still can not prove anything either!"
The musicians are laughing:
"Gotcha!
He's dating a wooden girlfriend!
Smart one, ha!"
I don't give a damn!
I am worthy!
"You know what, Violin?
Why don't we—
Move in together!
Ha?"[77]

declared Vladimir Mayakovsky, school dropout at fifteen, political prisoner at sixteen, art school matriculant at eighteen, published poet at nineteen, Bolshevik agitator at twenty-five, and deeply disillusioned suicide at thirty-seven.

After my death, thus shall you mourn me
There was a man—and see: he is no more!
Before his time did this man depart
And the song of his life in its midst was stilled
And alas! One more tune did he have
And now that tune is forever lost
Forever lost!
And great is the pity! For a violin had he
A living and singing soul
And this poet, whenever he voiced it
The inner secrets of his heart it expressed
All its strings his hand would make sing out.
Yet one hidden chord now is lost with him
Round and round it his fingers would dance
One string in his heart, mute has remained

Mute has remained—to this very day!
And great, oh great is the pity!
All its life this string would tremble
Silently quivering, silently trembling
To sound the tune that would set it free
Yearning, thirsting, sorrowing, desiring
As the heart sorrows for what fate has decreed
Though its tune was delayed—every day did it wait
And with unheard whisper begged it to come
Its time came and passed, and it never arrived
It never arrived!
And great, oh, how great is the pain
There was a man—and see: he is no more
And the song of his life in its midst is stilled
One more melody did he have
And now that song is forever lost
Forever lost!

wrote Chaim Nachman Bialik (1873–1934), a father of modern Hebrew
poetry, of himself.

One gentleman to another, Charles Valentine Le Grice, a classmate of
Coleridge and Charles Lamb and curate of St. Mary's, Penzance, composed
a sonnet "To a Gentleman, Who Presented the Author with a Violin":

. . . Oft in sorrow's saddest hour
The softest magic of thy power,
Shall sooth my troubled breast to peace,
Till the hushed storm shall seem to cease . . . [78]

Where class went, gender usually followed. In a package of quatrains
published in 1877, an anonymous bard contrasts the untaught virtues
of Mary, who "has but little learning," with Mirabel, "who's monstrous
clever," a Royal Academy grad, and plays the violin.[79] Where "Mirabel, on
music doting, comes it rather strong," and "Mary's voice is music, linking
soul to soul," it was clear where things were going.

Fifteen years later, a real-life Mirabel replied with verses of her own,
in this case a love sonnet addressed to her violin. Born like the versified
Mirabel in 1877, Marion Scott was the homeschooled child of a solicitor

father whose piano teacher had studied with Liszt. Home chamber music with the neighbors, themselves friends of Joachim, and the Rev. E. H. Moberly's Ladies String Orchestra led to the Royal College of Music, where she graduated in 1905. The same year, she published a slender volume, *Violin Verses*, whose contents range from a birthday sonnet to the Betts Strad to a collection of such practical tips as

> If you wish to acquire a brilliant staccato,
> Begin with a stroke that is almost legato
> Played at a tempo about moderato,
> Then sharpen the stroke till the whole thing's marcato . . . [80]

In 1896, the year that Scott entered the Royal College, James B. Kenyon (1858–1924), then a widely published and now a totally forgotten American poet, inadvertently showed how far things had come since Maribel:

> I would I were her violin,
> To rest beneath her dimpled chin,
> And softly kiss her swan-white throat,
> And breathe my love through every note.[81]

By now, more interesting poems and poets had taken up the theme in ways no American would match for decades. Set among images of sun, sky, flower, church, and melancholy waltzes, with "no hint of vice, of perversity, no blasphemy, no sympathy with darkness and death," as one analyst noted, a violin would take its place as early as 1857 when Charles Baudelaire reached for a sixteen-line Malayan verse form called the pantoum for "Harmonie du Soir" ("Evening Harmony"), one of his famously scandalous "Fleurs du mal," or "Flowers of Evil."[82] English-language translators struggled with the image of a violin that "frémit comme un coeur qu'on afflige" in the French original, successively rendering it as "quivers like a tormented heart," "like a heart palpitates," and "thrills like a tortured heart."[83] Irrespective of translation, "Harmonie du Soir" would become "one of the most eulogized and anthologized French poems."[84]

Another classic, not only of French literature but of modern poetry, Verlaine's "Chanson d'Automne"[85] goes back to 1866, when the poet was twenty-two. The often-cited "sanglots longs des violons de l'automne" in its opening lines were a challenge to translators too. Versions lovingly collected by C. John Holcombe, himself a published poet with experience in mining research, finance, and numismatics,[86] ranged from

> When the sighing begins
> In the violins
> Of the autumn song. . . .

to

> Long moans on autumn's saxophones . . .

Michel Esnault, a retired Marseille postal official with a passion for local history and archaeology as well as literature, called attention to the poem's association of melancholy, fatalism, and time of year,[87] while overlooking or taking for granted that it may well have been the first time any one of these themes, let alone all three, had been associated with the violin.

Unsurprisingly in an age of fiddle worship, the instrument came in for its share of literary attention with a little hymn to Ole Bull's Stradivari in the prologue to Henry Wadsworth Longfellow's "Tales of a Wayside Inn."

> Exquisite was it in design,
> Perfect in each minutest part.
> A marvel of the lutist's art;
> And in its hollow chamber, thus,
> The maker from whose hands it came
> Had written his unrivalled name,—
> "Antonius Stradivarius."[88]

Two years after the famous South Kensington show of 1872, Mary Anne Evans, otherwise known as George Eliot, dedicated 151 lines of iambic pentameter to

> that plain white-aproned man, who stood at work
> Patient and accurate full four score years.

Her "soul was lifted by the wings to-day," thanks to Joachim, "the master of the violin," and "great Sebastian, who made that fine Chaconne," she reported. But neither Bach nor Joachim had "made our joy today."

> Another soul was living in the air
> And swaying it to true deliverance
> Of high invention and responsive skill.

The reflection leads to a dialogue between Stradivari, already nearing seventy, and Naldo,

> a painter of eclectic school . . .
> knowing all tricks of style at thirty-one,
> and weary of them.

who challenges the old man to justify his art.

> Stradivari is unmoved:
> . . . when any master holds
> 'Twixt chin and hand a violin of mine,
> He will be glad that Stradivari lived,

he answers coolly.

Yet not everyone saw it quite this way. In Amy Lowell's "Cremona Violin," first published in *Men, Women and Ghosts*, a mixed bag of poems that the author somewhat coquettishly introduces as "a book of stories,"[89] "a fine Cremona pattern" becomes the inadvertent party to a domestic triangle. It then becomes its victim. An unlikely iconoclast from a family of New England achievers, Lowell was more musical than most, a dedicated Boston Symphony subscriber who regularly invited friends to home musicales. Carl Engel, the Paris-born, German-educated musicologist-composer who would later head the Music Division of the Library of Congress, introduced her to the music of Stravinsky and Bartók decades before most Americans had even heard of them. He also introduced her to the French symbolist poets.[90] Composed only three years earlier, the second of Stravinsky's *Three Pieces for String Quartet* would also find its place in *Men, Women and Ghosts*.

> Pale violin music whiffs across the moon,
> A pale smoke of violin music blows over the moon,
> Cherry petals fall and flutter,
> And the white Pierrot,

Wreathed in the smoke of the violins,
Splashed with cherry petals falling, falling,
Claws a grave for himself in the fresh earth
With his finger-nails.

Unlike the music, which is still played, the poem has long since become an heirloom of the early twentieth century avant-garde.

"The Cremona Violin," on the other hand, still has scenario potential. Young Lotta is married to the somewhat older Theodore Altgelt, concertmaster of the Bavarian court orchestra, who plays "as few men can." But while "gentle and unambitious," Theodore is married to his Strad, leaving his wife to

. . . [rise] and softly, pit-a-pat,
[Climb] up the stairs, and in her little room
[Find] sighing comfort with a moon in bloom

when he comes home for tea and a nap after the afternoon rehearsal.

Lotta walks out to look at her garden and falls into conversation with Heinrich, a handsome passerby. Guileless as he is clueless, Theodore reports over lunch the next day that Frau Gebnitz, the great soprano currently singing with the orchestra, has taken up with a lover because

. . . Gebnitz is a stone,
Pores over books all day, and has no ear
For his wife's singing.

That afternoon, while window-shopping in town, Lotta runs into Heinrich in front of a jewelry store. He insists on buying her a locket. It is clear by now where this is going. And then: the young Mozart, not quite twenty-five, arrives for the premiere of his new opera.

"Idomeneo" was the opera's name,
A name that poor Charlotta learnt to hate.
Herr Altgelt worked so hard he seldom came
Home for his tea, and it was very late,
Past midnight sometimes. . . .
He practised every morning and her heart

> Followed his bow. But often she would sit,
> While he was playing, quite withdrawn apart,
> Absently fingering and touching it,
> The locket . . .

Torn between Heinrich's love and Theodore's Strad, Lotta considers suicide while washing dishes.

> . . . What kept her here, why should she wait?
> The violin she had begun to hate
> Lay in its case before her. Here she flung
> The cover open. With the fiddle swung
>
> Over her head, the hanging clock's loud ticking
> Caught on her ear. 'Twas slow, and as she paused
> The little door in it came open, flicking
> A wooden cuckoo out. . . . "Cuckoo!"
> Smashed on the grate, the violin broke in two.
>
> "Cuckoo! Cuckoo!" the clock kept striking on;
> But no one listened. Frau Altgelt had gone.

Lowell's contemporary, poet and Lincoln biographer Carl Sandburg, produced no fewer than three love letters in two years in collections that won him his first Pulitzer Prize. The first, "Bath," is addressed to the virtuoso Mischa Elman.

A MAN saw the whole world as a grinning skull and crossbones. The rose flesh of life shriveled from all faces. Nothing counts. Everything is a fake. Dust to dust and ashes to ashes and then an old darkness and a useless silence. So he saw it all. Then he went to a Mischa Elman concert. Two hours waves of sound beat on his eardrums. Music washed something or other inside him. Music broke down and rebuilt something or other in his head and heart. He joined in five encores for the young Russian Jew with the fiddle. When he got outside his heels hit the sidewalk a new way. He was the same man in the same world as before. Only there was a singing fire and a climb of roses everlastingly over the world he looked on.[91]

The second is dedicated to the virtuoso Jan Kubelik:

YOUR bow swept over a string, and a long low note quivered to the
  air.
(A mother of Bohemia sobs over a new child perfect learning to suck
  milk.)

Your bow ran fast over all the high strings fluttering and wild.
(All the girls in Bohemia are laughing on a Sunday afternoon in the
  hills with their lovers.)[92]

The third is dedicated to the virtuoso Fritz Kreisler:

SELL me a violin, mister, of old mysterious wood.
Sell me a fiddle that has kissed dark nights on the forehead where
  men kiss sisters they love.
Sell me dried wood that has ached with passion clutching the knees
  and arms of a storm.
Sell me horsehair and rosin that has sucked at the breasts of the
  morning sun for milk.
Sell me something crushed in the heartsblood of pain readier than
  ever for one more song.[93]

In the strenuous decades that followed, there would be plenty of great fiddling available to ever larger audiences. But not even Heifetz, the greatest
of them all, seems to have inspired anything comparable from Sandburg
or anyone else. Heifetz inspired awe. He even inspired Leo Durocher,
one of baseball's most colorful figures in thirty-four years as a major
league manager. Searching for measures adequate to describe his superlative center fielder, Willie Mays, Durocher reached for Joe Louis, the great
heavyweight, Sammy Davis Jr., the great entertainer, Nashua, the great
racehorse, and Heifetz.[94] But Heifetz did not inspire poetry, unlike Elman,
Kubelik, Kreisler, and Paganini. As the editor, essayist, poet, and talented
musical amateur Leigh Hunt reported after hearing Paganini in 1834:

> His hand . . . clinging to the serious chords
> With godlike ravishment drew forth a breath
> So deep, so strong, so fervid, thick with love—
> Blissful, yet laden as with twenty prayers—

That Juno yearned with no diviner soul
To the first burthen of the lips of Jove.[95]

Even sympathetic critics agreed that the poem was not Hunt at his best.[96] But it left no doubt, at least, that hearing Paganini was not an everyday experience. The Viennese dramatist Franz Grillparzer, who had personally signed Paganini's autograph book, needed no persuading to testify to the master's magic, either—in twelve lines of iambic pentameter published in 1872.[97]

Dann aber höhnst du sie und dich,
Brichst spottend aus in gellendes Gelächter?
Du wärst kein Mörder? Frevler du am Ich
Des eigenen Leibs, der eignen Seele Mörder!
Und auch der meine—doch ich weich' dir aus![98]

But then you thumb your nose at them and you,
Burst out in screaming peals of scornful laughter?
No killer you? Transgressor on yourself,
Killer of The soul and body that you call your own!
And also mine—but I won't let you catch me!

Almost a century and a half later, Paganini's magic still inspired Scott Emmons, a PhD in classics, whose online collection of light verse, *The Daily Rhyme* (www.thedailyrhyme.com), supplemented his day job as a writer of greeting card texts for Hallmark.[99]

Paganini, Paganini,
Mortal, demon, witch or genie,
Mephistophelean maestro
Of the mystic violin!
With the sting of your staccato
And your prickly pizzicato,
When you'd diddle on your fiddle
It was little short of sin!

Paganini, Paganini,
Lean and lanky like linguine,
With a manner that was manic

And satanic when you played,
How your haunting hint of Hades
Would inflame the local ladies!
You were fiery, you were wiry,
You were very often laid![100]

PROSE

"MUSICAL NOVELS ARE not absolutely new, but they are still too rare to be hackneyed," an anonymous *New York Times* reviewer noted as late as 1878. It was another few decades before the flirtation of fiddle, fiddler, and fiction settled into a stable relationship. From then on, the relationship would be both flexible and durable, as novelists great and small, good, bad, and ugly, nurtured, cherished, and exploited its potential. "We have numberless pieces of fiction having to do with fiddles," another anonymous reviewer reported in 1896.[101]

As a couple of good quartet novels would prove, the trope could even be made to work in chamber ensembles. A bit of *Rashomon*, a bit of *Art of the Fugue*, Nathan Shaham's *Rosendorf Quartet*[102] counterpoints the many-leveled culture shocks of the ensemble's German Jewish characters as they struggle with their identities, histories, and one another in Mandatory Palestine during the Arab Uprising of 1936–39. The young players of Vikram Seth's *An Equal Music*,[103] coping concurrently with the open-ended challenges of their art, their livelihood, and their emotional lives in a London as remote from the golden age of Hill's as it is from Queen Victoria's Diamond Jubilee, are clearly recognizable to any quartet player.

The trope could also play out with success on an orchestral scale. Credible, articulate, and occasionally hilarious, the chess-playing music stand partners of Wolfgang Camphausen's *Eine kleine Schachmusik* are creations of a professional violinist whose decades of experience included seventeen summers in Bayreuth. Even their game, a nominal time-killer during a rehearsal break, is based on a careful study of the Hungarian grand master Géza Maróczy's anthology of a hundred great matches.[104] Meanwhile, implacable as bullfighters, they reflect on life, art, history, politics, Mozart, Wagner, sex, money, their wives, children, colleagues, conductors, audiences, and their considerable reservations about themselves and one another. "It's surely unnecessary, but necessary, to mention that the musicians, conductors, board members, women, children and even stage directors who appear in this book don't exist in reality," the author adds with what has to be a wink. "Similarities should be accepted with tolerance."

Still, in prose as in verse and image, the solo violin exercised a gravitational pull no other instrument or combination of instruments could match. Tropes devised triumphantly for the lending library, for ladies' magazines, and for the Yiddish theater were just as adaptable a century later to movie, TV, and computer screens, airport bookstores and e-book readers. Professor Moriarty came and went. Sherlock Holmes, an "eccentric" but "very capable performer of no ordinary merit," proud owner of a Strad "worth at least five hundred guineas," acquired "at a Jew broker's in Tottenham Court Road for fifty-five shillings," and a fan of Sarasate and Neruda, was still standing.[105] But some motifs were inevitably more popular than others.

Unsurprisingly, the misplaced or stolen, but usually recovered, Old Master was a perennial favorite, and Britain was its natural venue. Published in the golden age of Hill's, Edward Heron-Allen's novella *A Fatal Fiddle*, Walter Mayson's *The Stolen Fiddle*, and Charles Allen's *Papier Mâché* are early benchmarks.[106]

All three authors are as English as afternoon tea. Each is at home in a world where class is to society as north is to compass. Insiders themselves, all three write for readers who shop or would like to shop at Hill's.

Though *A Fatal Fiddle* was conceived and published in the United States, where Heron-Allen was on a three-year tour as an expert in palmistry, its milieu could hardly be less American. Despite his modest middle-class origins, Harold, a junior official in H. M. Department of Waste Paper and Sealing Wax and an accomplished amateur violinist, aspires to the department's top career job. Opportunity knocks when his superior, a devoted violin collector, invites him to a Foreign Office reception. Eager to shine, Harold spots a del Gesù among the clutter. He borrows it for the evening, makes a dazzling impression, and gets his promotion. Tipsy with success, he then leaves it on the train.

When a slippery French dealer finds him another del Gesù at a hair-raising £900, the desperate Harold borrows what he needs from "the Jews," then joins his brother-in-law's prospering haberdashery business to pay off the loan. A generation later, he meets his former patron for the first time since his resignation. "What a tragedy!" his patron exclaims when he realizes what happened. It appears that he had really owned a del Gesù but had loaned Harold a cheap copy. He then unknowingly sold the original twice, first for £700 to Harold's dealer, again for £7 when he assumed that Harold had returned the copy.

Mayson's story, too, plays out among the great and good. But his essentially guileless story is wrapped in a patriotic statement. The scene is a country house in the Lake District. An amateur quartet includes an earl as cellist; his sister, who owns and plays a Strad; a baronet's heir who drops by to show off his new English violin; and a violist neighbor who also collects instruments. A crooked butler's assistant, his brother, and "a singularly shrewd" foreign dealer, "whether German, Italian or French, I am not going to tell you," are the worms in their collective apple. Mr. Jones, a private detective who chases the burglars over a picturesque landscape in a picturesque costume, connects the story lines.

The intervening pages cover Wordsworth's grave, dialect jokes, a Christmas celebration where "all for the time [are] socially equal and sincerely well-disposed one to the other," and a Diamond Jubilee festivity "where the deserving poor or middle class felt proud to be asked." The high point is the courtroom scene, where it turns out that the "Strad" the singularly shrewd dealer sold the violist neighbor for £450 is the stolen English violin the baronet's nephew bought for £25. As the novel ends, "the Queen is so much struck by the fact of a modern Englishman being able to produce an instrument declared to be the work of Stradivarius," that she confers "the honour of knighthood" on its maker.

Characterized in an early twenty-first-century catalogue as "a detective novel involving the theft of a Stradivarius, written by an author who had misread too much Henry James,"[107] Charles Allen's version is hard to confuse with *The Golden Bowl* or *Portrait of a Lady*. But the narrative elements—a missing Strad, a burglar and a crooked maker, and a son who risks loss of the family title and estate if the instrument is stolen—are familiar. The action also migrates to Australia, where the narrative elements are taken in hand by the long arm of coincidence. In the end, virtue and true love come out ahead as the burglar's son ends up with the Strad and the titled young man ends up with both his title and the violin maker's daughter. "A good sound moral," said the *New York Times*'s reviewer.

A century later, the genre remained as fresh as ever. But this time, a quintet of global titles—Paul Adam's *Sleeper*, marketed in the United States as *The Rainaldi Quartet*; Douglas Preston and Lincoln Childs's *Brimstone*; Joseph Roccasalvo's *Portrait of a Woman*; Jô Soares's *A Samba for Sherlock*; and Gerald Elias's *Devil's Trill*—marked its progress.[108]

For a start, the genre, like so many things, had crossed the sea. Americans who had found one another at New York's American Museum of Natural History, Preston and Childs were potboiler auteurs of novel-a-year industriousness whose "airport ubiquitous" titles, as one admiring reader described them, could be "consumed in one sitting like a bag of cookies." Roccasalvo, also American, was a Harvard PhD and professor of comparative religion as well as a Roman Catholic priest. His four novels and two novellas between 1995 and 2007 seemed likelier to have been written for fun than for profit. Adam, an ex-journalist with nine novels in twelve years, was British but had worked in Rome and his native northern England.[109] The Brazilian Soares, in his late fifties when he took to writing novels, had already made a career as an entertainer and TV talk-show host.[110] Elias, another American, had aspired in his Long Island childhood to play first base for the New York Yankees but settled for violin lessons. He studied with Galamian and played for thirteen years with the Boston Symphony before taking a job as associate concertmaster of the Utah Symphony. His Utah job allowed him to teach, perform, conduct from Australia to Peru, take his family to Italy for a year, and learn a few useful things about Japan.[111]

Like Mayson and Heron-Allen, Elias not only spoke Violin with native fluency; he wrote it with the dedicated glee of a man with a lifetime of scores to settle. The others, though fluent in languages including Murder, Sex, Wines, Fine Dining, even Art History, had clearly learned Violin as a foreign language.

For Soares, like Charles Allen and Conan Doyle, Stradivari is essentially a brand name. His missing Strad, stolen from the emperor's lady friend on the threshold of chapter one and purportedly one of only two in Brazil, is immediately put to imaginative use in the murder of the first of four prostitutes. But it has neither history nor provenance. Preston and Child's missing Strad, ostensibly "played by Franz Clement at the premiere of Beethoven's violin concerto . . . by Brahms himself at the premiere of his Second Violin Concerto and by Paganini at the first Italian performance of all twenty-four of his caprices,"[112] has both. They're just fanciful in ways that would have made Mayson's and Heron-Allen's eyes roll.

Yet hints of current events suggest that they at least had an occasional look at the newspapers. Tomaso, Adam's luthier victim, is apparently on a collision course with a high-profile British dealer in hot pursuit of a Messiah clone. The crucial difference is that the luthier is believed to be without an enemy in the world, while the dealer stops at nothing. The search leads to coded portraits of Count Cozio and his proxy, Anselmi di Briata, a London auction, the batty heir to a dead collector, alone in a houseful of cats, and the Stradivari artifacts in the Cremona museum. In the end, a lost Maggini is reunited with its owner, and a collection of golden age masters, left orphaned by the murder of its Venetian owner, is turned into a charitable foundation for young players. Relieved and contrite, Gianni, the surviving maker, incinerates the del Gesù copy he once sold to the murdered Venetian as Ludwig Spohr's long-lost original.

Buoyed by their success, Gianni and his buddy Antonio, the cello player/cop, return for a reprise five years later in *The Ghost of Paganini*.[113] So does the ever-popular motif of the missing Strad, a fictional gift from Catherine the Great to Viotti that reportedly reached Paganini as a gift from Napoleon's formidable sister, Elisa, before disappearing after the death of Rossini's first wife, the soprano Isabella Colbran.

There are few surprises en route to the eventual recovery and decent Italian lunch at which the last loose ends are finally tied. But two scenes at least enhance the author's credibility. In the first, a dazzlingly gifted Russian prizewinner is amazed to meet people who play for no other reason than personal satisfaction. In the second, he joins the surviving members of Rainaldi's quartet in the fifth, the cavatina, movement of Beethoven's op. 130 in their friend's memory.

Soares, with no larger purpose than fun, has Sarah Bernhardt bring Sherlock Holmes to Rio de Janeiro a year before his literary birth. In quick order he dazzles the natives with Portuguese acquired in Guinea, wows a soubrette while inadvertently saving her from murder, and attends a Yoruba séance where Watson does his best to channel the wanted killer. Sherlock also takes up pot smoking, nearly capitulates to the host country's explosive cuisine, and performs brilliantly on Brazil's only other Strad. As expected, he also performs prodigious feats of deduction, all of them hopelessly off the mark. He meanwhile misses every possible clue before returning to England, serenely unaware that the serial killer he missed in Brazil is aboard the same ship, en route to London to resume his career as Jack the Ripper.

With an assist from Preston and Childs, even Stradivari's varnish gets a curtain call. Their Brimstone Strad has not been seen since the eve of World War I, when tertiary syphilis swept away the libidinous Italian virtuoso who was its last publicly visible owner. It resurfaces in the manichean world of President Ronald Reagan and the physicist Edward Teller. Its owner has a powerful hunch that Stradivari's legendary preservative might be the key to developing a nuclear reentry vehicle capable of beating a Star Wars defense. In the end, he falls victim to a bit of ingenious devilry by an heir to the original owner.

Roccasalvo follows Preston and Childs as good cop follows bad. Once again, the varnish is at the heart of the story. But this time it appears with harp and wings. Philip, an agnostic Harvard PhD candidate, already has one blockbuster novel under his belt. He now spends weekends in the well-recommended quiet of a Benedictine convent working on the next one. There he falls under the spell of Mother Ambrose, née Beatrice Stradivari, and gets up his nerve to ask her for the legendary formula. "It's critical to a book I'm writing," he explains. She confirms that it's real, "But what is missing is essential: how the varnish is applied to the violin parts." She then explains how the varnish, like divine grace, "is the same for all but varies in its application." They agree that the formula will be put up for auction, with the proceeds going to an appropriate charitable foundation.

By any standards, and certainly Roccasalvo's, Elias's story is conventionally earthy and implacably earthly, despite a sympathetic parish priest who plays Watson to the author's Holmes and a cantankerous Jewish violin teacher who is blinded by a rare genetic disorder. Like generations of his predecessors, Elias plays the Strad card. But this Strad is three-quarter size, built for an invented midget virtuoso known as Piccolino, who was born on February 29 in a mid-seventeenth-century leap year.

According to a nominal contemporary source, Piccolino was also the proud owner of another instrument, this one full-sized and a particular hit with the ladies. Among them is the Strad's donor, a duchess who orders the violin as a present on the occasion of her diminutive lover's thirteenth (that is, fifty-second) birthday. To both her own and Piccolino's misfortune, neither instrument is of any help when the duke returns unexpectedly, sword in hand. Named for its dedicatee, the Piccolino Strad has been bad news ever since.

Rediscovered some two hundred years later by an itinerant American millionaire, it has meanwhile become the linchpin of a competition held every thirteen years for prodigies under the age of thirteen. Enter the difficult hero, a onetime competitor who suspects that the competition's current board is running both a tax scam and a barely sanitized version of kiddie porn. In due course, the violin vanishes and the queen-bee violin teacher is strangled with a G string. Prime suspect of both the theft and the murder, Elias's hero takes off for Kyushu, Japan's most southwesterly main island, accompanied by a green-eyed local protégée and his faithful sidekick, an African-American cellist turned insurance claims adjuster. They return with the violin to solve the murder and await the author's second novel.

A couple of late twentieth-century products show how the instrument itself can carry a story. John Hersey's *Antonietta*[114] features a fictional Strad, nominally inspired by the fifty-five-year-old maker's impending marriage to his second wife, Antonia Maria Zambelli. The work of an accomplished professional in the sixth decade of a distinguished career, the novel's five chapter-length "acts" and four mini-lecture "intermezzi" carry the instrument from baroque Cremona on the eve of the eighteenth century to baroque Martha's Vineyard on the eve of the twenty-first, with stopovers in Paris and Lausanne, where Mozart, Berlioz, and Stravinsky can also appreciate its possibilities.

Hersey had studied seriously in China with a White Russian émigré as a schoolboy.[115] "This book was written for the fun of it," he announced preemptively. But there is never any doubt that the author, who had homes in Key West and Martha's Vineyard, knew what he was talking about. The payoff includes a Cremonese lunch menu and bread recipe, the tools needed for the thicknessing of Antonietta's maple back, a respectable English-language approximation of the potty-mouthed whimsy the twenty-two-year-old Mozart reserved for his cousin in Augsburg, and Berlioz's reverence for Gluck and despair at the academicians who repeatedly passed him over for the Prix de Rome. A guide to the Russian émigré scene in Lausanne during World War I, with reminiscences of the legendary Paris premiere of "Le Sacre du Printemps," is also included.

But the last "act," with its pitch-perfect ear for dialogue, high-definition eye for culture and couture, and virtuoso display of pickled tongue in cheek, suspends any residual disbelief that the book is meant for fun. A cadenza in the form of a shooting script, it follows Spenser Ham, who "buys and sells companies, you know, that sort of thing," as he wheels and deals between his Saarinen summer house on Martha's Vineyard and his Grand Bahama Island money laundry. When a designer guest tells him that he has no music in his soul, he boards the next London-bound Concorde and buys Antonietta. Reminded that a Strad, "like a great Arabian stallion . . . has to be *exercised*," he hires a pair of eye-catching young women, a violinist and pianist with a passion for Schoenberg, Hindemith, and Bartók, to show the summer people what Antonietta can do. The sweetener, for guests of more conservative taste, is a postrecital drawing with $25,000 as first prize. Responding to a call for volunteers to draw the winning ticket, a federal prosecutor and an investigator from the Securities and Exchange Commission march to the front of the room, serve papers, and lead the host away in handcuffs. As "the room vibrates with frustrated avarice," the novel ends and the players restore calm with a piano reduction of the Schoenberg concerto.

The biography of a rather different fictional violin, Kees van Hage's *Verstreken Jaren*[116] (*Times Gone By*) appeared a year later in Amsterdam. Like Hersey's, van Hage's story line extends over multiple generations. But unlike Hersey's, there are no translations, a serious disservice to a technically accomplished, historically informed, and richly imagined historical novel whose credible, multidimensional, and frequently funny characters deserve to be known beyond Holland, half of Belgium, and Suriname.

The only known celebration of a Markneukirchen violin in all of world literature, van Hage's novel begins with its creation by a dedicated hunchback who is appalled by the easy capitulation of his neighbors and colleagues to a cottage industry version of mass production. With the town on fire behind him,[117] he carries it off to Leipzig, where Mendelssohn, Schumann, and Ferdinand David appear in the story. From there, it passes via Mendelssohn's protégé Johannes Verhulst to the concertmaster of the Diligentia Orchestra in The Hague, who watches fascinated as the conservative Verhulst politics his way to an appointment as the orchestra's conductor. The next owner, an Amsterdam maker-dealer, is so put off by his brother's self-righteous socialism that he slips him a copy and makes off with the original. Its next owner leaves it behind in Berlin as he reports to his induction center in 1916 for a one-way ticket to the front. It returns to Holland with a German-Jewish violin teacher on the eve of World War II; he also leaves and doesn't come back. In swingy postwar Amsterdam a generation later, the violin is wrenched away by muggers as its latest owner and his pianist-fiancée make their way home after a triumphant graduation recital. The story ends—where else?—in post-unification Markneukirchen, where a West German brother, not averse to a bit of a currency scam as the West German mark replaces the East German mark, brings it back to his East German brother for restoration.

Now and then, authors have let the instrument speak for itself. Maud des Champs de la Tour's obscurely produced and conceivably pseudonymous *History of a Violin*,[118] a strong contender for worst novel ever published in English, begins with the arrival of a sycamore in Stradivari's workshop, where "Madame Stradivari poured out the chocolate and liqueurs for the guests, while her lovely daughter Zerlina, carried around the sweet cakes and confetti, aided by young Joseph Guarnerius—Antonio's pupil." Things move downhill from there.

Over the next 274 pages, the instrument born of the sycamore is walled up in a cupboard, lost in the snow, rediscovered in Paris, and dropped down a flight of stairs. But whatever the vicissitude, the challenge at every step is the same: keeping it away from or recovering it from the clutches of "old Abramo, the Jew-broker," "signor Isacco," who peddles junk as Strads and Amatis, "the Jew-boy we have all seen lurking about the village for some time," a "little Jew-girl," "two villainous-looking Jew-men," a "crafty Jewess," "a sullen, haggard-looking Jewess," and generally "my hated and irrepressible enemies, the Jews."

Over a century would pass before Thomas Marrocco, a California musicologist and quartet player, showed what a knowledgable musician could do with a retirement project and a vanity press. His talking Strad[119] may be an invention. It may even be androgynous, as it preemptively points out on the first page. But like few violins in fiction, it has an ear for language, an eye for the ridiculous, a feel for history, and an insider's understanding of the trade.

The charm, virtues, and, above all, the credibility of the story are already clear within three pages. "I have been caressed, fondled, treasured and worshipped," the narrator begins. "I have also been bought, sold, abused, pawned, stolen, imitated, neglected, traded and even put in solitary confinement in a bank vault." And then comes the clincher, "I was scratched and beaten black and blue during the premiere performance of Schoenberg's violin concerto."

The rest is a joy ride: sales to Vivaldi, Tartini, and almost to Viotti; a bumpy tour with an heir to the Duke of Northumberland who is forced to sell after losing an arm at the battle of Trafalgar; acquisition by Henry Lockey Hill; and the horrified discovery by 1830 that "I was a collectible." These events lead, in turn, to encounters with Vuillaume and Paganini; a near miss by a thief who substitutes a copy; resale by Achille to Teresina Tua; a near meltdown on a concert tour of Cairo; theft by a local garbage collector, tipped off by his chambermaid wife, followed by recovery and restoration in Naples by Vincenzo Gagliano. The latest in a five-generational clan, Gagliano, of course, sees his chance to make a copy with a Strad label.

The real fun begins on the threshold of the twentieth century, when the instrument passes to Ysaÿe in time to survive the San Francisco earthquake. Soon afterward, an Iowa farmer who has somehow acquired the Gagliano copy innocently tries to sell it as a Strad. The litigation, laid out in loving detail, ends with Ysaÿe's original acknowledged as authentic and Gagliano's copy authoritatively identified as the work of the Torinese Giovanni Francesco Pressenda.

Once more led astray, the narrator passes through a Marseille pawnshop, becomes an inadvertent accessory to the heroin trade, and joins an all-Strad quartet in German-occupied Rome. The violin is hidden from marauding Waffen-SS in a toilet, is traded for hard currency in postwar Zurich, and turns up, in a particularly nice, local touch, at Hans Weisshaar's shop in Los Angeles during the heroic restoration of the Red Diamond Strad. As might be expected, it then returns to Hill's, and eventually Sotheby's, where it worries with reason about becoming a hedge against inflation, an amateur's toy, or a tax-deductible charitable contribution, before settling down in a glass case in Paganini's Villa Gaione. At least, it consoles itself, it will be safe there from another round of Schoenberg.

Compared with Marrocco's fictional Strad, Jean Diwo's altogether real Milanollo Strad[120] has every reason to be a happy fiddle. Certified previous owners include the great G. B. Viotti, the double bass virtuoso Domenico Dragonetti, and the twentieth-century masters Christian Ferras and Pierre Amoyal, as well as Milanollo herself, the prodigy the instrument is named for.[121] Its latest owner at the time of writing was department head at a major Swiss hospital with a mantelful of awards and publications. He took exquisite care of it. He also wanted it played.[122]

Its current player, still young, with a respectable career ahead of him, liked Mozart, Fauré, and Wieniawski.[123] Diwo's publisher, France's fourth largest, turns out seven hundred titles a year.[124] The author himself, by now a nonagenarian, had been a senior editor at *Paris Match* and founding editor of *Télé 7 Jours*, France's *TV Guide,* before his retirement in 1982. He then produced best seller after best seller, including a book on his family's Paris neighborhood that sold a million copies.[125]

As might be expected, he had a feel for people who actually knew the Milanollo: Etienne Vatelot, the dean of Paris dealers, Christian Ferras, the formidable talent who succumbed to depression and alcohol at forty-nine, and Amoyal, the Heifetz protégé torn between reverence for the memory of his friend, admiration for the Milanollo, and his need for a serious instrument while trying to recover his own 1717 Kochanski Strad after it was stolen.

His feel for history, on the other hand, including claims to a Milanollo-Bach encounter at the court of Anhalt-Köthen, a Haydn-Viotti encounter in London, and a Ferras-Menuhin encounter in a recording studio, inclined to the casual. Neither his publisher nor his readers seemed terribly concerned that Bach left Anhalt-Köthen five years before the Milanollo was built, Haydn left London a month before Viotti arrived, and the violinists Ferras and Menuhin were an unlikely pair to record the Brahms concerto for violin and cello. "Known and appreciated, therefore carefree about tomorrow and unworried about the future, I am, and am comfortable being, a philosopher-violin," Diwo's Milanollo concludes philosophically.[126]

Now and then, as in Balzac's "Gambara,"[127] Grillparzer's "Der arme Spielmann," ("The Poor Fiddler"),[128] and Herman Melville's "The Fiddler,"[129] the medium actually approaches philosophy. Contemporaries of Beethoven, both Balzac and Grillparzer were fully aware of what he represented. Balzac had also fiddled as a child, and Grillparzer had wanted to until family fears of scoliosis put a stop to it.[130] Though Gambara is an instrument maker-composer, and Grillparzer's poor fiddler a player, an interest in how and why musicians do what they do is the common motif. The essential message of both is the power of art and the limits of human endeavor.

A native Cremonese whose father performed, composed, and built instruments, Gambara follows his path. It leads to a Venetian patron and a Venetian wife. But nothing works, and the couple settles miserably among the Italian diaspora in Paris, where Gambara's wife supports him by working as a seamstress for the local hookers.

Though actually interested in Gambara's wife, a young Milanese count seems an interested listener as Gambara lays out the theory and design of his projected masterpiece, a trilogy on the life and eventual triumph of Mohammed. Certain that he's listening to a madman, the count comes around after Gambara performs the score on the panharmonicon, the extraordinary synthesizer he hopes will make his fortune.

A few drinks bring Gambara around to unaccustomed moderation. But he only regrets it on sobering up in the morning. Writing off the wine therapy as a failure, the count decamps for Italy with Mme. Gambara, who has also despaired of Gambara after fifteen years of marriage.

Six years later, she returns, emaciated and aged. Gambara has been forced to auction his panharmonicon and sell his extraordinary score to the neighborhood vendors for wrapping fish and fruit. Since instrument repair pays too little, they now moonlight on the Champs-Élysées, performing passages from Gambara's operas, accompanied by Gambara's guitar.

"It is my misfortune to have heard the chorus of angels, and believed that men could understand the strains," Gambara explains to a principessa who takes pity on them. Moved to tears by her gesture, he invents an aphorism to cover his desperation and embarrassment. "L'eau est un corps brûlé"; "Water is a burning body," he says, as he wipes his eyes.

Grillparzer's story is equally bleak, and his Jacob in many ways a Viennese Gambara. But the differences matter, too. Gambara is middle-aged, thinks big, is a musician by choice and training, as well as by inheritance, and has a wife. Jacob is around seventy, thinks little, is a musician by default, and has regrets.

Still, the affinities are strong. Jacob hears the angel chorus as clearly as does Gambara. His contemporaries are just as insensible to it. "They play Wolfgang Amadeus Mozart and Sebastian Bach, but nobody plays God," he tells the narrator sadly. Resolved as best he can to educate listeners he considers both distracted and misguided, he divides his day in a routine as regular as the seasons. In the morning he practices. In the afternoon he earns his miserable living. In the evening he plays for himself and God. He succeeds only in turning off a handful of kids who want a waltz from a player with no idea how to play one. He tests the patience of a neighbor who asks from the middle of the street whether the fiddling from the window above will ever stop. The attention of the narrator, an oddly dispassionate "passionate friend of mankind," moved by "anthropological" curiosity to take down and report Jacob's story, is his closest approximation of success. By any standards, Jacob's approach to music is curious. Harmony is everything. His reverence for the harmonic series is impervious to the tempered scale. His violin with its multiple cracks is a trial for anyone within earshot. His obsession with perfect intervals suggests that he plays in tune. Rhythm, on the other hand, means nothing to him. With the significant exception of the song that attracts him to the one woman in his life, he seems disinclined, even unable, to carry a tune.

Music links Jacob to the world as it links Gambara. It also separates him from it as it separates Gambara. The middle son of a senior civil servant, Jacob fails in school, but his father says no to a trade. When he takes a job, like Melville's Bartleby, as an unpaid human copy machine, his father makes sure that he is passed over for promotion. At sea when his father finally dies, he allows his father's secretary to swindle him out of his inheritance, leaving him penniless.

One day, sitting alone at the window, Jacob hears Barbara, the girl next door, singing in the courtyard. Her song so moves him that he has it transcribed on paper. For once in his life, he even masters a tune. Overcoming his shyness, he pursues Barbara till she slaps him hard, kisses him remorsefully, and retreats to the next room. As she bars the door, he kisses the glass between them. Though touched by his innocence, she accedes to a loveless but practical marriage to a butcher, but names her first child Jacob, and even invites the senior Jacob to give him violin lessons. Although the boy only practices on Sundays, he manages to master the tune that drew Jacob to his mother. Meanwhile, with no other option in view, Jacob takes to the street with his violin.

Recalling their meeting in the wake of a Danube flood a few months afterward, the narrator learns from the landlady that Jacob now plays with the angels. After saving children from the rising water, he returned to save his landlord's business records. He then took sick and died. The narrator finds Barbara alone with the coffin. A few days later, he asks for Jacob's battered violin as an excuse for a follow-up visit. Tears streaming down her cheeks, she tells him that it now belongs to her son.

Melville's story, by an author whose masterpiece, *Moby-Dick*, published three years earlier, had not even sold out its modest first edition, takes the same basic motifs—unrecognized genius, public scorn, a failed musician—and adds two more, humility and hope, that lead things in a different and unexpected direction.

Helmstone, a writer whose poem has just gotten a bad review, bumps into his friend Standard, who is full of enthusiasm for a clown he recently watched at the circus. Standard's friend Hautboy, a cheerfully boyish forty-something, proposes that they head for the afternoon performance and have dinner afterward. Helmstone is as moved by Hautboy's unaffected enjoyment as he is by the "excellent judgment" and "exact line between enthusiasm and apathy" that Hautboy shows at dinner. But brilliance is nowhere in sight till Hautboy invites them to his apartment, and Standard agrees on the condition that Hautboy play his fiddle for them. Helmstone soon realizes that their host is no ordinary player. On their way home, Standard connects the dots. Hautboy was once a celebrated child prodigy. The fame is now long gone. Yet *"with* genius and *without* fame," as Standard emphasizes in italics, the grown-up Hautboy "is happier than a king." He then returns to the painful subject of Helmstone's bad review.

Helmstone gets the message as Gambara and Jacob don't. "Next day," he reports, "I tore all my manuscripts, bought me a fiddle, and went to take regular lessons of Hautboy."[131]

By the end of the nineteenth century, makers, composers, but most often players were as familiar in literature's Filene's basement as they were on Fifth Avenue. In Horatio Alger's brave new world, grit, courage and concern for others unfailingly pay off in the attentions of a WASP benefactor, a heaven-sent change of fortune, and induction into the middle class. It works for Ben, the Luggage Boy, Dan, the Detective, and Grit, the Young Boatman. It works just as well for Phil, the Fiddler, the little Italian immigrant fleeing servitude to his father.[132] Kate Douglas Wiggin, best known for *Rebecca of Sunnybrook Farm*, had a go at the violin genre in a story published in the *Atlantic* in 1895. With the help of *The Practical Violinist*, by "Jacob Augustus Friedheim, Instrument Maker to the Court of the Archduke of Weimar," her poor but kindly "Village Stradivarius"[133] builds a violin and teaches himself to play it before losing his sight as a young adult. He pairs off in middle-age with a warmhearted, music-loving neighbor, condemned till now to spinsterhood because of a childhood accident that scarred her face. The "glad game" turned the title character of Eleanor H. Porter's *Pollyanna* into a gold standard for goody-goodness. It works just as well for the title character of *Just David*, a best seller in 1916. A mysterious, nameless orphan who speaks French dukes it out with the local bullies, loans his inherited Amati to a little blind boy, offers a luckless neighbor tips on how to play the Brahms concerto, and saves his stern but loving adoptive parents from foreclosure. He then returns to a presumably brilliant future in the concert world his distraught father forsook after his wife's death.[134]

A violinist in his early years, even John Philip Sousa got into the literary act. *The Fifth String*, a novella of 120 small pages, appeared in 1902. It reportedly sold fifty thousand copies at $1.25, and it can still be accessed online a century later.[135] Diotti, a young, dashing Italian and the world's greatest violinist, is smitten on arrival in New York by the glorious Mildred. But Mildred is a glacier. In despair, Diotti escapes his next concert for the Bahamas, where Satan in person presents him with a violin that will thaw Mildred. But the violin has a supplementary fifth string that Diotti is warned to avoid at pain of instant death. He returns to New York, where the violin does what is expected of it, and Mildred, unaware of the consequences, demands that he play on the fifth string. The result is as expected. "A mystery story fan of today almost wishes Diotti had played the fatal string on page fifty," a later reviewer would write.[136]

As usual, the music-loving E. T. A. (the last initial is for "Amadeus") Hoffmann was a pacesetter for the occult and the uncanny. A remarkable figure where few non-German contemporaries would have thought to look for one, he began adult life as a Prussian official assigned to provincial law courts as far east as Warsaw. The daily routine of provincial officialdom left plenty of room for music criticism, piano teaching, even composition of music that was actually performed. Then came 1807 and Prussia's co-optation as a French satellite. Unwilling to work for the French, he settled for a job as theater director in Bamberg and began writing to support his family. It took only a few years for stories like "Councillor Krespel"[137] to make "Hoffmannesque" a literary quality as recognizable as "Kafkaesque."

A lawyer-diplomat, interchangeably weird and quaint, the title figure has so impressed the minor league prince who employs him that the prince rewards him with a house. Designed to Krespel's specifications, the house is built in his garden within a day. But violins are his real passion. If made by himself, he plays them once and only once. If old and Italian, he collects and dissects them. His passion takes him to Italy, where his virtuosity leads to a difficult marriage with Venice's reigning soprano. When his pregnant wife smashes his Cremonese violin in a fit of artistic temperament, he pitches her out the window, takes off for Germany, resumes his solitary life, and rediscovers his daughter, born of his marriage, and now herself of marriageable age.

At first, Krespel is delighted with the girl's composer-fiancé. He then notices an alarming symptom: a feverish flush when she sings when accompanied by himself on the violin and her fiancé at the piano. Realizing that singing will literally be the death of his daughter, he chases the young man out of her life. Given the choice of dying while singing with her fiancé or living silently with her father, she opts for the latter and helps him dissect violins, while bonding with a particularly fine instrument that she persuades him to spare.

One night, Krespel dreams that he hears her sing again. As he rushes to her room to find her dead, the soundpost of her favorite violin gives way in sympathy. Krespel buries the violin with his daughter. He returns from the cemetery in inexplicable good humor, smashes the bow, and announces that he's free. But free of what? The barely sublimated need to dominate things and people? The pursuit of unattainable artistic perfection? The vanity of human ambition? The futility of human striving? In principle, there are as many answers as there are doctoral candidates to deconstruct it.[138]

John Meade Falkner's first novel *The Lost Stradivarius*[139] is Victorian England's answer to Krespel. Like Hoffmann, Falkner was a polymath with collateral interests in local history, paleography, demonology, and early Anglican church music. Just out of Oxford, he parlayed a job as tutor to the sons of a senior executive into lifetime employment and board membership at Armstrong, Whitworth, a major arms manufacturer.[140] His three novels, written after hours between 1895 and 1903, were still in print and online a century later.

In a reader's guide to the ghost story published shortly before Falkner's death, the medievalist M. R. James, a master of the genre, spelled out its essentials: the "pretense of truth," which allows the reader to suspend disbelief; "a pleasing terror"; minimal sex and violence; as little detail as possible on how the spooky parts of the story really work; and proximity enough to the reader's time and place that he/she can feel at home with the scene and characters.[141] A morality story with glimpses of unmentionable evil, peopled by old Etonians and Oxford undergraduates who vacation in Rome and celebrate Christmas in ancient country houses with minimal heat and family portraits "attributed to Holbein," Falkner's scenario checks all the boxes.

The story is an extended flashback passed on to Sir Edward Maltravers, Bart., an Oxford undergraduate, by his Aunt Sophia, who wants him to learn about "certain events" in his father's life from a reliable source. The introductory facts seem harmless. Sir John, an old Etonian and an impassioned amateur violinist, has lucked into a congenial pianist classmate just back from a Roman holiday with a collection of baroque Neapolitan manuscripts. Reaching for his Pressenda violin, John starts reading one and immediately senses a ghostly presence in the room when he plays a particular gagliarda. So does his friend when they repeat it.

Serendipity leads John to find an unreconstructed 1704 Strad in a wall cupboard, as well as the diaries of the young man who occupied the room a century earlier. London's leading expert, George Smart, an obvious allusion to George Hart, confirms that the Strad is real. He also notices an enigmatic second label, "Porphyrius Philosophus," possibly a dedication to the neo-Platonic author of the anti-Christian *Adversus Christianos*, in Stradivari's hand. John decides to keep the Strad.

On a visit to his fiancée's home, he is startled to see the ghostly apparition he first encountered in Oxford in a flash of lightning. He then spots the apparition's portrait in the family gallery and learns that the young man was handsome, gifted, a prodigious violinist, and somehow rotten to the core.

Now married and a father, he leaves his wife and child to set off on the apparition's trail till finally his sister and an old college friend bring him home—pasty-white and barely functional. His wife has died in his absence. John dies, too, on Christmas day, after a somnambulant reprise of the fateful gagliarda. Under stress from modern strings and the dying man's wish to go to church, the fateful Strad implodes.

In a postscript to the flashback, his friend reports how the apparitional young man built a villa in Naples, dabbled in neo-Platonism, engaged in nameless pagan frolics including the fateful gagliarda, and was eventually stabbed to death. Whatever the apparition did, John evidently did, too. He died before disclosing the whereabouts of the crucial diary pages. His friend and Aunt Sophia control the damage by burning the diaries and the remains of the Strad. Its burning scroll reveals a grinning profile of Porphyrius.

Paolo Maurensig's *Canone Inverso*[142] is late twentieth-century Europe's answer much as Anne Rice's *Violin*[143] is late twentieth-century America's answer to Hoffmann and Falkner. Both were also best sellers—with six-figure sales in Maurensig's case, and nine-figure sales in Rice's.

The Cecchi Gori group, a major Italian company, hired Ricky Tognazzi, an actor-director of vast energy and some artistic ambition, to turn *Canone Inverso* into a film with the alternative title *Making Love*. They even engaged the inexhaustibly resourceful Ennio Morricone, godfather of Italian film music, to compose a real mirror canon—a two-voice composition whose second voice is an exact inversion of the first—in the spirit of the novel's title.[144] With similar hopes for a spin-off, Philips engaged Leila Josefowicz, a very good violinist and a MacArthur Fellow, as well as a favorite of the author's, to record a collection of greatest hits marketed as *Violin for Anne Rice*. Loosely connected to the novel, the CD includes tracks by Ysaÿe and Sting, the British rock guitarist, as well as the Tchaikovsky concerto, Sarasate's *Carmen* Fantasy, and the "Méditation" from *Thaïs*.[145]

But the commonalities end fairly abruptly. A longtime office worker who actually played, as well as restored, baroque instruments, Maurensig was born in Gorizia, the northeasternmost corner of Italy, where the long shadow of Vienna meets the long shadow of Venice. He was already in his fifties before he found a publisher. Rice, a New Orleans native who left and returned to the Catholic church, was a Hollywood favorite and full-time pro who published her first novel at thirty-five and just kept going. If Maurensig might plausibly be a character in a story by Hoffmann, Rice, with twenty-seven titles in thirty-two years, four of them pseudonymous erotica, might as plausibly be a character in a novel of her own.[146]

While only two years separate their authors, Maurensig's and Rice's stories are as distant from one another as each is distant from Falkner and Hoffmann. Falkner's take on James's "pleasing terror" is essentially a campfire entertainment, a late Victorian version of good gothic fun. Maurensig's terror is the real thing. Even in Italian, the narrative voice is Central European, precociously wise, sober, and basically illusionless. Rice wears her biographical heart on her literary sleeve. Her default position is the narcissism of the TV talk show, a genre as foreign to Maurensig as it would be to Hoffmann. If Maurensig has drifted away from "pleasing terror," Rice has decoupled from James's rule about sex and violence, though the traditional themes of guilt and salvation, even death and transfiguration, can still be spotted in her tangled narrative.

In barely two hundred pages, Maurensig's narrative is as economical and contrapuntal as Rice's is rhapsodic and self-indulgent. His novel's inspiration goes back to Stainer, the great Tyrolean violin maker, hounded in his lifetime by the Counter-Reformationist thought police and eventually done in by mental illness. The mirror canon of his title is more than a figure of speech.

The story begins with the voice of an unidentified first narrator, the winning bidder at a Christie's auction in the 1980s on a Stainer violin with an unmistakable and portentously diabolical head. He is pursued to his hotel room by the second voice, that of a writer eager to explain why he, too, had wanted the instrument. The explanation leads to a third voice, the derelict player who was the Stainer's previous owner. In the convenient sanctuary of an all-night café, the previous owner spells out to the fascinated writer why he, a concert-quality performer with a concert-quality violin, lives by passing the hat in Viennese wine locales.

His story, the novel's center of gravity, leads to three more contrapuntal episodes before the mysterious violinist wanders off again, leaving no apparent trace. The first episode, told so discreetly as to be barely noticeable, is the story of Central Europe slipping into madness between 1914 and 1945. The second describes the rise and fall of a friendship. The last describes the rise and fall of a family. As the third voice fades, it gives way to the second, which then fades, too, after the writer's search for the missing player ends inconclusively in a Hungarian village cemetery. At last, as theory prescribes, the first voice returns with the final cadence that resolves all narrative dissonances in the final pages.

In contrast to Maurensig, Rice barely pretends to the "pretense of truth." Her first-person narrator is frumpy, overweight, and middle-aged. She grieves for an art historian spouse who recently died of AIDS, leaving her bundles of money and a house in New Orleans. So distraught that days pass before she can even bring herself to have him buried, she dutifully attends to the publication of his *chef d'oeuvre* on St. Sebastian. All the while, guilty recollections of dead sisters, the alcoholic mother she let die unattended, and the daughter whose death from cancer broke up a previous marriage mingle with fantasies of violin playing, memories of Isaac Stern performing the Beethoven concerto, and a passion for the second movement of the Ninth Symphony that she remembers as a march, although it isn't one.

Redemption appears in the person of a ghost violinist, Russian, Byronic, and aristocratic. He first plays a local recital, then plays another for her alone, until she seizes his Strad and refuses to return it. He responds with an all-expense, time-travel tour of his earthly life as a Vienna-based protégé of Beethoven who aspired to study with Paganini and almost made it. Unfortunately, the idea so upsets his father that he decides to return to St. Petersburg with his son's Strad and sell it with the rest of the family collection. In the row that follows, the father smashes the son's fingers. The son counters by killing the father, only to be shot, in turn, when returning, as expected, to recover the Strad.

At this point, the narrator regains the initiative and makes her way back to real-time Vienna as a performance artist. Her new career takes her not only to Rio de Janeiro but Manaus, the scene of *Fitzcarraldo*, Werner Herzog's 1982 film about an opera-loving rubber baron, resolved to drag a 320-ton steamship across the narrow isthmus between parallel tributaries of the Amazon to reach the parcel he hopes will make his fortune. Returning the Strad to its spectral owner, she continues her tour with a Guarneri somehow acquired en route.

AND THEN, OF course, came the novels of sex, or, at least, of gender. Once again Britain blazed the literary trail. In 1888, Mrs. Humphry Ward published *Robert Elsmere*, a novel in three volumes about an Anglican rector who loses his faith in orthodox Christianity. Within five months it went through seven editions, was pirated in the United States and Canada, and was translated into several languages. W. E. Gladstone, the great reform prime minister and the novel's highest-profile reviewer, was so shaken by it that he asked for two long meetings with its author.[147]

Although the story unfolds over 561 pages, notice of what is to come is clear from the beginning. "In a stranger coming upon the house for the first time . . . the sense of a changing social order and a vanishing past . . . would have been greatly quickened by certain sounds which were streaming out on to the evening air," the author announces in the fifth paragraph of page one. The source of the sounds, it appears a few sentences later, is the rector's daughter playing the violin. A serious amateur, she has spent the afternoon practicing Ludwig Spohr.

A half generation later, the same portentous trifecta of woman, violin, and changing times would show up across the North Sea in *Buddenbrooks*, the chronicle of generational decline that made Thomas Mann a star at twenty-six.[148] Thomas Buddenbrook, the founding father's grandson and head of the family business, has married Gerda Arnoldsen, who not only owns but plays a Strad. Gerda hires the church organist to give their sickly son piano lessons. She even gets the organist to transcribe the "Liebestod" from Wagner's *Tristan*, only recently premiered. From here on, any contemporary reader could see the slippery slope only steps away.

By this time, though without Mann's art, let alone his irony, the special relationship of woman (especially New Woman) and violin covered the pages of popular magazines and filled the shelves of British lending libraries. The theme seemed particularly appealing to pioneer feminists on the threshold of the twentieth century. Of nine representative titles recovered from the attic by Paula Gillett, a Californian student of Victorian society on the threshold of the twenty-first, most are wistful, sad, or baleful. But almost all are cautionary.

In three of them, bad things happen to women players. In one, a daughter capitulates to a loveless marriage after her vengeful mother pitches her Strad into the fire. In another, an aspiring virtuosa, advised to quit by her teacher, pitches her violin in the fire, runs out the door, and inadvertently drowns. In a third, a viola graduate of the Royal Academy whose quartet plays for its members' parents' at-homes kills herself with a drug overdose.

In two of the novels, the outcome is resignation, after a spouse's death causes one player to resume her career and the other to end it. In two more, gender is the common denominator. In the earliest of Gillett's titles, published in 1880, a German professor agrees for the first time to take on a promising girl violinist on the condition that she pretend to be a boy. In one of the latest, published in 1910, a brilliant and beautiful mother sacrifices her own career as a violinist to dedicate her formidable talent to a prodigious son, on the grounds, says Gillett, that "great music must be made by men." The single exception, by Mrs. Francis Blundell, an upper-class Anglo-Catholic who produced fifty novels as M. E. Francis before her death in 1930, is the story of a Franco-Hungarian violin virtuosa who lays an outdoor musical ambush for a Hungarian piano virtuoso in Wiesbaden with such brilliant success that the two get married and live happily ever after. None of the authors, Gillett notes, even hints at the existence of Wilma Neruda, whose union of career, marriages, and motherhood might have been a real-life model.[149]

By the mid-twentieth century, the professional status of fictional women, like most other things, had changed dramatically on both sides of the Atlantic. Ian McEwan's Florence Ponting, a child of upscale North Oxford, is attractive, gifted, and on the threshold of adulthood at a meticulously observed Royal College of Music in Macmillan-era Britain.[150] An attentive father and academic mother have seen to skiing lessons, flying lessons, and foreign travel in addition to a first-rate musical education.

Sex education for Florence, on the other hand, has been weak in theory and nonexistent in practice. Where innumerable predecessors were famously instructed to shut their eyes and think of England, Florence shuts her eyes and thinks of the opening bars of Mozart's magnificent D Major viola quintet. It doesn't help. A critical mass of mutual inexperience turns her wedding night, the axis of the narrative, into a disaster for both parties. Edward, the appalled young man, goes on to a life of rock reviews, modest commercial success, and a second failed marriage. Florence's quartet records boxed sets of Schubert and Beethoven. A pillar of the music scene, it is still active and eminent some forty years after the failure of her first and only marriage.

Inez in San Francisco, a creation of Bart Schneider, the son of a violinist in the San Francisco Symphony, is attractive, gifted, and concurrently coping, like Florence in London, with music and sex.[151] Like countless real-life predecessors, she was also harassed in her student days by her teacher, in this case the concertmaster of the San Francisco Symphony, who is now her father-in-law. She has meanwhile grown up to be a front-desk first violinist and even occasional soloist in what was once her teacher's orchestra.

With her 1770 Landolfi and a job most of her peers would envy, she has reached a professional promised land that would have seemed to her Victorian predecessors as remote as women's suffrage. On the other hand, her Swedish American family has a history of suicide; her sister, now in a mental institution, has stitched her fingers together for the love of Jesus, and her marriage is not working. Hit on by a lesbian groupie who demonstrates pianos in a music store showroom, she finds momentary happiness and then kills herself.

Augie Boyer, the narrator and principal character of Schneider's follow-up novel, is male, heterosexual, and physically, if not culturally, a long way from the Golden Gate. When not working, he talks knowledgeably about art and plays quartets with a buddy, an uncommonly dapper St. Paul police detective with a passion for contemporary poetry. Though his career as a private eye and his private life as a deserted spouse have exposed him to the heartache and the thousand natural and not-so-natural shocks that flesh like his is heir to, he is not at all suicidal. His client, on the other hand, a distant echo of Inez, is again an aggravated case. Relocated like Augie to Minnesota's Twin Cities, she, too, is a professional violinist, and apparently a very good one. She also has a fragile personality; a creepy spouse who deals in violins, once Nazi plunder that a creepy uncle collects; and a creepy therapist.

In the climactic scene on the grounds of the Minnesota state capitol in the shadow of the Republican National Convention, a right to life rally converges with a freedom of choice rally. Thanks to a tip from his violinist client, Augie arrives at the pro-choice rally just in time to take a couple of shots aimed at his daughter, a high-profile rock singer, but survives. His wife has since borne a child by the friend she ran off with, but marital reconciliation is distantly conceivable. The violinist vanishes.[152]

Claire Kilroy's Daniel, an abruptly unemployed Peruvian investment banker with a violin case in his hand, has vanished by the end of her novel[153] too, with Interpol presumably on his heels. So has Alexander, a giant hustler and freelance mafioso, first spotted in a lower Manhattan singles bar, done up, the author notes, like the owner's impression of a KGB officer. Chechen, not Russian, he insists, he has now disappeared again somewhere between the Brooklyn Bridge and the Republic of Ingushetia, after unloading a totally undocumented but startling powerful violin for an unlikely price on twenty-something Eva, who is Irish, like the author, and the novel's first-person narrator.

Eva is a one-woman argument for the proposition that even paranoids have enemies, and truth is so precious that it must be used sparingly. Gifted, self-absorbed, accident-prone, but unfailingly resilient, she has just made her New York solo debut despite a miscarriage. For obvious reasons, she's paid Alexander in cash. Much of it comes from her missing father's estate, more from the sale of her Vuillaume to an aspiring student. A quarter is from Daniel, her sometime lover, who wants a piece of what a dubious Brooklyn dealer believes might be a del Gesù but which was sold as a Strad. That still leaves Alexander seriously angry about $70,000 that Eva somehow forgot to pay him.

She has, meanwhile, crisis-managed a soundpost crack overlooked in the original transaction, fended off a pointed inquiry about the nominal Strad from a hypertrophic version of the *Entente Internationale des Luthiers et Archetiers*, outflanked a threatened suit from the heir of a Polish-Jewish virtuoso for recovery of what she claims was her father's instrument, as well as Daniel's intended larceny, and publicly swatted the Monégasque friend and colleague who annexed her previous boyfriend, who was Czech. Eva is not only left standing at the end of the yo-yo scenario and any number of bumpy rides over the Atlantic and the East River; she seems still in secure possession of her uninsured and unauthenticated violin, is reunited with her loyal Siamese cat, as well as her favorite conductor, and she looks forward to an interesting career.

Natasha Darsky, Yael Goldstein's early twenty-first-century heroine, may have it best of the group, but not by much. A thoroughly secularized child of New York's high-rent Upper East Side, she has at least learned where babies come from—and don't come from—as a fifteen-year-old at summer camp. She also shows a precocious aptitude for the violin and pairs off with a charismatic classmate in her composition class at Harvard. Though her interest in composition falls victim to her partner's patriarchal conviction that only men compose, a second-place finish in a major competition, a well-developed figure, and a *Vanity Fair* cover pay off in a respectable concert career, a fling with an iconic Polish-Jewish movie director, and single motherhood.

Alex, the daughter, is precocious too, a little pianist who follows her mother on tour and plays a Beethoven cycle at fourteen. But as adolescents do, she turns rebellious. Estranged from her mother and rejected by a boyfriend, she enrolls at Indiana University's A-list music school, where, sure enough, her mother's old flame, now half crank and half cult figure, is professor of composition. Unaware of his link to her mother, Alex enrolls in his class. This relationship fails, too, leading to an equivocal reconciliation at her mother's farewell appearance at Carnegie Hall. Now an old pro, Natasha performs the Brahms concerto with her accustomed virtuosity. When the audience demands an encore, she responds in her daughter's presence with her daughter's improvisatory piece for solo violin.[154]

A satyr play to the others' postfeminist Sturm und Drang, Mayra Montero's *Deep Purple*[155] is elaborately and purposely funny. The fun begins with the author herself, a forty-eight-year-old Cuban-born Puerto Rican in literary drag as Augustín Cabán, a priapic male music reviewer determined to anthologize his liaisons with every itinerant virtuosa in a memoir and how-to manual. "There is," he observes, "no more noble service to fine music, no more imperishable support one can offer a soloist, than to throw her facedown on a bed."

His quest, at once reminiscent of Dr. Kinsey and *Dr. Tatiana's Sex Advice to All Creation*, leads him to—among others—a celesta player, a clarinetist, a horn player with a pet bat, and a male pianist. Above all, it leads to two violinists, one Antiguan and one German Portuguese. To the narrator's regret, the former is involved with her lesbian manager. To his alarm, the latter is a volcanically emancipated Donna Elvira, ready and eager after 150 years of denial, disdain, and humiliation to throw Don Giovanni facedown on a bed. Her furious passion reminds him of a string snapped against the fingerboard Bartók-style. A woman violinist has at last come out on top.

Her progress and ultimate success could be measured against a baseline and a sequence of benchmarks extending back seventy years to *The First Violin*,[156] a best seller by Jessie Fothergill, 26. Declared "sensational and immoral" by the American Library Association on its publication in 1877, the first edition was followed by at least another thirty-five.[157] The scandalous story line is personified in May, who is seventeen, English, and keen to try her luck as a concert singer in Germany, a country where people take their music seriously. A New Woman waiting to happen, she escapes marriage to a sadistic squire by signing on as companion to an elderly lady who is en route to a town on the lower Rhine for medical treatment.

Virtually on arrival, she crosses paths with Eugen, the title figure and concertmaster of the local orchestra. Eugen is gallant and English-speaking. He is also the single parent of a precocious little boy and is conveniently at hand when May runs short of cash, falls through thin ice while skating, and is nearly swept down the Rhine when a pontoon bridge breaks up in a storm. Chapters will pass before it becomes clear that Eugen is a gentleman, compelled to work for a living after voluntarily taking the hit for a forged check drawn on his father's account by his Italian ex-wife.

The story ends as might be expected, with May and Eugen married, the child again in a two-parent family, and domestic order restored. But May is far from a passive accessory. If Eugen's eyes "shock with a kind of tameless freedom," May's, too, sometimes glow with a "subdued fire . . . that removed her from the category of spiritless beauties."

The conjunction of male and violin that energizes May and Eugen would energize three major writers over the next six years. The first, Sholem Aleichem, published his novella *Stempenyu* in 1888. The title character, named for his home village, is a figure of Paganinian talent but also Paganinian libido. He inevitably casts his eye on the gorgeous Rochalle. Intoxicated like everyone by his playing, Rochalle is interested in him too. Her marriage is a bore. Her mother-in-law's solicitousness drives her nearly to distraction. Stempenyu's domestic scene is not exemplary either. His wife, Freidel, had managed to turn serial infatuation into a singular commitment, and this into a loveless marriage. What Freidel loves is money. She is also possessed of an unanticipated gift as well as a lust for business.

To this point, the story shows promise of becoming a Yiddish *Madame Bovary*. Speculating on the taste of Lower East Side theatergoers on his way to America some years later, Sholem Aleichem even rewrote it as one, with a tryst, a kiss, and a suicide. But the original story ends quite differently. Put off by Stempenyu's attentions, Rochalle says no, returns to her husband, and moves to another city, where their marriage perks up. Stempenyu returns to Freidel. Virtue wins. Happiness finishes a distant second.[158]

The male-violin dynamic also animates Leo Tolstoy's famous novella *The Kreutzer Sonata*,[159] published a year later. But it drives the story to a very different outcome. Among the most famous rants in world literature, it was published—and censored—in Russia in 1889. It appeared in Britain and the United States a year later.

The story begins as a conversation among strangers on a train who reflect on love and marriage. As talk turns to the recent case of Pozdnis-cheff, a man acquitted of killing his wife in a fit of jealousy, a fellow trav-

eler joins in, introducing himself as Pozdnischeff. He then explains what
he did and why he did it.

In a shrewd critique for American readers, Robert G. Ingersoll, a
prominent lawyer, active Republican, professed agnostic, and star of the
Chautauqua circuit, explained the writer's problem. A "man of genius"
and a Christian, Tolstoy believed "that beneath every blossom lies a coiled
serpent."[160] It just happened that Pozdnischeff had co-opted a good violinist as an unwitting serpent to test his conviction that creature instincts
corrupt both men and women.

As expected, the violinist guest and hostess hit it off musically, but
only musically, with Beethoven's Kreutzer sonata, a demanding masterpiece never known before or since to drive anyone crazy with desire. Yet for
Pozdnischeff, the first movement alone could be the second act of Wagner's
Tristan. Regarding music as nothing more than foreplay and fornication by
other means, he returns from a meeting early and unannounced, arms himself with a dagger from his study, and bursts into the dining room shoeless
to find the suspect couple sitting innocently. Crazed with rage, he kills
his wife anyway. He meanwhile allows the violinist to escape rather than
risk looking silly by pursuing him without shoes. Yet even acquittal gives
him no satisfaction. Remarkably, America's postmaster-general banned *The
Kreutzer Sonata* from the mails, though the ban was quickly overruled.[161]

Thomas Hardy's story "The Fiddler of the Reels," first published in
Scribner's, an upper-end American monthly, followed Tolstoy's novella by
three years. It was recycled in a Hardy sampler called *Life's Little Ironies.*[162]
The anthology's title did the story justice. In contrast to Tolstoy's respectable Russians, Hardy's Britons are essentially Shakespearean rustics. But
once again, the union of violin and male, and its effect on everyone in
earshot, bridges all intervening distances, and this time the heavy breathing is real.

The story is deceptively simple. Car'line's head, as does her family, tells
her to marry Ned, "a respectable mechanic" with a decent income. But her
heart belongs to Mop, the village fiddler. Like Don Giovanni, he pursues
anyone in a skirt. He also plays "so as to draw your soul out of your body
like a spider's thread till you felt as limp as withywind and yearned for
something to cling to."

Ned takes off for London where he helps build the 1851 Exhibition's
famed iron and glass Crystal Palace. Car'line proposes that she join him
but neglects to mention the three-year-old, Mop's child, she now leads by
the hand.

Dead game, Ned makes an affectionate home for both wife and child till a slumping economy causes them to return to their village. While Ned inquires about jobs, Car'line and the child trudge home, stopping to rest at the village pub, where the regulars are dancing to Mop's fiddle. A few drinks later, Car'line is again unable to resist. She joins in till she and the child are the last on the floor, whereupon she faints from fatigue. Ned arrives in time to revive her. But Mop and the child are gone—"to America was the general opinion." There, it is assumed, the child will be properly trained to support him as a dancer.

In the wake of World War II, the irresistible violinist appears in a fourth literary landmark, Thomas Mann's *Doktor Faustus*,[163] though the narrative context is actually the 1920s. Rudi Schwerdtfeger, the handsome, gifted, ingratiating concertmaster of a local orchestra, has been co-opted by a Munich salon. Ines, the hostess's elder daughter, is desperate to have him as her lover. Instead, Rudi falls for Marie, a Swiss costume designer. Marie finds him irresistible, too, and the couple prepares for a new life in Paris.

Once again, the critical combination of male and violin leads to a calamitous fallout. After his last Munich appearance, Rudi boards a tram filled with homebound concertgoers, among them Ines. High on morphine, crazed with jealousy, and armed with a revolver, she shoots him.

In 1977, Harold C. Schonberg, the *New York Times*'s chief music reviewer, recalled Fothergill's Eugen with his brooding secret, his "indescribable grace, ease and negligent beauty . . . a person accustomed to giving orders and seeing them obeyed without question." Why, Schonberg asked, though not altogether seriously, did the current concertmasters of the great American orchestras no longer measure up to such standards?[164] Although the answer took another generation to arrive, it was worth the wait. If attracting women was the goal, Frank Almond reported in a letter to the editor in 1999, his "comprehensive and painstaking research" as concertmaster of the Milwaukee Symphony only confirmed that a Strad was no match for an electric guitar. The guitar was also cheaper.[165]

But reports of a literary genre's death were arguably premature. Since the middle of the nineteenth century, more and more history, as well as music history, seemed to happen between Germany and Russia, where at least 70 percent of the world's Jews lived ever more precariously and the violin seemed to come as naturally to the heirs and spiritual family of Joseph Joachim as it did to the *badkhen*, the village entertainer. It was probably no coincidence that Jews and violins showed up increasingly in both Jewish and non-Jewish fiction, or that their story became ever more emblematic of a musical experience that extended far beyond music.

"As far back as I can remember, my heart has gone out to the fiddle," a later Sholem Aleichem narrator reminisces in the faux artless voice of a man who knows his audience down to their DNA. He recalls how the rabbi smacked him for playing air violin in religious school; how he drove his father wild, scavenging a derelict sofa for cedarwood to make an instrument; how he scraped together a ruble for lessons from the patriarch of a sprawling family orchestra, who explains that the first violinists were Methuselah, King David, and Paganini, "also a Jew"; and how his engagement nearly crashed when his presumptive father-in-law caught him hanging out with the local bandmaster when he was supposed to be in synagogue.[166]

A very different reminiscence by a writer whose command of sadness is matched only by Sholom Aleichem's command of artful artlessness, Chekhov's "Rothschild's Violin" is the story of a Jew, a violin, and a gesture.[167] Yakov, a Russian, lives in a nowhere town, where his day job is making coffins. But since its old people "died so seldom that it was positively painful," he also moonlights with a Jewish orchestra as a locally respected session fiddler. The cumulative impact of an exhausted wife, a one-room cabin, oppressive poverty, and the flautist, Rothschild, who plays everything as though it were a lament, have turned him into an anti-Semite as well as a misanthrope.

When his wife takes ill she dies unprotestingly, even gratefully, after reminding him that they had once had a child and been briefly happy. Feeling his own death approaching, Yakov regrets a half century of neglect. Asked by the priest if he has any confession to make, he recalls his unhappy wife and the wretched Rothschild. "Give Rothschild the fiddle," he says. Abandoning the flute, Rothschild tries to play it as Yakov did—with such success that everyone cries, and "wealthy traders and officials never fail to engage Rothschild for their social gatherings."

The alternative to the Old World was the New World, where Fannie Hurst was born in 1889 into a German-Jewish family that had settled in Ohio by 1860. A kind of immigrant American Fothergill, Hurst left for New York at twenty-one, where she worked as a waitress and acted bit parts in the theater. She really wanted to be a writer; but even editors who acknowledged that she was "basically a fairly corny artist" appreciated the stir-fry of social conscience, sympathetic characters, and overwrought prose that would make stories like "Humoresque,"[168] first published in 1919, prime-time entertainment for readers of the hugely popular *Saturday Evening Post*, and would make its author "Queen of the Sob Sisters," a best seller, and a friend of Eleanor Roosevelt.[169]

With its three episodes, "Humoresque" covers almost all bases but home. In the first, Mama Sarah Kantor tends to her huddled brood and the Lower East Side shop, while Papa Abrahm Kantor struggles to find a birthday present in dollar range for little Leon. But Leon insists on a four-dollar violin. Abrahm is frantic, but Sarah is in heaven. With three dollars she has somehow managed to save, she marches out and returns "disheveled, and a smudge of soot across her face, but beneath her arm, triumphant, a violin of one string and a broken back."

In the second episode, Leon, now twenty-one, has been a star and a Strad owner since he was eighteen. He is about to play for a house packed with "his people." The superstar impresario is pounding on his door, eager to sign him up for fifty concerts at $2,000 each, two to four times what the world's best-paid industrial workers earned in a year.[170] Gina Berg, née Ginsberg, a rising star at the Met whose father was once Abrahm's customer, drops by to wish him well. Leon plays the Mendelssohn concerto and the inevitable transcription of *Kol Nidrei* with Dvořák's "Humoresque" for an encore. Suddenly it is August 1914.

The third episode might have been inspired by real life. An immigrant kid from Rochester, New York, Lt. David Hochstein studied with Ševčík and Auer and played a successful New York recital before joining the army at twenty-five in October 1917. A few weeks before the armistice, he was killed in action. A last letter to his family arrived after his death.[171]

Hurst's Leon has also heeded President Wilson's call. It is now November 1917, and the family is gathered to see him off to France. Gina is there, too, deeply moved by Leon's setting of "I Have a Rendezvous with Death," a poem by Alan Seeger, a native New Yorker killed in action the year before. As Leon leaves, Sarah clings to the violin with one string and a broken back. Fade.

A half-generation later, Ernst, a co-protagonist of Eugene Drucker's novel *The Savior*,[172] finds himself in the onrushing Nazi headlights at just the moment he should be leaving the conservatory to start his career in Germany. More outraged than frightened, he departs for Britain, leaving his friend and classmate Gottfried, who would like to do the same but gets cold feet. Well into the war, a concentration camp commandant of intel-

lectual bent co-opts Gottfried to test whether music can bring around an
audience of the unresistingly apathetic inmates who ordinarily died within
weeks of arrival. The experiment succeeds so well that Gottfried dares to
play the most iconic piece in the repertory, the chaconne from Bach's solo
partita in D minor. With his curiosity satisfied and the Allies approaching, the commandant ends the experiment by killing the prisoners.

Dovidl, the centerpiece of Norman Lebrecht's *The Song of Names*,[173]
might appear lucky by comparison. Thanks to a prescient father and a
London concert presenter willing to take him in, Dovidl has evaded physical destruction. But that leaves him, his family's only survivor, to face the
challenges of survival as a prodigy. Trained to precocious virtuosity like a
little Flesch protégé, he skips out on his heavily promoted sold-out debut
recital the day of the concert, leaving his devastated foster father holding
the uninsured bag.

Decades later, Dovidl's quasi-brother, the impresario's son Martin,
finds himself judging a deeply provincial school competition in which a
modestly talented player's improbable and unmistakable rubato catches
his attention. The search for her teacher leads, of course, to Dovidl, who is
found in a Hassidic community that took him in the day he fled his debut
concert.

Furious, Martin totes up the accrued interest on decades of moral debt
and pushes Dovidl to return to London and make good on the recital he
scuttled. This time Dovidl fakes suicide. But at least he returns the borrowed Guadagnini he never paid for, along with a letter explaining why
he ran and hid. Meanwhile, a Polish whiz kid takes up the slack and saves
Martin's company.

Gordon Pape and Tony Aspler's novel *The Music Wars*[174] is none the
better for its authors' Canadian media experience as an investment guru
and a wine guru, respectively. But Aspler's experience reporting the 1978
Tchaikovsky Competition for the Canadian Broadcasting Corporation,
combined with the violinist Erick Friedman's real-life experience in 1966,
is a major comparative advantage.[175]

Like Friedman, the authors' David Solomon is brilliant, young, of
course Jewish, and as innocent as a lab mouse about what awaits him at
the world's most politicized competition. Like countless other visitors, he
has also been targeted by the KGB for bugging, harassment, manipula-
tion, and entrapment by specialists of every kind, from the hotel concierge
to the inevitable playmate from Intourist.

This is also the era of the Helsinki Accords, the refusenik, and the Jackson-Vanik Amendment, linking trade liberalization to emigration rights. David's grandfather fled the Ukraine after the Bolshevik Revolution. His father works for a New York Yiddish newspaper. David himself is filmed by a KGB photographer leaving Juilliard in the middle of an anti-Soviet demonstration. His manager then asks him to smuggle back a Guarneri in Moscow for its owner's nephew in New York. Warming to the task, David manages with Boy Scout resourcefulness and the help of both the usual and unusual suspects to get a human rights dissident as well as the Guarneri aboard the return flight to New York. From here to the obligatory surprise finale, the breathless idiom of Cold War fiction is itself the message.

Daniel Silva's experience at United Press International and CNN allowed him to take early retirement and write eleven novels between 1997 and 2008. But an unanticipated conjunction of life and art allowed the third of them, *The English Assassin*, with a first printing of one hundred thousand copies and an ad budget of $100,000, to hit the jackpot.[176] The art, personified in Gabriel Allon, a Swiss-based restorer, Mossad agent, and killer with a conscience, was Silva's contribution.

What the Swiss had done and not done during the Nazi years, and the exhaustive negotiations that led to a $1.25 billion settlement of Holocaust-related claims against Swiss banks in 1999, was pure windfall for a novelist in search of material.

The book begins with two bangs. The wife of a Swiss art collector shoots herself in the garden while her brilliantly talented thirteen-year-old daughter practices on her Strad upstairs. As the daughter realizes what's happened, the violin crashes to the floor. Engaged by her guilt-ridden father to locate plundered art, Allon arrives to find his client murdered and himself a suspect. The daughter, by now a world-class performer, helps Allon evade an English hit man and performs Tartini's *Devil's Trill* Sonata in Venice while Allon recovers the plundered art and nabs the accessory conspirators.

Seasoned lightly with magical realism, Jonathan Levi's *The Scrimshaw Violin*[177] is equally baroque and rather more artful.[178] Like Silva's, his principal character, Alexander Abba Lincoln, is Jewish. But he is also American, a violinist, a secular-minded rabbi, a medical examiner with elaborate forensic skills, and an occasional contributor to the *New York Times* op-ed page, where his piece on a so-called Jewish gene so impresses the Jewish summer people of Nantucket that they invite him to Shabbos dinner.

On arrival, he is much taken by the island but especially by his hostess and her house. A local product, descended from generations of "whalers, pirates and not so genteel Semitophobes," she shows him a roomful of scrimshaw, including a violin with a lovingly sculpted fingerboard, and introduces him to her mother, who brought it with her when she arrived decades earlier as a French war bride.

Dinner is so successful that the mother asks Lincoln to play the violin. As he complies with the last movement of the Bach G minor solo sonata, his educated fingers tell him that the fingerboard, far from whalebone, had once been the humerus of a "young mother, five feet three . . . who had known terrible agony at the end." The Bach turns into a *nigun*, a Jewish tune understood as a prayer for the dead. He finishes without a smile, walks out to the harbor, gives the violin a proper burial, and leaves.

Humor is not entirely unknown, and Jews have their share of it. Infatuated with music since his childhood discovery of a summer bandstand, Thomas Mann's Felix Krull, a title character like the Buddenbrooks, learns early how to mimic violinists with two sticks, an energetic vibrato, phantom position shifts, and an inward expression. His performance is such a triumph that his father decks him out in the era's obligatory sailor suit and patent leather shoes, buys him a cheap fiddle, and prophylactically smears the bow with Vaseline to be sure it produces no sound. He then persuades the bandmaster to let his little prodigy fiddle-synch a Hungarian dance. The audience, both elegant and plebeian, goes wild. Hauled off in triumph by upscale hotel guests, Felix emerges with a lyre-shaped diamond broach presented to him in a cascade of unintelligible French by an elderly Russian princess, is rewarded with chocolate cream cake at three different tables, and is even invited to play croquet with the rich kids. His father wisely begs off demands for a reprise.[179]

Clyde Small, the eponymous not quite hero, not quite antihero of Deane Narayn's novel *The Small Stradivari*,[180] is as American as Felix is European. Felix lives by his wits. Clyde lives by the rules to the extent, at least, that he understands them. A small-town high school teacher on the threshold of middle age, Clyde is a henpecked spouse at home. He also owns an heirloom violin of uncertain make with a Strad label. But with no heir in sight, and no violinist in the family, his wife, with her eyes on the country club, wants him to sell. As usual, Clyde does what he is told.

The quest predictably leads to New York and the funniest novel yet written about the violin trade by an Anglo-Indian author with an insider's familiarity presumably gained from his wife, the daughter of an Armenian-American collector in Flint, Michigan.[181] Clyde chases a certificate. Dealers chase one another. Everyone, including one dealer's nubile ward and another's nubile daughter, chases Clyde. Of course, each dealer finds a customer and offers him a Strad. But it's the same customer and, in each case, Clyde's Strad, assuming that it is one. In the end, Clyde himself is the buyer. He returns home and puts his experience to use by attending to an heir.

An Edge of Pride, Narayn's second and last novel,[182] leaves no scam unturned as it covers the same terrain from the other side of the counter. Guy, possessor of a law degree, struggles with his brother Maurice for control of the business, the soul of the profession, and some satisfaction from Maurice's secretary, bad-girl Kay, who does what it takes to get a sale. Guy makes up for lost time with good-girl Nina, whose virtuoso brother suspects that Maurice has sold him a faux Guadagnini. Good-guy Guy saves the day, gets the girl, and inherits the firm.

If Guy ends up as an innocent winner, Harry Belten, the title figure of Barry Targan's 1975 Iowa Short Fiction award winner, makes his way as a winning innocent.[183] A fiddle-crazed hardware salesman from upstate New York, Harry wants to play the Mendelssohn concerto in public after eighteen years of closeted practice. As his wife wrings her hands and friends watch in dismay, Harry not only takes out a second mortgage, he persuades the best teacher in the area to give him lessons. He then books a hall, sells tickets, and hires the Oswego Symphony for two rehearsals and a concert. To everyone's relief and amazement, he makes it to the end without disaster. But there is no suggestion of any plan to move on, for example, to the Beethoven.

MOVING PICTURES WORTH
A THOUSAND WORDS

IT WAS EVIDENT as early as 1607, when Monteverdi wrote it into *Orfeo*, that the violin had theatrical potential. The potential was unmistakable by the time that John Joseph Merlin, an eighteenth-century Belgian clock and instrument maker, reportedly crashed into a mirror while playing a violin on roller skates of his own design.[184]

In February 1848, Arthur Saint-Léon, both an accomplished violinist and the era's leading male dancer, raised the bar with his *Le Violon du Diable*, also known as *Tartini, Il Violinista*. By contemporary standards, it was notable enough that he both choreographed *Le Violon du Diable* and danced the lead. But a dancer who also played the violin was truly remarkable.[185] Nothing would come close to matching it till 1991, when the British violinist Anthony Marwood did a reprise of sorts with a choreographed version of Ysaÿe's A minor solo sonata he called *Obsessus*. Dancing and fiddling at the same time was "exhilarating," he reported.[186]

That the violin as its chosen vehicle made it big in the Yiddish theater a half century later was no surprise. In 1897, Joseph Lateiner's *David's Violin*, music by Sigmund Mogulescu, opened on New York's Lower East Side. With a score and libretto adaptable to virtually any stage, budget, ensemble, or venue from Odessa to Buenos Aires, it was soon on its way around the Jewish world. In 1917, Columbia recorded the last-act hit, "A generation goes, a generation comes." As late as 1927, it was produced in Detroit.[187]

With its cut-out characters, easy laughs, glatt kosher schmaltz, reminiscences of the Book of Job, and even a father-daughter scene out of Verdi, the story was as predictable as rhyming "June" and "moon." But no one for a moment would have thought less of it for that. Solomon eyes Evie. Evie eyes Tevye. Itsele eyes Yankele. Tevye, Yankele, and Keyla Beyla eye Tabele. Any number of characters eye Tevye's fortune. David, who is Tevye's brother and Yankele's uncle, has been on the family blacklist for fifteen years since running off to play the violin. What was not to like?

For an act or two, things look dark. Tevye nearly marries the gold-digging Evie. Solomon makes off with Tevye's money, wiping him out. Itsele and Keyla Beyla refuse to help. But it all turns out for the best. David, who returns in the guise of a street fiddler, offers to share the fortune he made. He and Tevye sing the show's big hit with obbligato violin cadenza. Tevye is transformed. Yankele and Tabele, now married, are seen with a baby behind a scrim. Solomon is forgiven and sent to music school. The various gold diggers are swept out the door. Tevye explains that it was David's violin that brought them back together. Everybody sings.

Three years later, Jacob Gordin's *God, Man and Devil* picked up where Lateiner and Mogelescu had left off. Performed in German and Polish, filmed in 1950, and revived as late as 1975, it became an instant classic. High-minded and earnest, the piece includes the traditional repertory company of familiar types, including the inevitable *badkhen*. But entertainment was no more a priority for Gordin, creator of the "Yiddish King Lear," than it was for Shakespeare. His goal, on the contrary, was nothing less than a Yiddish *Faust* with a hint of Job, transported to Dubrovne, a little town in White Russia, where Satan, known here as Mazik, picks Hershel, a pious, hardworking, and virtuous Torah scribe, to win his bet with G-d on the endless possibilities of human corruptibility.

Sure enough, the uncorrupted Hershele is a violinist who observes the fifth night of Chanukah in Act I by accompanying his family in the Twenty-third Psalm. The violin is also a casualty of his progressive corruption and ruthlessness, as he turns a lottery ticket into a fortune, the fortune into a prayer shawl factory, the factory into a sweatshop, and his marriage into a disaster. "Play for me just one more time," his niece begs in Act III. "I don't think I'll ever play again," he replies. But he does. Overcome by remorse at the end of Act IV, he plays the Twenty-third Psalm once more, then hangs himself with a bloodied talit.[188]

In 2001, a chamber opera version of Levi's *The Scrimshaw Violin*, libretto by Levi, score by Bruce Saylor, opened at New York's 92nd Street Y.[189] An art that was simple, cheap, and heartfelt in 1897, and unabashedly didactic in 1900, was now filtered through multiple generations of global and post-immigrant experience, including the Shoah and the gulag, as well as Juilliard, where Saylor had studied, and Yale and Cambridge, where Levi had.

Gil Morgenstern, cofounder with Levi of the Nine Circles Chamber Theater, which commissioned and produced the opera, had studied with Galamian. His parents were Viennese refugees, class of 1938.[190] Saylor's score paired hints of jazz and klezmer with solo Bach in ways that Lateiner and Mogulescu could never have imagined. Yet the violin was still the central character, New York was still New York, *The Scrimshaw Violin* was as authentically Jewish American musical theater as *David's Violin*, and "Generations come, generations go" with obbligato violin cadenza was still being acted out in real life.

Three years later, the violin was central again in *The Guest from the Future*. With music by Mel Marvin, who had directed *The Scrimshaw Violin*, the scenario this time was the famous postwar meeting of Isaiah Berlin, the Oxford philosopher-historian, and Anna Akhmatova, the Russian poet. "We wanted to work in a cross-disciplinary way and investigate the theatrical and dramatic possibilities of a concert experience," Morgenstern told an interviewer. "Along the way, we have also been exploring how the violin in particular can communicate without text."[191]

There was a role model for the taking in Edgardo Cozarinsky, a native Argentinean whose gravitational field extended from great-grandparents who originated in Kiev and Odessa to the Dirty War at home that caused him to leave Buenos Aires for Paris in 1974. In 1997, Cozarinsky's film *Rothschild's Violin* was released to general acclaim and a succession of international film festivals. "Music says what words don't dare," mutters the clearly agitated Benjamin Fleischman, a character in the film, as his composition class joins its professor, Dimitri Shostakovich, in a discussion of the *yurodivy*, the holy fool, in Mussorgsky's *Boris Godunov*.

Like Morgenstern's, Cozarinsky's project combines artfully imagined narrative, an uncut chamber opera, several levels of historical memory, and the iconic violin. It also subsumes them in a film within a film, financed with French money, and cast with Russian, Hungarian, and Baltic actors. Shot on locations from Budapest to St. Petersburg, the film is laced with extraordinary archival material showing people pretending to be tank treads and ball bearings, stunt fliers spelling out S-T-A-L-I-N in the sky, and Western fellow travelers like Paul Robeson and Lion Feuchtwanger testifying to the glories of Soviet humanism.

Artistic as well as entrepreneurial and managerial top billing deservedly went to the director, a literary-cinematic polymath. But credits, acknowledged or implied, reach back to Chekhov, whose story appeared in 1894; to Fleischmann, the composition student who saw its potential in the late 1930s; to Shostakovich, who preserved and completed his student's powerful score in 1943–44, after Fleischmann died fighting with a civil defense unit; and to Solomon Volkov, the violin student turned musicologist who directed the opera's first staged production in Leningrad in 1968 before publishing an unauthorized and hotly debated biography of Shostakovich in the United States in 1979.[192]

At least one commentator was reminded of Russian nesting dolls.[193] The innermost is obviously Chekhov's haunting story. The outermost is Shostakovich, neither martyr nor hero, and drawn increasingly and recurringly to Jewish themes.[194] But inseparable from all of them is the violin itself. Triumphantly carried away by Rothschild, the title character of an opera shut down within a day of its premiere by a regime that declared Israel and all things Jewish non grata, it reappears in the movie's last scene, now in Chagallian blue, in the hands of a young player under a St. Petersburg lamppost. "A potent image of freedom, Cozarinsky's violin is a timeless symbol of the indomitability of the artistic spirit," said one British reviewer. To a degree unusual in film criticism, this was neither hyperbole nor understatement.[195]

Golden oldies dating back to the early days of TV were mercifully forgotten. In the season of 1959–60, BBC, National Telefilm Associates of America, a distant ancestor of America's Public Broadcasting System,[196] and British Lion Film Corporation had the bright idea of bringing Harry Lime, the famous Orson Welles character from Carol Reed's classic *Third Man*, back from the dead for two thirty-nine-episode seasons and international syndication.

In *Broken Strings*, broadcast on July 1, 1960,[197] a Soviet virtuoso dazzles all of Paris with his Tchaikovsky and his state-owned del Gesù. But he also moonlights as a Western agent, and the neck of his violin has been cunningly retooled as a secret cache. With the help of his manager, the bad guys steal the violin from his dressing room. Lime recovers it while wearing a tuxedo, getting hit over the head with a pistol, and gazing deep, deep into the eyes of the gorgeous, American-accented French intelligence agent who offered him $100,000 to do the job.

Hollywood's contribution was a series of half-hour episodes called *Shotgun Slade*, about a cowboy private eye whose weapon of choice is a hybrid long gun, built to fire a 12-gauge shotgun shell and a .35 caliber rifle bullet from its respective barrels. In episode twenty-six, aired on May 15,

1960, a Denver insurance company hires Slade to look after a Strad priced at $40,000, whose owner is a Viennese maestro on a vaudeville tour with two nifty nieces. In the twenty-two minutes of action between commercial breaks, Slade is brained by a falling sandbag, brushes off a measure or two of the Brahms concerto, exchanges the obligatory roundhouse punches with the company's sharpshooter and its strong man, is nearly, but not quite, distracted by the nieces, and finally foils the insurance fraud that is the nieces' real purpose.[198]

But it was the movies, with their global reach and resources, that would become and remain the master medium. All that was needed was sound. In August 1926, with all twelve of New York's major dailies in attendance, Western Electric introduced Bell Laboratories' Vitaphone, a process that coordinated a film projector with a sixteen-inch disk and turntable. The debut was a thundering success.[199] "The future of this new contrivance is boundless," the *New York Times* reported.[200]

Between 1926 and 1930, when Vitaphone gave way to the modern sound track, Warner would produce multiple feature films and some two thousand short features, among them single-take mini-recitals by Mischa Elman playing Dvořák's "Humoresque" and Gossec's "Minuet" and Efrem Zimbalist playing the second movement variations of Beethoven's Kreutzer sonata. Both were enthusiastically received. "Whether it was a note from the piano or the plucking of the violin strings, it was audible throughout the theatre and just as inspiring as if Mr. Zimbalist and Mr. Bauer had themselves been before the audience," the *New York Times*'s reporter noted.

In 2007, forty years after Elman's death and twenty-two after Zimbalist's, a twenty-two-year-old Vietnamese student at an aeronautics institute in Moscow, located and uploaded the ancient films to YouTube. Once aimed at local theaters too small to hire an orchestra but large enough to support Vitaphone, Elman's "Humoresque" and Zimbalist's Beethoven were now accessible anytime, anywhere, to anyone who wished to watch them.[201]

The filmed recital would return from the recesses of memory for a brief reprise after World War II. In 1947, Paul Gordon, a Hollywood producer, organized a company called Concert Film Corporation for a series called Concert Magic. Billed as "The First Motion Picture Concert," it featured Yehudi Menuhin, who agreed to play for a minimal advance. It was assumed that the royalties would follow when the films caught on. But they didn't. Half a century later, the films would be rediscovered and marketed as DVDs.[202] In 1948 they barely made it to release.

A year later, Rudolph Polk, another producer, and the actor Sam Jaffe signed Polk's longtime friend and associate Jascha Heifetz as well as the cellist Gregor Piatigorsky, the pianist Artur Rubinstein, the tenor Jan Peerce, and the contralto Marian Anderson, for a two-a-year series of six short film portraits at $5,000 each. Assisted by four writers, two directors, and a co-producer, he also produced *Of Men and Music*, a quartet of performer features held together by Deems Taylor, a composer, music critic, and gifted essayist known to millions of radio listeners as the intermission voice of the New York Philharmonic. It was released by 20th Century–Fox, a major Hollywood studio in 1950.[203] As usual, the unapproachable Heifetz was the supreme challenge. Interviewers and interviewee agreed to a token show of sailing, tennis, ping-pong, gardening, the family car, and his wife and a child. But the unmistakable message was that the only Heifetz that mattered was the one with the violin.

Confident as Menuhin was that the medium had a future, Heifetz even bought 350 of the Polk company's preferred shares, over 10 percent of the total. Recovered from the warehouse in 1977, the documentaries were released on cassette, turned into DVDs, and eventually marketed on Amazon. But like Gordon's product, they, too, were a contemporary bust. The company was declared bankrupt, the vindictive Heifetz actually sued, and Polk died soon after of a heart attack.[204]

The feature film, a thing of perennial fantasy and wonder, showed more promise with Paganini, of course, an irresistible candidate for cinematic treatment. In 1922–23, Conrad Veidt, en route from one benchmark role as Cesare, the somnambulant medium in *The Cabinet of Dr. Caligari*, to another as Major Strasser in *Casablanca*, stopped off to play Paganini in Heinz Goldberg's silent film of the same name. A single scene, archived at Gosfilmofond in Moscow, is its only known survivor. But its six minutes and 38 seconds are packed with long shadows, implied menace, artfully edited Venetian ambience, and armies of elaborately costumed extras. With Veidt himself as a statuesque Paganini in the era's obligatory eye makeup, hints that Liszt and Berlioz also show up in the story, and a winning child actor who can only be playing the little Achille,[205] the viewer can only wish that more had survived.

In the mid-1920s, Paul Knepler, a Viennese publisher, showed Franz Lehár a manuscript novel, *very* loosely based on the life of Paganini, called *Hexenmeister (The Wizard)*. A good violinist himself, the composer was so taken with the scenario that he immediately began turning it into the operetta that would become his twenty-eighth work for the stage. Retitled

Paganini, it premiered to a mixed response in Vienna in October 1925. But it took off in Berlin a few months later when the thirty-two-year-old Richard Tauber, Central Europe's tenor of choice, became available to play the twenty-something title character.

Already notable for the composer's signature tunes and the leading man's signature high notes, the score featured two prominent violin solos. Ufa, Alfred Hugenberg's version of a Hollywood studio, was in full flower in Berlin's western suburbs. Tauber, at the top of his form, was top box office. Talkies were just over the horizon. There was no shortage of fiddlers available to take on Lehár's cadenzas. But nothing cinematic came of it.

Twenty years would pass before Paganini resurfaced, this time at Gainsborough Studios, J. Arthur Rank's[206] wannabe Hollywood on the south bank of the Thames. Distilled from a novel by Manuel Komroff, a tirelessly prolific and successful pop novelist,[207] *The Magic Bow* was evidently just what its producers ordered for a new postwar audience. For Britain's leading producer of cinematic bodice-rippers, Stewart Granger, the son of a professional army officer and great-great-grandson of a Neapolitan opera singer, was just the man for the leading part.

Granger's Paganini is masterfully self-assured, scornful of the idle rich, dashingly handsome in open-necked Byronic décolleté, and unmistakably thirty-three, when the few meandering cues in the script would suggest that the actual character was somewhere between thirteen and twenty. Like actors before and after, he took violin lessons to prepare for the part. But serious playing was left to Menuhin. While Granger held his arms behind his back, an assistant director thrust a violin under his chin and a pair of professional players bowed and fingered for the camera. Menuhin would later recall the script without exaggeration as "vulgar and nonsensical" beyond anything he had ever read.[208] But he welcomed the chance to get together with Diana Gould, who would become his second wife a year later. His contract specified noninterference with music, which included Paganini's 24th caprice tricked out as a violin concerto, the second theme from the first movement of the D Major violin concerto tricked out like a dance band arrangement of Rachmaninov, and a *Reader's Digest* reduction of the last movement of the Beethoven concerto, a piece Paganini is not known to have played. "Interruptions on a theme of Paganini," a contemporary headline writer called it.[209]

Klaus Kinski's *Paganini* forty years later could be called shapeless, plotless, narcissistic, pornographic, surprisingly if selectively knowledgeable, and, in spots, even brilliant. But it was not boring. Famed as a specialist in transgressive characters who had never met a piece of scenery he didn't want to chew, Kinski had already played the poets François Villon and Arthur Rimbaud, the conquistador Aguirre, the quietly desperate every-man Woyzeck, and Count Dracula. He now set out to play Paganini. He even engaged his son Nikolai as Paganini's son, Achille.

When his longtime director, Werner Herzog, called his script unfilm-able, Kinski directed it himself, his only appearance as director in some 120 films. Characteristically, he also filmed himself in his X-rated and exuberantly polyglot performance as director. For good measure, he edited the film, though the version released for a single screening in Paris was reedited by the producers. It was not hard to guess why, though the col-lateral damage included loss of a wicked takeoff on the title figure by the veteran mime Marcel Marceau. The film was released commercially in Japan, where it was delicately classified as "pink,"[210] the category reserved for upscale pornography.

In a second spin-off film, Kinski's friend, the parfumier Andreas Frey-tag von Loringhoven, happily recalled the debut screening. The whole French cabinet had showed up and then sheepishly ducked out again, leav-ing only Jack Lang, the minister of culture, and Danielle Gouze, wife of President Mitterrand, to see it to the end. The reedited version earned one of Kinski's trademark tantrums, also filmed, when the movie was shown in Cannes. Another decade had passed, and Kinski had died before the film finally appeared to uneven reviews in Germany. The full collection—Kinski's version, the producers' version, Kinski as director, the interview with the parfumier, and the tantrum in Cannes, 341 minutes in all—was then marketed as a European (PAL) DVD. There was also a memoir, more accurately a tirade, packaged as a book.[211]

In its reductionist obsession with sex, music, money, misanthropy, and the artist's consuming dedication to his son, the film rolls over and past the historical Paganini. Still, as Gerhard Koch noted in the *Frankfurter Allgemeine*, even if it gets three-quarters wrong, it gets a quarter right.[212] Someone had obviously done some serious reading. Kinski's haunted Paga-nini comes galaxies closer to Delacroix's portrait of the man in black than does the famously handsome Granger. Little Nikolai Kinski, no mean actor himself in his show of grief and desperation as his father dies, is care-fully costumed like the real Achille. The music, spectacularly performed by Salvatore Accardo, is real Paganini. The threshold hysteria as Paganini performs in a Parma theater, the ineffable Watsons hauling a burned-out Paganini along behind them, the dying man's meandering fantasies of "Russia and America," let alone the tragicomedy of his burial—all can be watched without suspension of disbelief. Most remarkable of all is a scene in which Paganini, out walking by himself, takes the fiddle out of the hands of a kid on the street, tosses off a few dazzling variations on the Austrian national hymn, passes his hat, returns the violin and the hat's contents to the boy, extends his regards to the astonished listeners, turns on his heel, and leaves the scene. There are actual reports of a generous Paganini. There are few such reports of an understated Kinski.

In sympathetic hands, the maker, even the instrument, could astonish. With the help of Busby Berkeley, the instrument literally glows in the dark in Warner Bros.' *Gold Diggers* of 1933. A white violin first appears in the hands of a white tail–suited Dick Powell. The chorus has white violins, too. Clad in white lily-pad costumes that show off a lot of leg, the chorus immediately picks up Powell's tune while arranged on a vast spiral staircase. It then forms a giant flower before regrouping as a violin outline that lights up as the house goes dark, limning the seemingly disembodied instruments in neon.

King Vidor, a director unfazed by *War and Peace*, could even make a point of the violin by turning the player into an accessory. In *Our Daily Bread*, his Depression-era saga of a cooperative farm improvised by unemployed Californians, a violinist appears no fewer than three times: in teacher mode, giving lessons to the Italian shoemaker's son; in hoedown mode, accompanied by an accordion and harmonica player; and, perhaps most interestingly, in workingman mode, lined up with a plumber, a carpenter, and a stonemason, all applying for membership in the co-op. That Heifetz at the time was Vidor's son-in-law may or may not have mattered. But it clearly mattered to Vidor that the violinist, like the others in the line-up, was a man who worked with his hands.

The accessory violinist—in fact, a whole section of them—shows up again in *Here Come the Coeds*, a low-budget vehicle for the comedy team of Bud Abbott and Lou Costello in wartime 1944, and rereleased in peacetime 1950. This time the scene is an embattled women's college, where Phil Spitalny's all-girl orchestra, known to network radio listeners as the Hour of Charm Orchestra, seems to run the music program, and the music appreciation class features a performance of Sarasate's *Zigeunerweisen* by Spitalny's wife, Evelyn Klein, a Juilliard graduate, known to network radio listeners as Evelyn and Her Magic Violin. The accessory violinist is there again in Carol Reed's postwar classic *The Third Man*, when Ernst Deutsch, as the ingratiatingly slithery "Baron" Kurtz, apologizes sheepishly to Joseph Cotten when he is discovered in a frayed tuxedo, earning his shabby living as a strolling violinist in a Viennese café.

Now and then, the violin itself could be the star. In *Stradivari*, one of three films produced in Germany in 1935 by the Hungarian-born Géza von Bolváry, the title refers to the instrument, a fictitious but presumably bona fide Strad passed on to Sándor, a dashing young Hungarian officer and virtuoso violinist, by his uncle. Meanwhile, Sándor falls in love with Maria, an Italian music education student whose teacher identifies the Strad as the masterpiece it is. Supposedly made in 1672, the instrument is thought to be under a curse placed on it by Stradivari himself when he was turned down by Nicolò Amati's daughter. Pursuing its provenance, Maria discovers that the curse has since made life miserable for generations of owners, from Cosimo de Medici to a French general who took it to Russia in 1812. Long believed lost, it was only recovered in 1895 by a Russian princess, who sold it to a Gypsy.

Undeterred, the couple are about to marry and tour the United States when World War I breaks out and Sándor has to join his regiment. He naturally takes the violin along. As years pass without news, Dr. Pietro Rossi courts Maria back in Milan. Then both Sándor and the Strad reappear. Seriously wounded, Sándor has been taken prisoner by the Italians and brought to Rossi for life-saving surgery. Seemingly no worse for wear, the Strad has been recovered, too, and sold to Rossi by a soldier who claims to have found it beside a dead Hussar. Rossi presents it to Maria, who naturally recognizes it, assumes that Sándor is dead, and agrees to marry Rossi. But Rossi knows better. He magnanimously allows the Strad to reunite Maria with Sándor, though whatever luck it now brought would run out spectacularly for Germans, Hungarians, and Italians alike over the next decade. After a three-year pause, von Bolváry returned for a modestly successful postwar career in Italy and West Germany. *Stradivari*, included for no very obvious reason in the military government's list of banned films after 1945, eventually made its way to the Berlin Cinémathèque.[213]

A half century later, François Girard's *Red Violin* was also supposed to be a product of Cremona's golden age. But this time, the fictions include the maker as well as the instrument and the adventures that follow it. The adventures begin at its creation, when the maker's wife dies young in child-birth, as foretold by a tarot card–reading fortune-teller. Grief-stricken, the master mixes a few drops of her blood into the varnish, assuring that his masterpiece will be indelibly and unmistakably red, and paints it on the instrument with a brush made from her hair. The red violin turns out to be his final work. Donated to a Tyrolean monastery, it is soon on its way across the globe and the centuries. From his point on, *The Red Violin* turns increasingly purple.

En route from Cremona to an auction house improbably located in Montreal, the violin literally bounces off a couple of floors and walls, is buried with a former player, and comes within a matchstick of being incinerated in China. In the end, it attracts the expert attention of an African-American expert. All the while, it passes from hand to ever unlikelier hand: an Austrian orphan, drilled until he drops dead of stress before a select audience; a generation or two of Gypsies; a Victorian gran-dee, part Byron, part Paganini, who uses it as a four-stringed aphrodisiac; and Red Guards, high on the Cultural Revolution. No wonder that the Canadian auctioneers send it straight to a shop fitted out like an acoustics lab for badly needed restoration.

For viewers with an ear for musical form, the story line is a classic rondo, whose recurring themes—the fortune-teller in Cremona, the auction in Montreal—alternate with the changing scene. John Corigliano's score, a chaconne, makes the same point. In the end, the film unites two of the medium's classic tropes, the violin as picaresque hero, and the ever-popular bait-and-switch scam, in which a ringer is substituted for the original.[214]

As the Mexican director Francisco Vargas would prove in 2005 with *The Violin*, the medium could not only name a film for a violin without a name, but it could even find a leading role for its battered case. The incongruously named Plutarco, memorably played by the octogenarian Angel Tavira, is a desperately poor peasant farmer who roams his corner of desperately poor southern Mexico as a street fiddler, accompanied by his son and grandson. All three generations are concurrently engaged in the perennial war of conquerors and the conquered, stretching back to Cortés, and the insurgents have buried ammunition in Plutarco's cornfield.

Betting on his age, instrument, and credibility to get him past the soldiers standing between him and the ammunition, Plutarco mortgages the next year's crop to his landlord to get a donkey and exchanges personal history with the soldiers' music-loving captain to gain his confidence. He then recovers the ammunition, packs it in his violin case, and leaves the violin. When Plutarco returns with the empty case, the violin is gone. The captain challenges him to play the violin, an obvious impossibility, since it's the captain who has it. Meanwhile, his troops have seized the insurgents, including Plutarco's son. A fadeout shot shows his grandson on the road with his little sister and a guitar that is presumably his father's.[215]

The maker-dealer might seem a still unlikelier candidate for stardom. Yet a couple of late twentieth-century European directors not only found possibilities there too. In a three-hour cine-bio made for TV in 1989, Giacomo Battiato even managed to find, or infer, a bit of drama in the life of Antonio Stradivari.

The large black holes and expansive white spaces in the life of a man who barely wrote, didn't fight, and is not known to have traveled are inevitably a challenge. But they are also an opportunity for Italian writers to imagine plausible scenes from a long life in a messy and colorful time and place. Money was clearly no object for the film's four-company consortium of Franco-Italian producers.[216] The production values include good taste, a sly sense of humor, and an uncommon degree of historical literacy. There is some wonderful violin playing by Salvatore Accardo. Cremona was, and remains, a rewarding film location.

Of course, a familiar, compelling, even charismatic lead doesn't hurt. With some seventy films and roles from Quasimodo to Zorba the Greek behind him, the seventy-two-year-old Anthony Quinn plays Stradivari as a single-minded perfectionist, intermittently narcissistic, unfailingly authoritarian, but essentially lovable. In a series of flashbacks, he persuades Nicolò Amati that he really wants to make violins by sneaking out of his orphanage at night to steal a pattern, and slips an intended rib of his first instrument into the only readily available steam bath, the orphanage soup. On the threshold of adulthood, he bumbles into a hilarious opera performance in which a trio of castrati, suspended over the stage on wires, throw a hissy fit, while his presumptive father-in-law tries and fails to make time with a young female in his loge. He copes with local authorities who are disposed to slug first and ask questions later, as well as temperamental customers, and the formalities of Spanish and Austrian occupiers. He experiences the illness and death of his first wife after the doctor's portentous Latin and quack prescriptions, followed by an egregious bill and the bizarre and useless ministrations of the neighborhood wise woman. He bullies his elder sons. He takes his second wife for a cruise on the Po with water music provided by a red-headed priest who looks suspiciously like Antonio Vivaldi. Above all, he works. "I make violins, I don't make music," Battiato has him say.[217]

Strictly speaking, Stéphane, the grimly unromantic luthier in Claude Sautet's unrelievedly bleak and very French *Un Coeur en Hiver* (*A Heart in Winter*) three years later, doesn't make violins or music. But he comes close enough to catch the attention of Camille, a very good violinist on the threshold of a serious career, and a regular at the most credible violin shop yet seen on film. Camille has become the special other of Stéphane's partner, Maxime, who is as good in the front room as Stéphane is in the back.

As interested in Stéphane's ear as she is in his bench skills, Camille wants him to set up her Vuillaume. But she also wants him at her rehearsal for a recording of the Ravel piano trio, a piece significantly warmer than any of the three principals. Her interest leads, of course, to a relationship. But the relationship is elliptical. Stéphane is polite, considerate of apprentices, and can establish friendships with women as well as men. Unlike his other friends, he's even willing to assist his terminally ill mentor and closest friend commit suicide. But he doesn't, won't, and perhaps can't, do love. With the shop as collateral damage, his rejection destroys not only his relationship to Camille but both his and her relationship to Maxime. Ravel's luminous score and Jean-Jacques Kantorow's lovely violin playing stand out among the devastation like orchids in an ice storm.[218]

With its open-ended, feel-good potential, the teacher-pupil relationship was a natural for movie treatment. A first, tentative circumnavigation of its possibilities, *They Shall Have Music* began in 1938 as an agreement with the producer Samuel Goldwyn to pay $40,000 up front, to accede to Heifetz's insistence on an educational message, and to make a still unspecified future film with Heifetz cast as Heifetz. First came the sound track, all repertory of the artist's choice; the Los Angeles Philharmonic served as backup. Then came the camera, with Heifetz in hundreds of takes, playing in synchrony with his recorded self. Four weeks later, Heifetz was the most comprehensively filmed violinist in history. In the end, 1,500 of 50,000 feet would actually be used.[219]

The footage was originally planned for a Warner Bros. project called *The Confessions of a Nazi Spy*, a film that was actually produced and released in 1939. A better option turned up in a story by the screenwriter Irmgard von Cube, herself only recently arrived from Europe. The saga of a neighborhood music school pressed to pay the rent, it was passed on to the screenwriter John Howard Lawson, Hollywood's premier Communist, and the director Archie Mayo, who had already directed Mae West, Bette Davis, Humphrey Bogart, and Gary Cooper, and would later direct the Marx Brothers. Like life imitating art, a Los Angeles neighborhood school happened to find itself in the same fix as the New York school of von Cube's story. Better still, large numbers of its graduates moved on to the California Junior Symphony Orchestra, a well-known incubator of professional talent created in 1936 by Peter Meremblum, a former Auer pupil. The school was still in operation some seventy years later. Goldwyn quickly hired forty of Meremblum's kids, and the cameras began rolling in earnest.

The plot was gratifyingly conventional. Frankie, on the brink of delinquency, lucks into a Heifetz performance at Carnegie Hall. Transfixed, he resumes practicing on a violin left by his late father, but he runs away from home, accompanied by his dog, after his stepfather smashes it. The kindly director of the settlement house music school takes pity on them. But the pitiless music store proprietors who own the property are resolved to collect the rent or foreclose on the eve of the big concert. Frankie proposes an impromptu fund-raiser in front of Carnegie Hall. Heifetz, arriving by coincidence, expresses interest and gives Frankie his card. When the director's presumptive son-in-law claims Heifetz as a school patron in a frantic effort to stave off foreclosure, Frankie deputizes his friends to find Heifetz. They fail to turn him up, but they find and steal his violin. While a phalanx of neighborhood mothers hold off the cops, a desperate Frankie manages to locate Heifetz's manager. Already on the scene, the movers are carrying away instruments when Heifetz pulls up in a blare of police sirens. He identifies his violin, joins the school orchestra for a triumphant last movement of Mendelssohn, and incidentally saves the day. The real-life Heifetz, not known as demonstrative, presented each player a dedicated photo.[220]

Two years later, RKO released *Melody for Three*, a sixty-seven-minute entr'acte of near-zero specific gravity, featuring a perfectly normal small-town American prodigy, a superstar American conductor, a live radio orchestra in Chicago, and an unhappy family. What renders it unexpectedly interesting is the improbable combination of Fay Wray, who had once played King Kong's love interest, and Jean Hersholt, a Danish immigrant known to contemporary radio listeners as the kindly, resourceful

Dr. Christian. Toscha Seidel, an Auer protégé who made good in Hollywood, serves up a tossed salad of Brahms's Hungarian dances. Schuyler Standish, cast as the prodigy, seems actually to have played the violin.[221] Dr. Christian, of course, is just the man to set a broken family. En route to the inevitable happy end, dazzled studio tourists are introduced to sound effects and possibly the first glimpse on film of the next broadcast wonder, television.

Carnegie Hall, a Heifetz reprise of sorts, followed in postwar 1947. For those who knew where to look for it, there was plenty of drama. But most of it was in the opening credits. The film's coproducer, Boris Morros, was a onetime cello prodigy from St. Petersburg who had come to America in 1922, conducted the orchestra at New York's Rivoli Theater, and worked his way up to music director and talent booker for Paramount Pictures. A Soviet agent since 1934, he embarked on a new career as counterspy for the FBI in 1947,[222] the year of *Carnegie Hall*'s release. Edgar Ulmer, the film's director, was a Central European veteran of the Weimar and Yiddish film work with a long Hollywood résumé. By a convenient coincidence, the cellist Gregor Piatigorsky was a childhood friend and the conductor Fritz Reiner was his daughter's godfather.[223] Both make cameo appearances in *Carnegie Hall*.

For the normal moviegoer, the product is a union of ladies' magazine and B movie convention, with an occasional long shadow borrowed from F. W. Murnau, the Weimar master who brought Ulmer to Hollywood, and a fine shot of the pianist Artur Rubinstein from high above the stage. Like Tarzan swinging from tree to tree, the story line leaps and swoops from cameo to cameo, as the great ones of the day—Jan Peerce, Ezio Pinza, Lily Pons and Risë Stevens, Bruno Walter, Leopold Stokowski, Artur Rodzinski and Reiner, Rubinstein, Piatigorsky, and above all, Heifetz—sing, play, conduct and occasionally act. Linking their appearances is Nora, who heard Tchaikovsky conduct the opening night concert when she was nine and who was prematurely widowed when her husband, a gifted but irascible pianist, drank too much in a fit of self-pity and fell down the stairs. Over the course of the film, Nora works her way up from cleaning Carnegie Hall to managing it. Meanwhile, she raises her son, Tony, to be a more serious pianist than his father by taking him across the street from their Fifty-seventh Street apartment, where she introduces him to role model after role model. Finally rebellious after years of meeting, hearing, even occasionally playing with the great ones of the era, he takes a job with Vaughan Monroe's big band, where he can play "modern music." To his mother's surprise, he appears on the Carnegie Hall stage as composer-conductor-pianist in a crossover Fifty-seventh Street Concerto, with Harry James, another pillar of the big band era, as solo trumpet.[224]

In fact, the joke is on Tony. Within a few years of the film's release, the big band had lost out to a very different ensemble, and Vaughan Monroe was gone and forgotten. Carnegie Hall, on the other hand, was declared a National Historic Landmark after a near miss by the wrecker's ball in 1960, and Heifetz's abridged but Olympian performance of the first movement of the Tchaikovsky concerto, lifted straight from the film, might reasonably have qualified as a National Historic Landmark itself. Uploaded to YouTube in December 2006, it had already been viewed nearly a half-million times by September 2008.[225]

DECADES PASSED BEFORE the teacher-pupil scenario reappeared. The occasion was President Nixon's rediscovery of China in 1972. Seven years later, Isaac Stern and the pianist David Golub discovered China too. Murray Lerner's heartfelt and shrewdly edited *From Mao to Mozart* is as close as film comes to providing a culture-to-culture experience in which learning and teaching are reciprocal and continuous. Curious and impressed, the visitors are also exasperated, deeply moved, and occasionally shaken by the warmth, talent, enthusiasm, resourcefulness, bloody-mindedness, ineptitude, and memories they encounter. But as the hosts intend and hope, they leave their own mark as well.

There are easily a dozen memorable scenes. But three stand out among the best of the best. In one, Tan Shu-zhen, who has clearly seen hell close-up as associate director of the Shanghai Conservatory during the Cultural Revolution, answers Stern's question about the puzzling difference between the youngest and the middle generation of Chinese players. The answer, spelled out in slow, articulate, and devastatingly understated English, is obviously the terrible decade when Tan himself was locked in a closet and consigned to cleaning toilets. Even the normally irrepressible Stern is momentarily silent.

The second is a confrontation about the piano, alleged to be the best in Shanghai. Golub finds it unplayable. This time Stern takes charge. If nothing better is available, he announces, he'll just have to call Beijing and demand that another be flown to Shanghai on a military plane. A playable piano shows up in short order.

The third scene takes place at a master class before a large audience.

The player, a girl in her teens, is desperate to do the right thing. Taut as an E string, she's also on the spot as never before or, in all likelihood, again. Stern stops her firmly but kindly. At once elfin, avuncular, and seductive, he persuades her to sing her piece, then play it again as she's just sung it. She does as he asks and suddenly produces music. Stern beams. The girl beams. The audience applauds.

In the meanwhile, the Suzuki method, now visible even as dot-dot-dot-dot-dash-dash (. . . . - -) on suburban bumper stickers, had not only made it to America's Main Streets but to East Harlem's mean streets. Allan Miller's charming documentary *Small Wonders* did the rest, preserving, packaging, and marketing the magical Roberta Guaspari for posterity and for anyone else curious to see what she did and how she did it, while incidentally delivering a real-life, late twentieth-century version of *They Shall Have Music*.

Feel-bad elements are implied but not allowed to compromise the feel-good theme. The bean counters at the Board of Education who cut off Guaspari's funding, eliminators of "frills in a no-frill world," as Sam Donaldson of ABC News refers to them in a 1991 TV clip, get no opportunity for excuse or rebuttal. The viewer can only guess how much—or little—money is actually involved. Though one little boy backs off tearfully when Guaspari warns that she expects hard work, there is little indication of dropouts. Remarkably, Suzuki is never mentioned.

The feel-good elements, on the other hand, are treated with genuine respect and affection. Miller's camera delivers a powerful sense of the city's diversity and energy, Guaspari's recruitment pitch, the annual lottery for admission to the program, and the whooping delight of the pint-sized winners. In preparation for the big concert, a little boy named José is seen practicing earnestly in his room, and then in the bathtub before being packed into his white recital shirt by his adoring parents and supportive family. There is the Knicks game at the Garden where Guaspari marshals her charges for the opening "Star-Spangled Banner" like an NBA coach preparing his team for the play-offs. Above all, there is Guaspari herself, demonstrating, admonishing, encouraging, cajoling, or wearily schlepping little violins. "I like the way you talk to them," a mother assures her over coffee and cookies at a support group meeting straight out of Norman Rockwell. "It's just like home."

Remarkably, *Music of the Heart*, the studio film that was its sequel, was not only as good as its documentary predecessor, it even made money: $79 million gross revenue on production costs of $7 million.[226] Its quality, let alone its success, was all the more amazing for the principals involved. A master of the horror movie, the director Wes Craven was best known for creating Freddy Krueger, a serial killer who attacks his victims from inside their dreams. The pop icon Madonna was the original choice to play Guaspari but dropped out. She was replaced by the brilliant Meryl Streep, whose talent might persuade even the crowd at the popcorn stand to consider the Suzuki method. Both actresses reportedly made a good-faith effort to hold, even play a violin believably. But it was clear that Streep had also studied Guaspari. The extra effort pays off in dimensions only hinted at in Miller's film. "There was a time when a movie like this would have had to end with a prize or a big victory, a sense of somebody's having gone for the gold," Janet Maslin noted in her review. "The reward here is simpler: just an affirmation of the power of music to provide beauty, pleasure and a sense of accomplishment."[227] How often had anyone said that about a Hollywood movie?

On the QT, released the same year, is as cringe-inducingly high-minded and unintentionally funny as *Music of the Heart* is affecting and plausible. Original in part for pairing a young white man with a black mentor and father figure, it is also the rare studio film dedicated to buskers. Sam Ball, as Jari, the pupil, is a twenty-five-year-old from Michigan's Upper Peninsula who wants to matriculate at a fictitious New York Academy of Music. Meanwhile, he struggles to make a living in the subway. James Earl Jones, already a veteran of some eighty films, is Leo, the teacher, a busker and session player who plays virtually anything, anywhere, at any time.

Jari has to find his own voice, Leo tells him. He needs to play the Sibelius concerto with soul. He leads Jari into an unused subway tunnel, produces an English horn, plays him the solo from Sibelius's *Swan of Tuonela*, and quotes a few translated lines from the German poet Rainer Maria Rilke.

Jari learns only after his mentor's death that Leo ended up in the subway because he turned down a scholarship from Juilliard years earlier, believing it was not for black people. At his audition, he honors Leo's memory by playing Sibelius with feeling, including a cadenza where none is indicated. It was inspired by Rilke, he explains.

Released three years later, Chen Kaige's *Together* carries the pupil-teacher trope to a new world and a new century. Once more, driven parent and talented kid depart the sticks to take on the big city. But the scene is a China barely recognizable as the country Stern and Golub visited only a generation earlier, where the director, a survivor of the Cultural Revolution, is still haunted by his teenage betrayal of his father.[228]

Cheng, smarmy, loquacious, essentially good-hearted and tough as barbed wire, is a short-order cook who wants the best for his son, Xiaochun, a teenage violinist of stupendous promise. A competition in Beijing ends with a dubious fifth-place finish. But it also leads to Professor Jiang, a gifted but depressive teacher who lives off the beaten track with a houseful of cats and Lili, a gold digger with a heart of gold.

Though awash in self-pity and seemingly incapable even of changing his socks, Jiang brings Xiaochun along as a musician. A force of nature unprecedented in his early adolescent life, Lili almost unconsciously becomes the boy's surrogate big sister, while his father scrambles to meet the bills in a restaurant kitchen, on a building site, and as a bicycle courier.

Things now turn complicated. Cheng persuades the young and swingy Professor Yu Shifeng to teach his son. Yu not only agrees. He invites Xiaochun to move in with him and another pupil, Lin Yu, while he decides which of them to enter in a major international competition. Xiaochun wins. But as he prepares to leave, he learns that he was taken in as a foundling after Cheng discovered him at the local train station with a violin and an attached note from his mother.

Stretched to breaking between art and life, love and ambition, old China and new China, Xiaochun races tearfully for the train station and home, while his support group searches frantically for him. As the movie ends, Lin is heard playing the Tchaikovsky concerto at the competition, while Xiaochun does the same as a kind of positioning signal in the crowded middle of the station concourse. As implausible a finale as any since the Goldwyn era,[229] the scene is still memorable for the playing by Lin Chuan Yun, a Sassmannshaus protégé who made his own Beijing debut at five.[230]

And then, of course, comes love, the trope for all seasons. Boy meets girl, love meets violin—and vice versa. All that was needed was sound, and Hollywood was ready for it with Fox's *Caravan* in 1934. Where Hollywood went, Europe followed two years later with *"Die Liebe des Maharadscha"* (*The Maharajah's Love*), an Austro-Italian co-production with two directors, alternate casts, and an alternate title, *"Una donna fra due mondi"* (*A Woman between Two Worlds*).

Neither film can be accused of being art. "As balmy a narrative as the cinema has arranged . . . in recent months," a contemporary reviewer called

Caravan on its release. "The tragedy of 'A Woman between Two Worlds' seemed as nothing compared with that of a woman between two directors," Isa Miranda, the film's Italian leading lady, recalled of a set where alternate directors filmed alternate versions scene by scene.[231] Yet, like the era's Ford or Chevrolet, each film is an affordable family-friendly product, with at least an obbligato role for the violin.

With a book by Samson Raphaelson, a favorite of the great Ernst Lubitsch, and Robert Liebmann, who co-authored the Weimar classic *The Blue Angel*, *Caravan* opened at New York's still shiny new Radio City Music Hall in 1934. Like his colleagues, the director, Erik Charell, né Erich Karl Löwenberg, was a veteran of Germany's super studio, Ufa, and a fugitive from Hitler.

In his first Hollywood leading role, en route to becoming America's favorite French actor, Charles Boyer even got to sing.[232] Cast as Latzi, a Hungarian gypsy, opposite a very young Loretta Young, Boyer is impetuously hired by the young Countess Wilms to marry her by midnight, so she can comply with the terms of her inheritance. She then falls in love with the dashing young Lieutenant von Tokay, who is himself in love with Latzi's gypsy sweetheart, Tinka. A surviving still shows the improbably costumed Boyer gazing into the eyes of a kittenish Young while clutching a violin.[233]

Though its Austrian director Arthur Maria Rabenalt and German composer, Franz Grothe, each made his arrangements with the Third Reich,[234] no one would know it from *The Maharajah's Love*. In the style of the era, the film tippy-toes between the glamour of a brooding maharajah and the era's squeamishness about miscegenation with a European. For a Depression-era audience still decades away from mass tourism, exotic was its own reward, and intermarriage as much a no-no in Hollywood as it was in Babelsberg. It was also easy to deal with. Gustav Diessl, a Central European heartthrob, was hired to play the lovesick Indian in a Savile Row suit, and the writers made sure that the titillation stopped at foreplay. The directors focused on such hardy perennial themes as comical Englishmen, fun in the sun, and the lives of the rich and famous. There are even a few licks of swing.

The scenario is Fred and Ginger without dancing. An itinerant piano quartet shows up at the Italian Riviera hotel where the exiled maharajah is fending off a flamboyant English gold digger while negotiating his return to India. Though he doesn't even like music, he's transfixed by the pianist, a spitting image of his mysteriously lost wife. When the violinist, her love since conservatory days, fires her in a fit of preemptive jealousy, she takes up ambivalently with the maharajah, even allowing herself to be fitted for the costume department's version of a sari. But she soon returns to the violinist, now working joylessly at a nightclub. As the band blasts a Glenn Milleresque welcome, the reunited couple exchange radiant smiles and fall into one another's arms.

Save for one qualification, the story line could be generic. But the violinist, in his only feature film appearance, is the Czech virtuoso Váša Príhoda, who had actually played in cafés in his student days. The script even allows him a bit of dialogue and a few close-ups. But above all, it offers him an opportunity to play Léon de Saint-Lubin's transcription of the sextet from Donizetti's *Lucia*, one of the literature's classic knuckle-busters, while the maharajah makes eyes at the pianist.

The same year, the full-time concert player made his movie debut in Gustav Molander's *Intermezzo*, with Gösta Ekman, the darling of Swedish film and a pillar of the Swedish theater, conspicuously top-billed as the great violinist over a supporting cast that included the young Ingrid Bergman. With the help of Kay Brown, an agent and talent scout as prodigious as himself, the producer David O. Selznick then acquired both Bergman and the rights for a Hollywood makeover.[235] This time, with World War II just over the horizon, the violinist role went to Leslie Howard, the willowy British heartthrob who was almost concurrently at work as the doomed Ashley Wilkes in Selznick's *Gone with the Wind*.

Returning from a picture-perfect concert tour to a picture-perfect home, wife, children, even dog, Howard's character soon finds himself at the apex of a domestic triangle in a cold climate. With his pianist about to retire, he joins Bergman, his pianist's protégé and daughter's piano teacher, in a spontaneous transcription of the Grieg piano concerto as party guests look on. They then segue to the film's theme tune, Heinz Provost's "Intermezzo," a soupy period piece later recorded by Heifetz, but played here by an unacknowledged Seidel. As a concert tour leads to a montage of breaking ice, flowering trees, Sinding's *Rustles of Spring*, and a Mediterranean holiday, Howard's old friend and pianist shows up with divorce papers for him and a Paris scholarship for his protégée.

Can one person's happiness be built on the unhappiness of another? A self-denying Howard draws a deep breath, leaves for Paris, returns home to a reproachful son, and stands guilt-ridden and anxious at his daughter's bedside after she's been struck by a car as she runs to greet him. But punishment has its limits. Backlit by the sun, he is at last welcomed home by his loyal dog and loyal wife as Max Steiner's score jogs along with a generous sampler of Grieg, including *The Last Spring*.

If the Grieg in *Intermezzo* is Hollywood's version of strong emotion and wistful resignation, the rehearsals of Beethoven's Ninth that frame Ingmar Bergman's *Till Glädje* (*To Joy*) are the thirty-one-year-old director's version of irony. Like *Intermezzo*, his film is an album of scenes from a musical marriage. But unlike Howard, Stig, Bergman's angry young man, is a provincial orchestra player whose ambitions exceed his modest talent, while his wife, Marta, is a colleague who first came to his attention when the orchestra's crusty but kindhearted conductor introduced her—"a woman in the orchestra, sort of silly and against nature, but she is reasonably talented"—as a new member of the second violin section.[236]

Untouched by Hollywood's so-called Hays Code, Bergman's film, which was never formally released in the United States, approaches real life in ways that Hollywood didn't and couldn't. As it opens, Stig takes a phone call informing him that Marta has been killed by an exploding kerosene stove, leaving him alone with their twins. In the flashbacks that follow, they meet and mate, despite his rudeness, insecurity, and Napoleonic sense of self. A disastrous debut as soloist ends with the conductor's consolation that the world needs its second-raters too. With money tight, Stig drinks too much, lets a colleague's predatory wife seduce him, bangs his hand in frustration, and punches Marta. He then feels contrite and sees her off for a country holiday with the kids and a kerosene stove. Again in the present, the film ends as one of the children slips into the rehearsal as the conductor delivers a little speech on the Ninth Symphony as an expression of joy beyond understanding.

What Hollywood could manage was melodramas, three of them alone between 1939 and 1954 with a violinist, a superstar actress, and a climactic shootout between art and temptation as common denominator. The earliest, *Golden Boy*, a movie version of Clifford Odets's thumpingly successful Broadway play of 1937, is the story of Joe Bonaparte, who decides that the ring at Madison Square Garden is a more promising launching pad than the recital platform at Town Hall. No less a postwar product than it was a generation earlier, *Humoresque*, a film version of Fannie Hurst's story, followed in 1946. In *Rhapsody*, the last of the trilogy, postwar noir literally gives way to Technicolor, and love finally gets a bit of a break.

As played by the young William Holden, Odets's Joe is touched, but unmoved, by the $1,500 Ruggieri that his loving father, played by Lee J. Cobb, buys him for his twenty-first birthday. Instead, he persuades Tom, a minor league manager played by Adolphe Menjou, to give him a chance as a fighter. Tom, who needs the money so he can divorce his wife and marry Lorna, a self-styled "tramp from Newark," played by Barbara Stanwyck, agrees.

Despite Tom's pleas, Joe avoids the big punch, preferring to win on points, till Eddie Fuseli, a major league mobster, takes over both his career and Tom's. Lorna progressively loses her heart to Joe, while Joe, increasingly fond of silk shirts and supercharged Duesenbergs, risks losing his soul to Fuseli. Finally at the Garden, just a step from the middleweight championship, he knocks out the Chocolate Drop, the pride of Harlem, in the second round. But he also kills him and incidentally breaks his own hand. "You've made me a killer," the horrified Golden Boy tells Fuseli. "I only wish I'd killed a no-good gutter rat like you."

In the stage version, an unseemly squabble between Fuseli, the contending managers, and trainers ends with a phone call reporting that Joe and Lorna have died in a car crash in Babylon, on Long Island. On screen, Joe returns home to a tearful father, the Ruggieri, and a new life, with Lorna by his side. "A great violinist with a broken hand?" Joe asks. "It'll heal," says Lorna.[237]

Taken for given at the time, the sound track includes a full-throated, original-text *Funiculì, Funiculà* to confirm the warm Italian immigrant family values of its Jewish actors. There are hints of the Brahms concerto as Joe tries out the birthday Ruggieri, allusions to the inevitable Méditation from *Thaïs*, and echoes of Beethoven's Seventh at a concert in the park as something big makes its entrance in the relationship of Joe and Lorna.

While distantly recognizable as Hurst's story, Hollywood's *Humoresque* is as remote from the *Saturday Evening Post* as the postwar world of 1946 is from the postwar world of 1921. Though mentioned in the credits, even the author herself finishes a distant third behind Joan Crawford and John Garfield in a scenario retrofitted as "the most vibrant love story ever told." This time the studio is Warner Bros., and the real golden boy is the twenty-six-year-old Isaac Stern, employed to fiddle for a reported $25,000 at a time when Strads sold for less and the average American earned around a tenth as much in a year.

Famed before the Hays Code for its satisfyingly realistic presentation of sex and violence, Warner Bros. was now heavily invested in melodrama. Crawford, too, was in transition after a well-publicized bust-up with MGM. Clifford Odets, author of *Golden Boy*, the play, but conspicuously absent from *Golden Boy*, the movie, was invited to cowrite *Humoresque*. John Garfield, Odets's original choice for Joe Bonaparte on stage, now appeared in *Humoresque* as its charismatic violinist.

Though Hollywood's version, like Hurst's, is located on New York's Lower East Side, little Leon is now a slightly more assimilated Paul, and the Kaplans have become ethnically indeterminate Borays. Even the price of cheap violins, at $8.00, has doubled since Hurst. But Papa is still dismayed and mama delighted that little Paul wants a fiddle for his birthday, while Paul practices "because he wants to," and works his way up through the neighborhood conservatory where Gina, still the girl next door, but now a cellist in the orchestra, continues to have a crush on him.

As in 1917, the hero is still a work in progress. But it's now the Depression. With help from his friend, Sid, played by the pianist-composer Oscar Levant, Paul lucks into a session with the studio orchestra at a local radio station. But he fails to see eye to eye with the conductor. Sid then takes him along to a society party where a very drunk guest demands that Paul prove he's not a boxer. Reaching for his violin, Paul fires off the inevitable *Zigeunerweisen* with such bravura that he gets the attention of Joan Crawford as Helen, the hard-drinking hostess, who favors snappy insults as the best way to get acquainted.

Sobered up and contrite, Helen shows up at the family grocery the next morning to leave him an expensive cigarette case. The cigarette case leads to a mating dance in a cocktail lounge, an elegant tailor, a manager with an office in Rockefeller Center, a tame conductor, and a new apartment. As the couple splashes in the sea and gallops around on horses, even Paul shares his mother's concern. At his orchestra debut, he nonetheless aims Edouard Lalo's *Symphonie Espagnole* at Helen, alone in the balcony, while his clueless father applauds in the front row, and Gina, aware that her childhood loyalty is going nowhere, leaves. Paul then stands up the family party for his patron's. The reviews are sensational.

When her long-suffering spouse gallantly offers a divorce, Helen hurries to pass on the good news to Paul at a rehearsal of Franz Waxman's virtuoso *Carmen Fantasy*. For the first time, she's really in love, she pleads. But this time it's Don José, not Carmen, who backs off.

Back at her beach house on Long Island, Helen picks up the era's emblematic white telephone to tell Paul that she won't make it to the concert but plans to hear it on the radio. As he pours out his soul in an unlikely arrangement of the "Liebestod" from *Tristan* for orchestra and solo violin, she gives herself to the crashing waves.

If *Rhapsody* is full of familiar motifs, its scenario is again a palimpsest. This time the ur-text, still faintly visible beneath the screenplay, is *Maurice Guest*, a very large and ambitious novel, published in London in 1908.[238] The author, Henry Handel Richardson, in real life Ethel Florence Lindesay Richardson, was an expatriate Australian who lived in Germany before settling in England and studied piano at the Leipzig Conservatory.

At least in principle, Louise, her enigmatic heroine, is in Leipzig to study piano too. But, measured by contemporary standards, the novel is at least as much about sex in a remarkable variety of permutations as it is about music. A contemporary of Hedda Gabler with a passion for *Walküre* and *Tristan*, the Australian Louise is crazy about the German Schilsky, a violinist and composer of dazzling talent and Nietzschean disposition. But Schilsky's priority is seducing the American Ephie, while the British Maurice, a modest talent, is crazy about Louise. Within three months of its British publication, the book had been reviewed at least fifty-eight times, and within a year of its American publication another forty-one. Multiple editions and translations would follow. In 1919, James Gibbons Huneker, the era's bellwether music and art critic, declared it nothing less than "the most satisfying musical fiction in the English language." "This novel has been claimed by many for the gallery of the great, and it belongs there," the Nobel Prize winner Doris Lessing proclaimed seventy-three years later. As early as 1935, there was talk of a movie version. There were even rumors that Greta Garbo might play Louise.[239] But it was 1954 before it finally made its way to Hollywood.

By this time, it had come a long way from Leipzig in every sense, with the prodigious Michael Rabin, 18, and the veteran pianist Claudio Arrau as crucial accessories. As Louise, Elizabeth Taylor, glorious at twenty-one, cruises what claims to be an Alpine landscape in a Cadillac convertible. Less than a decade after World War II, with Leipzig firmly behind the Iron Curtain, the action has moved to prosperous, well-fed, and neutral Zurich. There is even a production number for Vittorio Gassmann as the irresistible violinist, again known as Paul. Just back from a summer job at a French casino, he rejoins his classmates at MGM's version of the Olde Worlde tavern. "Is there a fiddle in the house?" he demands. He grabs the first instrument in reach, gazes soulfully at Taylor, and launches into the usual *Zigeunerweisen*, while his classmates grab instruments including a piano, bass, harp, and possibly a cimbalom, and pitch in, too.

But the most interesting makeover is the story itself. Rediscovered as a benchmark of Australian literature and postcolonial criticism a century or so after her creation,[240] Richardson's Louise is a New Woman, a bundle of "love, suffering, sensual abandonment" who lives in "the closed world of an artist of love."[241] Elizabeth Taylor's Louise is a spoiled rich kid used to getting what she wants from her indulgent papa, the debonair Louis Calhern. Intent on adding Paul to her collection, she follows him back from the summer break and matriculates pro forma as a piano student at his conservatory. But Paul's eye is on the annual competition and his career. He finds it distracting to have his ear nibbled while warming up on Paganini. Solo practice is the obvious solution. He dazzles in the usual Tchaikovsky, then leaves for Rome with a less demanding classmate as Louise looks on in disbelief.

Louise first tries to kill herself. She then turns to James Guest, the penniless ex-GI and aspiring pianist from next door, and marries him as revenge on Paul. In short order, she turns him into the elegantly tailored, self-loathing drunk Paul rediscovers in the bar of the Paris Ritz. As Paul prudently heads for the exit, James buys passage to New York on a slow boat from Marseille while Louise returns to her father. Don't kick a man when he's down, he tells her. Take James back to Zurich and see him back to independence. And so she does, sitting by like a Suzuki mother as he practices, till James, too, is ready to dazzle in the usual Rachmaninov Second. Louise and Paul again meet briefly, but the magic is gone. With Betty Friedan's landmark *The Feminine Mystique* still nine years over the horizon, it can be argued whether its lessons speak from the heart of mid-twentieth-century America. But there's no question that they speak from the heart of MGM. Real men make careers. Real women make men.

If the first time was soap opera, the second was farce. It took till 1959 for Ernest Pintoff's seven-minute gem *The Violinist* to reach American screens. But it was worth the wait. A twenty-eight-year-old former jazz trumpeter, Pintoff found a new vocation at the wonderfully innovative United Productions of America. He then established his own company with a fellow secessionist, the twenty-six-year-old Jimmy T. Murakami. In Murakami's inspired animation, Harry the violinist is a little fireplug in a green suit and porkpie hat. Not a genius, just normal, as Carl Reiner's voiceover explains, he neither plays Tchaikovsky nor *Zigeunerweisen*. He just chases birds, talks to people, and plays at bus stops, where Felix, a dog, is his only fan. But Felix also speaks truth to Harry's modest powers. "They're right, Harry," Felix tells him, when even a hardhat in a manhole points out that Harry's playing lacks warmth. Harry turns himself over to Professor Feelinger, a specialist, who explains that an artist has to suffer. Harry not only stops chasing birds and talking to people, he stops shaving and eating. Even the hardhat is impressed. But people now find the scraggly, emaciated Harry so ugly as to be funny. Realizing that only he can make himself happy, Harry returns to chasing birds, eating bear meat in the subway, talking to people, and playing the violin. Pintoff's first independent production, *The Violinist* was nominated for an Academy Award.

As another new century dawned, resourceful directors still found expressive material in printed form. Set in Cornwall, Charles Duke's film *Ladies in Lavender* is based on a slight but graceful story by William J. Locke.[242] Genteely indestructible, unmarried, and aged forty-eight and forty-five, Janet and Ursula live uneventful lives in a cottage inherited from their naval captain father—until an Atlantic storm casts up a young Pole on their beach. The village doctor sets the young man's broken ankle. The sisters take charge of his recuperation. Young and handsome, the stranger even kisses hands. He speaks no English. Janet establishes contact in schoolgirl German.

As the young man recovers, the sisters feel increasingly proprietary, even competitive. Enter music via Janet at the parlor piano. Touched by her good intentions but appalled by her art, the young man pantomimes a violin and reveals himself as a professional musician. With a violin borrowed from the doctor, he produces Paganini's variations on *The Carnival of Venice*. A summer visitor passing by outside the window makes contact and leads him off to London to advance his career without his leaving so much as a farewell note. Villagers crowd around a radio in their Sunday best to hear his broadcast debut. The sisters, who are there in person, are gratefully, if belatedly, acknowledged before they go home. Although they may not have reached love's promised land, at least they've caught a glimpse of it. Joshua Bell, recruited for yet another sound track, fiddles with his usual authority.

If Duke's scenario enhances Locke's wistfully autumnal story, Tognazzi's version of *Canone Inverso*, with its conflations of Nazis in Vienna and Russians in Prague, the predictable nude scene in a Turkish bath, and a bizarre family tableau set in Treblinka, only diminishes Maurensig's dark and ingenious

one. But two very different directors, Joe Wright, a dyslexic native Londoner who made his career filming Jane Austen and Ian McEwan, and Dai
Sijie, a middle-aged Chinese expatriate based in Paris, show how directors who want to can even enhance nonfiction. Wright's spin-off from a
book by Steve Lopez is itself spun off from a series of columns in the *Los
Angeles Times*.[243] Dai, a survivor of Mao's Cultural Revolution, opts for a
semi-autobiographical scenario by himself. But both spot violins in unexpected places, understand why they matter, show an informed respect for
Beethoven unique in the history of film, and examine the world from the
bottom up.

Born of a daily newspaper columnist's perennial search for material,
The Soloist begins in Los Angeles's Pershing Square in the shadow of the
Beethoven statue, where Lopez strikes up a conversation with Nathaniel
Ayres, a derelict violinist, already remarkable for making do with two
strings. The conversation first inspires Lopez's curiosity and interest. It
then inspires concern, friendship, and a sense of mission.

No beginner, Ayres is a onetime bass player who took up the cello at
Juilliard. Clearly schizophrenic, he is also in love with his art. Since he
now lives on the street, where a cello, let alone a bass, is too much for his
superstuffed shopping cart, he has taught himself to play the violin. At
the intersection of homelessness, squalor, and madness, just blocks from
the *Los Angeles Times* office, he introduces Lopez to a whole curriculum—
classical repertory, psychoactive drugs, urban survival skills—not usually
taught in journalism schools.

With help from Jamie Foxx and Robert Downey Jr., highly professional actors with their own complicated histories, Wright turns Lopez's
cacophony of mental breakdown, dysfunctional families, race in America,
civic neglect, heroic volunteers, spontaneous generosity, professional ethics,
even the concurrent implosion of newspaper journalism, into cinematic
polyphony. But real people—Los Angeles's mayor, Antonio Villaraigosa, a
platoon of LA Philharmonic players, their conductor, Esa-Pekka Salonen,
and a contingent of homeless extras, also do their part. The medium itself
allows Wright to submerge a thoughtful Downey and blissful Foxx in a
long shot of an audience caught up in the slow movement of Beethoven's
Ninth, and to superimpose a fragment of the "song of thanks on recovery
from an illness" from Beethoven's op. 132 quartet on an armada of white
pigeons, launched into a bright blue sky. He considered himself very fortunate to have worked on the film, Downey told Lopez.[244]

Starting with his autobiographical novel,[245] Dai locates *Balzac and the*

Little Chinese Seamstress at the confluence of love, music, and contemporary history. Love comes fairly effortlessly in his scenario in which the nameless seamstress plays a kind of village Eliza Doolittle to the two young men from the city who not only make themselves her two-headed Henry Higgins but see her through an illegal abortion. Music, too, comes fairly naturally, at least to Wa, 17, a violinist of commitment and talent at an unlikely place and time.

Born to a dentist and a family of doctors, Luo, 18, and Wa are just in time to find themselves in the path of another great twentieth-century convulsion. Relegated to a mountain village for re-education, they are received by a commissar awed by Wa's ancient wind-up alarm clock, outraged by his bourgeois cookbook, and baffled by his violin. Like the cookbook, the violin seems destined for the fire till Luo intervenes in the nick of time. It's not a toy, it's a musical instrument, he explains. He proposes that Wa demonstrate. Unconvinced, the commissar wants to know what he's just heard. "Mozart," Wa stammers. "Mozart what?" the headman asks suspiciously. "'Mozart Is Thinking of Chairman Mao,'" Luo answers in a flash of inspiration. *Swan Lake*, ostensibly composed as an homage to Lenin, gets the same treatment.

In the end, the Party discovers capitalism and transforms China. The seamstress, transformed from village Eliza Doolittle to peasant Rastignac by the Balzac novels the boys have read her from a secret cache, demonstratively leaves by herself to take on the city. Luo returns to college and makes good as a dentist like his father. Wa, like Dai himself, moves to Paris, where he joins a string quartet.

All kinds of cultural revolutions are implied in this, but none is of the kind Mao had in mind. "Man is born free, but is everywhere in chains," Rousseau declared of the human condition. "There is no instrument from which one obtains a more varied and universal expression," he declared of the violin. One can only wonder what he might have made of Wa playing late Beethoven in Paris, or a nouveau régime in Beijing that allowed Dai to make his film in China but not show it there.[246]

CODA

E VEN AFTER FIVE centuries, violin history can be summarized in a few sentences. The instrument appeared from nowhere in particular. Like none before or after, it proved adaptable to almost anything short of a drum and bugle corps. It fit any budget. A few thousand specimens identified as works of art, were coveted, marketed, copied, and occasionally stolen like works of art. From the sixteenth century on, the best gravitated unfailingly to money and power. For better or worse, nearly anyone could move a bow across the strings. But a few, who played very, very well, were celebrated and rewarded like singers, pianists, and conductors, if not quite like athletes, rock stars, and hedge fund managers.

In its first century, composers and players discovered and royalty began collecting the violin. In its second, composers and players began developing its solo potential. By its third, much of Western music was already built on or around it. In its fourth, repertory, virtuosity, orchestras, audiences, conservatories, and concert halls grew as Europe grew. By its fifth, it was established on at least five continents.

The rest, as Hillel says in a much-cited tractate of the Babylonian Talmud, is commentary. But even in 2003, on the threshold of its sixth century, Byambasuren Davaa's and Luigi Falorni's charming *Story of the Weeping Camel* was a metaphor as irresistible as the myth of Orpheus.

A tribute to the power of the bowed string, the film shows a multigenerational family of Mongolian herders trying in vain to reconcile a mother camel with the white calf she rejected at birth. Finally, they bring in a local musician whose two-string *morin khuur* succeeds where all else has failed. Tears come to the eyes of the audience as well as the mother camel as mother and calf are reunited.

Though tearless, the thoroughly Victorian exchange between William

Ewart Gladstone, Britain's only four-term prime minister, and Edward Seymour, Duke of Somerset, was at once a testimonial to the age and the instrument. A few days before Christmas 1872, Gladstone was invited back to his hometown, Liverpool, to deliver a speech at a Liverpool College convocation. Established in 1840 to "maintain indissolubly the connection between sound religion and useful learning,"[1] the school was a natural platform for a famously high-minded public figure with firm views on virtually everything and a message for the year's prizewinners.

In the rolling periodic sentences contemporary audiences adored, the prime minister pointed with pride, viewed with alarm, endorsed sound religion and useful learning, applauded the astonishing industrial growth of his country and his native city, deplored materialism and skepticism, and cautioned his audience against overestimating themselves while underestimating the past. He then reached the peroration. "To perfect that wonder of travel, the locomotive," Gladstone reminded his audience, "has perhaps not required the expenditure of more mental strength and application, than to perfect that wonder of music, the violin."[2]

Speaking to a local audience in his native Devon a few days later, the Duke of Somerset was unimpressed. "Men have been scraping on these squeaking strings for the last three hundred years, but what good has the world gained by it?" he demanded. Equally unimpressed by the duke, *The Musical World*, a trade paper, needed only a week after the prime minister's speech to point with a mix of concern and innocent merriment to the duke's "veriest twaddle" before an audience of "grinning rustics." *Musical World* knew better, its editor noted. But the duke was representative of "a powerful class," and his ignorance went "a long way to account for the neglect of art shown by our governors."

"The railroad and the locomotive are going, not only through Europe, but they have gone into Japan," the duke continued. "I should like to know what fiddle has ever done the same?"[3] Little more than a century later, as thousands of parents around the Western world bought little violins made in China for children learning to play from a method made in Japan, it was hard to read the duke's remarks without a sense of irony, and the editor's reply without a sense of déjà vu.

Meanwhile, remarkably, an answer to the duke's question arrived, after a four-month lag, from another country halfway around the world. The country had only existed as a self-governing colony for twenty years. The real question, according to the *Waikato Times* of New Zealand's northern island, was: "What wealth was good for"? The writer found it interesting that it was not the duke but the middle-class Gladstone who got the answer right. Nobody wanted a locomotive for its own sake, the editor reminded his readers. "But hundreds of thousands gladly pay . . . for the sake only of the exquisite pleasure which those strings afford."

The popularity of violins and violinists led predictably to reflections on the public interest. In the high summer of Victorian high seriousness, the answer came as no surprise. On the one hand was "The shearer, who knocks down his cheque at the nearest public-house," on the other "The working man who spends the same amount of his earnings in attending the theatre or concert room." The locomotive represented "the means of acquiring wealth with rapidity and ease." The violin represented "the expenditure of that wealth in a manner of which an intelligent, cultured man need not be ashamed."

It was fine for a black man to "work hard to earn a gaudy scarf or a white waistcoat," the editor noted, again in the spirit of the age. But he wanted it understood that it was "not a less good thing that a white man should work equally hard to visit a picture gallery or hear an opera." Less than a century later, after Gandhi, Martin Luther King, and Nelson Mandela, this was hard to read without cringing. The fine arts "do not permit men to sink to the level of beasts,"[4] he added firmly. Less than a century after Auschwitz and the gulag, it was hard to read this, too, without cringing.

Yet even after Auschwitz and the gulag, there were violins just as there was still poetry. If no longer an avatar of virtue, the violin was at least an avatar of aspiration for countless young Asians as it had been for countless young Jews, and the violin remained the instrument of hope and consolation for countless Westerners of all ages, still unmatched and unchallenged by any other.

Half a century after the end of World War II, in three of the most eloquent pages ever dedicated to the violin, Aldo Zargani recalled how his father, a professional player driven to silence by persecution and war, had resumed practicing in April 1945. Word of a real violinist soon got around the Alpine corner that had sheltered the family from the Germans and the paramilitaries of Mussolini's vicious little satellite republic. A few days later, the neighbors—partisans, peasant farmers, and herders—appeared in the barnyard and demanded that "the professor" play them "something beautiful." Zargani's father went in the house, returned with his violin, and, surrounded by listeners sitting or squatting in anticipation of their well-deserved concert, played what he called "the air of Bach," the opening adagio and fugue from the G Minor sonata for violin solo. "He then bowed silently, acknowledging the applause and comments of the unlikely audience that understood perfectly the solitary hymn of triumph and suffering, and went back in the house, streaming with perspiration from the galley slave labor that is playing the violin."[5] In much the same spirit, the great Russian cellist Mstislav Rostropovich played solo Bach at the Berlin Wall after it opened in 1989.

In 1941, Mieczyslaw Weinberg (Moishei Vainberg), a young composer of great promise, lost his family to the Nazis. In 1948, he lost his father-in-law, the great Jewish actor Solomon Mikhoels, to Stalin. In early 1953, he was himself arrested as an alleged accessory to the alleged Jewish Doctors' Plot. He almost certainly owed his survival to Stalin's death a few weeks later.[6] It was 1963 before he was at last allowed to grieve in a powerful Sixth Symphony scored for large orchestra and boys' chorus. Three of its five movements include texts. Two are by Yiddish poets, Leib Kvitko and Samuil Galkin, both of them further victims of Stalin, the third by the Russian poet Mikhail Lukonin. Galkin's verses are about the murder of children, while Kvitko's,[7] composed around their own little concerto, are about a boy, his homemade fiddle, and the birds and animals he plays for. "Sleep, people, rest, violins will sing of peace on earth," says Lukonin's text, as a solo violin takes up the fanfare theme originally introduced by two trumpets.

Jennifer Koh, already under contract to play with Washington's National Symphony in September 2001, agreed without hesitation to proceed with the concert after the attacks on the Pentagon and the World Trade Center. An all-Beethoven program simplified the choice. Bomb scares at or near the Kennedy Center complicated rehearsals but had no deterrent effect on the concert. "It was completely sold out, and after I finished playing people were just weeping," Koh remembered. New Yorkers responded similarly a week later to a performance of Brahms's German Requiem by Kurt Masur and the New York Philharmonic, and again five years later as the psychiatrist Oliver Sacks "saw and joined a silent crowd who sat gazing out to sea and listening to a young man playing Bach's chaconne in D minor on his violin" as he approached Battery Park on his morning bike ride.[8]

In January 2010, after an earthquake devastated Port-au-Prince, Haiti, Romel Joseph, a Juilliard-trained violinist, kept himself alive for eighteen hours beneath the wreckage of the five-story school where his wife already lay dead—by playing a Mozart concerto, the Brahms concerto, and César Franck's great violin sonata in his head.[9] In October 2010, the Boston-born Lynn Chang, a Galamian protégé and Paganini Prize winner, represented Liu Xiaobo, the imprisoned winner of the year's Nobel Peace Prize, at the awards ceremony in Oslo. "An artist plays to educate, to entertain, to illuminate, but here it's a much deeper purpose," he told National Public Radio's Melissa Block. "We're trying to finish in music where words left off."[10]

At a regular Thursday night concert at New York's Avery Fisher Hall, two early modern masterpieces framed an intimation of the century to come. A shocker in 1892, Debussy's *Prelude to the Afternoon of a Faun* was by now as reassuringly familiar as Rossini's Overture to *William Tell*. Sibelius's violin concerto, considered more effort than it was worth as late as 1930, had long become standard repertory. The novelty *Kraft*, by the Finnish composer Magnus Lindberg, was scored for an ensemble including gongs, drums, helium tanks, plastic tubes, bowls of water, and assorted auto parts that merged at least once in a chord of seventy-two notes. "The ovation was long and enthusiastic," Anthony Tommasini reported in the the *New York Times*. Of 897 words, thirty-three went to Debussy, eighty-seven went to Sibelius, ten to Joshua Bell's "lustrous tone, temperament and command."[11]

A few months later, Hahn-Bin, 22, Korean and a protégé of Itzhak Perlman, appeared for a recital at New York's Morgan Library. But this time the review appeared in the Fashion & Style section of the paper. Dressed in a black sleeveless kimono with heavy eye makeup and a Mohawk, he stood out, as he clearly intended to, in a crowd whose expectations of concert dress had not advanced appreciably since the Congress of Berlin. There would be three costume changes before the evening was over. "The classical-music world needs to be shaken up a little bit," said his manager, Vickie Margulies, of Young Concert Artists, Inc. "It's not like he is following a trend right now," Perlman added. "He is setting the trend."[12]

Christoph Poppen, a very good violinist, teacher, and conductor, was equally at home with the music of the baroque and the music of his late twentieth-century contemporaries. Like most of his colleagues, he looked to Asia as the future. But he didn't see this as the end of the Western market. The Western tradition had its roots in dance and the church, he reflected. It was true that neither was what it used to be. He still saw a place for the bank director who came to be moved and entertained, and occasionally was even known to cry. The violinist-artisan had once been the peer of the butcher, baker, and candlestick maker. The violinist-artist was now a combination of social worker, doctor, and priest who might not make people better but could at least make them feel better.[13]

Would this still be true in another ten or another hundred years? Who could say? But it was hardly the first time the question had been asked. Born in 1896, raised in a Vienna nearly crazed with music, Rudolf Kolisch was heir to the First Viennese School and present at the creation of the Second. A confidant of Bartók and Schoenberg, he had played the premieres of countless twentieth-century classics. By the time he died, at eighty-two, he had seen many things come and go, from whole countries to the diatonic scale. One day late in life, en route to lunch off Harvard Square, he was asked where he thought music was going. "I don't know," he replied as traffic swirled around him. There was a thoughtful pause. "But if you'd asked me that in Schumann's time, I couldn't have answered either," he said.

NOTES

ACKNOWLEDGMENTS

1. Tully Potter, "Paganini's Spirited Pupil," *The Strad*, December 1993.

2. David Schoenbaum, "Rudolf Kolisch at 82: A link to Old Vienna," *High Fidelity/Musical America*, August 1978.

3. David Schoenbaum, "The Glory of the Violin," *New York Times Book Review*, January 28, 1973.

INTRODUCTION: THE GLOBAL INSTRUMENT

1. Oxford English Dictionary, Second Edition 1989, OED Online.

2. Ben S. Bernanke, "Global Economic Integration: What's New and What's Not," Jackson Hole, Wyoming, August 25, 2006, http://www.federalreserve.gov/boarddocs/speeches/2006/20060825/default.htm, accessed August 27, 2006

3. Quoted in David Boyden, *The History of Violin Playing from Its Origins to 1761*, London 1974, p. 494.

4. Peter Cooke, "The Violin—Instrument of Four Continents," in Robin Stowell, ed., *The Cambridge Companion to the Violin*, Cambridge 1992, pp. 239–40.

5. "The Violin, Extra-European and Folk Usage," in Laura Macy, ed., *Grove Music Online*, www.grovemusic.com.

6. Johannes Wilbert, *Mystic Endowment*, Cambridge, Massachusetts 1993, pp. 247ff.

7. Quoted by Karl Moens, "Vuillaume et les premiers Luthiers," in *Violons, Vuillaume: Un maître luthier français du XIXe siècle, 1798–1875,* exhibition catalogue, Cité de la Musique/Musée de la musique, Paris, October 23, 1998–January 31, 1999, pp. 130–38, 160–62.

8. "Some Famous Old Violins," *New York Times*, March 15, 1880.

9. Sir James Beament, *The Violin Explained*, Oxford 1997, pp. v, 238–39.

10. Edward Dent, Historical Introduction, in William Henry Hill, Arthur F. Hill, and Alfred Ebsworth Hill, *The Violin-Makers of the Guarneri Family*, New York 1989, p. xxvii.

11. Anne Midgette, "A Swing and a Hit for Violinist," *Washington Post*, July 4, 2009, http://www.youtube.com/watch?v=n9LXHrzOVYA, accessed August 13, 2009.

12. Dan Ephron, "The Stradivari of Ramadi," *Newsweek*, July 16, 2007; John Gerome, "He's Not Fiddling Around," *Washington Post*, August 31, 2007.

13. Clair Cline, "The Prison Camp Violin," *Guidepost*, January 1997.

14. Thomas Marrocco, *Memoirs of a Strad*, New York, Los Angeles, Chicago 1988, pp. 138ff.

15. www.hweisshaar.com/2007_FallNewsletter.pdf, accessed March 8, 2008; http://www .cozio.com/Instrument.aspx?id=1039, accessed March 8, 2008; http://news.bbc.co.uk/go/pr/ fr/-/1/hi/magazine/7244441.stm, accessed March 8, 2008; "Virtuoso's Trip Destroys Priceless Stradivari," *Independent*, February 13, 2008.

16. Beament, *The Violin Explained*, p. 61.

17. Judith Thurman, "Wilder Women," *The New Yorker*, August 10, 2009.

18. "Violin, Sing the Blues for Me," CD, Old Hat Enterprises, Raleigh, North Carolina 1999. Cf. Paul A. Cimbala, "Black Musicians from Slavery to Freedom," *Journal of Negro History*, 1995, pp. 15–29.

19. William Shakespeare, *Much Ado about Nothing*, Act 2, Scene 3.

20. *The Beggar's Opera*, Act II, Scene 3, in John Gay, *The Beggar's Opera and Other Works*, Halle (Saale) 1959, p. 120.

21. Peter Holman, *Four and Twenty Fiddlers*, Oxford 1993, Ch. 4.

22. Lawrence Libin et al., "Instruments, Collections of," in *Grove Music Online*, accessed September 10, 2004, http://www.grovemusic.com.

23. Nicholas Kenyon, "The Baroque Violin," in Dominic Gill, *The Book of the Violin*, Oxford 1984, p. 60.

24. Helen Cripe, *Thomas Jefferson and Music*, Charlottesville, Virginia 1974, pp. 12–13, 43–47, Appendix III.

25. Brian W. Harvey, *The Violin Family and Its Makers in the British Isles*, Oxford 1995, p. 122.

26. "Fleet-Fingered Crowe," *The Strad*, January 2004.

27. Richard McGrady, *Music and Musicians in Early Nineteenth Century Cornwell*, Exeter 1991.

28. Gordon Swift, "Exploring Carnatic Violin," *Strings*, February 2005; Ken Hunt, "The Perfect Ingredient," *The Strad*, August 2006.

29. V. N. Jog, interview with the author, Iowa City, Iowa, March 28, 1998.

30. "Contests: Cookie and Pinky Come Through," *Time*, May 26, 1967.

31. Max Weber, *Die rationalen und soziologischen Grundlagen der Musik*, Tübingen 1972; *The Rational and Social Foundations of Music*, Carbondale, Illinois, 1958.

32. *The Strad Directory 2001*, Harrow, Middlesex, 2000.

33. David Templeton, "Soul Song," *Strings*, October 2008, http://www.arvelbird.com/, accessed September 30, 2009.

34. See www.buskaid.org/za/Sponsors.htm.

35. Theodore Levin, *The Hundred Thousand Fools of God*, Bloomington and Indianapolis, Indiana 1996, p. 184.

36. Yoshimasa Kurabayashi and Yoshiru Matsuda, *Economic and Social Aspects of the Performing Arts in Japan*, Tokyo 1988, p. 4.

37. "Global Strings," *The Economist*, August 16, 1997.

38. Interview with the author, *Commonwealth Secretariat*, London, July 7, 1997.

39. Sheila Melvin and Jingdong Cai, "The Shanghai Symphony: An Orchestra with a Political Accompaniment," *New York Times*, March 5, 2000.

BOOK 1: MAKING IT

1. Boyden, *The History*, p. vii.

2. Lloyd Moss, *Zin! Zin! Zin! A Violin*, New York 1995.

3. See http://www.vor.ru/culture/cultarch293_eng.html, accessed November 19, 2004; http://www.mmoma.ru/en/exhibitions/gogolevsky/iskusstvo_russkih_masterov/, accessed November 17, 2011.

4. See http://www.musolife.com/musical-instruments-collection-at-the-victoria-and-albert-museum-set-to-close.html, accessed January 21, 2010.

5. See http://www.vam.ac.uk/collections/furniture/musical_instruments/history/carl_engel/index.html, accessed January 21, 2010; Catalogue of the Special Exhibition at South Kensington, p. 13, in George Dissmore, *Violin Gallery*, Des Moines, Iowa 1890.

6. Carl Engel, *Researches into the Early History of the Violin Family*, London 1883.

7. Interview with the author, London, June 17, 1999.

8. Carl Peters, *Lebenserinnerungen*, Munich and Berlin 1943, p. 58.

9. L'abbé Odon Jean Marie Delarc, *L'Eglise de Paris pendant la Révolution*, Paris 1895–97, Tome I, pp. 428–29, 443, Tome II, p. 370; Sébastien-André Sibire, *L'Aristocratie négrière, ou Réflexions philosophiques et historiques sur l'esclavage et l'affranchissement des Noirs*, Paris 1789; *Discours civique et chrétien au sujet de la paix générale de l'Europe*, Paris 1802; *Le Portrait de Buonaparte, suivie d'un discours sur le nature et les effets des conquêtes*, Paris 1814.

10. Sébastien-André Sibire, *Le Chélomonie ou le parfait Luthier*, Paris 1806.

11. François-Joseph Fétis, *Notice biographique sur Nicolò Paganini*, Paris 1851; Antoine Stradivari, *Luthier célèbre*, Paris 1856.

12. George Hart, *The Violin: Its Famous Makers and Their Imitators*, London 1885, p. 341.

13. Federico Sacchi, *Il Conte Cozio di Salabue*, London 1898, pp. 18ff.

14. Quoted by Stewart Pollens and Henryk Kaston, *François-Xavier Tourte, Bow Maker*, New York 2001, p. 21.

15. Dominic Gill, *The Book of the Violin*, Oxford 1984, pp. 14–15.

16. See http://atdpweb.soe.berkeley.edu/2030/jmoriuchi/violin-pictures.html.

17. See http://library.thinkquest.org/27110/instruments/violin.html, accessed June 29, 2012.

18. Moens, "Vuillaume et les premiers luthiers," in *Violons, Vuillaume*.

19. Henry Saint-George, *The Bow, Its History, Manufacture and Use*, New York and London 1922, p. 32.

20. Viz. Beament, *The Violin Explained*, p. 58.

21. Brian W. Harvey, *The Violin Family and Its Makers in the British Isles*, Oxford 1995; Brian Harvey and Carla J. Shapreau, *Violin Fraud*, Oxford 1997.

22. Duane Rosengard, *Giovanni Battista Guadagnini*, Haddonfield, New Jersey 2000.

23. Carlo Bonetti et al., *Antonio Stradivari, Notizie e Documenti*, Cremona 1937.

24. Bernhard Zoebisch, *Vogtländischer Geigenbau*, Markneukirchen 2000.

25. W. Henry Hill, Alfred F. Hill, and Arthur E. Hill, *Antonio Stradivari*, Mineola, New York 1963, and *The Violin-Makers of the Guarneri Family*, Mineola, New York 1989.

26. Margaret L. Huggins, *Gio. Paolo Maggini: His Life and Work*, compiled and edited from material collected and contributed by William Ebsworth Hill and his sons William, Arthur, and Alfred Hill, London 1892, republished 1976.

27. Roger Hargrave, "The Failure of Brotherly Love?," *The Strad*, May 1995, p. 475.

28. Flavio Dasseno, "Per una identificazione della scuola bresciana," in Flavio Dassenno and Ugo Ravasio, *Gasparo da Salò e la Liuteria Bresciana tra Rinascimento e Barocco*, Brescia 1990, p. 11.

29. Sylvette Milliot, "La famille Chanot-Chardon," Tome 1, *Les Luthiers Parisiens aux XIXe et XXe Siècles*, Spa, Belgium, 1994.

30. Interview with the author, Richmond, England, June 17, 1999.

31. Interview with the author, London, June 18, 1999; e-mail July 10, 2002.

32. Smithsonian Institution Research Reports, No. 92, Spring 1998; Mark Levine, "Medici of the Meadowlands," *New York Times Magazine*, August 3, 2003.

33. W. Henry Hill et al., *Antonio Stradivari*, p. 226.

34. Stewart Pollens, "Ornamental Ornithology," *The Strad*, October 2007.

35. Harry Haskell, *The Early Music Revival*, New York and London 1988, passim; James Gollin, *Pied Piper: The Many Lives of Noah Greenberg*, Hillsdale, New York 2001, passim.

36. Joanna Pieters, "History Man," *The Strad*, February 2002.

37. Samuel Zygmuntowicz, "A Copyist's Credo," *The Strad*, April 1995, interview with the author, Bremen, December 9, 1997. Cf. John Marchese, *The Violin Maker*, New York 2007, pp. 77–80.

38. Christopher Hogwood, The Academy of Ancient Music, Haydn, "The Creation," L'Oiseau-Lyre digital 430 397-2, 1990.

39. John Dilworth, "Origins of the Species," *The Strad*, January 2001.

40. Annette Otterstedt, e-mail to the author, July 1, 2002.

41. Boyden, *The History*, p. 8.

42. Olga Adelmann and Anita Otterstedt, *Die Alemannische Schule*, Berlin 1997, p. 36.

43. Viz. Klaus Osse, "Die Wurzeln des professionellen Streichinstrumentenbaus im mittleren Europa," in *Zum Streichinstrumentenbau des 18. Jahrhunderts: Bericht über das 11. Symposium zu Fragen des Musikinstrumentenbaus*, Michaelstein 1990. Cf. A. L. Kroeber, *Anthropology*, New York 1948, pp. 445–51.

44. Thomas Drescher, "Der Nürnberger Geigenbau als Exempel," in Klaus Martius, *Leopold Widhalm und der Nürnberger Lauten- und Geigenbau im 18. Jahrhundert*, Frankfurt 1996, pp. 12ff. Cf. Richard Goldthwaite, *The Building of Renaissance Florence*, Baltimore, Maryland, and London 1980, pp. 106, 401–2.

45. Sandro Pasqual and Roberto Regazzi, *Le Radici del Successo della Liuteria a Bologna*, Bologna 1998, p. 41.

46. Osse, "Die Wurzeln," in *Zum Streichinstrumentenbau*, p. 17.

47. Martius, *Leopold Widhalm*, p. 14. Cf. Thomas Riedmiller, "Lehrzeit-Wanderjahre-Meister-werkstattt," in *Alte Geigen und Bogen*, Cologne 1997, pp. 57–59.

48. Theodore Levin, *The Hundred Thousand Fools of God*, Bloomington and Indianapolis, Indiana 1996, passim. Cf. James Keough, "Kamancheh Meister," *Strings*, April 2004.

49. Annette Otterstedt, *Die Gambe*, Kassel 1994, p. 17.

50. Karl Moens, "Geiger in der Münchner Hofkapelle zur Zeit Lassos," in Ignace Bossuyt et al., eds., *Orlandus Lassus and his Time*, Yearbook of the Alamire Foundation, Leuwen 1995.

51. Holman, *Four and Twenty Fiddlers*, pp. 14–15.

52. Moens, "Violes ou Violins?" in *Musique-Images-Instruments II*, 1996.

53. Moens, "Geiger in der Münchner Hofkapelle," in *Musique-Images-Instruments II*, 1996.

54. Moens, "Die Frühgeschichte der Violine im Lichte neuer Forschungen," in *Lauten, Harfen, Violinen*, exhibition catalog, Herne 1984; "De Viool in de 16de eeuw," Deel II, in *Musica Antiqua* XI/1, 1994.

55. Andrew Dipper, "By Royal Appointment," *The Strad*, June 2005.

56. Andrew Dipper, "Historical Background to the Instruments of the Amati Family at the French Court, 1500–1600," in *E furono Liutai in Cremona dal Rinascimento al Romanticismo*," Cremona 2000.

57. Moens, "Les Instruments Attribués à Andrea Amati," *Musique-Images-Instruments*, unpublished.

58. Dipper, "Historical Background," p. 31; Carlo Chiesa, "Un introduzione alla vita e all'opera di Andrea Amati" in Fausto Cacciatori, ed., *Andrea Amati*, Cremona 2007, p. 17; Renzo Meucci, "Gli strumenti di Andrea Amati," in *Andrea Amati*, p. 33.

59. Roger Hargrave, "Artistic Alliance," *The Strad*, August 2000, p. 835.

60. Moens, "Les Instruments attribués à Andrea Amati," "De viool in de 16de eeuw, Deel I: de vroegste bronnen," f. 3.

61. Boyden, *The History*, op. cit., pp. 20, 22, 91; Osse, "Die Wurzeln"; Moens, "Geiger in der Münchner Hofkapelle," "De viool in de 16de eeuw, Deel II, Der frühe Geigenbau in Süddeutschland," p. 360.

62. Quoted by Boyden, *The History*, op. cit., pp. 31ff.

63. Jean-Frédéric Schmitt, "Venise, Lutherie et Histoire," in *Les Violins, Lutherie Vénitienne, Peintures et Dessins*, Paris 1995, p. 20.

64. Cf. Henry Raynor, *A Social History of Music*, New York 1978, pp. 75ff.

65. Holman, *Four and Twenty Fiddlers*, p. 13.

66. Ibid.

67. Lewis Lockwood, *Music in Renaissance Ferrara, 1400–1505*, Cambridge 1984, pp. 121–51.

68. Holman, *Four and Twenty Fiddlers*, p. 19.

69. Moens, "Geiger in der Münchner Hofkapelle."

70. Boyden, *The History*, op. cit., pp. 59ff.

71. Annette Otterstedt, "What Old Fiddles Can Teach Us," *Galpin Society Journal*, April 1999, pp. 226–27.

72. Moens, "Violes ou Violons?"

73. Moens, "Geiger in der Münchner Hofkapelle."

74. Moens, "Der frühe Geigenbau in Süddeutschland," p. 378.

75. Pasqual and Regazzi, *La Radici*, pp. 44ff.; Gerhard Stradner, "Beziehungen zwischen dem norditalienischen und dem süddeutsch-österreichischen Geigenbau" in *Zum Streichinstrumentenbau des 18. Jahrhunderts*, pp. 22ff.

76. Elia Santoro, *Violini e Violinari: Gli Amati e i Guarneri a Cremona tra Rinascimento e Barocco*, Cremona 1989, pp. 7, 12–13.

77. Pasqual and Regazzi, *La Radici*, pp. 70–71.

78. Felix Gilbert, "Macchiavelli" in Peter Paret, ed., *Makers of Modern Strategy*, Princeton 1986; Geoffrey Parker, *The Military Revolution*, Cambridge 1988; Garrett Mattingly, *Renaissance Diplomacy*, Boston 1955.

79. Luigi Barzini, *The Italians*, New York 1977, pp. 14–41.

80. Ibid., pp. 210ff.

81. Niccolò Machiavelli, *Il Principe*, Milan 1991, Chs. 12–13.

82. Michael Howard, *War in European History*, London, Oxford, and New York 1976; Richard Goldthwaite, *Wealth and the Demand for Art in Italy, 1300–1600*, op. cit., pp. 29ff.

83. W. Henry Hill et al., *Antonio Stradivari*, pp. 160–61; Ravasio, "La Liuteria Bresciana tra Rinascimento e Barocco," in Dassenno and Ravasio, op. cit., p. 25.

84. Carlo M. Cipolla, *Money, Prices and Civilization in the Mediterranean World*, New York 1967, p. 55.

85. Ravasio, "La Liuteria Bresciana," p. 24. Cf. Martha Feldman, *City Culture and the Madrigal at Venice*, Berkeley, California 1995, pp. xixff., 3ff.

86. Dassenno, "Per una identificazione," p. 12.

87. "Brescia," *Encyclopædia Britannica*, http://80-www.search.eb.com.proxy.lib.uiowa.edu/eb/article?eu=16601.

88. Huggins, *Paolo Maggini*, p. 11.

89. Dassenno, "Per una identificazione," p. 12.

90. Richard Goldthwaite, *The Building*, p. 33; Pasqual and Regazzi, op. cit., p. 22.

91. Huggins, *Paolo Maggini*, pp. 15ff. Marco Bizzarini and Giocamo Fornari, "Liuteria e Composizione Musicale," in Dassenno and Ravasio, *Gasparo da Salò*, pp. 81–82.

92. Ravasio, "La Liuteria Bresciana," in Dassenno and Ravasio, *Gasparo da Salò*, pp. 19–20.

93. Huggins, op. cit., pp. 52ff.

94. Luigi Faccini, *La Lombardia fra '600 e '700*, Milan 1988, p. 21.

95. Charles Beare, "Guarneri del Gesù's Place in Cremonese Violin Making," in Charles Beare, Bruce Carlson, and Andrea Mosconi, *Joseph Guarnerius de Gesú*, Cremona 1995, p. 19; W. Henry Hill et al., *Antonio Stradivari*, pp. 241–43, quoted by Dassenno, "Per una identificazione," in Dassenno and Ravasio, *Gasparo da Salò*, p. 16; Charles Beare, "Guarneri del Gesù's Place in Cremonese Violin Making," in Beare et al., *Joseph Guarnerius*, p. 19.

96. Emanuel Jaeger, "Lutherie et tradition musicale à Venise au xviiie siècle," in *Les Violins, Lutherie Vénitienne, Peintures et Dessins*, pp. 8–9.

97. Carlo Chiesa and Duane Rosengard, "Guarneri del Gesù, A Biographical History," in Peter Biddulph et al., *Giuseppe Guarneri del Gesù*, London 1998, vol. 2, pp. 15–16; Dennis Stevens, "Music of the Amati Age," *The Strad*, April 1995, p. 471. Cf. "Cremona," *Enciclopedia Italiana XI*, Milan and Rome 1931–39, p. 829; "Cremona," *Dizionario Enciclopedico Italiano III*, Roma 1956, p. 625.

98. Domenico Sella, *Italy in the Seventeenth Century*, Harlow, Essex 1997, pp. 60ff.

99. Antonio Leone, "La Città della Musica," in *Cremona, Liuteria e Musica in una Città d'Arte*, Cremona 1994, p. 37; Santoro, *Violinari e Violini*, op. cit., pp. 36–41; Santoro, "Collezione civica del Commune di Cremona," in Leone, op. cit.

100. Simone F. Sacconi, *'I Segreti' di Stradivari*, Cremona 1972, p. 186.

101. Santoro, "Collezione civica del Commune di Cremona," in Leone, op. cit.

102. Carlo Bonetti, *Gli Ebrei a Cremona*, Cremona 1917, pp. 5–15.

103. Carlo Bonetti, *La Genealogia degli Amati Liutai e il Primato della Scuola Liutistica Cremonese*, Cremona 1938, pp. 15–16.

104. Ibid., p. 36.

105. Roger Hargrave, unpublished manuscript.

106. Chiesa in Cacciatori, *Andrea Amati*, pp. 22–24.

107. Stevens, "Music."

108. Carlo Cipolla, *The Economic Decline of Empires*, London 1970, pp. 204–5. Cf. Domenico Sella, *Italy in the Seventeenth Century*, pp. 36ff.

109. Sella, *Seventeenth Century Italy*, pp. 2–3.

110. Stevens, "Music." Howard Mayer Brown and Naomi Joy Barker, "Agostino Licino," in *Grove Music Online*, accessed December 7, 2002, http://80-www.grovemusic.com.proxy.lib.uiowa.edu; Santoro, *Violinari e Violini*, p. 93; Bonetti et al., *Antonio Stradivari*, p. 36.

111. Quoted by Thomas Drescher, "Nürnberger Geigenbau als Exempel," in Martius, *Leopold Widhalm*, p. 13.

112. William Henry Hill, Arthur F. Hill, and Alfred Ebsworth Hill, *The Violin-Makers of the Guarneri Family, 1626–1762*, New York 1998, p. 6; Santoro, *Violinari e Violini*, pp. 17ff., 59ff.

113. For a schematic map, see Bonetti et al., *Antonio Stradivari*, p. 33.

114. Roger Graham Hargrave, "The Working Methods of Guarneri del Gesú," in Biddulph et al., *Giuseppe Guarneri del Gesú*, vol. 2, p. 137.

115. William Henry Hill, et al., *The Violin-Makers of the Guarneri Family*, pp. 9ff.; Santoro, *Violinari e Violini*, pp. 116ff.

116. Carlo Chiesa and Philip J. Kass, "Survival of the Fittest," *The Strad*, December 1996; Philip

J. Kass, "The Stati d'Anime of S. Faustino in Cremona: Tracing the Amati Family, 1641–86," Violin Society of America 1999.

117. W. Henry Hill et al., *Antonio Stradivari*, pp. 25–31. Cf. Bonetti et al., *Antonio Stradivari*, pp. 31–32.

118. Bonetti et al., *Antonio Stradivari*, p. 25.

119. W. Henry Hill et al., *Antonio Stradivari*, p. 286.

120. Renzo Bacchetta, *Stradivari non è nato nel 1644*, Cremona 1937, pp. 32–34.

121. W. Henry Hill et al., *Antonio Stradivari*, p. 8.

122. Charles Beare and Bruce Carlson, *Antonio Stradivari, The Cremona Exhibition of 1987*, London 1993, p. 26.

123. William Henry Hill et al., *The Violin-Makers of the Guarneri Family*, p. 26; Carlo Chiesa and Duane Rosengard, "Guarneri del Gesù: A Biographical History," in Biddulph et al., *Giuseppe Guarneri*, vol. 2, pp. 12–13.

124. Kass, "The Stati d'Anime," entry for 1659.

125. Bonetti et al., *Antonio Stradivari*, pp. 51–54

126. W. Henry Hill et al., *Antonio Stradivari*, pp. 10–11; Chiesa and Rosengard, "Giuseppe Guarneri," p. 11.

127. W. Henry Hill et al., *Antonio Stradivari*, pp. 15–21; Bonetti et al., *Antonio Stradivari*, pp. 57–64.

128. Carlo Chiesa and Duane Rosengard, *The Stradivari Legacy*, London 1998.

129. W. Henry Hill et al., *Antonio Stradivari*, pp. 221–26.

130. Aldo De Maddalena, *Dalla Città al Borgo*, Milan 1982, pp. 216ff.; Domenico Sella, *Crisis and Continuity*, Cambridge and London 1979, pp. 176ff.; Faccini, *La Lombardia,* pp. 65, 262ff.

131. Sacconi, *I 'Segreti.'*

132. Berend C. Stoel and Terry M. Borman, "A Comparison of Wood Densities between Classical Cremonese and Modern Violins," *PLoS ONE*, July 2008.

133. Lloyd Burckle and Henri D. Grissino-Mayer, "Stradivari, Violins, Tree Rings, and the Maunder Minimum," *Dendrochronologia* 21/1, 2003, pp. 41–45.

134. Michael D. Lemonick, "Stradivari's Secret," *Discover*, July 2000.

135. Joseph Alper, "The Stradivari Formula," *Science* 84, March 1984; Wm C. Honeyman, *The Violin: How to Choose One*, Dundee, Scotland 1893; Henri D. Grissino-Mayer et al., "Mastering the Rings," *The Strad*, April 2002; Thierry Maniguet, "Savart et Vuillaume," in *Violons, Vuillaume*, pp. 60–65.

136. Beament, *The Violin Explained*, passim; J. Meyer, "Zum Klangphänomen der altitalienischen Geigen," *Acustica* 1989; Martin Schleske, "Wired for Sound," *The Strad*, October 2002; Martin Schleske, "High Fidelity," *The Strad*, November 2002; Jeremy S. Loen and A. Thomas King, "Thick and Thin," *The Strad*, December 2002; Kevin Coates, *Geometry, Proportion and the Art of Lutherie*, Oxford 1985, pp. 167ff.

137. Martin Schleske, "On the Acoustical Properties of Violin Varnish," *CAS Journal*, November 1998.

138. Roger Millant, *J.B. Vuillaume, sa Vie et son Oeuvre*, London 1972, pp. 20, 88–89; W. Henry Hill et al., *Antonio Stradivari*, Chs. 7 and 12.

139. Harvey, *The Violin Family*, pp. 37ff.

140. Joseph Curtin, "Stradivari's Varnish: a Memoir," *Brick Magazine*, Winter 2004. Cf. Roger Graham Hargrave, "The Working Methods of Guarneri del Gesù," in Biddulph et al., *Giuseppe Guarneri*, vol. 2, p. 155.

141. Henry Fountain, "What Exalts Stradivarius? Not Varnish, Study Says," *New York Times*, December 4, 2009; Nathaniel Herzberg, "Un des secrets de Stradivarius dévoilé," *Le Monde*, December 5, 2009; Jean-Philippe Echard et al., "The Nature of the Extraordinary Finish of Stradivari's Instruments," *Angewandte Chemie*, international edition, 2009, No. 48, pp. 1–6.

142. Sacconi, *I 'Segreti,'* p. 1.

143. Bruno Caizzi, *Industria, Commercia e Banca in Lombadia nel XVIII Secolo,* Milan 1968, pp. 7ff.; Cipolla, "The Economic Decline of Italy," pp. 202ff.

144. Bonetti et al., *Antonio Stradivari,* pp. 60–63, Chiesa and Rosengard, *The Stradivari Legacy,* p. 19.

145. Chiesa and Rosengard, *The Stradivari Legacy,* p. 79.

146. William Henry Hill et al., *The Violin-Makers of the Guarneri Family,* pp. 32–43.

147. Viz. Eleanor Selfridge-Field, *Venetian Instrumental Music,* New York 1994, passim. Cf. Jaeger, "Lutherie et tradition musicale," pp. 8–14.

148. William Henry Hill et al., *The Violin-Makers of the Guarneri Family,* p. 147.

149. Roger Graham Hargrave, "The Working Methods," in Biddulph et al., *Giuseppe Guarneri,* vol. 2, p. 142.

150. Chiesa and Rosengard, "Guarneri del Gesú," in Biddulph et al., *Giuseppe Guarneri,* pp. 20–21. Cf. Hargrave, "The Working Methods," pp. 151–52.

151. Chiesa and Rosengard, "Guarneri del Gesú," in Biddulph et al., *Giuseppe Guarneri,* p. 17.

152. William Henry Hill et al., *The Violin-Makers of the Guarneri Family,* p. 99; interview with the author, Chicago, Illinois, April 3, 1998.

153. Brian Yule, "Del Gesù at the Met," *The Strad,* April 1995; Roger Hargrave, interview with the author, December 9, 1997.

154. Chiesa and Rosengard, "Guarneri del Gesù—A Brief History," in *Joseph Guarnerius del Gesù,* Cremona 1995, p. 37.

155. William Henry Hill et al., *The Violin-Makers of the Guarneri Family,* pp. 89–92.

156. Chiesa and Rosengard, "Guarneri del Gesú: A Biographical History," pp. 8–20.

157. Dmitri Gindin with Duane Rosengard, *The Late Cremonese Violin Makers,* Cremona 2002.

158. Quoted by Stevens, "Music," p. 470.

159. Elia Santoro, *Traffici e Falsificzioni, dei Violini di Antonio Stradivari,* Cremona 1973, p. 76.

160. Viz. Paolo Lombardini, *Cenni sulla celebre Scuola Cremonese degli Strumenti ad Arco non che sui Lavori e sulla Famiglia del Sommo Antonio Stradivari,* Cremona 1872, p. 27; Bonetti et al., *Antonio Stradivari,* pp. 83–85. Cf. Victoria Finlay, *Color,* New York 2002, p. 197.

161. Bacchetta, *Stradivari non è nato,* p. 116.

162. Finlay, *Color,* p. 172.

163. The photo can be found in William Henry Hill et al., *The Violin-Makers of the Guarneri Family,* p. 126.

164. Kass, "The Stati d'Anime of S. Faustino in Cremona"; "The Parish of S. Faustino," op. cit.

165. Elia Santoro, ed., *Le Celebrazioni Stradivariane a Cremona 1937–49,* Cremona 1996, pp. 29ff.

166. Elia Santoro, ed., *Stradivariane a Cremona 1937–49,* Cremona 1996, pp. 27–29; cf. Alfredo Puerari, introduction, in Sacconi, *I 'Segreti,'* p. xiv. Herbert K. Goodkind, *Violin Iconography of Antonio Stradivari,* Larchmont, New York 1972, pp. 723ff.; Ariana Todes, "City of Hope," *The Strad,* Cremona supplement 2008, p. 7.

167. Stefano Pio, "Giorgio Serafin and his Bottega 'alla Cremona,'" quoted from *Liuteri & Sonadori: Venezia 1750–1880,* Venice 2002, www.maestronet.com/m_library/maestro_mag/Giorgio %20Serafin.cfm.

168. "Venise ou la filiation" in *Les Violins,* pp. 23ff.

169. Pio, "Giorgio Serafin."

170. Santoro, *Traffici e Falsificazione,* pp. 23ff.

171. Alberto Conforti, *Il Violino,* Milan 1987, p. 66.

172. Vannes, *Dictionnaire Universel des Luthiers,* 2 vols., Brussels 1951–59.

173. Walter Kolneder, *Das Buch der Violine,* Zurich 1972, pp. 146ff.

174. Rosengard, *Giovanni Battista Guadagnini*, passim.

175. Ibid., p. 62. Cf. Mariangela Dona, "Milan," in *Grove Music Online*, accessed February 10, 2003, http://80-www.grovemusic.com.proxy.lib.uiowa.edu.

176. Charles Beare et al., "Guadagnini," in *Grove Music Online*, accessed February 7, 2003, http://80-www.grovemusic.com.proxy.lib.uiowa.edu.

177. Rosengard, *Giovanni Battista Guadagnini*, pp. 93ff.

178. Philip J. Kass, "Italy's Import," *The Strad*, May 1998, pp. 482–84.

179. Rosengard, *Giovanni Battista Guadagnini*, p. 128.

180. Arnold Gingrich, *A Thousand Mornings of Music*, New York 1970, p. 173n.

181. Philip J. Kass, "Guadagnini Re-evaluated," *The Strad*, October 1997.

182. Charles Beare et al., "Guadagnini."

183. Fred Lindeman, "De Viool in de Nordelijke Nederlanden," in *400 Jahr Vioolbouwkunst in Nederland*, Amsterdam 1999, p. 122; Johan Giskes, "Vier Eeuwen Nederlandse Vioolbouw," in ibid., p. 56. Cf. *Société Comptoir de l'Industrie Cottonière Etablissments Boussac v. Alexander's Department Stores, Inc.*, No. 125, Docket 26881, United States Court of Appeals Second Circuit.

184. Giskes, "Vier Eeuwen Nederlandse Vioolbouw," in ibid., p. 55; Lindeman, "De Viool in de Noordelijke Nederlanden," p. 121.

185. Holman, *Four and Twenty Fiddlers*, pp. 48, 97–99, 121; cf. Holman, "The Violin in Tudor and Stuart England," in *The British Violin*, Oxford 1999, p. 4.

186. Giskes, "Vier Eeuwen Nederlandse Vioolbouw," in ibid., p. 57; Lindeman, "De Viool in de Noordelijke Nederlanden," p. 118.

187. Giskes, "Vier Eeuwen Nederlandse Vioolbouw," in ibid., p. 55.

188. Giskes, "Vier Eeuwen Nederlandse Vioolbouw," in ibid., pp. 60ff.

189. Giskes, "Vier Eeuwen Nederlandse Vioolbouw," in ibid., pp. 63ff.

190. Charles Beare, "Johannes Theodorus Cuypers," in *Grove Music Online*, accessed February 28, 2003, http://80-www.grovemusic.com.proxy.lib.uiowa.edu.

191. Suzanne Wijsman et al., "Violoncello," in *Grove Music Online*, accessed June 1, 2003, http://80-www.grovemusic.com.proxy.lib.uiowa.edu.

192. Pearce, *Violins and Violin Makers*, London 1866, p. 33.

193. Arthur Hill diary, unpublished, entry for February 8, 1911.

194. Nathan Milstein, *From Russia to the West*, New York 1990, p. 207.

195. Charles Beare, Introduction, *The British Violin*, p. 2.

196. Mace quoted in J. L. Boston, "Musicians and Scrapers," *Galpin Society Journal*, June 1956, pp. 51–57. John Milton, "The Passion," c. 1645, http://www.slpatech.com/scrap%20book/Christmas/on_the_morning_of_christs_nativi.htm, accessed July 5, 2005.

197. J. Wilson, ed., *Roger North on Music*, London 1959, p. 233.

198. Ibid., p. 235.

199. Beare, Introduction, *The British Violin*, p. 2.

200. Andrew Fairfax, "The British Violin," *Dartington Violin Conference 2000*, British Violin Association 2001, p. 41; John Walter Hill, "Gasparo Visconti" and William C. Smith et al., "Hare," in *Grove Music Online*, accessed May 2, 2003, http://80-www.grovemusic.com.proxy.lib.uiowa.edu.

201. Kenneth Skeaping, "Some Speculations on a Crisis in the History of the Violin," *Galpin Society Journal*, March 1955.

202. Harvey, *The Violin Family*, p. 18.

203. Charles Beare, John Dilworth, and Philip J. Kass, "Vincenzo Panormo," in *Grove Music Online*, accessed May 2, 2003, http://80-www.grovemusic.com.proxy.lib.uiowa.edu.

204. Otterstedt, *Die Gambe*, pp. 42ff.

205. Wilson, ed., *Roger North on Music*, p. 300.

616   NOTES TO PAGES 48–59

206. Pearce, *Violins and Violin Makers*, p. 95.

207. Wilson, ed., *Roger North on Music*, p. 294.

208. Fairfax, "The British Violin," pp. 38, 41; Henry Fielding, *Joseph Andrews*, London 1947, pp. vii, 7.

209. Quoted by Fairfax, "The British Violin," p. 46, from Charles Reade, "Jack of All Trades," in *Cream*, London 1858.

210. Harvey, *The Violin Family*, pp. 222ff. Cf. Charles Beare and Philip J. Kass, "Lott," in *Grove Music Online*, accessed June 21, 2003, http://80-www.grovemusic.com.proxy.lib.uiowa.edu; Ida Haendel, *Woman with Violin*, London 1970, pp. 159ff. Humphrey Burton, *Menuhin*, London 2000, pp. 207–8. E-mail to the author from Charles Beare, May 20 and 24, 2002, and from Robert Bein, May 21, 2002. Peter Zazofsky, interview with the author, Iowa City, Iowa, May 15, 2000.

211. Meredith Morris, *British Violin Makers*, London 1926.

212. John Milnes, draft biography, unpublished [BVMA 2005?].

213. Albert Cooper, "A Tale of Copies and Collusion," *The Strad*, January 1993; Harvey and Shapreau, *Violin Fraud*, p. 17.

214. John Milnes, e-mail to the author, May 22, 2002.

215. Meredith Morris, *Walter Mayson*, Maesteg 1906, passim; Harvey, *The Violin Family*, pp. 242ff.

216. Edward Heron-Allen, *Violin-Making as It Was and Is*, London 1884.

217. Interview with the author, Richmond, June 17, 1999; e-mail to the author, December 28, 2003.

218. George Orwell, "Charles Reade," in Sonia Orwell and Ian Angus, eds., *The Collected Essays, Journalism and Letters of George Orwell*, Vol. 2, pp. 50–54

219. Brian W. Harvey and Carol Fitzgerald, eds., *Edward Heron-Allen's Journal of the Great War*, Chichester 2002.

220. Harvey, *The Violin Family*, pp. 270ff.; "Eminent Victorian," *The Strad*, February 2003.

221. In author's presence, Aspen, Colorado, July 29, 1998.

222. Edward Ball, "Mass Markies," *The Strad*, March 2003.

223. J. H. Clapham, *Economic Development of France & Germany*, Cambridge, UK 1961, pp. 166–67, 200–1.

224. Phyllis Deane, *The First Industrial Revolution*, Cambridge, UK 1965, pp. 197, 255; Clapham, *Economic Development*, pp. 159–63.

225. Julie Bunn and Lydia Rose Seiber, "Music, Makers and Markets," *The Strad*, August 1997, p. 840. The guild charter can be found in *The Strad*, August 1997, p. 845.

226. Milliot, "La famille Chanot-Chardon," pp. 13ff.

227. Benoît Rolland, "Bow Heirs," *The Strad*, April 2003; Evelyne Bonétat in Paul Childs, *The Bow Makers of the Peccatte Family*, Montrose, New York 1996, pp. 9ff.

228. Kolneder, *Das Buch der Violine*, p. 171; Bonétat in Childs, *The Bow Makers*, pp. 9ff.

229. The discussion below is primarily based on Milliot, *Histoire de la Lutherie parisienne du XVIIIᵉ siècle à 1960*, Spa 1994, Tome I, pp. 13ff.

230. Milliot, "Violinistes et luthiers parisiens au XVIIIᵉ siècle" in Florence Gétreau, *Instrumentistes et Luthiers parisiens*, Paris 1988, pp. 99ff.

231. Milliot, *Histoire*, Tome I, pp. 20–21.

232. Ibid., p. 111.

233. Ibid., pp. 117–25.

234. Charles Beare and Sylvette Milliot, "Nicolas Lupot," in *Grove Music Online*, accessed July 28, 2003, http://80-www.grovemusic.com.proxy.lib.uiowa.edu.

235. Malou Haine, *Les Facteurs d'Instrument de Musique à Paris au XIXᵉ Siècle*, Brussels 1985, p. 317.

236. Milliot, "Jean-Baptiste Vuillaume, L'Histoire d'une Reussité," in *Violons, Vuillaume*, p. 49.

237. Milliot, "Les Luthiers au XIXᵉ siècle," in Gétreau, *Instrumentistes*, p. 201.

238. Haine, *Les Facteurs*, pp. 71, 137.

239. Ibid., pp. 134ff.; Kolneder, *Das Buch*, p. 171; Edward H. Tarr, "Thibouville," in *Grove Music Online*, accessed August 2, 2003, http://80-www.grovemusic.com.proxy.lib.uiowa.edu.

240. Emanuel Jaeger, "La baleine de la lutherie," in *Violons, Vuillaume*, pp. 18ff.

241. Alberto Conforti, *Il Violino*, Milan 1987, p. 67.

242. "Violin Acquired to Honor Usher Abell," *National Music Museum Newsletter*, Vermillion, South Dakota, May 2003, p. 7.

243. Alain Giraud, "A Thwarted Revolution?," *The Strad*, September 2004.

244. Millant, *J.B. Vuillaume*, p. 103.

245. Philippe Thiébaut, "Copies et pastiches dans les art du décor," in *Violons, Vuillaume*, p. 126.

246. Milliot, "Les Luthiers au XIXᵉ siècle," in Gétreau, *Instrumentistes*, pp. 197ff.

247. Milliot, "Jean-Baptiste Vuillaume," in *Violons, Vuillaume*, pp. 52ff.

248. Millant, *J.B. Vuillaume*, p. 83.

249. Letter of August 26, 1857, *Violons, Vuillaume*, pp. 21–25.

250. David Laurie, *The Reminiscences of a Fiddle Dealer*, New York and Boston 1925, pp. 45ff.

251. Haine, *Les Facteurs*, p. 156.

252. Edward Neill, "Storia del violino di Nicolò Paganini," in *Il Violino di Paganini*, Genoa 1995, pp. 16–17; cf. Milliot, "Jean-Baptiste Vuillaume," in *Violons, Vuillaume*, p. 51.

253. Amnon Weinstein, "Great Minds," *The Strad*, January 2002.

254. Charles Beare, Jaak Liivoja-Lorius, and Sylvette Milliot, "Vuillaume," in *Grove Music Online*, accessed August 8, 2003, http://80-www.grovemusic.com.proxy.lib.uiowa.edu.

255. *Violons, Vuillaume*, pp. 36–37.

256. Millant, *J.B. Vuillaume*, p. 23.

257. Milliot, "Jean-Baptiste Vuillaume," in *Violons, Vuillaume*, pp. 52ff.

258. Ibid., p. 132; Louis P. Lochner, *Fritz Kreisler*, London 1951, pp. 346ff.

259. Carlo Marcello Rietman, *Il Violino e Genova*, Genoa 1975, p. 75; Morel quoted in *Violons, Vuillaume*, pp. 37–39.

260. Letter to Fétis of September 26, 1834, quoted by Pietro Berri, *Paganini*, Milan 1982, p. 54.

261. Malou Haine, "Jean-Baptiste Vuillaume, Innovateur ou Conservateur," in *Violons, Vuillaume*, pp. 68–77.

262. Beare et al., "Vuillaume," and Millant, *J.B. Vuillaume*, p. 112.

263. Milliot, "Jean-Baptiste Vuillaume," in *Violons, Vuillaume*, p. 57.

264. Milliot, "La famille Chanot-Chardon," pp. 97ff.

265. Ibid., pp. 162–64 passim.

266. Ibid., p. 55.

267. Ibid., pp. 100ff.

268. Ibid., p. 58

269. Quoted by Milliot, "La famille Chanot-Chardon," p. 136.

270. Interview with Ingeborg Behnke, Berlin, December 2000.

271. Interview with Martin Eifler, Berlin, December 2000.

272. Walter Senn and Karl Roy, *Jakob Stainer*, Frankfurt 1986, p. 52.

273. Ibid., pp. 22, 472–73.

274. Senn and Roy, "Jakob Stainer," in *Grove Music Online*, accessed September 22, 2003, http://www.grovemusic.com.

275. Senn and Roy, *Jakob Stainer*, pp. 47ff.

276. Skeaping, "Some Speculations."

277. Riedmiller in *Alte Geigen*, pp. 9–14, 57–59.

278. Drescher, "Nürnberger Geigenbau," in Martius, *Leopold Widhalm*, pp. 12ff.; Klaus Martius, "Abermals vermehrte Nachrichten von Nürnberger Geigenbauern," in Martius, *Leopold Widhalm*, p. 17.

279. Martius, "Abermals vermehrte Nachrichten," in Martius, *Leopold Widhalm*, p. 26.

280. Dieter Krickeberg, "Bemerkungen zur gesellschaftlichen Stellung der Geigen- und Lautenmacher in Nürnberg des 18. Jahrhunderts," in Martius, *Leopold Widhalm*, pp. 43ff.

281. Walter Senn, "Klotz (Familie)," in *Musik in Geschichte und Gegenwart*, Kassel et al., 1958, Vol. 7, pp. 1250–57. Cf. Charles Beare and Karl Roy, "Klotz (Kloz)," in *Grove Music Online*, accessed October 4, 2003, http://www.grovemusic.com.

282. Julius Maçon, "Die Entwicklung der Geigenindustrie in Mittenwald," Erlangen 1913, pp. 60–69.

283. Maçon, "Die Entwicklung," pp. 71ff.

284. Cf. www.geigenbauschule-mittenwald.de/wir-über-uns/wir-über-uns.html, October 11, 2003, www.matthias-klotz.de/framesdt/framesetdt.html.

285. *Festschrift, 325 Jahre Geigenmacherinnung Markneukirchen*, Markneukirchen 2002, p. 20.

286. Peter Schubert, "Zur Entwicklungsgeschichte des Vogländischen Streichinstrumentenbaus," in *Zum Streichinstrumentenbau*, pp. 37ff.

287. Interview with Heidrun Eichler, Markneukirchen, May 8, 2003; Zoebisch, *Vogtländischer Geigenbau*, p. 1.

288. Ibid., pp. 9–11.

289. Zoebisch, *Vogtländischer Geigenbau*, Vol. 1, p. 15.

290. *Festschrift, 325 Jahre*, pp. 14–15, Peter Schubert, "Zur Entwicklungsgeschichte des Vogländischen Streichinstrumentenbaus," in *Zum Streichinstrumentenbau*, pp. 26ff.

291. Kolneder, *Das Buch*, p. 172.

292. Zoebisch, *Vogtländischer Geigenbau*, Vol. 1, p. 14.

293. Ibid., pp. 4ff.

294. "What She Plays," *Strings*, February–March 2002, http://www.macfound.org/site/c.lkLXJ8MQKrH/b.2066197/k.3F6D/2006_Overview.htm, accessed September 19, 2006.

295. Schubert, "Zur Entwicklungsgeschichte," pp. 38ff.

296. Margaret Mehl, "Made in Japan," *The Strad*, May 2008.

297. Akten Betreffend: Stiftung der Fa Suzuki, Staatliche Akademische Hochschule für Musik in Berlin, Archive of the Hochschule der Künste, Berlin.

298. Ian de Stains, "Making Masters," *The Strad*, August 1997.

299. Review in *The Strad*, December 2006, p. 42.

300. See http://www.matsudaviolin.com/, accessed April 22, 2011.

301. Sheila Melvin and Jindong Cai, "An Orchestra with a Political Accompaniment," *New York Times*, March 5, 2000.

302. Mia Turner, "The Odyssey of a Master Chinese Violin Maker," *International Herald Tribune*, April 21, 2000.

303. Kevin McKeough, "Made in China," *Strings*, October 2003; Nancy Pellegrini, "The Rise and Rise of Chinese Lutherie," *The Strad*, March 2010.

304. Annette Otterstedt, "Brave New World," *The Strad*, September 2000.

305. Adelmann and Otterstedt, *Die Alemannische Schule*, p. 11.

306. Ibid., p. 32.

307. Ibid., p. 42.

308. John Dilworth, "Mr. Baker the Fiddell Maker," *The Strad*, May 1995.

309. Cited by Adelmann and Otterstedt, *Die Alemannische Schule*, p. 32.

310. Interview with the author, Oxford, July 6, 1997.

311. *Import and Export Guide; Every Species of Authentic Information Relative to the Shipping, Navigation and Commerce of the East Indians, China and All Other Parts of the Globe*, London 1834, p. 57.

312. Ibid.

313. John Koster, "Inventive Violin Making," *America's Shrine to Music Museum Newsletter*, August 2001, and "Recent Acquisitions," *National Music Museum Newsletter*, August 2003.

314. Patrick Sullivan, "Metal Mania Has Rocked String World for Decades," *Strings*, November 2010.

315. Hugh Davies, "Stroh Violin," in *Grove Music Online*, accessed November 23, 2002, http://www.grovemusic.com.

316. Translated as *On the Sensations of Tone as a Physiological Basis for the Theory of Music*, London 1885.

317. James Christensen, "Dr. Stelzner's Original Instruments," *The Strad*, October 2001. Cf. Margaret Downie Banks, "A Physicist's Unfulfilled Prophecy," *America's Shrine to Music Museum Newsletter* 26, No. 2, May 1999.

318. Paul R. Laird, "The Life and Work of Carleen Maley Hutchins," *Ars Musica Denver*, Vol. 6, No. 1, Fall 1993.

319. Margaret Downey Banks, "Graphite, Gruyère, and a Pig Named Susie," *National Music Museum Newsletter*, February 2003; Emily Langer, "Violin Maker's Instruments Rivaled the Storied Stradivarius," *Washington Post*, August 16, 2009.

320. "The Strads of Montclair," *Time*, June 15, 1962; "The Physics of Violins," *Scientific American*, November 1962.

321. Kyle Gann (with Kurt Stone),"Henry Brant," in *Grove Music Online*, accessed November 27, 2003, http://www.grovemusic.com.

322. Marcia Manna, "A Variety of Violins," *San Diego Union-Tribune*, March 17, 2002.

323. Howard Klein, "Unusual Violins in Recital Debut," *New York Times*, May 21, 1965.

324. *The New York Album*, Sony CD 57961.

325. Richard Lipkin, "To Build a Better Violin," *ASAP*, September 3, 1994; Manna, "A Variety."

326. John Schelleng, "The Violin as a Circuit," *Journal of the Acoustical Society of America* 35, 1963, pp. 326–38.

327. Quoted in Laird, "Carleen Maling Hutchins."

328. Darol Anger, "Shattering the Mold," *Strings*, July–August 1996.

329. Joseph Curtin, "Chip Off the Old Block," *The Strad*, November 2000

330. Margalit Fox, "Pain Relief, Strings Attached," *New York Times*, August 4, 1997.

331. Anger, "Shattering the Mold."

332. Eric Chapman, "Rivinus and the Pellegrina," *Journal of the American Viola Society*, 2004.

333. Steven L. Shepherd, "A New Golden Age," *Strings*, July–August 1998.

334. Anger, "Shattering the Mold."

335. E-mail to the author, December 12, 2003.

336. James C. McKinley Jr., "Famed Guitar Maker Raided by Federal Agents," *New York Times*, August 31, 2011; Kathryn Marie Dudley, "Luthiers: The Latest Endangered Species," *New York Times*, October 25, 2011; Raffi Khatchadourian, "The Stolen Forests," *The New Yorker*, October 6, 2008; "Nation Marks Lacey Act Centennial," http://www.fws.gov/pacific/news/2000/2000-98.htm, "Background Information: The Lacey Act Amendments in the Farm Bill," http://www.ncbfaa.org/Scripts/4Disapi.dll/4DCGI/cms/review.html?Action=CMS_Document&DocID=11480&MenuKey=pubs, accessed November 25, 2011.

337. Erin Shrader, "Future Shock," *Strings*, April 2007, p. 68.

338. Interview with the author, Bonn, December 1, 2000.

339. Interview with the author, Ann Arbor, Michigan, June 9, 1998; Joseph Curtin, "Weinreich and Directional Tone Colour," *The Strad*, April 2000.

340. John Dilworth, "Nocturnal Activities," *The Strad*, November 2003; *Journal of the Violin Society of America*, 1976–; British Violin Making Association, annual conference transcripts 1995–.

341. Laird, "Carleen Maling Hutchings."

342. Walter Sullivan, "Confession of a Musical Shelf-Robber," *New York Times*, February 2, 1975.

343. David Nicholson, "The Science of Music," Newport News, Virginia, *Daily Press*, February 28, 1999.

344. Patrick Sullivan, "Open Studio," *Strings*, April 2003, John Dilworth, "Meeting of the Makers," *The Strad*, November 2003.

345. See http://www.violin-maker.co.uk, accessed May 27, 2005.

346. Gabriel Gottlieb, "Making It Together," *The Strad*, March 2001.

347. Ethan Winter, "From Sawdust to Sine Waves," *The Strad*, July 1994.

348. Stewart Pollens, "Curtains for Cremona," *The Strad*, November 1995.

349. *Strad Directory* 2004, London 2003.

350. Helen Wallace, "The Violin Making School Boom—20 Years On," *The Strad*, February 1992; Juliette Barber, "Reluctant Hero," *The Strad*, April 1999.

351. Pollens, "Curtains for Cremona."

352. Timothy Pfaff, "Man with a Mission," *Strings*, December 1998; interview with the author, Des Moines, Iowa, September 30, 1999.

353. For examples, see John Milnes et al., *The British Violin*, Oxford 2000; Giovanni Accornero, *Annibale Fagnola*, Turin 1999; Ramon C. Pinto, *Los Luthiers Españoles*, Barcelona 1988; Eric Blot and Alberto Giordano, *Liuteria Italiana 1860–1960*, Cremona 1994; Peter Bedenek, *Violin Makers of Hungary*, Munich 1997.

354. E-mail to the author, December 18, 2003.

355. Interview with the author, December 17, 2003. Cf. Margalit Fox, "René A. Morel, Master Restorer of Rare Violins, Dies at 79," *New York Times*, November 19, 2011.

356. Natasha Randall, "Double Acts," *The Strad*, January 2004.

357. E-mail to the author, January 10, 2004.

358. Interview with Robert Bein, Chicago, April 3, 1998.

359. Alberto Bachmann, *Encyclopedia of the Violin*, New York 1966, p. 49.

360. Thomas Wenberg, *The Violin Makers of the United States*, Mt. Hood, Oregon 1986, passim. Steven L. Shepherd, "Thomas Wenberg and the Making of an American Classic," *Strings*, December 1998.

361. Paul Berman, *A Tale of Two Utopias*, New York 1996, p. 9.

362. E-mail to the author, January 5, 2004.

363. E-mail to the author, December 28, 2003.

364. E-mail to the author, July 10, 2001.

365. Interview with the author, Ann Arbor, Michigan, June 9, 1998.

366. Interview with Samuel Zygmuntowicz, *PBS Online News Hour*, February 19, 2001.

367. Telephone interview with the author, December 14, 2003.

368. Interview with the author, Ann Arbor, Michigan, June 9, 1998.

369. Interview with the author, Minneapolis, Minnesota, May 16, 1998; e-mail December 15, 2003.

370. Herman van der Wee, *Prosperity & Upheaval*, Berkeley and Los Angeles 1987, Chs. 4–6.

371. Janet Banks, "News of Newark," *The Strad*, February 1992.

372. Ibid.

373. E-mail to the author, December 10, 2003.

374. "If This Wood Could Talk," *Los Angeles Times Magazine*, August 31, 1997.

375. E-mail to the author from Charles Beare, January 14, 2004.

376. "Der Rückzug," *Wirtschaftswoche*, March 12, 1992; Karl Pröglhöf, "Kremser enttarnte 'Millionengeige,'" *Niederösterreichische Nachrichten*, March 16, 1992.

377. Andrew C. Revkin, "String Theory," *New York Times*, November 28, 2006; Sam Zymunto-wicz, "A Scanner in the Works," *The Strad*, January 2009.

378. Martin Schleske, "Wired for Sound," *The Strad*, October 2002; "High Fidelity," *The Strad*, November 2002. Cf. Jeanne Rubner, "Geigenbau mit Kopf und Bauch," *Süddeutsche Zeitung*, April 4, 1996.

379. Joanna Pieters, "Masters of the Bel Canto," *The Strad*, March 2002.

380. Steven L. Shepherd, "The Mysterious Technology of the Violin," *American Heritage of Invention and Technology*, Spring 2000.

381. See http://www.josephcurtinstudios.com/news/tech/www/reciprocal_bow.htm.

382. Joseph Curtin, "Space-Age Stradivari," *The Strad*, April 1999. Cf. Paul Kotapish, "New Chips Off the Old Block," *Strings*, April 2002, http://www.macfound.org/programs/fel/fellows/curtin_joseph.htm, accessed October 28, 2005.

383. *Import and Export Guide*, p. 57.

384. James Reel, "Same Old Song," *Strings*, April 2003.

385. Interview with the author, Ann Arbor, Michigan, June 9, 1998.

386. Telephone interview with the author, December 14, 2003.

387. "South Korean College Students Learn Economics the Hard Way," *Baltimore City Paper*, March 4–10, 1998.

388. See http://www.philharmonia.org/musicians.html, accessed July 5, 2005.

389. "News and Events," *The Strad*, March 2005, p. 8.

390. Haskell, *The Early Music Revival*; James Gollin, *Pied Piper: The Many Lives of Noah Green-berg*, Hillsdale, New York 2001.

391. Interview with the author, St. Petersburg, November 22, 1997.

392. E-mail to the author, January 6, 2004.

393. E-mail announcement, June 24, 2006.

394. E-mail to the author, January 4, 2004.

395. Mirka Zemanová, "Like Father Like Son," *The Strad*, September 1991.

396. Mark Landler, "Germany's East Is Able to Prevent Industrial Flight to Third World," *New York Times*, November 21, 2003.

397. Zoebisch, *Vogtländischer Geigenbau*, Vorwort.

398. David Schoenbaum, "Mark Two," *The Strad,* April 2004.

399. Henry Saint-George, *The Bow*, preface.

400. Philip Kass, "Industry Meets Art," *Strings*, November 2010.

401. Mary Anne Alburger, *The Violin Makers*, London 1978, pp. 189ff.

402. Richard E. Sadler, *W. E. Hill & Sons*, London 1996, p. 108.

403. Jeremy Eichler, "The Bow of Bach's Dreams? Not Quite," *New York Times*, August 10, 2003. Cf. David Boyden, "Bow," in *Grove Music Online*, accessed June 6, 2004, http://www.grovemusic.com; Haskell, *The Early Music Revival*, p. 88.

404. Manuel Komroff, *The Magic Bow*, New York and London 1940; *The Magic Bow*, Gainsborough Pictures 1946.

405. Childs, *The Bow Makers*, p. xix.

406. Robin Stowell, *Violin Technique and Performance Practice in the Late 18th and Early 19th Century*, Cambridge 1985, p. 19; Boyden, *The History*, p. 328, n. 23.

407. Alburger, *The Violin Makers*, p. 194.

408. Andrew Bellis, "Of Wood and Whiskers: A Guide to Bow-Making," University of Oxford Faculty of Music, n.d., p. 6.

409. "Nonagenarian Still Going Strong," *Strings*, October 2000; Stewart Pollens, "An Eye for Detail," *The Strad*, July 2005.

410. Boyden, *The History*, p. 328; W. Henry Hill et al., *Antonio Stradivari*, p. 209.

411. Boyden, *The History*, p. vi.

412. Boyden, *The History*, p. 45.

413. Cf. Julian Clark, "L'évolution de l'archet à la fin du XVIIIᵉ siècle," in Gétreau, *Instrumentistes*, pp. 111ff.

414. Peter Walls, "Bow," in *Grove Music Online*, accessed June 7, 2004, http://www.grovemusic.com.

415. Boyden, "Bow," op. cit.

416. Cf. Boyden, *The History*, p. 328; Stowell, *Violin Technique*, p. 1; Stewart Pollens and Henryk Kaston, *François-Xavier Tourte, Bow Maker*, New York 2001, pp. 31ff.

417. Pollens and Kaston, *François-Xavier Tourte*, pp. 81–82.

418. Ibid., p. 27.

419. Stowell, *Violin Technique*, pp. 11ff.

420. Saint-George, *The Bow*, p. 40; Robert Pierce; "The Big Issue," *The Strad*, August 2002.

421. Boyden, *The History*; Stowell, *Violin Technique*, p. 14; Saint-George, *The Bow*, pp. 31–32.

422. Pollens and Kaston, *François-Xavier Tourte*, pp. 27–30, 76.

423. Stowell, *Violin Technique*, pp. 19–23.

424. Pollens and Kaston, *François-Xavier Tourte*, pp. 46ff.

425. Bachmann, *Encyclopedia of the Violin*, p. 122; Saint-George, *The Bow*, pp. 36ff.; Charles Beare and Philip J. Kass, "John (Kew) Dodd," in *Grove Music Online*, accessed June 20, 2004, http://www.grovemusic.com.

426. Pollens and Kaston, *François-Xavier Tourte*, pp. 55ff.

427. Quoted by Etienne Vatelot in "Paris, Capital de l'Archèterie au XIXᵉ Siècle," in Gétreau, *Instrumentistes*, pp. 209ff.

428. Saint-George, *The Bow*, pp. 40–41. Cf. Pollens and Kaston, *François-Xavier Tourte*, pp. 31ff.

429. Vatelot, "Paris, Capital de l'Archetrie," in Gétreau, *Instrumentistes*, pp. 209ff.

430. Alfred Hill to Harrison Bowne Smith, December 21, 1933, unpublished.

431. Pollens and Kaston, *François-Xavier Tourte*, pp. 31–55.

432. Ibid., p. 46.

433. Saint-George, *The Bow*, p. 35; Harvey, *The Violin Family*, pp. 124–31; Philip J. Kass, "The Tubbs Bow," *World of Strings*, Autumn 1980.

434. Bunn and Seiber, "Music, Makers and Markets."

435. See http://www.arcobrasil.com/PernambucoWood/pernambuccowood.html, accessed February 26, 2000.

436. Childs, *The Bow Makers*, p. 48.

437. Bunn and Seiber, "Music, Makers and Markets."

438. Kass, "The Tubbs Bow"; Finlay, *Color*, p. 179.

439. Harvey and Georgeanna Whistler, "Nikolaus Ferder Kittel," *Music Journal*, May–June 1966.

440. Ayke Agus, *Heifetz as I Knew Him*, Portland, Oregon 2001, p. 68.

441. http://www.filimonovfineviolins.tk/, accessed February 13, 2009.

442. Alfred Hill to Harrison Bowne Smith, October 4, 1933, unpublished.

443. Sadler, *W. E. Hill & Sons*, pp. 60–61, 69, 110

444. Bunn and Seiber, "Music, Makers and Markets."

445. Benoît Rolland, "Bow Heirs," *The Strad*, April 2003

446. Tully Potter, "David Oistrakh," *The Strad*, October 1984, p. 413.

447. Russ Rymer, "Frogs Among Whales," *The Strad*, November 2003, http://www.violinist
.com/blog/caeli/20067/5458/, accessed May 15, 2007.

448. Rolland, "Bow Heirs"; Russ Rymer, "Back to the Future," *The Strad*, May 2004; Russ
Rymer, "Saving the Music Tree," *Smithsonian*, April 2004.

449. Rymer, "Saving the Music Tree."

450. Hélène Pourquié, "Les Archetiers s'engagent pour le bois," Bois-Fôret.info, December 20,
2002.

451. Robert Pierce, "The Big Issue," *The Strad*, August 2002; News and Events, *The Strad*, February 2003.

452. Quoted by Rymer, "Saving the Music Tree."

453. Arian Sheets, "An American Company's Exploration of Flexible Steel Tubing," *National
Music Museum Newsletter*, May 2004.

454. Heather Kurzbauer, "Science Friction," *Strings*, October 2002; Ellen Pfeifer, "Violin Bows
Go High-Tech," *Wall Street Journal*, November 13, 2002.

455. Catherine Nelson, "Sticks and Tones," *The Strad*, January 2009.

BOOK 2: SELLING IT

1. Albert Berr, *Geigengeschichten*, Konstanz 1984, pp. 1430–44.

2. H. R. Haweis, *Old Violins and Violin Lore*, London 1923, p. 136.

3. Charles Beare, "Hart," in *Grove Music Online*, accessed September 3, 2004, http://www
.grovemusic.com.proxy.lib.uiowa.edu.

4. David Laurie, *The Reminiscences of a Fiddle Dealer*, Boston and New York 1925, pp. xiii–xiv.

5. W. Henry Hill et al., *Antonio Stradivari*, p. 265.

6. James M. Fleming, "The 'Court' Stradivari," in Goodkind, *Violin Iconoraphy*, pp. 88ff.

7. Carlo Ginzburg, "Spie, Radici di un Paradigma Indizario," in *Miti, Emblemi, Spie*, Tirom
1992, pp. 158ff.

8. Ibid.

9. Interview with Charles Beare, London, June 2, 1998.

10. Finley Peter Dunne, *Mr. Dooley in Peace and War*, Boston 1898, p. xiii.

11. Haweis, *Old Violins,* pp. 134–35.

12. "The late Rev. H. R. Haweis," *Westminster Review*, May 1901.

13. Haweis, *Old Violins*, p. 214.

14. Sadler, *W. E. Hill & Sons*, p. 101.

15. Interview with the author, Chicago, Illinois, April 4, 1998.

16. David Schoenbaum, "Nearing Endgame in the Violin Trade," *New York Times*, February
11, 2001.

17. Arnold Ehrlich, *Die Geige in Wahrheit und Fabel*, Leipzig 1899, p. 12.

18. Ibid., pp. 1–6

19. Alfred Hill to Harrison Smith, April 13, 1932.

20. Henri Temianka, *Facing the Music*, New York 1973, p. 137.

21. Sears, Roebuck catalogue, New York 1969, p. 192.

22. See http://www.usd.edu/smm/FAQ.html#Strad, accessed September 8, 2004.

23. Interview with Dietmar Machold, Vienna, October 5, 2000.

24. Margarete Heise-Sapper, "Mit Stradivaris ein Neues Image Erworben," *Handelsblatt*, September 16–17, 1994.

25. Interviews with Dietmar Machold, Vienna, October 5, and Roger Hargrave, Bremen, December 22, 2000.

26. Laurie Niles, "The Milstein Strad Moves to Pasadena," http://www.violinist.com/blog/laurie/20067/5475/, accessed October 12, 2008; http://company.monster.com/brighton/, accessed October 13, 2008; Jerry Kohl, e-mail to the author, October 12, 2008; Dave Fulton, e-mail to the author, October 13, 2008.

27. Interview with the author, London, June 2, 1998.

28. Joseph Wechsberg, "Trustee in Fiddledale-I," *The New Yorker*, October 17, 1953.

29. Interview with the author, Bremen, September 12, 1997.

30. Frances Gillham, phone interview with the author, February 28, 2001.

31. Joe Drape and Howard W. French, "Flamboyant Owner Finds a Horse," *New York Times*, May 19, 2000.

32. "Edvard Munch's 'The Scream' fetches $120M at Auction," http://www.cbsnews.com/8301-201_162-57426665/edvard-munchs-the-scream-fetches-$120m-at-auction/, accessed July 2, 2012; Carol Vogel, "A Rubens Brings $76.7 Million at London Auction," *New York Times*, July 11, 2002; Carol Vogel,"Long Suspect, a Vermeer Is Vindicated," *New York Times*, July 8, 2004; Carol Vogel, "Price for a Klimt Soars to $29 Million," *New York Times*, November 6, 2003; Carol Vogel, "Mantegna Mystery," *New York Times*, January 24, 2003.

33. Chiesa and Rosengard, *The Stradivari Legacy*, pp. 37–39.

34. Etienne Vatelot, "Le Stradivarius français," in *Violons, Vuillaume*, pp. 52ff.; Philippe Blay, "Pages d'un Album," in *Violons, Vuillaume*.

35. "Derek Jeter's Mansion Completed with Price Tag of $7.7 Million in Tampa's Davis Islands," http://www.nesn.com/2011/02/derek-jeters-77-million-tampa-mansion-completed-after-year-of-construction.html, accessed April 26, 2011.

36. Jennifer Gould Kiel, "It's a 'Hugue' Place, http://www.nypost.com/p/news/business/realestate/residential/it_hugue_place_b9IXuvEDnuVkv3a4SRKEfK#ixzz1ok5BFiYt; Eamon Murphy, "Reclusive Heiress Leaves Behind 5 Homes Worth $180 Million," http://realestate.aol.com/blog/2012/03/09/huguette-clark-reclusive-heiress-leaves-behind-55-million-apa/, accessed March 2, 2012.

37. Interviews with the author in 1993 and 1997.

38. Marie-France Calas, "Au-delà d'une Première Exposition Temporaire," in *Violons, Vuillaume*, p. 15.

39. Frederic C. Howe, *Socialized Germany*, New York 1916, p. 75.

40. Elena Ferrari Barassi, "Antonio Stradivari's Musical Environment" in Beare and Carlson, *Antonio Stradivari*, pp. 29–37.

41. Barassi, "Stradivari's Musical Environment," in Beare and Carlson, *Antonio Stradivari*, p. 33.

42. W. Henry Hill et al., *Antonio Stradivari*, pp. 75–79; Santoro, *Traffici e Falsificazione*, pp. 23ff.

43. Chiesa and Rosengard, *The Stradivari Legacy*, p. 57.

44. Claire Wilson, "New Baby Boomers are Digging Guitars as Pricey Collectibles," *New York Times*, September 24, 2004.

45. "Paganini and the Stradivarius," *The Strad*, October 1982.

46. Herbert K. Goodkind, *Violin Iconography*, p. 752.

47. For a list, see http://www.cozio.com/Owner.aspx?id=841, accessed October 13, 2004; http://www.vor.ru/culture/cultarch293_eng.html, accessed November 19, 2004.

48. Greg King, *The Man Who Killed Rasputin*, Secaucus, New Jersey 1995, p. 203.

49. Ibid., pp. 236ff.

50. Tully Potter, "David Oistrakh," *The Strad*, October 1984, p. 412.

51. Denise Yim, *Viotti and the Chinnerys*, Aldershot, UK, and Burlington, Vermont 2004, p. 143.

52. Jann Pasler, "Countess Greffulhe as Entrepreneur," in William Weber, ed., *The Musician as Entrepreneur, 1700–1914*, Bloomington and Indianapolis, Indiana 2004, pp. 221ff.; http://www.cozio.com/Owner.aspx?id=170, accessed March 13, 2005; W. Henry Hill et al., *Antonio Stradivari*, p. 124.

53. *The Times* (London), December 29, 1917.

54. See http://www.sankt-magnus.de/Knoop.html, accessed September 22, 2004.

55. Stuart Jeffries, "Kindness of Strangers," *Guardian*, November 21, 2002.

56. Asa Briggs, *Victorian Things*, Chicago and London 1989, pp. 184–85.

57. Peter Gay, *Pleasure Wars*, New York and London 1998, p. 172; cf. http://icbirmingham .icnetwork.co.uk/expats/pastpres/content_objectid=13706966_method=full_siteid=50002_ headline=-Pen-maker-who-Turner-couldn-t-brush-off-name_page.html, accessed September 22, 2004.

58. W. Henry Hill et al., *Antonio Stradivari*, p. 264.

59. Jeannie Chapel, "The Papers of Joseph Gillott," *Journal of the History of Collections*, 2007, pp. 1–48.

60. Hart, *The Violin*, pp. 354ff.; George Hart, *The Emperor Stradivari*, London 1893.

61. Harvey, *The Violin Family*, pp. 219–22; Milliot, *Les Luthiers Parisiens*; Milliot, "La famille Chanot-Chardon," p. 74; http://www.cozio.com/Owner.aspx?id=320, accessed October 22, 2004; W. Henry Hill et al., *Antonio Stradivari*, p. 264; Chapel, "The Papers of Joseph Gillott."

62. G. D. H. Cole and Raymond Postgate, *The Common People*, London 1966, p. 354.

63. Robert Bein, e-mail to the author, September 19, 2002.

64. W. Henry Hill et al., *Antonio Stradivari*, pp. 273–78.

65. Albert H. Pitkin in *The Hawley Collection of Violins*, Chicago 1904, p. 15.

66. Ernest N. Doring, *How Many Strads?*, Chicago 1945, pp. 53–55.

67. Ibid., pp. 75–78. Cf. *Musical Courier*, May 26 and June 2, 1909, and January 6, 1916.

68. John Conway, "Celebrating the Birth of Texas Oil," http://www.texas-ec.org/tcp/101oil .html, accessed February 7, 2005.

69. "Young Buys His Daughter Million Dollar Collection," *Beaumont Enterprise*, undated, courtesy of Grey Riley.

70. Program of March 7, 1931, courtesy of Greg Riley.

71. Doring, "Collecting Violins, the Yount Collection," *Violins and Violinists*, April 1938.

72. Gisela Hammig kindly let the author see her grandfather's order book, Berlin, December 5, 1997.

73. E. Millicent Sowerby, *Rare People and Rare Books*, London 1967, p. 36.

74. Cited from propaganda ministry documents in the Bundesarchiv, Potsdam. E-mail to the author from Martin Eifler, Federal Commission for Culture and Media, January 16, 2001. E-mail to the author from Charles Beare, December 29, 2008. Cf. Charles Beare, "Walter Hamma," *The Strad*, October 1988.

75. Joanna Pieters, "Stranger than Fiction," *The Strad*, August 2001.

76. Cyrilla Barr, *Elizabeth Sprague Coolidge*, New York 1998, pp. 158–65.

77. Nat Brandt, *Con Brio*, New York and Oxford 1993, pp. 19–20.

78. Carol June Bradley, "Edward N. Waters: Notes on a Career," *Notes*, December 1993, pp. 487–88.

79. See http://www.loc.gov/rr/perform/guide/instru.html, http://www.whittalllodge.org/biography.html, October 14, 2004; Paul Hume, "Gertrude Clarke Whittall Dies," *Washington Post*, June 30, 1965; Lochner, *Fritz Kreisler*, pp. 312ff. Barr, *Elizabeth Sprague Coolidge*, pp. 245–47; Bradley, "Edward N. Waters."

80. William D. Mangam, *The Clarks, An American Phenomenon*, New York 1941, pp. 55–80; http://www.senate.gov/artandhistory/history/common/contested_elections/089William_Clark.htm, accessed November 30, 2011.

81. Claude Lebet, *Le Quatuor Stradivarius Nicolò Paganini*, Spa, Belgium 1994, pp. 15ff.

82. "Corcoran to Receive Famous Instruments," *Washington Post*, January 27, 1964.

83. Ibid., p. 19.

84. See http://www.koanart.com/judy.html, accessed November 6, 2004.

85. Howard R. Bowen to David Lloyd Kreeger, January 25, 1967, President's Correspondence, Box 61c, University of Iowa Archives.

86. Vineeta Anand, "Stradivarius Quartet Plays Endowment's Kind of Music," *Pensions & Investments*, September 19, 1994, http://www.nmf.or.jp/english/instrument/instruments.html; Margarete Heise-Sapper, "Mit Stradivaris ein neues Image Erworben," *Handelsblatt*, September 16–17, 1995.

87. See http://www.cozio.com/Owner.aspx?id=1886, http://www.stradivarisociety.com/InvestInInstrument.htm, accessed November 9, 2004; Robert Bein, e-mail to the author, September 19, 2002, interview with Geoffrey Fushi, Chicago, Illinois, April 4, 1998; interview with Charles Beare, London, July 9, 1997; Goodkind, *Violin Iconography*, appendix.

88. Melinda Bargreen, "Exquisite Strings," *Seattle Times*, July 14, 2002.

89. Bill Dedman, "Who Is Watching Heiress Huguette Clark's Millions?," http://www.msnbc.msn.com/id/38733524/ns/business-huguette_clark_mystery/, accessed September 8, 2010.

90. Honeyman, *The Violin: How to Choose One*, pp. 9–11.

91. E-mail to the author, August 29, 2004.

92. Santoro, *Traffici e Falsificazione*, p. 8.

93. Ibid., p. 9.

94. Ibid., pp. 60–61.

95. Ibid., pp. 14 and 73; Bacchetta, *Stradivari*, pp. 41ff.

96. Cristina Bordas Ibañez, "The Stradivari of the Royal Palace in Madrid," in Shin'ichi Yokoyama, *The Decorated Instruments of Antonio Stradivari*, Tokyo 2002.

97. Giovanni Iviglia, "Il Carteggio di Cozio di Salabue," in Santoro, ed., *Le Celebrazioni*, pp. 267ff.

98. Bacchetta, *Stradivari non è nato*, pp. 77–78; Rosengard, *Giovanni Battista Guadagnini*, pp. 107ff.

99. Santoro, *Traffici e Falsificazioni*, p. 73.

100. Ibid., p. 55. Cf. Rosengard, *Giovanni Battista Guadagnini*, p. 112; Charles Beare and Carlo Chiesa, "Cozio di Salabue," *Grove Music Online*, accessed September 5, 2002, http://www.grovemusic.com.

101. Cf. Carlo Chiesa, "Cozio's Carteggio: The Confusion," *The Strad*, August 2001.

102. Quoted in Emmanuel August Dieudonné Las Cases, *Mémorial de Sainte-Hélène*, preface by Jean Tulard, Paris 1968, p. 155.

103. Elia Santoro, ed., *L'epistolario di Cozio di Salabue*, Cremona 1993; Cozio di Salabue, *Carteggio*, Milan 1950.

104. Sacchi, *Il Conte Cozio*, pp. 14ff.

105. Bacchetta, *Stradivari non è nato*, p. 102. Cf. Sacchi, *Il Conte Cozio*, pp. 18ff.

106. Santoro, *Traffici e Falsificazione*, p. 73; Berri, *Paganini*, pp. 141–42, 462.

107. Charles Beare, "Luigi Tarisio," *Grove Music Online*, accessed September 5, 2002, http://www.grovemusic.com; Santoro, *Traffici e Falsificazione*, pp. 74ff.

108. Quoted by Beare, "Luigi Tarisio."

109. Etienne Vatelot, "Le Stradivarius Français," in *Violons, Vuillaume*, pp. 30–32; Milliot, "Jean-Baptiste Vuillaume," in *Violons, Vuillaume*, p. 50.

110. Hart, *The Violin*, pp. 335ff.

111. Millant, *J. B. Vuillaume*, pp. 123ff.

112. Quoted in *Violons, Vuillaume*, pp. 32ff.; Milliot, "Jean-Baptiste Vuillaume," ibid., p. 50.

113. W. Henry Hill et al., *Antonio Stradivari*, p. 263.

114. Milliot, "La famille Chanot-Chardon," pp. 57–59.

115. Milliot, "Jean Baptiste Vuillaume," in *Violons, Vuillaume*, p. 55. Cf. Lebet, *Le Quatuor Stradivari*, p. 15; Sadler, *W. E. Hill & Sons*, pp. 21–22.

116. Milliot, "La famille Chanot-Chardon," p. 51.

117. Etienne Vatelot, "Le Stradivarius français," in *Violons, Vuillaume*, p. 22.

118. Lebet, *Le Quatuor Stradivarius*, passim.

119. Vatelot, "Le Stradivarius français," in *Violons, Vuillaume*, p. 35; Milliot, "La famille Chanot-Chardon," p. 52.

120. Milliot, "La famille Chanot-Chardon," p. 52.

121. Ibid., p. 55.

122. Arthur Hill's diary, March 23, 1891; February 2, 1892; March 29, 1893; June 13, 1894.

123. W. Henry Hill et al., *Antonio Stradivari*, p. 225.

124. Frank Howe and Christina Bashford, "Walter Willson Cobbett," *Grove Music Online*, http://www.grovemusic.com.proxy.lib.uiowa.edu, accessed January 17, 2005; "The Chamber Music Life," *Cobbett's Cyclopedic Survey of Chamber Music*, Oxford and Toronto 1929, pp. 254ff.; http://www.scandura.net/profile/history/, accessed January 17, 2005.

125. Quoted by Cyril Ehrlich, *The Music Profession in Britain*, Oxford 1985, p. 156.

126. Charles Wilson, "Economic Conditions," in *The New Cambridge Modern History*, Vol. 11, Cambridge 1970, p. 62.

127. Cf. Ehrlich, *The Music Profession*, pp. 100ff.

128. Alberto Bachmann, "Violin Makers in America," *An Encyclopedia of the Violin*, New York and London 1925, New York 1966, pp. 49–54.

129. Harvey, *The Violin Family*, p. 124.

130. Nicholas Faith, *Sold*, London 1985, pp. 21ff.

131. All are mentioned in Arthur Hill's diary, January 6 and 7, 1891; October 13 and December 10, 1891; January 25, 1892; January 26, March 2, June 25, and September 14, 1894; May 10 and November 13, 1895; February 28 and May 6, 1896.

132. Alan Kidd, *Manchester, A History*, Lancaster 2006, pp. 12, 15–24, 224; Robina McNeil and Michael Nevell, *The Industrial Archaeology of Greater Manchester*, Coalbrookdale, UK 2000.

133. Wilson, "Economic Conditions," pp. 49ff.

134. Ehrlich, *The Music Profession*, pp. 104ff.

135. Edmund Fellowes, *Memoirs of an Amateur Musician*, London 1946, pp. 8–9.

136. Hill's diary, December 20, 1890.

137. Ehrlich, *The Music Profession*, pp. 156ff.

138. A. Victor Murray, "Education," *New Cambridge Modern History*, Vol. 11, pp. 197–98.

139. February 27, July 22, 1890, April 1, 1892.

140. Hill's diary, January 3, January 5, January 14, February 3, May 8, 1894; "Henry Holmes," in *The New Grove Dictionary*, vol. 8, p. 657. Cf. Ehrlich, *The Music Profession*, p. 112.

141. Hill's diary, December 13, 1894, and May 18 and September 18, 1896.

142. Quoted in Harvey, *The Violin Family*, p. 199.

143. Pepys's diary, February 17 and March 5, 1660; R. C. Lathym and W. Matthews, *The Diary of Samuel Pepys*, Vol. 1, London 1995, pp. 58 and 76. Cf. Harvey, *The Violin Family*, pp. 189ff.

144. Sadler, *W. E. Hill & Sons*, p. 122.

145. For auction prices, see www.maestronet.com.

146. Hill's diary, January 11 and October 26, 1894; March 31, 1897.

147. Ibid., November 1, 1890; June 2 and October 26, 1891; May 9 and December 16, 1892; July 17, 1894; March 29, July 1, and September 18, 1895.

148. Ibid., February 27 and May 28, 1894.

149. H. R. Haweis, *Old Violins and Violin Lore*, London c. 1898, pp. 133–42.

150. Jane Horner, "Double Trouble," *The Strad*, February 1995, p. 162.

151. Haweis, *Old Violins*, p. 142.

152. Hill's diary, February 25, 1892. Hill reports insuring the Betts Strad against all contingencies for £1,500, at an annual premium of £7/10s.

153. W. Henry Hill et al., *Antonio Stradivari*; William Henry Hill et al., *The Violin-Makers of the Guarneri Family*.

154. W. Henry Hill et al., *Antonio Stradivari*, p. 277.

155. Hill's diary, September 29, 1890; May 12, 1891; January 29, 1894; November 5, 1894.

156. Ibid., January 27, 1890.

157. Ehrlich, *The Music Profession*, p. 51.

158. Ibid., pp. 142ff.

159. Harvey, *The Violin Family*, pp. 154–55.

160. Hill's diary, October 29, 1890; January 20, 1892; and September 13, 1890.

161. Jane Horner, "Double Trouble," *The Strad*, February 1995; Alburger, *The Violin Makers*, pp. 189ff.

162. Hill's diary, November 11, 1892.

163. Ibid., February 18, 1892.

164. Cited by Harvey, *The Violin Family*, p. 216.

165. Hill's diary, March 31, 1894.

166. Sadler, *W. E. Hill & Sons*, p. 23.

167. Hill's diary, August 19–September 4, 1890; July 22–September 3, 1892.

168. Interview with the author, Chicago, Illinois, April 4, 1998.

169. Hill's diary, March 24, May 24, July 16, August 7, and October 1, 1894.

170. Ibid., May 5, 1891.

171. Fridolin Hamma, *Meisterwerke alter italienischer Geigenbau-Kunst*, Stuttgart c. 1933, pp. 1, 19ff. Cf. Albert Berr, *Geigengeschichten*, Konstanz 1948.

172. Hill's diary, March 3, 1891.

173. Ibid., March 12 and May 1, 1891.

174. Hill's diary, June 8 and December 30, 1890; January 1 and May 8, 1891; March 3 and June 24, 1892; November 2, 1895; February 1, 1898.

175. Sadler, *W. E. Hill & Sons*, p. 23.

176. Charles Loch Mowat, *Britain Between the Wars*, London 1955, pp. 203ff.; Frank Herrmann, *Sotheby's, Portrait of an Auction House*, New York and London 1981, pp. 205ff.

177. Alfred Hill to Harrison Bowne Smith, July 22, 1926, unpublished letter.

178. Charles Reade, *Readiana: Comments on Current Events*, London 1883.

179. Alfred Hill to Harrison Bowne Smith, June 20 and October 5, 1934, unpublished letters.

180. Ibid., January 22, 1924.

181. Ibid., August 30, 1927.

182. See http://www.vadimgluzman.com/violin.html, http://www.cozio.com/Instrument.aspx?id=77, accessed February 5, 2005.

183. Alfred Hill to Harrison Bowne Smith, October 5, 1934, unpublished letter.

184. Ibid., August 25, 1927.

185. Ibid., June 20, 1934.

186. Ibid., October 27, 1933, and December 18, 1934.

187. Kenway Lee, "Jascha Heifetz's Carlo Tononi Violin, 1736," *The Strad*, January 1995.

188. Exchange rates from http://www.sammler.com/coins/inflation.htm, accessed September 11, 2005.

189. Wechsberg, "Trustee in Fiddledale-I"; Burton, *Menuhin*, pp. 86ff.

190. Peter Herrmann, interview with the author, Berlin, November 7, 1997.

191. Wechsberg, "Trustee in Fiddledale-I," p. 38.

192. Wechsberg, "Trustee in Fiddledale-II," p. 48; Doring, *How Many Strads?*, pp. 121, 149; http://www.cozio.com/Owner.aspx?id=200 and http://www.hfmgv.org/exhibits/pic/1999/99.feb .html, accessed February 23, 2005.

193. Stuart Pollens, "Travelling Apprenticeship," *The Strad*, December 1986.

194. Kenneth Warren, "Rembert Wurlitzer: An Appreciation," *The Strad*, December 1963; Charles Beare, "Wurlitzer, Rembert," *Grove Music Online*, accessed February 21, 2005, http:// www.grovemusic.com.proxy.lib.uiowa.edu.

195. Pollens, "Travelling Apprenticeship."

196. Beare, "Wurlitzer, Rembert."

197. *New York Times*, October 22, 1963, p. 37; *Time*, "Milestones," November 1, 1963.

198. Stuart Pollens, "Morel Responsibility," *The Strad*, June 1986.

199. E-mails to the author, February 23–24, 2005.

200. Douglas Martin, "Jacques Francais, 80, Dealer in String Instruments, Dies," *New York Times*, February 8, 2004.

201. Interview with the author, London, July 9, 1997.

202. Interview with the author, London, September 21, 2000.

203. Tony Faber, *Stradivari's Genius*, New York 2004, p. 197.

204. Harold C. Schonberg, "Record $200,000 Is Bid for a Strad," *New York Times*, June 4, 1971; Geraldine Keen, "Record £84.000 Paid for a Stradivari Violin," *Times* (London), June 4, 1971.

205. Herman Van der Wee, *Prosperity and Upheaval*, Berkeley and Los Angeles 1987, p. 260.

206. Paul Kennedy, *The Rise and Fall of the Great Powers*, New York 1987, pp. 432, 436.

207. Data from Society of Motor Manufacturers and Traders' Yearbooks, 1950, http://imvp.mit .edu/papers/93/Graves/graves-1.pdf, accessed March 1, 2005.

208. Van der Wee, *Prosperity*, pp. 128–29.

209. Ibid., pp. 133, 85–87.

210. Robert Lacey, *Sotheby's: Bidding for Class*, Boston 1998, pp. 105–7.

211. Peter Horner, interview with the author, London, June 17, 1999.

212. Graham Wells, interview with the author, London, July 7, 1997.

213. Deborah Brewster, "Violins Can Add Value to a Finely Tuned Portfolio," *Financial Times* (U.S. edition), April 11, 2003.

214. Christopher Mason, *The Art of the Steal*, New York 2004, p. 251.

215. Interview with the author, London, June 17, 1999.

216. E-mail to the author, March 18, 2005.

217. Neil Grauer, "Heavenly Strings," *Cigar Aficionado*, http://www.cigaraficionado.com/Cigar/ Aficionado/goodlife/fm1295.html, accessed March 18, 2005.

218. Interview with the author, London, June 18, 1999.

219. "The Highly Strung Market for Violins," *Economist*, June 27, 1998.

220. Interview with the author, London, June 1, 1998.

221. "Art Records Tumble at Christie's HK Auction," Reuters, May 25, 2008.

222. See http://www.violin-fund.ru/eng/partners/, accessed November 25, 2005; e-mail to the author from Regina Imatdinova, Violin-Fund, Moscow, December 5, 2005.

223. Sophia Kishkovsky, "Rare Violin in the Spotlight," *New York Times*, November 21, 2005; Maria Levitov, "$1M Violin Bought by Russian," *St. Petersburg Times*, November 4, 2005.

224. See http://www.legalintel.ru/eng/, accessed November 25, 2005.

225. See http://www.rfu.ru/english/index.asp, accessed November 25, 2005.

226. Levitov, "$1M Violin."

227. Dalya Alberge, "Richest Sounding Violin Sells for a Record-Breaking Price," *Times* (London), February 14, 2008; Helen Womack, "Prized Violin Again Plays for Moscow's Elite," *Guardian*, March 24, 2008; Sophia Kishkovsky, "A Treasure Is Restored," *New York Times*, May 8, 2008.

228. Goodkind, *Violin Iconography*, p. 27.

229. Faber, *Stradivari's Genius*, New York 2004, pp. 196ff.

230. Charles Beare and Margaret Campbell, "Beare," *Grove Music Online*, accessed April 9, 2005, http://www.grovemusic.com.proxy.lib.uiowa.edu; "Beare Move," *The Strad*, February 2000, p. 117.

231. John Willman, "The Big, the Small and the Extra-Nifty," *Financial Times*, April 21, 2008.

232. Naomi Sadler, "The Wow Factor," *The Strad*, April 2005, p. 39.

233. Interview with the author, London, July 9, 1997.

234. Charles Beare, *Capolavori di Antonio Stradivari*, Milan 1987.

235. Interview with the author, London, June 2, 1998.

236. "Warum André Rieu die Stradivari kaufte," *Welt am Sonntag*, November 25, 1998.

237. Michael van Eekeren, "Kartel Houdt Macht over Stradivarius-Onderzoek," *Volkskrant*, January 29, 1999.

238. Anne-Catherine Hutton, "Christoph Landon, Luthier: un artisan en quête du Graal," *La Scena Musicale*, May 1999.

239. "Meister-Geiger Rieu gibt Stradivari zurück," *Welt am Sonntag*, December 20, 1998.

240. Interview with Willem Bouman, The Hague, June 23, 1999.

241. *Journal of the Violin Society of America* 17, no. 3, 2001, pp. 203–4.

242. E-mail to the author, May 3, 2005.

243. *The Strad*, December 1994, p. 1193.

244. "Rieu Hat wieder eine Stradivari," Associated Press Worldstream, September 30, 2001.

245. James M. Fleming, "The 'Court' Stradivari," reprinted in Goodkind, *Violin Iconography*, pp. 88ff.

246. Hill's diary, January 22, 1897.

247. Anne Inglis, "The Flying Fiddle," *The Strad*, October 1991.

248. Ibid.

249. Alix Kirsta, "Fiddles," *Guardian*, August 30, 2002.

250. John Dilworth, e-mail to the author, November 8, 2004.

251. Inglis, "The Flying Fiddle."

252. Andrew Hooker, *Mr. Black's Violins*, Boston 2009, passim.

253. Kirsta, "Fiddles."

254. Inglis, "The Flying Fiddle."

255. Michael Peppiatt, "The Art of The Deal," *New York Times Book Review*, September 19, 2004.

256. E-mail to the author, April 26, 2005.

257. See http://www.oursites.org/robertbein/myself.htm, accessed May 13, 2005.

258. "Sex and Music," *Playboy*, April 1998.

259. Kirsta, "Fiddles"; Howard Reich and William Gaines, "Dealers Gain Collector's Trust," *Chicago Tribune*, June 17, 2001.

260. Reich and Gaines, "Dealers Gain."

261. Interview with the author, Chicago, Illinois, April 3, 1998.

262. Christopher Reuning, Expert's Report Served on Behalf of the Defendant in the Case between the Claimants Timothy Douglas White and Wilson Peter Cotton, and defendant Peter Biddulph, January 5, 2001, p. 18, unpublished.

263. Robert Bein, interview with author, Chicago, Illinois, September 9, 2000.

264. Charles Beare, "Robert Bein 1950–2007," *The Strad*, July 2007.

265. Ted C. Fishman, "The Chinese Century," *New York Times Magazine*, July 4, 2004.

266. Bein & Fushi Inc., Special China Edition, no. 16, p. 8.

267. Roger Hargrave, "Machold Remembered," *The Strad*, April 1995.

268. Interview with the author, Bremen, December 9, 1997.

269. Ibid.

270. Carsten Holm, "How the World's Top Stradivarius Dealer Misplayed," *Der Spiegel*, May 10, 2012.

271. David Schoenbaum and Elizabeth Pond, *The German Question and Other German Questions*, Basingstoke, London, and New York 1996, pp. 113–19.

272. See http://www.scctv.net/Entrepreneur.asp, accessed May 24, 2005.

273. "The Foresight Saga, Continued," *Economist*, January 4, 2003.

274. Kristin Suess, "Violins as Investment," College-Conservatory of Music and College of Business Administration, University of Cincinnati, March 13, 1999, unpublished.

275. Philip E. Margolis, "Investing in Old Italian String Instruments," Cozio Publishing, June 2006.

276. Diary, September 13, 1892, unpublished.

277. See http://www.thebullionexchange.com/austrian_philharmonic_gold_coins.htm, accessed May 23, 2005.

278. Wolfgang Höritsch, Austrian National Bank, interview with the author, Vienna, October 5, 2000; cf. catalogue, "Der klingende Schatz der Oesterreichischen Nationalbank," Vienna, December 20–21, 1996, p. 9.

279. See www.energytech.at/(de)/sanierung/results/id2513.html, accessed May 24, 2005.

280. Carsten Holm, "Der Tiefe Fall des Stradivari-Dealers," *Der Spiegel*, April 15, 2011.

281. Interview with the author, Cambridge, July 10, 1997.

282. Antony Thorncroft, "Bank on a Strad," *Financial Times*, August 13, 1995.

283. Interview with the author, Cambridge, September 19, 2000.

284. E-mail to the author from Martin Eifler, Federal Commission for Culture and Media, Berlin, January 17, 2001.

285. See http://www.soundpostonline.com/archive/spring2002/page4.htm, accessed May 25, 2005.

286. See http://www.cozio.com/Instrument.aspx?id=121, accessed May 25, 2005.

287. Koh Huiting, "Pulling Strings," *Business Times* (Singapore), April 15, 2000.

288. Susan Elliott, "Musician and 15 Partners Join Forces to Aquire a Multimillion-Dollar Violin," *New York Times*, February 6, 2001.

289. Press release, Long Term Capital Company, Westport, Connecticut, December 8, 2004.

290. Telephone interview with the author, June 6, 2005.

291. "Protecting Capital with an Austrian Twist," *Chamber News*, United States–Austrian Chamber of Commerce, October 2003.

292. David Schoenbaum, "Washington, Stradivarius Capital," *Washington Post*, October 21, 2011.

293. Auction Preview, Winter 2004, http://www.actecfoundation.org/newsletter/Foundation .pdf, accessed May 25, 2005.

294. Interview with the author, Minneapolis, Minnesota, May 15, 1998.

295. Kay Miller, "Working Like a Dog," *Minneapolis Star-Tribune*, June 18, 2003.

296. Mary VanClay, "Mysteries of the Market," *Strings*, November 1996, pp. 18–20.

297. See http://www.givensviolins.com/about/privacy.asp, accessed May 30, 2005; "La Voce," Newsletter of Claire Givens, Inc., Fall 1998. Cf. Susan M. Barbieri, "An Elegy for Ethics," *Strings*, May–June 2002.

298. Interview with the author, Ann Arbor, Michigan, June 6, 1998.

299. See http://www.wheaton.edu/learnres/ARCSC/collects/sc32/bio.htm, accessed May 31, 2005.

300. See http://www.ups.com/content/us/en/about/history/1980.html, accessed June 1, 2005.

301. http://www.alalm.org/Articles/Article3.htm, accessed June 1, 2005.

302. See "At the Auctions: Are Major Changes Under Way?," *Soundpost*, Fall 2000, http://www .soundpostonline.com/archive/fall2000/page11.html, accessed June 12, 2005.

303. Lauren Foster, "Art Buyers Urged to Be Aware as Internet Auction Fraud Soars," *Financial Times* (U.S. edition), April 25, 2003.

304. Erin White, "When a Strange Pursuit Becomes a Career Path," *Wall Street Journal*, July 19, 2005.

305. Prospectus for Lady Blunt sale, May 2011.

306. Laurinel Owen, "Virtually Yours," *The Strad*, November 2003.

307. See http://www.tarisio.com/auction_results/auction_results_sort.php?q_type=6&kws=Odd one,%20Carlo%20Giuseppe&TPS=10, accessed June 12, 2005.

308. Deborah Brewster, "Violins Can Add Value," *Financial Times*, April 11, 2003.

309. Norman Lebrecht, "On the Fiddle," January 5, 2005, http://www.scena.org/columns/ lebrecht/050105-NL-fiddle.html.

310. Stewart Pollens, "Eye for Detail," *The Strad*, July 2005.

311. "Stern Lawsuit Settled," *Strings*, August–September 2005; Noreen Gillespie, "Children of the Late Violinist Isaac Stern Challenge Handling of Father's Estate," Associated Press Worldstream, December 8, 2004; Dan Glaister, "Children in Court Battle over Isaac Stern's Estate," *Guardian*, December 9, 2004; Lawrence Gelder, "Arts Briefly," *New York Times*, May 6, 2005.

312. See http://www.violinist.com/discussion/response.cfm?ID=3952, April 21–22, 2004.

313. "EU fines Sotheby's for Price-Fixing," *Guardian*, October 30, 2002; Jennifer Dixon, "Taubman convicted," *Detroit Free Press*, December 5, 2001.

314. OED Online, accessed July 13, 2005.

315. Pasqual and Regazzi, *Le Radici*, p. 74.

316. Carlo Chiesa, "Violin Making and Making on the Contrada Larga in Milan," *Violin Society of America* 14, no. 3, 1996.

317. Duane Rosengard, "Rugeri," *The Strad*, November 2006, p. 96.

318. Chiesa and Rosengard, "Giuseppe Guarneri," in Biddulph et al., *Giuseppe Guarneri*, vol. 2, pp. 37ff.

319. "Twalf Jaar Geëist Wegen Roofmord op Vioolbouwer in Huizen," *NRC Handelsblad*, February 9, 1990; "Straffen Tot Tien Jaar na Doden van Vioolbouwer," *NRC Handelsblad*, September 14, 1990.

320. "Der süße Ton der Stradivari," *Der Spiegel*, November 18, 1996.

321. "Der Fall 'Stradivari,' Beobachtungen bei der Bremer Mordkommission," Radio Bremen TV, May 28, 1997, http://www.radiobremen.de/tv/daecher/archiv/105.html, accessed July 18, 2005. Cf. "Blick auf den Bildschirm: Fernsehkrimis sind Anders," *Neue Zürcher Zeitung*, July 31, 1997.

322. "Drei von Vier Entflohenen Geschnappt," Associated Press Worldstream, February 10, 1997; Kerstin Schneider, "Lebenslänglich trotz Freispruchs," *Taz*, November 7, 1998.

323. Jakob und Wilhelm Grimm, "Die Bremer Stadtmusikanten," *Kinder- und Haus Märchen*, Darmstadt 1955, Vol. I, p. 151.

324. "Strassenmusiker in Europa," interview with Vasile Darnea, Radio Bremen, June 2, 2003, http://www.radiobremen.de/online/gesellschaft/strassenmusik.html, accessed July 19, 2005.

325. Sonia Simmenauer, *Muss Es Sein?*, Berlin 2008, p. 23.

326. Johannes Willms, "Die Räuber," *Süddeutsche Zeitung*, April 16, 1999; Willem de Vries, *Sonderstab Musik*, Cologne 1998, p. 76; Shirli Gilbert, *Music in the Holocaust*, Oxford 2005, p. 130.

327. U.S. National Archives and Records Administration, Record Group 242, Roll, M1949, Roll 20.

328. Interview with Martin Eifler, Office of the Federal Commissioner for Culture and Media, Berlin, December 15, 2000.

329. Alan Riding, "Your Stolen Art? I Threw It Away, Dear," *New York Times*, May 17, 2002; Todd Sechser, "Financing Nuclear Security," Proliferation Brief, Carnegie Endowment for International Peace, December 7, 1999.

330. Mirka Zemanová, "Like Father Like Son," *The Strad*, September 1991.

331. Pasqual and Regazzi, *Le Radici*, pp. 110ff.

332. William K. Rashbaum, "An Upper West Side Mystery: The Vanished Stradivarius," *New York Times*, April 13, 2002; William Hoffman, "Case of the Missing Strad," *Dallas Business Journal*, September 27, 2002; Michael Markowitz, "Owner of the Missing Strad Sues Dealer That Lost It," Andante.com, September 26, 2002; Roy Appleton, "Stolen Fiddle Has Yielded a Fiddle Battle," *Dallas Morning News*, November 17, 2002; Michael Collins, Bickel & Brewer, Dallas, Texas, telephone interview with the author, August 30, 2005.

333. Pasqual and Regazzi, *Le Radici*, pp. 110ff.

334. Daniel Pearl, "Stradivarius Violin, Lost Years Ago, Resurfaces but New Owner Plays Coy," *Wall Street Journal*, October 17, 1994.

335. Carla Shapreau, "The Adventures of the Duke of Alcantara," *The Strad*, May 1996. Cf. Harvey and Shapreau, *Violin Fraud*, pp. 107ff.; University of California, Los Angeles, press release; http://www.cozio.com/Instrument.aspx?id=1405, accessed July 24, 2005.

336. See http://www.amromusic.com/violin_adventure.htm, accessed July 22, 2005; Chip Averwater, e-mail to the author, July 27, 2005.

337. Louis Spohr, *Selbstbiographie*, Cassel and Göttingen 1860, Vol. 1, pp. 55–56, 69–71.

338. Maurice Solway, *Recollections of a Violinist*, Oakville, New York, and London 1984, p. 47.

339. Arthur Train, "The Lost Stradivarius," in *True Stories of Crime from the District Attorney's Office*, New York 1908; http://www.cozio.com/Instrument.aspx?id=528, accessed June 12, 2008.

340. "Huberman Violin Stolen at Carnegie," *New York Times*, February 29, 1936.

341. Henry Roth, "Bronislaw Huberman," *The Strad*, December 1982; Nadine Brozan, "Chronicle," *New York Times*, June 11, 1993.

342. Charles Beare, "Lost and Found," *The Strad*, December 1987.

343. Carla Shapreau, "Did He or Didn't He?" *The Strad*, January 1998; James Pegolotti, "The Gibson Stradivarius: From Huberman to Bell," http://www.joshuabell.com/, accessed July 25, 2005.

344. Mark Wrolstad, "A Famed Violin's Fantastic Journey," *Dallas Morning News*, October 28, 2001.

345. Pierre Amoyal, *Pour l'Amour d'un Stradivarius*, Paris 2004, passim.

346. W. Henry Hill et al., *Antonio Stradivari*, pp. 211, 243–44.

347. Edward Heron-Allen, "Old Violin Frauds," *The Strad*, October 1890.

348. Hill's diary, February 4, 1890; Frederic C. Howe, *Socialized Germany*, New York 1916, p. 77; Gordon Johnson, *University Politics*, Cambridge 1994, p. 13.

349. Milliot, "La famille Chanot-Chardon," pp. 95ff.

350. "Dispute Regarding a Violin," *The Strad*, June–September 1890.

351. Hill's diary, September 24 and December 5, 1890; June 11 and July 4, 1891; February 18, 1892.

352. Ibid., January 15–16, 1890.

353. Ibid., March 12, 1895.

354. Ibid., June 29, July 7, and July 16, 1891.

355. Ibid., October 27, 1891.

356. Santoro, ed., *Le Celebrazioni*, pp. 19ff.

357. *Neue Zürcher Zeitung*, November 28, 1958.

358. Giovanni Iviglia, *Cremona Wie Es nicht Sein Soll*, Bellinzona-Lugano 1957, pp. 70, 78–79.

359. *Neue Zürcher Zeitung*, December 21, 1958.

360. Ibid., November 27, 1958.

361. Ibid., December 7, 1958.

362. Ibid., December 5, 1958.

363. Ibid., November 26, 1958.

364. Ibid., December 7, 1958.

365. Ibid., December 12, 1958. Cf. Frank Arnau, *Kunst der Fälscher, Fälscher der Kunst*, Munich and Zurich 1964, p. 364.

366. Memorandum of Decision, *Raymond A. Russell v. Kristina Lee Anderson*, Superior Court of California, County of Santa Cruz, No. CV 139974.

367. Jonathan Lopez, *The Man Who Made Vermeers*, Boston and New York 2009; "Kunstfälscher Muss Sechs Jahre in Haft," *Der Spiegel*, October 27, 2011.

368. Martin Bailey, "Rembrandt Research Project Ended," *The Art Newspaper*, February 24, 2011.

369. "Streit um Stradivari," *Süddeutsche Zeitung*, February 7, 1997; Matthias Oloew, "Alte Geigen—ein Schönes DDR-Erbe," *Der Tagesspiegel*, October 8, 1997; Hans-Jörg Heims, "Stradivari-Klänge beim Stabswechsel," *Süddeutsche Zeitung*, October 29, 1998.

370. Interview with Martin Eifler, Berlin, December 15, 2000; interview with Ingeborg Behnke, Berlin, November 28, 2000.

371. Carol Vogel, "The Case of the Servant with the Fur Collar," *New York Times*, September 22, 2005.

372. I. Bernard Cohen, "Faraday and Franklin's 'Newborn Baby,'" *Proceedings of the American Philosophical Society*, June 1987.

373. R. Bruce Weber, "Seeking Violin's Secrets with CAT Scan," *New York Times*, December 8, 1997; Erica R. Hendy, "Scanning a Stradivarius," *Smithsonian*, May 2010; http://www.bbc.co.uk/news/technology-15926864 (November 20, 2011); http://www.npr.org/2011/11/30/142949546/ct-scans-re-create-307-year-old-violin, accessed November 30, 2011; Brian Vastag, "Smithsonian's Scan Man in High Demand," *Washington Post*, December 12, 2011; e-mails from Gary Sturm, August 22, 2011; Joseph Curtin, August 24, 2011; Roger Hargrave, November 19, 2011.

374. Dieter Schorr, "Ein Himmel Voller Falscher Geigen," *Stuttgarter Nachrichten*, January 11, 1973.

375. Alain le Garsmeur, "Tuned for Battle," *New York Times Magazine*, September 10, 1972.

376. Schorr, "Ein Himmel"; Charles Beare, review of *Alte Meistergeigen: Beschreibungen, Experti-*

sen: Venezianischer Schule, Verband Schweizer Geigenbaumeister, Frankfurt 1978; *Early Music,* January 1978.

377. *Alte Meistergeigen* I–VIII, Frankfurt 1978–1996.

378. Charles Beare to the author, March 2005, with attached letter from Japanese correspondent of July 1999.

379. Douglas Heingartner, "A Computer That Has an Eye for Van Gogh," *New York Times,* June 13, 2004.

380. Roger Hargrave, "Identity Crisis," *The Strad,* July 2005.

381. See http://www.talkorigins.org/faqs/piltdown.html, accessed August 7, 2005.

382. Leslie Sheppard, "The 'Balfour' Strad," *The Strad,* January 1981.

383. Harvey and Shapreau, *Violin Fraud,* pp. 17ff.; e-mail from Charles Beare and telephone interview with Robert Bein, September 1, 2005.

384. Hargrave, "Identity Crisis."

385. See http://www.abcviolins.com/fidfad.html, accessed December 8, 2011.

386. Claudia Fritz et al., "Player Preferences among New and Old Violins," *Proceedings of the National Academy of Sciences,* www.pnas.org/cni/doi/10.173/pnas.1114999109; http://www.spiegel .de/wissenschaft/technik/0,1518,806748,00.html; http://www.npr.org/blogs/deceptivecadence/2012/ 01/02/144482863/double-blind-violin-test-can-you-pick-the-strad, accessed January 3, 2012; Joseph Curtin, "The Indianapolis Experiment," *The Strad,* February 2012.

387. Laurinel Owen, "Leading Light," *The Strad,* November 2004; "Presentation on How the Bow Produces Sound from the String," *Bulletin of the Southern California Association of Violin Makers,* July 1994.

388. Henry Grissino-Mayer, "A Familiar Ring," *Journal of the Violin Society of America* 17, no. 3, 2001, pp. 93ff.

389. Lesley Bannatyne, "Trees and Logs Have Tales to Tell," *Christian Science Monitor,* March 8, 2005, http://users.ox.ac.uk/~arch0050/; Aegean Dendrochronology Project, http://users.ox.ac .uk/~arch0050/, accessed August 20, 2005; http://en.wikipedia.org/wiki/Andrew_E._Douglass; Micha Beuting and Peter Klein, "The Technique of Dendrochronology as Applied to Stringed Instruments of the Orpheon Foundation," http://www.mdw.ac.at/I105/orpheon/Seiten/educa tion/DendroBeutingText.htm, accessed August 22, 2005.

390. W. Henry Hill et al., *Antonio Stradivari,* p. 61.

391. Ibid., p. 64.

392. Philip J. Kass, "Violin Making in Turin," *Journal of the Violin Society of America* 17, no. 3, 2001, p. 174; "Holes in History," *The Strad,* August 2001.

393. Roger Starr, "The Hidden Rooms Behind Museum Displays," *City Journal,* Spring 1995.

394. Stewart Pollens, *The Violin Forms of Antonio Stradivari,* London 1992.

395. Panel Discussion on the Messiah Stradivari, *Journal of the Violin Society of America* 17, no. 3, 2001, pp. 208–9; Jim McKean and Colin Macfarlane, "Strad Keeper Bows to Fake Claims," *Scotland on Sunday,* May 17, 1998.

396. Stewart Pollens, "Le Messie," *Journal of the Violin Society of America* 16, no. 1, 1999.

397. Stewart Pollens, "'Messiah' on Trial," *The Strad,* August 2001; e-mail to the author, August 22, 2005.

398. W. Henry Hill et al., *Antonio Stradivari,* pp. 64–65.

399. Faber, *Stradivari's Genius,* pp. 32, 52–57, 210ff.

400. Bacchetta, *Stradivari,* pp. 77ff.

401. Pollens, "'Messiah' on Trial."

402. Giles Whittell, "A Stradivarius Riddle," *Times* (London), October 27, 2000.

403. John Topham and Derek McCormick, "A Dendrochronological Investigation of Stringed

Instruments of the Cremonese School (1666–1757), including 'The Messiah' Violin Attributed to Antonio Stradivari," *Journal of Archaeological Science* 27, 2000, pp. 183–92.

404. Panel Discussion on the Messiah Stradivari, pp. 192–93. Cf. http://www.sound postonline. com/archive/fall2000/page17.html;   http://soundpostonline.com/archive/winter2001/page7.html, accessed August 28, 2005; Kristen Thorner, "Into the Woods," *The Strad*, August 2001.

405. "Oxford 'Messiah' Branded a Fake," *Times* (London), March 15, 1999; "Famous Violin Comes Under Fresh Scrutiny," *Wall Street Journal*, March 11, 1999; "Stradivari's Masterpiece May Be Fake," *Independent*, March 20, 1999.

406. Panel Discussion on the Messiah Stradivari, p. 182.

407. Ibid., p. 191.

408. Ibid., p. 154.

409. Ibid., p. 210.

410. Henri D. Grissino-Mayer et al., "Mastering the Rings," *The Strad*, April 2002; Henri D. Grissino-Mayer, Paul R. Sheppard, and Malcolm K. Cleaveland, "Dendrochronological Dating of Stringed Instruments," *Journal of the Violin Society of America* 18, no. 2, 2003; Henri D. Grissino-Mayer, Paul R. Sheppard, and Malcolm K. Cleaveland, "A Dendrochronological Reexamination of the 'Messiah' Violin and Other Instruments Attributed to Antonio Stradivari," *Journal of Archaeological Science* 31, 2004.

411. Interview with the author, Oxford, December 16, 2009.

412. Grissino-Mayer, "Mastering the Rings," p. 415.

413. John Dilworth, "Pure Thrill," *The Strad*, August 2001, p. 843.

414. Philip J. Kass, e-mail to the author, August 19, 2005.

415. Samuel Applebaum and Henry Roth, *The Way They Play*, Vol. 8, Neptune, New Jersey 1980, p. 185.

416. Interview with the author, Chicago, Illinois, April 3, 1998.

417. See http://www.fritz-reuter.com/reports/, accessed September 10, 2005.

418. Giacomo Leopardi, *Pensieri*, New York and Oxford 1981, p. 28.

419. Geoffrey Fushi, interview with the author, Chicago, Illinois, April 4, 1998; "Be Careful What You Say About a Competitor," *Music Trades*, September 1992; "The Battle Rages," *Strings*, January–February 1993, p. 9.

420. "Die unreinen Töne des Violinisten Yoshio Unno," *Neue Zürcher Zeitung*, December 12–13, 1981; Geraldine Norman, "Many a New Fiddle," *Times* (London), May 27, 1982.

421. Ibid.; Dick Cooper, "Dealer Accused of Blocking Probe," *Philadelphia Inquirer*, March 11, 1982; "Violin Maker Sentenced," *Philadelphia Inquirer*, September 23, 1982.

422. Decision of Interest, *New York Law Journal* 231, February 3, 2004, p. 19.

423. Ibid.

424. Ibid.

425. Michael D. Sorkin and Philip Kennicott, "Indicted Dealer Must Face the Music," *St. Louis Post-Dispatch*, June 14, 1997.

426. Telephone interview with Kurt Sassmannshaus, February 5, 2002.

427. Michael D. Sorkin and Philip Kennicott, "Violin Dealer Leaves Trail of Angry Victims," *St. Louis Post-Dispatch*, March 3, 1997.

428. Michael D. Sorkin and Philip Kennicott, "Violin Dealer Is Sentenced to 2 Years for Fraud," *St. Louis Post-Dispatch*, December 12, 1997.

429. Michael D. Sorkin, "Lawyers Ask Judge to Force Violin Thief to Repay," *St. Louis Post-Dispatch*, February 13, 1998.

430. Ibid.

431. Michael D. Sorkin, "I'm Sorry: Violin Thief Vows to Repay Victims," *St. Louis Post-Dispatch*, February 27, 1998.

432. For example, "Discovery Rules Override Policy to Protect Settlement Disclosure," *Federal Discovery News*, January 14, 2002.

433. Gwendolyn Freed, "Lawsuit Frays Strings of Trust in High-Priced, Secretive World," *Minneapolis Star-Tribune*, February 20, 2000.

434. Declaration of Timothy Douglas White, No. 99 C 1740, United States District Court, Northern District of Illinois, Eastern Division, July 7, 1999.

435. Ibid.

436. Reich and Gaines, "Dealers Gain."

437. Robert Bein, interview with the author, Chicago, Illinois, September 9, 2000.

438. Ibid.

439. Cited in Declaration of Timothy White.

440. Cited in Interim Report, In the High Court of Justice, Ch 1997, W No. 1651, May 22, 1998, http://hrothgar.co.uk/YAWS/ch_g/pt26.htm#case-02, accessed October 8, 2005.

441. Ibid.

442. Ibid.

443. Cited in Memorandum Opinion and Order, No. 99 C 1740, United States District Court, Northern District of Illinois, Eastern Division, January 14, 2000.

444. See http://www.mgrewal.com/anton.htm; http://en.wikipedia.org/wiki/Anton_Piller_order, accessed October 6, 2005.

445. Cited in Memorandum Opinion and Order, No. 99 C 1740, United States District Court, Northern District of Illinois, Eastern Division, January 14, 2000.

446. Ibid.

447. Cited in Interim Report, In the High Court of Justice, Ch. 1997, W. No. 1651, May 22, 1998.

448. Kirsta, "Fiddles."

449. Interim report, In the High Court of Justice, Ch. 1997, W. No. 1651, May 22, 1998.

450. Kirsta, "Fiddles."

451. See http://www.naxos.com/scripts/Artists_gallery/artist_pro_new.asp?Artist_Name=Anthony, %20Adele, accessed December 2, 2005.

452. Kevin McKeough, "Power Play," *Strings*, April 2002.

453. Kirsta, "Fiddles."

454. HC 1997 01651, In the High Court of Justice, Chancery Division, Mr. Justice Evans-Lombe, February 15, 2001.

455. "Biddulph on the Move," *The Strad*, November 2005.

456. Reich and Gaines, "Dealers Gain."

457. Judge Wayne R. Andersen, United States District Court, Northern District of Illinois, Case No. 99C 1740, January 13, 2005.

458. *The Strad*, June 2002.

459. Mark Mueller, "US Senate Checking NJSO Violin Deal," *Newark Star-Ledger*, June 24, 2004; Lynnley Brown, "Senate Committee Questions Actions by Smithsonian," *New York Times*, June 24, 2004; Jacqueline Trescott, "Smithsonian Benefactor Arrested in Germany," *Washington Post*, June 17, 2004.

460. Mark Levine, "Medici of the Meadowlands," *New York Times Magazine*, August 3, 2003.

461. Mark Mueller, "False Notes," *Newark Star-Ledger*, August 1, 2004.

462. Alix Kirsta, "Orchestra Manoeuvres in the Dark," *Guardian*, June 11, 2005; Levine, "Medici of the Meadowlands"; "One of Our Vice Presidents Is in Trouble," Federation of British Aquatic Societies, April 2003, http://www.fbas.co.uk/herbert.html, https://www.njsymphony.org/GoldenAge/goldenageframe.htm, accessed February 23, 2003

463. Levine, "Medici of the Meadowlands."

464. Dr. Herbert R. Axelrod, ed., *Heifetz*, Neptune City, New Jersey 1990, p. 9.

465. Stefan Hersh, "Problem Children," http://www.soundpostonline.com/archive/summer2004/page4.htm, accessed October 26, 2005.

466. Mueller, "False Notes."

467. New Jersey Symphony Orchestra fact sheet, https://www.njsymphony.org/GoldenAge/goldenageframe.htm, February 14, 2003.

468. Jennifer Fried, "Financing in D Major," *American Lawyer*, September 2003.

469. Kirsta, "Orhestral Manoeuvres."

470. Mueller, "False Notes."

471. Ibid.

472. Fried, "Financing."

473. Gwendolyn Freed, "A Violin Bargain, Strings Attached," *Wall Street Journal*, March 4, 2003; Fried, "Financing"; Mueller, "False Notes"; Levine, "Medici of the Meadowlands."

474. www.investor.prudential.com/MediaRegister.cfm?MediaID=7294, accessed February 23, 2003; "New Jersey Symphony to Purchase Stradivarius Violins," *Bloomberg News*, February 19, 2003.

475. "The 60 Largest American Charitable Contributions of the Year," *Chronicle of Philanthropy*, www.slate.com/id/2094847/, accessed October 29, 2005.

476. "Report: US Fugitive Relaxing in Cuba," Associated Press, April 25, 2004; Ronald Smothers, "Fraud Charges Greet Charitable Collector," *New York Times*, June 17, 2004.

477. Originaltext-Service, Vienna, June 20, 2004, http://www.presseportal.at/meldung.php?schluessel=OTS_20040620_OTS0003&ch=medien, accessed October 30, 2005.

478. Mueller, "False Notes."

479. Levine, "Medici of the Meadowlands."

480. Ronald Smothers, "Violin Collector Known for Sale to Orchestra Is Sentenced to 18 Months in Tax Fraud," *New York Times*, March 22, 2005.

481. See http://www.legal-dictionary.org/legal-dictionary-u/Unjust-Enrichment.asp, accessed November 5, 2005.

482. Mark Mueller, "Axelrod Admits Guilt to Tax Fraud Charge," *Newark Star-Ledger*, December 9, 2004.

483. Daniel Wakin, "Report Faults Orchestra Officials," *New York Times*, December 18, 2004.

484. Telephone interview with the author, January 7, 2010.

485. Paul Cox, "NJ Symphony Sells Its Ill-Fated Strings to Twin Investment Bankers," *Newark Star-Ledger*, November 23, 2007; Daniel Wakin, "Orchestra Will Sell a Collection in Dispute," *New York Times*, November 24, 2007.

486. All figures from www.tarisio.com, accessed January 8, 2010.

487. Roger Altman, "The Great Crash, 2008," *Foreign Affairs*, January–February 2009; Tami Lubhi, "Americans' Wealth Drops $1.3 Trillion," CNNMoney.com, June 11, 2009.

488. Philip J. Kass, "A Famed Fiddler Parts with the Fabled 'Kochanski,'" *Strings*, February 2010, p. 56; Caroline Gill, "A Bargain at $18M," *The Strad*, December 2009, p. 20.

489. Richard Osley and Kate Salter, "Fall of the Russian Billionaires," *Independent*, February 15, 2009; "Number of Russian Billionaires Halves," *Telegraph*, February 14, 2009; "The Russian Billionaire's Guide to London," July 2, 2008, http://www.youtube.com/watch?v=Sn6B45Ukexo, accessed January 10, 2010.

490. Gill, "A Bargain."

491. Ibid.

492. See http://www.violinist.com/blog/SMSHCT/20101/10827/, accessed January 12, 2010.

493. "Machold Quites New York to Go West," *The Strad*, April 2006, p. 10.

494. Carsten Holm, "Der Stradivari-Wahn," *Der Spiegel*, December 10, 2007.

495. Daniela Filz, "Schlossherr in Geldnöten," *Niederösterreichische Nachrichten*, November 2, 2010; "Eröffnete Insolvenzen," *Wirtschaftsblatt*, November 3, 2010; Carsten Holm, "Ein Reicher Mann Vergeigt Sein Schloss," *Der Spiegel*, November 28, 2010; David Schoenbaum, "Das Griechenland der Musikwelt," *Frankfurter Allgemeine Zeitung*, December 22, 2010.

496. Josef Kleinrath and Daniela Filz, "Schlossbesitzer in Haft," *Niederösterreichische Nachrichten*, March 28, 2011; Renate Graber, "Millionen mit Stradivaris Vergeigt," *Der Standard*, March 31, 2011; Mark Mueller, "Violin Broker Probed in New Jersey Symphony Orchestra Deal Now Faces Fraud Charges in Austria," *Newark Star-Ledger*, April 3, 2011.

497. Interviews with the author, New York, October 15, 2009, and Chicago, Illinois, December 14, 2009.

BOOK 3: PLAYING IT

1. William Henry Hill et al., *The Violin-Makers of the Guarneri Family*, pp. xxx–xxxiii; Chiesa and Rosengard, "Guarneri del Gesù," in Biddulph et al., in *Giuseppe Guarneri*, vol. 2, p. 17.

2. Joseph Baretti, *An Account of the Manners and Customs of Italy: with Observations on the Mistakes of Some Travellers, with Regard to That Country*, London 1768, vol. 1, p. 150.

3. Quoted by M. Alexandra Eddy, "American Violin Method-Books and European Teachers," *American Music*, Summer 1990, p. 188.

4. William B. Boulton, *Thomas Gainsborough: His Life, Work, Friends and Sitters*, Chicago and London 1907, pp. 121–22. Cf. Mary Cyr, "Carl Friedrich Abel's Solos: A Musical Offering to Gainsborough?" *Musical Times*, June 1987, pp. 317–21.

5. Helen Cripe, *Thomas Jefferson and Music*, Charlottesville, Virginia 1974, pp. 12ff.

6. Richard Metternich, *Memoirs of Prince Metternich*, London 1880, Vol. 1, p. 363; Geraldine de Courcy, *Paganini: The Genoese*, Norman, Oklahoma 1957, Vol. I, pp. 193–94.

7. See http://www.paulkleezentrum.ch/ww/en/pub/web_root/act/musik/paul_klee_und_die _musik.cfm, accessed December 15, 2008.

8. Michele Leight, http://www.thecityreview.com/matpic.html, accessed December 15, 2008. Cf. Martin Boyd, "Pleasure Seekers," *The Strad,* April 1998, pp. 356–61.

9. Lochner, *Fritz Kreisler*, pp. 1ff.; Amy Biancolli, *Fritz Kreisler*, Portland, Oregon 1998, p. 26; Oliver Sacks, *Musicophilia*, New York 2007, pp. 320–23.

10. See http://www.surgical-tutor.org.uk/default-home.htm?surgeons/billroth.htm~right, accessed December 17, 2008; F. William Sunderman, "Theodore Billroth as Musician," *Bulletin of the Medical Library Association*, May 1937; Benjamin Simkin, Reader's Letter, *The Strad*, October 2001.

11. Douglas Martin, "F. William Sunderman, Doctor and Scientist, Dies at 104," *New York Times*, March 17, 2003.

12. Henri Temianka, *Facing the Music*, New York 1973, pp. 83–85, 110.

13. Kenneth Chang, "Martin D. Kamen, 89, a Discoverer of Radioactive Carbon-14," *New York Times*, September 5, 2002; Pearce Wright, "Martin Kamen," Guardian.co.uk, September 9, 2002.

14. Arthur Hill, letter to Harrison Bowne Smith, unpublished, February 7, 1935; Arthur I. Miller, "A Genius Finds Consolation in the Music of Another," *New York Times*, January 31, 2006; Roy Malan, *Efrem Zimbalist*, Pompton Plains, New Jersey 2004, p. 155.

15. Dave Wilbur, "Robert Byrd, Mountain Fiddler," in John Lilly, ed., *Mountains of Music*, Urbana, Illinois 1999.

16. See http://www.thehenryford.org/exhibits/pic/1999/99.feb.html, accessed February 22, 2005.

17. See http://www.archives.gov/global-pages/larger-image.html?i=/publications/prologue/2007/

spring/images/schoolhouse-rn-violin-l.jpg&c=/publications/prologue/2007/spring/images/ schoolhouse-rn-violin.ca, accessed December 31, 2008.

18. See http://en.wikipedia.org/wiki/Nicholas_Longworth, accessed December 19, 2008; Clara Longworth de Chambrun, *The Making of Nicholas Longworth*, New York 1933, pp. 210ff.; Carol Felsenthal, *The Life and Times of Alice Roosevelt Longworth*, New York 1988, p. 151; "Longworth to Fiddle," *New York Times,* June 15, 1912; Malan, *Efrem Zimbalist*, p. 155.

19. Laura Kalman, *Abe Fortas*, New Haven, Connecticut 1990, pp. 9–10, 193–94; "Chief Confidant to Chief Justice," *Time*, July 5, 1968.

20. Helen Rappoport, *Joseph Stalin: A Biographical Companion*, Santa Barbara, California 1999, pp. 298–300; Shimon Naveh, "Tukhachevsky," in Harold Shukman, ed., *Stalin's Generals*, London 1993, pp. 257–58; Laurel E. Fay, *Shostakovich*, New York 2000, p. 27.

21. Christer Jorgensen, *Hitler's Espionage Machine*, Guilford, Connecticut 2004, p. 46; David Kahn, *Hitler's Spies*, New York 1978, pp. 61, 232; http://www.youtube.com/watch?v=rV25q UZcZt8, accessed December 21, 2008.

22. E. Millicent Sowerby, *Rare People and Rare Books*, London 1967, p. 36. Cf. Anthony Read, *The Devil's Disciples*, New York 2004, p. 396.

23. Jonathan Petropoulos, *Art as Politics in the Third Reich*, Chapel Hill, North Carolina 1996, pp. 203, 260, 363 n. 130.

24. Harvey Sachs, *Music in Fascist Italy*, London 1987, pp. 11ff.

25. Beverly Smith, "Kreisler, Einstein, Mussolini," *Musical Observer*, May 1931.

26. Ariane Todes, "Charlie Chaplin," *The Strad*, December 2008.

27. Frank Cullen, Florence Hackman, and Donald McNeilly, *Vaudeville, Old and New*, New York 2007, p. 88.

28. Mervyn Rothstein, "Henny Youngman, King of the One-Liners, Is Dead at 91 after 6 Decades of Laughter," *New York Times*, February 25, 1998.

29. See https://www.cia.gov/news-information/featured-story-archive/marlene-dietrich.html, http://home.snafu.de/fright.night/musicalsaw1.htm. Cf. http://www.musicianguide.com/biogra phies/1608002307/Marlene-Dietrich.html, accessed December 27, 2008.

30. Graham Robb, *Balzac*, New York 1994, p. 10.

31. Wilborn Hampton, "Alfred Kazin, the Author Who Wrote of Literature and Himself, Is Dead at 83," *New York Times*, June 6, 1998.

32. Frank Kermode, *Not Entitled*, New York 1995, pp. 96ff.

33. Elna Sherman, "Music in Thomas Hardy's Life and Work," *Musical Quarterly*, October 1940.

34. Barbara Reynolds, *Dorothy L. Sayers: Her Life and Soul*, New York 1993, passim.

35. Juliet Barker, "Laurence Edward Alan Lee," *Oxford Dictionary of National Biography*, Oxford 2004, Vol. 33, pp. 89ff.

36. Anthony Trollope, *The Tireless Traveler*, Berkeley and London 1978, p. 164.

37. Fellowes, *Memoirs*, passim.

38. Catherine Drinker Bowen, *Friends and Fiddlers*, Boston 1937, pp. 47ff.

39. Ibid., p. 87.

40. Ibid., pp. 112–13.

41. Wayne Booth, *For the Love of It*, Chicago 2000, p. 209.

42. *ACMP Newsletter*, December 2002.

43. "For the Joy of It," *Time*, December 24, 1965; Karen Campbell, "Playing for the Fun of It," *Christian Science Monitor*, March 21, 1997; Daniel J. Wakin, "Devoted to Playing the Small Classics," *New York Times*, August 1, 2000; http://www.acmp.net/about, accessed December 29, 2008.

44. Bruno Aulich and Ernst Heimeran, *Das Stillvergnügte Streichquartett*, Munich 1936.

45. Lester Chafetz, *The Ill-Tempered String Quartet*, Jefferson, North Carolina, and London 1989.

46. See http://www.scandura.net/profile/history/, accessed January 17, 2005; http://www.bba aviation.com/about/grphistory26.htm, accessed December 31, 2008.

47. *Cobbett's Cyclopedic Survey of Chamber Music*, 2 vols., Oxford and Toronto 1929–30.

48. Ibid., Vol. 1, pp. 539ff.

49. Carl Flesch, *Die Kunst des Violinspiels*, Berlin 1928, Vol. 2, p. 73.

50. Bowen, *Friends and Fiddlers*, p. 249.

51. Holman, *Four and Twenty Fiddlers*, pp. 124–27.

52. Heinrich W. Schwab, "The Social Status of the Town Musician," and Dieter Krickeberg, "The Folk Musician in the 17th and 18th Centuries," in Walter Salmen, ed., *The Social Status of the Professional Musician from the Middle Age to the 19th Century*, New York 1983, pp. 34–35, 106, 119.

53. Christoph-Hellmut Mahling, "The Origin and Social Status of the Court Orchestral Musician in the 18th and early 19th Century in Germany," in Salmen, ed., *The Social Status*, passim.

54. Holman, *Four and Twenty Fiddlers*, p. 39.

55. Christoph Wolff et al., "Johann Sebastian Bach," in *Grove Music Online*, accessed January 11, 2009, http://www.grovemusic.com; Michael Talbot, "Vivaldi, Antonio," ibid., accessed February 10, 2009.

56. Boris Schwarz, *Great Masters of the Violin*, New York 1983, p. 49; Michael Talbot, "Arcangelo Corelli," in *Grove Music Online*, accessed January 12, 2009, http://www.grovemusic.com; Maynard Solomon, *Mozart*, New York 1995, p. 22.

57. Martha Feldman, *City Culture and the Madrigal at Venice*, Berkeley and London, 1995.

58. Francesco Geminiani, *The Art of Playing on the Violin*, David Boyden, ed., London 1952, p. xi.

59. Eddy, "American Violin-Method Books," p. 170.

60. Boris Schwarz, *Great Masters*, pp. 83–86; C. M. Sunday, "Francesco Geminiani—The Art of Playing the Violin," Connexions Module 13325, February 19, 2006, http://cnx.org/content/m13325/latest/, accessed January 16, 2009.

61. Leopold Mozart, *Versuch einer Gründlichen Violinschule*, Hans Joachim Moser, ed., Leipzig 1956, facsimile of Augsburg 1787 edition, p. 92.

62. Aristide Wirsta, Introduction, in L'Abbé Le Fils, *Principes du Violon*, 1761 edition, Paris 1961, p. viii.

63. Neal Zaslaw, "L'Abbé le fils," in *Grove Music Online*, accessed January 17, 2009, http://www.grovemusic.com; http://fr.wikipedia.org/wiki/Joseph-Barnab%C3%A9_Saint-Sevin_dit_L%27Abb%C3%A9_le_Fils, accessed February 1, 2009.

64. Wirsta, Introduction, in L'Abbé le fils, *Principes du Violon*, pp. viiiff.

65. Boyden, *The History*, p. vi.

66. Ibid., p. 361.

67. Ibid.

68. Mozart, *Versuch*, p. 221; David Boyden, "The Missing Italian Manuscript," *Music Quarterly*, July 1960, p. 316.

69. *A Letter from the Late Signor Tartini to Signora Maddalena Lombardini (now Signora Sirmen), Published as an Important Lesson to Performers on the Violin, translated by Dr. Burney*, London 1779, reprinted London 1913.

70. Robin Kay Deverich, "How Did They Learn?" http://www.violintutor.com/historyofviolinpedagogy.pdf, accessed May 13, 2009, pp. 12–13.

71. Eddy, "American Violin-Method Books," pp. 191ff.

72. Enrico Fubini, *Gli Enciclopedisti e la Musica*, Turin 1991, passim.

73. Ibid., p. 95.

74. Cynthia M. Geselle, "The Conservatoire de Musique and National Music Education in France, 1795–1801," in Malcolm Boyd, ed., *Music and the French Revolution*, Cambridge, UK, New York, and Victoria, Australia 1992.

75. Robin K. Deverich, "The Maidstone Movement," *Journal of Research in Music Education,* Spring 1987, pp. 39–55.

76. Deverich, "How Did They Learn?" pp. 17–22.

77. See http://www.uvm.edu/~mhopkins/string/?Page=history.html, accessed October 25, 2005.

78. Interview with the author, Aspen, Colorado, July 28, 1998.

79. Boris Schwarz, *Music and Musical Life in Soviet Russia*, Bloomington, Indiana 1983, pp. 397–98.

80. Miriam Morton, *The Arts and the Soviet Child*, New York 1972, pp. 139–44; John Dunstan, *Paths to Excellence and the Soviet School*, Windsor, Berks, UK 1998, pp. 59–80; Joseph Horowitz, "The Sound of Russian Music in the West," *New York Times*, June 11, 1978.

81. Yehudi Menuhin, *Unfinished Journey*, New York 1997, pp. 373–94.

82. Deverich, "How Did They Learn?" p. 24.

83. Evelyn Hermann, *Shinichi Suzuki*, Athens, Ohio 1981, passim.

84. Shinichi Suzuki, *Nurtured by Love*, Smithtown, New York 1969, pp. 78–79.

85. Margaret Mehl, "Land of the Rising Sisters," *The Strad*, May 2007.

86. See http://wapedia.mobi/de/Karl_Klingler, accessed May 22, 2009.

87. Staatl. Akademische Hochschule der Musik, Aufnahmeprotokoll, Violine und Bratsche, Sommerhalbjahr 1923.

88. "Every Child Can Become Rich in Musical Sense," reprinted in Hermann, *Shinichi Suzuki*, p. 140.

89. "Fiddling Legions," *Newsweek*, March 25, 1964.

90. Henri Temianka, *Facing the Music*, New York 1973, p. 69.

91. Interview with the author, Tokyo, September 24, 1992.

92. Sheryl WuDunn, "Shinichi Suzuki Dies at 99," *New York Times*, January 27, 1998; Anne Turner, "Shinichi Suzuki: Master of the Musical Method," *Guardian,* January 27, 1998; James Kirkup, "Shinichi Suzuki," *Independent,* January 27, 1998; "Shinichi Suzuki," *Economist*, February 7, 1998.

93. Interview with the author, Hong Kong, October 22, 2001.

94. E-mail to the author, May 18, 2009.

95. "The Law of Ability and the 'Mother Tongue Method' of Education," in Hermann, *Shinichi Suzuki*, p. 181.

96. Efrain Hernandez Jr., "The Violin as Bridge," *Boston Globe*, July 16, 1990; Joe McGonegal, "Violin Students Show Their Musical Stuff," *Wicked Local*, May 2, 2007.

97. E-mail to the author, May 18, 2009.

98. Evelyn Nieves, "Fiscal Cuts May Still Harm Harlem Pupils," *New York Times*, April 3, 1991; Allan Kozinn, "Musical Notes; Violinists to Play So Youngsters Can String Along," *New York Times*, July 6, 1993.

99. Richard Harrington, "A Violin Teacher's Unstrung Heroes," *Washington Post*, October 26, 1996; Meredith Kolodner, "Inauguration Thrill for Young Violinists, *New York Daily News*, December 3, 2008; http://www.petrafoundation.org/fellows/Roberta_Guaspari/index.html, accessed May 25, 2009.

100. Alex Ross, "Learning the Score," in *Listen to This*, New York 2010.

101. Geoff Edgers, "High Honors for Letting Music Go Free," http://www.boston.com/news/local/

rhode_island/articles/2010/10/20/high_honors_for_letting_music_go_free/, accessed October 25, 2010.

102. Megan Hall, "MacArthur 'Genius' Uses Music to Bring Social Justice," *All Things Considered*, National Public Radio, October 11, 2010; Ross, "Learning the Score."

103. Otto Pohl, "Helping Soweto Youth Make the Music of Their Lives," *New York Times*, November 22, 2003.

104. "South Africa 5th Sept 2010 Prt 2," http://www.youtube.com/watch?v=nO9nq5I9s9I&NR=1, accessed October 26, 2010.

105. Bob Simon, "The Strings of Soweto," *60 Minutes*, part 2, http://www.cbsnews.com/stories/2004/05/07/60II/main616247.shtml, accessed October 26, 2010; Tristan Jacob-Hoff, "The Joie de Vivre of Soweto's Young Musicians," http://www.guardian.co.uk/music/musicblog/2008/jan/31/sowetostringsnalden, accessed October 26, 2010.

106. Elaine Dutka, "Sound Out of Soweto," *Los Angeles Times*, April 4, 2001.

107. Chris Hawley, "Venezuela Drug Trade Booms," *USA Today*, July 21, 2010.

108. Jonathan Govias, "Inside El Sistema," *The Strad*, September 2010; "Se Está Borrando la Frontera Entre Música Clásica y Popular," *El Mundo,* June 25, 2008.

109. Richard Morrison, "True Class," *Times* (London), February 15, 2007.

110. Andreas Obst, "Allmacht Musik," *Frankfurter Allgemeine Zeitung*, August 9, 2006; "The Abreu Fellows Program," http://www.youtube.com/watch?v=Nwlj6YtaGk4, July 14, 2010, accessed November 4, 2010; Geoff Edgers, "Sour Note for Music Program," *Boston Globe*, January 3, 2011; Jeremy Eichler, "At NEC, a Missed Opportunity," *Boston Globe*, January 9, 2011; Daniel J. Wakin, "Conservatory Is to Cut Ties to Children's Music Project," *New York Times*, January 21, 2011.

111. Mark Churchill, emeritus dean of New England Conservatory, director of El Sistema USA, telephone interview with the author, October 29, 2010; Eric Booth, "Thoughts on Seeing El Sistema," unpublished, May 26, 2008; Arthur Lubow, "Conductor of the People," *New York Times Magazine*, October 28, 2007.

112. Interview with Elena Dolenko, Caracas, January 31, 2008; http://encontrarte.aporrea.org/creadores/musica/82/a14496.html, accessed November 3, 2010.

113. Rory Carroll, "Chávez Pours Millions More into Pioneering Music Scheme," *Guardian*, September 4, 2007; Lubow, "Conductor of the People."

114. Jane Baldauf-Berdes, *Women Musicians of Venice*, Oxford 1993, p. 107.

115. Helen Geyer, "Die Venezianischen Konservatorien im 18. Jahrhundert," in Fend and Noiray, eds., *Musical Education*, pp. 40–41.

116. Talbot, "Vivaldi, Antonio"; Baldauf-Berdes, *Women Musicians*, p. 236.

117. Elsie Arnold and Jane Baldauf-Berdes, *Maddalena Lombardini Sirmen*, Lanham, Maryland, and London 2002, pp. 7–34.

118. Schwarz, *Great Masters*, pp. 70–71; Pierluigi Petrobelli, "Tartini, Giuseppe," Oxford Music Online, accessed August 23, 2012.

119. Emanuel Hondré, "La Conservatoire de Musique de Paris," in Fend and Noiray, eds., *Musical Education*, pp. 81ff.

120. Lynne Heller, "Das Konservatorium für Musik in Wien," in Fend and Noiray, eds., *Musical Education*, pp. 205ff.; Richard Evidon, "Joseph Hellmesberger"; Boris Schwarz, "Joseph Boehm"; "Gesellschaft der Musikfreunde," in *Grove Music Online*, accessed February 24, 2009, http://www.grovemusic.com; Joseph Sonnleithner, *Allgemeine Deutsche Biographie*, Vol. 34, Leipzig 1892, pp. 640–41.

121. W. W. Cazalet, *The History of the Royal Academy of Music*, London 1854, pp. x–xi.

122. Ehrlich, *The Music Profession*, pp. 79ff.; Bernarr Rainbow and Anthony Kemp, "London (i), VIII," in *Grove Music Online*, accessed February 25, 2009, http://www.grovemusic.com.

123. Hill's diary, March 3, 1894.

124. "Royal College of Music," *New York Times*, May 3, 1894.

125. Rebecca Grotjahn, "Musik als Wissenschaft und Kunst," in Arnfried Edler and Sabine Meins, eds., *Musik, Wissenschaft und Ihre Vermittlung*, Augsburg 2002, pp. 353–54; "Die höhere Ausbildung in der Musik," in Fend and Noiray, eds., *Musical Education*, pp. 301ff.; Dietmar Schenk, *Die Hochschule für Musik zu Berlin*, Stuttgart 2004, pp. 25–26.

126. Boris Schwarz, "Interaction between Russian and Jewish Musicians," in Judith Cohen, ed., *Proceedings of the World Congress on Jewish Music, 1978*, Tel Aviv 1982.

127. Lyudmila Kovnatskaya, "St. Petersburg"; Vincent Duckles and Eleanor F. McCrickard, "Domenico Dall'Oglio," in *Grove Music Online*, accessed March 21, 2009; Schwarz, *Great Masters*, pp. 408–13.

128. I. M. Yampolsky and Rosamund Bartlett, "Moscow," in *Grove Music Online*, accessed March 21, 2009.

129. Lynn Sargeant, "A New Class of People," *Music and Letters* 85, no. 1, 2004.

130. Lynn M. Sargeant, "Ambivalence and Desire," in Fend and Noiray, eds., *Musical Education*, pp. 257ff.

131. Andreas Moser, *Joseph Joachim*, Berlin 1910, Vol. 2, pp. 144ff.

132. Bruno Walter, *Thema und Variationen*, Frankfurt 1960, pp. 34ff.

133. Dietmar Schenk, "Das Stern'sche Konservatorium der Musik," in Fend and Noiray, eds., *Musical Education*, pp. 275ff.

134. Schenk, *Die Hochschule*, p. 31.

135. Joseph Joachim, letter to his wife, July 15, 1870, cited in Beatrix Borchard, *Stimme und Geige*, Vienna, Cologne, and Weimar 2005, p. 346.

136. Schenk, *Die Hochschule*, pp. 31ff.; Borchard, *Stimme und Geige*, pp. 294ff.

137. Letter of April 17, 1869, Acta Betreffend den Director Professor Dr. Joseph Joachim, archive, Hochschule der Künste, Berlin.

138. Joseph Joachim, letter to his wife, June 21, 1869, quoted by Borchard, *Stimme und Geige*.

139. Siegfried Borris, *Hochschule für Musik*, Berlin 1964, p. 10.

140. Schenk, *Die Hochschule*, pp. 309–11; Borris, *Hochschule*, p. 12.

141. Laura Carter Holloway Langford, "Francis B. Thurber," in *Famous American Fortunes and the Men Who Have Made Them*, Philadelphia 1884, pp. 407ff.

142. Clarence D. Long, *Wages and Earnings in the United States, 1860–1890*, Princeton, New Jersey 1960, chapter 3.

143. "National Conservatory Concert," *New York Evening Post,* February 22, 1899.

144. Emanuel Rubin, "Jeannette Meyers Thurber and the National Conservatory of Music," *American Music*, Autumn 1990, pp. 294–325.

145. Gregor Benko and Terry McNeill, "Josef Hofmann," http://www.marstonrecords.com/hofmannv6/hoffmannv6_liner.htm, accessed April 17, 2009; "In Philadelphia," *Time*, June 13, 1927; Carl Flesch, *Erinnerungen eines Geigers*, Freiburg and Zurich 1960, pp. 178–79.

146. See http://historicaltextarchive.com/sections.php?op=viewarticle&artid=419, accessed April 18, 2009.

147. James Oestreich, "Innovative New Baton Keeps a School's Faculty Aquiver," *New York Times,* April 16, 1998.

148. "Gives $5,000,000 to Advance Music," *New York Times*, June 27, 1919.

149. Andrea Olmstead, *Juilliard, A History*, Urbana and Chicago, Illinois 1999, passim.

150. Ibid., p. 137.

151. Lisa B. Robinson, *A Living Legacy: Historic Stringed Instruments at the Juilliard School*, Pompton Plains, New Jersey 2006.

152. George M. Logan, *The Indiana University School of Music*, Bloomington and Indianapolis, Indiana 2000, pp. 25–26.

153. Ibid., p. 109; Thomas D. Clark, *Indiana University*, Vol. 3, Bloomington, Indiana, and London 1977, p. 487.

154. Logan, *The Indiana University School of Music*, p. 154.

155. Ibid., p. 223.

156. Arthur Pougin, *Notice sur Rode*, Paris 1874, p. 10.

157. Ibid., pp. 32–33.

158. P. Baillot, *L'Art du Violon, Nouvelle Méthode, Dédiée à ses Elèves*, Mainz and Antwerp c. 1834, pp. 1–10.

159. Charles Dancla, *Notes et Souvenirs*, Paris 1893, p. 7.

160. Albert Mell and Cormac Newark, "Charles Dancla," *Grove Music Online*, accessed June 5, 2009.

161. Dancla, *Notes*, pp. 10ff., 30–32, 125.

162. Carl Flesch, *Erinnerungen eines Geigers*, Freiburg and Zurich 1960, p. 56.

163. Henri Temianka, *Facing the Music*, New York 1973, p. 3.

164. Interview with the author, London, July 9, 1997.

165. Heinrich Ehrlich, *Modernes Musikleben*, Berlin 1895, pp. 172–74.

166. Richard Stern, *Was Muß der Musikstudierende von Berlin Wissen?*, Berlin 1914.

167. Flesch, *Erinnerungen*, p. 33.

168. Waldemar Meyer, *Aus einem Künstlerleben*, Berlin 1925, pp. 21, 58; Brigitte Höft, ed., *Mein Lieber Spiering*, Mannheim 1996, p. 9, http://www.csporter.com/spiering.shtml, accessed March 19, 2006.

169. Andreas Moser, *Joseph Joachim: Ein Lebensbild*, Vol. 2, Berlin 1910, p. 184.

170. Leopold Auer, *Violin Playing as I Teach It*, New York 1921, p. 23.

171. Flesch, *Erinnerungen*, pp. 35ff.; Ovide Musin, *My Memories: A Half-Century of Adventures and Experiences and Global Travel, Written by Himself*, New York 1920, p. 61.

172. Joseph Joachim and Andreas Moser, *Violinschule*, Berlin 1902–05.

173. Enzo Porta, *Il Violino nella Storia*, Turin 2000.

174. Cited in Paolo Peterlongo, *Il Violino di Vecsey*, Milan 1977, pp. 152–54.

175. Flesch, *Erinnerungen*, pp. 37, 108.

176. E. James, *Camillo Sivori*, London 1845, pp. 10–11.

177. Schwarz, *Great Masters*, p. 442. Cf. Ayke Agus, *Heifetz as I Knew Him*, Portland, Oregon 2001.

178. Schwarz, *Great Masters*, pp. 415–16.

179. Leopold Auer, *My Long Life in Music*, New York 1923, p. 356.

180. Interview with Elman, in Frederick Martens, *Violin Mastery, Talks with Master Violinists and Teachers*, New York 1919.

181. Arthur Weschler-Vered, *Jascha Heifetz*, London 1986, p. 47; Axelrod, ed., *Heifetz*, p. 126.

182. Nathan Milstein, *From Russia to the West*, New York 1990, p. 26.

183. Malan, *Efrem Zimbalist*, p. 23.

184. Auer, *Violin Playing as I Teach It*, pp. 58–63.

185. Schwarz, *Great Masters*, pp. 414ff.; Porta, *Il Violino*, pp. 169–74.

186. Flesch, *Erinnerungen*, p. 148.

187. Auer, *My Long Life*, pp. 320ff.; Allan Kozinn, *Mischa Elman and the Romantic Style*, Chur, Switzerland 1990, pp. 36ff.

188. Malan, *Efrem Zimbalist*, pp. 141ff.

189. Ibid., pp. 178ff.; Henri Temianka, "Flesch Start," *The Strad*, July 1986.

190. Carl F. Flesch, biographical notes for record project, undated, Rostal Papers, Folder "I. Fassung und Verschiedenes," Universität der Künste, Berlin.

191. Flesch, *Erinnerungen*, pp. 199ff.

192. Ibid., p. 73.

193. Rosa Fain, interview with the author, Düsseldorf, December 1, 2000.

194. "Cry Now, Pay Later," *Time*, December 6, 1968.

195. Arnold Steinhardt, *Indivisible by Four*, New York 1998, p. 28.

196. Interview with the author, March 26, 2003.

197. Elizabeth A. H. Green, *Miraculous Teacher*, Ann Arbor, Michigan 1993, p. 37.

198. Telephone interview with Henry Meyer, March 26, 2002.

199. Green, *Miraculous Teacher*, pp. 75ff.; Porta, *Il Violino*, pp. 203–04.

200. See http://www.brainyquote.com/quotes/authors/v/vince_lombardi.html, accessed July 5, 2009; Schwarz, *Great Masters*, p. 550.

201. David Blum, "A Gold Coin," *The New Yorker*, February 4, 1991.

202. Ibid.

203. Katie Robbins, "2010 Indianapolis Violin Competition Gets Under Way," *Strings*, September 2010.

204. Green, *Miraculous Teacher*, p. 93.

205. Mary Budd Horozaniecki, "Gingold, Virtuoso Teacher," *String Notes*, Fall 2007.

206. E-mail to the author, May 28, 2009.

207. Interviews with the author, Aspen, Colorado, July 28–29, 1998, and Hanover, Germany, November 17, 2000.

208. Cf. "Zakhar Bron, Thoughts on This Master Teacher," http://www.violinist.com/discussion/response.cfm?ID=8561, accessed July 21, 2009.

209. Carlos Maria Solare, "Quest for Artistry," *The Strad*, September 1996.

210. See http://www.violinist.com/blog/laurie/200911/10686/, accessed November 12, 2010.

211. Interview with the author, Aspen, Colorado, July 29, 1998.

212. Cf. David Schoenbaum, "Striking a Chord," *Washington Post*, May 6, 2000; "Building a New Conservatory the American Way," *New York Times*, June 4, 2000.

213. David Barboza, "Isaac Stern's Great Leap Forward Reverberates," *New York Times*, July 1, 2009.

214. "Heinrich Ehrlich," in *Neue Deutsche Biographie*, Vol. 4, Berlin 1959, p. 363.

215. Heinrich Ehrlich, "Das Musikproletariat und die Konservatorien," in *Modernes Musikleben*, Berlin 1895.

216. Norman Lebrecht, "End of the Road for Opera's Lovers," http://www.scena.org/columns/lebrecht/070207-NL-road.html, accessed February 27, 2010.

217. Daniel Wakin, "The Juilliard Effect," *New York Times*, December 12, 2004.

218. Kristina Singer, master's thesis, University of Vienna, February 2007, http://www.josephwechsberg.com/html/joseph-wechsberg-biography.html, accessed August 22, 2009; William Shawn, obituary, *The New Yorker*, April 25, 1983; Joseph Wechsberg, *The First Time Around*, New York 1970, pp. 86–92.

219. Catherine S. Manegold, "At Home With: Yeou-Cheng Ma," *New York Times*, March 10, 1994.

220. Molly O'Neill, "George Lang Tells His Story, Bottom to Top," *New York Times*, April 22, 1998; Matt DeLucia, "George Lang—His Amazing Journey to Café des Artistes," *New York Restaurant Insider*, March 2007; George Lang, *Nobody Knows the Truffles I've Seen*, New York 1998, pp. 278–80.

221. Charles Loch Mowat, *Britain between the Wars*, London 1959, p. 491; Ehrlich, *The Music Profession*, table p. 237.

222. Ernst Rudorff to Joseph Joachim, December 18, 1881, quoted in Barbara Kühnen, "Ist die kleine Soldat nicht ein ganzer Kerl?," in Elena Ostleitner and Ursula Simek, eds., *Ich fahre in mein Liebes Wien*, Vienna 1996, pp. 144ff.

223. Ehrlich, *The Music Profession*, pp. 156ff.

224. John H. Mueller, *The American Symphony Orchestra*, Westwood, Connecticut 1951, p. 308; Ehrlich, *The Music Profession*, pp. 161, 186ff.

225. Matthew A. Killmeier, "Race Music," in *St. James Encyclopedia of Popular Culture*, Detroit, Michigan 1999.

226. Bálint Sárosi, *Gypsy Music*, Budapest 1971, pp. 238ff.

227. Moser, *Joseph Joachim*, pp. 124ff.

228. Yoshimasa Kurabayashi and Yoshiro Matsuda, *Economic and Social Aspects of the Performing Arts in Japan*, Tokyo 1988, p. 9.

229. Sheila Melvin and Jindong Cai, "An Orchestra with a Political Accompaniment," *New York Times*, March 5, 2000.

230. Eugene Goossens, *Overture and Beginners*, London 1951, p. 110.

231. Ehrlich, *The Music Profession*, p. 201.

232. Robert D. Leiter, *The Musicians and Petrillo*, New York 1953, pp. 56–57, http://eh.net/ency clopedia/article/Smiley.1920s.final, accessed December 1, 2009.

233. Edwin Evans, "Music and the Cinema," *Music and Letters*, January 1929; Ehrlich, *The Music Profession*, p. 205.

234. Anne Mischakoff Heiles, "Golden Fiddlers of the Silver Screen," *The Strad*, November 2009; Leiter, *The Musicians and Petrillo*, p. 57.

235. Louis Kaufman, *A Fiddler's Tale*, Madison, Wisconsin, and London 2003, pp. 112ff.; S. Stevenson Smith, "The Economic Situation of the Performer," *Juilliard Review*, Fall 1955.

236. Anne Midgette, "Can the iPod Kill these Radio Stars?" *New York Times*, October 29, 2006.

237. Norman Lebrecht, *When the Music Stopped*, London 1997, pp. 380–88.

238. See http://www.bach-cantatas.com/Bio/Philadelphia-Orchestra.htm, accessed November 16, 2009.

239. Norman Lebrecht, "Look Who's Been Dumped," *La Scena Musicale*, http://www.scena.org/columns/lebrecht/031231-NL-recording.html, accessed December 31, 2003.

240. Anne Midgette, "Critic's Notebook: Urge.com and Online Classical," *New York Times*, May 19, 2006.

241. Joseph Szigeti, *Szigeti on the Violin*, New York and London 1969, pp. 21ff.

242. Ibid., pp. 22–23.

243. See www.miraclesofmodernscience.com, accessed December 23, 2011; "Miracles of Modern Science," *Weekend Edition Sunday*, National Public Radio, December 11, 2011.

244. Allan Kozinn, "A Man of Many Talents," *New York Times*, October 5, 2008.

245. Greg Cahill, *Making Your Living as a String Player*, San Rafael, California 2004; Angela Myles Beeching, *Beyond Talent: Creating a Successful Career*, New York 2005.

246. Walter Salmen, "The Musician in the Middle Ages," in Walter Salmen, ed., *The Social Status of the Professional Musician from the Middle Ages to the 19th Century*, New York 1983.

247. Richard Stites, *Serfdom, Society and the Arts in Imperial Russia*, New Haven, Connecticut, and London 2005, pp. 71ff.

248. Faubion Bowers, *Scriabin*, Mineola, New York 1996, p. 52.

249. Paul A. Cimbala, "Musicians," in Randall M. Miller and John David Smith, eds., *Dictionary of Afro-American Slavery*, Santa Barbara, California 1997, pp. 508ff.; "Fortunate Bondsmen," *Southern Studies*, 1979, pp. 291–303; "Black Musicians from Slavery to Freedom," *Journal of Negro History* 80, 1995, pp. 15–29.

250. Cited by Heinrich W. Schwab, "The Social Status of the Town Musician," in Salmen, ed., *The Social Status*, p. 33.

251. John Spitzer and Neal Zaslaw, *The Birth of the Orchestra: History of an Institution, 1650–1815*, New York 2004, pp. 428–29.

252. Tanya Kevorkian, *Baroque Piety*, Farnham, Surrey, UK 2007, pp. 195ff.

253. Spitzer and Zaslaw, *The Birth*, pp. 72ff. Cf. Robert L. Weaver, "The Consolidation of the Main Elements of the Orchestra," in Joan Peyser, ed., *The Orchestra*, New York 1986, pp. 11–16.

254. Spitzer and Zaslaw, *The Birth*, p. 75; Milliot, "Violonistes et luthiers," in Gétreau, *Instrumentistes*, pp. 83ff.

255. Boyden, *The History*, p. 227.

256. Quoted by Spitzer and Zaslaw, *The Birth*, p. 180.

257. Jerôme de la Gorce, "Lully, Jean-Baptiste," in *Grove Music Online*, accessed August 31, 2009; Spitzer and Zaslaw, *The Birth*, pp. 88–104.

258. Arnold Schering, *Musikgeschichte Leipzigs von 1650 bis 1723*, Leipzig 1926, pp. 257ff., 342, 405; Pippa Drummond, "Pisendel, Johann Georg," in *Grove Music Online*, accessed September 7, 2009.

259. Spitzer and Zaslaw, *The Birth*, p. 130.

260. Milliot, "Violinistes et luthiers," in Getreaú, *Instrumentistes*, p. 87; Spitzer and Zaslaw, *The Birth*, pp. 201–2.

261. Quoted by Holman, *Four and Twenty Fiddlers*, pp. 78–79.

262. Ibid., pp. 39–51.

263. Spitzer and Zaslaw, *The Birth*, pp. 270–71.

264. Holman, *Four and Twenty Fiddlers*, p. 299.

265. Ibid., p. 418; Spitzer and Zaslaw, *The Birth*, p. 272.

266. Holman, *Four and Twenty Fiddlers*, pp. 291–96.

267. John Timbs, *Curiosities of London*, London 1867, p. 136.

268. Wilson, ed., *Roger North on Music*, pp. 309, 355ff. Cf. Harvey, *The Violin Family*, pp. 26ff.

269. Wilson, ed., *Roger North*, pp. 300, 355ff.

270. Baretti, *An Account of the Manners and Customs of Italy*, Vol. 1, p. 150.

271. Wilson, ed., *Roger North*, p. 309. Cf. Jamie C. Kassler, "North, Roger," in *Grove Music Online*, accessed September 30, 2009.

272. Quoted by Michael Broyles, "Ensemble Music Moves Out of the Private House," in Peyser, ed., *The Orchestra*, p. 124.

273. Karl Geiringer, *Haydn*, Berkeley and Los Angeles 1968, pp. 115–16.

274. Rebecca Harris-Warrick and Julian Rushton, "Philidor 3: Anne Danican Philidor," *Grove Music Online*, accessed October 3, 2009.

275. http://www.musicologie.org/sites/c/concert_spirituel.html, accessed October 3, 2009; Peyser, ed., *The Orchestra*, pp. 52–54; Spitzer and Zaslaw, *The Birth*, pp. 197–201.

276. Milliot, "Violinistes et luthiers," in Getreaú, *Instrumentistes*, p. 89.

277. Gabriel Banat, *The Chevalier de Saint-Georges*, Hillsdale, New York 2006, pp. 116–19, 262–65; http://musicmac.ifrance.com/docs/societes.html, accessed October 4, 2009.

278. Geiringer, *Haydn*, p. 45.

279. Mahling, "The Origin and Social Status," in Salmen, ed., *The Social Status*, passim.

280. Spitzer and Zaslaw, *The Birth*, pp. 250–56.

281. Maynard Solomon, *Mozart*, New York 1995, p. 139; Floyd K. Grave, "Holzbauer, Ignaz," in *Grove Music Online*, accessed October 8, 2009.

282. Solomon, *Mozart*, pp. 139–40.

283. Spitzer and Zaslaw, *The Birth*, pp. 432–33; Margaret Menninger, "Art and Civic Patronage

in Leipzig," Harvard dissertation, 1998, pp. 216ff.; Anna Amalie Albert and Thomas Bauman, "Hiller, Johann Adam," and George B. Stauffer, "Leipzig," in *Grove Music Online*, accessed October 12, 2009; Hans-Joachim Nösselt, *Das Gewandhausorchester*, Leipzig 1943, passim.

284. Cyril Ehrlich, *First Philharmonic*, Oxford 1995, p. 25.

285. Nicholas Kenyon, *The BBC Symphony Orchestra*, London 1981.

286. Ehrlich, *First Philharmonic*, p. 52.

287. Ibid., p. 200.

288. Ibid., p. 120.

289. Flesch, *Erinnerungen*, p. 61.

290. Clemens Hellsberg, *Demokratie der Könige*, Vienna 1992, passim.

291. Herta Blaukopf and Kurt Blaukopf, *Die Wiener Philharmoniker*, Vienna 1992, pp. 57ff.

292. Herbert Haffner, *Die Berliner Philharmoniker*, Mainz 2007, pp. 11–12.

293. Peter Muck, ed., *Einhundert Jahre Berliner Philharmonisches Orchester*, Tutzing 1982, pp. 393ff.

294. Edith Stargardt-Wolff, *Wegbereiter grosser Musik*, Berlin and Wiesbaden 1954, Vol. II, p. 30.

295. Berta Geissmar, *Musik im Schatten der Politik*, Zurich 1945, passim.

296. Haffner, *Die Berliner*, pp. 94–136.

297. Norman Lebrecht, "The Monster and His Myth," January 30, 2008, http://www.scena.org/columns/lebrecht/080130-NL-Monster.html, accessed November 9, 2009.

298. Joseph Horowitz, *Classical Music in America*, New York 2005, pp. 73–75.

299. Leiter, *The Musicians and Petrillo*, p. 130.

300. Jessica Gienow-Hecht, *Sound Diplomacy*, Chicago and London 2009, p. 190.

301. Christine Ammer, *Unsung*, Portland, Oregon 2001, pp. 39–40.

302. Bliss Perry, *Life and Letters of Henry Higginson*, Boston 1921, p. 308.

303. Janet Baker-Carr, *Evening at Symphony*, Boston 1977, p. 126.

304. Barbara Nielsen, "Musician Involvement in the Governance of Symphony Orchestras," Polyphonic.org, April 7, 2008.

305. Spitzer and Zaslaw, *The Birth*, pp. 398ff.

306. Julia Moore, "Beethoven and Musical Economics," Ph.D. dissertation, University of Illinois, 1987.

307. Spitzer and Zaslaw, *The Birth*, p. 412.

308. Simon McVeigh, "Felice Giardini," *Music and Letters*, October 1983; Simon McVeigh, *The Violinist in London's Concert Life, 1750–1784*, London and New York 1989; Spitzer and Zaslaw, *The Birth*, p. 413.

309. John Rosselli, *Music and Musicians in 19th Century Italy*, Portland, Oregon 2000, pp. 72ff.

310. Henry William Byerly Thomson, *The Choice of a Profession*, London 1857, p. 3.

311. Andrew King, "Army, Navy, Medicine, Law," *Nineteenth-Century Gender Studies*, Summer 2009.

312. William Martin, *Les Conditions de Vie et de Travail des Musiciens*, Geneva 1923, Vol. 1, p. 5.

313. Hellsberg, *Demokratie*, p. 136.

314. Ibid., pp. 313–15.

315. Baker-Carr, *Evening*, p. 138.

316. See http://www.victorianweb.org/history/work/nelson1.html, accessed November 29, 2009; Goossens, *Overture*, p. 91.

317. Ehrlich, *The Music Profession*, pp. 120ff.

318. Martin, *Les Conditions de Vie*, Vol. 1, pp. 42ff.

319. Ibid., Vol. 2, pp. 3ff.

320. Ibid., Vol. 2, pp. 18ff.

321. Edward Arian, *Bach, Beethoven and Bureaucracy*, Alabama 1971, p. 14; Mueller, *The American Symphony Orchestra*, p. 156.

322. Harry Ellis Dickson, *Beating Time*, Boston 1995, pp. 49–58.

323. NARA Records of the Reich Ministry for Propaganda 1936–44, T70 87, Proposed Contract, August 24, 1937; Rüdiger Hachtmann, "Beschäftigungslage und Lohnentwicklung in der deutschen Metallindustrie, 1933–49," p. 54; http://hsr-trans.zhsf.uni-koeln.de/hsrretro/docs/artikel/hsr/hsr1981_33.pdf, accessed December 3, 2009.

324. Leiter, *The Musicians and Petrillo*, pp. 113–19. Cf. Menuhin, *Unfinished Journey*, pp. 162–65.

325. Dickson, *Beating Time*, pp. 69–71; Leiter, *The Musicians and Petrillo*, pp. 119–31.

326. "Leader Praises Petrillo," *New York Times*, December 15, 1942.

327. S. Stephenson Smith, "The Economic Situation of the Performer," *Juilliard Review*, Fall 1955.

328. *RCA v. Whiteman et al.*, 114 Fed (2nd) 86; 311 US 712 (1940); Erik Barnouw, *The Golden Web*, New York 1968, p. 217.

329. "Current Population Reports," Bureau of the Census, Series P-60, No. 24, Washington, April 1957.

330. Horowitz, *Classical Music*, p. 483.

331. Julie Ayer, *More Than Meets the Ear*, Minneapolis 2005, p. 33.

332. Julie Ayer, "The Birth of ICSOM," *Polyphonic*, September 17, 2007, http://www.polyphonic.org/article.php?id=128, accessed January 18, 2010.

333. Harold C. Schonberg, "The Sound of Money," *New York Times*, October 22, 1965.

334. "Comparative Growth in Orchestra Annual Salaries," *Senza Sordino*, March 2001.

335. Charles Michener, "Onward and Upward with the Arts," *The New Yorker*, February 7, 2005; Horowitz, *Classical Music*, pp. 483–84; Blair Tindall, "The Plight of the White-Collar Worker," *New York Times*, July 4, 2004; http://www.census.gov/Press-Release/www/releases/archives/income_wealth/002484.html, accessed December 10, 2009.

336. Jutta Allmendinger and Richard Hackman, "The Survival of Art or the Art of Survival," unpublished, March 1991; "Organizations in Changing Environments," *Journal of Administrative Science*, September 1996; Günther G. Schulze and Anselm Rose, "Public Orchestra Funding in Germany," *Journal of Cultural Economics* 22, 1998, pp. 227ff.; Ayer, *More Than*, p. 149.

337. Lawrence Van Gelder, "Arts Briefing," *New York Times*, September 13, 2004; e-mail to the author, September 14, 2004.

338. Interview with the author, London, July 11, 1997.

339. Interview with the author, Berlin, January 29, 1997.

340. Jutta Allmendinger and J. Richard Hackman, "The More, the Better?" *Social Forces*, December 1995, pp. 428–29.

341. J. Richard Hackman, *Leading Teams*, Cambridge, MA 2002.

342. Allmendinger and Hackman, "The Survival of Art or the Art of Survival," p. 7.

343. Jutta Allmendinger, J. Richard Hackman, and Erin V. Lehman, "Life and Work in Symphony Orchestras," *Musical Quarterly* 80, 1996, pp. 6ff.

344. Haffner, *Die Berliner*, p. 259.

345. Seymour and Robert Levine, "Why They're Not Smiling," *Harmony*, April 1996.

346. Charlotte Higgins, "Orchestras Throw a Lifeline to Musicians," *Guardian,* January 28, 2006; Blair Tindall, "Better Playing through Chemistry," *New York Times*, October 17, 2004; James R. Oestreich, "The Shushing of the Symphony," *New York Times*, January 11, 2004; Eleanor Blau, "Taking Arms Against Stage Fright," *New York Times,* September 20, 1998.

347. "Bonn Violinists Drop 'More Pay for More Notes' Lawsuit," *Agence France Presse*, May 27, 2004; "'Paid by the Note? Don't be Ridiculous,'" *Guardian*, March 25, 2004.

348. Ayer, *More Than*, p. 76.

349. See http://prescriptions.blogs.nytimes.com/2010/01/17/an-economist-who-sees-no-way-to-slow-rising-costs/, accessed January 25, 2010; Allan Kozinn, "Strike in Philadelphia," *New York Times*, September 17, 1996.

350. Sarah Bryan Miller, "Symphony Strike Echoes across US," *Christian Science Monitor*, January 20, 2005; Ben Mattison, "St. Louis Symphony Musicians Approve New Contract," http://www.playbillarts.com/news/article/1510-St-Louis-Symphony-Musicians-Approve-New-Contract-Ending-Two-Month-Work-Stoppage.html, accessed January 28, 2010.

351. John von Rhein, "Orchestra, Lyric Opera in Tune," *Chicago Tribune*, December 5, 2009; Daniel Wakin, "Cleveland Settles Orchestra Strike," *New York Times*, January 19, 2010; Andrew Manshel, "Too Big to Succeed?" *Wall Street Journal*, January 23, 2010; Janet I. Tu, "Seattle Symphony, Management Reach Tentative Agreement," *Seattle Times*, January 10, 2010; e-mail to the author, January 30, 2010.

352. Philip Boroff, "Bankruptcy Alert," http://www.bloomberg.com/news/2011-05-02/bankruptcy-alert-the-philadelphia-orchestra-declared-it-so-who-s-next-.html, accessed June 28, 2011.

353. "Global Strings," *Economist*, August 16, 1997.

354. "The World's Greatest Orchestras," *Gramophone*, December 2008.

355. Deems Taylor, *Music to My Ears*, New York 1949, p. 106.

356. Conversation with the author, Bologna, 1993.

357. Manshel, "Too Big to Succeed?"; http://espn.go.com/mlb/teams/salaries?team=cle, accessed February 15, 2010.

358. Robert Frank, "Higher Education: the Ultimate Winner-Take-All Market," Forum for the Future of Higher Education, Aspen, Colorado, September 27, 1999, http://inequality.cornell.edu/publications/working_papers/RobertFrank1.pdf, accessed February 6, 2010.

359. Don Olesen, "Are Women Sour Notes in Orchestras?" *Milwaukee Journal*, April 19, 1970.

360. Ayer, *More Than*, p. 123; Mueller, *The American Symphony Orchestra*, pp. 258ff.

361. Haffner, *Die Berliner*, pp. 245–48.

362. Evelyn Chadwick, "Of Music and Men," *The Strad*, December 1997.

363. James R. Oestreich, "An Agent of Change Keeps Stretching," *New York Times*, February 24, 2009; Rory Williams, "Women Still Fight for Seat in Major Orchestras Worldwide," *Strings*, October 2010.

364. Ayer, *More Than*, pp. 113–22.

365. Nikolai Biro-Hubert, *Dirigierdschungel*, Berlin 1997, pp. 163–64.

366. Claudia Goldin and Cecilia Rouse, "Orchestrating Impartiality," *American Economic Review*, September 2000, pp. 715ff.

367. Allmendinger et al., "Life and Work," p. 208.

368. Daniel J. Wakin, "The Philharmonic Denies Bias," *New York Times*, July 26, 2005; Dareh Gregorian, "Philharmonious End to Lawsuit," *New York Post*, September 4, 2007.

369. Lowell Noteboom, "A Champion for Orchestras," *Symphony*, July–August 2006, pp. 55ff.

370. George Booth, "Saddened Woman, with Violin Resting on Floor, Sits Quietly on Stool," *The New Yorker*, September 24, 2001, http://www.cartoonbank.com/2001/Saddened-woman-with-violin-resting-on-floor-sits-quietly-on-stool/invt/121064, accessed March 5, 2010.

371. Charles Michener, "Onward and Upward with the Arts—The Clevelanders: Can an Orchestra Survive Its City?" *The New Yorker*, February 7, 2005.

372. Lawrence B. Johnson, "Stalled Talks and Money Woes Major Threat to DSO," *Detroit News*, August 19, 2010.

373. Patricia M. Fergus, "Factors Affecting the Development of the Orchestra and String Program," *Journal of Research in Music Education*, Autumn 1964; Michael Hopkins, "Elevation of the School Band and Decline of the School Orchestra," http://www.uvm.edu/~mhopkins/string/his

tory/stringed/01.html, http://www.childrensmusicworkshop.com/advocacy/musicedinca.html, accessed February 28, 2010.

374. Helen Pellegrini, "The Rise and Rise of Chinese Lutherie," *The Strad*, March 2009.

375. Daniel Wakin, "The Face-the-Music Academy," *New York Times*, February 18, 2007.

376. Anne Midgette, "Classical Artists such as Hilary Hahn Chart Big on Billboard with Little Sales," *Washington Post*, January 30, 2010.

377. National Endowment for the Arts, *2008 Survey of Public Participation in the Arts*, pp. 79ff., http://www.artsjournal.com/sandow/2006/05/new_book_episode_and_allan_koz.html.

378. "Forty Years after Woodstock," Pew Research Center, August 2009, pp. 14–15.

379. Greg Sandow, "Age of the French Classical Audience," http://www.artsjournal.com/san dow/2009/12/age_of_the_french_classical_au.html, https://www.cia.gov/library/publications/ the-world-factbook/geos/fr.html, accessed March 19, 2010.

380. Greg Sandow, "New Book Episode," http://www.artsjournal.com/sandow/2006/05/new_ book_episode_and_allan_koz.html, accessed May 30, 2006.

381. Allan Kozinn, "Check the Numbers," *New York Times*, May 28, 2006; Norman Lebrecht, "Will Music Be Safe in Their Hands?" http://www.scena.org/columns/lebrecht/051221-NL -theirhands.html, accessed December 21, 2005; "End This Downloads Ban," http://www.scena .org/columns/lebrecht/090225-NL-downloads.html, accessed February 25, 2009.

382. Norman Lebrecht, "When Times are Tough, Classical Music Blooms," June 7, 2009, http://www.bloomberg.com/apps/news?pid=20670001&sid=a_kEJSPKJ5ao, accessed March 12, 2010.

383. Paul Gleason, "The Maximalist Matt Haimovitz Takes the Cello to New Places," *Harvard Magazine*, October 31, 2008; John von Rhein, "Matt Heimovitz Turns Classical Cello into a Switched-On Lounge Act," *Chicago Tribune*, October 29, 2009.

384. Anthony Tommasini, "Feeding Those Young and Curious Listeners," *New York Times*, June 17, 2009.

385. Orchestra Spotlight: Milwaukee Symphony Orchestra, February 2007, http://www.poly phonic.org/spotlight.php?id=58, accessed March 18, 2010; http://www.siahq.org/conference/ sia2005/images/MilwPoster800.gif, accessed March 18, 2010.

386. See http://www.macfound.org/programs/fel/fellows/dworkin_aaron.htm, http://www.answers .com/topic/aaron-p-dworkin, http://www.sphinxmusic.org/programs/competition.html, accessed March 16, 2010; John von Rhein, "Sphinx Looks to Change Makeup of US Orchestras," *Chicago Tribune*, October 3, 2008; Sphinx Organization, *Year in Review 2008–09*, Detroit, Michigan, and New York n.d., pp. 20–21.

387. Anthony Tommasini, "Ten Years of Opening the Tent," *New York Times*, January 3, 2010.

388. Alex Ross, "The Evangelist," *The New Yorker*, December 5, 2005.

389. See http://www.acjw.org, accessed March 18, 2010.

390. "Trip to Asia," Boomtown Media International 2008; Tommasini, "Ten Years."

391. Andrew L. Pincus, *Musicians with a Mission*, Boston 2002, pp. 230ff.; Chester Lane, "Join-ing Hands," *Symphony*, May–June 2006; Andrew Rooney, "Opening Doors," *The Strad*, April 1997; Henry Fogel, "Midori and the Orchestra Residency," http://www.artsjournal.com/onthe record/2008/10/midori_and_the_orchestra_resid.htm, accessed March 18, 2010.

392. Daniel Wakin, "Getting to Carnegie via YouTube," *New York Times*, December 2, 2008; Michal Shein, "My Experience Performing with the YouTube Symphony," *Polyphonic*, April 23, 2009; Anne Midgette, "YouTube's Un-Harmonic Convergence," *Washington Post*, April 16, 2009; Anthony Tommasini, "To Get to Carnegie Hall? Try Out on YouTube," *New York Times*, April 17, 2009; Greg Sandow, "YouTube (sigh) Symphony," *Wall Street Journal Arts Journal*, http://www.artsjournal.com/sandow/2009/04/you tube_sigh_symphony.html, accessed March 19, 2010.

393. Jacob Hale Russell and John Jurgensen, "Fugue for Man & Machine," *Wall Street Journal*, May 5, 2007.

394. Interview with the author and e-mail to the author, February 10–March 3, 2010.

395. De Courcy, *Paganini*, Vol. I, p. 272; Vol. II, pp. 46, 294.

396. "Czech Quartet," in Michael Kennedy, ed., *The Oxford Dictionary of Music*, 2nd ed. rev., *Oxford Music Online*, http://www.oxfordmusiconline.com.proxy.lib.uiowa.edu/subscriber/article/opr/t237/e2661, accessed February 18, 2011.

397. Quoted by John Gibbens, "Shelf Life," *Telegraph*, September 24, 2006.

398. "De Coppet Musicians to Play," *New York Times*, February 13, 1905.

399. Steinhardt, *Indivisible by Four*, p. 166.

400. Viz. http://www.loc.gov/pictures/item/99405878/, accessed July 21, 2012.

401. Steinhardt, *Indivisible by Four*, p. 185.

402. Interview with the author, Berlin, September 27, 1997.

403. Sonia Simmenauer, *Muss Es Sein?*, Berlin 2008, p. 16.

404. Anne Midgette, "Music That Thinks Outside the Chamber," *New York Times*, June 24, 2007.

405. Brandt, *Con Brio*, p. 163.

406. Norman Lebrecht, "Comment," *The Strad*, November 2010.

407. Friedrich Wilhelm Riemer, ed., *Briefwechsel zwischen Goethe und Zelter*, Berlin 1834, letter of November 9, 1829, p. 305.

408. Emma Pomfret, "The Stormy, Intimate Life of the String Quartet," *Times* (London), February 8, 2008.

409. *The New Yorker*, April 4, 1963.

410. Martin Kettle, "Broken Strings," *Guardian*, October 6, 2000; Chris Kahn, "Lawsuit Rocks Virginia String Quartet," Associated Press, June 8, 2001; Daniel Wakin, "The Broken Chord," *New York Times*, December 11, 2005; "2 Musicians in a Legal Dispute Will Keep Their Instruments," *New York Times*, January 11, 2006.

411. See http://www.rmahome.com/c/faculty/35-faculty/3-david-ehrlich, accessed February 19, 2011.

412. Christoph Poppen, interview with the author, July 14, 1997.

413. Pomfret, "The Stormy, Intimate Life."

414. Martin, *Les Conditions de Vie*, Vol. 2, pp. 4ff.

415. Lebrecht, "Comment."

416. Steinhardt, *Indivisible by Four*, p. 7.

417. Ibid.

418. Quoted by Boyden, *The History*, p. 32.

419. Robin Stowell, "The Sonata," in Robin Stowell, ed., *The Cambridge Companion to the Violin*, Cambridge and New York 1992, pp. 168ff.

420. Nona Pyron and Aurelio Bianco, "Farina, Carlo," *Grove Music Online*, accessed April 13, 2010.

421. Elias Dann and Jiří Sehnal, "Biber, Heinrich Ignaz Franz von," *Grove Music Online*, accessed April 15, 2010.

422. See http://www.hoasm.org/VIIA/Matteis1.html, accessed June 14, 2010.

423. Johann Kuhnau, *Der Musikalische Quack-Salber*, edited by K. Benndorf, Berlin 1900, p. 242.

424. Michael Talbot, "Corelli, Arcangelo," *Grove Music Online*, accessed April 16, 2010.

425. E-mail to the author from Cho-liang Lin, October 3, 2003.

426. Quoted by Simon McVeigh, "The Violinists of the Baroque and Classical Periods," in Stowell, ed., *The Cambridge Companion*, p. 51.

427. Quoted in Schwarz, *Great Masters*, p. 102.

428. Michael Talbot, "Vivaldi," *Grove Music Online*, accessed July 21, 2012.

429. Winton Dean and Carlo Vitali, "Cuzzoni, Francesca," *Grove Music Online*, accessed April 23, 2010; http://pierre-marteau.com/wiki/index.php?title=Prices_and_Wages_%28Great_Britain%29#Wages, accessed April 24, 2010.

430. Raymond F. Glover, ed., *The Hymnal 1982, Companion Volume Three A*, New York 1994, p. 678.

431. Simon McVeigh, "Felice Giardini," *Music and Letters*, October 1983; McVeigh, *The Violinist*, passim; Christopher Hogwood and Simon McVeigh, "Giardini, Felice," *Grove Music Online*, accessed April 23, 2010; David Golby, "Giardini [Degiardino], Felice," *Oxford Dictionary of National Biography Online*, accessed April 23, 2010.

432. Remo Giazotto, *Giovan Battista Viotti*, Milan 1956, p. 42.

433. http://www.hymnary.org/tune/italian_hymn_giardini.

434. François-Joseph Fétis, "Viotti," in *Biographie universelle des musiciens*, facsimile of 1878 original, Paris 2006, p. 360.

435. Warwick Lister, *Amico*, New York 2009, p. 69; Georges Cucuel, "Le Baron de Bagge et Son Temps," in *L'Année Musicale*, Vol. 1, Paris 1911; C. Stanford Perry, "Baron Bach," *Music & Letters*, April 1931.

436. Quoted in Robin Stowell, *Violin Technique and Performance Practice in the Late Eighteenth and Early Nineteenth Centuries*, Cambridge 1985, p. 270 n. 14.

437. Arthur Pougin, *Viotti et l'École Modern de Violon*, Paris 1888, pp. 24–25; "Mara, Mme. Giovanni Battista," in Highfill et al., eds., *A Biographical Dictionary of Actors, Actresses, Musicians, Dancers, Managers, and Other Stage Personnel in London, 1660–1800*, Carbondale, Illinois 1984, Vol. 10, pp. 77–87.

438. Fétis, "Viotti," p. 362.

439. Giazotto, *Giovan Battista Viotti*, pp. 99–101.

440. Ibid., pp. 71ff.

441. Yim, *Viotti*, pp. 29–30.

442. Giazotto, *Giovan Battista Viotti*, p. 121.

443. Yim, *Viotti*, pp. 120ff., 137.

444. Michael E. Scorgie, "The Rise and Fall of William Bassett Chinnery," *The Abacus* 43, no. 1, 2007; Lister, *Amico*, p. 264.

445. Yim, *Viotti*, pp. 217ff.

446. Lister, *Amico*, pp. 317ff.

447. Yim, *Viotti*, pp. 249ff.; Lister, *Amico*, pp. 348ff., http://westminster.gov.uk/services/environment/landandpremises/parksandopenspaces/paddington-street-gardens/, accessed May 21, 2010.

448. Lister, *Amico*, p. 395; W. Henry Hill et al., *Antonio Stradivari*, p. 54.

449. Giazotto, *Giovan Battista Viotti*, p. 13.

450. Lister, *Amico*, pp. 334–35.

451. Berri, *Paganini*, pp. 295ff., 491, verses in author's translation. *Violons, Vuillaume*, p. 99.

452. Quoted in de Courcy, *Paganini*, Vol. I, p. 157; Berri, *Paganini*, pp. 132–33.

453. Stendhal, *Vie de Rossini*, Paris 1922, Vol. 2, p. 116; Berri, *Paganini*, p. 226.

454. Berri, *Paganini*, pp. 287ff., de Courcy, *Paganini*, pp. 416ff.

455. Albert Mell, review of de Courcy, *Paganini*, *Musical Quarterly*, October 1958, pp. 524–27.

456. Ibid.; Carlo Marcello Rietmann, *Il Violino e Genova*, Genoa 1975, p. 23; de Courcy, *Paganini*, Vol. I, pp. 38–43.

457. P. Berri, "Fasti e nefasti genovesi dell' 'Elixir Le Roy,'" *Minerva Medica*, November 17, 1956, pp. 808–11.

458. Berri, *Paganini*, p. 57.

459. Ibid., p. 49.

460. Ibid., pp. 77ff., 131; de Courcy, *Paganini*, Vol. I, pp. 109–10.

461. See http://oce.catholic.com/index.php?title=Pope_Leo_XII, accessed June 10, 2010.

462. Berri, *Paganini*, pp. 405–6.

463. Ibid., p. 405.

464. P. de Wailly, "Boucher de Perthes et Paganini," *Revue de Musicologie*, August 1928, pp. 167–68.

465. Ibid., pp. 127ff.

466. De Courcy, *Paganini*, p. 392.

467. Ibid., pp. 168–69.

468. Rietmann, *Il Violino*, p. 32.

469. De Courcy, *Paganini*, pp. 115–16.

470. H. Reich, "Paganini, Napoléon des Violonistes," *Therapiewoche* 30, 1980, pp. 1731–35.

471. Carl Guhr, *Ueber Paganini's Kunst die Violine zu Spielen*, Mainz, Antwerp, and Brussels 1829, p. 42; Elizabeth A. H. Green, *Miraculous Teacher*, Ann Arbor, Michigan, and Bryn Mawr, Pennsylvania 1993, p. 69.

472. Heinrich W. Schwab, *Konzert*, Leipzig 1971, Band 4, p. 53; Pierre Baillot, *L'Art du Violon*, Mainz and Antwerp 1834, p. 5.

473. Charles Chadwick, "The Minor Star and the Comet," *The Strad*, July 1997.

474. de Courcy, *Paganini*, pp. 762ff.

475. Berri, *Paganini*, pp. 328ff.; de Courcy, *Paganini*, Vol. II, pp. 35ff.

476. Berri, *Paganini*, p. 369.

477. De Courcy, *Paganini*, Vol. II, p. 46.

478. Berri, "Fasti e nefasti."

479. Hugh McGinnis Ferguson, "No Gambling at the Casino Paganini," *American Scholar*, Winter 1994.

480. De Courcy, *Paganini*, pp. 304–6; W. Henry Hill et al., *Antonio Stradivari*, p. 271.

481. http://en.wikipedia.org/wiki/Caprice_No._24_%28Paganini%29#Variations_on_the_theme, accessed July 1, 2012.

482. Berri, *Paganini*, p. 354.

483. http://www.youtube.com/watch?v=NHkX0URELfQ.

484. Warren Kirkendale, "Segreto Communicato da Paganini," *American Musicological Society Journal*, Fall 1965, p. 394.

485. Viz. Rietmann, *Il Violino*, pp. 53–79.

486. Viz. M. W. Rowe, *Heinrich Wilhelm Ernst*, Farnham, Surrey 2008, passim.

487. Meir A. Goldschmidt, "A Norwegian Musician," *Cornhill Magazine* 6, October 1862, pp. 514ff.

488. Schwarz, *Great Masters*, p. 232; http://verifiable.com/app#/data_sets/925, accessed July 4, 2010.

489. A. T. Andreas, *History of Chicago*, Chicago 1884, Vol. 1, p. 499.

490. Ibid., pp. 171ff.

491. Eduard Hanslick, *Music Criticisms*, Harmondsworth, Middlesex, UK 1963, p. 69.

492. Adrian Williams, *Portrait of Liszt*, Oxford 1990, pp. 554–56.

493. Flesch, *Erinnerungen*, p. 39.

494. Camilla Cay, "Myth-Making Fiddler," *The Strad*, January 1996.

495. Haugen and Cay, *Ole Bull*, pp. 115ff.; "Oleanna" on *Folksongs of Four Continents*, Folkways Records FW 6911.

496. Talbot, "Vivaldi, Antonio," accessed July 9, 2010; Robin Stowell, *Beethoven*, pp. 30ff.

497. Dagmar Hoffmann-Axtholm, "Bilderbetrachtung," *Basler Jahrbuch für historische Musikpraxis* 30, 2006, pp. vii–xxiv.

498. Moser, *Joseph Joachim*, Vol. 1, p. 223.

499. Borchard, *Stimme und Geige*, pp. 368ff.

500. George Bernard Shaw, *Shaw's Music*, London 1981, Vol. 1, p. 993.

501. "Joseph Joachim Is Dead, Age 76," *New York Times*, August 16, 1907.

502. Borchard, *Stimme und Geige*, p. 18.

503. Moser, *Joseph Joachim*, Vol. 2, pp. 351–52.

504. Alessandro Barrico, *L'Anima di Hegel e le Mucche del Wisconsin*, Milan 1993, p. 19.

505. Alex Ross, *The Rest Is Noise*, New York 2007, p. 129.

506. George Francis Dawson, *The Republican Campaign Text-Book for 1888*, New York, Chicago, and Washington 1888, pp. 114ff.; http://oregonstate.edu/cla/polisci/faculty-research/sahr/sahr.htm, http://wiki.answers.com/Q/Average_salary_in_1930, accessed July 30, 2010.

507. See http://www.bls.gov/opub/cwc/cm20030124ar03p1.htm, accessed July 31, 2010; Axelrod, ed., *Heifetz*, p. 10–11; http://www.williamwalton.net/articles/concertos.html, accessed August 1, 2010.

508. See http://www.bls.gov/opub/uscs/1950.pdf, accessed August 1, 2010.

509. Harlow Robinson, *The Last Impresario*, New York 1994, pp. 287–90; http://bber.unm.edu/econ/us-pci.htm, accessed August 1, 2010.

510. Paolo Peterlongo, *Il Violino di Vecsey*, Milan 1977, pp. 200ff.

511. Borchard, *Stimme und Geige*, p. 115; Gidon Kremer, *Obertöne*, Salzburg and Vienna 1997, pp. 80–81.

512. Daniel Wakin, "Violinist Cancels Recital over Detroit Strike Tension," *New York Times*, October 12, 2010.

513. E-mail from Zina Schiff, December 13, 2003.

514. See http://perso.club-internet.fr/jszulman/Christian_Ferras/; http://perso.club-internet.fr/jszulman/Christian_Ferras/interviews.html, accessed August 23, 2010; Thierry de Choudens, *Christian Ferras*, Geneva 2004, pp. 189ff.

515. Klaus Weiler, *Gerhard Taschner, das vergessene Genie*, Augsburg 2004, passim.

516. Menuhin, *Unfinished Journey*, p. 105.

517. John Richard, *A Tour from London to Petersburgh, and from Thence to Moscow*, Dublin 1781, p. 47.

518. Musin, *My Memories*, pp. 105ff.

519. Lochner, *Fritz Kreisler*, pp. 23ff.

520. Peterlongo, *Il Violino*, p. 200.

521. John and John Anthony Maltese, "The Heifetz War Years," *The Strad*, December 2005.

522. Axelrod, ed., *Heifetz*, pp. 520–38.

523. Paul Cohen, "I Am the Violin," IDTV Amsterdam 2004; Benedict Mirow, "Hilary Hahn, a Portrait," Deutsche Grammophon 2007.

524. Antoine Ysaÿe and Bertram Ratcliffe, *Ysaÿe*, London and Toronto 1947, p. 17.

525. See http://www.henrykszeryng.net/en/main.php?page=timeline_part_3, accessed August 2, 2010.

526. John Rockwell, "Girl, 14, Conquers Tanglewood with 3 Violins," *New York Times*, July 28, 1986; Tim Page, "Unpretentious Prodigy Puzzled by All the Fuss," *New York Times*, July 29, 1986; Barbara Lourie Sand, *Teaching Genius*, Portland, Oregon 2000, p. 151.

527. See http://www.godowsky.com/Biography/humor.html, accessed August 6, 2010.

528. Gidon Kremer, *Kindheitssplitter*, Munich 1993, p. 173.

529. Solomon, *Mozart*, p. 47.

530. Dancla, *Notes et Souvenirs*, p. 65.

531. Tully Potter, "Paganini's Spirited Pupil," *The Strad*, December 1993.

532. Saul Elman, *Memoirs of Mischa Elman's Father*, New York 1933; Moshe Menuhin, *The Menuhin Saga*, London 1984.

533. Interview with the author, Berlin, February 1, 1997.

534. Menuhin, *Unfinished Journey*, pp. 20–21.

535. Louise Lee, "Prodigies," *Wall Street Journal*, July 23, 1996.

536. Sand, *Teaching Genius*, p. 150.

537. Interview with the author, Berlin, December 23, 1997.

538. Kremer, *Kindheitssplitter*, pp. 22, 67.

539. See http://www.ruggieroricci.com/images/achieve.jpg, http://www.ruggieroricci.com/images/sixfamous.jpg, accessed August 9, 2010.

540. "Ricci Custody Decree Lauds Two Teachers," *New York Times*, December 31, 1930.

541. Folder "I. Fassung und Verschiedenes," Draft Vorwort I, photo album, Rostal Papers, Universität der Künste, Berlin.

542. Burton, *Menuhin*, p. 3.

543. Lee, "Prodigies."

544. Peterlongo, *Il Violino*, p. 180.

545. Christopher Fifield, *Ibbs and Tillett*, Aldershot, Hants, UK 2005, p. 19; Ida Haendel, *Woman with Violin*, London 1970, pp. 79ff.

546. Menuhin, *Unfinished Journey*, p. 166.

547. Winthrop Sargeant, "Prodigy's Progress," *The New Yorker*, October 8 and 15, 1955.

548. Norman Lebrecht, "Yehudi Menuhin—So Much Love for Man, So Little for Us," *La Scena Musicale* 5, no. 7, April 2000.

549. Pierre Amoyal, *Pour l'Amour d'un Stradivarius*, Paris 2004, pp. 38–41; Agus, *Heifetz*, p. 35.

550. "Music in Review," *New York Times*, January 4, 1937; "Shoots Wife, Child and Kills Himself," *New York Times*, December 29, 1939; Noel Straus, "Miriam Solovieff in Violin Recital," *New York Times*, February 24, 1940; Noel Straus, "Miss Miriam Solovieff, Violinist, at Best in Tartini Work at Carnegie Hall Recital," *New York Times*, January 12, 1948; http://www.musimem.com/obi-0703-1203.htm, accessed August 20, 2010.

551. Einfach Midori, *Einfach Midori*, Berlin 2004.

552. Tim Page, "Midori at 21," in *Tim Page on Music*, Portland, Oregon 2002, pp. 153ff.

553. Dennis Rooney, "Opening Doors," *The Strad*, April 1997.

554. Anthony Feinstein, "The Psychiatrist's Chair," *The Strad*, December 1997.

555. Anthony Feinstein, *Michael Rabin*, Milwaukee, Wisconsin 2005, passim.

556. Interview with the author, Iowa City, Iowa, April 13, 2000.

557. Marie Brunfaut, *Jules LaForgue, les Ysaye et Leur Temps*, Brussels 1961, p. 111.

558. Ellen Freilich, "The 'Naumburg'—Still a Force," *New York Times*, June 14, 1981.

559. See http://www2.census.gov/prod2/popscan/p60-137.pdf, accessed August 26, 2010.

560. "Contests: Cookie and Pinky Come Through," *Time*, May 26, 1967; Joseph Horowitz, *The Ivory Trade*, New York 1990, pp. 70–77.

561. Temianka, *Facing the Music*, pp. 27–29; Yakov Soroker, *David Oistrakh*, Jerusalem 1982, pp. 22–24; Haendel, *Woman with Violin*, pp. 50–51; "Electrofonic Violin," in *Oxford Dictionary of Music*, New York 2004, p. 223.

562. Michel Stockhem, "The Queen Elisabeth Competition," http://www.concours-reine-elisabeth.be/en/historique/estouest.php, accessed August 29, 2010; Soroker, *David Oistrakh*, pp. 26ff.

563. Phone interview with the author, November 23, 1997.

564. "Violinist from Iowa, 27, Wins Wieniawski Contest in Poznan," *New York Times*, November 19, 1962.

565. Interview with the author, Des Moines, Iowa, September 30, 1999.

566. Maya Pritsker, "The Tchaikovsky Competition Takes Some Halting Steps Back to Respectability," Andante.com, June 27, 2002.

567. Stockhem, "The Queen Elisabeth Competition"; Eugene Drucker, e-mail to the author, August 24, 2010.

568. Agus, *Heifetz*, p. 69; Jessica Duchen, "Staying on Top," *The Strad*, January 1995.

569. Szigeti, *Szigeti on the Violin*, p. 14.

570. Thelma Shifrin, "Worlds Apart," *The Strad,* May 1986; interview with the author, Cologne, September 25, 1997.

571. Axel Brüggemann, "Hammer und Sichel auf dem Goldenen Vorhang," *Welt am Sonntag*, December 12, 2004; http://www.violin-fund.ru/eng/competition/comp5/juri/, accessed August 31, 2010; http://www.legalintel.ru/history.php?lang=eng, accessed February 5, 2011.

572. Interview with the author, Hanover, Germany, November 30, 2000.

573. Phone interview with the author, June 30, 2004.

574. "Violinist Marsick Arrives," *New York Times*, October 21, 1895; Bowen, *Friends and Fiddlers*, pp. 49ff.; Ruth Railton, *Dare to Excel*, London 1992, pp. 63ff.

575. E-mail to the author from James Murphy, Director of Communications, National Youth Orchestra, October 13, 2010.

576. Bowen, *Friends and Fiddlers*, pp. 49ff.; Railton, *Dare to Excel*, pp. 63ff.; Humphrey Maud, e-mail to the author, September 23, 2010.

577. Kozinn, *Mischa Elman*, pp. 7ff.

578. Interview with the author, London, June 17, 1999; Gene Weingarten, "Pearls before Breakfast," *Washington Post*, April 8, 2007.

579. Meyer, *Aus einem Künstlerleben*, pp. 76ff.

580. Directive of October 25, 1939, addressed to Goebbels, Minister of Propaganda, NARA Records of the Reich Ministry for Propaganda, 1936–44, T70 58.

581. Interview with the author, Berlin, October 10, 1997.

582. Quoted in Albrecht Roeseler, *Grosse Geiger unseres Jahrhunderts*, Munich 1996, p. 314.

583. Joachim Kaiser, *Erlebte Musik*, Hamburg 1977, pp. 619ff.; "Mein Image Interessiert Mich Nicht," *Frankfurter Rundschau*, December 13, 2002.

584. Fellowes, *Memoirs*, pp. 79ff.; Faber, *Stradivari's Genius*, pp. 155ff.

585. Thomas Beecham, *A Mingled Chime*, New York 1976, pp. 132–33; William Primrose, *Walk on the North Side*, Provo, Utah 1978, pp. 36–39; "Albert Edward Sammons," *The Strad*, August 1986.

586. David Tunley, *The Bel Canto Violin*, Aldershot, Hants, UK 1999, pp. 67ff.

587. Anne Mischakoff, *Khandoshkin and the Beginning of Russian String Music*, Ann Arbor, Michigan 1983, pp. 1–15.

588. Menuhin, *Unfinished Journey*, pp. 284–85.

589. Margaret Mehl, "Japan's Early Twentieth-Century Violin Boom," *Nineteenth-Century Music Review* 7, no. 1, 2010; Yoshimasa Kurabayashi and Yoshiro Matsuda, *Economic and Social Aspects of the Performing Arts in Japan*, Tokyo 1988, pp. 4–5.

590. Margaret Mehl, "Land of the Rising Sisters," *The Strad*, May 2007.

591. See http://www.kna-club.com/kna/kna-archiv/q_kna-concert06.html, http://www.psywar.org/page.php?detail=1944NFDTT051, accessed September 28, 2010.

592. Kurabayashi and Matsuda, *Economic and Social Aspects*, pp. 121–22.

593. Anne Midgette, "Music: A No-Frills Label Sings to the Rafters," *New York Times*, October 7, 2007.

594. Choong-sik Ahn, *The Story of Western Music in Korea*, eBookstand Books 2005, pp. 57–62.

595. David Brand, "Education: The New Whiz Kids," *Time*, August 31, 1987.

596. See http://app1.chinadaily.com.cn/star/history/00-04-11/w01-chung.html, accessed October 4, 2010; Barbara Rowes, "Tiny Kyung-wha Chung Is No Dragon Lady," *People*, November 8, 1982.

597. Sand, *Teaching Genius*, pp. 161ff.

598. Wen-Hsin Yeh, *The Alienated Academy*, Cambridge, MA 1990, p. 56; Barbara Mittler, *Dangerous Tunes*, Wiesbaden 1997, p. 26.

599. Ken Smith, "From East to West and Back," *The Strad*, September 1995; Benjamin Ivry, "In a Galaxy of Violinists, Cho-liang Lin shines Bright," *Strings*, November–December 2001.

600. Sheila Melvin and Jindong Cai, *Rhapsody in Red*, New York 2004, pp. 189–90.

601. Sheila Melvin, "An Orchestra with Political Accompaniment," *New York Times*, March 5, 2000.

602. Richard Kurt Kraus, *Pianos & Politics in China*, New York and Oxford 1989, p. 153.

603. Barbara Koh, "With Strings Attached," *Financial Times*, January 20, 2007; Joseph Kahn and Daniel Wakin, "Classical Music Looks toward China with Hope," *New York Times*, April 3, 2007; Elisabetta Povoledo, "Chinese Orchestra Performs for the Pope," *New York Times*, May 8, 2008; Daniela Petroff, "Chinese Orchestra Performs for Pope Benedict at Vatican," http://ap.google.com/article/ALeqM5h4low64OvnoS4hKG-Cq9_Joi0BtAD90GV8C01, accessed May 7, 2008.

604. Josephine R. B. Wright, "George Polgreen Bridgetower," *Musical Quarterly*, January 1980.

605. Betty Matthews, "George Polgreen Bridgetower," *Musical Review*, February 1968.

606. Banat, *The Chevalier de Saint-Georges*, pp. 12–13.

607. Douglas Fulmer, "String Band Traditions," *American Visions*, April/May 1995; Paul A. Cimbala, "The Fortunate Bondsmen," *Southern Studies* 18, 1979; "Black Musicians from Slavery to Freedom," *Journal of Negro History* 80, 1995.

608. John B. Judis, "Maximum Leader," *New York Times Book Review*, August 18, 1996.

609. "Farrakhan, in Libya, to Get Rights Award," *New York Times*, August 30, 1996.

610. Michael Daly, "Speaks Like a Devil, Plays Like an Angel," *New York Daily News*, October 15, 1995; Bernard Holland, "Sending a Message, Louis Farrakhan Plays Mendelssohn," *New York Times*, April 19, 1993.

611. Geoffrey Fushi, e-mail to the author, October 20, 2010.

612. *All Things Considered*, National Public Radio, February 16, 2002.

613. Interview with Linda Johnson, Cincinnati, Ohio, December 1999; interview with Gareth Johnson, Dubuque, Iowa, November 2008.

614. Sherrie Tucker, "West Coast Women: A Jazz Genealogy," *Pacific Review of Ethnomusicology*, Winter 1996/97.

615. Anthony Barnett, "The Gingervating Ginger," *The Strad*, November 2010.

616. A. G. Basoli, "Paganini's Violin Encounters Jazz," *New York Times*, January 2, 2002; Susan M. Barbieri, "Motown Maverick," *Strings*, February–March 2002; http://www.macfound.org/site/c.lkLXJ8MQKrH/b.2070789/apps/nl/content2.asp, accessed October 24, 2010.

617. Katie Toms and Hermione Hoby, "Why Are Our Orchestras So White?," *Guardian*, September 14, 2008.

618. Von Rhein, "Sphinx Looks to Change Makeup of U.S. Orchestras"; Linda S. Mah, "Diversity Needed in American Orchestras," *Kalamazoo Gazette*, February 18, 2010.

619. Ljiljiana Grubisic and Jill Blackledge, "In Memoriam: Eudice Shapiro," *USC News*, September 12, 2007.

620. Interview with the author, Ann Arbor, Michigan, June 9, 1998.

621. Inge Kjemtrup, "A World of Musical Wonder," *Strings*, June 2001.

622. Interviews with the author, Lübeck, August 12, 1997; Iowa City, Iowa, April 17, 2001.

623. See http://soysionista.blogspot.com/2010/04/el-violin-un-invento-sefardi.html, accessed November 12, 2010; Elana Estrin, "Did Jews Invent the Violin?," *Jerusalem Post*, August 20, 2010.

624. Roland Al Robboy, "Reifying the Heifetz-Trotsky Axis," *Los Angeles Institute of Contemporary Art Journal*, June–July 1978.

625. Isidor Loeb, "Le Nombre des Juifs de Castille et d'Espagne," *Revue des Études Juives* 14, 1887, pp. 161–83; Henry Kamen, "The Mediterranean and the Expulsion of Spanish Jews in 1492," *Past & Present*, May 1988; Santoro, *Violinari e Violini*, pp. 34–35.

626. Meucci, "Gli strumenti," in Cacciatori, ed., *Andrea Amati*, pp. 33–34.

627. Holman, *Four and Twenty Fiddlers*, pp. 15, 82ff.; Roger Prior, "Jewish Musicians at the Tudor Court," *Musical Quarterly*, Spring 1983.

628. Alfred Sendrey, *The Music of Jews in the Diaspora*, Cranberry, New Jersey, and London 1970, pp. 319ff.

629. Sendrey, *The Music*, pp. 345ff.; Moshe Beregovski, "Jewish Instrumental Folk Music" (1937), in *Old Jewish Folk Music*, Philadelphia 1982, pp. 530ff., Mark Slobin, *Fiddler on the Move*, New York 2000, passim.

630. David Sorkin, *The Transformation of German Jewry*, New York and Oxford 1987, pp. 107ff.

631. Marsha L. Rozenblit, *The Jews of Vienna*, Albany, New York 1983, pp. 99ff. Cf. Steven Beller, *Vienna and the Jews*, Cambridge and New York 1989, pp. 148ff.

632. Barbara von der Lühe, "Ich bin Pole, Jude, freier Künstler und Paneuropäer," *Das Orchester* 10, 1997; Botstein, *Judentum und Modernität*, Vienna and Cologne 1991, p. 143.

633. Botstein, *Judentum*, pp. 133–34; Steven J. Zipperstein, *The Jews of Odessa*, Stanford, California 1985, pp. 65–66.

634. Flesch, *Erinnerungen*, p. 60.

635. James Loeffler, *The Most Musical Nation*, New Haven, Connecticut, and London 2010, pp. 46, 97, 120–21.

636. Isaac Babel, "Awakening," in *The Collected Stories*, New York 1955, pp. 305ff.

637. Jonathan Karp, "Of Maestros and Minstrels," in Barbara Kirshenblatt-Gimblett and Jonathan Karp (eds.), *The Art of Being Jewish in Modern Times*, Philadelphia 2008, p. 68.

638 See http://www.thepeaches.com/music/composers/gershwin/MischaJaschaToschaSascha.htm, accessed December 27, 2008.

639. Emily Barton, "6 Rms, Riv vu," *New York Times Book Review*, June 2, 2002.

640. Eduard Hanslick, *Wiener Tagblatt*, February 27, 1897, quoted in Kühnen, "Ist die Kleine Soldat . . . ," p. 149.

641. *The Nation*, December 7, 1899.

642. Henry C. Lahee, *Famous Violinists of To-day and Yesterday*, Boston 1899, p. 300.

643. Elsie Arnold and Jane Baldauf-Berdes, *Maddalena Lombardini Sirmen*, Lanham, Maryland, and London 2002, passim.

644. Solomon, *Mozart*, pp. 294, 314.

645. Susan Kagan, "Camilla Urso," *Signs*, Spring 1977, p. 728.

646. Quoted in Karen Shaffer and Neva Greenwood, *Maud Powell*, Arlington, Virginia, and Ames, Iowa 1988, p. 277.

647. Lahee, *Famous Violinists*, p. 322.

648. Shaffer and Greenwood, *Maud Powell*, p. 140; Ammer, *Unsung*, pp. 33ff.; Camilla Urso Collection, Claremont College, http://www.oac.cdlib.org/data/13030/9d/kt4w10339d/files/kt4w10339d.pdf, accessed December 5, 2010.

649. Lahee, *Famous Violinists*, p. 324.

650. Francesca Oding, "Violins, Bows and Various Objects from the Teresina Tua Collection,"

in *Gallery of Musical Instruments: Notes for a Guided Visit*, Turin n.d., http://www.assamco.it/guidainglese.pdf, accessed December 5, 2010.

651. Shaffer and Greenwood, *Maud Powell*, p. 277; Sergei Bertensson et al., *Sergei Rachmaninov*, Bloomington, Indiana 2001, p. 67; Flesch, *Erinnerungen*, p. 49; "Signorina Teresina Tua," *New York Times*, October 18, 1887.

652. John Clapham, "Wilma Neruda," in *Grove Music Online*, accessed December 7, 2010.

653. Paula Gillett, *Musical Women in England 1870–1914*, New York 2000, p. 82.

654. Quoted in Shaffer and Greenwood, *Maud Powell*, p. 277.

655. Barbara Kühnen, "Ist die Kleine Soldat . . .," in Ostleitner and Simek, eds., *Ich Fahre in Mein Liebes Wien*, p. 137.

656. Hermann Klein, "An Annual Critical Report of Important Musical Events," *Musical Notes*, 1889, p. 26.

657. Tully Potter, "Brahms's Understudy," *The Strad*, December 1996.

658. Quoted in Shaffer and Greenwood, *Maud Powell*, p. 318.

659. Amy Fay, "Music in New York," *Music*, December 1900.

660. Alan Walker, *Franz Liszt*, Ithaca, New York 1996, p. 472.

661. "Her $5000 Stradivarius," *New York Times*, January 28, 1893; Misc Rep 210, Gemunder et al. T. Hauser, City Court of New York, General Term, December 8, 1993.

662. "Promenade Concerts, Queen's Hall," *Musical Times*, October 1, 1900.

663. "Leonora von Stosch in Her Own Words," *The Strad*, June 1998.

664. "Society in the Berkshires," *New York Times*, September 10, 1893.

665. "American Girl Wins a Prize," *New York Times*, October 2, 1897; http://lcweb2.loc.gov/service/music/eadxmlmusic/eadpdfmusic/mu2005.wp.0053.pdf, accessed December 10, 2010.

666. "The Philharmonic Society," *New York Times,* January 6, 1900.

667. "Lincolns Entertain the Tafts," *New York Times*, September 8, 1913.

668. Wayne Warren, "District of Columbia's Largest Residence Pipe Organ Saved from Demolition," *Tracker*, July 1, 2004; Peter Quinn, "Race Cleansing in America," *American Heritage Magazine*, February/March 2003.

669. See http://lcweb2.loc.gov/service/music/eadxmlmusic/eadpdfmusic/mu2005.wp.0053.pdf, accessed December 11, 2010.

670. Shaffer and Greenwood, *Maud Powell*, pp. 300–1.

671. Ibid., p. 319.

672. "Fail to Steal Rare Violin," *New York Times*, July 14, 1911; Scott Nearing, "Wages and Salaries Organized Industry," *Popular Science Monthly*, May 1915, p. 487.

673. See http://www.cozio.com/Instrument.aspx?id=2699, accessed December 16, 2010; "George Gemunder Dead," *New York Times*, January 17, 1899.

674. "Gets Maud Powell Violin," *New York Times*, February 23, 1921.

675. "Noted Baritone and Violinist to Broadcast on Thursday," *New York Times*, February 8, 1925.

676. Karen Shaffer, e-mail to the author, December 19, 2010.

677. "Erica Morini, 91," *New York Times,* November 3, 1995; Margaret Campbell, "Obituary: Erica Morini," *Independent*, November 10, 1995; Tully Potter, "Connoisseur's Choice," *The Strad*, March 1996.

678. Joseph Macleod, *The Sisters d'Aranyi*, London 1969, passim.

679. Peter Quantrill, "Guila Bustabo," *Guardian*, June 12, 2002.

680. Jessica Duchen, "Handled with Care," *The Strad*, December 1986.

681. Haendel, *Woman with Violin*, p. 159.

682. Interview with the author, London, September 20, 2000.

683. Axelrod, ed., *Heifetz*, pp. 10–12.

684. Richard Newman with Karen Kirtley, *Alma Rosé*, Portland, Oregon 2000, passim.

685. "Phil Spitalny, Leader of All-Girl Orchestra, Dies at 80," *New York Times,* October 12, 1970.

686. Sherrie Tucker, *Swing Shift*, Durham, North Carolina, and London 2000, pp. 70ff.

687. Josef Hofmann to Eudice Shapiro, December 5, 1939.

688. Interview with the author, Los Angeles, California, March 10, 2000.

689. Chris Pasles, "Eudice Shapiro, 93; Violinist Who Made History in Hollywood," *Los Angeles Times*, September 25, 2007.

690. Shaffer and Greenwood, *Maud Powell*, pp. 134ff., 282ff.

691. Quoted in Ammer, *Unsung*, pp. 140ff.; *La Vie Musicale*, February 1, 1912.

692. Lara St. John, "An Interview That Pissed Me Off," http://www.larastjohn.com/essays/pissedinterview.html, accessed April 2002; Lynne Walker, "The Allure of the Violin," *Independent*, April 19, 2005.

693. Michael White, "Tasmin Little: The Violin Star from Next Door," *New York Times*, November 9, 2003.

694. James R. Oestreich, "As Complex as the Music She Plays," *New York Times,* November 11, 2010.

695. Anne Midgette, "The Curse of Beauty for Serious Musicians," *New York Times*, May 27, 2004.

696. Interview with the author, Berlin, December 19, 1997.

697. Norman Lebrecht, "Ida Haendel—The One They Don't Want You to Hear," June 22, 2000, http://www.scena.org/columns/lebrecht/000621-NL-IdaHaendel.html.

698. Telephone interview with the author, November 3, 2005.

699. Robinson, *The Last Impresario*, pp. 29ff., 103.

700. Cited by William Weber, *The Rise of Musical Classics in Eighteenth Century England*, New York 1992, p. 5.

701. Cited by William Weber, *Music and the Middle Class*, London 1975, pp. 18ff.

702. Alessandra Comini, *The Changing Image of Beethoven*, Santa Fe, New Mexico 2008, p. 144; Weber, *Music and the Middle Class*, p. 45; Lebrecht, *When the Music Stopped*, pp. 43ff.

703. Lebrecht, *When the Music Stopped*, pp. 98–99.

704. Heinrich Ehrlich, "Konzertgeber und Konzertagenten," in *Modernes Musikleben*, Berlin 1895, p. 9.

705. Constance Hope, "Dr. Jekyll and Mr. Heifetz," cited in Axelrod, ed., *Heifetz*, pp. 145ff.; Mary R. Bowling, "Such Interesting People," *Columbia Library Columns*, November 1976.

706. Heinrich Ehrlich, "Die Modernen Konzertreisen," in *Modernes Musikleben*, p. 5.

707. Lebrecht, *When the Music Stopped*, p. 84.

708. Flesch, *Erinnerungen*, p. 93.

709. Heinrich Ehrlich, *Dreissig Jahre Künstlerleben*, Berlin 1893, pp. 311–12.

710. John Bainbridge, "S. Hurok," *Life*, August 28, 1944.

711. Bosley Crowther, "Tonight We Sing," *New York Times,* February 13, 1953.

712. "Music: S. Hurok," *Time*, March 18, 1974.

713. Interview with the author, Iowa City, Iowa, April 10, 2000.

714. William Berlind, "Ronald Wilford, Steel-Fisted Manager of Virtuosos, Trashes his Board," *New York Observer*, March 22, 1998.

715. Norman Lebrecht, "Could Silver Fox, the Manager of Maestros, Be Losing His Grip?," http://www.scena.org/columns/lebrecht/010124-NL-silverfox.html, accessed January 24, 2001; www.cami.com, accessed January 2, 2011.

716. Lebrecht, *When the Music Stops*, p. 444.

717. Tim Rogers, "How a Dallas Hedge Fund Manager Got Caught Up in a World of Fraud," *D Magazine,* June 2009.

718. Cf. Drew McManus, "IMG Artists Chairman Guilty of Securities Fraud," *Adaptistration*, April 16, 2009; "Additional Fallout from the IMG Artists Scandal," *Adaptistration*, May 5, 2009.

719. Keith J. Fernandez, "Part of the Manager's Job Is to Bring Money into the Arts," *Emirates 24/7,* March 27, 2008.

720. Nicholas Confessore, "For a Low-Budget Comedy, an Unexpected Second Act," *New York Times,* March 22, 2009; Brendan Case, "Dallas Hedge Fund Exec Barrett Wissman Pleads Guilty to Securities Fraud," *Dallas Morning News,* April 16, 2009; Norman Lebrecht, "IMG Artists Adrift After Wissman Plea," *Bloomberg News*, May 1, 2009; Tomoeh Murakami Tse, "Ex-Official David Logisci's Plea Advances N.Y. State Pension Probe," *Washington Post*, March 11, 2010.

721. Temianka, *Facing the Music*, pp. 205ff.

722. William Primrose, *Walk on the North Side*, Provo, Utah 1978, pp. 41–42.

723. Haendel, *Woman with Violin*, pp. 84ff., 108ff.

724. Temianka, *Facing the Music*, p. 217.

725. Artur Holde, "Glanz und Elend der Solisten in den USA," *Neue Zeitschrift für Musik*, February 1957.

726. Lebrecht, *When the Music Stops*, pp. 138–40; Wolfgang Sandner, "Fast ein Staatskünstler," *Frankfurter Allgemeine Zeitung*, September 30, 2000.

727. Ralph Blumenthal, "Discord over Concerts in the Heartland," *New York Times*, March 10, 2003.

728. Evan Eisenberg, *The Recording Angel*, New York 1988, p. 16.

729. Erik Østergaard, "The History of Nipper and His Master's Voice," http://www.erikoest.dk/nipper.htm, accessed January 9, 2011.

730. Shaffer and Greenwood, *Maud Powell*, pp. 214ff., 263, 380.

731. Axelrod, ed., *Heifetz*, pp. 650ff.

732. "Vivaldi für das Volk," *Frankfurter Allgemeine Zeitung*, June 16, 2007.

733. Anne Midgette, "Classical Artists Such as Hilary Hahn Chart Big on Billboard with Little Sales," *Washington Post*, January 30, 2010.

734. "Vanessa-Mae Tops Young-Rich List," April 21, 2006, http://news.bbc.co.uk/2/hi/business/4927490.stm; "Crossover Is Key, Says Pop Violinist David Garrett," August 12, 2009, http://www.dw-world.de/dw/article/0,,4557458,00.html, accessed January 11, 2011.

735. Norman Lebrecht, "Young, Gifted and Left to Go It Alone," February 14, 2007, http://www.scena.org/columns/lebrecht/070214-NL-gifted.html; Malcolm Hayes, "Seriously Thrilling," http://www.ruthpalmer.com/photos/classic-fm-review.jpg, accessed January 11, 2011.

736. Anne Midgette, "A No-Frills Label Sings to the Rafters," *New York Times*, October 7, 2007.

737. Interview with the author, Hong Kong, October 22, 2001.

738. Telephone interview with the author, February 15, 2011.

739. Interview with the author Hamburg, December 10, 1997.

740. Interview with the author, Hanover, Germany, November 30, 2000.

741. Interview with the author, Amsterdam, March 26, 1999.

742. Arthur Lubow, "Movement," *New York Times Magazine,* June 19, 2005; John Hiscock, "Carnegie Hall: Knight Who Conquered New York," *Telegraph,* August 5, 2009.

743. "Ariama.com Announces Partnership Agreements with Key Classical Institutions," PR Newswire, December 14, 2010.

744. Jeff Lunden, "Juilliard, Carnegie Join Together to Teach More than Music," http://m.npr.org/news/NPR+Music+Mobile/132491657?singlePage=true, January 2, 2011.

745. Klaus Harpprecht, "Musik ist Menschlich, in jeder Hinsicht," *Neue Gesellschaft/Frankfurter Hefte* 11, 1997.

746. Richard Kurt Kraus, *Pianos & Politics in China*, New York and Oxford 1989, pp. 154–57.

747. Ross, *Listen to This*, p. 164.

748. "Orchestra Important in Rebuilding Iraq," Associated Press, November 14, 2003; Barbara Jepson, "The Battle of the Bands Is Peaceable," *New York Times*, December 7, 2003; Lynn Neary, "Iraqi Orchestra Visits Washington," *All Things Considered*, National Public Radio, December 9, 2003; Edward Wong, "And the Orchestra Plays On," *New York Times*, September 28, 2006; Sam Enriquez, "Iraqi Orchestra Finds Harmony amid War," *Los Angeles Times*, September 23, 2007; Steven Lee Myers, "National Symphony Orchestra," http://baghdadbureau.blogs.nytimes.com/2009/07/22/national-symphony-orchestra/.

749. Robert Fisk, "These Iranian Troubadours Show How Music Can Corrupt the Soul," *Independent*, December 5, 2009.

750. Schenk, *Die Hochschule*, p. 62.

751. Ernest Newman, "The War and the Future of Music," *Musical Times*, September 1, 1914.

752. Acta Betreffend den Lehrer Professor Henri Marteau, Königliche akademische Hochschule für Musik zu Berlin, Universität der Künste, Berlin.

753. Fritz Kreisler, *Four Weeks in the Trenches*, Boston and New York 1915.

754. Biancolli, *Fritz Kreisler*, pp. 97ff.; Lochner, *Fritz Kreisler*, pp. 138ff.; "Fritz Kreisler in a Statement of Great Frankness Tells of His Conduct in the War," *New York Times*, November 25, 1917; "Kreisler Calls on Hillis to Retract," *New York Times*, November 27, 1917.

755. Juri Jelagin, *The Taming of the Arts*, New York 1951, pp. 179ff.

756. Harri Körvits, *Eduard Soermus*, Leipzig 1978, passim.

757. See http://holocaustmusic.ort.org/politics-and-propaganda/third-reich/havemann-gustav/, http://www.havemann.com/havemann_gustav.html, accessed January 23, 2011.

758. Flesch, *Erinnerungen*, p. 173.

759. Albrecht Dümling and Peter Girth, *Entartete Musik*, Düsseldorf 1993, pp. 84–86.

760. Cited in Barbara von der Lühe, "Ich bin Pole, Jude, Freier Künstler und Paneuropäer," *Das Orchester*, October 1997.

761. Frederick T. Birchall, "Hubermann Bars German Concerts," *New York Times*, September 14, 1933.

762. Temianka, *Facing the Music*, pp. 61–62; Tully Potter, *Adolf Busch*, London 2010, Vol. 1, pp. 637–43.

763. Rep 80, Acc. 3223, Nr. 163/1, Landesarchiv Berlin, personnel file, Hochschule der Musik Hanns Eisler.

764. Cited in Dümling and Girth, *Entartete Musik*, p. 223.

765. "Hidden 84 Years, Concerto Is Heard," *New York Times*, November 27, 1937.

766. Olin Downes, "Schumann Concerto," *New York Times*, December 5, 1937.

767. Potter, *Adolf Busch*, p. 656.

768. Erik Palmstierna, *Horizons of Immortality*, London 1937; Sir Oliver Lodge, "Baron Palmstierna's Book," *Observer*, September 26, 1937.

769. Olin Downes, "Music of the Times: A Schumann Concerto Found," *New York Times*, August 22, 1937.

770. Macleod, *The Sisters D'Aranyi*, pp. 186ff.

771. Cited in Downes, "Music of the Times."

772. Potter, *Adolf Busch*, p. 656.

773. Ibid., pp. 483ff.

774. Weiler, *Gerhard Taschner*, pp. 33–34.

775. Prof. Georg Kulenkampff, personnel file, Universität der Künste, Berlin.

776. Joachim Hartnack, *Große Geiger unserer Zeit*, Zurich 1993, p. 145.

777. Fred K. Prieberg, *Musik in der Sowjetunion*, Cologne 1965, pp. 15 and 461.

778. Kremer, *Kindheitssplitter*, p. 95.

779. "Inspired Minds," interview with Deutsche Welle 2003, http://inspiredminds.de/detail.php?id=35, accessed February 19, 2011.

780. Interview with the author, Cologne, September 25, 1997.

781. Bruno Monsaingeon, "Oistrakh: Artist of the People?," Warner Music Vision 1994.

782. Mstislav Rostropovich and Galina Vishnevskaya, *Russia, Music and Liberty*, Portland, Oregon 1983, p. 102.

783. David Rounds, "Quartet-Tradition, Russian Style," *The Strad,* June 1995.

784. Tully Potter, "Eclipsed Genius," *The Strad*, April 1997.

785. Schwarz, *Music and Musical Life*, pp. 95ff.

786. Interview with the author, Düsseldorf, December 1, 2000.

787. Monsaingeon, "Oistrakh."

788. Jelagin, *Taming of the Arts*, p. 226.

789. Rosa Fain, interview with the author, Düsseldorf, December 1, 2000; Soroker, *David Oistrakh*.

790. Interviews with the author, St. Petersburg, November 21, 1997; Düsseldorf, December 1, 2000.

791. Dubinsky, *Stormy Applause*, New York 1989, p. 5.

792. Ibid., p. 27.

793. Soroker, *David Oistrakh*, p. 128.

794. Monsaingeon, "Oistrakh: Artist of the People?"

795. Interview with the author, Cologne, September 25, 1997.

796. Monsaingeon, "Oistrakh: Artist of the People?"

797. Quoted by Peter Pulzer, e-mail to the author, May 26, 2002; Kozinn, *Mischa Elman*, p. 251; Milstein, *From Russia*, pp. 218ff.

798. Dmitri Paperno, *Notes of a Moscow Pianist*, Portland, Oregon 1998, p. 153.

799. "Man Muss als Künstler ein Risiko Tragen," *Der Spiegel*, December 17, 1979.

800. Soroker, *David Oistrakh*, p. 124.

801. Dubinsky, *Stormy Applause*, p. 22.

802. Milstein, *From Russia*, p. 223; interview with Dmitri Sitkovetsky, Cologne, September 25, 1997; interview with Rosa Fain, Düsseldorf, December 1, 2000.

803. Soroker, *David Oistrakh*, p. 111.

804. Dubinsky, *Stormy Applause*, pp. 262ff.

805. Louis Rapoport, *Stalin's War Against the Jews*, New York 1990, pp. 176ff.

806. Interview with the author, Düsseldorf, December 1, 2000.

807. Monsaingeon, "Oistrakh: Artist of the People?"

808. Gidon Kremer, *Obertöne*, Salzburg and Vienna 1997, p. 220.

809. "Man Muss als Künstler . . . "; Carla Hall, "Defection Reported," *Washington Post,* August 20, 1980; Eleanor Blau, "Soviet Puzzle," *New York Times*, August 27, 1980.

810. "Sich Umdrehen und Weggehen—Das War der Letzte Mögliche Protest," *Frankfurter Allgemeine*, May 6, 1982.

811. Faber, *Stradivari's Genius*, pp. xvi–xvii; Veli-Pekka Lappalainen, "Finnish Journalist

Reveals Role in Mullova Defection 25 Years Ago," *Helsingen Sanomat*, September 14, 2008; Joe Klein, "From Russia with Talent," *New York*, August 6, 1984.

812. Brüggemann, "Hammer und Sichel"; "Russian Violinists, Asian Strings," *Economist*, February 21, 1998.

813. William Harvey, "Playing for the Fighting 69th," *Juilliard Journal*, October 2001, http://www.aolnews.com/2010/08/09/wielding-a-violin-for-change-in-afghanistan/; interview with Scott Simon, "An American Musician, an Influence in Afghanistan," *Weekend Edition Saturday*, National Public Radio, December 3, 2010.

BOOK 4: IMAGINING IT

1. Conrad Aiken, "Music I Heard," in Harriet Monroe, ed., *The New Poetry: An Anthology*, New York 1917.

2. Harold D. Dickerson Jr., "The Music of *This* Sphere in Keller's *Romeo und Julia auf dem Dorfe*," *German Quarterly*, January 1978.

3. Dorothy Adelson, "The Vinteuil Sonata," *Music and Letters* 23, 1942, pp. 228ff. Cf. André Coeuroy, "Music in the Work of Marcel Proust," *Musical Quarterly* 12, 1926, pp. 132–51; Walter A. Strauss, review, *SubStance*, Special Issue, 1993, pp. 361–64.

4. Malcolm Boyd, "Dance of Death," *Grove Music Online*, accessed October 23, 2006, including hyperlink to illustration.

5. Pierluigi Petrobelli, *Tartini, le sue idee e il suo tempo*, Lucca 1992, p. 99.

6. Ibid., pp. 6, 33–34.

7. Joseph Jérome Lalande, *Voyage d'un François en Italie*, Paris 1770, Vol. 8, pp. 188–90.

8. Claudio Casini, *Paganini*, Milan 1982, pp. 109–10.

9. Ivor Guest, *Fanny Cerrito*, London 1974, pp. 55–56, 128–29, 136; Biddulph et al., *Giuseppe Guarneri*, p. 35.

10. Peter Burwasser, "Symphony of Destruction," *Philadelphia Citypaper*, March 18–24, 2004.

11. See http://www.gospelmusic.org.uk/other_music/devil_went_to_georgia.htm, accessed October 28, 2006; Charlie Daniels, "The Devil Went Down to Georgia," Atlanta 1985, http://en.wikipedia.org/wiki/The_Devil_Went_Down_to_Georgia#Parodies, accessed November 6, 2006.

12. Boyden, *The History*, pp. 7–12.

13. See http://www.appliedmicrowave.com/PrintAds.htm and http://www.rareads.com/scans/9615.jpg, accessed October 14, 2006.

14. Viz. Jeremy Montagu, "Musical Instruments in Hans Memling's Paintings," *Early Music*, 2007, pp. 505–24.

15. Max Sauerlandt, *Die Musik in Fünf Jahrhunderten der Europäischen Malerei*, Königstein and Leipzig 1922, p. iii.

16 Ildikó Ember, *Music in Painting*, Budapest 1989, plate 20.

17. Marc Le Bot, "L'âme du violon," in *Les Violons, Lutherie Vénitienne, Peinetures et Dessins*, Paris 1995, pp. 216ff.

18. Ibid., plate 35.

19. Ibid., plate 32; Annalisa Bini, Claudio Strinati, and Rossella Vodret, *Colori della Musica*, Geneva and Milan 2000, pp. 153 and 157.

20. Bini et al., *Colori della Musica*, pp. 231 and 233.

21. Sauerlandt, *Die Musik in fünf Jahrhunderten der Europäischen Malerei*, p. 93.

22. Gilles Lambert, *Caravaggio*, Cologne 2000, p. 8.

23. Sylvia Ferino-Pagden, *Dipingere La Musica*, Milan 2000, p. 202.

24. Budapest Museum of Fine Arts; see http://commons.wikimedia.org/wiki/Image:Benjamin_Gerritsz._Cuyp_001.jpg, accessed November 11, 2006.

25. Ferino-Pagden, *Dipingere*, p. 230.

26. Ibid., pp. 260–61; see http://www.itc-belotti.org/basch4a/bascheni.htm, accessed November 3, 2006.

27. Bini et al., *Colori della Musica*, p. 212.

28. See http://www.art.nl/journal/article.aspx?ID=3, accessed November 9, 2006.

29. See http://www.franshalsmuseum.collectionconnection.nl/FHM/franshals_fs_e.aspx?i=eos%2075-332.JPG&m=e-os%2075-332.JPG.

30. See http://commons.wikimedia.org/wiki/Image:Januarius_Zick_005.jpg, accessed December 7, 2006.

31. See http://commons.wikimedia.org/wiki/Image:Januarius_Zick_001.jpg, accessed December 7, 2006.

32. See http://www.getty.edu/museum/conservation/partnerships/bouguereau/, http://www.metafilter.com/mefi/32533, http://en.wikipedia.org/wiki/Image:Bouguereau_Seule-au-monde.jpg, accessed November 19, 2006.

33. See John Rockwell, "A German Who Cast a Sharp Eye on His Countrymen," *New York Times*, June 16, 1996; http://www.berlinonline.de/berliner-zeitung/archiv/.bin/dump.fcgi/1998/0729/feuilleton/0019/index.html.

34. See http://www.carlspitzweg.de/, accessed November 22, 2006.

35. Frederick C. Moffatt, "Barnburning and Hunkerism," *Winterthur Portfolio*, Spring 1994.

36. See http://en.wikipedia.org/wiki/George_Caleb_Bingham, accessed November 13, 2006.

37. Albert TenEyck Gardner, "Harnett's 'Music and Good Luck,'" *Metropolitan Museum of Art Bulletin*, January 1964; Carol J. Oja, "The Still-Life Paintings of William Michael Harnett," *Musical Quarterly*, October 1977; Laurence Libin, "Still Life with Violin and Music," *BBC Music*, August 1, 2002; http://www.sheldonartgallery.org/collection/index.html?topic=extension&clct_artist_full_name=Frank+Tuchfarber&clct_id=6365, accessed November 17, 2006; http://www.nga.gov/cgi-bin/pinfo?Object=78129+0+note, accessed November 23, 2006.

38. Paul Ripley, http://www.victorianartinbritain.co.uk/tissot_hush.htm, http://www.victorianartinbritain.co.uk/biog/tissot.htm, accessed November 26, 2006.

39. M. Therese Southgate, "The Cover," *Journal of the American Medical Association*, January 10, 2001, p. 137; http://www.nga.gov/collection/gallery/gg90/gg90-46354.0.html, accessed November 23, 2006.

40. Boyden, *The History*, plates 37 and 39.

41. See http://www.npg.org.uk/live/search/portrait.asp?search=sp&sText=D11509&rNo=0, accessed November 26, 2006; Stewart Deas, "Arcangelo Corelli," *Music and Letters*, January 1953, p. 3.

42. Jonathan Swift, *Gulliver's Travels*, part 4, chapter 10, in *Selected Prose Works of Jonathan Swift*, London 1949, p. 367.

43. See http://www.hung-art.hu/kep/d/donat/muvek/bihari.jpg, accessed November 26, 2006; Bence Szabolcsi, *A Concise History of Hungarian Music*, Budapest 1974, chapter 6.

44. James D. Herbert, "A Picture of Chardin's Making," *Eighteenth-Century Studies* 34, no. 2, p. 260.

45. See http://www.royalcollection.org.uk/eGallery/object.asp?theme=ARTS&object=407298&row=3.

46. Schwab, *Konzert*, Vol. 4, p. 82, plate 52.

47. Berri, *Paganini*, p. 159.

48. Aileen Ribiero, *Ingres in Fashion*, New Haven, Connecticut, and London, 1999, passim.

49. Nina Athanassaglou-Kallmyer, "Blemished Physiologies," *Art Bulletin*, December 2001.

50. Boris Schwarz, "Heinrich Wilhelm Ernst," *Grove Music Online*, accessed December 2, 2006, http://www.grovemusic.com.

51. *Vanity Fair*, January 5, 1905.

52. William J. McCloskey, *Man with Violin, 1920*, Bowers Museum of Cultural Art, Santa Ana, California.

53. Lawrence Ferlinghetti, "Don't Let That Horse," in *A Coney Island of the Mind*, New York 1958.

54. John Russell, "Farewell to Chagall," *New York Times*, April 7, 1985; http://www.suite101.com/article.cfm/graphic_artists_retired; http://mahalanobis.twoday.net/topics/art/, accessed December 3, 2006; e-mail to the author from John Malyon, December 4, 2006; www.artcyclopedia.com, accessed December 5, 2006.

55. André Kertész, *Hungarian Memories*, Boston 1982; Ben Shahn, http://lcweb2.loc.gov/cgi-bin/query/D?fsaall:7:./temp/~pp_xdii, accessed May 23, 2007.

56. See http://www.wakeling.demon.co.uk/page5-photo-essay.htm, accessed June 17, 2008.

57. See http://commons.wikimedia.org/wiki/Image:Marconi_Gaudenzio_-_Nudo_accademico_femminile_con_violino.jpg, accessed June 17, 2008.

58. See http://cgfa.sunsite.dk/hughes/p-hughes42.htm, accessed June 17, 2008; cf. Gillett, *Musical Women in England*, pp. 101–4.

59. Draft introduction, p. 4, in Rostal papers, 1905–91, Folder "I. Fassung und Verschiedenes," Hochschule der Künste, Berlin.

60. Lebrecht, "Yehudi Menuhin—So Much Love."

61. *Economist*, June 23, 2007, p. 73.

62. "Bond Quartet Hits US High Note," BBC News, April 18, 2001, http://news.bbc.co.uk/2/hi/entertainment/1284270.stm, accessed December 8, 2006.

63. See http://www.answers.com/topic/bond-string-quartet, accessed February 9, 2010.

64. See http://www.emersonquartet.com/artist.php?view=dpk, accessed December 8, 2006.

65. Molière, "Le Bourgeois Gentilhomme," act 2, scene 3, in Maurice Rat, ed., *Théatre Choisi*, Paris 1954.

66. See http://drama.eserver.org/plays/medieval/gammer-gurton.txt, act 2, scene 3, accessed April 14, 2007.

67. Holman, *Four and Twenty Fiddlers*, pp. 58ff.

68. Quoted by J. L. Boston, "Musicians and Scrapers: An Eighteenth-Century Opinion," *Galpin Society Journal*, June 1956.

69. William Wordsworth, "The Waggoner," London 1819, Canto Second, lines 297–98, 374–75.

70. William Wordsworth, "The Power of Music," in *The Poetical Works of William Wordsworth*, Vol. 2, Oxford 1952, pp. 217–19.

71. *Joseph von Eichendorffs Werke*, Leipzig 1924, p. 6; Anton Wilhelm Florentin von Zuccalmaglio et al., "Der bucklichte Fiedler," *Deutsche Volkslieder*, Berlin 1840; Thomas Hardy, "At the Railway Station, Upways," in *Late Lyrics and Earlier*, London 1922; William Butler Yeats, "The Fiddler of Dooney," *The Wind Among the Reeds*, New York and London 1899.

72. Archibald Lampman, "The Violinist," *Poems of Archibald Lampman*, Toronto 1900.

73. Joyce H. Cauthen, *With Fiddle and Well-Rosined Bow*, Tuscaloosa and London 1989, pp. 19–40.

74. See http://www.npr.org/templates/story/story.php?storyId=128172325 and http://www.wvculture.org/goldenseal/Fall10/byrd.html, accessed September 28, 2012.

75. Anne de Noailles, "Les Violins Dans le Soir," *Les Eblouissements*, Paris 1907.

76. Rainer Maria Rilke, "Der Nachbar," *Das Buch der Bilder*, Munich 1902.

77. M. Jouravel, "Violin and a Little Nervous," *The First Rendezvous: Translation of Select Collection of Russian Poetry*, SPb: Renome; 2003, p. 228. See http://www.chernomore.net/Poetry/Vladimir_Mayakovsky.htm.

78. Charles Valentine Le Grice, "To a Gentleman, Who Presented the Author with a Violin," http://www.radix.net/~dalila/violinpoems.html, accessed June 10, 2007.

79. "True Music," *Fun*, April 18, 1877.

80. Marion Scott, *Violin Verses*, London 1905.

81. James B. Kenyon, "Her Violin," *Magazine of Music*, May 1896.

82. Charles Baudelaire, *Les Fleurs du Mal*, Paris 1857.

83. Respective translations by Walter Aggeler, Roy Campbell, Lewis Piaget Shanks, Geoffrey Wagner, http://fleursdumal.org/poem/142, accessed April 19, 2007.

84. Ignace Feuerlicht, "Baudelaire's 'Harmonie du Soir,'" *French Review*, October 1959, p. 17.

85. Paul Verlaine, "Chanson d'Automne," in *Poèmes Saturniens, Oeuvres Poétiques Complètes*, Paris 1957, p. 56.

86. See http://textetc.com/workshop/wt-verlaine-1.html, accessed April 16, 2007.

87. See http://verlaineexplique.free.fr/poemesat/chanson.html, accessed April 16, 2007.

88. Henry Wadsworth Longfellow, *Tales of a Wayside Inn*, Boston 1863.

89. Amy Lowell, preface, *Men, Women and Ghosts*, New York 1916.

90. William C. Bedford, "A Musical Apprentice: Amy Lowell to Carl Engel," *Musical Quarterly*, October 1972.

91. Carl Sandburg, "Bath," *Chicago Poems*, New York 1916.

92. Sandburg, "Jan Kubelik," ibid.

93. Carl Sandburg, "Kreisler," *Cornhuskers*, New York 1918.

94. George Plimpton, *Out of My League*, Guilford, Connecticut 2003, p. 44.

95. "Paganini, Poetical Works 1822–59," in Robert Morrison and Michael Eberle-Sinatra, eds., *Selected Writings of Leigh Hunt*, Vol. 6, London and Brookfield, Vermont 2003.

96. Percy M. Young, "Leigh Hunt—Music Critic," *Music and Letters*, April 1944, p. 94.

97. Johannes Brockt, "Grillparzer and Music," *Music and Letters*, July 1947, p. 242.

98. Franz Grillparzer, "Paganini," in Rudolf von Gottschall, ed., *Grillparzers Sämtliche Werke*, Vol. 2, Hamburg n.d., p. 130.

99. See http://www.writersblock.ca/winter1999/feature2.htm, accessed June 15, 2007.

100. Scott Emmons, "Paganini!" http://www.wordchowder.com/Geniuses.html, accessed June 14, 2007.

101. "New Publications," *New York Times*, November 17, 1878; "Rests on a Strad," *New York Times*, March 4, 1896.

102. Nathan Shaham, *The Rosendorf Quartet*, trans. Dalya Bilu, New York 1987.

103. Vikram Seth, *An Equal Music*, London 1999.

104. Wolfgang Camphausen, *Eine Kleine Schachmusik*, Cologne 1999, p. 33.

105. Ted Friedman, "Music of Sherlock Holmes," *Topical Time*, November–December 1998, pp. 32–33; http://www.trussel.com/detfic/friedmus.htm, accessed January 12, 2008. Cf. Carl Heifetz, "The Case of the Jewish Pawnbroker," *Plugs and Dottles*, January 1996, http://www.sherlock-holmes.com/featur5.htm, accessed July 13, 2008.

106. Edward Heron-Allen, *A Fatal Fiddle*, Chicago, New York, and San Francisco 1886; Charles Allen, *Papier Mâché*, New York and London 1896; Walter Mayson, *The Stolen Fiddle*, London and New York 1897.

107. See http://www.telinco.co.uk/RobertTemple/Dmstr1.htm, accessed February 12, 2008.

108. Paul Adam, *Sleeper*, London 2004; Douglas Preston and Lincoln Childs, *Brimstone*, New York and Boston 2004; Joseph Roccasalvo, *Portrait of a Woman*, San Francisco 1995; Jô Soares, *O Xangô de Baker Street*, Saõ Paulo 1995, translation of *A Samba for Sherlock*, New York 1997; Gerald Elias, *Devil's Trill*, New York 2009.

109. See http://en.wikipedia.org/wiki/Paul_Adam_(English_novelist), http://tubious.com/paul-adam-novelist, http://www.prestonchild.com/bios/index.html, accessed January 20, 2008; Joann Laviglio, "Preston, Child Collaboration Continues with New Novel," Associated Press, June 28, 2006; http://en.wikipedia.org/wiki/J%C3%B4_Soares, accessed February 3, 2008.

110. See http://madstopreading.wordpress.com/2007/12/14/digging-into-the-preston-child-myst ique/, accessed January 24, 2008.

111. See http://www.geraldelias.com/bio.html, accessed February 7, 2010.

112. Preston and Childs, *Brimstone*, p. 335.

113. Paul Adam, *Paganini's Ghost*, New York 2009.

114. John Hersey, *Antonietta*, New York 1991.

115. John Hersey, "The Art of Fiction," *Paris Review*, Summer–Fall 1986.

116. Kees van Hage, *Verstreken Jaren*, Amsterdam 1992.

117. *Consular Reports, Commerce, Manufactures, Etc.,* May, June, July, August 1895, Washington, D.C., p. 277.

118. Maud des Champs de la Tour, *The History of a Violin*, Lymington 1878.

119. W. Thomas Marrocco, *Memoirs of a Stradivarius*, New York, Los Angeles, Chicago 1988.

120. Jean Diwo, *Moi, Milanollo*, Paris 2007.

121. See http://www.cozio.com/forum/Topic125-3-1.aspx, accessed May 20, 2008.

122. See http://www.xigenpharma.com/management_governance.htm, accessed May 20, 2008.

123. Patricia Boccadoro, "Interview: Corey Cerovsek," November 5, 2006, http://www.culture kiosque.com/klassik/intervie/corey_cerovsek.html, accessed May 20, 2008.

124. See http://editions.flammarion.com/editeurs/?flam, http://www.rcsmediagroup.it/wps/por tal/mg/business/books/flammarion?language=en, accessed May 20, 2008.

125. See http://www.actualitedulivre.com/interview.php?sur=Jean%20Diwo, http://www.lire.fr/ critique.asp/idC=50710&idTC=3&idR=218&idG=3, accessed May 21, 2008.

126. Diwo, *Moi, Milanollo*, p. 387.

127. Honoré de Balzac, "Gambara," trans. Clara Bell and James Waring, Penn State Electronic Series, 2002, http://artfl.uchicago.edu/cgi-bin/philologic31/getobject.pl?c.74:1.balzac, accessed May 26, 2008.

128. Franz Grillparzer, "Der Arme Spielmann," in Rudolf von Gottschall, ed., *Grillparzers Sämtliche Werke*, Vol. 2, pp. 177ff.

129. Herman Melville, "The Fiddler," *Harper's New Monthly*, September 1854.

130. Franz Grillparzer, "Biographisches," *Grillparzers Sämtliche Werke*, Vol. 2, pp. 377, 388–89.

131. R. K. Gupta, "Hautboy and Plinlimmon," *American Literature*, November 1971.

132. Horatio Alger, *Phil the Fiddler*, Philadelphia and Boston 1872.

133. Kate Douglas Wiggin, "A Village Stradivarius," *Atlantic Monthly*, January–February 1895.

134. Eleanor H. Porter, *Just David*, New York and Boston 1916.

135. John Philip Sousa, *The Fifth String*, Indianapolis, Indiana 1902.

136. See http://www.wgpark.com/page.asp?pid=10, accessed December 21, 2010.

137. In E. T. A. Hoffmann, *Rat Krespel, Die Fermate, Don Juan*, Stuttgart 1966.

138. Cf. James M. McGlathery, "Der Himmel Hängt Ihm Voller Geigen," *German Quarterly*, March 1978; Birgit Röder, "'Sie Ist Dahin und das Geheimnis Gelöst,'" *German Life and Letters*, January 2000; Christof M. Stotko, "Die Adaption der Weiblichen Gesangstimme als Mittel der Dominanz Musikalischer Produktion in E. T. A. Hoffmann's *Rat Krespel*," seminar paper, University of Munich, July 15, 2002.

139. John Meade Falkner, *The Lost Stradivarius*, Edinburgh and London 1895.

140. Sir William Haley, "John Meade Falkner," in N. Hardy Wallis, ed., *Essays by Divers Hands*, Vol. 30, London 1960; "J. Meade Falkner," http://www.hertford.ox.ac.uk/main, accessed March 16, 2007.

141. "Excerpts from 'Some Remarks on Ghost Stories,'" http://ednet.rvc.cc.il.us/~fcoffman/103/ Horror103/MRJamesRemarks.html, accessed June 8, 2008.

142. Paolo Maurensig, *Canone Inverso*, Milan 1996.

143. Anne Rice, *Violin*, New York 1997.

144. See http://it.movies.yahoo.com/c/canone-inverso-making-love/index-368854.html, accessed November 8, 2008.

145. Philip Anson, "Leila Josefowicz, Portrait of a Woman with a Violin," *La Scena Musicale* 4, no. 5, February 1, 2000; http://www.amazon.ca/Vln-Anne-Rice-Sting/dp/B000004lO3, accessed June 9, 2008.

146. See http://home.nikocity.de/contrasto/Mauren.htm, http://en.wikipedia.org/wiki/Anne_Rice; http://en.wikipedia.org/wiki/Paolo_Maurensig, accessed June 9, 2008.

147. Mrs. Humphry Ward, *Robert Elsmere*, London 1888; http://www.1911encyclopedia.org/Mary_Augusta_Ward, http://www25-temp.uua.org/uuhs/duub/articles/maryaugustaward.html, accessed June 18, 2008.

148. Thomas Mann, *Buddenbrooks*, Frankfurt 1960, part 8, chapters 6–7.

149. Gillett, *Musical Women in England*, pp. 115–35.

150. Ian McEwan, *On Chesil Beach*, New York 2007.

151. Bart Schneider, *Beautiful Inez*, New York 2005.

152. Bart Schneider, *The Man in the Blizzard*, New York 2008.

153. Claire Kilroy, *Tenderwire*, Orlando, Florida 2006.

154. Yael Goldstein, *Overture*, New York 2007.

155. Mayra Montero, *Deep Purple*, New York 2003, originally published as *Púrpura Profundo*, Barcelona 2000.

156. Jessie Fothergill, *The First Violin*, London 1877.

157. Helen Debenham, "Almost Always Two Sides to a Question," in Kay Boardman and Shirley Jones, eds., *Popular Victorian Women Writers*, Manchester and New York 2004.

158. Sholem Aleichem, *Stempenyu: A Jewish Romance*, New York 2007; Joshua Walden, "The 'Yidishe Paganini': Sholem Aleichem's Stempenyu and the Music of Yiddish Theater," unpublished, 2012.

159. Count Leo Tolstoy, "The Kreutzer Sonata," trans. Benjamin R. Tucker, in *The Kreutzer Sonata and Other Stories*, http://ebooks.adelaide.edu.au/t/tolstoy/leo/t65k/; *Epilogue to the Kreutzer Sonata*, trans. Leo Wiener, http://www.geocities.com/cmcarpenter28/Works/epilogue.txt, accessed June 26, 2008.

160. Robert G. Ingersoll, "Tolstoi and 'The Kreutzer Sonata,'" *North American Review*, September 1890.

161. "Count Tolstoy Not Obscene," *New York Times*, September 25, 1890.

162. Thomas Hardy, "The Fiddler of the Reels," *Scribner's*, May 1893; Thomas Hardy, *Life's Little Ironies*, London 1894.

163. Thomas Mann, *Doktor Faustus*, Frankfurt 1967.

164. Harold C. Schonberg, "Miss Fothergill's 'First Violin,'" *New York Times*, August 14, 1977.

165. Frank Almond, letter, Arts & Entertainment, *New York Times*, September 5, 1999.

166. Sholom Aleichem, "The Fiddle," in Robert N. Linscott, ed., *The Old Country*, New York 1946.

167. "Rothschild's Fiddle," in *The Stories of Anton Tchekov*, New York 1932.

168. Fannie Hurst, "Humoresque," in *Humoresque: A Laugh on Life with a Tear Behind It*, New York and London 1919.

169. See http://www.ohioana-authors.org/hurst/index.php, accessed July 2, 2008.

170. Albert Rees, *Real Wages in Manufacturing, 1890–1914*, Princeton 1961, chapter 3.

171. "David Hochstein's Recital," *New York Times*, November 20, 1915; "Camp Life Makes Men Over," *New York Times*, March 10, 1918; "David Hochstein Killed," *New York Times*, January 28, 1919; Gdal Saleski, *Famous Musicians of a Wandering Race*, New York 1927, p. 197; "David Hochstein," *The Violinist*, February 1919.

172. Eugene Drucker, *The Savior*, New York 2007.

173. Norman Lebrecht, *The Song of Names*, London 2002.

174. Gordon Pape and Tony Aspler, *The Music Wars*, New York 1982.

175. Dennis Rooney, "Peaks and Pitfalls," *The Strad*, January 1990; cf. Dennis Rooney, "His Master's Pupil," *The Strad*, November 2004.

176. Daniel Silva, *The English Assassin*, New York 2002; http://en.wikipedia.org/wiki/Daniel_Silva, accessed July 13, 2008; *Cahner's Business Information 2002*; http://www.amazon.com/English-Assassin-Daniel-Silva/dp/0451208188, accessed July 13, 2008.

177. Jonathan Levi, "The Scrimshaw Violin," *Granta,* Winter 1997.

178. See http://www.jonathanlevi.com/home.php?pgsel=Biography&clk=1, accessed July 4, 2008.

179. Thomas Mann, *Bekenntnisse des Hochstaplers Felix Krull*, Berlin 1956, pp. 20–22.

180. Deane Narayn, *The Small Stradivari*, New York and London 1961.

181. See http://www.cozio.com/Owner.aspx?id=1072, accessed April 13, 2009.

182. Deane Narayn, *An Edge of Pride*, London 1964.

183. Barry Targan, "Harry Belten and the Mendelssohn Violin Concerto," *Esquire*, July 1966. Cf. Michael Kardos, "Mr. Lost Classic," *Missouri Review* 1, 2004, pp. 186–88.

184. Harvey, *The Violin Family*, p. 93, http://www.uh.edu/engines/epi630.htm, accessed August 28, 2008.

185. Maiko Kawabata, "Virtuosity, the Violin, the Devil," *Current Musicology*, Spring 2007, n. 32; http://www.balletmet.org/Notes/SaintLeon.html, http://en.wikipedia.org/wiki/Cesare_Pugni, accessed August 30, 2008.

186. *The Strad*, June 2001, p. 601.

187. Mark Slobin, ed., *Yiddish Theater in America, "David's Fiddle" and "Shloyme Gorgl,"* New York 1994; Nina Warnke, "Going East," *American Jewish History*, March 2004, pp. 1ff.; Irving Howe, *World of Our Fathers*, New York 1976, pp. 463–67.

188. Jacob Gordin, "God, Man and Devil," in Nahma Sandrow, ed. and trans., *God, Man and Devil*, Syracuse, New York 1999. Cf. Howe, *World of Our Fathers*, pp. 467–71.

189. Allan Kozinn, "An Old Violin Whose Music Is Peculiarly Haunting," *New York Times*, December 7, 2001.

190. Jeremy Eichler, "Discovering the Soul in a Mystical Setting," *Newsday*, December 2, 2001; Allan Kozinn, "An Old Violin Whose Music Is Particularly Haunting," *New York Times*, December 7, 2001.

191. Johanna Keller, "Violin as Player," *The Strad*, November 2004.

192. Cf. Alex Ross, "Unauthorized," *The New Yorker*, September 6, 2004.

193. Boris Vladimsky, "Rothschild's Violin Matryoshka," San Francisco Jewish Film Festival 1998, http://www.sfjff.org/public_html/sfjff18/filmmakers/d0718b-a-i.html, accessed November 15, 2008.

194. Cf. James Loeffler, "Hidden Sympathies," http://www.nextbook.org/features/feature_shostakovich.html, accessed November 29, 2008.

195. Paul Cutts, "Rothschild's Violin," *The Strad*, March 1998, p. 305.

196. See http://en.wikipedia.org/wiki/WNET, accessed September 2, 2008.

197. Ronald Waldman, "The Third Man," *Radio Times*, September 25, 1959.

198. See http://www.scott-brady.com/slade/shotgunslade.htm, http://en.wikipedia.org/wiki/Shotgun_Slade, accessed September 2, 2008.

100. Donald Crafton, *The Talkies*, Berkeley 1999, pp. 76–81; http://en.wikipedia.org/wiki/Vitaphone, accessed September 7, 2008.

200. Mordaunt Hall, "Vitaphone Stirs as Talking Movie," *New York Times*, August 7, 1926.

201. See http://www.youtube.com/watch?v=NSNfkX9Qmp4, http://www.youtube.com/watch?v=PKAM5acK4D8, accessed September 8, 2008.

202. Tully Potter, liner notes, "Yehudi Menuhin Plays Mendelssohn Violin Concerto," Euroarts DVD 2054618, 2005.

203. Bosley Crowther, "'Of Men and Music,' in Which Leading Artists Display Their Talents," *New York Times*, February 15, 1951.

204. Axelrod, ed., *Heifetz*, pp. 629ff. Cf. "Teva Man," http://www.amazon.com/Heifetz-Piatigorsky-Historic-Performance-Footage/dp/B000A4T8MC, accessed September 9, 2008; Louis Kaufman, *A Fiddler's Tale*, Madison and London 2003, pp. 141–42.

205. See http://www.film-zeit.de/Film/2449/PAGANINI/Crew/, accessed February 20, 2011.

206. See http://en.wikipedia.org/wiki/J._Arthur_Rank, accessed October 5, 2008.

207. Komroff, *The Magic Bow*; "Manuel Komroff Is Dead at 84," *New York Times*, December 11, 1974.

208. Menuhin, *Unfinished Journey*, pp. 183–85.

209. See http://www.screenonline.org.uk/film/id/441045/index.html, accessed October 6, 2008.

210. See http://en.wikipedia.org/wiki/Pink_film, accessed October 7, 2008.

211. Klaus Kinski, *Paganini*, Munich 1992.

212. Gerhard R. Koch, "Vampir mit Violine," *Frankfurter Allgemeine Zeitung*, October 8, 1999.

213. See http://www.films.pierre-marteau.com/hist_filme/1935_d_stradivari.html; http://www.deutscher-tonfilm.de/s2.html, accessed August 6, 2008; http://www.filmportal.de/film/stradivari_39566cb231cd4dcd8c218eb33928fa76, accessed August 14, 2008; http://de.wikipedia.org/wiki/G%C3%A9za_von_Bolv%C3%A1ry, accessed September 11, 2001; http://de.wikipedia.org/wiki/Liste_der_unter_alliierter_Milit%C3%A4rzensur_verbotenen_deutschen_Filme, accessed September 11, 2008.

214. David Schoenbaum, "Trauma and Tragedy Follow Many a Fine Fiddle," *New York Times*, August 22, 1999.

215. Justin Chang, "The Violin," *Variety*, May 24, 2006; Manohla Dargis, "Songs in the Street, Revolution in the Air," *New York Times*, December 5, 2007; http://moviessansfrontiers.blogspot.com/2006/12/29-mexican-film-el-violin-2005-by.html, http://twitchfilm.com/interviews/2007/12/the-violininterview-with-francisco-vargas.php, accessed July 22, 2012; http://www.film-forward.com/theviolin.html, accessed August 1, 2008.

216. See http://www.hollywood.com/movie/Stradivari/162357, accessed September 17, 2008.

217. Henry Mitkiewicz, "Stradivari Biography Plays Down Violins," *Toronto Star*, March 4, 1999. Cf. Robert Suro, "Maestros in the Movies," *New York Times*, October 25, 1987.

218. Jorn K. Bramann, "Socrates: The Good Life," in *Educating Rita and Other Philosophical Movies*, http://faculty.frostburg.edu/phil/forum/Winter1.htm, accessed July 30, 2008; Janet Maslin, "Good with Violins, Not People," *New York Times*, June 4, 1993; http://worldfilm.about.com/library/films/blcoeur.htm, accessed July 30, 2008.

219. Arthur Weschler-Vered, *Jascha Heifetz*, London 1986, pp. 96ff.

220. Deems Taylor, "Jascha, That's My Baby," in Axelrod, ed., *Heifetz*, p. 354.

221. See http://www.tahgallery.com/Standish.htm, accessed October 2, 2008.

222. Boris Morros obituary, *New York Times*, January 10, 1963; http://en.wikipedia.org/wiki/Boris_Morros, accessed September 24, 2008; Boris Morros, *My Ten Years as a Counterspy*, New York 1959.

223. See http://en.wikipedia.org/wiki/Edgar_G._Ulmer, accessed July 13, 2008; Geoffrey McNab, "Magic on a Shoestring," *Guardian*, August 5, 2004.

224. Bosley Crowther, "'Carnegie Hall,' In Which an Array of Musical Talent Is Seen," *New York Times*, May 3, 1947.

225. See http://www.youtube.com/watch?v=kFaq9kTlcaY, accessed September 25, 2008.

226. See http://en.wikipedia.org/wiki/Music_of_the_heart, accessed October 4, 2008.

227. Janet Maslin, "A Director Trades in the Hatchets for Violins," *New York Times*, October 29, 1999.

228. Kimberly Chun, "'Together' in Harmony," *Asianweek*, June 4, 2003.

229. Roger Ebert, "Together," *Chicago Sun-Times*, June 6, 2003.

230. See http://www.violinmasterclass.com/bio_content.php?bio=chuan, accessed October 5, 2008.

231. André Sennwald, "Caravan," *New York Times*, September 28, 1934; Orio Caldiron and Matilde Hochkofler, *Isa Miranda*, Rome 1978, pp. 61–62.

232. See http://movies.msn.com/movies/movie-synopsis/caravan.4/, accessed October 15, 2008.

233. André Sennwald, "'Caravan,' Erik Charell's Musical Romance of the Tokay Country," *New York Times*, September 28, 1934.

234. See http://derstandard.at/3052193/Regieverbot-und-Erotik?_lexikaGroup=11, accessed January 3, 2010; Ernst Klee, *Das Kulturlexikon zum Dritten Reich*, Frankfurt 2007, p. 202.

235. Derek Granger obituary, *Independent*, January 31, 1995.

236. See http://www.darkskymagazine.com/2008/04/21/to-joy-till-gladje/.

237. Frank S. Nugent, "Columbia Presents Clifford Odets' 'Golden Boy,'" *New York Times*, September 8, 1939.

238. Henry Handel Richardson, *Maurice Guest*, St. Lucia, Queensland, Australia 1998, p. xxvi.

239. Ibid., pp. lvi–lxv.

240. See http://www.adb.online.anu.edu.au/biogs/A110392b.htm, accessed October 31, 2008; Margaret K. Butcher, "From Maurice Guest to Martha Quest," *Journal of Postcolonial Writing*, Summer 1982.

241. Carmen Callil, "Agony by Agony," *Guardian*, August 23, 2008.

242. William J. Locke, "Ladies in Lavender," in *Far-Away Stories*, London, New York, Toronto 1919.

243. Steve Lopez, *The Soloist*, New York 2008.

244. "Robert Downey Jr. Talks with Steve Lopez," *Los Angeles Times*, January 11, 2009.

245. Dai Sijie, *Balzac et la Petite Tailleuse Chinoise*, Paris 2000; *Balzac and the Little Chinese Seamstress*, New York 2001.

246. A. O. Scott, "Is Mozart Thinking of Chairman Mao?" *New York Times*, July 29, 2005.

CODA

1. See http://www.charitycommission.gov.uk/SHOWCHARITY/RegisterOfCharities/Regis.terHomePage.aspx, accessed February 22, 2011.

2. W. E. Gladstone, *Address Delivered at the Distribution of Prizes in the Liverpool College*, London 1872, p. 27.

3. *The Musical World*, December 28, 1872.

4. "The Locomotive and the Violin," *Waikato Times*, May 3, 1873.

5. Aldo Zargani, *Per Violino Solo*, Bologna 1995, pp. 17–20.

6. Robert R. Reilly, "Light in the Dark," http://www.music-weinberg.net/biography1.html, accessed February 26, 2011.

7. Leib Kvitko, *Dos Fidele*, National Yiddish Book Center, Amherst, MA n.d.

8. Interview with Bruce Duffie, http://www.bruceduffie.com/koh2.html, accessed February 26, 2011; Anthony Tommasini, "Brahms and Masur Touch the Heart of the Matter," *New York Times*, September 22, 2001; Sacks, *Musicophilia*, p. 329.

9. Michael Salla, "Out of 'a Grave,' Haitian Violinist Keeps Music in His Heart," *Miami Herald*, January 20, 2010; *All Things Considered*, National Public Radio, January 15, 2011.

10. *All Things Considered*, National Public Radio, November 23, 2010.

11. Anthony Tommasini, "A Night for a Rhapsodic Violin and an Old Brake Drum," *New York Times*, October 8, 2010.

12. Alex Hawgood, "Hahn-bin Straddles Classical Music and Fashion," *New York Times*, February 24, 2011.

13. Interview with the author, Berlin, July 14, 1997.

INDEX